DEFEATING ISIS

DEFEATING
ISIS

WHO THEY ARE, HOW THEY FIGHT,
WHAT THEY BELIEVE

MALCOLM NANCE

Skyhorse Publishing

Skyhorse Publishing books may be purchased in bulk at special discounts for sales promotion, corporate gifts, fund-raising, or educational purposes. Special editions can also be created to specifications. For details, contact the Special Sales Department, Skyhorse Publishing, 307 West 36th Street, 11th Floor, New York, NY 10018 or info@skyhorsepublishing.com.

Skyhorse® and Skyhorse Publishing® are registered trademarks of Skyhorse Publishing, Inc.®, a Delaware corporation.

Visit our website at www.skyhorsepublishing.com.

10 9 8 7 6 5 4 3 2 1

Library of Congress Cataloging-in-Publication Data is available on file.

Cover design by Brian Peterson

ISBN: 978-1-5107-1184-6
Ebook ISBN: 978-1-5107-1185-3

Printed in the United States of America

CONTENTS

Dedicated to the men and women of RAID, BRIO and BAT and especially the police dogs Diesel and Akil who gave their lives to save others.

FOREWORD

ISIS is a cult that wants to transform Islam at gunpoint, and to defeat it the world must understand the group on its own terms, according to Malcolm Nance. As an analyst, historian, and counterterrorism expert, Nance explains that ISIS has deep roots, stretching back to the earliest days of Islamic history. He's absolutely clear, however, that it was a very modern event that allowed ISIS to burst onto center stage and show off its brutality for the world to see.

"The invasion of Iraq," he writes, "was not just an exhausting failure, unsuccessful in stamping out insurgency and terrorism, it actually created the entire legion of terror and tyranny that we know as the Islamic State."

In his detailed and informed study Nance argues that, in effect, America's War on Terror created a new breed of vicious terrorists who wear the mask of Islam like actors in a Kabuki theatre while carrying out horrifically un-Islamic acts like posing for selfies during battle, and burning a hostage alive.

But as William Shakespeare scoffed, "the Devil can cite scripture for his purpose."

—Richard Engel
December 23, 2015

ACKNOWLEDGMENTS

A collection of notables contributed to this book, including the members of the Terrorist Asymmetric Project on Strategy, Tactics and Radical Ideology (TAPSTRI), which was formed in Hudson, New York for the very purpose of observing and creating counter-ideology and violent extremism defeat strategies for the US intelligence community and the greater counterterrorism effort. TAPSTRI terrorism media researcher Chris Sampson is arguably one of the world's preeminent experts on ISIS and social media. He has not only compiled TAPSTRI's thousands of videos from ISIS and al-Qaeda, but he has also worked tirelessly to take down over a thousand ISIS websites and Twitter feeds. Scriven King is an internationally renowned security professional who provided a great deal of the analysis on ISIS tactics and combat operations. Sergei-Beliveau-Dubois is a French-speaking maritime/combat archaeologist and specialist in cultural crimes and heritage protection, who documented the atrocities of cultural cleansing. "RJ" is a former US Air Force intelligence operator who provided numerous sources for ISIS combat tactics and intelligence structure. Information related to blood antiquities and strategies to defeat them come from Major Tommy Lavoti, Katie Paul, and Deborah Lehr of the Antiquities Coalition. Other contributors include Hosam, an Egyptian-American patriot who provided much of the day-to-day materials on Egypt's fight with the Ansar Beit Maqdis, and Doctor John Bedolla, MD, an Assistant Professor University of Texas at Austin Dell Medical School and Miguel Bedolla MD, PhD, MPH, who provided valuable research on the ISIS medical system.

Additional thanks go out to the staff and advisory board of the International Spy Museum. They stand as a public monument to all of those who follow in their footsteps of the greats and who silently serve this nation fighting in the shadows.

Skyhorse Publishing editor Jay McCullough made this book possible from beginning to end. Our decade-long friendship started with my first book, *Terrorist Recognition Handbook*. He is one of the best editors in the business.

Finally, a note of thanks to my wife Maryse, who was the driving force behind this book. While working with her in Iraq as she risked her own life to manage oil security projects. She saw first hand the beginnings of ISIS, and brought clarity and a wife's passion to this book as she helped me focus on how to defeat this group at all costs.

COMMON ISLAMIC TERMS

Here is a convenient reference for the many terms you may encounter when studying this subject. Although these words and phrases may be common in Islamic practice and jurisprudence, it is important to note that adherents of ISIS often distort or overemphasize many of Islam's most important tenets or misapply them *in extremis*; they are extremists.

Allah: The One True God

Allahu Akbar: "God is Greatest," a phrase also known as the takbir

Al-Wala Wal Bara: The ultra-orthodox Salafist practice of swearing to live one's life for God and rejecting all things that are ungodly or un-Islamic; ISIS takes this practice to a literal extreme in all aspects, except weapons, vehicles, and electronic technology

Ansar al-Sunnah: Literally, "helpers of the teachings of the Prophet;" in practice, the congregation of Islam

Aqeed: Creed; Strength of faith and Belief in the One God

Ba'ya, Ba'yat (pl): Sworn oath

Dar al-Islam: "The house (lands) of Islam"; all regions under ISIS control

Dar al-Kuffar: "The house (lands) of the unbelievers/Infidels"; all regions outside of ISIS control

Dawa'/Dawah: "Religious invitation"; evangelism or working to bring the word of Allah to all

Fardh Ayn: (Arabic) The individual religious obligation or duty of every Muslim that are Charity, Fasting, Prayer, Pilgrimage to Mecca and Witnessing that "There is No God But God and Mohammed is His Messenger." Jihadi cultists believe that Jihad and death (Martyrdom) are also obligations which are not specified in Islam.

Fatwa: Religious ruling from an authorized religious body, the Ulema

Fi Sabilillah: "In the path of God"

Fiqh: Islamic passing of judgement

Forsan al-Khalifa: Knights of the Caliphate; euphemism for ISIS terrorists overseas

Hadiths: Interpretive texts of the Qur'an written by Islamic scholars

Haramayin: The cities of Mecca and Medina, home of the two Holy Shrines of the Grand Mosque & Kaaba (Mecca) and the Tomb of the Prophet Mohammed (Medina)

Hijab: Literally meaning "screen," this can refer to physical coverings used by Muslim women or, more generally, a given standard of modesty

Hijrah: Emigration; the path of the Prophet Mohammed from Mecca to Medina (Yathrib) to found Islam in 622; Used by ISIS/al-Qaeda to signify abandoning past lives and moving to ISIS controlled territory or mentally departing from family/friends/Muslims to carry out terror attacks without their knowledge

Hud, Hudud (pl): Punishments reserved for perceived "crimes against religion," like adultery, stealing, apostasy, and homosexuality

Iblis: Demons or minions of the Devil

Imama: Islamic Political leadership

Imarah: Islamic Leadership

Jammah: To gather

Jihad: "Struggle"; Islamic term for struggle of knowing one's self (the Greater Jihad); common parlance for a defensive Holy War (lesser jihad); this is *not* a religious obligation in Islam but in ISIS's cultist practice it is a life-long obligation to be carried out until death

Jund al-Khalifa: Soldiers of the Caliphate; euphemism for ISIS Middle East terrorists

Kafir, Kufr: "Infidel," "unbeliever"; those who have live in ignorance of Islam

Kalifah: The Caliphate of the self-appointed "Islamic State"

Khanzir: "Pig"; terms used by ISIS for enemy Muslim Soldiers or Shia Muslims; people to be slaughtered by beheading

Millah: Path of Righteousness

Muhajirun/Mujhajirat: Men/Women who have chosen to abandon their past lives and "Emigrate" from the Land of the Disbelievers to the Caliphate/ISIS controlled territory; "mental Muhajirun" are those who cannot physically leave but mentally separate themselves from family/friends/ infidels and other Muslims to live like those in the caliphate, a common practice among those planning a terror attack

Mujahid/Mujahideen (pl): One who is involved in a holy struggle or jihad

Munafiq, Munafiqun (pl): Person who professes faith in Islam but conceals dissent against the cause; a hypocrite or traitor

Murtadd/Murtaddin (pl): Apostate, rejectionist, one who leaves Islam for another religion; often used for Muslim enemies

Mutaweyun: Collaborators; those who work with America or its allies in espionage or government

Muwahidun: Those who are believers in Monotheism, belief in the One God

Quds: Jerusalem, home of third holiest shrine in Islam, Dome of the Rock (Al-Aqsa mosque)

Rafida: Apostates; Muslims who have left Islam. Used by ISIS adherents to arbitrarily declare any Muslim as a heretic and worthy of death

Ramadan: A month in the Islamic calendar during which fasting is a way to focus on the worship of God

Ribat: Islamic historical term for a combat outpost or small mud/dirt fort, from the desert skirmishes of the Prophet Mohammed

Sahabah: The immediate friends and companions of the Prophet Mohammed at the founding of Islam in the seventh century; considered the best role models for Muslims

Sahwat: Traitors; any Muslim military personnel that does not defect to ISIS

Salafi/Salafist: Ultra orthodox practice of persons who live their modern lives in the manner of the seventh-century *Sahabah,* or friends and companions of the Prophet Mohammed; Salafists are extremely orthodox in prayer, dress, diet, and lifestyle

Sama': "To listen"

Sayarah Mufakha: Booby-trapped car bomb; suicide Vehicle-Borne Improvised Explosive Device (SVBIED)

Selibi/Selibiyeen: "Those who carry the cross"; Crusaders; Westerners, particularly military and government workers

Shaheed: Death as a martyr in a just war; this is *not* an obligation in Islam but in ISIS's cultist practice all adherents must strive to martyr themselves in jihad

Sharia: Islamic law

Shaytan: Satan

Shirk: The practice of idolatry or polytheism; belief in a god who is not Allah, or in many gods

Shuhidah (Amiliyah Shuidah): "Suicide Operation" or "Suicide Bombing"

Sunnah: the way of life prescribed to Muslims on the basis of Muhammad's teachings and interpretation of the Qur'an.

Ta'ah: Obedience

Takbir: A call to recognized the greatness of God; followed by "Allahu Akbar"

Takfir: to declare or accuse another person of being a Kafir, or unbeliever; in ISIS practice, this is a preliminary sanctification of, and justification for murder

Tajwid: The rules for recitation of the Qur'an

Taqwa: The spiritual self-guidance found within adherents that leads one to accept and fear of God. Piety.

Tawaghit: Tyrants; used to describe Muslim regimes not aligned with ISIS

Tawhid: Belief in the oneness of God; monotheism

Ulema (Ulama): The highest body of scholarship in Islamic law and jurisprudence.

Ummah: the collective word for the Muslim people

INTRODUCTION

The Islamic State of Iraq and Syria—"ISIS," or "the caliphate of the Islamic State"—has become the single most dangerous threat to global security since al-Qaeda. It is more than just a threat to America and the West, because it also poses an existential threat to Islam: its goal is to coopt or enslave 1.8 billion Muslims.

I predicted in my 2007 book, *The Terrorists of Iraq*, that "the potential to create an Iraqi franchise of al-Qaeda or other terrorist groups of far more sophistication and with greater global reach than the Afghanistan-trained al-Qaeda under the Taliban is extremely high." This has come to pass in the form of the terrorist monster created from three components: thirty thousand former Ba'athist intelligence officers—essentially commandoes and spies; al-Qaeda's most ruthless branch; and a foreign legion of fresh young fighters numbering in the tens of thousands.

ISIS must be stopped at all costs, and the first step toward that goal is to identify who they are, where they are, and how they fight. In these pages I detail the strategy, tactics, internal organization, weapons, and techniques used by the most deadly terrorist group in the world. It begins with the historical development of terrorist actions and weapons over history, analyzes the structure of its subordinate "States" or wings to the terrorist organization, identifies the terrorists with individual profiles, and illuminates their various covert operating procedures in use throughout the world. It is equally important to clear up the many general misperceptions about ISIS and its tenuous relationship to Islam.

Having spent the past thirty-four years as an intelligence and combat veteran, with the majority of that time devoted to studying the Global Jihad, al-Qaeda, and now ISIS, I hope my insider's view will shed light on how ISIS organizes, fights, and spreads its ideology. I've survived their suicide bomb attacks, I've seen their defeats. Here, I've set out to show how ISIS's street-level tactics led to their rapid victories, as well as the strategies and tactics that will demonstrate how badly they can lose.

PART I: WHO THEY ARE

CHAPTER 1

THE OLD HISTORY OF THE NEW CALIPHATE

THE TERRORIST CIVIL WAR TO DESTROY TRADITIONAL ISLAM AND CONQUER THE WORLD

In June 2014, the Iraqi-based terrorist group called the Islamic State for Iraq and al-Sham—more commonly known as ISIS—stormed across Iraq and Syria and bore down toward the gates of Baghdad. Many casual observers were stunned that the Iraq war was still in progress. In three swift offensives, ISIS columns of tan Toyotas under the black flag took large swaths of eastern Syria, as well as northern and western Iraq. The Syria offensives occurred in 2012 and 2013; by early 2014 the campaign in Iraq commenced. These attacks were largely overlooked by the news media, but US intelligence recognized that the creeping seizure of terrain would culminate into a final blitz. The invasion saw the Iraqi army collapse as ISIS careened towards Baghdad, capturing billions of dollars' worth of American-supplied weapons and equipment. The world looked on in shock as the group claimed numerous oilfields and tens of millions of dollars in banks. After seizing the cities of Mosul, Tikrit, Qaeim, Fallujah, and Ramadi, they reveled in an orgy of mass beheadings, crucifixions, rapes, and summary executions. Spectacles of disembowelment, stoning, and live immolation of a captive pilot in a cage—all captured in high-definition video and broadcast to a horrified world—heralded their arrival as the world's first terrorist-run nation.

America fought the fathers and brothers of ISIS—then called Al-Qaeda in Iraq—and tens of thousands of Saddam loyalists nonstop between 2003 and 2011. The brutal counter-insurgency pitted almost the entire might of the US armed forces against men with rifles, roadside bombs, and suicide car bombs. We are fighting the exact same terrorists, and two new generations of their sons, in the exact same cities and neighborhoods where they fought the US Army and Marines. We lost approximately five thousand service members in that fight.

Unlike its parent, al-Qaeda, the newest generation of Jihadis was not waiting for the local Muslims to accept their beliefs or their efforts. They would take the Middle East by storm. Soon after, the terrorist leader Abu Bakr al-Baghdadi declared the formation of an "Islamic State" and gave himself the grandiose title of "Caliph Ibrahim."[1] The world was informed this was the only legitimate Muslim nation on earth. The world's 1.8 billion Muslims were told to answer only to ISIS's commands, to abandon their lives, and to emigrate to Iraq and Syria as citizens of the new Islamic Caliphate.

Apparently in the eyes of many in the news media, political world, and academia, the sky had broken open and a new group, far more powerful and capable than al-Qaeda, had mysteriously descended from thin air—something completely new under the sun. The chattering classes breathlessly explained that like al-Qaeda, ISIS was led by an enigmatic Muslim madman who believed in an apocalyptic ideology that was previously unknown to anyone in the West. It was a good story and it played well, particularly after the *Charlie Hebdo* attacks in Paris, but in fact very little of the ISIS narrative is new. Once ISIS went on their social media rampage, they successfully created the appearance that ISIS was greater, more powerful, and completely different from al-Qaeda. However, it is the same as it ever was, and has been known by many names, such as al-Qaedism or Islamic Jihadism, though little consensus exists about what it should be called officially.

The "Islamic State," al-Qaeda, and the dozens of affiliated terrorist groups did not instantaneously coalesce ex nihilo, nor did their brutality and inhumanity begin a mere year ago. The world has been exposed to its relentless bloodletting for decades, watching the ebb and flow of al-Qaeda through the terror spectacles of the 9/11 attacks in New York, the March 11, 2004 attacks on the Madrid subway, the 7/7 attacks in London in 2005. Jihadists took different names such as ISIS, Boko Haram, al-Qaeda of the Islamic Maghreb, al-Murabitoun, ISIS in Libya, Ansar al-Sunnah, al-Qaeda of the Indian Sub-Continent, al-Qaeda of the Arabian Peninsula in Yemen, al-Shaabab; a list seemingly without end. In short, any small group of like-minded followers in the name of Jihad can take a photograph with the ISIS or al-Qaeda banner and be considered a grave threat to the global order. Alternatively, an endless parade of journalists, terror experts, scholars, and politicians will argue that ISIS is not al-Qaeda, or that the Nigerian group Boko Haram has no allegiance or connection to al-Shaabab in Somalia, and that girls from Britain who join ISIS in Syria to become brides have nothing to do with Osama bin Laden.

From 2003, ISIS was formerly known to the world as al Qaeda-in-the Land Between the Two Rivers (Mesopotamia) or Al-Qaeda in Iraq (AQI).[2] Under the command of the Jordanian-born Abu Mussab al-Zarqawi, AQI started their multiyear rampage by blowing up the United Nations headquarters in Baghdad and slaughtering Iraqis, Americans, and civilians wherever the opportunity presented itself. Working in concert with Saddam's ex-Ba'athist terror army, and in league with dozens of micro-jihadist groups both Iraqi and foreign, the United States had eight years of nearly nonstop fighting and massive sectarian bloodletting. Iraq's "liberation" unleashed a Pandora's box of local, regional, and international hatreds, as thousands of suicidal jihadi recruits flowed into Iraq with the desire to kill an American and die a hero's death. For nearly 3100 days, as many as fifty thousand terrorist insurgents supported or fought in urban combat against a massive combination of American and Iraqi firepower. On numerous occasions US Intelligence considered AQI and its sister groups neutralized, their leadership decimated, and manpower pools near extinction. However, Iraqi government missteps allowed it to revive, and by 2011, AQI commenced another region-wide terror campaign that has yet to abate in Iraq or Syria.

For the original followers of al-Qaeda's ideology of jihad, written by Osama bin Laden himself, the war in Iraq was about leaping from the cold dirty caves in mountains of Afghanistan and into the heart of the historic Muslim world to fight the Western armies and die in a glorious holy war. Each would get their chance. For the leadership, the US invasion of Iraq would be central to the ideology that was launched in 1988 and built upon the teachings of others who sought to bring Islam to a new destination in its history.

Before 9/11, a fledging global jihadi movement of small, fragmented groups tried desperately to gain traction, attention, and recruiting. If the 9/11 attacks were designed to be a spectacular demonstration that the cool, cunning, and sacrifice of a small band of cultists could change the world, then it was an incredible success, if only for one day. After

9/11 they had sufficient notoriety as the United States tried to stamp out each one with force, but the invasion of Iraq drew terror recruits to bin Laden's ideology in a way that even 9/11 could not. The invasion offended many Muslim sensibilities and sparked outrage among those who interpreted the events as the Muslim world under attack. It did not help that virtually the entirety of American political rhetoric from the right verified for the would-be jihadist that America was going to war with Islam—all Islam—and confirmed their suspicions that Osama bin Laden had been proven correct. Tens of thousands of jihadists flowed in and became enamored with the cult belief that the highest form of worship to God was to die in a suicide bombing against the enemies of Islam.

Just as 9/11 changed everything, the same could be said for the ISIS invasion of Iraq. In one day the entire balance of power in the Middle East shifted. It would be a very new phase in the global war on terrorism that was not only entirely predictable, but wholly made from one historic geopolitical error: the American invasion of Iraq.

ISIS WAS BORN FROM THE INVASION OF IRAQ

In 2003, President George W. Bush invaded Iraq on the pretext that Saddam had real viable weapons of mass destruction, or the ability to make them in short order, including potentially nuclear weapons. Although UN weapons inspectors found nothing but scraps, that didn't matter to the Bush administration, which ordered the invasion in an effort to change the entire strategic balance of the Middle East by toppling Saddam Hussein.

American politicians did not help dispel the belief by the jihadists that they were going to change the Middle East by force. At virtually every turn after 9/11, the administration of President George W. Bush and Vice President Dick Cheney projected the grand fantasy that America alone could rid the Middle East of dictators and give the Muslim world the beacon of freedom and democracy by means of the edifying effects of cruise missiles. This vision was backed by a group called the Project for a New American Century, which espoused a neoconservative vision of a US military that would asymmetrically tear through Arab lands, wrest weapons of mass destruction and oil from the control of dictators, and be showered with glory and adulation by the local Arab crowds. Iran would cower in fear. America would assure Israel's safety by installing moderate, democratic, American-friendly Arab governments. These beliefs had no basis in the intelligence community, or anyone with a basic understanding of the Middle East.

The Bush administration expected a victory on par with the Israeli victory against three Arab armies in the 1967 war, or at least an effort that would exceed Norman Schwarzkopf's defeat of multiple Iraqi army corps during the 1991 Gulf War. The Iraqi people would be eternally grateful as we removed a strategic enemy of Israel. The next stop would be to disarm Iran.

For George W. Bush, Dick Cheney, Condoleezza Rice, Donald Rumsfeld, and Paul Wolfowitz, the post–9/11 world was to have been born anew through the American vision of freedom and democracy in the Middle East. Stationed permanently in Iraq, the US Army and Air Force would protect and control Iraqi oil. It would act as a counterbalance to Saudi Arabia and the Gulf states, and stifle the nuclear intentions of Iran. The war was also supposed to demonstrate the results of applied American strength and Presidential resolve to both Russia and China.

When Saddam was finally toppled, all the regulating structures that had held the personal, tribal, and religious tensions in stasis since 1917 suddenly disappeared. George W. Bush and his national security staff overturned a century of fragile glassmaking, smashing it to pieces without the slightest thought to what would happen to the region, or the world.

Iraq's dictator, Saddam Hussein, was aware of the possibility that a war would be swift and that the Iraqi army would betray him. Apart from his Republican Guard units, Saddam had no faith that his regular army would be successful in stopping an American advance. It is widely believed that he was delusional in his assertion that the UN Security Council would stop the Americans, but someone on his staff was aware of the American and British forces massing on the Kuwait border. His sons Uday and Qusay, in collaboration with General Izzadin al-Durri, formed and led the terrorist commando force called the Saddam Fedayeen.

When the invasion started, the Iraqi army, once the fourth largest in the world, simply chose not to show up for the war. As Saddam's generals had predicted, the Shi'ites and Kurds abandoned the country to the invaders. During the major combat phase of the war, very few of the Iraqi Regular Army's major units stood up and fought the Americans. With rare exceptions, they disbanded in the face of American combat power, abandoned their positions and uniforms, and walked home to await the outcome. The remaining units of the Iraqi army were devastated by the US Army. As many as six thousand soldiers of the Saddam Fedayeen and other regime loyalists died in action, but this was a relatively modest number in light of the firepower delivered by the Americans.

On the other hand, the delaying actions of the Saddam Fedayeen transformed from major combat and large-scale engagements into the low-level terrorism and guerrilla attacks that became the hallmarks of the insurgency. After twenty-one days of combat, President George W. Bush declared "Mission Accomplished." But Sad-dam Hussein had prepared well in advance. Six months before the invasion, he had laid out an asymmetric strategic battle plan to attack the American military's weaknesses: vulnerability to terrorism and suicide attacks.

Before the invasion the Iraqi high command staff and intelligence agencies had developed a battle plan they called "Mogadishu on the Tigris" or "Project 111." Saddam's forces fully intended for the United States to meet an insurgent army after they had settled in to occupy Iraq. They would dissolve into the shadows and fight from their hometowns. They had the ultimate home-field advantage, as they would hide in the narrow alleys, brick homes, and flat roofs of the streets where they grew up.

Like clockwork, on or about April 19, 2003, almost

Saddam Fedayeen march in suicide commando parade uniform.

all of the former regime loyalist fighters who were engaged in combat disappeared back into the population overnight. The US Army and Marines spread throughout Iraq in pursuit and occupied Baghdad. It was generally acknowledged that the regime was finished when US Marine Corps combat engineers grappled the enormous statue of Saddam Hussein, his right hand aloft, and pulled it to the ground in the middle of Firdous Square. A joyous rapture filled Iraq and people flooded into the streets to celebrate . . . and loot. Iraqis erupted into a wild frenzy. That frenzy was the perfect cover that Saddam needed to destroy his criminal records.

Days later, mysterious fires started throughout all of the most sensitive Iraqi ministries. Within a few days the bonfires had destroyed the bulk of the documentary history of Saddam's government. Any chance to know the true organizational depths of the regime was lost. Within days of ordering the US Army to stop the looting, an atmosphere of normalcy returned. The Coalition was gradually reimposing security throughout Iraq. The Iraqi people ceased looting and gave way to a tenuous civil control.

At the end of that period the administration under President George W. Bush was flush with success. Yet this victory was spoiled almost immediately with the a lack of a coherent policy, a staggering series of governance missteps, a contempt for prudent planning, and strategic political errors, salted throughout with hubris and a crippling arrogance. By the end of major combat the American coalition had lost 139 soldiers. The trickle of soldiers who began to die at the hands of the new insurgents were killed by men whom Secretary of Defense Donald Rumsfeld derisively called "Dead Enders." The were anything but dead. Sometime around mid-May 2003, Saddam Hussein, in hiding near his hometown of Tikrit, sent word out to the former regime loyalists to begin the Iraq insurgency. From that day until their withdrawal in 2011, American would lose 4,493 dead, 32,000 wounded.

AQI prepares to behead western hostage in 2004.

On the other side of the ledger, the United Nations has estimated there have been 155,000 deaths caused from the invasion of Iraq. That number is conservative.

Saddam was not the only one with a plan for the invasion of Iraq. Osama bin Laden prepared for an Afghan-style insurgency there to fight alongside the Ba'athists if need be. After winning victory over the Americans, Iraq would become an Islamic Principality, or Emirate. Al-Qaeda would launch its doctrinal theories and encourage emigration of millions of Muslims to a perfect land of fighters and lovers of God. Al-Qaeda would indoctrinate them into their beliefs and use technology to lure in new followers. Although the invasion of Iraq did not create bin Laden's cult, it may prove to be one of the single greatest politico-military mistakes in American history. President George W. Bush and his staff clearly sought to use the opportunity presented by 9/11 to fundamentally change the face of the Muslim world. Unfortunately, what they did not know was that the invasion would validate the entirety of Osama bin Laden's cultist rhetoric in a way that the 9/11 attacks never could. It was always part of Osama bin Laden's plan for America to overreact to the attacks, though he surmised that an American invasion of Afghanistan would spark yet another a battle between his variant of Islam and democracy. He viewed Western democracy as corrupting, worldly, and ungodly. Just as he felt the Soviet loss of Afghanistan destroyed Soviet communism, Osama bin Laden believed that defeating America in Afghanistan, and draining them of money and blood, would likewise destroy the West economically and politically.

ISIS's belief system did not originate in Iraq; it is, and always has been, deeply rooted in a strategic plan initiated by bin Laden and subsequently executed by the Jordanian Al-Qaeda in Iraq leader Abu Mussab al-Zarqawi. Nor did Zarqawi develop the plan for the caliphate. In the 1980s, Zarqawi was a petty criminal who traveled to Afghanistan to fight the Soviets, but was too late. He did learn more about the neo-Salafist movement, and while there he met with bin Landen, who encouraged him to return to his own country and start his own branch of the jihad. On his way through Iraqi Kurdistan, he also met with leaders of the Kurdish jihadist group Ansar al-Islam. In Jordan the charismatic ex-felon started the group Monotheism and Holy War or Jama'at al-Tawhid wal-Jihad. While under arrest on explosives charges, he and his men dressed like Afghans in prison, and devoted themselves to destabilizing Jordan for the global jihad movement. With these early associations with al-Qaeda, and adoption of their ideology, he was a perfect candidate to lead the Iraq insurgency.

Zarqawi and Tawheed wal-Jihad crossed into Iraq in March 2003 under cover of Saddam Hussein's call to defend Iraq from the American invasion. Zarqawi set up his command in Fallujah and patiently waited for his hosts to be destroyed. During that time, jihadis flocked to Iraq through Syria from across the Muslim world and were supported by al-Qaeda's global facilitators. Dozens of small Salafist extremist groups formed and by 2006 were consolidating under AQI's control. Al-Qaeda fought under different names over time in an effort to combine its predominantly foreign fighter base with dozens of Iraqi insurgent groups. Bin Laden wanted all of the Islamic terror cells to combine into a single cohesive terror command that would ultimately form an Islamic nation in the heart of Iraq. Initially it was called the Islamic Emirate of Iraq (IEI), but they settled for the Islamic State of Iraq (ISI).

With the death of Zarqawi on June 7, 2006, AQI decided to branch out and create a dual command organization led by an Egyptian, Abu Ayyub al-Masri, and an Iraqi, Abu Umar al-Baghdadi. AQI took on the mantle of a terror coordination and advisory committee called the Mujahideen Shura Council (MSC). Despite al-Qaeda's best efforts to hide the dual command through deception and lies, American counterintelligence discovered the location of the pair and killed them both in a single airstrike.[3] Their deputy Iraqi Abu Bakr al-Baghdadi took command and formally adopted the name change to the Islamic State of Iraq (ISI).[4] In 2007 he formed an alliance of Islamic insurgent groups to counter the increasingly popular anti-al Qaeda group called Sons of Iraq. Al-Baghdadi's terror alliance called itself the Coalition of the Nobility.

By the end of the first four years of the Iraq insurgency, a handful of former military and religious extremists tied America down so badly that soldiers needed to wear full body armor to use the latrine. In 2006, the Abu Ghraib scandal broke when photographs emerged depicting American soldiers torturing and sexually humiliating Iraqi captives, in the very prison where Saddam Hussein had committed similar crimes. After Abu Ghraib, the reasons for the invasion of Iraq started to unravel and would ultimately be discovered as false. Despite command of the entire country, coalition forces never found weapons of mass destruction. The ties between Saddam Hussein and 9/11 were found to be entirely fabricated or rhetorically conflated. All of these errors caused a new wave of foreign men to join al-Qaeda against the US.

On a certain level, American combat operations themselves lent to the belief, among US citizens and politicians, that anywhere the United States applied its massive combat power was essentially the equivalence of victory. The terrorists in the jihadist world used a very simple metric for success: When you withdraw we will win. When you stay we will win—by killing you.

To their great satisfaction, the headlines after major combat operations in Fallujah read along the lines of "After leveling city, US tries to build trust."[5] The insurgents would ensure that no trust could ever be built, through propaganda campaigns that needed little input from their media communications people, as the Americans seemed to do all of the damage themselves.

The Washington propaganda about the insurgency created a dangerous mindset about combating al-Qaeda and the belief that an increase in forces introduced in 2008, "the Surge," directly resulted in a "victory" against AQI. In fact, the insurgents simply vanished or went back to their Syrian safe havens. Despite a lack of metrics, the Americans assumed that if they were winning sharp battles in ground combat and few insurgents were present, then they must be in their final throes. If all of those were true, then one would be close to achieving victory. But victory never came.

By 2007 the call for the removal of US troops

AQI plants their flag in a destroyed M2A3 Bradley Fighting Vehicle—Baghdad 2005.

accelerated. The American people grew weary of the political spin, the Bush administration started making small signals that the withdrawal of forces was not only possible, but probable. Wildly fluctuating and seemingly amazing statements about the readiness of the Iraqi security forces went from only two battalions ready for war to the President claiming over 200,000 men were ready to relieve US forces in the insurgency. By 2008, President Bush could not get a signed status of forces agreement with Iraq to protect American soldiers who would be stationed or working in the nation. In fact, the Iraqi Prime Minister Nuri al-Maliki did not want any US forces in Iraq past 2011. He demanded that the US leave the nation to the new government. Maliki explained that the American invasion created a new a sovereign nation with the ability to choose its own destiny. That destiny would be to corral the Sunnah minority and its terrorists without the intervention of Americans. Freedom in Iraq would be freedom for the Shi'ite majority. As far as Nuri al-Maliki was concerned, this was the only benefit of the American invasion.

In December 2011, the last US heavy units formed into convoys and over a 24-hour period quietly withdrew to Kuwait for a sea voyage back to America. The terrorists of ISI had many targets to choose from, but they didn't raise a finger. America was gone, and in essence, Iraq was now their playground.

Almost immediately the al-Maliki government ruled Iraqi in such a way that all the guarantees and assurances that the Americans had promised vanished almost overnight. Al-Maliki sought to crush Sunni and Kurdish aspirations of any kind. By the withdrawal of US forces in 2011, AQI and its sister groups were moribund, its leadership decimated and manpower pools near extinction. They moved their operations in Syria and attacked points of weakness in Iraq until political bloody-mindedness of Iraqi Prime Minister Nuri al-Maliki became too much for the Sunnah ex-Saddamists. They turned back to terror and opened their arms to join AQI, now named ISIS.

Since that time the insurgency has never stopped and from its ashes rose "The Islamic State."

Yet ISIS, as a terror organization, is not comprised strictly of foreign fighters. Since its inception, it was always bin Laden's intention that younger Iraqis take over leadership of the group. In fact, since ISIS's "liberation" of the Iraqi Sunnah regions, it has survived by expert manipulation of the local tribalism, an appeal to Sunnah nationalism, and a thick layer of fanatical religious piety. ISIS's transformation into the most feared terror group in the world was an ingenious veil of an unwavering Islamic cultism cast over the ruthless, covert Ba'athist counter-intelligence structure. Not only could they detect and eliminate their enemies; the entire population could be kept under the dual heels of insane Islamic interpretations coupled with summary execution. ISIS based its population control tools on Saddam, which in turn had an organizational structure and training much like the infamous East German Stasi. This amalgamated organization of highly skilled terrorists, coupled with Saddam's former commando, intelligence, and espionage officers, now dominate the center of the Middle East and seek to conqueror the Muslim world.

The current confusion about ISIS stems from a clash of dueling perceptions. ISIS has mastered the world of modern social media and easily consumed video clips for a society that does not give much time to the day-to-day affairs of the Middle East. The alternative is the sober but media-unfriendly reporting that reveals the hard realities of the people who are enslaved under their tyranny. ISIS wants the viewer to not only fear them, but dares the viewer to intercede and face the same fate. They challenge the dispossessed, the susceptible, the mentally defective, and the faithful to join them and take riches and spoils in both this world and the next. Who the terrorists of ISIS really are, and who they are not, what they want, and what they may achieve, becomes difficult to discern in light of superficial news media organs, the bigoted mischaracterizations of calculating politicians, and the woo-woo of conspiracy theorists in social media. In many respects, the portrayal of ISIS, like al-Qaeda before them, is of cartoonish, ten-foot-tall terrorist ogres who can be best avoided by hiding under our beds. But this plays directly into their goals; they are terrorists.

It is true that ISIS participants are younger, a less professional generation of jihadist than the traditional al-Qaeda terrorist. A more apt description is that they resemble a terror mob, but what they lack in professional skill they make up for in an almost berserker-like frenzy of passion to slaughter anyone who stands in their path, including their own.

The invasion of Iraq was not just an exhausting failure, unsuccessful in stamping out insurgency and terrorism; it actually created the entire legion of terror and tyranny that we know as the Islamic State. Had the invasion not toppled the existing social, political, and tribal structure of Mesopotamia, there would be no ISIS to fight. Al-Qaeda might well have died slowly in the mountains of Pakistan. Today however, the global jihad movement under the aegis of a newly minted ISIS has reinforced their ranks and even provided the old-guard al-Qaeda with enough recruits to conduct terrorist acts across such a widely diverse number of regions that the world is adjusting to the circumstances in what is becoming the "new normal."

At this date, many pundits and politicians shun the prospect of being tied to the strategic debacle that was the Iraq war. Over the decade they have attempted to launder their reputations and demur at the mere mention of ever claiming to tie Iraq to WMDs and the 9/11 attacks on America. But now they want a new war. Not only in Iraq but in Syria, in an effort to cleanse the Middle East of ISIS—al-Qaeda Generation 5.0. Many say bringing justice to the deaths of the 3,000 Americans who were murdered on September 11 was our highest goal in Iraq. In that respect the mission missed its mark. ISIS may not yet have the operational capacity to perform a 9/11–style attack, but their ability to recruit and inspire may cause this to occur sooner rather than later.

The Sahwah Campaign

The request to the former regime insurgents was direct and to the point—we wanted them to agree to a cease-fire and during that time they were to eliminate or turn over all foreign fighters and Al-Qaeda in Iraq (AQI) members—to the last man. With the Sahwah campaign many did just that, and the Sunnah tribes revolted and ran AQI out of many parts of the Northern and Western governorates. The plan was simple. Once these tribes had proved that the overwhelming number of foreign fighters were gone, the US Army would have no reason to remain in Iraq. Simply put, in exchange for a greater share of governance in Iraq, the Iraqi insurgents had to neutralize Zarqawi's followers and destroy or compromise the AQI cells in their communities.

FROM AL-QAEDA TO ISIS: THE FIVE GENERATIONS

AQ Generation 1.0: 1988–1991

The original Arab nationals that fought the Soviet Union in Afghanistan gathered together in Peshawar, Pakistan in 1988. Osama bin Laden disagreed with his mentor, Abdullah Azzam, about what to do at the end of the war. Bin Laden and his lieutenants had designed a plan to establish an Islamic Caliphate across the Muslim world and prepare for the prophesied return of the savior and the prophet Jesus. To this end he formed a professional terror cadre to provoke America and the West to invade Afghanistan, where the US would be defeated militarily and economically like the Soviet Union. Bin Laden killed off Azzam and seized control of the vast number of foreign fighters who were about to depart Afghanistan at the end of the Soviet war. He formed a new group, Tenzim al-Qaeda al-Jihad ("Headquarters of the Holy War Organization") and spread his ideology through books, audiocassettes, and pamphlets.

AQ Generation 2.0: 1991–1996

The followers of bin Laden and his new deputy, Egyptian Islamic Jihad leader Ayman al-Zawahiri, set up operations in Khartoum, Sudan. Soon after they carry out their first attacks against Western targets in Aden, Yemen. After defeating the regional warlords in Afghanistan, the Taliban invite bin Laden to establish his base of operations in Kabul. Here he cultivates select terror professionals to carry out attacks against the West, including bombing the World Trade Center in 1993, plans to blow up twelve airliners over the Pacific Ocean, assassinate the Pope, and fly a bomb-laden airplane into CIA headquarters.

AQ Generation 3.0: 1997–2003

Using newer, more inventive young terrorists, with older mentors, al-Qaeda attacked the American embassies in Kenya and Tanzania after bin Laden issues an official declaration of war on the United States and the West. The US retaliates with cruise missiles, almost killing bin Laden at the Zawar Kili terrorist base camp. An al-Qaeda suicide bomb boat successfully struck the USS *Cole* in Yemen harbor. The decade-long effort culminated with the 9/11 attacks on New York City and Washington DC, killing almost 3,000 citizens. America invaded Afghanistan. Inexplicably, President George W. Bush invaded Iraq, creating a new failed state for al-Qaeda to attack. Al-Qaeda rapidly professionalized.

AQ Generation 4.0: 2003–2011

The US invasion of Iraq shocked the Muslim world. Al-Qaeda calls for young men to fight America in Iraq. Al-Qaeda conducted mass-casualty terror attacks against civilians in Madrid, London, Moscow, and Mumbai. Hundreds of thousands die in Iraq. Saudi Arabia crushed a direct insurgency in the heart of the Kingdom by al-Qaeda of the Arabian Peninsula (AQAP). The Arab Spring of 2011 led to the Syrian civil war. Al-Qaeda in Iraq (AQI), now called the Islamic State of Iraq, seizes eastern Syria and forms ISIS.[6]

AQ Generation 5.0 (ISIS Gen 1.0): 2011–Present

The withdrawal of US forces from Iraq and the death of Osama bin Laden led to the Iraq insurgency as the center of terrorism in the Middle East. Al-Qaeda and its nominal leader, Ayman al-Zawahiri, found itself gradually sidelined to Yemen, Somalia, and the Saharan desert. In 2014 ISIS seized large parts of Iraq and combined them with captured regions of Syria, declaring a new Islamic Caliphate to be called the "Islamic State." Former al-Qaeda loyalist groups in Egypt, Nigeria, Yemen, Afghanistan, and Libya swore loyalty to Abu Bakr al-Baghdadi, the self-proclaimed Caliph Ibrahim. Attacks on Russia, Tunisia, and Paris led to the formation of a global coalition to destroy them.

CHRONOLOGY OF SIGNIFICANT HISTORICAL EVENTS

2006
Al-Qaeda in Iraq (AQI) announces creation of the terrorist group Islamic State of Iraq (ISI).

April 2010
ISI Leader Abu Omar al-Baghdadi killed in April 2010. Abu Bakr al-Baghdadi takes over the organization.[7] The leadership of ISIS takes a new shape in 2010, filling its ranks with former Ba'athist Iraqi military officers and members of the Iraqi secret services.[8]

January 2011
Abu Bakr al-Baghdadi sends fighters to join rebel forces in Syria in 2011, which provides them with battle skills and helps them gain traction with Syrian Sunnis. Recruitment jumps.[9]

2012
ISI launches the terror campaign named Operation Breaking the Walls, a plan to conduct massive raids on Iraqi prisons to free hundreds of hardened AQI fighters and bring them into ISI.

2013
ISI attacks Abu Ghraib prison, freeing the most-wanted criminals and terrorists in Iraq.[10]

April 2013
Al-Baghdadi releases an audio message announcing that ISI and al-Nusra Front (ANF) are now one organization, and thus ISI's new name will become the Islamic State of Iraq and al-Sham.[11] In the message, al-Baghdadi claimed that the al-Nusra Front in Syria was a fully funded branch of ISI.[12] Al-Nusra leader Abu Mohammad al-Julani refuses to accept this.[13] As a result of the dispute, al-Qaeda emir Ayman al-Zawahiri issued a statement that ISI should confine its activities to Iraq. ISIS refused the order to vacate Syria.[14] Al-Qaeda breaks with ISIS in February 2014.[15]

May 2014

The State Department added the following aliases to the Islamic State of Iraq and the Levant (ISIL): the Islamic State of Iraq and al-Sham (ISIS), the Islamic State of Iraq and Syria (ISIS), ad-Dawla al-Islamiyya fi al-'Iraq wa-sh-Sham, Daesh, Dawla al Islamiya, and Al-Furqan Establishment for Media Production.[16]

June 2014

ISIS blitz campaign "Lion of God al-Balawi" allows them to take control of a large swath of land across northern Syria and Iraq.[17] The city of Mosul, the third largest in Iraq,[18] falls to ISIS in June.[19] Land under ISIS control runs from Aleppo to Fallujah to Mosul.[20] On June 29, 2014, ISIS declares a new Islamic caliphate, to be referred to as "The Islamic State."

July 2014

ISIS seizes the largest oilfield in Syria.[21]

August 2014

ISIS posts a video on social media showing the beheading of American journalist James Foley.[22] US launches airstrikes on ISIS targets in Kurdish regions of Iraq.[23]

September 2014

ISIS posts the video of the beheading of another American journalist, Steven Sotloff. It appears that both Foley and Sotloff were beheaded by the same man, later identified as British subject Mohammed Emwazi, a.k.a. "Jihadi John."[24]

March 2015

ISIS claims Nigerian Terrorist group Boko Haram ("Western Education is forbidden") pledged their allegiance to the Islamic State.[25]

May 2015

Thirty-five global terror groups in total have sworn allegiance.[26]

October 2015

Ansar Beit al-Muqadis, an Egyptian ISIS group, claims responsibility for blowing up a Russian airliner over the Sinai Peninsula, killing 255 passengers.[27]

November 2015

ISIS terror cell launches multiple suicide attacks on Paris, killing 130.[28]

CHAPTER 2

THE ISIS CALIPHATE'S LEADERSHIP AND MEMBERS

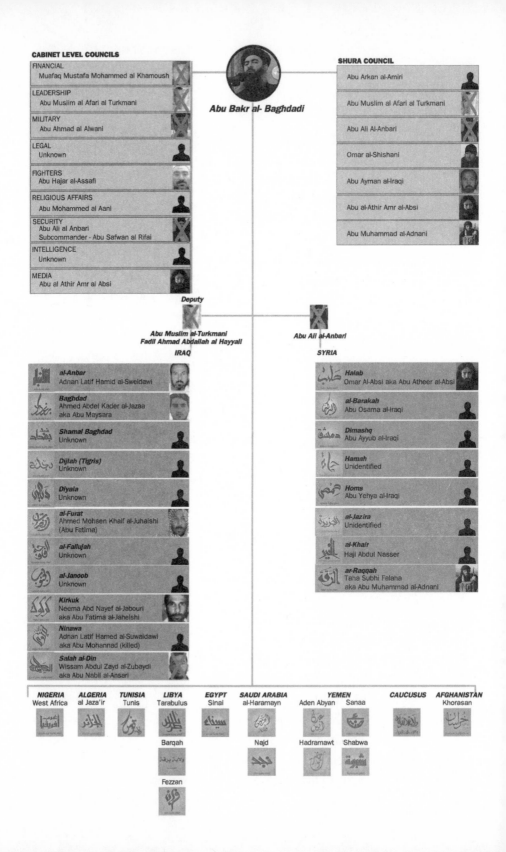

"THE CALIPH" ABU BAKR AL-BAGHDADI

(A.k.a. Caliph Ibrahim, Ibrahim Awwad Ibrahim Bou Badri bin Armoush, Dr. Ibrahim 'Awwad, Ibrahim 'Ali al-Badri al-Samarrai', Ibrahim 'Awad Ibrahim al-Badri al Samarrai, Dr. Ibrahim, Dr. Abu Dua)

"Abu Bakr al-Baghdadi" is a nom de guerre. Among his fellow terrorists he was known as Abu Bakr, named after the first Caliph of Islam. The surname "al-Baghdadi" indicates that he claims to be from Baghdad. To the US Army he was detainee US9IZ-157911CI, and held under his real name: Ibrahim Awwad Ibrahim al-Badri bin Armoush, or just Ibrahim al-Badri. To the rest of the world he is the one terrorist who has almost equaled Osama Bin Laden in achievements, but not in name recognition. He is ISIS.

Not much is known about al-Baghdadi's early life. Many argue this is by design, as Baghdadi took a lesson from the deaths of his two predecessors who suffered an early retirement via laser-guided missiles.[29] He is an Iraqi citizen born in Samarra, Iraq, in 1971. The name on his birth certificate was Ibrahim Awwad Ali al-Badri al-Samarrai.[30]

According to the declassified prison file developed by the US Army and Iraqi intelligence, he is

"[ISIS has] a statement to make that will cause the world to hear and understand the meaning of terrorism."
—Abu Bakr al-Baghdadi

from the Bu Badri tribe. Other parts of his resume are apocryphal. He is said to have a PhD in Islamic studies from Baghdad Islamic University. Some say he was a Sharia professor and a Salafi preacher.[31, 32] He claims to be a Sayyed or a direct descendent from the bloodline of the Prophet Mohammed; others claim he was raised a Sufi, a mystical sect hated by jihadists like ISIS. In an interview with *The Telegraph*, a man named Abu

Ali, from Baghdad's Tobchi neighborhood and reportedly a contemporary of Baghdadi's, saw a different view of the young man than the hagiography painted by the ISIS media. When asked about a widely circulated biography of Baghdadi portraying him as a wise scholar and preacher who toured multiple mosques around Iraq, Ali recalled things more humbly. "He wasn't a preacher as people say . . . The mosque here had its own imam. When he was away, religious students would take his place. [Baghdadi] would sometimes lead the prayers but not give any sermons." He was a severe religious conservative who once fought with his imam and distained mixing of sexes and dancing at weddings. [33]

While in college at Baghdad's Islamic University, Baghdadi, according to some sources, was more interested in playing soccer than in studying.[34] ISIS maintains that Baghdadi has a doctorate in Islamic Studies and that he is descended from the Quraysh tribe, which is the tribe of Prophet Mohammed.[35] This latter point is a stipulation of Sunni law—which imposes a set of conditions on any would-be caliph, including that he be a Qurayshi.[36] This aspect of Baghdadi's background is hotly disputed by those who know the family and the man; falsely claiming such lineage to seize control of Islam is tantamount to apostasy.

Whatever his origins, al-Baghdadi's extremism was stoked by the American invasion of Iraq and forged in the terror resistance. At the start of the occupation he remained close to the Saddam Fedayeen and Ba'ath party members who were fighting America underground with their military and intelligence skills.[37] In 2004, Baghdadi was detained at Camp Bucca on suspicion of being an al-Qaeda supporter. Camp Bucca was located near Umm Qasr, Iraq, deep in the Shi'ite south, where a Sunni escapee like himself would find no welcome or assistance. Baghdadi remained in American custody for about ten months before being released in late 2004.[38]

During his incarceration at Camp Bucca, nicknamed by US Intelligence as the Jihadi War College, he met the terror professionals who used the internment as a sabbatical and education center for a new generation of leaders. On his release Baghdadi wholeheartedly joined in the insurgency. In 2005 he formed the Iraqi terrorist group Jaysh al-ahli al-Sunnah wal Jamaa or "Army of the Family of the Sunnah and the Mosque."[39],[40] This group announced in its formation communique that they were fighting in retaliation against the heavy-handedness of the Iraqi security forces and to remove America from Iraq. While in this role he may have served as a go-between for Abu Umar al-Baghdadi, the joint commander of Al-Qaeda in Iraq (AQI) and the Mujahideen Shura (advisory) Council (MSC). In that position he was a sure bet for filling the shoes as leader of Al-Qaeda in Iraq when Abu Umar was killed by US forces. The MSC went so far as to even announce the establishment of a Sunni Iraqi mini-Caliphate called "The Islamic State" in 2006. The name and concept never took, but al-Baghdadi kept it in his pocket until 2014.

According to ISIS's official biography, in 2007 al-Baghdadi had assumed shadow leadership as executive officer of the al-Qaeda followers, now named the Islamic State of Iraq (ISI). He was Emir of ISI's Sharia committees. With al-Baghdadi's help, bin Laden's mandate to transition the foreign-fighter-led AQI to all-local Iraqi leadership was assured. After the death of Abu Umar al-Baghdadi and his Egyptian co-commander Abu Ayyub al-Masri, his chance would come. On May 16, 2010, al-Baghdadi was announced as ISI's Emir al-Mujahideen, prince of the holy warriors.[41]

According to one ISIS defector, Baghdadi's appointment took many by surprise, and that his rise was orchestrated by Haji Bakr, a former colonel of the Iraqi Revolutionary Guard and later "the architect of the Islamic State" who oversaw its occupation of Northern Syria.[42] Abu Bakr's move was allegedly designed to put a Sayyed's Qurayshi lineage, prestige, and religious face on an Iraqi who, like Saddam, would seize control of all Islam. Being Iraqi, he was familiar with how to harness the power and control of a police state like Saddam Hussein's to bring Islam under its dictatorial control. That would require a Caliph who would foster a Saddam/bin Laden hybrid monster to retain absolute control within his Caliphate. That Caliph would be expected to carve out of Syria and Iraq a Sunnah nation-state and use bin Laden's template of al-Qaeda terror expeditions to reach across the Muslim world and seize the rest.

In 2011, after the Syrian rebellion started, al-Baghdadi sent his fighters to join rebel forces in Syria. He named this group the Jebhat al-Nusra. This provided ISI with opportunity to acquire weapons, safe installations, and battle skills. Their presence helped them gain traction with Syrian Sunnis, and fed ISIS recruitment.[43] It also ultimately precipitated the al-Qaeda–ISIS split, as Jehbat al-Nusra was made the official branch of al-Qaeda in Syria. Al-Baghdadi was furious and seized their best manpower and tried to kill their leaders. He then announced that he was changing the name of the group to the Islamic State of Iraq . . . and Syria.[44] He realized that listening to Dr. Ayman al-Zawahiri, an old man cowering in Afghanistan, was a loser's game. He would take charge of the entire al-Qaeda global machine. He killed al-Qaeda's emissaries and announced that he would no longer follow Zawahiri's orders. He would transform it from the Iraq-centered terror force to a far grander vision— an Islamic State—and reintroduce an Islamic Caliphate with himself as the Caliph.[45]

In June 2014, Abu Bakr al-Baghdadi declared the formation of the caliphate.[46] To mark the event, he emerged to preach a sermon in Mosul. Wearing a freshly stolen Rolex, he came out of hiding to proclaim himself the ruler of all Muslims and exhorted all who follow Islam to abandon their lives and come live in the only religiously sanctioned Muslim land . . . or else.[47]

> . . . the Islamic State—represented by ahlul-halli-wal-'aqd (its people of authority), consisting of its senior figures, leaders, and the shūrā council—resolve[s] to announce the establishment of the Islamic khilāfah, the appointment of a khalīfah for the Muslims, and the pledge of allegiance to the shaykh (sheikh), the mujāhid, the scholar who practices what he preaches, the worshipper, the leader, the warrior, the reviver, descendant from the family of the Prophet, the slave of Allah, Ibrāhīm Ibn 'Awwād Ibn Ibrāhīm Ibn 'Alī Ibn Muhammad al-Badrī al-Hāshimī al-Husaynī al-Qurashī by lineage, as-Sāmurrā'ī by birth and upbringing, al-Baghdādī by residence and scholarship. And he has accepted the bay'ah (pledge of allegiance). Thus, he is the imam and khalīfah for the Muslims everywhere. Accordingly, the "Iraq and Shām" in the name of the Islamic State is henceforth removed from all official deliberations and communications, and the official name is the Islamic State

from the date of this declaration.[48]—Abu Bakr al-Baghdadi, June 29, 2014

Seizing the heart of the Middle East and carving out a Sunnah homeland from Damascus to Baghdad are the kinds of actions that have made al-Baghdadi far more effective than al-Zawahiri and the staid al-Qaeda leadership.[49] In contrast to the leadership structure for al-Qaeda, which has always been covert, al-Baghdadi's ISIS is an expeditionary Islamic army on the march; they have decided to be the ones kicking down the doors instead of waiting for theirs to be flattened. Al-Baghdadi is a directive commander and the organization is centralized exactly along the lines of Saddam Hussein's Ba'ath party. Its henchmen do exactly what they're told, when they're told, and they will kill anyone or eliminate anything that opposes them.

THE ORIGINAL GANGSTERS

OSAMA BIN LADEN: "THE FOUNDER"

The ideology and plan to restore the caliphate and bring on the apocalypse was developed well before ISIS existed; it was the fever dream of Osama bin Laden. When he formed al-Qaeda al-Jihad, "Headquarters of the Holy War," he envisoned ISIS-like organizations all over the Middle East and seeded his organization in every Muslim nation. ISIS and its future variants will continue to be a vindication of the plan established a quarter century ago. Bin Laden's challenge to any and all jihadists who followed was to work toward three goals: (1) Fight and die to establish a neo-Islamic Caliphate; (2) Re-engineer Islam to topple the existing power structures through terror and insurgency; (3) Provoke the West into a ground fight in order to economically break them and convert the rest of the world to fulfill the prophecies of the Islamic End of Days.[50]

ABU MUSSAB AL-ZARQAWI: "THE SLAUGHTERER"

Before ISIS, the most experienced foreign Mujahideen in Iraq were the professional terrorists under the leadership of bin Laden protégé Ahmed Fadhil Nazzar Khalaya, a young Jordanian also known by his cover name, Abu Musab al-Zarqawi. Zarqawi was an al-Qaeda follower trained in Afghanistan who led the Islamic extremist terrorist group Tawhid Wah Al Jihad, "Unity and Holy War." When the Americans invaded Iraq, he brought his small band to the city of Fallujah. They filled several safe houses with weapons and explosives and let Saddam's rule fall. Then they implemented their terror campaign to kill Americans. Zarqawi started by blowing up the United Nations headquarters. From there they would not stop attacking US forces for the entire three thousand days that US forces were in the country. Zarqawi was the point man for giving the Americans a Jihad like they had never seen before. With nearly unlimited weapons, Zarqawi would organize and take command of Al-Qaeda in Iraq (AQI) and wage a guerrilla war alongside the Saddam Fedayeen commandoes and Ba'ath party loyalists that the Americans would regret. Zarqawi popularized video images of his victims being beheaded and executed on social media. The "Prince of the Holy Warriors" died after bombs were dropped on his safe house during a Special Forces mission in 2005.

ABU AYYUB AL-MASRI: "THE PROFESSIONAL"

When Abu Mussab al-Zarqawi was killed, al-Qaeda needed an immediate successor with combat experience. Bin Laden agreed that

Zarqawi's second-in-command, a former Egyptian army Special Forces officer named Abu Hamza al-Muhajir (a.k.a. Abu Ayyub al-Masri, "the Egyptian"), would take command. Al-Masri was a former member of the Egyptian Islamic Jihad terrorist group and a student of Dr. Ayman al-Zawahiri, the secondary al-Qaeda terrorist leader. Al-Masri was previously assigned to coordinate Jihadi volunteer operations in Europe and the Middle East. He was sent to Iraq to assist Zarqawi and professionalize their terror operations. Additionally, he was to groom Iraqi leadership to take command of AQI and establish the Caliphate in the heart of historic Islam. He would work toward that goal with Abu Umar al-Baghdadi till both were killed by the same US missile in 2010.

ABU UMAR AL-BAGHDADI: "THE FIRST EMIR OF THE ISLAMIC STATE"

Abu Umar al-Baghdadi was Iraqi-born Hamid Dawud Mohamed Khalil al Zawi. He was an Iraqi member of the Mujihdeen Shura Council (MSC) along with Abu Musab al-Zarqawi, spiritual advisor Sheikh Abd al-Rahman, and AQI operations officers Abu Ayyub al-Masri and Abu Shaheed, the Iraqi who was the AQC's liaison to AQI.[51] Abu Umar was highly successful at staying out of the line of fire, even as he was enemy number one to US forces in Iraq. Unlike Zarqawi, he led operations from the rear, maintained a high level of operational security, and managed the ISI like a CEO.

During this period Abu Umar was tasked to create an umbrella organization that would bind all Iraqi and foreign Islamic extremist groups under al-Qaeda. They called themselves Khalf al-Mutayibee, the "Coalition of Nobility." In 2006, this group, with Abu Umar at the helm and Abu Bakr al-Baghdadi helping, would carve Iraq into an "Islamic State." Abu Umar was elected as the first Emir of the Islamic State. In 2007 the MSC released a communiqué that proclaimed the establishment of a Sunnah Caliphate in Iraq. They delineated its boundaries and asked all to swear loaylity to its new Emir, Abu Umar al-Baghdadi. The announcement of the "Islamic State" read:

> Your brothers announce the establishment of the Islamic State in Baghdad, Anbar, Diyala, Kirkuk, Salah al-Din, Ninawa, and in other parts of the governorate of Babel, in order to protect our religion and our people. Further, the Mujahid delivers a special call to the tribal heads in Iraq, and to all Sunnah Muslims in that country, to pledge loyalty to the Emir of the Believers, Abu Umar al-Baghdadi, by their adherence and obedience. [52]

This announcement was lost in the tides of combat and the Islamic State tried other names, including the "Islamic Emirate of Iraq," but settled on a new name, "The Islamic State of Iraq (ISI)." On April 17, 2010, a special reconnaissance unit observed a safe house containing al-Masri and al-Baghdadi. They called in that the signature of the residence indicated high-value targets and that the two leaders might be inside. A special operations force led by the Iraqi Special Forces and backed by US Army Rangers attacked the residence. The occupants fought, and helicopters with rockets and Hellfire missiles pummeled the building. The troops pulled the crushed corpses of al-Masri and the first Emir of the Islamic State, Abu Umar, from the rubble. Their identities were later confirmed by DNA. These deaths turned the entire mission of seizing an Islamic State into the hands of Abu Bakr al-Baghdadi.

HAJI BAKR: "THE SPY"

Abu Bakr al-Baghdadi did not rise to power on the shouders of Al-Qaeda in Iraq alone. During his internment at Camp Bucca he met, slept, and broke bread with many Sunnah members of the former Saddam regime loyalists who were fighting in the largest insurgent contingent, the Army of the Mujahideen. These men were almost exclusively the Saddam Fedayeen, the Special Republican Guard, and the five Ba'ath intelligence agencies, just now in civilian clothes. While there, Abu Bakr al-Baghdadi not only renewed his belief in Salafist Islam, but developed an appreciation for Saddam Hussein's centralized power structure to control people and resources. One of the men he met was named Samir Mohammed Abdul al-Khlifawi, a.k.a. Haji Bakr. Haji Bakr was a former Lieutenant Colonel in the Internal security apparatus of the Air Force. That was meaningless, as it was just a cover name the counterintelligence men designated to hunt down armed services members who were suspected of disloyalty to Saddam. He was the worst kind of spy—the one detested by all intelligence officers—an internal spy catcher. Usually to prove one's worth under Saddam a spy catcher had to catch spies, and in an intelligence agency that meant turning in one's friends and family. Haji Bakr was accomplished at intelligence work, but when the Americans invaded he went underground with all the other intelligence officers and started supporting the insurgency in civilian guise. Upon his release, Abu Bakr al-Baghdadi was now a senior man in AQI and Haji Bakr was invited to bring his intelligence experience and organizational skills to improve the relations with the Ba'athists.

One thing Haji Bakr excelled at was human terrain. He understood how Ba'ath intelligence used information collected in Stasi-like

---

Camp Bucca, Iraq[54]

Camp Bucca was the principal detention facility for the bulk of the Iraqi extremist insurgents captured in the five previous years. Despite the best efforts of American security forces, the detention of so many suspected and real insurgents at Camp Bucca had inadvertently created a concentrated ideas and team-building environment. This location allowed the guilty, the innocent, and the unlucky, to convalesce, strengthen relationships, and hobnob among the terror elite. Camp Bucca allowed the lowest key insurgents to meet, share lessons and knowledge, and conduct terror practicums on what each different group had learned from dealing with a large-scale professional force such as the Americans. The detainees knew they would eventually be released and that the Iraqi army would just be a hollow, well-equipped shell of the US Army that designed it."

meticulousness to hunt and harm the opposition, real or imagined. He also knew that any future Sunnah nation would need such skills and he brought them to Abu Bakr al-Baghdadi. In 2011 he was sent to Syria to use his experienced relationships with Syrian intelligence during the insurgency to seize whatever he could and carve out a safe haven. He was the right man for the job, and with his support ISI managed to form and enter Syria with a force called the Jebhat al-Nusra, made up of Syrian AIS members and foreign fighters. They seized major military bases, intelligence, weapons stores, and equipment that gave Haji Bakr an instant covert spy agency with government-level high-tech weapons and equipment. While in Syria and commanding ISI troops, he sketched out the state management structure for the leadership. In January 2014, he was killed by members of the Syrian Martyrs Brigade in the Syrian town of Tal Rifaat. *Der Spiegel* magazine received his handwritten notes. His notes and charts organized a top-to-bottom-level spy agency with dossiers containing every detail of everyone's life,
for use against them. Haji Bakr has been called "Baghdadi's Brain" or even "Baghdadi's Ba'athist," but the German magazine called him "The Architect of ISIS."

Most ISIS leaders, like Haji Bakr, come directly from the ranks of Al-Qaeda in Iraq, where they joined their skills with Saddam Hussein's former Ba'athist political and intelligence officers.[53]

THE DEPUTIES

Abu Arkan al-Amiri (or Abu Arkan al-Ameri)

Head of Shura Council: Abu Arkan is a murky figure; such key facts as his birthplace and birthdate are unknown.[55] He was appointed to the Shura Council, ISIS's top advisory council[56] by Baghdadi himself, and thus heads the one group that (in theory, at least) could overrule the caliph's dictates and overthrow the caliph himself.[57] In the event that Baghdadi for any reason ceased operating as caliph, this council would determine his successor.[58] If that occurred, some sources count Abu Arkan as a strong contender for the position.[59][60] As part of daily operations, the Shura Council's main function is to communicate commands from Baghdadi and his two top deputies, as well as to recommend governors.[61]

Sheikh Abu Mohammad al-Adnani: "The Voice of the Caliph"

Official Spokesperson, Member of Shura Council, Governor of Raqqa: Abu Mohammad al-Adnani was born Taha Sobhi Falaha[62] in 1977 in Banash, Syria.[63] He was detained at Camp Bucca for five years, between 2005 and 2010 under the name of Yasser Khalaf Hussein Nazal al-Rawi.[64],[65] In 2013, al-Adnani was reportedly head of Syrian operations.[66] Al-Adnani achieved prominence as ISIS's spokesman, thus serving as the voice behind such pronouncements ISIS's creation of a caliphate,[67] and in September 2014, a speech encouraging ISIS supporters to kill Westerners, including the following widely quoted excerpt:[68]

> If you can kill a disbelieving American or European—especially the spiteful and filthy French—or an Australian, or a Canadian, or any other disbeliever from the disbelievers waging war, including the citizens of the countries that entered into a coalition against the Islamic State, then rely upon Allah, and kill him in any manner or way however it may be. Smash his head with a rock, or slaughter him with a knife, or run him over with your car, or throw him down from a high place, or choke him, or poison him.

However, it is not his job as spokesman that makes him significant to the organization—ISIS relies much more on unofficial "crowdsourcing" of messages than al-Qaeda does.[69] However, he possesses an understanding of the inner circle's aims, born from his close relationship with ISIS leaders.[70]

Al-Adnani also serves as governor of Raqqa.[71] ISIS took control of the Syrian town in 2014, transforming it into the capital of the Islamic State.[72] In January 2016, he was reported wounded in an air strike.

Fadl Ahmed Abdullah al-Hiyali (Abu Muslim al-Turkmani)

Fadl Ahmed Abdullah al-Hiyali was known by many names. Abu Muslim al-Turkmani was his nom de guerre, while he was also known as Abu Mutaz al-Qurashi and as Haji Mutazz.

Before his death, Al-Turkmani was said to be the second-in-command of ISIS in Iraq. In 2013, he was made deputy Emir of Iraq and Syria by Baghdadi; US officials reported that he wasn't an executive officer, but high on the hierarchical ladder nonetheless.[73] After the deaths of Abu Abdulrahman al-Bilawi and Baghdadi's Deputy Samir al-Khlifawi in January of 2014, al-Turkmani became the senior-most ISIS leader under Baghdadi.

As Emir of Iraq, he was reported to be in charge of overseeing Iraqi Provinces under ISIS's control. In this position he managed ISIS military operations, finances, media, operations, and logistics, and had sub-Emirs reporting to him on all province-wide events.

As a former Lieutenant Colonel in the Iraqi Army under Saddam Hussein, he served the regime's intelligence apparatus and was said to have served in the Iraqi Special Forces and the Special Republican Guard. After the invasion of Iraq in 2003, he joined the Sunni insurgency against the coalition forces. It's unknown whether he was arrested for being part of the insurgency or because he was a loyal Ba'athist member and close to Saddam Hussein and Izzat al-Douri. Either way, he was imprisoned and served inside a US-operated prison believed to be Camp Bucca.[74] He was born in Tal Afar, Nineveh Governance, to a family of Sunni Muslims.

Despite numerous reports of Abu Muslim al-Turkmani's death in the past, US officials are confident that al-Turkmani died on August 18, 2015, when a drone struck the car he was driving near the occupied Iraqi city of Mosul.[75] Official ISIS spokesman Abu Mohammad al-Adnani confirmed his death.

Abu Ali al-Anbari: Deputy Emir, Emir of Syria

Abu Ali al-Anbari served as a deputy Emir to Baghdadi and as Emir of Syria. In addition, he sat on the ISIS intelligence and security councils.[76] He directed Syrian operations and also administered the governors who manage finances, weaponry, legal issues in the twelve Syrian provinces.[77] [78]

Al-Anbari was an ethnic Turkman,[79] was born in Mosul, Iraq, and resided in Raqqa, Syria.[80] Like many senior members of ISIS, Abu Ali al-Anbari served in the military under Saddam Hussein at the rank of Major General. During the invasion of Iraq in 2003, Anbari joined Al-Qaeda in Iraq after being ejected from the Ansar al-Islam terrorist group for financial corruption.

After an airstrike allegedly left the Caliph Abu Bakr al-Baghdadi with injuries, Abu Ali al-Anbari took over the role as acting Caliph until Baghdadi recovered. He was also positioned as successor in the event al-Baghdadi died.[81] The Pentagon reported in December 2015 that Abu Ali al-Anbari was killed in November 2015 during an air raid, along with fifteen other terrorists.[82]

Tarkhan Tayumurazovich Batirashvili, a.k.a. Omar al-Shishani, a.k.a. Omar the Chechen

Military Commander, Member of Shura Council: Al-Shishani is a Chechen who was born in 1986 in a region of Georgia known as the Pankisi Gorge, a breeding ground for separatist rebels[83] where unemployment is 90 percent.[84] He is rumored to be ISIS's second-in-command and is the top commander of ISIS's Syrian military arm, a post he assumed after his predecessor, Abu Abdul-Rahman al-Bilawi al-Anbar, was killed in Mosul in June 2014.[85] Known as a "tactical mastermind," he commands about 1,000 Chechen fighters who were instrumental in ISIS's successes in Syria and Northern Iraq (and who are seen as some of the most brutal combatants in the Syrian conflict).[86] Al-Shishani was once a sergeant of the Georgian army, where he served in the 2008 war with Russia.[87] He was discharged from the army in 2010 after contracting tuberculosis.[88] He spent at least two years in prison on a weapons possession charge,[89] which is where his extremist ideology developed.[90] According to his father, who is Christian (Shishani's late mother was Muslim), al-Shishani was not particularly interested in religion in his youth.[91]

His rise has been precipitous in ISIS. In March 2012, al-Shishani arrived in Syria, transferring his loyalty to ISIS in May 2013, and was elevated to head of Northern Syria later that year.[92] He has since been featured in so many ISIS videos he has become "the face of the ISIS conquests."[93]

Abu al-Athir Amr al-Absi: "The Propagandist to God"

Shura Council Member, Head of Media Council: Al-Absi is a Syrian national who was born in 1979 in Saudi Arabia.[94] As head of ISIS's media operations, al-Absi is considered by some to be among the top five most important members of ISIS leadership, and a serious candidate as Baghdadi's successor.[95] In fact, he is credited with bringing Omar al-Shishani to Baghdadi.[96]

Al-Absi marshals a large number of full-time media personnel, and through his efforts, ISIS has gained a reputation as "the first organization of this kind [to understand] the impact of social media,"[97] deploying strategies such as "Twitter bombs" to drive recruitment online, especially among foreign fighters and younger fighters.[98] In addition to social media, al-Absi relies on a host of (largely anonymous) bloggers[99] and in July 2014 launched *Dabiq*, a high production value, glossy-style online magazine.

In late summer 2012, his older brother, the ISIS fighter Firas al-Absi (a.k.a. Sheikh Abu Mohammed al-Absi), was killed in Syria by other rebel forces.[100],[101] This event prompted al-Absi to join up with al-Baghdadi for whom he previously served as ISIS's governor of Aleppo.[102],[103] In this capacity, sources speculate that he was responsible for many of the group's kidnappings in Syria.[104] Al-Absi is also responsible for engaging with important regional religious leaders and other significant players.[105]

Jihadi John—Mohammed Emwazi: "The Face of ISIS"

For many, a black-hooded Mohammed Emwazi is the image that comes to mind when thinking of ISIS. He was the ISIS Lord High Executioner nicknamed "Jihadi John."

Emwazi was born in born in al-Jahra, Kuwait in 1988 to Kuwaiti parents, and raised in North Kensington, London. He was known to have wanted to play for the Manchester United football team. One of his teachers described him as "reasonably hard working," and noted he had been bullied. He would become the iconic voice and face of the ISIS death cult.[106]

After graduating from University of Westminster in 2009 with a degree in computing, he went to Tanzania under an assumed name, "Muhammad ibn Muazzam." Upon returning, he said he had been interrogated by British authorities, who suggested he was involved with the al-Qaeda–backed al-Shabaab militia.[107] He denied being involved with al-Shabaab, but according to hostages who met Emwazi he was obsessed with Somalia and forced them to watch videos about Somalia. After he successfully returned to England, he met with Asim Qureshi of the London-based CAGE, a human rights advocacy group, and told him "that he had been very unfairly treated" by British authorities.[108]

He later moved to Kuwait and worked in business. After a few trips back and forth between Kuwait and London, British authorities held him once again. He disclosed to Qureshi that he was frustrated at how he was being scrutinized, saying "I feel like a prisoner, only not in a cage, in London." He then disappeared.

"Jihadi John" would become infamous after Aug 19, 2014, when a video called "A Message to America" depicting the graphic beheading of kidnapped journalist James Foley was broadcast worldwide. Then came "A Second Message to America," which ended with the beheading of

American journalist Steven Sotloff. He took part in beheading British citizens David Haines, then Alan Henning, twenty-one Syrian soldiers, and then Peter Kassig. In January 2015, "Jihadi John" was featured in the execution videos of Haruna Yukawa and then Kenji Goto.

Emwazi was part of a crew that would guard Western hostages in the Syrian town of Idlib. Here his captives nicknamed the four British captors "the Beatles." The hostages used the name to keep track of who was present and they had named Emwazi "John" after John Lennon.

Speculation on the identity of "Jihadi John" was rampant until February 2015, when friends of Emwazi identified him to the *Washington Post*, stating "He was like a brother to me . . . I'm sure it was him." His mother claimed she knew it was him."[109]

British intelligence pulled out all of the stops to locate and neutralize "the Beatles" and kill Emwazi in particular. British intelligence operated American MQ-9 Reaper drones to identify and kill high-value ISIS commanders. Somehow, Emwazi appeared to intelligence operators, allowing them to identify him through drones and track his movements. On November 12, 2015, a drone identified him leaving a building and entering a car in Raqqa, Syria. He was instantly vaporized.[110]

AN AMERICAN IN ISIS—THE LIFE AND DEATH OF DOUGLAS MACARTHUR MCCAIN

Douglas McArthur McCain was born in Chicago, Illinois on January 29, 1981. He frequently moved between Chicago and New Hope, a suburb of Minneapolis. He attended Robbinsdale Cooper High School and Robbinsdale Armstrong High School, played on the basketball team, and was known as a "fun guy to be around" according to his friends. In high school, he was best friends with Troy Kastigar, who went to fight and die with al-Shabaab in Somalia.

After he dropped out of high school, McCain accumulated a criminal record with misdemeanor theft, marijuana possession, disorderly conduct, obstruction of public official, driving without a license, and other charges starting in 2000.[111] He eventually moved from the Minneapolis area to San Diego around 2004. Somewhere during that move he converted to Islam. A tweet posted on May 14, 2014 said "I reverted to Islam 10 years ago and I must say In sha Allah I will never look back the best thing that ever happen to me."

He attended San Diego City College[112] and worked for a Somali restaurant named "African Spice" in the City Heights area of San Diego. A local who saw him at the restaurant claimed he smoked and was not very religious. "He was just a regular American kid."[113] He claimed on Facebook that he worked for the Dawah-Calling to Allah.[114] In San Diego, he attended the Masjid Nur mosque in City Heights. Attendees were quoted in local reports as being surprised at the reports of his death and association with ISIS.

After his conversion, McCain went to Sweden to compete in a rap battle. Those who interacted with him during this trip said he was very clearly devoted to Islam, but as one person, Kevin Kohlin, noted, "He respected my Christianity."[115]

His Facebook account was under the name "Duale ThaslaveAllah;" on Twitter he was "Duale Khalid" with "It's Islam over everything" as his tag line.[116] He also reposted from this account a prayer for ISIS: "It takes a warrior to understand a warrior. Pray for ISIS." In another tweet he said, "Ya allah, when it's my time to go have mercy on my soul have mercy on my bros."[117] A subsequent tweet republished the entire translation of a speech given by ISIS spokesman, Abu Mohammad al-Adnani.

He travelled to Syria via Istanbul. Locals who remember him said he travelled with the name "Duale" and was eager to talk about basketball.[118] On June 9, 2014, he told another Twitter user "I'll be joining you soon." A

Arrest photo by Anoka County Sheriffs, Minnesota 2003

Arrest photo by Hennepin County Sheriffs 2008

day later he would post another tweet on June 10, 2014, saying "I'm with the brothers now," perhaps indicating when he crossed the border and joined ISIS.

He was killed in Syria in August 2014, in a skirmish between ISIS and the Free Syrian Army. He was easily identified by his tattoos. He was found with $800 and his US passport (see below).[119] He was one of fifteen young men to join ISIS from the Minnesota area.

MANPOWER POOL OF THE CULT INTERNATIONAL

HOW MANY MEMBERS?

There's no exact headcount as to how many fighters are in the ranks of ISIS. This happens not only because any estimate is based on guesswork, but also because ISIS has grown rapidly since its self-proclamation as a caliphate: countless people around the world joined it daily. Depending on the source, there are wildly different numbers: 9,000–18,000 (US intelligence), 20,000–31,000 (CIA), 50,000 in Syria alone (Syrian Observatory for Human Rights), 70,000 (Russian General Staff), 100,000 (Baghdad-based security expert Hisham al-Hashimi), and 200,000 (the chief of staff to Kurdish president).[120]

Most fighters are, understandably, from Syria and Iraq. A Reuters report based on an inside source claims that 90 percent of fighters in Iraq are Iraqi and 70 percent of fighters in Syria are Syrian.[121] Still, many of ISIS's most effective fighters are foreigners from around the world. A UN Security Council report from March 2015 estimated that some 22,000 fighters from 100 different nations have traveled to Syria and Iraq to support ISIS.[122]

In December 2015, the Soufan Group released a report entitled "Foreign Fighters—An Updated Assessment of the Flow of Foreign Fighters into Syria." The data was drawn from a variety of sources, including official numbers presented by governments and estimates by various organizations, regional specialists, or from news sources.

Soufan calculated that between 27,000 and 31,000 people from 86 countries have left their homes to join ISIS or other jihadist groups. By contrast, in June 2014, when ISIS declared itself a Caliphate, the Soufan Group estimated in "Foreign Fighters in Syria" that the initial number was around 12,000 fighters from 81 countries.

Additionally, they noted that thus far the efforts to limit fighters show limited impact. However, the increase in fighters is not uniform. Western Europe saw double the fighters since June 2014. North America saw no change, whereas Russia and Central Asia experienced a significant rise, an estimated 300 percent increase since June 2014. They speculate that the rate of return to the West may be as high as 20–30 percent.

In light of admissions that the existing insurgents have an ability to rapidly regenerate at a consistent rate, any numbers projected on their manpower could quickly become unreliable.

The US Combined Joint Task Force estimates ISIS has lost 23,000 soldiers and defectors since the air campaign began in June 2014. Rates of defections are also said to have increased. In November 2015, ninety fighters surrendered to Kurdish forces. Twenty-two surrendered that same month during an offense near Ramadi.

THE FIGHTERS

The Americas

Canada: Canadian officials place the number of fighters in Syria/Iraq at 130.[123] One Canadian, André Poulin, was killed in Syria after being filmed for an al-Hayat video called "The Chosen Few of Different Lands." Also Damian Clairmont, 22, died fighting with ISIS in Syria in January 2014.

USA: The House Homeland Security committee says around 250 Americans have traveled to Syria/Iraq to fight. October 21, 2015, FBI Director Comey said the rate of recruitment is down. Official: 150. Unofficial: 250+. Director of National Intelligence James Clapper stated in March 2015 that forty have returned to the US. [124]

Brazil: Official: 3.[125]

Chile: One fighter from Chile has died in Syria: Bastian Vazquez, known as Abu Sifayya.

Trinidad and Tobago: After the Paris attacks, Trinidad confirmed that eighty-nine citizens had joined ISIS.[126]

Western Europe

Austria: Official: 300. Unofficial: 233. Returnees: 70.[127]

Belgium: The Belgian government suggested that there are 180–190 fighters in Syria/Iraq, with 60–70 killed. The official return count by the government is 118 as of July 2015. Belgian researcher Pieter Van Ostaeyen calculated 516 Belgians in ISIS.[128]

Britain: British police said that 700 or more people had joined ISIS. There are an estimated 350 who have returned home.[129]

Denmark: Danish Security and Intelligence Service put the number of Danes joining the fight in Iraq/Syria at 125. [130]

France: Official: 1,700. Returnees: 250 (May 2015).[131]

Finland: According to Veli-Pekka Kivimaki at Finnish National Defence University, there are seventy Finns fighting in Syria/Iraq, whereas fifteen have been killed and twenty returned home. [132]

Germany: Interior Minister Thomas de Maiziere stated that 760 Germans, many with dual citizenship, have joined ISIS, 120 have been killed, and that 200 have returned.[133]

Ireland: Alan Shatter, former Minister of Justice, said that there were around forty Irish fighters and that they associate with the British fighters. He noted that they were "perfect snipers." [134]

Italy: In September 2015, Italian Minister of Defense Roberta Pinotti stated that eighty-seven Italians are in the fight in Iraq/Syria[135]. *Il Giornale* reported ten fighters had returned to Italy in early 2015.[136]

Netherlands: Officials said that an average of five "jihadists" leave every month and as of October 1, 2015, a total of 220 had left to join ISIS. They believe around forty have returned home. The death count in Syria Iraq is "very likely" forty-two. They estimate that 140 fighters are left.[137]

Norway: Official: 81.[138]

Portugal: In early 2015, after the death of a boy named Abu al-Faruq and his father Abu Juwairiya al-Portughali, Lisbon officials give the estimate that twelve to fifteen citzens of Portugal have joined ISIS.[139]

Spain: Official: 133. Unofficial: 250.[140]

Sweden: Säpo (Swedish Security Service) official Anders Thornberg states around three hundred Swedes have travelled to Iraq/Syria to fight with ISIS. Forty have been killed. The Swedish Security Service has identified 115 returnees. [141]

Switzerland: FIS states that there are seventy-one cases on record, fifty-seven who went to Syria/Iraq, fourteen who went to Somalia, Afghanistan, and Pakistan. It is believed that fifteen are dead including eight confirmed. There are seven confirmed returnees.[142]

Balkans

Albania: ICSR-International Center for the Study of Radicalisation and Political Violence published a report tracking foreign fighters suggesting ninety fighters; other estimates push the range up to one hundred.[143]

Bosnia: Official: 330. Unofficial: 217. Returnees: 51.[144]

Kosovo: The Minister of Internal Affairs stated in February 2015 the estimate number of fighters is around three hundred.[145]
Serbia: Unofficial: fifty to seventy.[146]

Russia and Eastern Europe

Azerbaijani: Official: 104+. Unofficial: 216. Returnees: 49.[147]
Georgia: Georgian officials say that fifty or more citizens have joined ISIS. The Integration Foundation of Caucuses People put the number closer to two hundred.[148]
Macedonia: Official: 146. Unofficial: 100.[149]
Moldova: 1+.[150]
Montenegro: The government of Montenegro hasn't confirmed any numbers, but Radio Free Europe claimed a CIA document numbered thirty fighters in Syria/Iraq.[151]
Romania: 1+.[152]
Russia: Official: 2,400. [153]

Central Asia

Afghanistan: Unofficial: 50. [154]
Kazakhstan: Official: 300.[155]
Kyrgyzstan: Unofficial: 500.[156]
Tajikistan: Official: 386.[157]
Turkmenistan: Unofficial: 360.[158]
Uzbekistan: While Tashkent claims 500 Uzbeks are fighting in Iraq/Syria, the Crisis Group suggests that the number is closer to 2,500.[159]

Near East and Levant

Jordan: Official: 2,000+. Unofficial: 2,500.[160]
Lebanon: Official: 900.[161]
Turkey: Officia: 2,000–2,200. Returnees: 600+.

Arabian Gulf States

Saudi Arabia: The Brookings Institute has reported the number of Saudi fighters as 2,500.[162]
UAE: Unofficial: 15.[163]
Qatar: Unofficial: 10.[164]
Kuwait: Unofficial: 70.[165]

North Africa
Algeria: Official: 170. Unofficial: 200–250.[166]
Egypt: Official: 600+. Unofficial: 1,000.[167]
Libya: Unofficial: 600.[168]
Morocco: According to a study by the German Institute for International-al Security and Affairs, the growth of Moroccan fighters jumped from 1,122 in June 2014 to over 1,500. This does not include Europeans of Moroccan ancestry, which would add another 1,000.[169]
Tunisians: More than 6,000, Unofficial: 7,000. Returnees: 625+.[170]

Sub-Saharan Africa (Does Not Include Nigeria)
Somalia: Unofficial: 70.[171]
South Africa: In May 2015, Al Jazeera reported that twenty-three or more families went to Iraq/Syria. Two South Africans have been killed fighting in Syria. Official: 1.[172]
Sudan: The Ministry of Interior stated that around seventy Sudanese have traveled to Libya and Syria to join ISIS. [173]

East and Southeast Asia
Cambodia: Official: 1.[174]
China: A Chinese state-run newspaper announced that around three hundred Uigurs have joined ISIS. China says fighters are coming from the East Turkestan Islamic Movement (ETIM), though some have said ETIM is a regional interest not tied to ISIS.[175]
India: India has acknowledged twenty-three Indian citizens have joined ISIS, many going through Pakistan first. India says ISIS has no footing in India, but that 150 youth are under surveillance. [176]
Indonesia: Official: 700. Unofficial: 500. Returnees: 162.[177]
Japan: Former Air Force official Toshio Tamogami stated that Israeli for-eign ministry official Nissim Ben Shitrit reported nine Japanese citizens were in Syria/Iraq.[178]
Madagascar: Official: 3+.[179]
Malaysia: Official: 100. Returnees: 5+.[180]
Maldives: Despite the size of the country, the Maldives has an estimated two hundred fighters who joined ISIS. [181]
Pakistan: Official: 70. Unofficial: 330.[182]

Philippines: Former President Fidel Ramos stated the total of Filipinos who had joined ISIS was around one hundred. The most recent report comes only after a few months of the establishment of "The Islamic State." (Aug 2014)[183]

Singapore: Official: 2.[184]

Australasia

Australia: Assistant Secretary Cameron Gifford said that around 120 Australians are engaged in fighting in Syria/Iraq. Between 32 and 42 have been killed. He said approximately 30 Australians have returned home and that 170 people are providing material support.[185]

New Zealand: Official: 5–10. Unofficial: 6.[186]

CHAPTER 3

THE CALIPHATE ORGANIZATIONAL STRUCTURE

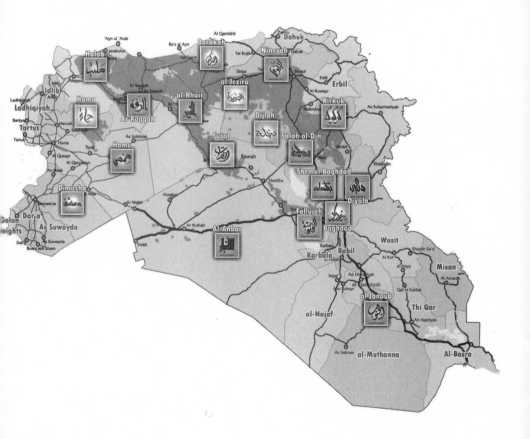

CALIPHATE LEVEL—LEADERSHIP

CALIPH

Caliph Ibrahim al-Qureyshi (Abu Bakr al-Baghdadi)

DEPUTY POSITIONS

Deputy/Emir of Syria
Abu Ali al-Anbari (KIA December 12, 2015)

Deputy/Emir of Iraq
Abu Muslim al-Turkmani. Real name: Fadil Ahmad Abdallah al-Hayyali (KIA August 18, 2015)

CABINET-LEVEL COUNCILS

Financial Council
Muafaq Mustafa Mohammed al-Khamoush (KIA)

Leadership Council
Abu Muslim al-Afari al-Turkmani

Military Council
Walid Mohammed al-Alwani, a.k.a. Abu Ahmad al-Alwani
Deputy to Alwani: Omar al-Shishani[187]
Feres Reif al-Naima (Chief of Logistics and Supplies)[188]
Abdul Rahman al-Afari (Oversees Martyr's families)[189]
Khairy Abed Mahmoud al-Taey a.k.a. Abu Kifah (Supervises IED deployment)[190]
Abdullah Ahmed al-Mashhadani (Supplies Foreign Fighters)[191]
Previous Heads of Military Council:
Adnan Latif Hamid al-Sweidawi (KIA November 7, 2014 in Mosul)
Adnan Ismail Najm al-Bilawai al-Dulaimi a.k.a. Abu Abdulrahman al-Bilawi (KIA June 4, 2014 in Mosul)

Sharia Council
Abu Mohammed al-Ani

Internal Security
Abu Ali al-Anbari (possible KIA)

Intelligence
Unknown

Media Council
Abu al Athir Amr al Absi

SHURA COUNCIL

Abu Arkan al-Amiri (Head of Shura Council)
Abu Muslim al-Afari al-Turkmani
Abu Ali al-Anbari
Omar al-Shishani
Abu Ayman al-Iraqi
Abu al-Athir Amr al-Absi
Abu Muhammad al-Adnani

Border
Ridwan Taleh Hussein Ismail Hamduni (Abu Jarnas)

Other ISIS Leaders
Wahib Shaker al-Fahdawi (Abu Wahib)
Lafadarim Mohaskari (Abu Abdullah al-Kosovi)
Abu Khutab al-Kurdi (Led Kobani campaign)
Abu Hazifa al-Yamani
Abu Omar (the boxer)
Ahmed Abu Samra (American-Syrian)
Turki al-Banali (Abu Himam al-Athari), referred to as Emir of North
Africa in some reports
Bashar Ismail al-Hamdani (Abu Mohammed)—prisoner control
Abdul Wahed Khudair Ahmed (Abu Luay)—general security official
Mohammed Hamid al-Dulaimi (Abu Hajer al-Assafi)—mail official
Auf Abdul Rahman al-Afawi (Abu Saja)

Ahmed Abousamra (Media Center Work)

THE SYRIAN COMMAND

DEPUTY/EMIR OF SYRIA

Abu Ali al-Anbari (KIA-December 12, 2015)

ALEPPO (HALAB)

Governate Overview
Aleppo (Halab) is the most populous region in Syria, located in the semi-arid Aleppo Plateau with 10 districts, 32 towns, 1430 villages. The district borders Turkey along key entry points such as Gaziantep. The main cities are Aleppo, Manbij, As Safirah, Al-Bab, Ayn Al-Arab, Afrin, A'zaz, Dayr Hafir, Jarabulus and Atarib. Population: 4.9 million.

Organization
Wali: Omar Al-Absi a.k.a. Abu Atheer al-Absi (possibly removed)[192]

Army Leadership
Abu Osama al-Tunisi

Additional Commanders
Hassan Aboud al-Sarmini

Estimated Fighter Count
4,000[193]

Campaigns/Battles
Battle of Aleppo 2012–Present: The battle of Aleppo, also known as the "mother of battles," began on July 19, 2012 and is still ongoing. The al-Nusra Front have about two thousand[194] of the estimated 6–15 thousand rebel fighters[195] [196] from a vast array of secular and not-so-secular groups, which are widely outnumbered by the other side: 28–30

thousand members of the pro-Assad Syrian forces accompanied by Hezbollah.[197]

As for the "outcome" of this seemingly unending conflict, it is impossible to say who has won or lost. At this point, the city and its surrounding area are held, variously, by the Syrian Army, the Kurds, and the opposition, while the immense "state within a state" that is now under the sway of ISIS is less than 15 km from the Old City. At the same time, control of some of the other parts of the city and its environs are often more or less in play.[198]

Other Battles

Kuweires Offensive—September 14, 2015–November 16, 2015: ISIS held the Kuweires Military Airbase for two years. The Syrian Arab Army fought to uproot ISIS control of Kuweires Airbase with cooperation from the National Defense Forces and the Al-Ba'ath Battalion. Additionally, the operation notably involved support from the Iranian Quds force and from Russian airstrikes.[199]

Siege of Kobane: September 13, 2014–March 15, 2015: ISIS started its offensive against Kobane on September 13, 2015 with a massive campaign to overwhelm the local forces. Using freshly captured tanks, they took twenty-one Kurdish villages in twenty-four hours. Within two more days they had a total of sixty villages under their control. Forty-five thousand people fled to Turkey. By late September, ISIS was within 10 km of Kobane and was shelling the city from the outskirts. [200] By early October, ISIS had control of 350 villages.[201] On October 5, ISIS began to enter the city of Kobane with the capture of Mistanour Hill, and then on further into the streets of the south side of the city. On October 6, ISIS raised its flag in the southeastern area of the city.[202] The gains made on October 6, were reversed by Kurdish forces the next day with help from American airstrikes. Over the coming days, however, ISIS would continue its push until it captured the headquarters of the Kurdish forces on October 10, 2014.[203]

Over six months, the People's Protection Units (YPG) would battle with ISIS through the city until they pushed ISIS out of both the city of Kobane by January 26, 2015 and recaptured the villages by March 15, 2015. The YPG and allies lost 1,405 people. Up to two thousand ISIS mujahideen died, with eighteen tanks destroyed.

BARAKAH A.K.A. AL-HASAKAH

Province Overview
Cities: Al-Hasakah, Jaza, Kahtanieh, al-Maabadah, al-Mnajeer, Tel Baydar, Tel Erphan, Tel Hamees. The population is approximately 1.5 million.

Organization
Wali: Abu Osama al-Iraqi[204]

Army Leader
Top Commander may be Abdul Mohsen al-Zaghilani al-Taresh[205]

Fighter Count
6,000

Notable Leaders
Ahmed Alaqqal was emir over Tel Abiad and Hesba. He was beheaded in Suluk after ISIS found him to be a drug dealer. The Alaqqal family was key to establishing ISIS. Their family is very involved in ISIS with lots of members as senior leaders. Hadi Alaqqal is a founder of al-Nusra Front.[206]

Campaigns
The Battle of Ras al-Ayn, November 8, 2012[207] – July 17, 2013[208]: The Syrian army left the city of thirty thousand inhabitants[209] in mid-November 2012 and an armed conflict broke out between the Kurds of the YPG and rebel forces.[210]

At one point in the battle, around two hundred fighters from the al-Nusra Front and one hundred fighters from an FSA faction, Ghuraba al-Sham, some of whose members favor a secular state and some of whom are Islamist, faced off with around four hundred Kurdish combatants.[211] After two earlier ceasefires,[212] the second of which included the participation of the FSA,[213] the third and final phase of the battle ended in July of 2013 with a victory for the Kurdish militia, and the division of the city into an eastern half and a western half: one under Arab control and the other under Kurdish control, as well as the expulsion of the jihadis from the city.[214],[215] This eventual division of the city occurred in spite of an attempt on the part of Kurdish PYD to foster unity in January of 2013 by raising the FSA flag alongside the PYD flag at a plenary meeting of the Kurdish militia. This was somewhat surprising, since the fighters of the YPG militia had been known to kidnap or attack those who dared to raise the FSA colors in their territory.[216]

Battle of Markadah, March 21–31, 2014: In a direct attack on the al-Nusra front, ISIS laid siege to Markadahin in late March 2014. The ISIS fighters drove al-Nusra front into a local hospital and local Mt. Markadah. Eventually, ISIS fighters drove the remaining al-Nusra front fighters and Omar al-Faruq al-Turki was killed.[217] The town seizure gives ISIS control over very important weapons and a route between al-Hasakah and Deir ez-Zor, or al-Mayadin.

DIMASHQ

Governorate Overview
Capital: Damascus. Population: 2,836,000. Located in the Southwestern part of Syria, Wilayat Dimashq borders Lebanon and Jordan.

Organization
Wali: Abu Ayyub al-Iraqi[218]
Fighter Count: around 1,500[219]

Campaigns/Battles
Yarmouk Camp: Yarmouk Camp was overtaken by ISIS in April 2015. After first attempting to overrun the camp, the ISIS fighters were repelled before they successfully overtook the camp on April 4, 2014.[220] The fighting saw a clash between three different alliances, with ISIS and al-Nusra fighting against Aknaf Bait al-Maqdis, Free Syrian Army, and Jaysh al-Islam fighters and the alliance of Syrian Armed Forces, Palestine Liberation Army, Popular Front for the Liberation of Palestine (PFLP) and Fatah al-Intifada. Within days, the Palestine Liberation Army joined with their allies to attack ISIS. Despite a small advance against them, ISIS remained in control. Then came the attacks from Jaysh al-Islam on April 12. There were small and steady advances, but more important

were the changes in alignments of the groups involved on both sides. The Aknaf Bait al-Maqdis cease to exist as the members joined the Syrian regime forces. Many members of al-Nusra Front left to join ISIS.[221] Though ISIS retreated by late April, the fighting continued until by June 8, 2015, when ISIS was driven from the camp. The camp's population is around 18,000 civilians. [222]

GEZIRA

History-Province Overview
Wali: Unknown

Campaigns/Battles

HAMA

Wali: Unknown
Army Commandeder: Unknown

Battles
Major combat occurred in Hama, including the siege of the city by Syrian Arab Army forces in 2011 and three major offensives by the rebel forces in 2012–2014, led by the Free Syrian Army and an alliance including the Jebhat al-Nusra. At this juncture the JAN was no longer a branch of ISIS.

HOMS

Organization
Wali: Abu Yehya al-Iraqi

Campaigns/Battles
Battle of Homs, May 2011–May 2014: the siege of Homs pitted the rebels against the SAA and its allies, among whom was Hezbollah.[223] At some point after January 2012, the new ISIS-created al-Nusra Front[224] [225] [226] [227] would become one of the rebel forces active in the siege, using

bombs or fighting alongside the FSA and the other rebels or on the periphery of the city.[228] By May 8, 2014, Bashar al-Assad was able to lay claim to a major victory, after having succeeded in driving the rebels out of a city with a million citizens that had earlier been seen as the "cradle of the revolution."[229] In the two years before they were expelled, around two thousand rebels may have been killed.[230] Some SAA soldiers went over to the rebel side, only to be routed after a long fight.

The sectarian and political violence that occurred during the siege of Homs was at times "exemplary." For instance, on July 17, 2011, three supporters of the Assad regime were kidnapped and then dismembered, while the pieces of their bodies were then sent back to their families as a reminder.[231] The Arab League, some of whose members were aiding the rebels, tried to intervene to little or no avail.[232] For its part, the Assad regime was taken to task by Ban Ki-moon for torture and summary executions.[233]

Battle of Sadad, October 21-28, 2013: (Syrian Army Victory)

First Battle of the Shaer Gas Field, July 16–26, 2014

Battle of Arsal, August 2–7, 2014: The war spills into Lebanon (see chapter 4)

Battle of Mahin, October 31, 2015: On October 31, 2015, ISIS launched two VBIED attacks on the eastern side of Mahin, killing four from the National Defense Force and two from the Palestine Liberation Army. After the night attack the NDF and PLA forces retreated to Sadad. The NDF attempted to drive ISIS from Mahin early in November but failed.[234] On November 23, 2015, SSNP, NDF from Sadad, Desert Hawks Brigade, and Gozarto Protection Forces joined together to uproot ISIS from Mahin. [235]

Battle of Al-Qaryatayn, August 5–10, 2015: Victory for ISIS. Al-Qaryatayn came under ISIS assault after successfully staying out of the civil war for four years. After years of successfully remaining engaged but neutral between government and rebel forces, ISIS began its advance to take over the town of forty thousand with suicide attacks on local checkpoints.[236]

AL-KHAIR (DEIR EZ-ZOR)

Organization
Wali: Haji Abdul Nasser[237]
Army Leader: Ahmed al-Mohammed al-Obaid (Abu Dijana al-Zer)[238]
Fighting Force: around 9,000

Campaigns/Battles
Battle of Deir ez-Zor, July 2011–July 14, 2014: The Syrian Army arrived in July of 2011 in order to secure the city during what came to be known, nationwide, as the "Ramadan massacre."[239] The mêlée in Deir ez-Zor continued for many months and included a partial retreat by the SAA, defections from the army, the killing of SAA forces by defectors,[240] a rebel attack on an army base in which twelve SAA infantry were killed,[241] a car bomb that took the lives of nine people outside an SAA intelligence complex,[242] and a cease-fire arranged by the U.N. By May of 2012 many towns and villages in Deir ez-Zor province were in the hands of the rebels,[243] among whom was the al-Nusra Front.[244] The clashes resumed, becoming more intense, with shelling by the SAA,[245] along with advances and retreats, and the seizure of the key Siyasiyeh Bridge over the Euphrates by the rebels on January 29, 2013, thereby cutting off SAA supply lines to the province of Hasakah.[246] On May 3, 2013, the Deir Ez-Zor suspension bridge was shelled by the FSA and destroyed. That left the Siyasiyeh Bridge as the only major link to the province of Hasakah (it too was blown up by the SAA in September 2014).[247]

The fighting as well as the stalemate at Deir ez-Zor continued with Assad's forces retaining control of part of the city. ISIS executed its major offensive there from April 10–July 14, 2014 in order to vanquish the other rebel forces that were still active in the Deir-ez-Zor governorate. It succeeded rather decisively. Among the National Coalition forces that ISIS routed was, ironically, the al-Nusra Front,[248] of which ISIS had earlier been a part, along with the FSA and the Islamic Brigades.[249] After three months of violent clashes, ISIS had gained hold of almost the entire Deir ez-Zor governorate, one of the largest in Syria.[250] Around half of the city of Deir ez-Zor[251] and the SAF airport remained in the hands of the SAA, which did not take part in the inter-rebel fighting.[252] Heavy clashes then went on for months between the SAA and the Islamic State.

AR-RAQQA

Organization
Wali: Taha Subhi Falaha a.k.a. Abu Muhammad al-Adnani- ISIS Spokeman
Army Commander: Ali al-Hamoud a.k.a. Ali Moussa al-Shawakh[253]
Fighting Force: Around 11,000
Additional leaders in Raqqa:
Ali al-Hamoud, "Ali Moussa al-Shawakh"
Abdullah al-Shoukh
Todab al-Barij al-Abdul Hadi—Tribal issues
Abdul Rahman al-Sahu—Security
Abu Hamza al-Riyadiyat—Security
Abu Hassan al-Furati—Security

Campaigns/Battles
2014 Eastern Syria Offensive: July 23–August 28, 2014
Battle of al-Taqba Air Base: August 10–28, 2014
Seizure of Raqqa, 2013: There was an armed conflict outside the city of Raqqa that may have served as a prelude to the battle of Raqqa, which began on March 4, 2013.[254] As the uprising began to spread across the landscape of Syria, twenty people, eight of them children and three women, were killed in late December 2012 in the village of Qahtaniya, not far from the city of Raqqa, when the village was shelled by Syrian army tanks. According to the Syrian Observatory for Human Rights, no al-Nusra fighters were in Qahtaniya at the time. The deaths of these twenty people had followed the earlier advance across the region of Syrian rebel forces.[255]

By early 2013, the rebels had taken over a lot of the northern part of country, but had failed to secure a single major city. They began to plan an attack on Raqqa.

The seven thousand rebel fighters during the battle were led by the al-Nusra Front, along with elements of the FSA and Ahrar al-Sham, the major Islamic rebel group in Syria at the time.[256] The rebels approached the city from the north[257] and took on the Syrian security forces in violent clashes around the city's government offices. On March 4, 2013, when they seized the main square in the city, the police and border guards were seen leaving, without being harried in any way by the rebels. This occurred after Assad's forces at the eastern gate of the city had already left and handed over the entire eastern district to the rebels without a fight. Raqqa, the first major city to be taken by the opposition, fell in only a few hours. Some of military and security officers who decided to fight to the end were killed and then mutilated.[258] After a little shove by the rebels, the golden statue of Hafez, Bashar's father fell onto the main square.[259] More than three hundred members of the Ba'athist security forces were captured with nearly equal ease.[260] A new tyranny would soon begin as the city was designated as the new capital of the "Islamic state." The Syrian regime called in air strikes soon after the al-Nusra-led victory.[261] [262]

THE IRAQ COMMAND

Deputy/Emir of Iraq:
Abu Muslim al-Turkmani. Real name: Fadil Ahmad Abdallah al-Hayyali (KIA August 18, 2015)

ANBAR

Province Overview
Anbar is the largest of the Iraqi wilayat. Its capital was Ramadi. Its estimated population was just above 1.5 million. It lies west of Fallujah and Haditha. It is

overwhelmingly Sunni and the largest tribe is the Duliami. It is divided into seven districts.

Wali: Adnan Latif Hamid al-Sweidawi (KIA November 7, 2014 in Mosul)

Campaigns/Battles

Anbar Campaign, December 30, 2013–June 25, 2014: The Dulaimis had been holding demonstrations against the Maliki government following the arrest of a Sunni finance minister the year before. Protests had also spread to Ramadi, Samarra, Tikrit and beyond. Al-Qaim, Abu Ghraib are also seized.

Fall of Fallujah, December 30, 2013–January 4, 2014: For a year, protesters in Anbar had raised their voices in opposition to Maliki's Shi'ite-dominated government. But after authorities arrested a prominent Sunni lawmaker, the tensions boiled over. On December 30, 2013, as many people in the area reacted in anger at the arrest, army patrols on the highway to Ramadi came under fire from militants.[263] Within two days ISIS gained more control over the town.

The Iraqi Army withdrew after fighting. A majority of police walked away from their posts. To compound that problem, one hundred inmates were freed from a local prison. By January 4, 2014, Iraqi security official in Anbar announced that Fallujah had fallen to ISIS control.[264]

Northern Iraq Offensive, Jun 5–25, 2014: ISIS captures Saqlawiya on June 15, 2014.

The Siege of Saqlawiya[265], September 14–22, 2014: Camp Saqlawiya had been locked down after being surrounded by ISIS fighters for a week. The soldiers in the camp were hopeful for reinforcements when ISIS fighters arrived. Instead of help, ISIS hit them with two SVBIED attacks. The militants were dressed as soldiers according to survivors. The Humvees they were driving detonated along with three SPBIEDs. Those who survived the attack were rounded up and massacred. Between three hundred and five hundred soldiers were killed.[266]

The Battle of Ramadi, November 21, 2014–May 17, 2015: Though ISIS had partially controlled Ramadi before, the government held control over the city until late in the year, when ISIS announced its new Wilayat in Anbar. In November, ISIS launched a four-front assault on

Ramadi using mortars, VBIEDs, and run-and-gun attacks that killed twenty soldiers.[267] Fighting continued between ISIS fighters and government forces as ISIS sought to gain control of the government buildings. Repeatedly, local tribal forces and government forces would repel the attacks, which were heavy and sustained, for months.

By January 2015, Iraqi forces launched operations to "cleanse" the area of ISIS fighters. But on March 11, ISIS attacked again with car bombs and SPBIED attacks and again government forces kept them at bay. Despite the efforts of the government forces in April of 2015, it would be an attack on May 14, 2015, that would turn the tables. Using heavily armored bulldozers and ten SVBIEDs, they rammed the gates of the government complex and captured the police headquarters and the Ramadi Great Mosque. They then raised the ISIS flag on the provincial government building.[268] By May 17, 2015, ISIS had complete control over Ramadi as Iraqi forces abandoned the city.[269] In December 2015, ISIS would lose the city and hundreds of fighters to a re-energized Iraqi army.

Events
March 4, 2013: Akashat ambush— ISIS claims a cross border attack on Syrian soldiers and Iraqi guards.[270]
October 2, 2014: The town al-Hit in western Iraq falls to ISIS.[271]
Aug 27, 2015: ISIS deploys an SVBIED attack that kills General Abdel Rahman Abu Ragheef, deputy commander of operations for Anbar and Brig Safeen Abdel Majeed.[272]

BAGHDAD

Organization
Wali: Ahmed Abdel Kader al-Jazaa (Abu Maysara)[273]

Battles
Aug 13, 2015: SVBIED attack kills 75 and injures 212.

DIJLAH/TIGRIS

Organization
Wali: Unknown

DIYALA

Province Overview
Diyala Governorate is in the northeast of Iraq along the Iranian border. There are six districts: Ba'quba, Al-Muqdadiya, Khanaqin, Al-Khalis, Kifri, and Balad Ruz. The population is estimated around 1.4 million.

Organization
Wali: Unknown

Campaigns
Northern Iraq Offensive (June 5–25, 2014)
June 15, 2014: ISIS takes control of Adhaim just north of Baghdad.
June 15, 2014: ISIS kills forty-four prisoners at Baqubah police station.
July 17, 2015: Khan Bani Saad bombing: 120–130 killed.

EUPHRATES

Organization
Wali: Ahmed Mohsen Khalf al-Juhaishi (Abu Fatima)

FALLUJAH

GEZIRA

Wali: Aasi ali Nasser al-Obeidi (KIA: January 10, 2016)

JUNOUB

Province Overview
Located in the south of Iraq, Basra, Nasiryyah, Suq al-Shuyukh, Faw, Al-Jabasiyya, Al-Medina, al-Zubayr, al-Huwayr, Al-Hammar, Al-Islah, Al-Samahwah, Al-Shafi, Abu al-Khasib, Al-Harithah, and Zawb'a.

KIRKUK

History-Province Overview
Located in the north of Iraq, Kirkuk has four districts, Al-Dibs, Daquq, Al-Hawijia, and Kirkuk. It has an estimated population of 1.4 million.

Wali: Ni'ma Abd Nayef al-Jabouri a.k.a. Abu Fatima al-Jaheishi[274]

Battles
Battle of Kirkuk: December 2014
Second battle of Kirkuk: January–February 2015

NINEVAH

Province Overview
Located on the northwestern border of Syria, Ninevah is a very diverse region with thirty districts, Mosul being the capital and most-populated district. The population is around 3.3 million.

Wali: Adnan Latif Hamed al-Suwaidawi a.k.a. Abu Mohannad (killed) replaced by unknown[275]

Campaigns/Battles
Northern Iraq Offensive, June 6, 2014
Battle of Mosul ("Battle of the Lion of God al-Bilawi"), June 5–25, 2014: Starting June 6, ISIS engages checkpoints on the west side of Mosul at 2:30 a.m. and advances into city. ISIS seized Mosul on Tuesday, June 10, by taking over the police stations, governor's headquarters,

airport, and military bases in the area. By the end of the day ISIS had raised its flag in town.[276] They released more than a thousand prisoners whom the Iraqi government claimed were al-Qaeda or ISIS members.[277]
Jun 15, 2014: ISIS captures Tal Afar and local airbase.[278]
Aug 1-4, 2014: Battle of Zumar—ISIS vs Peshmerga
Mosul Dam, Aug 6–16, 2014: ISIS seized the Mosul Dam on August 7, 2014. The United States, Iraqi, and Kurdish forces fought to recapture the dam and a local town nearby. With a combination of US airstrikes and Kurdish ground assault on the surrounding fighters' positions, three days later Iraqi and Kurdish forces announced the dam was no longer under ISIS control.[279]

The Sinjar Offensives: On August 3, 2014, ISIS began its campaign to seize Sinjar with an early morning raid.[280] For the next several months it would maintain control over the area and force the Yazidi populace to flee the area or seek refuge in the Sinjar mountains. ISIS massacred between two thousand and five thousand Yazidis and twenty thousand were displaced. In late October 2014, ISIS launched an effort to control the area around Mount Sinjar, thus stranding Yazidis on the mountain top without an avenue of escape. Starting on December 17, 2014, Peshmerga forces with US airstrike support began the first of two campaigns to break the "siege" of Mount Sinjar. After breaking the siege, Peshmerga forces then went on to clear the local area of ISIS, forcing them back to Tal Afar or Mosul. Though the Peshmerga forces were able to take back Sinjar and other villages, they were not able to uproot ISIS from Tal Afar. Between November 12 and 14 2015, Peshmerga forces again returned to clear ISIS from the Sinjar area.

NORTH BAGHDAD

Province Overview
Created by ISIS, this area contains parts of Baghdad, Taji, Husseiniyya, Saba' al-Bor, and Tagiyyat.

SALAHUDDIN

Province Overview
Samarra, Baiji, Tikrit, Hajjaj Village, Al-'Awjah, Al-Dur, Al-Mukishiyyafah, Al-Ishaqi, Al-Duluwiyyah, Balad, Siniyyah

Wali: Wissam Abdul Zayd al-Zubaydi a.k.a. Abu Nabil al-Ansari[281]

Campaigns
Northern Iraq Offensive (June 5–25, 2014)
June 5, 2014: Samarra attacked as part of Northern Iraq Offensive.
June 11, 2014: Tikrit attacked as part of Northern Iraq Offensive. ISIS called this battle "Battle of the Lion of God al-Bilawi." Tikrit falls to ISIS on June 11, 2014.[282]

Battles
June 11, 2014: ISIS attacks in Baiji.
June 11, 2014: ISIS kills over a thousand Iraqi Air Force members at Camp Speicher.[283]
Siege of Amirli, June 11, 2014: ISIS tries to lay siege to Amirli and is repelled by both militia forces and Iraqi government.[284]
The Camp Speicher Massacre, June 12, 2014: As military cadets were leaving their base to go on break see family, buses full of ISIS members pulled up and kidnapped them. They were taken to al-Qusour al-Re'asiya and nearly seventeen hundred were massacred. Photos and video released later shows the cadets by ISIS as they tied them up, and took them to be executed. Survivors told about playing dead and escaping after dark.[285] ISIS attacked the air base late on July 17, 2014, using SPBIEDs and snipers. [286]
First Battle of Tikrit, June 26–30, 2014: After ISIS had taken control of Tikrit, the Iraqi government launched an assault to remove ISIS from the city. In the first days, the Iraqi military engaged ISIS fighters around the University of Tikrit with helicopters and ground forces, including Iranian-trained militia members. Fighting lasted for four days until Iraqi forces retreated and left Tikrit in the hands of ISIS.
Second Battle of Tikrit: March 2–April 17, 2015

First Battle of Bajji, October 29–December 21, 2014: After ISIS captured large sections of northern Iraq in its June 2014 offensive, the Iraqi military with coalition assistance fought to drive ISIS out of the Baiji and the Baiji Oil Refinery. In the end, ISIS would remain in charge of Baiji.

Second Battle of Baiji, December 23, 2014: After the failure to drive ISIS from Baiji, Iraqi forces along with a coalition of local militias began a new campaign to drive ISIS from Baiji. The battles over the next several months would see an ebb and flow of ISIS control over Baiji, but ultimately the group held control. In April 2015, ISIS drew in hundreds of fighters from Syria to help hold the oil refinery.[287]

The battle for the refinery became a strategic objective for both ISIS and the government of Iraq. Thousands of Iraqi security forces and Shi'ite militiamen assaulted the facility for months. By May 2015, the Iraqis had ISIS out of the main complex. In September 2015, ISIS launched a fierce counterattack which partially displaced some Iraqi units. By January 2016, ISIS would finally be pushed out the contested ruins.

PART II:
WHERE THEY ARE

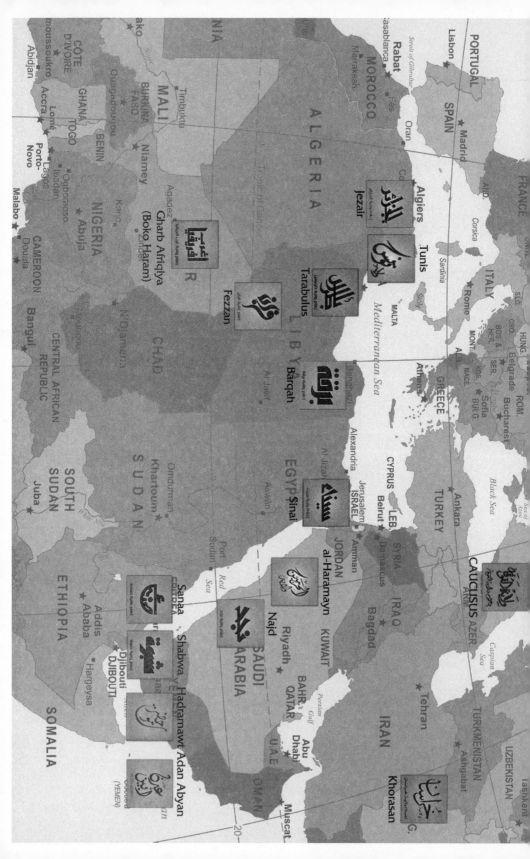

CHAPTER 4

ISIS IN THE LEVANT

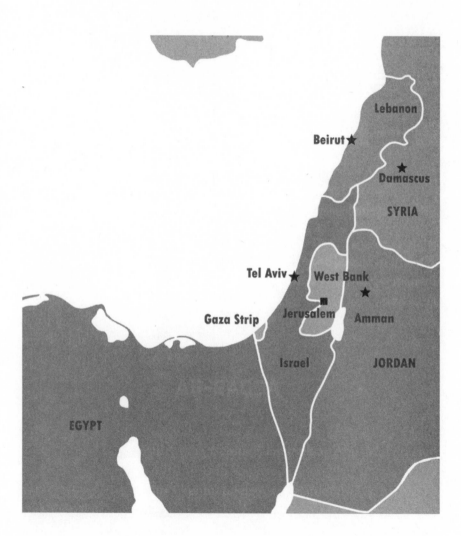

ISIS IN LEBANON

HISTORY

As a consequence of Lebanon's long civil war and raw sentiments among its participants generally along religious lines, Lebanon's Shi'ite population backed Syrian President Bashar al-Assadin the 2011 Syrian civil war.[288] The Iranian-backed Lebanese Shi'ite group Hezbollah became involved in the Syrian civil war in 2013, on the side of the Syrian government.[289] Many in Lebanon's non-Sunni population fear the turmoil that ISIS may spread and are arming themselves or expressing a desire to fight ISIS.[290] In Ras Baalbek, the Christian Militia and Hezbollah have made an unlikely mutual defense pact in the event of ISIS incursion.[291]

Due to Hezbollah's involvement in Syria, Lebanese Sunni elements have retaliated by bombing Hezbollah areas in Lebanon through 2013–2014, but it is unclear whether those elements were ISIS-affiliated.[292]

In 2014, ISIS led assaults on the Lebanese border city of Arsal and in Tripoli.[293] According to Major General Abbas Ibrahim, head of the Lebanese Directorate of General Security, ISIS troops infiltrated villages and areas around the Qalamoun Mountains bordering Syria in late 2014 and early 2015 to obtain advantageous positions for the fighting in Syria.[294] While ISIS has expressed a desire to invade Lebanon, its rival Jabhat al-Nusra does not want to fight the Lebanese government, as many of its fighters' families are refugees just over the Lebanese border.[295] There are 1.1 million Syrian refugees in Lebanon at this time.[296] Relations between al-Nusra and ISIS in that area are respectful due to a personal relationship between al-Nusra's Abu Malek al-Telli and Abu Bakr al-Baghdadi, and a tentative cease-fire with the Lebanese government remains, al-Nusra's influence in the area is waning.[297] Jabhat al-Nusra's Lebanese ally is the Abdallah Azzam Brigade.[298]

Major General Ibrahim has stated that there are more than a thousand ISIS fighters in Lebanon, drawing from the country's disaffected Sunnis, Syrian civil war veterans, and from Free Syrian Army units based in Homs.[299]

An invasion and subjugation of Lebanon could be said to be aspirational for ISIS, since Hezbollah's presence, and Iranian government backing, would be a serious obstacle to this goal.

ISIS PLEDGE OF ALLEGIANCE

In June 2014, the "Free Sunnis of Baalbek" pledged allegiance to the Islamic State via Twitter:

> We announce our allegiance, with all pride, to the Mujahid Abu Bakr al-Baghdadi as Caliph of the Muslims . . . We also announce our full support for what [ISIS] is doing for Islam . . . [it is] the duty of all Muslims to work toward finding a caliph who can set up rule by sharia law.[300]

ISIS ORGANIZATION

ISIS leadership has not formally recognized a Lebanese affiliate at this date.[301] There is speculation that Sheikh Abu Abdulah al-Maqdisi is the ISIS "Emir" of Lebanon.[302] According to Lebanese security forces, ISIS was forming a military committee to undertake a military campaign in Lebanon, and the effort was supervised by Syrian ISIS commander Khalaf al-Zeyabi, a.k.a. Abu Musaab Halous.[303]

CAMPAIGNS

ISIS led a joint campaign with al-Nusra in August 2014 to take the Lebanese border city of Arsal, in retaliation for the arrest of Imad Ahmad Jomaa, a former al-Nusra commander who had defected to ISIS. The Lebanese Army retook the lost terrain after five days.

On November 12, 2015, ISIS operatives conducted a series of suicide bombings in Beirut against civilians, killing 43 and wounding 239. A day later, ISIS operatives conducted the infamous terrorist attacks in Paris. It is unclear whether this is the beginning of a sustained suicide bombing campaign.

OTHER SIGNIFICANT EVENTS

November 2013

Iranian Embassy in Beiruit is struck by two ISIS suicide bombers of the Abdullah Azzam Brigade, killing twenty-three and wounding 160.[304]

January 2014

ISIS claims responsibility for a suicide bombing against Hezbollah in the Haret Hreik district of Beirut, which killed four people. The bomber was a nineteen year old from Northern Lebanon.[305]

The "Free Sunnis of Baalbek Brigade" threatens to kill Maj. Suzan al-Hajj, Internal Security Forces chief of Cyber Crime and Intellectual Property bureau. The Free Sunnis of Baalbek Brigade pledged their allegiance to ISIS in late June 2014.

Lebanese soldiers relay ISIS demand to release prisoners from Roumieh prison. If the prisoners were not released in three days they would be executed.

June 2014

A suicide bomber attempts and fails to assassinate Major General Abbas Ibrahim, head of Lebanese Intelligence, the Directorate of General Security.[306] ISIS declares the intention to expand into Lebanon, among other countries.[307]

August 2014

Lebanese security forces arrest al-Nusra–affiliated commander Imad Ahmad Jomaa, a.k.a. Emad Gomaa. In retaliation, al-Nusra and ISIS storm the Lebanese border city of Arsal and take dozens of Lebanese Army soldiers as prisoner.[308] After five days, the forces withdraw from Arsal.[309]

August 30, 2014

ISIS releases a video recording of Lebanese soldier Ali al-Sayyed, a Sunni captured during the fighting around Arsal earlier that month. Another video posted later depicted nine of al-Sayyed's comrades begging for their lives, with instructions to protest against the Lebanese government's incarceration of ISIS militants, including ISIS commander Imad Ahmad Jomaa, a.k.a. Emad Gomaa.

December 3, 2014
Lebanese authorities announce the arrest of Saja al-Dulaimi, a purported former wife of Abu Bakr al-Baghdadi.[310]

January 2015
ISIS states the intention to declare an Islamic State of Lebanon.[311]

February 23, 2015
Lebanon's *Daily Star* cites Lebanese security sources as saying that ISIS was recruiting suicide bombers for targets against Shi'ites in Beirut, "as well as French and Western interests."[312]

March 2015
ISIS shells a Christian church in Ras Baalbek during a wedding ceremony. The event precipitates a mutual-defense pact between Hezbollah and the Christian militias in Ras Baalbek.[313]

November 12, 2015
ISIS claims responsibility for two bombings in the southern Beirut suburb of Burj al-Barajneh, a Hezbollah territory, killing 43 and wounding 239. One attack was a conducted by a suicide bomber on a motorcycle outside a Shi'ite mosque, while the other detonated himself outside a bakery, within fifty yards of the first bomber. A third bomber died after losing his legs from the detonation of the second bomber's explosives; the third bomber was unable to carry out his attack. All three bombers wore explosives vests.[314]

December 1, 2015
The Lebanese Army conducts a prisoner exchange with the al-Nusra Front in Labweh, a village in the Bekaa Valley. Under negotiations mediated by Qatari officials, sixteen Lebanese security personnel were released for twelve al-Nusra militants, as well as Saja al-Dulaimi, a purported former wife of Abu Bakr al-Baghdadi.[315]

CASE STUDY: ISIS SUICIDE BOMBING IN BEIRUT

At approximately 6:00 p.m. on November 12, 2015, a motorcyclist stopped his bike outside a Shi'ite mosque on Hussaineya Street in the Burj al-Barajneh neighborhood of Beirut and detonated a suicide bomb. Approximately five minutes later, as neighborhood residents attempted to help bomb victims, a second suicide bomber detonated his vest in a bakery about twenty meters away from the first blast.[316] Adel Termos, a thirty-two-year-old auto mechanic, tackled the second bomber before the suicide bomber detonated his vest, thereby possibly sparing many lives. He died from the subsequent explosion. Termos was married and had two children.[317] Another victim of the second bomb was a third bomber nearby, who lost his legs and expired before detonating his explosives vest.[318]

ISIS claimed responsibility in an online statement. The intention was to kill Shia with the first bomb, then cause as many casualties as possible among responders with the next bombs. [319] Among the 43 dead and over 160 injured were several children.

Lebanese security forces arrested eleven people in connection with the attack within forty-eight hours of the detonations. Nine were Syrian and two were Lebanese. The Syrians had been in a Palestinian refugee camp in Burj al-Barajneh. One of the suspects was identified as a smuggler, who secreted the terror cell across the Syrian border. Another suspect had intended to become a suicide bomber.[320]

According to Lebanese Interior Minister Nuhad Mashnuq, the bomb makers prepared the explosives belts at an apartment in the Ashrafieh district of Beirut. The planners had intended for five of their number to detonate suicide bombs at a hospital in the Burj al-Barajneh neighborhood, but the high state of security led them to detonate their bombs in a busy street instead.[321]

ISIS IN JORDAN

HISTORY

Jordan's government has been allied with the US for decades and its US-supplied military is strong and disciplined, making the kingdom a difficult military target for ISIS. In 2014, the Jordanian military repulsed a tentative incursion by ISIS forces into the kingdom. ISIS forces attempted to cross the border and seize the Turabil/Karame border post.[322] Despite the kingdom's alliances and military strength, the population has a low opinion of the US, and was internally susceptible to the ISIS message, until the burning death of a Jordanian pilot. ISIS has now stirred Jordanian outrage. Zarqa a poverty-stricken city north of Amman, remains a hotbed of unemployed young men and Islamic radicals.[323] Ma'an and Rusayfa are similarly sympathetic to Jihadi sentiments.[324] Although over three thousand Jordanians have traveled to Syria to fight, many have joined ISIS's rival al-Nusra Front.[325]

JORDANIAN PLEDGE OF ALLEGIANCE

According to an ISIS-affiliated Twitter account on May 7, 2015, the "Shahids Battalion of Ma'an in Jordan pledged allegiance to the Caliphate around a year ago." If this occurred, it deviates from the customary video recordings of ISIS pledges and subsequent acknowledgment by Abu Bakr al-Baghdadi, during which al-Baghdadi announces leadership of the new group.

ORGANIZATION OF ISIS IN JORDAN

Little is known about the ISIS command structure in Jordan, or whether it is informal. Jordanian security forces appear to have successfully suppressed overt participation in ISIS. Since Jordan has supplied many recruits for the fight in Syria, it stands to reason that ISIS has recruiters in the area, as well as facilitators to transport recruits across the border.

Despite this, there have been remarkably few ISIS-sponsored attacks in the kingdom.

OTHER SIGNIFICANT EVENTS

January 3, 2015
Jordanian pilot First Lieutenant Muath al-Kasasbeh is immolated alive in a cage. ISIS releases a video depicting the event on February 3, 2015.[326] On news of his death, the pilot's tribe erupted in protest chants against King Abdullah II.

February 4, 2015
Jordan executes Iraq-born suicide bomber Sajida al-Rishawi in retaliation for the execution of pilot Muath al-Kasasbeh.[327]

Early February, 2015
Jordan deploys a large contingent on the border with Iraq as a show of force and to stem infiltration. The Jordanian Air Force begins to fly twenty sorties a day to bomb ISIS targets in Syria.[328]

ISIS Al Furqan Media Foundation released "Healing The Believers' Chests" after murdering Jordanian pilot Muath al-Kasasbeh.

April 25, 2015
The Al-Minbar al-I'lami al-Jihadi web forum announces that "The Lone Lions in the Ma'an Province," an ISIS-affiliated group, conducted an attack on a military intelligence facility.

May 7, 2015
The Al-Minbar al-I'lami al-Jihadi web forum announces that "The Lone Lions in the Ma'an Province," an ISIS-affiliated group, stole a pickup truck from Jordanian security forces. During the operation, three police were injured, and the truck destroyed by burning.

WEAPONS AND EQUIPMENT ORDER OF BATTLE

The only weapons used thus far in attacks by ISIS-affiliated groups have been small arms, though proximity to the conflict zone may give access to assault rifles and heavier materiel.

ISIS IN GAZA

HISTORY

The Gaza Strip has a long history of Salafist jihadi organizations and support. Although many such Salafists may be ISIS sympathizers, few have traveled to Syria to fight, and the Hamas authorities have been quick to stamp out any overt support for ISIS.

ISIS operatives appear to play Hamas against Israel, especially by firing impotent rockets into Israeli territory. Whereas Hamas sees ISIS as a threat in Gaza, it may coordinate with ISIS in the Sinai peninsula to traffic arms across the Egyptian border. In late 2015, the ISIS beheading of an Hamas leader at the Yarmouth Palestinian refugee camp in Syria set off a tit-for-tat series of reprisals between ISIS and Hamas in Gaza.

Although little is known about ISIS's strength in Gaza, the increasing number of attacks against Hamas indicate that it may be growing in popularity in the region, and may pose a threat to both Hamas and Israel.

ISIS PLEDGE OF ALLEGIANCE

The Mujahideen Shura Council in the Environs of Jerusalem issued a statement on February 2, 2014, stating that they were "committed to helping ISIS and bolstering its ranks," and that internal conflicts within the jihad in Syria were due to "an unfair view toward ISIS and its emir, the Prince of Believers Abu Bakr al-Baghdadi."[329] Ansar Beit al-Maqdis pledged allegiance to ISIS in November 2014, changing its name to "Sinai Province."[330]

ISIS ORGANIZATION

ISIS in Gaza is the self-styled "Gaza District of the Islamic State." Little is known of senior membership; Abu Qatadah al-Filistini appeared in a video calling on Gazans to "join the convoy of the mujahideen and to join the State of the Caliphate." Another Gazan, Abu Azzam Al-Ghazzawim, appeared in the same video.[331] Ansar Beit al-Maqdis is affiliated with ISIS.[332]

CAMPAIGNS

ISIS has not conducted a concerted campaign in Gaza. Most of the recruitment for fighters in Syria appear to be over the Internet, followed by travel to Turkey.

OTHER SIGNIFICANT EVENTS

April 2015
ISIS beheads captives from Yarmouk Palestinian refugee camp in Syria, including a Hamas leader.[333]

April 7, 2015
Hamas arrests Salafist imam Adnan Khader Mayat from the Bureij refugee camp in Gaza.[334] ISIS retaliates by bombing Hamas's Internal Security Headquarters at Sheikh Radwan in Gaza, though there are no casualties.[335]

May 4, 2015
Hamas arrests Salafist Sheikh Yasser Abu Houli, and demolishes a mosque in Almtahabin used by Ansar al-Bayt al-Maqdis, a group that has pledged allegiance to ISIS.[336]

May 31, 2015
ISIS militants assassinate Hamas commander Saber Siam by car bomb. A statement on the killing read that Siam was "a partner in a declared war against religion and against Muslims, working for the heretical government in Gaza," also warning Gazans of future bombings at Hamas facilities.[337]

August 19, 2015
ISIS-affiliated group Ansar Beit al-Maqdis, or "Province of Sinai," asserts that Egyptian Intelligence has abducted four Hamas naval commandos, Abed al-Daim al-Bassat, Said Abdullah Abu Jbin, Yasser Fathi Zanun, and Hussein Hamis al-Thbada, from a tour bus.[338] The abductors wore shalwar kameezes, characteristic Pakistani apparel, and checked the passenger manifest on laptops.[339]

WEAPONS AND EQUIPMENT ORDER OF BATTLE

ISIS militants in Gaza have fired rockets into Israel. They have also successfully used car bombs against Hamas personnel, as well as bombings against Hamas buildings and offices. In videos, they pose with AK-style assault rifles.

CHAPTER 5

ISIS IN NORTH AFRICA

ISIS IN EGYPT

HISTORY

The Arab Spring transforms Egypt

After the 2011 Arab Spring, many active extremist groups in Egypt received very little oversight as the post-Mubarak power struggles ensued. Al-Qaeda's ties through the region are well-documented; its current leader is the Egyptian Dr. Ayman al-Zawahiri. After the fall of Mubarak, the government released prisoners, and many of these Egyptians added experienced fighters back into the pool.[340]

First Signs of the Islamic State in Egypt: October 2014

By November 2014, one of these active groups, Ansar Beit al-Maqdis (ABM), "Supporters of the Holy House of Jerusalem", would align itself with ISIS. The origins of ABM predate the Arab Spring, it was formally established in 2011 after members of Jama'at al-Tawhid wal-Jihad (TWJ) joined with other, smaller Salafist groups to form ABM.[341]

There are some suggestions that the reason ABM joined ISIS was the Egyptian crackdowns in 2014, including the loss of their leader, Tawfiq Mohammad Faraj (Abu Abdullah). Faraj was killed March 11, 2014 by Egyptian authorities along with Muhammad Al-Sayyid Mansur Al-Turki a.k.a. Abu Ubayda. The US State Department recognized Ansar Beit al-Maqdis as a terrorist organization on April 4, 2014.[342] After the loss of the ABM leadership, ISIS sent representatives to develop ties with them. The group was inconsistent about its support for a short period of time but eventually they decided that it was in their interest to join the movement that had the most energy and star

ISIS fighter in the July 1, 2015 "Operation Sheikh Abu Suhab al-Ansari" against Egyptian forces.

power. Shadi al-Menei became the leader of ABM until he too was killed May 23, 2015.[343] ABM was estimated to have as many as two thousand fighters spread across its operational regions, but the majority of its combat power was in the Sinai peninsula before the Egyptian army's "Operation Martyr's Right" in September 2015, which reduced ABM's fighting force by as much as 50 percent.

The Pledge/No Pledge Conundrum

For a period of time there was internal dissension as to whether the ABM should align itself with ISIS. ABM's members were historically close to al-Qaeda, but ISIS made a strong case that they were the most capable organization and could assist ABM directly.

In June 2014, a false loyalty oath to ISIS appeared on an ABM-associated Twitter account. Soon afterward a post stating that this tweet was false was posted on another account.[344] This created a situation where ISIS needed to make contact with ABM leadership and get them onboard and break their affiliation with al-Qaeda. In September 2014 the Kuwaiti newspaper *al-Shahed* reported that ISIS sent Musa'id Abu Qatmah as a representative to Sinai through the Gaza tunnel systems to convince the Egyptians to side with al-Baghdadi.[345] That same month, men carrying three letters from a Libya-based ISIS representative named Abu Ahmad

ISIS fighter shows off weapons cache in video released by Wilayat Sinai.

al-Libi were dispatched to Sinai. Al-Libi encouraged the Sinai group to unite under ISIS in exchange for a massive influx of guns and funds. On November 3, 2014, another loyalty oath appeared online, but was quickly rejected by other ABM-related accounts. This indicated that the internal dissent in ABM was reaching a peak, and members were taking the matters into their own hands. ABM was on the verge of splitting between junior members, who wanted to join ISIS, and the senior members, who were consulting their Shura council. After Egyptian newspapers reported on the pledge, an ABM-related account demanded that the media "check the accuracy of their sources and to stick to ABM's official statements." [346]

Ansar Beit al-Maqdis Finally Pledges Loyalty to ISIS

On November 11, 2014, ABM officially swore its loyalty oath to ISIS leader Abu Bakr al-Baghdadi in an audio recording released online and announced via Twitter.[347] The pledge was published in ISIS's *Dabiq* magazine, number 5:

> Allah—the Exalted—said, "And hold firmly to the rope of Allah all together and do not become divided" [Āl 'Imrān: 103]. And Allah's Messenger (sallallāhu 'alayhi wa sallam) said, "Whoever dies while not having a pledge of allegiance, dies a death of jāhiliyyah" [Sahīh Muslim on the authority of

ISIS continued brutality in Egypt with yet another execution.

'Imrān]. Therefore, in obedience to the order of Allah ('azza wa jall) and in obedience to His Messenger (sallallāhu 'alayhi wa sallam), ordering not to divide and to stick to the jamā'ah, we declare the bay'ah to the Khalīfah Ibrāhīm Ibn 'Awwād Ibn Ibrāhīm al-Qurashī al-Husaynī, pledging to selflessly hear and obey, in times of hardship and ease, and in times of delight and dislike. We pledge not to dispute the matter of those in authority except if we see obvious kufr concerning which we have proof from Allah. We call the Muslims everywhere to give bay'ah to the Khalīfah and support him, in obedience to Allah and actualization of the unheeded obligation of the era.

Abu Bakr al-Baghdadi accepted their pledge in an audio recording entitled "Despite the Disbelivers' Hate" via al-Furqan that also accepted pledges of allegiance from Yemen, Algeria, and Libya.[348] Shortly after, *Dabiq* laid out historical ties between Sinai and the "land of Sham" so as to lay claim to the region. It explained that Sinai was "a front against the Jews, and important step towards the liberation of Bayt ul-Maqdis." Unlike previous oaths, there was no follow-up denial. The oath to ISIS still deeply divides ABM. [349]

ORGANIZATION OF ISIS IN EGYPT

Emir: Abu Osama al-Masri[350]

Al-Masri is a forty-two-year-old former scholar from al-Azhar University in Cairo who ran a clothing import company in Egypt before joining ABM.[351]

ISIS/ABM controls several regional cell networks:

Religious "Criterion" Cell: Led by Mohammed Nar Mohammed, Deputy: Hani Mustafa Amin Amer

Greater Cairo and Central Region: Mohamed el-Sayed Mansour Hassan

Ismailia cell: Led by Mahmoud Mohammed Salman, Deputy: Mahmoud Abdul Aziz Ahmed al-Araj

Dakahlia cell: Ahmed Rahman Mr. Awad

Beni Suef cell: Mohamed Taha Mustafa Ashour
Fayoum Cell: Saad Abdul Aziz Abdul Majid
Qena cell: Mohamed Mansour
Implementation Group: Hassanein Gharabli
Monitoring and Tracking group: Mohammed Bakri Aaron
Engineering Committee: Abdul Rahman Mohammed Sayed Mohamed Aboul Einein
Safehouses/Escape & Evasion/Armory: Mr. Mohammed Mansour Hassan Ibrahim
Logistical Support Group: Imad Saeed
Media Group: Obuamad

Known members of ABM/ISIS-Sinai
Ahmed Muhammad Abdel Aziz al-Sigini
Ashraf Ali Hasanain al-Gharablys: Killed by Egyptian forces, he was accused of being behind attacks along Libya border and the beheading of Tomislav Salopek. [352]
Muhammad Ali Afifi Bedawi Nasif: Executed with others[353]
Muhammad al-Said Hassan Ibrahim al-Toukhi (more commonly known as Abu Obayda)
Shadi al-Mani: ABM leader killed by head of Menaei tribe, Sheikh Abdel Meguid al-Menaei, after assassination attempt.[354]
Walid Waked Attallah: Arrested Oct 17, 2014. Responsible for blast in October 2014 aimed at police. [355]

ISIS-SINAI ACTIVITIES

Ongoing: ABM carried out twenty-six attacks on fuel lines between February 2011 and January 19, 2015, including a gas pipeline attack in Sinai[356] on February 4, 2011 and an Egyptian gas pipeline attack[357] on July 4, 2011.

August 18, 2011
ABM targets an Egged busline in the Israeli city of Eilat, killing eight off-duty Israeli soldiers. Israeli forces chase them across the border and accidentally kill eight Egyptian soldiers. Also struck in this attack were a passenger vehicle and military patrol.[358]

August 2012

Rockets fired to Israeli town of Eilat.[359]

September 12, 2012

In response to a controversial anti-Islamic film, "Innocence of Muslims," ABM attacks Israeli border guards in a "disciplinary attack against those

Fighter in Sinai plans his SVBIED attack.

who insulted the beloved Prophet," [360] and release a video[361] alleging that the "Innocence of Muslims" video was put out by a Jewish filmmaker. It is later revealed that the filmmaker was an Egyptian Copt in California, Nakoula Bassely Nakoula.[362]

September 2013

ABM attempts to assassinate Interior Minister Muhammad Ibrahim.[363]

December 24, 2013

Mansoura Security Directorate attacked, sixteen killed (mostly police officers) and 134 injured in by truck bomb. [364] The city's security directorate was the target of ABM. ABM claims responsibility. [365]

January 2014

ABM downs Egyptian MH-17 military chopper near Sheikh Zuwaid city with a surface-to-air missile and releases a video of fighters firing the weapon. Five soldiers are killed.[366]

January 24, 2014

Cairo hit by car bombs, damaging a museum.[367]

February 16, 2014

ABM attacks tourists on a bus in Taba with a suicide bombing to damage the tourism industry. Three South Korean tourists and an Egyptian driver are killed.[368]

August 18, 2014

ABM releases video of the beheading of four Egyptians accused of being Israeli spies. This is the first beheading video for ABM.[369]

October 2014

Sheta al-Ma'atqa killed early October 2014 by Egyptian military forces. Twenty-one other ISIS members killed with him between October 3–October 9. Mohamed Samir, military spokesman, said al-Ma'atqa was ABM Emir in Sadat and Wefeq in Rafah. [370]

October 2014

Abu Osama al-Masri travels to Syria in Oct 2014, strikes deal for ABM to become part of ISIS and issues a statement in favor of ISIS.[371]

October 20, 2014

Walid Atallah, a military Emir, captured.[372]

October 24, 2014

ABM carried out attack at the Karm al-Qawadis checkpoint on orders from ISIS, and released video of the attack on November 11, 2014.[373] ISIS supplied weapons and funding via Palestinian groups.

October 24, 2014

ABM attacks checkpoint at Sheikh Zuweid, then attacks responding security forces with IEDs. Additionally, ABM launches gun attack on Arish checkpoint. Thirty-three are killed.[374] The attack indicates ISIS-Sinai knew the movements of senior officers.[375]

November 12, 2014

ISIS Sinai hijacks Egyptian missile boat in order to attack Israeli vessels and offshore gas rigs. The Ambassador III–class missile ship was in the middle of a "combat exercise" when ISIS-Sinai members commandeered the ship, after faking an accident with the ship. When the ship didn't respond to the Egyptian fleet, attackers eventually used the communications system and gave themselves away. Egyptian naval commandos stormed the vessel and recovered it. [376]

December 2014

ISIS Sinai kills American oil worker William Henderson.[377]

January 29, 2015

Compound attack in el-Arish, Sheikh Zuweid, and Rafah. Forty-four killed in a series of attacks on security buildings, a military base, a news office, checkpoints, a local hotel, and a police club. Tactics used: car bombs, suicide bombers, run-and-gun, and mortars. The first strikes were aimed at the al-Arish police office and Battalion 101.[378]

March 10, 2015

Forty-two wounded when a fuel tanker turned into a SVBIED fails to strike police barracks in Arish and explodes short of the target. [379]

April 2, 2015

ABM carries out gun attacks at Sheikh Zuweid and Arish, killing five Egyptian soldiers and two civilians.[380]

April 12, 2015

Six killed on a highway. Car bomb attack in Arish at police station. Gun attack at Rafah checkpoint, killing three.[381]

May 21, 2015

ABM leader Abu Osama al-Masri calls for the killing of judges. "It is wrong for the tyrants to jail our brothers . . . Poison their food . . . surveil them at home and in the street, destroy their homes with explosives if you can."[382]

William Henderson's identification cards and passport were posted to Twitter by ISIS Sinai branch after they claimed to have executed him.

June 3, 2015

Daytime attack near pyramids of Giza kills two police officers. The gunmen attacked via motorcycle. [383]

June 10, 2015

Two militants killed in an attempted attack in Luxor. Three men sought to enter the Karnak Temple but one died by premature self-detonation of his suicide vests and the other was shot in the head. The third was injured and captured.[384]

ISIS releases statement detailing "Operation Sheikh Abu Suhab al-Ansari" from July 1, 2015 in the Sinai area of Sheikh Zuweid, Rafah, and Arish.

Tamislov Salopek is captured and shown in hostage video from ISIS Wilayat Sinai, August 5, 2015. He was beheaded and subsequent video released.

June 29, 2015

ISIS kills Egypt's top prosecutor, Hisham Barakat, by car bomb, likely via a remote-controlled IED. [385]

July 1, 2015

ISIS attacks the Sinai in Operation "Sheikh Abu Suhab al-Ansari."

July 2, 2015

Egyptian Army AH-64 Apache shot down by surface-to-air missile.

July 6, 2015

Egyptian Army says the situation in North Sinai under control after airstrikes and that it has killed 241 terrorists over past week. [386]

July 16, 2015

ISIS-Sinai claims to have attacked Egyptian naval vessel. Egypt says the ship exchanged fire with attackers off north Sinai coast but denies the claim that the ship suffered more than a fire on the ship and no fatalities. ISIS claims it killed everyone on board. [387]

July 24, 2015

Tamislov Salopek, Croatian, kidnapped.

August 5, 2015

ISIS-Sinai releases video on August 5 of Salopek with a threat to kill him if Egypt doesn't release all female Muslim prisoners, followed by an August 12 video of Salopek being beheaded.[388]

September 2015

ISIS kills Major General Khaled Kamal Osman and Brigadier General Ahmed Abdel Satar in separate attacks. ISIS claims responsibility later on Twitter.[389]

October 1, 2015

Sawarka tribal leader, Khaled el-Menaei, killed by ISIS-Sinai.[390]

October 31, 2015

Russian Metrojet Flight 9268 is bombed over Sinai as it departs from Sharm el-Sheikh, killing 224.. ISIS releases statement that it knows how the plane has been destroyed, that it is responsible, and that it will reveal how the bombing was conducted. Within days, ISIS releases video claiming responsibility.[391] A photo allegedly showing a soda can bomb is published in *Dabiq* 12 shortly afterward.

BATTLES

ISIS Operation "Sheikh Abu Suhab al-Ansari"

July 1, 2015: ISIS launches a massive attack against Egyptian forces in the cities of Sheikh Zuweid, Rafah, and Arish in an attempt to cut the Sinai peninsula off from Egypt and establish a foothold along the Israeli border. The attacks struck over 21 major bases and left 21 Egyptian soldiers and 241 attackers dead.

Egyptian Army: Operation "Martyr's Right"

September 8, 2015–Sept 23, 2015: The Egyptian military launched a major offensive to clear out militants in North Sinai, killing 535 ISIS-Sinai members and arresting 578 others.[392],[393]

ISIS IN LIBYA

HISTORY

From the end of Qaddafi to the pledges to ISIS

In the ruins of the post-Qaddafi Libya, the country fairly quickly fell into chaos and under the rule of militias throughout the country. While jihadist groups have been active in Libya for many years, new groups quickly emerged after the fall of the disgraced dictator in an effort to assert control over regional interests. In addition to trafficking,[394] porous borders, and a long history of jihadist networks, Libya's failed state was a perfect power vacuum for the rise of two groups in the area, al-Qaeda and ISIS,[395] who have recruited Libyans for fighting in the Syrian civil war. There were enough Libyans fighting in Syria to establish a Libyan battalion under al-Mahdi al-Harati.[396] The power vacuum in the country also allows militias and other groups room to establish training camps free from the oversight found in neighboring countries like Egypt, Tunisia, and Algeria.[397]

Libyan fighters in Syria announce the formation of the Al-Battar Brigade in a video posted on YouTube.

The Post-war Chaos that led to ISIS

After the Libyan civil war ended the country was governed by the representative General National Congress. The GNC took power over from the Transitional National Council, the governing body formed during the war. The GNC led for two years but did not meet its mandate to form a new permanent Parliament. A faction named themselves the New GNC. It was made up of Islamist members and backed by the Libya Central Shield (LCS) and the Libyan Revolutionary Operations Room (Gorfa 'Amiliat Thuwar Libiya) militias. The New GNC along with other Islamist groups including the Eastern Libya Shura Council of Benghazi Revolutionaries (SCBR) comprised of the Ansar al-Shari'a militia, the 17 February Martyrs Brigade, the Rafallah Sahati Brigade, and Libya Shield 1 militia, created their own governmental structure. The SCBR council even attempted to declare Eastern Libya an Islamic Emirate in 2014. The internationally recognized Libyan government refused to recognize these groups, so they formed their own rival government and settled into clashes with the Libyan Army. Libya split into essentially four parts: Libya Dawn militia and other allied forces controlled Libya from Ras an Nuft to the western border and the Capitol Tripoli; the Libyan Army and Operation Dignity forces controlled from Ras al Nuf to the Egyptian Border to the East including Benghazi, Tobruq.

As the battle between two major campaigns ensued in Libya, other players in the region were taking sides, including neighboring countries. Egypt and UAE were supportive of the efforts of General Haftar and former Prime Minister Abdullah al-Thani, and Qatar, Sudan, and Turkey backed the various Islamist groups comprising the "Libya Dawn" coalition.

At the beginning of Libya's post-Qaddafi era, the Islamic State was of little concern compared to al-Qaeda. [398] Al-Qaeda–linked groups like Libyan Islamic Fighting Group (LIFG) have been active since the mid-1990s and were mostly controlled by Qaddafi until his fall.[399] With the failed Libyan state, al-Qaeda had the opportunity to exploit the power vacuum with its existing ties to local groups. Despite al-Qaeda's activity and networking resources in the area, it wasn't long before delegations from a newly formed ISIS would begin to cultivate Libya as part of its planned expansion. Fighters were flowing between Syria and Libya and the Islamic State to fight the Syrian civil war.

Among these fighters were a group known as "The Battar Brigade," who fought alongside ISIS fighters in Deir Ez-zor and in Mosul before returning home to Libya.[400] These fighters returned and began to work to unite the various factions in Derna and encourage them to join the Islamic State. When they met opposition to their plan, they would kill their critics.[401]

FIRST SIGNS OF THE ISLAMIC STATE IN LIBYA

Ansar al-Sharia Militia

The Ansar al-Sharia (AAS) formed in 2012 from an amalgam of small Islamic militias in Benghazi Libya. They coalesced into an armed opposition group with a political platform to bring Sharia law to Libya and oppose democracy, despite the fact that most Libyans fought for this in the revolution against Qaddafi. Their claim to fame was when their members found and killed Mummar Qaddafi in Sirte's District 7, bringing to an end his regime in 2011. AAS quickly occupied Sirte and ran it as their own militia city. They leaned on charity and Islamic law as their pathway into the local's good graces. They also started to eliminate all remnants of Sufi Islam by destroying shrines and imposing the ISIS-brand interpretation of Islam on the locals.

AAS Attack on American Diplomatic Facility

On 11 September, 2012 members of AAS stormed the American Diplomatic Mission in the eastern city of Benghazi and then the nearby CIA annex. During the initial attack they killed the US Ambassador Chris Stevens and Foreign Service Information's management officer Sean Smith. Later that night two CIA contractors Tyrone Woods and Glen Doherty would be killed during a mortar attack. Ansar al-Sharia leader Ahmed Abu Khattala was blamed for planning and leading the attack. He would be brought to the USA after a US Special Forces raid in Libya captured him in 2014.

The AAS fought the Libyan Government forces of General Haftar after he launched Operation Karamah (Dignity) in a bid to remove the Islamist militias from Benghazi. AAS leader al-Zawahiri was killed in fighting after receiving mortal wounds in 2014. For a while Benghazi fell under the control of the AAS but was eventually routed. Soon after many of its fighters and leaders fled and joined ISIS in Sirte early 2015.

In April 2014, the Shura Council of Islamic Youth (MSSI) emerged and announced that it was establishing "Islamic Courts" followed by a parade of fighters through the streets of Derna.[402] The new group announced they would take over as the security force for Derna and institute punishments, including executions and floggings.[403] Additionally, the group promised to eliminate any opposition in Derna, which manifested in targeted assassinations of judges, local community leaders, and rival militia members.

In September 2014, ISIS sent leaders to Libya to discuss expansion in the region. The delegation included former Ba'athists, including Abu Nabil al-Anbari, Abu Habib al-Jazrawi (Saudi), and Abu al-Baraa el-Azdi (Yemeni).[404]

LIBYA PLEDGES LOYALTY TO ISIS

On October 5, 2014, MSSI and other militants pledged their support for ISIS. On October 30, 2014, a large gathering from different factions arrived in Derna to swear allegiance to Abu Bakr al-Baghdadi. In an audio recording released November 13, 2014, al-Baghdadi accepted the pledges from many groups in the region, including Libya, Yemen, Egypt, Algeria, Saudi Arabia, and Afghanistan.[405] ISIS's *Dabiq* magazine, issue 5, featured a section that celebrated the expansion of the Caliphate:

> Meanwhile, the Islamic State announced the expansion of the Khilāfah to Sinai, Libya, Yemen, Algeria, and the Arabian Peninsula, accepting the bay'āt of the mujāhidīn in those lands[406] . . . Glad tidings, O Muslims, for we give you good news by announcing the expansion of the Islamic State to new lands, to the lands of al-Haramayn and Yemen . . . to Egypt, Libya, and

Algeria. We announce the acceptance of the bay'ah of those who gave us bay'ah in those lands, the nullification of the groups therein, the announcement of new wilāyāt for the Islamic State, and the appointment of wulāt for them[407] . . . On the 17th of Muharram 1436, the world heard announcements from the mujāhidīn of the Arabian Peninsula, Yemen, Sinai, Libya, and Algeria, pronouncing their bay'āt to the Khalīfah of the Muslims, Abū Bakr al-Husaynī al-Baghdādī[408]. . . Again, like other lands, the Islamic State uprooted methodologies in Libya that allowed for the consolidation of murtaddīn—the allies of the crusaders—by ordering to directly target them, despite what might be said by the weak-hearted and sick-hearted, those who claimed that Libya should only be a land for "da'wah" immediately after the killing of Gaddafi despite the abundance of arms and the condition of tawahhush (mayhem) then ideal for jihad . . . The Islamic State here in Libya is still young. It is in great need of every Muslim who can come, especially medical, shar'ī, and administrative personnel, in addition to fighters.[409]

ORGANIZATION OF ISIS IN LIBYA

After al-Baghdadi accepted the pledges of allegiance from Libya it was announced that Libya would be divided into three provinces or wiliyat. These would be al-Barqa (East), Tarablus (West) and al-Fazzan (South). There are estimates of up to 3,000 ISIS terrorists of multiple nationalities in Libya.[410]

ISIS-Libya Emirate
Emir: Abul-Mughirah al-Qahtani.[411]

Barqa Govenorate
Emir: Abu Nabil al-Anbari as Emir of Wilayat al-Barqa [412]
Capitol city is Derna; members claim operations in three major cities: Derna, Bengahzi, Nawfaliyah.

The Libya Wilayats according to ISIS photo release, Barqah (Cyrenaica), Tarablus (Tripoli), and Fezzan.

Derna
Emir: Abu Al-Baraa el-Azdi (Yemeni from Azd tribe) [413]
Head Judiciary: Abu Habib al-Jazrawi (Saudi) [414]
Qadhi Derna: Abu Maryam al-Misri
Shar' Derna: Abdul-Hamed Al-Qasimi
Benghazi
Emir: Covert Member
Judiciary: Abu Abdullah al-Libi
Nawfaliyah
Emir: Ali Qarqaa (Abu Humam al-Libi)[415]
Judiciary: Abu Dujanah al-Libi (KIA)[416]

Trabulus Governorate
The capital of this governorate is the city of Sirte.
Emir of the Trabalus: Abu Talha al-Tunisi (Tunisian) [417]
Emir of Sirte: Usama Karami
Judiciary of Sirte: Mufti Hassan al-Karami [418]

Fezzan Governorate
Capital city: Sebha.

CAMPAIGNS

Battle for Control of Derna: October 5, 2014–present
The ISIS campaign to take Derna began in early October 2014 as a group pledged loyalty to ISIS and celebrated their announcement with a parade of over sixty trucks through the town.[419] At the end of the month, local ISIS supporters held a forum in the city to call residents and other fighters to swear loyalty to Abu Bakr al-Baghdadi.[420]

On November 12, 2014, pro-government airstrikes on Derna were launched after two ISIS car bomb attacks. Libyan Forces surrounded ISIS in Derna.[421] By December 12, the Libyan government approved a ground campaign to take back Derna from ISIS.[422] In December 2014, Salim Derby of the Libyan Islamic Fighting Group brought together members of Ansar al-Sharia Derna, Jaysh al-Islam and Abu Salim Martyrs Brigade to form the "Shura Council of

Mujahideen in Derna" which was opposed to ISIS control. They placed themselves under Gen Haftar and "Operation Dignity" forces. ISIS subsequently assassinated Salim Derby and another leader, Nasser Akr. [423] In late March 2015 Gen Haftar organized a siege on Derna which predictably produced immediate conflicts between the Libyan commanders and local tribes involved in the operation.[424] In June 2015, the Shura Council of Mujahideen Derna announced that local fighters had pushed ISIS out of Derna, and that many ISIS fighters had surrendered. [425] By end of July, the council said it had driven all ISIS fighters from Derna.[426]

The Fall of An Nawfaliyah: February 8–9, 2015

ISIS sent a convoy of thirty-five armed vehicles from their secret camps near Sirte to take Nawfaliyah. At the outskirts, they held a forum called "The First Forum of the Islamic State," with appeals for locals to repent. This action increased ISIS's influence over east-west travel along the coastal road and gave them a launching point toward Ras Lanuf and Ajdabiyah. [427]

Battle of Sirte: March 14–September 23, 2015

In March 2014, ISIS made its move to finally seize a Libyan city and execute the divide and conquer plan that worked well in Iraq and Syria. However, with the Libyan Dawn army to the west and the Operation Dignity forces to the east would require they seize a city where neither had significant influence. They wisely chose the strategically important city of Sirte.

Mortar attack photo released by Wilayat Barqah.

ISIS chose Sirte for a multitude of opportunities it offered. They could capitalize on the weakness between the two rival governments as Sirte was the seam that held Libya together. From there ISIS could attack in any direction, destroy each rival government piecemeal and quickly capture the nation's number one economic export, oil.

Sirte (also known as Sidra) sits on the southwest side of the bowl that comprises the Gulf of Sidra. It was the stronghold, birthplace and execution spot of Colonel Qaddafi. He was captured and killed there by the Ansar al-Sharia militia. Its population had seen better days before the revolution. But after Qaddafi, the loyalist locals hated both the Tripoli-Misratah-dominated Libyan Dawn and the Benghazi-based Operation Dignity forces. The AAS had been working to ingratiate themselves with them and found they were ripe to be exploited then dominated.

All of this occurred during a period when the AAS had been moving toward joining ISIS. On ISIS's advice they infiltrated the city in small numbers, established a network of safe houses and identified the key people to be coopted or assassinated when the moment came to seize the city.

Sirte was also home to one of the largest military bases in the country, Gardabiyah airbase. ISIS seized it on May 29, 2015, after government-backed forces withdrew. Even though most of the aircraft there were derelict or destroyed by NATO forces, the military base and its defensive infrastructure would be a boon to those who held it. The Libyan government said the base had been emptied of equipment, but it gave ISIS a foothold and defense center to operate freely.[428]

Wilayat Fezzan members carry out night attack and abduct local tribal leader for execution.

ISIS also seized the national power plant and electrical distribution hub that split power between Eastern and Western Libya.

In Libya ISIS applied the Syria-Iraq playbook to exploit greed and larceny. They seduced and coopted those with a reason to want to operate in a secure environment, including arms merchants, criminals, and human traffickers from the Southern tribes. The criminal class would be allowed to continue their activities so long as they paid a percentage of their profits. This way ISIS would gain income and use the smugglers to bring in manpower and weapons from across the Sahara to their stronghold. The population didn't have it so easy. In late September 2015, ISIS in Sirte again demanded local residents pledge their loyalty. They imposed strict Syrian-Iraqi style civil controls on the population, including orders for women to cover 100 percent of themselves.[429] The locals and immediate tribes quickly supported ISIS but were shocked when ISIS demanded loyalty pledges, and that they recant their past lives and accept the foreign-led oppression that would surpass Qaddafi.

In a blitz of finely honed Byzantine politics, appeals to religious piety and sensitivity of the desires of influential individuals would allow ISIS established their headquarters in the Qaddafi's Ouagadougou conference center and proclaimed Sirte as the 'Raqqa" of Mediterranean North Africa.

Battle for the Libyan Oil "Crescent": January 2016

After consolidating its victories in Sirte and successfully splitting the two opposing governments forces, ISIS planned to damage the dysfunctional opposition forces even further and take away from the Libyan government their ability to produce and ship oil, Libya's principle revenue. Their strategy was to seize the coastal highway from Sirte to Ajdabiyah and then cut Benghazi off from Tobruk by eventually taking the Ajdabiyah-Tobruk road.

In early 2015 ISIS had entered Nawfaliyah about twenty kilometers from Ben Jawad and it allowed them to launch into Sirte. Now with Sirte in hand, weapons flowing in and over 3,000 fighters they could carry out their economic decapitation plan. On 4 January 2016 ISIS seized Ben Jawad and launched an attack to take control of the Sidra oil terminal twenty-three kilometers to the east. They started their attacks with suicide bombers and conducted pre-attack reconnaissance with drones. With the capture of this facility the major transshipment center for oil produced in the Gulf of Sidra basin would fall under the control of the terrorist group. ISIS was well aware of this as they posted in their January 2016 newsletter Al-Naba' that ISIS's was taking control of Libya's "Oil Crescent". ISIS calls the southern half of the Gulf of Sidra, the "Oil Crescent" due to the geography's shape resembling the crescent moon which is also significant in Islam.

OTHER SIGNIFICANT EVENTS

November 2014
ISIS Derna claims to have attacked Libyan security forces around Benghazi with nine suicide bombers from Libya, Egypt, and Tunisia. [430]

November 12, 2014
Tobruk and al-Bayda bombings. SVBIED attack in Tobruk kills one. Attack was near Tobruk city's Intelligence HQ. SVBIED in Al Bayda outside air base kills four.[431]

November 13, 2014
SVBIED attack in Tripoli near the Egyptian and UAE embassies.

December 1, 2014
Mohammed Battu and Sirak Qath, human rights activists, are found beheaded. They had been kidnapped from Derna November 6, 2014.[432]

January 3, 2015
ISIS Fezzan claims responsibility for attack on Sokhna checkpoint.[433]

January 8 2015
ISIS Barqah claims to have killed Sofien Chourabi and Nadhir Ktari, Tunisian journalists. The two were kidnapped in September 2014.[434]

January 27, 2015
Corinthia Hotel in Tripoli attacked with SVBIED and gunmen. Ten people killed. Wilayat Tripoli claims responsibility in retribution for death of Abu Anas al-Libi.[435]

February 3, 2015
ISIS attacks French-Libyan oil field outside of Mabruk. Twelve people are killed. Employees include Filipinos and Ghanaians.

February 15, 2015
Al-Hayat propaganda unit releases video showing the execution of Egyptian Christians.[436][437]

February 20, 2015
Islamic State kills forty in al-Qubbah. The targets were a petrol station, a police station, and Agila Salah, the parliamentary speaker. ISIS took responsibility and stated it was retaliation for Egyptian airstrikes after the beheading video aired.[438]

March 10, 2015
ISIS releases video of destruction of Sufi shrines in Libya.[439]

March 18, 2015
Senior ISIS commander, Ahmed Rouissi, killed by Libyan forces near Sirte. The Tunisian militant was a member of Tunisia's Ansar al-Sharia.[440]

March 24, 2015
ISIS claims responsibility for suicide bombing killing seven in Benghazi. Posted photos show attack and bomber.[441]

Il ne faisait ni de bien ni de mal pourquoi il ne se défend pas ?

ISIS carries on its campaign against Sufi shrines in Libya.

April 5, 2015
Wilayat Tripoli claims responsibility for SV-BIED attack killing four people in Misrata, with twenty-one wounded. Al-Bayan, ISIS radio, said the attacker was named Abu Dujana. [442]

April 13, 2015

Bomb attack at Moroccan embassy gate in Tripoli. Gunmen attack South Korea's mission on the same day. ISIS claims responsibility on Twitter. [443]

April 19, 2015

Al-Hayat releases another video of thirty Ethiopian Christians beheaded and shot, possibly in Wilayat Fazzan. [444]

April 27, 2015

ISIS kills Libyan journalists and leaves their bodies in the Green Mountain forests. Their throats were slit. They

The Al-Hayat video *"A Message Signed with Blood to the Nation of the Cross"* featured the mass execution of Coptic Christians from Egypt.

had been covering the inauguration of the newly elected parliament. [445]

June 9, 2015

ISIS kidnaps eighty-eight Eritrean Christians south of Tripoli and releases a video. Muslims and Christian women were separated from the captured group. [446]

June 10, 2015

ISIS kills senior AQ leader Nasser Akr. Akr was a member of the Derna Shura Council. Nine ISIS members are killed, and two Shura Council are killed, including Abu Salem Brigade commander Salim Derby. [447]

Suicide bomber before his SBVIED attack in Benghazi.

July 12, 2015

ISIS launches attacks on remote checkpoints along the Ajdibiyah–Tobruk road at the 200 km and 60 km gates. Seizing this highway would effectively cut off the major logistical line for Benghazi and give ISIS a strategic stranglehold over all other groups in Eastern Libya. Their attacks are repulsed.

ISIS in Libya kills more Christians in another video released by Al-Hayat.

August 14, 2015

Battles rage in Sirte leaving 150–200 dead. Libyan government attributes clashes to the ISIS assassination of Imam Khalid bin Rajab Ferjani, a local Salafist who had preached against ISIS the previous Friday. [448]

Libyan SPG-9 recoilless rifle on a technical in action.

November 13, 2015

The US launches airstrike to kill ISIS Wilayat Barqah leader Abu Nabil al-Anbari. Though US officials say he was killed, local Derna sources tell *Libya Herald* that he survived. [449]

The ISIS Toyota Truck Brigades parade through town.

ISIS fighters in Libya parade around with a Russian T-55 tank taken from base in Gardabiya.

WEAPONS AND EQUIPMENT ORDER OF BATTLE

Light Vehicles: Toyota Hilux pickup trucks, Land Rover Defender high-capacity pickup trucks.
BM-21 GRAD Multiple Rocket Launchers captured from Libyan National Army
UAE built Nimr Mine resistant armored vehicles captured from Libyan National Army
T-55 tanks captured from Libyan Militias—Gardabiya [450]

FINANCE

ISIS in Sirte started to collect taxes with penalty for failure to pay being death by beheading.[451] It also closed the banks in the area of Sirte, and ordered a shift to Sharia-compliant banking.[452]

ISIS IN TUNISIA

Tunisians are mainstay recruits of the foreign fighters in the Middle East terror world. As of June 2015, the Tunisian Ministry of Interior estimated the number of men who legally and illegally left the country to make their way to Iraq and Syria to join ISIS and al-Qaeda to be around three or four thousand. That makes Tunisians the largest body of foreigners in ISIS, second only to the native Iraqis and Syrians.[453] Tunisia is a hotbed recruiting ground for jihadists who rake the small villages and towns for the young, dispossessed, and aimless.

Tunisia may be the only "success story from the Arab Spring." It was in this country that a small personal protest against the corruption of the police started the "Jasmine Revolution," which led to mini-revolutions and the ouster of dictators such as Qaddafi and Mubarak and civil wars in Syria and Yemen.[454] These opposing images make Tunisia a nation of symbolic value for both sides on the war against terror. For those who stand with democracy, it represents the most viable opposition to ISIS in the realm of ideas: an Arab democracy, an achievable alternative to chaos and terror.[455] This is one of the reasons why, in November of 2015, Secretary of State John Kerry went to Tunisia to announce the US was extending loan guarantees to the country. It was an investment in the new democratic system, as well as an emblematic act in the fight against terror. [456]

On the other hand, ISIS has been trying to integrate its operatives back into Tunisia, a country that borders Libya and Algeria to become a central hub for expansion into the Maghreb regions of North Africa. A country with a peaceful and stable government does not provide the conditions necessary for ISIS to establish a foothold. ISIS thrives in chaos and expands in a political and security vacuum, so it has focused its terror effort on promoting civil unrest and political division by perpetrating terrorist attacks. Their seemingly odd choice of targeting tourism and tourists also has symbolic and practical value, as it undermines the economic basis of the country and destabilizes it.[457] Prior to the attacks in Tunisia, it had been one of the only North African countries (Morocco aside) with a major base of revenue from British and European visitors.

HISTORY OF ISIS IN TUNISIA

Since 2011, relations between terrorist groups operating from Libya and in Tunisia have only intensified. Some of these interactions date as far back as the 1980s. Many Tunisian jihadists trained in Libya with support of the Qaddafi regime and returned to organize several attacks on Tunisian soil. Tunisia, after the revolution, became a haven for terror groups. The Soufan Group identified the problem as "a security vacuum and porous borders." This has turned specific towns such as Bizerte and Ben Gardane into prime recruiting grounds for jihadists. Both al-Qaeda in the Islamic Maghreb (AQIM, led by Abdelmalek Droukdal, also known as Abu Musab Abdel Wadoud) and ISIS are believed to have presence in these locations and use them as smuggling crossroads.[458] Kasserine, with its proximity to the border with Algeria, makes a convenient location for remote meetings. With its mountainous terrains it can serve as cover for clandestine training camps. In one the poorer parts of town there is "Jihad Avenue," which earned that nickname after so many of the young men joined, and died, in terrorist operations. The poverty and lack of employment or future prospects makes the region's young men particularly susceptible to radicalization.[459]

Though al-Qaeda grew quickly after the 2011 Arab Spring in Tunisia, so has ISIS. The dilemma Tunisian terrorist groups face is in whether to remain loyal to AQIM or swear new allegiances to ISIS. Since many had already fought for ISIS in Syria, this transferred to their local loyalties as well. Propaganda was also a factor: ISIS promotes itself as louder and quicker, it creates the idea of momentum, and in the hands of a western media megaphone, its threats, no matter how minor, cannot be ignored. [460]

From December 2014 to July 2015, some eleven acts of terrorism have been attributed to AQIM or ISIS groups.[461] Many fear that this internal battle for power in the region between the groups may result in more high-profile attacks, causing the violence to escalate. This is true especially in Tunisia, where the tourism industry so vital to the economy has already become a target. Without decisive action from the Tunisian government and the international community, the dismantling of Tunisia's access to tourism capital is likely to continue through repeated attacks.

The country has a deep history with al-Qaeda going back to its founding in 1988, and some groups still remain loyal to them, though other terrorist branches in Tunisia lean towards an allegiance with ISIS, even if they have not yet declared their pledges or been accepted. What they have in common is their wish to disrupt the establishment of democracy in the country.[462]

In simple terms, the jihadists first appeared in Tunisia under President Zein el-Abidine Ben Ali, who attempted to impose highly unpopular secular measures on a highly religious populace, such as banning long beards and authorizing spying on mosques and religious groups. This created an underground resistance that eventually turned to violence. Ben Ali's rule ended with the revolution in 2011, but only when amnesty was given to those condemned under the old regime, so that they could return to public life. Subsequently, some groups transitioned from religious organizations into violent militias, and established connections to foreign terrorist groups, especially in Libya. After assassinations of leftist politicians, these groups went underground. [463]

In their wake came the Uqaba ibn Nafi Brigade, a Tunisian offshoot of AQIM led by Mohamad al-Arabi bin Mesoud (also known as Abi Yahya al-Jaza'iri). The Brigade's military leader is said to be Khalid al-Shaib (a.k.a. Lokman Abou Sakhr). They were responsible for most of the terrorist acts from 2012 up to the arrival of ISIS in 2014.

ISIS announced its presence in Tunisia in late 2014, in a video calling for Tunisians to "raise the flag of Islam and tear to shreds the flags of Charles de Gaulle and Napoleon." This order was taken up by some members of both Ansar al-Sharia and Uqaba ibn Nafi Brigade, in addition to two new groups: Jund al-Khailafa (Soldiers of the Caliphate) and T'alai Jund al-Khilafah. Most of these groups appear to be aware of each other and have cordial relations. According to Anouar Jamaoui from the Center of Research and Studies on Dialogue of Civilizations and Comparative Religions, "all of these groups have a shared ideological appeal based on a set of principles: Jihad in the name of God to establish Sharia law on earth, the establishment of a worldwide Islamic Caliphate, the belief that democracy and its associated trappings are forms of apostasy, and opposition to all secular regimes, the West, and all forms of political Islam."[464]

ISIS announced that it intended to form a new province to be called the Wilayat Ifriqiya—a throwback to the name of Tunisia in medieval era. This new province, which would include northeastern Libya and northwestern Algeria, and operating with ISIS's Tripoli Wiliyat, could challenge al-Qaeda's dominance in the region in yet another internal battle for power amongst extremist groups.[465, 466]

GROUPS WHO HAVE PLEDGED IN TUNISIA

Uqba ibn Nafi Battalion: Pledge of allegiance, May 28, 2015 via Twitter
Mujahidin of Tunisia al-Qayrawan-Bayat: Pledge via audio, May 18, 2015
Jund al-Khilafah Tunisia: March 31, 2015

Notable Tunisians in ISIS

Abu Aisha al-Tunisi: Algerian intelligence suggests he was communicating with ISIS spokesman Abu Mohammad al-Adnani about traffic of foreign fighters.
Abu Yahya al-Tunisi: Featured in Tarabulus Wilayat video telling fighters in Tunisia to join ISIS.

MAJOR TERRORIST ATTACKS

The Bardo Museum Attack

On March 18, 2015, two ISIS terrorists, Hatem Khachnaoui and Yassine Laabidi, infiltrated Tunisia from Libya and launched a terrorist attack against tourists visiting the Bardo Museum.

Most of the tourists were Europeans visiting the city on the cruise ships the MSC *Splendida* and the *Costa Fascinosa*, docked at the Port of La Goulette. Disembarked tourists usually travel to tourist spots in large shuttle buses. At the time of the attack there were over two hundred tourists in the area, principally from Poland, the UK, Germany, Spain, and Italy, accompanied by Tunisians visiting the museum.

The attack started with assault rifles and grenades at the Tunisian National Assembly. Two gunmen rammed the gate of the government building and opened fire on the guards

Security footage of ISIS terrorists Hatem Khachnaoui and Yassine Laabidi as they shot their way through the Bardo Museum. (Tunisian Brigade Antiterrorisme)

and armored vehicles blocking the road. A later audio report took claim for this attempt: "A normal sunny day, the beautiful weather and mild . . . Each carrying a weapon and grenades and sneaked toward the council [parliament] and the museum, apostates of the police and guards of the presidency who were carrying weapons did not intervene."

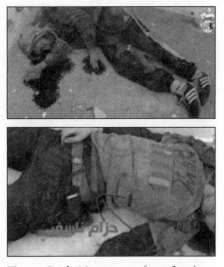

The two Bardo Museum attackers after the attack. The Arabic on the left indicates the suicide bomb belt. (Tunisian Brigade Anti-terrorisme)

Seeing the assault would fail, the attackers moved to their secondary target, the Bardo Museum, shooting eight tourists dead as they came off a tour bus. The terrorists chased down tourists and local security who were using the museum for shelter, killing eleven more. The attackers were specifically looking for foreign tourists. The security response was slowed because only one of the four guards was at work while the others were on break. Within minutes Tunisian SWAT teams—the Brigade Antiterrorisme (BAT) Armed Tunisian tactical units—made entry and engaged the attackers while rescuing most of the hostages. They cornered Laabidi and Kachnaoui and shot them dead, but not before coming under attack with RGD-1 hand grenades and killing a police dog. Twenty-one foreign tourists and Tunisians were killed in the attack. Both terrorists were wearing suicide bomb belts with Zero-fused grenade pin detonators.

ISIS took responsibility for the museum attack in *Dabiq* magazine number 8:

In the city of Tunis, two soldiers of the Islamic State carried out an assault on kāfir tourists in the Bardo National Museum. The two mujāhidīn, Abū Zakariyyā at-Tūnusī and Abū Anas at-Tūnusī, were sent on their mission after having trained with their brothers in Libya and having declared their bay'ah to the Khalīfah (hafidhahullāh). They returned to Tunisia, bravely advanced towards the security quarter in Tunis, entered the museum—located across from the Tunisian parliament—and poured terror on the kuffār inside, killing more than 20 of them and injuring a dozen others. They then faced off against the local murtadd security forces with their AK assault rifles, hand grenades, and explosive belts, and were killed fi sabīlillāh. The operation succeeded in bringing anguish to a number of the nations involved in the crusader coalition (Italy, France, Britain, Japan, Poland, Australia, Spain, and Belgium), after some of their own citizens became prey for the soldiers.

The Sousse Beach Attack

June 26, 2015: Thirty-eight people died in an attack on the Riu Imperial Marhaba Hotel in Port el-Kantaoui, located on the outskirts of Sousse, Tunisia carried out by a single ISIS gunman. The shooter was Seifeddine Yacoubi (a.k.a. Saifeddine Rezgui), a 23-year-old Kairouan University electrical engineering student from the town of Gaafour in the governorate of Siliana.

The attack took place around noon and started when the terrorist landed on the beach using a small boat and drew an AK-47 rifle hidden in a large umbrella. Rezgui attempted to blend into his environment in order to avoid early detection by law enforcement and eyewitnesses in the area. He was seen wearing common beach attire with a small bag attached to his person and an umbrella. The bag was later found to have multiple magazines for the AK-47 and small handmade explosive charges. An eyewitness noted they say saw Rezgui pull the AK-47 from a parasol and from there walked along the beach and resort area firing at his targets. ISIS released a statement on this attack on June 26, 2015:[467]

Death and injury of dozens of nationals of the Crusader coalition in a high quality raid in the city of Sousse in Muslim: Tunisia. In a high quality raid, whose basis for success was prepared by Allah, a soldier of the caliphate, the devout knight [Abu Yahya al-Qayrawani] went to attack unclean nests, nests of immorality, abomination and heresy against Allah, in the city of Sousse. In spite of the stringent [security] measures that were taken around these nests on the Al-Qantawi beach, our brother managed to reach the target at the [Imperial] Hotel and, with the help of Allah, he managed to make his way to cause the infidels immense sorrow, nearly forty dead and a similar number of wounded, most of them nationals of countries of the Crusader coalition that is fighting against the Caliphate State. This was a painful blow and a message painted in blood to those in Tunisia who have rejected Islam and to those who are behind them, their masters in the Crusader alliance [i.e. the West]. With Allah's help, they will find out what will hurt them in the days ahead. In Muslim Tunis there are devout men who do not condone exploitation and [have first-hand knowledge of] the battlefields of jihad in Iraq, Syria, Libya, and elsewhere. We ask Allah to accept our brother to the group of shahids and turn his blood into light that will illuminate the path of the believers, especially of Allah, wherever they may be.

November 24, 2015

ISIS carried out a suicide bombing against a bus containing soldiers of the Presidential Guard on a main road in Tunis. Twelve officers died, while sixteen were wounded. This was the third major attack by the group on Tunisian soil. ISIS named the attacker as Abu Abdallah al-Tunisi. Tunisia's government identified him as Hussam al-Abdelli. Neighbors had witnessed his transformation from a local vendor who loved soccer to a person of isolation. It is common for ISIS terrorists to socially withdraw, once they have become radicalized.[468] He had previously been held by the government on suspicion of association with terrorist organizations.

Since the start of these attacks, the government has attempted to fight these threats, with some measure of success. Police and security forces were deployed and carried out over 700 operations and made arrests of over 120 suspects. The president has also announced that it will close down mosques that are operating illegally and fostering extremism. However, there is only so much the Tunisian government can do, being as it is in such close proximity to other countries where ISIS presence is strong.

OTHER SIGNIFICANT EVENTS

In July 2015, the Tunisian government announced plans to build a 100-mile-long wall along the Libyan border. This would help protect the country from terrorist militants coming and going to Libya. Even so, the border—which is three times as long as the proposed wall—is hard to patrol in desert land were militants can still roam with some freedom. The gunman at Sousse and two gunmen from the museum, for example, trained together in Sabratha, Libya, after crossing the border illegally.

ISIS IN ALGERIA

HISTORY

Algerian terrorist groups had not drawn much attention until September 14, 2014, when they pledged their allegiance to ISIS.[469] A week later, on September 21, they encountered fifty-five-year-old Herve Gourdel, a Frenchman and a tour guide, hiking in a national park. Only a few days after capturing Gourdel, they released a video titled "A Message with Blood to the French Government," which showed Gourdel's severed head and corpse.[470] Gourdel's capture and brutal execution were the ticket to terrorism fame. It was the first country other than Syria to have witnessed the beheading of a Western hostage[471]

ISIS video from Algeria shows Herve Gourdel before being beheaded in September 2014.

This act of terrorism against a foreigner in Algerian territory was said to be an act of obedience to ISIS, who orders their followers to attack members of countries that oppose them. It was also an answer to France's airstrike attacks on ISIS.

Jund al-Khilafa started out as is a splinter group from AQIM (al Qaeda in the Islamic Maghreb), which, for its part, gained force during the civil war in the 1990s, which involved Algerian Islamist groups. The group's name is not exclusive: it means "soldiers of the caliphate" and they share it with other radical groups in different countries.

JUND AL-KHILAFA PLEDGES LOYALTY TO ISIS

Jund al-Khilafa in Algeria officially broke from al-Qaeda in September 2014, through a communication by leader Abdelmalek Gouri (also known as Khaled Abu Suleiman). In this communication, he took an oath of allegiance to ISIS, claiming AQIM had "deviated from the right path." He pledged his loyalty to ISIS

In Algeria, Jund al-Khilafa releases video pledging its loyalty to ISIS.

leader Abu bakr al-Baghdadi: "You have in the Islamic Maghreb men. If you order them, they will obey you."[472] [473]

This pledge was recognized only in November, through a communiqué by ISIS accepting this bayah from Jund al Khilafa in Algeria at the same time as other elements in Saudi Arabia, Yemen, Libya, and Sinai. The news, as it pertains to Algeria, did not signify another province, or wilayat, for the group there does not control territory at this point.[474]

Since their pledge and recognition by ISIS, Jund al-Khilafa has suffered a series of setbacks. Agence France-Presse reported in December 2014 that the Algerian army had killed their leader, Abdelmalik Gouri. He died in Sidi Daoud alongside two other members of the group. The local army has also killed other several militants and seized weapons, ammunition, and explosives in a continuing series of aggressive combat operations and ambushes.[475] The government estimated at that point, fifty-six JAK terrorists had already been killed that year. [476]

This fierce retaliation from the army made the group go silent, and they were not heard from until March 2015, but even then only in the form of a statement praising a new allegiance to ISIS, that of Boko Haram.[477] This lack of activity in Algeria may indicate ISIS playing a long game, preparing a future jihad. However, in Algeria, signs of action have petered off after the death of their leader and their apparent inability to gain territory or organize campaigns. The beheading of Gourdel was before ISIS accepted their pledge, and there are no reported governance activities—dawas—in the region. [478]

The United States designated Jund al-Khilafa as a terrorist organization on October 1, 2015.[479]

ORGANIZATION OF ISIS IN ALGERIA

Emir: Khaled Abu Suleimane, whose real name was Gouri Abdelmalek, killed December 22, 2014, by the Algerian army.[480]
Judiciary: Unknown
Shura Council: Covert Membership
Sharia Council: Covert Membership
Military Council: Covert Membership
Security Council: Covert Membership

ISIS IN MALI

HISTORY

Mali's terror war has only recently come to the attention of Western media after a November 20, 2015 hotel attack left twenty-two people dead.[481] While authorship for the attack has been claimed by al-Qaeda in the Islamic Maghreb (AQIM) and its offshoot al-Mourabitoun, many proposed that this attack had a roundabout link to ISIS, as it may have been a competitive response to ISIS's November 13, 2015 attacks in Paris.[482]

The Paris and Mali attacks betray an intense rivalry between ISIS and al-Qaeda. Mali's northern region is essentially a vast, ungoverned desert, and the country shares borders with Algeria and Libya, who have long been al-Qaeda territory. The group, however, has lately been losing ground to ISIS. At the time of the Paris attacks, security experts said there was no proof of ISIS presence in Mali. [483] This rivalry between al-Qaeda and ISIS had been brewing long before 2015, but was heightened once the crisis in Mali took place, with much online activity from members of both groups "jostling" each other on social media. As the *New York Times* put it, the Mali attack could be seen as an attempt of one-upmanship for "bragging rights."[484]

The northern region of Mali has become one of the most dangerous places for UN workers.[485] In October 2015, the Malian Foreign Minister had appealed to the UN for international forces to reinforce the peace-keeping missions, as Mali "again runs the risk of becoming the destination of hordes of terrorists who have been forced out of other parts of the world." [486]

Mali had shown promises of a democracy until 2012, when Tuareg separatists got their hands on weapons smuggled from a post-Qaddafi Libya and attempted to declare independence. This insurgency met little resistance from the government and for a while, in 2012, the group effectively controlled the northern part of the country. [487] This insurgency was eventually hijacked by al-Qaeda and smaller groups like Ansar Dine and the Movement of Oneness and Jihad in West Africa (MUJAO). The Tuareg rule gave way to Sharia law.[488]

Worried about the situation, the French sent troops and launched airstrikes in 2013.[489] This military offensive resulted in the scattering of fighters away from the main towns. The UN also arrived en force in 2013, with nine thousand troops at its peak.[490] The dispersal of jihadists, however, did not mean the end of terrorism in Mali. The violence spiked after French troops drew down from forty-five hundred soldiers to around one thousand. With little help from the government, the UN now stands as the lone player in the battle against extremist groups, even without the necessary tools to do so, such as training, intelligence, or equipment. [491]

Despite its well-established presence in Mali, al-Qaeda found itself in a weakened position internationally, having to prove itself to its followers—and the world at large.

This particular jihad for prominence in the Islamic world was first noted in an August 2015 al-Qaeda attack on a hotel, which left five UN staff and twelve others dead.[492] Then came the November attack following the Paris massacre, al-Qaeda's "answer to ISIS." This was then followed a few days later by a yet another al-Qaeda rocket attack at a UN base in the north, which killed three people.[493]

ALLEGIANCES AND CONFUSION

Al-Mourabitoun, or "the Sentinels," is al-Qaeda's main offshoot in the region and is also present in Libya and Niger. Through AQIM, it can also be linked to Ansar Dine in the Mali region. "The Sentinels" were formed from two other groups; the Movement for Oneness and Jihad in West Africa (MUJAO, led by Adnan Abu Walid Sahraoui) and the Masked Men Brigade (led by Mokhtar Belmokhtar).

MUJAO pledges Loyalty to ISIS

In May 2014, there was some confusion reagarding pledges to ISIS when a radio message purported to be from Adnan Abu Walid Sahraoui (the leader for the former MUJAO) pledged al-Mourabitoun's allegiance to ISIS's al-Baghdadi. The report came through news agency al-Akhbar, a common channel for terrorists to disseminate their desired information, and seemed to encompass the entirety of al-Mourabitoun. [494] This oath was rejected a short time later by Mokhtar Belmokhtar, which indicated a possible split in the group.

According to Belmokhtar, the pledge was invalid, since it had not been approved by the groups's shura council and could not therefore represent the will of al-Mourabitoun. Although Belmokhtar had once formed his own group (the previously mentioned Masked Men Brigade) separately from al-Qaeda, he still pledged allegiance to them by way of AQIM's leader, Ayman al Zawahri. In 2014, in fact, when ISIS sought to expand its so-called caliphate, Belmokhtar instead said he would not switch from AQIM (and his "emir" al Zawahiri) to ISIS (and "caliph" al Baghdadi). [495]

It is possible that this allegiance statement from May 2014 referred only to al-Sahraoui and MUJAO, and that they are now part of ISIS. This muddle at least shed some light into the leadership of al-Mourabitoun, which has an undefined hierarchy to outsiders. For a while, it was rumored that their leader was Abu Bakr al-Muhajir, also known as Abu Bakr al-Masri ("the Egyptian"), who was killed in April 2014. After his death, there were doubts regarding who his successor would be. The jumbled pledge of allegiance gave the initial appearance that al Sahraoui was the new leader, but Belmokhtar's reply showed that that was probably not the case.

After this debacle in May, a July 2015 online statement by al-Mourabitoun clarified that Belmokhtar was in fact the group's leader, a decision made by a shura council.[496] This statement of leadership was signed with yet another variant in the group's name: al-Murabitoun—Al Qaeda in West Africa. This signature makes the link between both organizations even more official. Al-Mourabitoun is considered by the US Department of State to be the greatest near-term threat in the region.[497]

So far, no response has come from ISIS to this situation or this (partial) pledge on the part of MUJAO.[498]

CHAPTER 6

ISIS IN WEST AFRICA: BOKO HARAM

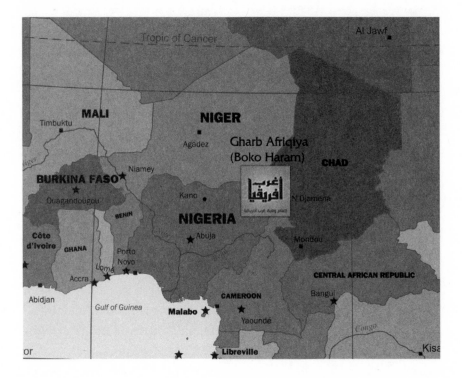

HISTORY

Before the high-profile abduction of three hundred Nigerian schoolgirls from the town of Chibok in 2014, Boko Haram was a little-known terror group outside Nigeria. When a few escaped girls revealed the horrific details of their abduction, the story of the ultra-violent religious cult stunned the world. Despite the precedents of mass murder set by ISIS and its associated groups, Boko Haram has eclipsed virtually every atrocity in Iraq and Syria conducted by caliphate forces.

Boko is a Nigerian dialect word that means "Western Education," *Haram* the Arabic word for something that is forbidden by Islam. Before its 2015 oath of allegiance to the Islamic State, Boko Haram's official name was Jama'atu Ahlis Sunna Lidda'await wal-Jihad—"People Committed to the Propagation of the Prophet's Teaching and Holy War." After the alliance, it was renamed Wilayat Gharb Afriqiya, or "Islamic State Province of West Africa."[499]

Neo-Salafist cleric Mohammed Yusuf, a follower of Osama bin Laden and the al-Qaeda cult variant of Islamic fundamentalism or Takfiri ideology, founded Boko Haram in 2002 in the city of Maiduguri, in the far northeastern part of Nigeria. In order to create closer ties with al-Qaeda, he dispatched some of his group's members to Afghanistan, Pakistan, and Sudan for terrorist insurgency training and strategic advice. He also sought funds to construct his own mosques and religious schools to further broaden the appeal of his preaching to a wider group of Nigerians.[500]

Nigeria is the largest Muslim country in Africa. Whereas the Muslim population of 160 million follow the Maliki school of Islam, the cult followers of al-Qaeda and ISIS in Nigeria (and their hostages) number approximately 10,000. Despite this miniscule 0.0016 percent representation of the population, Boko Haram's terrorist actions occupy almost 100 percent of the media's focus.

Mohammed Yusuf was inspired to create an ultraorthodox fundamentalist Islamic nation state along the lines of the Taliban in Afghanistan. He accepted the Saudi Salafist school of thought called al-Wala wal Bara, or "love of all things that are of God and detestation of all things un-Islamic." He believed, like the Taliban, that western practices in clothing, music, art, science, immunization, cultural diversity, and foods had corrupted the Muslim practice of sole devotion to the worship of God, to the exclusion of all else. He rejected that the earth was round, Darwinism, and evolution. Despite coming from a nation of Muslims, Yusuf taught his followers that Nigeria was actually secular and had been taken over by Western influence. As a result, the good Muslims who followed him would be compelled to band together and cleanse Nigeria of the bad Muslims. When he founded Boko Haram, they quickly acquired the appellation of the "Nigerian Taliban."[501]

In 2003, Boko Haram adopted the al-Qaeda (and now ISIS) practice of abandoning cities, moving to an uncontrolled space, and creating their own jihad zone after the fashion of the Prophet Mohammed when he left Mecca for Medina to start Islam. All ISIS adherents perform this rite by both physically leaving their lands and traveling to Iraq, Syria, Afghanistan, or to a local Hijrah zone to form up (Jamaa') and move away from their past and the unbelievers.

Many Boko followers left the city and went to the bush with Yusuf to start a new "Afghanistan." Like al-Qaeda and ISIS, a core component of this ideology is to cleanse Islam of all infidels (primarily Westerners) and apostates (all other Muslims) through perpetual jihad. Each follower must wage jihad until Islam is safe or until they die. To not be martyred may be the will of God, but it is a greater honor to die in jihad. To this end, Boko Haram armed its followers and launched a Taliban-style insurgency to purify or subjugate the rest of Nigeria.

In 2004 Boko initiated clashes with the government by following the classic Iraq and Afghanistan insurgency playbook. They started at a low level by attacking remote police stations to acquire arms. On occasion they would ambush the residences of local and regional officials and kill them and their families, in order to destabilize the social hierarchy. The Nigerian government responded by destroying their encampments, killing numerous followers and arresting others. But like all good insurgencies, stepping on them was like stepping on mercury; they broke up, went out into the desert, and reformed when the pressure was lifted.[502]

By 2009 they were ready to start their insurgency. Boko attempted to seize the city of Maiduguri and killed over a thousand civilians in the process. During the siege Boko Haram members hunted and summarily executed Christians.

In 2009 Mohammed Yusuf was said to be captured in Maiduguri and executed by police. Abu Muhammed Abn Muhammed Abu Bakr al-Shekau, Yusuf's arguably insane former deputy, succeeded him. Like many deputies who step into the shoes of a popular leader, Abu Bakr Shekau was Stalin-like in his personal ambition. Shekau would soon demonstrate a ruthlessness and passion for killing that made the good old days of Yusuf's reign seem benign. In time, Shekau transformed Boko Haram from a small terror force to a large-scale insurgent group along the lines of the Taliban.

Like Yusuf, Shekau adopted the bin Laden doctrine that all of the neo-Salafist jihad zones must form branches of a new caliphate and then spread in remote regions of a country until each connected and then collapsed the post-colonial host government. A new Islamic state would then replace the old government. Shekau learned these lessons quickly. Observing a tactic popularized by the Taliban and Al-Qaeda in Iraq, his men stormed Bauchi prison and freed seven hundred prisoners to gain experienced manpower.

In June 2011, Boko launched its first sustained terror campaign. They initiated the first suicide bombing in the history of Nigeria by trying to drive a vehicle packed with explosives into the national police headquarters, the Louis Edet House in Abuja. Only one policeman and the bomber were killed. This was followed by a gun attack on a beer

garden serving alcohol that killed twenty-five. Boko then mimicked the Al-Qaeda in Iraq attack on the United Nations headquarters in Baghdad with a suicide car-bombing campaign against the United Nations

Abu Bakr Shekau preaches the ISIS cult message to his followers.

headquarters in Abuja, killing twenty-one people. From that point Nigeria was truly at war.

Boko focused itself on mass terror massacres, particularly against Christian churches and towns that support the government. They killed 185 in attacks on churches in Kano, drove a suicide car bomb into a church on Christmas Day that killed 43, stormed the Mamudo government secondary school in Yobe State and slaughtered 41 school children, killed over 600 civilians in Christian villages in Gwoza and Gamboru in Borno state, and killed or displaced over 2,000 people in the siege of the city of Baga, which they burned to the ground.

Boko Haram attempted to carve out a mini-province by operating a remote zone that includes parts of northern Nigeria, southern Chad, northwestern Cameroon, and southern Niger. The Council on Foreign Relations reported that the territory controlled by the sect is approximately the size of Belgium.[503]

Since the insurgency started their killing spree in 2009, numerous civilians have been killed while millions more have been displaced. The number of civilians killed varies greatly. Some say the death toll is at ten thousand but could be as high as twenty thousand. Many deaths may have gone unreported by overwhelmed officials, due to the Islamic practice of rapid burial. While the number of people that were displaced from their houses by the conflict is unknown, UNICEF did report that the number of children who were displaced from the territories is at 1.4 million, with 1.2 million of those refugees coming directly from northern Nigeria.[504]

By 2016, Boko Haram held the title of "The World's Deadliest Terrorist Group," surpassing even ISIS. Watching from afar, the Islamic State found much to admire in the group's mayhem against the infidels of Nigeria. When Boko Haram leadership offered Abu Bakr al-Baghdadi allegiance, he quickly accepted.

PLEDGE OF ALLIANCE TO ISIS

On March 7, 2015, Abu Bakr Shekau changed Boko Haram's alliance from al-Qaeda and swore allegiance to ISIS's leader Abu Bakr

ISIS video style, copied by Boko Haram, now shows forced confessions followed by beheadings.

al-Baghdadi.[505] Shekau declared that all areas and territory under its control to be part of the Islamic state and dedicated the caliphate.

A month after the alliance, Boko Haram renamed itself as the "Islamic State–West Africa Province" (ISWAP). Boko quickly took up the ISIS practices of releasing videos depicting mass executions of civilians and security forces.[506]

ORGANIZATION OF BOKO HARAM

Little is known about the leadership of Boko Haram, but it resembles current ISIS and al-Qaeda organizations.

The Emir is Abu Bakr Shekau. In August 2015, Chadian President Idriss Deby alleged that Abu Bakr Shekau was replaced by Mahamat Daoud, another unknown figure. Shekau denied this on an audio recording, declaring that he was still alive and in command.[507]

Below Shekau is the thirty-member Shura (Advisory) Council. The council is the highest decision making body and commands the subordinate cells. Two unknown figures have appeared to take leading roles within the structure, Khalid al-Barnawi and Mamman Nur. They might have been responsible for expanding Boko Haram's outside connections with al-Qaeda of the Islamic Maghreb (AQIM), Somalis' al-Shabaab, the Jihad in West Africa Movement (MUJAO), and other smaller Salafist militant groups in Africa. Mamman Nur coordinated the bombing of the UN office in Abuja and it was reported that he might have been also responsible for the bombing of the churches in Nigeria.[508]

The subordinate combat operational cells are independent military departments. Each department has its own sets of specialization and responsibility, including:

- Direct combat against security forces
- Kidnapping, ransom, and torture

- Target Selection/Intelligence collection
- Suicide bombing
- IED planting team
- Vehicle acquisition teams (for SVBIEDs)
- Recruiting

Boko Haram is known to have two spokespersons called Abu Zaid and Abu Qaqa, but their true identities are unknown.

Because of the umbrella-like structure, the size and strength of Boko Haram is difficult to ascertain. Some put the number between 5,000 to 50,000 fighters, others put the numbers to an estimated 7,000 to 10,000 fighters with an additional 10,000 press-ganged into the group.[509] A median assessment, taking into account major losses in February of 2015, places them between 2,000–5,000 hardliners now trapped in the Sambisa forest.

Peter Dorrie, writing for *War is Boring*, noted that despite the fact that neighboring countries have sent 35,000 troops to fight an estimated 10,000 Boko Haram, numbers do not tell the whole picture, as the group relies on rough terrain and support from the local populace to survive. Thus far they have been holding on despite immense pressure.[510]

FEMALE SUICIDE BOMBING CAMPAIGN

Boko Haram has switched back and forth in its waves of attacks on Nigerian forces and the civilian populace. They would oscillate from frontal infantry assaults on cities to an asymmetrical approach using suicide bombers to attack both hard and soft targets.[511] As of this writing there have been nearly eighty-five women who have blown themselves up in bombings.

Boko has pioneered the use of children as young as eleven and teen girls as suicide bombers.[512] Professor Mia Bloom of the University of Massachusetts at Lowell believes that the bombers were either brainwashed and/or sexually exploited and tortured by Boko Haram. Due to the culture of shame in many tribal regions and Islamic communities, they may have felt no other option but to seek redemption though the cultist belief that suicide bombers go directly to heaven. The use of female suicide bombers also has the advantage of perfect concealment to blend in among other Muslim women of Nigeria. As a result, single women entering markets are now quickly eyed with suspicion by security forces.

PROPAGANDA

ISIS beheads captured Nigerian Police Force officer.

As with the ISIS main force, Boko Haram propagates by means of social networking and media. The group made numerous videos renowned for the brutality against civilians and military servicemen. A good example was the first Boko video of the execution of a captured soldier. The ten-minute video begins with combat footage of clashes with the Nigerian army and the Boko Haram, followed by images of dozens of dead soldiers. It ends with Boko Haram members beheading the soldier.[513] Just as with the slick media-ready videos of ISIS beheading soldiers and civilians, Boko Haram videotapes now depict identical beheading shots and show the executioner placing the head on the back of the dead body. Other videos show the shooting of injured Nigerian soldiers in the head, decapitation of a civilian, and the execution of two men believed to be spies.[514]

Kayode Akindele, a Nigeria-based financial, political, and risk analyst for TIA Capital, noted that after the loyalty oath to the caliphate, Boko has moved away from portraying its leader Abu Bakr al-Shekau as a mad African warlord and focused its media on the operations of its terrorists. This came after Boko released a video of Shekau saying that the three hundred abducted Chibok girls were converted to Islam and were all married to his men. [515] Additionally, his rant denouncing 90 percent of Islam as infidels did not help matters.

Due to this lack of focus on Shekau personally in propaganda videos, there is much speculation that he has been killed, injured, or deposed. The Nigerian military claimed countless times that he was killed but he always comes back in a video to refute those claims. It is quite possible that because he pledged alliance with the Islamic State he now must take a lower profile role in the IS chain of command and leave the pontificating to Abu Bakr al-Baghdadi.[516]

Boko Haram also uses social networks such as Twitter to post videos, announcements, battle reports, images of their child soldiers in training, or the capture of towns. They even used the application to announce their allegiance to ISIS. It was reported that after the opening of the account, Boko Haram gathered approximately five thousand followers. The account has since been shut down.[517]

SIGNIFICANT EVENTS

New ISIS West Africa video does not show Abu Bakr Shekau, leading to speculation that he's dead.

July 2009
Boko Haram carries out ten attacks in four provinces, killing 150 people during an uprising between Boko Haram and the police.[518] Founder Mohammed Yusuf executed while in police custody.

September 2010
Raid on a prison in Bauchi, Nigeria, frees over seven hundred prisoners.[519]

December 2010
Boko Haram claims responsibility for four detonation of IEDs killing thirty-eight people and injuring seventy-four more in Kalong shopping market.[520]

June 2011
Boko Haram's first suicide bombing takes place at Nigerian police headquarters in Abuja.[521]

June 2011

Eight to ten Boko Haram affiliates throw bombs and fire gunshots at a beer garden in Dala Kabompi, killing twenty-five civilians and injuring thirty more.[522]

August 2011

SVBIED (Suicide Vehicle-Borne Improvised Explosive Device) bombing at UN building in Abuja kills twenty-one and wounds sixty others.[523]

November 2011

Boko Haram militants attack six churches, four police stations, a military Joint Task Force office, the State Security Services building, a college, and local businesses, killing over sixty people.

December 2011

St. Teresa Catholic church bombing in Madalla kills thirty-seven people and injures fifty-seven.[524]

January 2012

Attacks across Kano kill 185 people.[525]

February 2012

Boko Haram militants open fire on civilians after planting bombs in a market in Maiduguri, killing thirty-eight people. Eight assailants subsequently killed by Joint Task Force.

April 2012

Car bomb near church in Kaduna kills about forty people.

September 2012

Twenty-one coordinated attacks on cell towers with explosives destroy thirty-one towers and kill fifteen.[526]

November 2012

A bus-borne SVBIED crashes into St. Andrew Military Protestant Church. A second SVBIED later detonates outside the church to target first responders. Both attacks leave thirty-two people dead and eleven others wounded.[527]

December 2012
Attacks on churches across Nigeria kill approximately forty.

February 2013
Boko Haram kidnaps seven French citizens in Cameroon's Waza National Park. Tanguy Moulin-Fournier, his wife, brother, and four children are freed in April 2013.[528]

August 2013
Attack on mosque in Konduga during prayer kills forty-four.[529]

September 2013
Militants dressed in military fatigues set checkpoints in Beni Shiek village, killing 142 people.

July 2013
Boko Haram sets fire to the Government Secondary School in Yobe state and shoot people fleeing the fire, killing forty-six and wounding four others.[530]

May 2013
Boko Haram militants in Bama Town launch a series of coordinated attacks on a military barracks, police station, prison, and several other government buildings, killing fifty-five people including the assailants.

September 2013
Attack on college in Gujba kills fifty teachers and male students.[531]

April 2014
Boko Haram kidnaps approximately three hundred female students from the Government Secondary School in the town of Chibok in Borno.[532]

May 2014
Attack in Gamboru Ngala, a town in Nigeria, kills three hundred people.[533]

April 2015
Boko Haram pledges alliance with ISIS.

July 2015

First beheading video since making alliance with ISIS.[534]

July 2015

Boko Haram militants gun down nearly 150 people as they pray in mosques during the holy month of Ramadan in Borno State.[535]

February 2015

Attack on Christian village in Izghe kills 121.[536]

September 2015

Militants on horseback ride to the village of Baanu in Borno State, Nigeria, kill seventy-nine people.[537]

September 2015

Militants kill 30 and wound 145 others in an attack on a market and infirmary in northern Cameroon.[538]

October 2015

Two teenage female suicide bombers blow themselves up in the village of Kangeleri, Cameroon, killing nine people and injuring twenty-nine others.[539]

October 2015

Five coordinated suicide bombings kill thirty-six and wound fifty others in Lake Chad.[540]

November 2015

Four suicide bombers blow themselves up in northern Cameroon, killing six and wounding twelve others.[541]

WEAPONS AND EQUIPMENT

Boko Haram's weapons are primarily stolen in raids on Nigerian and Chadian authorities, as well as purchased through the Central African black market in the four-country border region.[542] Caches seized by the Nigerian army reveal a wide mix of weapons, though predominantly from Nigeria's own army. The Libyan civil war led rebels to seize numerous weapons from the regime's bases and depots, which ended up on the black markets. According to Michael Leiter, a former director of the National Counter Terrorism Center, some of those weapons from the Libyan army stocks were smuggled down through Niger and Chad where the borders are unpatrolled, unmarked, and rife with illicit trade.[543] Some Nigerian servicemen in the military are sympathizers or more likely corrupt. For the right amount of money, an armory door can be left unlocked, or a truck full of ammunition may be left on the side of the road. A Nigerian military officer that was indicted for supplying numerous weapons to Niger Delta militants.[544]

Some of the weapons that have been documented in Boko Haram's arsenal were Toyota Hilux technicals mounted with ZPU-23-2 anti-air-craft guns. Boko Haram acquired heavy armor through combat actions; Nigerians have recaptured T-55 tanks and a Panhard ERC-90 "Sagaie" armored patrol vehicle from Boko Haram in Konduga.[545]

The standard rifle is the ubiquitous AK-47 Kalashnikov. They utilize Improvised Explosives Devices (IEDs), grenades, mortars, and land mines. Basic terror operatives use arson and petrol bombs to carry out attacks on churches and residences.[546] With conscripted former soldiers the group could master the skillsets needed to operate and run tanks and other heavy vehicles; T-55s are not sophisticated machines.

In one of his videos, Shekau claimed that his militants brought down a Nigerian military jet. On a still image, a Boko Haram militant is standing on the wreckage of a plane they claimed to have brought down.[547] Whether this video was propaganda and just desert wreckage from another time, or whether Boko Haram militants really brought down the plane, is unconfirmed. Another type of weapon used by the cult is assassination motorbikes, with an operator and a gunman. Since Boko Haram's weapons are similar to the weapons used by other terrorist groups such as ISIS in Iraq, Syria, and Libya and by

Boko Haram member displays weapons captured from Nigerian army.

the al-Qaeda affiliates, Boko Haram fighters can easily operate in other regions should the need arise.

There is speculation about how Boko Haram conducts maintenance and acquires spare parts for their materiel. The tanks and ACP's need diesel fuel, ammunition, and spare parts for them to be operational. The Council on Foreign Relations suggests that the maintenance of the heavy equipment is likely done by former military personnel, while the ammunition, fuel, and spare parts come from either Nigeria itself or from the war-torn country of Libya.[548]

The *Washington Post* reported on the "bunkering" of oil in Nigeria, the practice of cutting pipelines using hacksaws and other cutting implements. When the oil company sees the drop in pressure, they dial back the pressure long enough for thieves to attach spigots to the line. Once the pressure rises, the thieves simply divert the oil out of the line for resale or use.[549]

Boko Haram using captured Nigerian 25 pound field gun.

Aljazeera News also reported similar practices, but by means of storing the oil in boats and barges and by distilling it into diesel through improvised factories.[550] Boko Haram could use such approaches to fuel their tanks and other vehicles.

FINANCE

How Boko Haram finances its operations is relatively unknown. Some reporting suggests that the fundraising for the Boko began after the 9/11 attacks. Allegedly Osama bin Laden sent an aide with approximately $3 million to dispense among groups that have similar ideology as that of al-Qaeda, particularly to Yusuf's foundation.[551] Linda

Thomas Greenfield, US Assistant Secretary of State for African affairs, has suggested that they acquire funds through criminal activities such as kidnapping, robberies, forced donations, and extortion of the local populace.[552] When Boko Haram militants kidnapped three hundred female students from Chibok in 2014, Abu Bakr Shekau released a video offering to sell the girls as sex slaves and wives. Boko Haram also receives funding through strategic money paths and networks such as ISIS, al-Qaeda in the Land of Islamic Maghreb and from the militants of al-Shabaab from Somalia.[553] These groups have been known to train Boko Haram members.

CHAPTER 7

ISIS IN EUROPE, NORTH AMERICA, AND AUSTRALIA

تهاوت باريس

PARIS S'EST EFFONDRÉ

ISIS IN FRANCE

After the American invasion of Iraq in 2003, it quickly became apparent that French citizens were participating in the fight against the US forces as members of Al-Qaeda in Iraq (AQI). In 2003–2004 alone, the French intelligence service arrested 117 Frenchmen for activities associated with joining the Iraq insurgency.[554] The pathway from France to Iraq was known as the French Network. It was a group of likeminded activists, adventurers, and fanatics who joined al-Qaeda's call to defeat America in the center of historic Islam. Three French citizens of this network were Abdelhalim Badjoudj, Redouane el-Hakimand, and Tarek Ouinis. Badjoudj was killed as a suicide bomber in an October 2004 attack where he drove and detonated an SVBIED that injured two American soldiers and two Iraqi police officers. Hakimand was killed by an airstrike in Fallujah in 2004 while fighting as an insurgent, and Ouinis was killed in a firefight with US troops in the Sunni Triangle.[555] Numerous French fighters served in leadership and combat roles in AQI and those that remained past 2011 became members of ISIS. As of 2016, as many as 1,700 members of ISIS are French citizens.

ISIS understood the power of its call for Hijrah, emigration to an Islamic land, and Jamaa, gathering together to work and live in prayer. They also know how to manipulate the minds of the Europeans to reject their lives in the unholy land of the Crusaders, and to come live as an Islamic knight in a land made up solely of the best Muslims. They could be given a wife, take whatever riches they could, and kill with impunity like Rambo.

French fighter "Abu Suhayb al-Faranci" is profiled in a highly polished tribute by al-Hayat.

At the beheading of Peter Kassig and of the eighteen Syrian pilots, two French citizens were identified in connection with the decapitations. One was Maxime Hauchard; the second was identified as Michael Dos Santos.[556] Just as the British subject Jihadi

John decapitated the former US Army Ranger Kassig, the two French-men decapitated two of the eighteen Syrian captives. Twenty French citizens from the French town of Lunel have left for Syria; two were killed in combat fighting for ISIS, identified as Karim and Hamza.[557]

This appealed to many. However, those who could not make it to the jihad zone were encouraged to stay in France, and to mentally and physically alienate themselves from French society. They were to make symbolic attacks against French citizens wherever possible. France is an attractive target for ISIS due to its international appeal, and because it represents everything jihadists hate the most.

Mohammed Merah murdered seven people in southwest France in 2012 by conducting a motorcycle "run and gun" attack across the city of Toulouse. Riding a stolen Yamaha 500CC T-MAX motorcycle, he rode up to his victims and gunned them down. He shot and killed a French Muslim paratrooper, then killed two more Muslim French soldiers. He then attacked the Ozar Hatorah Jewish day school and murdered four, including Jewish children. Merah was said to have radicalized in prison and traveled to Pakistan and Afghanistan twice before carrying out this mission. Merah was found holed up in an apartment, armed with a fully automatic AK-47, a Uzi submachine gun, and six pistols. Explosives were found in his brother's car. After a thirty-six-hour siege where he sprayed the French RAID SWAT teams with automatic weapons fire, he was killed with a sniper bullet to the head.[558]

THE PARIS MASSACRE: ISIS DECLARES WAR ON FRANCE

On November 13, 2015, three teams of ISIS suicide bombers and gunmen conducted multiple, almost-simultaneous attacks throughout northern and eastern Paris. They killed 131 people and wounded 368 others. The attacks consisted of mass shootings, suicide bombings, and a suicide hostage barricade. The attacks started at 9:20 p.m., with two suicide bombers exploded at the Stade de France Soccer stadium.

A second team began running-gun attacks on the Rue Bichat, the Rue de la Fontaine-au-Roi, and the Rue de Charonne, and culminated with a suicide bombing at a restaurant on Boulevard Voltaire. At almost the same time, a third team of four terrorists wearing suicide vests entered the Bataclan theatre from the rear and began systematically shooting as many hostages as they could find.[559] French counterterrorism police prepared for a hostage barricade, but by midnight realized that the terrorists were killing hostages, and forced a dynamic entry and engaged the terrorists in a massive gun battle. The terrorists were killed when their bomb belts exploded or were shot dead by police. The siege ended at 1:00 a.m.[560]

The attack was reminiscent of the November 2008 Mumbai attacks that killed 162 people, where the Lashkar-e-Taiba teams hit multiple civilian targets with overwhelming firepower and suicide bombings almost simultaneously. The element of surprise at multiple locations provided attackers the ability to carry out the attacks without having to worry about police having enough resources to stop them early. Whereas the Mumbai attack was designed to last longer than the initial attack, the Paris aggressors calculated their attacks to achieve the maximum number of casualties as quickly as possible. This proved to be a better strategy than the one used by the Mumbai attackers, who faced an unprepared adversary; Paris is home to some of the world's best counterterrorism forces, and their immediate intervention had to be taken into account.

THE PARIS MASSACRE ATTACKS

The Stade de France Suicide Bomb Team

Bilal Hadfi, a 20-year-old French citizen who'd been living in Belgium, tried to gain entry to the Stade de France but self-detonated his explosive

"Stade De France Group
Left- Ukashah al-Iraqi aka M al-Mahmod; Middle- Bilal Hadfi aka Abu Mujahid al-Baljiki;
Right- Ahmad al-Muhammad aka Ali Al-Iraqi"

device nearby upon being turned away. He was supposed to be one of the more experienced attackers, as he fought with ISIS in Syria for over a year. Before the attacks, he posted pro-jihadist messages on the Internet and had communication with ISIS in Libya. Belgian officials received intelligence that he had gone to fight in Syria, but were unaware he had returned to Europe.[561]

Paris attack cell leader Belgian Abdelhamid Abaaoud featured in *Dabiq* magazine under his nom de guerre, Abu Umar Al-Baijiki.

The second suicide bomber, M. al-Mahmod, possibly a cover name, had entered the EU with Syrian refugees via the Greek island of Leros on October 3, 2015. He may have been infiltrated to central Europe by Abdelhamid Abaaoud, the cell leader.[562] Another ersatz refugee, Ahmad al-Mohammad, possibly an alias, was also registered on Leros in October upon his arrival by boat from Turkey. Fingerprints from that "refugee" also match the attacker's. It's possible that al-Mohammad's passport belonged to a dead Syrian soldier whose identity was stolen upon his death. ISIS and al-Qaeda have employed this kind of document exploitation in the Middle East and North Africa on several occasions in the past.[563]

Mobile Suicide Attack "Run and Gun" Team: Bar and Restaurant Attacks

Brahim Abdeslam, a thirty-one year-old French member of the Molenbeek terror cell living in Belgium, carried out the shootings in the 10th and 11th arrondissements. Shortly afterwards, he blew himself up at the Comptoir Voltaire restaurant on the boulevard Voltaire.[564] A second suicide bomber remains unidentified. The gunman for the attack was suspected to be the terrorist cell leader

Left - Chakib Akrouh aka Dhul Qarnayn al-Baljiki
Right - Brahim Abdesalam aka Abul Qa'qa' al-Baljiki

Abdelhamid Abaaoud, who drove the suicide bombers to their destinations.[565]

Bataclan Theater Suicide Hostage Barricade[566]

Three ISIS terrorists attacked the Bataclan theatre using AKM rifles and wearing suicide explosive vests and, once inside, took hostages. A concert was happening at the time. Samy Amimour, a twenty-eight year-old from Paris, was already wanted on terrorism-related charges and had fought in Yemen as a jihadist. Omar Ismail Mostefai, a twenty-nine year-old from the Parisian suburbs, was also wanted on terrorism charges, and had traveled to Syria in 2013 to fight with ISIS. After the attack Mostefai would be identified by his severed finger.[567] The third Bataclan attacker was Foued Mohamed-Aggad, a twenty-three-year-old from Strasbourg, who travelled to Syria in 2013 to join ISIS.

Target Bataclan
Left - Fouad Mohamed Fuad Aggad aka Abu Fu'ad al-Faranasi; Middle - Ismail Omar Mostefai aka Abu Rayyan al-Faranasi; Right - Samy Amimour aka Abu Qital al-Faranasi

Rescue operations resulted in the deaths of all three attackers. One was killed in the initial police assault on the building before the standoff occurred. The other two were killed by their explosive belts once law enforcement made entry. One of them was killed when his suicide vest exploded when gunfire from law enforcement rifle struck him.

ATTACK CASUALTIES

- Locations around the Stade de France (1 killed)
- Le Carillon bar and Le Petit Cambodge restaurant (15 killed)
- Casa Nostra pizzeria (5 killed)

- La Belle Equipe bistro (19 killed)
- Le Bataclan concert hall (91 killed)

ST. DENIS SAFEHOUSE RAID

As planned, the terrorist cell leader Abdelhamid Abaaoud survived the raid on the Paris streets and went to a safehouse at 8 Rue de Corbillion in the St. Denis area of the city. French intelligence and police had started observing the residences of people they suspected in the attacks. One surveillance team saw a man they believed to be Abaaoud enter an apartment block nearby. Abaaoud had been on the run from a massive manhunt that was carried out throughout all of France for four days. A large contingent of SWAT officers from both the French National Gendarme's *Recherece, Assistance, Intervention et Deterrence* (RAID) team—the equivalent of the FBI hostage rescue team—and the City of Paris's Research and Intervention Brigade (*Brigade de Recherche et d'Intervention*) surrounded the building. Snipers watched the apartment suspected of being the bomb factory. They observed two men and one woman inside. The men were wearing suicide bomb vests and carrying AK rifles. At 4:20 a.m., the RAID assault teams attempted to make entry, leading with an assault dog. An explosive breach failed because the terrorists had reinforced the door. Immediately, Abaaoud opened fire with a fusillade of automatic weapons fire, killing the police dog and wounding several RAID officers. The snipers had to switch from precision-aimed shots to bursts of full automatic fire to suppress the shooters. The woman terrorist, Hasna Aït Boulahcen, a relative of Abaaoud, tried to lure the RAID team to make a second entry, claiming she was a hostage. Snipers observed the terrorists behind her and realized she was a ruse to lure in the units. They opened fire on the terrorist behind her and detonated his explosive vest. She was killed in the blast. In the end, three terrorists were killed, including Abaaoud, Boulahcen, and an unidentified corpse so badly mangled that it took days to realize there had been a third person inside. However, fingerprints matching the man were found on an AK-47 that was used in the run-and-gun attacks on the restaurants. Five other men were arrested.

French authorities believed that Abaaoud and others were planning to strike other targets in Paris in the following days.

AFTERMATH OF THE ATTACKS

One terrorist, Salah Abdeslam, escaped the attacks. He may have had a crisis of faith and did not carry out his portion of the mission. His suicide bomb vest was found in a trash can along with a cellphone. His suicide bomb vest had been rendered safe by removing the detonator, which was not found. He was seen with Belgian Mohammed Abrini days before the Paris attacks and a massive multinational manhunt for the two unfolded. French police believed he was headed to Belgium, where Belgian officials carried out a series of raids. Somehow Abdeslam escaped.

ISIS CLAIMS RESPONSIBILITY

In video recordings released after the attacks, ISIS claimed responsibility. Using French citizens, they announced, "As long as you keep bombing you will not live in peace. You will even fear traveling to the market."[568]

French fighters threaten France in an al-Hayat video.

ISIS IN BELGIUM

The Belgian government suggested that there are 180–190 fighters in Syria/Iraq, with as many as 60–70 who have been killed in combat or suicide bombings. As of July 2015, the official government count of Belgians who have returned to the country from Syria/Iraq is 118, but Belgian researcher Pieter Van Ostaeyen estimates that there have been as many as 516 Belgians in ISIS, the highest rate per capita of all recruits in Europe.[569]

Mehdi Nemmouche, a French national, conducted the May 2014 assault rifle attack on the Jewish Museum of Belgium, killing four before being caught. He was a criminal with four convictions and a prison sentence before leaving for Syria to join ISIS. Nemmouche was said to be one of the ISIS prison guards who tortured hostages.

Abdelhamid Abaaoud and his Belgian fighter friends in *Dabiq* Magazine.

His nickname was Abu Omar the Hitter. He left Syria and returned to France in 2014 to carry out the Brussels attack.

On August 21, 2015, a Belgian of Moroccan origin, Ayoub El Khazzani, boarded the Thalys Eurostar high-speed train with an AKM-variant Kalashnikov, a 9mm Luger pistol, and a knife. He was foiled when three Americans and a British citizen charged him and stopped the potential massacre. It is believed that he was an ISIS-supported operative who planned the attack with Abdelhamid Abaaoud, mastermind of the Paris attack.

Abaaoud was a Belgian citizen of Moroccan origin and resided in Molenbeek. He had spent time in Syria and was a known member of ISIS. He was made famous for a French-language videotape of him dragging the bodies of dead Syrian army soldiers behind a captured Iraqi Humvee. He operated in the Deir Ez-zor combat zone. He may have planned the Paris attacks and acquired weapons in Molenbeek before he was killed by French BRI SWAT officers.

Despite the attack in Paris, Belgium may remain a safe haven for Jihadists returning from Syria and Iraq, especially in the Brussels suburb of Molenbeek. One of Brussel's nineteen districts, Molenbeek has a population of approximately 100,000, with 30 percent being of foreign nationality and 40 percent having foreign roots.[570] Young Muslims in Belgium are antagonized by racism and they have an astronomical rate of unemployment, exceeding 25 percent. The recruiters and radicalizers of ISIS and al-Qaeda play on these grievances and offer them a sense of purpose as well as adventure.

Molenbeek was a logistical and operational hub for ISIS attacks in France and Belgium. After the Paris massacre, Belgium placed the entire country on the highest state of alert and carried out hundreds of raids in an effort to stop what they believed was an imminent threat to carry out an attack in Brussels. Although the pressure was turned on after the Paris attack, it will remain a place where sympathies for ISIS may remain strong.

THE EUROPEAN WEAPONS NETWORK

Since the November 2015 Paris suicide bomb attacks, French police have conducted 2,700 raids, detained 23 people, and put 360 others under house arrest. Two people were also arrested for supplying weapons. One of those two suspects is Claude Hermant, who was arrested in Lille on suspicion of delivering a weapon to Amedy Coulibaly, the al-Qaeda attacker who was killed at the Porte du Vincennes hostage siege during the Charlie Hebdo attacks in 2015.

Unlike the United States, where guns can be purchased legally, or in Belgium, a country that is known as a treasure trove for illegal weapons, in France it's almost impossible to legally own anything larger than a shotgun or a hunting rifle. The weapons used in most French attacks were military-grade, fully automatic weapons that most likely came to Belgium via or eastern Europe. In 2009 alone, French authorities confiscated over 1,500 illegal weapons. In 2010 that number almost doubled to 2,700 weapons. The Paris-based National Observatory for Delinquency reported that the number of weapons coming into France from warzones and drug smugglers increased two-fold in the last several years.[571] In October 2014, raids on several houses in France found large caches of weapons, including machine guns, assault rifles, and pistols. Forty-eight people were detained.[572] It was noted that most if not all weapons found on the black market in France and other Western countries were likely acquired from countries where laws are poorly enforced or the weapons are leftovers from conflict zones such as the Libyan revolution or the conflicts in Syria and Iraq. The New York–based nonprofit Foreign Policy Association estimates that there are millions of weapons on the loose with little regulation by foreign government officials.[573]

Kathie Lynn Austin, an expert on firearms trafficking, remarked that the main reason that many Kalashnikovs make it to the black market is that Russia frequently upgrades its weapons, and obsolete weapons are pilfered or sold in large lots to the black market.[574] In the 1990s, before the collapse of the Soviet Union, Russian intelligence would give weapons to radical groups such as France's Action Directe and the German Red Army Faction, as well as armed militia groups in Bosnia, Serbia, and Kosovo. Even these older weapons find their way into the very lucrative arms market and from there into the hands of ISIS in Europe.

Before its demise, the "dark web" commerce website Silk Road offered many firearms for sale through the Internet, with payment by bitcoin, which makes tracing the sale of illegal guns difficult if not impossible. In some black markets, an AK-47 can cost as little as 700 Euros ($750).[575]

Belgium is a treasure trove for both dark web and street-level black market purchases. Returning jihadists facilitate the sale of weapons in Europe as a fundraising scheme. The weapons used in the Paris massacres of 2015 came from dealers in Brussels. Claude Moniquet, a former French intelligence officer and co-founder of European Strategic Intelligence and Security Centre, estimated that 90 percent of all weapons flowing into Belgium originated from the Balkans, where smuggling is a living tradition.[576]

ISIS IN TURKEY

HISTORY

Turkey is on the 900-km frontline of the war with ISIS. Thus far it has not been fully drawn into the fight, but has been in the middle for a while. Despite stated goals of reducing fighter flow to Iraq and Syria, or worse, from Iraq and Syria, Turkey remains a perfect conduit for foreign fighters, money, and materiel. Though there is no stated ISIS wilayat in Turkey, it is safe to say that ISIS has a very powerful presence.

The largest concern in Turkey is the traffic of foreign fighters to Iraq and Syria and the possibility that they will bring the cult of death from Turkey's doorstep and into its home. Turkey has both deported and denied entry to thousands of people. Additional concerns are the trafficking and availability of weapons, technology, and black market antiquities.

SIGNIFICANT EVENTS

November 29, 2014
Two suicide bombings (SVBIED and PBIED) kill thirty people. Turkey issues a denial that the bombers were Turkish.

December 1, 2014
Turkey allows the United States and coalition forces to use Incirlik air base to strike ISIS in Syria.

December 10, 2014
Turkey reaches an agreement with the UK to stop the flow of foreign fighters and increase intelligence sharing.

January 6, 2015
A married pregnant mother conducts a black-widow attack on an Istanbul police station by detonating the explosive vest she was wearing. One officer is killed. The bomber, Diana Ramazanova was an eighteen-year-old from Dagestan whose husband had been killed in Syria over a month earlier. The two were married after meeting on a dating site.

Suicide bomber Diana Ramazanova and her husband.

January 25, 2015
Turkish officials announce the discovery of a cell of operatives sent to Turkey to attack diplomatic missions, including the Belgian, French, and American

missions. Intelligence indicated that French national Sufian Yassin led the seventeen-man cell.

February 21, 2015
ISIS threatens to take over Suleyman Shah's tomb if Turkey does't give it up. Turkey evacuates the tomb, giving ISIS a victory.

May 2015
Konstantiniyye magazine released as the Turkish-language ISIS propaganda equivalent of the English-language publication *Dabiq*.

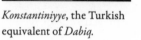

July 20, 2015
A young woman self-detonates in the Amara Cultural Center in Suruc, killing thirty and wounding over a hundred more.

July 24, 2015
Turkey launches first attacks on ISIS in Syria, including strikes on al-A'zaz, Tel al-Hawa, and Jarabulus.

Konstantiniyye, the Turkish equivalent of *Dabiq*.

August 26, 2015
After ISIS releases an edition of *Dabiq* discussing the minting of ISIS coins, Turkey seizes coin-making equipment in Gaziantep and arrests six connected with the operation.

August 29, 2015
Turkey strikes ISIS positions again, but this time by operating in the Syrian airspace.

October 10, 2015
Ninety-eight people are killed when two SPBIEDs detonate during a peace rally in Ankara.

November 24, 2015
Turkey shoots down Russian Sukhoi-24 along the border with Syria.

January 12, 2016
ISIS suicide bomber from Saudi Arabia blows up in the Sultan Ahmet district near an ancient Egyptian obelisk, killing nine German tourists and a Peruvian.

ISIS IN THE CAUCASUS

HISTORY

During the 1995 war against the Russian Federation thousands of foreign fighters from dozens of Islamic extremist groups fought to establish an independent Islamic Republic of Chechnya. There was heavy involvement of educated, Western "vacation jihadists," principally from the United Kingdom, along with a nascent propaganda effort through audio tapes, video, pamphlets, and books produced in the West. The practice of videotaping the decapitation executions of Russian soldiers began during the war in Chechnya. The Russian military forces finally enforced order on the breakaway republic with scorched-earth policies. Highly sophisticated Islamic-oriented Chechen militants departed in the region of Chechnya, Dagestan, and Ingushetia, and traveled down to Iraq and Syria.

Tarkhan Tayumurazovich Batirashvilli, a.k.a. Abu Omar al-Shishani, a.k.a. Omar the Chechen, was a sergeant in the Georgian Army who is now Emir of Northern Syria. He commands a force nearing one thousand strong and commands fear and respect.

Tarkhan Tayumurazovich Batirashvilli, a.k.a. Abu Omar al-Shishani, the Emir of Northern Syria.

The al-Qaeda–linked Islamic Caucasus Emirate (ICE) has been the primary jihad group in the area, but with the deaths of several top leaders, and the defections of several others, is losing ground to ISIS.[577] As many as two thousand Russian citizens have joined ISIS's war in Syria, according to the Deputy Secretary of the Russian Security Council, but other sources indicate that the number may be as high as five thousand.[578, 579]

Chechens also have a notable presence in the Russian black market and for involvement with organized crime in Russia and internationally.

CAUCASUS OATH OF ALLEGIANCE

On June 27, 2015, the Caucusus province issued its oath of allegiance to Abu Bakr al-Baghdadi. "Obeying the order of Allah, we are declaring our allegiance to Caliph Ibrahim ben Awwad ben Ibrahim al Badri al-Qoureishi al Husseini for obedience and subordination . . . We testify that all mujahideen of the Caucasus are united in this decision, and there are no disagreements among us on this issue."[580]

ORGANIZATION OF ISIS IN THE CAUCASES

Little is known of any formal organization by ISIS in the Caucasus region, other than that Abu Bakr al-Baghdadi conferred the title of Emir on Abu Muhammad al-Qadri for the United Wilayat of Kabarda, Balkaria, and Karachay.[581] Qadri may be Rustam Asilderov, who defected from ICE.

OTHER SIGNIFICANT EVENTS

September 3, 2014
ISIS releases a video depicting captured Syrian aircraft, made in Syria, with a threat to deploy them against Russia and to liberate Chechnya.[582] ISIS states the intention of including Chechnya and the Caucasus in the Caliphate.

October 2014
In a wiretapped phone conversation with his father, Omar al-Shishani says that ISIS will invade Russia.[583]

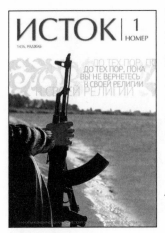

Istok, the Russian language version of *Dabiq*, is released in May 2015.

May 27, 2015

ISIS propaganda department al-Hayat, publisher of *Dabiq*, publishes a twenty-four-page Russian- language magazine called *Istok* ("outflow" or "origin"). One reference inside says that the writers of the magazine "have been fighting in the Caucasus against Russian tyrants."[584]

June 18, 2015

CIS Anti-Terrorist Center chief Andrei Novikov reports confirmed documentation that up to five thousand Russian Federation citizens are fighting for ISIS.[585]

June 27, 2015

ISIS spokesman Abu Mohammad al-Adnan issues an audio recording stating that Abu Bakr al-Baghdadi has accepted a pledge of allegiance by Caucasus jihadis, and that Abu Muhammad al-Qadri is the Emir of the United Wilayat of Kabarda, Balkaria, and Karachay.[586]

August 2, 2015

Russian FSB forces conduct a raid in a forest of the Sunzha district of Ingushetia, killing eight ISIS supporters. The FSB found a cache of assault weapons, grenades, IEDs, and ammunition.[587]

September 2, 2015

ISIS Caucasus claims responsibility for an attack on a Russian military barracks in Magharamakint, Dagestan.[588]

November 29, 2015

Three ISIS-affiliated militants killed by a special counterterrorism detachment of Russia's Federal Security Service (FSB) in Dagestan. One of the fighters had recently returned from Syria.[589]

WEAPONS AND EQUIPMENT ORDER OF BATTLE

With the apparent control of Russia over the Caucasus region, fighters from the region appear to be going to the conflict in Syria and Iraq, rather than staging another war against Russia. Attacks thus far have been distinctive hit-and-run ambush tactics with the same materiel used during the war, including Russian-made small arms, assault rifles, and RPGs. They also employ grenades and homemade bombs.[590] Chechen militants would sometimes capture and use military vehicles but preferred to destroy them.

ISIS IN CANADA

The ISIS presence in Canada appears to be minimal, and has thus far demonstrated a few inspirational attacks. There are no known ISIS groups or cells.

SIGNIFICANT EVENTS

October 20, 2014

At 11:30 a.m. in Saint-Jean-sur-Richelieu, Quebec, twenty-five-year-old Martin Couture-Rouleau ran his car into two officers in an insurance company parking lot. Police engaged in a chase, during which Couture-Rouleau called 911 to declare that his actions were taken in the name of Allah. Couture-Rouleau lost control of his car during the chase and flipped upside down into a ditch. He then exited the car and attempted to attack a police woman. When he charged toward her, he was shot to death by officers. In the end, one Canadian Army soldier, warrant officer Patrice Vincent, fifty-three, was

Canadian Andre Poulin under nom de guerre "Abu Muslim" in the al-Hayat video, "Al-Ghuraba: The Chosen Few of Different Lands."

Canadian Martin Couture-Rouleau, the 2014 Saint-Jean-sur-Richelieu attacker.

killed. The twenty-eight-year veteran had planned to retire.

Couture-Rouleau was known to the RCMP due to Internet postings and from relatives who had seen a personality shift since converting to Islam a year before. He was living with his parents. He changed his name to Ahmad LeConverti and often posted Qur'an verses on Facebook. His passport had been seized.[591]

October 22, 2014

At 9:52 a.m. at Parliament Hill in Ottowa, Michael Zehaf-Bibeau killed Corporal Nathan Cirillo, who was working as a sentry for the Canadian National War Memorial. Zehaf-Bibeau was shot by officers after he went to the Canadian Parliament building and engaged in a shootout with security, injuring three responding officers.[592]

The thirty-two-year old Libyan-Canadian from Montreal was considered mentally ill by his mother. She claimed he felt trapped by officials because his passport was being held. Despite earlier statements that he had intended to travel to Syria, he was intending to travel to Saudi Arabia. His mother also stated that he had been a severe drug addict.[593]

ISIS IN THE UNITED STATES

ISIS's activities in North America have been limited to aspirational attacks at most. No organized ISIS cells have conducted a major operation in America yet. There are currently dozens of cases before the Department of Justice of Americans who have either engaged in support or sought to engage support for ISIS. By the end of 2015, there were nine hundred active investigations throughout all fifty states, according to the FBI. Additionally, seventy-one cases are in the judicial system for individuals who have been charged with ISIS-related crimes.[594] No groups have sworn allegiance to ISIS.

MAY 2015

Garland, Texas: At an event dubbed the "First Annual Muhammad Art Exhibit and Contest," held at the Curtis Culwell Center, an arena and conference center in Garland, Texas, two gunmen attacked after getting out of a black sedan. They began shooting at police officers, who were guarding the event and had established a perimeter. The assailants wore body armor, carried assault rifles, and used the car as cover while shooting at the police officers. In less than twenty seconds, police killed both attackers, who were later identified as Elton Simpson and Nadir Soofi.[595]

Mugshot of Garland, Texas shooting suspect Elton Simpson.

The roommates had driven from Phoenix, Arizona. Soofi had a carpet cleaning business in Phoenix. The Texas native was born to a Pakistani father and American mother, and was raised as a Muslim. After his parents divorced he lived in Pakistan for six years, then returned to the US. The college dropout had a list of over twenty offenses on record and a failed pizza business that had just closed down months before.[596] His mother said Elton Simpson had indoctrinated her son.

Thirty-year old Elton Simpson had been engaging in contacts with ISIS members before the attack. Having converted to Islam in high school, the FBI first took note of him in 2007 after tracking the activities of Phoenix-area resident Hassan Abujihaad, a former Navy sailor who had been convicted on terror charges. Both had attended the Islamic Community Center of Phoenix.[597]

Simpson had been under investigation for years, with over 1,500 hours of secret recordings with an FBI informant. In those conversations he states, "I'm telling you man, we can make it to the battlefield." He was later charged for lying about his plans to travel to Somalia. During trial the recordings of his conversations were played and he said, "If you get shot, or you get killed, it's straightaway [to heaven]. That's what we're here for, so why not take that route?"[598]

Simpson also actively contacted the British pro-ISIS hacker from the CyberCaliphate, Junaid Hussain, a.k.a. Abu Hussain al-Britani, via

Twitter direct messages. He also was in contact with Minnesota resident Muhammad Abdullahi Hassan, who was a known recruiter for the jihad militant group al-Shabaab. Days before the attacks, Simpson tweeted about the Garland, Texas event with the question, "When will they ever learn?" Junaid Hussain then called on Simpson to "do their part" in a tweet response.[599] Simpson posted a tweet just before the attack reading, "May Allah accept us as mujahideen," which Junaid Hussain subsequently re-tweeted.

A third suspect, Abdul Kareem, a.k.a. Decarus Lowell Thomas from Philadelphia, was charged with conspiracy, false statements, and transport of firearms after allegedly supplying the attackers with weapons and ammunition.[600]

DECEMBER 2015

San Bernardino, California: Two American Muslims, American-born Sayed Farook and his Pakistani-born wife Tashfeen Malik, plotted and carried out a mass shooting at the Inland Regional Center, a social services center supporting the disabled in San Bernardino, killing fourteen people. Armed with AR-15 rifles, handguns and homemade pipe bombs they entered a Christmas party for staff and disabled in the office where Farook used to work. Before entering, Tashfee Malik left their six-month-old child with her husband's mother. She then posted a loyalty oath to ISIS on social media, just moments before committing the attack. The couple, dressed all in black, then entered the office party and shot 65–75

rounds of .223 rifle ammunition, killing fourteen and wounding twenty-two others. They left behind three pipe bombs wired to a remote detonator that failed to explode. The pair managed to elude a hasty police perimeter and return to their residence for eighteen minutes when surveillance officers saw them depart for an undetermined destination. Fearing they were enroute to another targets the police attempted to stop them. Tashfeen Malik engaged them with an AR-15 rifle from the backseat of the rented SUV while Farook drove. They were both killed in a fusillade of gunfire from a wide variety of police and SWAT officers. Both Farook and Malik were radicalized over some period of time and may have had similar beliefs when they met in Saudi Arabia. They successfully hid their intentions from their family, with the exception of a brother-in-law, Enrique Marquez, Jr., who discussed plots for both an attack on a regional university and a mass shooting on a highway.[601] ISIS praised the attack in their online magazine Dabiq 13 but did not take credit for the incident. They showed a photo of Farook and referred to him as a "Mujahid" or holy warrior:

> "As the operation took place, Tashfeen Malik made a post online reaffirming their bay'ah to Amīrul-Mu'minīn, Shaykh Abū Bakr al-Baghdādī (hafidhahullāh). She and her husband then engaged in a shootout with security forces and were killed, thereby attaining shahādah in the path of Allah. We consider them so, and Allah is their judge. Thus, the Khilāfah's call for the Muslims to strike the crusaders in their own lands was answered once more, but on this particular occasion the attack was unique. The mujāhid involved did not suffice with embarking upon the noble path of jihād alone. Rather, he conducted the operation together with his wife, with the two thereby aiding one another in righteousness and taqwā."[602]

ISIS IN AUSTRALIA

No known organizations in Australia have sworn bayat to ISIS. However, numerous Australians have joined and radicalized individuals carried out two noteworthy events. Cameron Gifford, the assistant secretary of the National Security Law and Policy Division of the Australian Federal Police, noted that around 120 Australians are engaged in fighting in Syria/Iraq, that somewhere between 32–42 have been killed in combat

Australian Abu Khaled al-Cambodi featured in an al-Hayat video.

or suicide bombings, that approximately 30 Australians have returned home, and that 170 people are providing material support.

Self-radicalization is the most emerging threat in Australia, followed by returning jihadis who inspire or plan attacks. Australia has suffered disproportionately from terrorist attacks.

SIGNIFICANT EVENTS

September 2014

Endeavor Hills stabbings: Eighteen-year-old Abdul Numan Haider stabbed an officer from the Joint Counter Terrorism team after arriving at the police station in Melbourne's Endeavor Hills suburb. Haider was

Australian Abdul Numan Haider posing for ISIS.

already known to authorities from previous threats against Tony Abbott, the Australian prime minister at that time.[603] Haider's parents migrated to Australia from Afghanistan around 2004. Authorities had previously visited with his family. He had been monitored by authorities for months and had planned to behead police officers.[604] He was carrying the ISIS shahada flag when he stabbed the officer. He was shot dead with one round.

December 2014

Sydney Hostage Crisis: Early on December 15, 2014, Man Haron Monis took eighteen people hostage—eight staff and ten customers—at the

Lindt Café in Sydney. The siege lasted sixteen hours and played out on national and international television, since it occurred directly across the street from the Seven Network studio.[605] Armed with a shotgun, Monis ordered to the hostages to hold up a black shahada flag. He claimed to have planted bombs around Sydney and ordered a hostage to tell the news media that "This is an attack by the Islamic State."

In the afternoon, five hostages managed to escape. Around 2:14 a.m., the Tactical Operations Unit stormed the cafe using stun grenade and M4A1 carbines.[606] In the end, two hostages died. Tori Johnson, manager of the café, was shot by Monis when he tried to take his gun, and employee Katrina Dawson was killed by police bullets.[607] Three other hostages were wounded during the raid by police gunfire. Monis was killed by officers during raid. Monis had a complex psychological pathology; he was diagnosed as schizophrenic by his doctors, and claimed to be a vast range of different characters, from a member of the Iranian intelligence services to a faith healer. While protesting at Parliament House, he called himself "Ayatollah Manteghi Boroujerdi."[608]

CHAPTER 8

ISIS IN AFGHANISTAN, THE GULF STATES, ARABIAN PENINSULA, AND ASIA

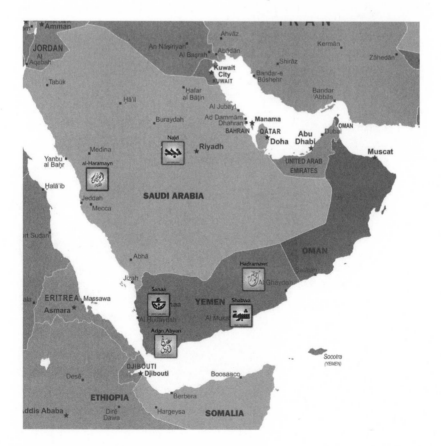

ISIS IN AFGHANISTAN (KHORASAN)

HISTORY

In 2012, militants associated with ISIS started recruiting jihadists, primarily from the terrorist group Lashkar-e-Jhangvi Said, in Pakistan.[609] In early 2014, ISIS began organizing and funding local groups in Afghanistan to compete with the Taliban and al-Qaeda.[610] By September 2014, two hundred militants had left Pakistan to join the Islamic State. In October 2014, five regional Pakistani Taliban commanders (Hafiz Khan Saeed, Hafiz Quran Daulat, Gul Zaman, Mufti Hassan, and Khalid Mansoor) switched allegiances from Afghan Taliban leader Mullah Omar and pledged loyalty to Abu Bakr al-Baghdadi.[611] Additional leaders pledged allegiance in a January 10, 2015 video, including Saad Emirati of Logar Province, Ubaidah al-Peshwari of al-Tawhid in Peshawar, Shekh Muhsin of Kunar province, Talha of Lakki Marwat, and Omar al-Malnsur of the Lal Masjid (Red Mosque). The group calls itself the Islamic State of Khorasan, comprising Afghanistan, Pakistan, and parts of India.

ISIS has sympathizers or open supporters in twenty-five of Afghanistan's thirty-four provinces. Much of the recruitment occurs due to ISIS's large bankroll and social media. ISIS fighters combat the Afghan army on a regular basis, but do not generally fight other militant Islamic groups, with one exception: for control of the drug trade in Nangarhar Province.[612] Although the Khorasan province cells may recruit small militant groups in the area as well as Taliban splinter groups, its competitor, the Taliban, is well entrenched and has experience dealing with such groups. Unless

Afghanistan ISIS members swear a Bayat, or loyalty oath, to Abu Bakr al-Baghdadi.

and until the Khorasan group is able to attract enough followers, they are unlikely to engage or prevail against the Afghan Taliban. However, many Pakistani militants have been impressed by ISIS's successes in Syria and Iraq.[613] Another com-

ISIS recruits test their stamina in a terrorist training camp in Nangarhar province, Afghanistan.

petitor for hearts and minds in the region is al-Qaeda of the Indian Subcontinent (AQIS); analysts speculate that this and other groups will conduct terror operations and atrocities to demonstrate a competitive effectiveness over ISIS.[614]

Khorasan operatives freely distribute pamphlets in the markets of large Pakistani cities such as Peshawar.[615] Little is known about ISIS's military coordination efforts with Afghan militants, or the Khorasan group's capabilities, but it is clear that they have routed the Taliban out of sections of Nangarhar province.[616] In turn, as of September 2015 the intelligence on ISIS in that province, which may be coming from the Taliban itself, has become so well developed that well over a hundred members were killed by Afghan Special Forces and airstrikes on their camps in less than sixty days.

AFGHANISTAN MILITANTS PLEDGE LOYALTY TO ISIS

"I show allegiance to the commander of faithful, Caliph Abu Bakr al-Baghdadi Qureshi al Hussaini, and will listen and obey every order of you and follow your orders regardless of what circumstances may be."—Shahidullah Shahid, (January 2015)

ORGANIZATION OF ISIS IN AFGHANISTAN/ KHORASAN

ISIS-Khorasan's control on the region is tenuous, and they have not announced a formal organizational structure. However, leaders of regional groups could be said to be "Emirs" of certain provinces, even if they have only a handful of followers, and do not control those provinces outright.

National Level
Emir: Hafiz Saeed Khan (reported killed July 10, 2015, status uknown)
Deputy: Abdul Raul Aliza (killed February 9, 2015)
Deputy: Hafiz Wahidi (killed March 18, 2015)

Regions
Kurram Agency
Emir: Hafiz Quran Daulat

Khyber Agency
Emir: Gul Zaman (died July 7, 2015)
Affiliated tribe: Qambar Khel tribe

Peshawar
Emir: Mufti Hassan
Affiliate: Ubaidah al-Peshwari, leader of the al-Tawhid and Jihad Group in Peshawar

Hangu District
Emir: Khalid Mansoor

Kunar Province
Emir: Qari Harun
Affiliate: Sheikh Muhsin

Logar Province
Emir: Saad Emirati

Lakki Marwat Province
Emir: Talha

Dir Province
Hudhayfah group

Other Affiliated Groups
Direct Support
Tehrik-i-Taliban Pakistan (TTP) (Spokesperson: Shahidullah Shahid)[617]
Ansar-ul-Khilafat Wal-Jihad
Pakistani Jundullah
Lal Masjid
Jamia Hafsa

Indirect Support
Jamat-ul-Ahrar[618] (Spokesperson: Ehsanullah Ehsan)
Lashkar-e-Jhangvisaid[619]
Ahl-e-Summat Wai Jamat

PROPAGANDA

The Khorasan group regularly distributes multiple-language recruitment pamphlets in large Pakistani cities. They are also stepping up the number of English-language communications, indicating an increasing degree of sophistication. They have also released videos depicting pledges of allegiance, which included the beheading of a Pakistani called "Manzoor,"[620] as well as a video showing the execution of four Afghan prisoners by blowing them up with land mines.

ISIS member in Afghanistan spreads the message of the cult of jihad.

ISIS Khorasan blows up group of Shiite Muslims for being "apostates." They placed explosives under each victim and fired it off with a linear detonation cord.

CAMPAIGNS

The Islamic State of Khorasan has an ongoing recruitment campaign throughout the region, consisting of word-of-mouth, pamphleteering, and bribery of top commanders.

Khorasan group militants regularly conduct isolated bombings and ambushes, but not in a coordinated campaign.

In September 2015, the Khorasan group also conducted a successful military campaign against the Afghan Taliban in the Achin, Dih Bala, and Nazyan districts of Nangarhar Province. They conducted operations against Afghan security forces in this area for the first time. The area provides access to agricultural drug products, as well as the smuggling routes of the border area to Pakistan.

WEAPONS AND EQUIPMENT ORDER OF BATTLE

Little is known of ISIS's arsenal or capabilities in Afghanistan. However, as ISIS's Khorasan group consists mainly of former Taliban splinter groups, the equipment and training of Khorasan militants would likely resemble that of what has generally been associated with traditional Taliban fighters, including light arms, machine guns, RPGs, IEDs. Although anecdotal, an Afghan militant in Peshawar estimated that ISIS training "is much more advanced than ours and it's good for us to learn those techniques."[621]

FINANCE

Khorasan leadership has cultivated tentative ties to local Islamic militant groups through bribes, presumably from ISIS coffers. The Khorasan group's fight against Taliban leaders in Nangarhar Province appears to be an attempt to control the revenue from the drug trade in those areas.

OTHER SIGNIFICANT EVENTS

2012
Militants later associated with the nascent group that would be called ISIS begin recruiting followers in Pakistan.

November 2012
Dozens of Pakistani fighters from Lashkar-e-Jhangvisaid embark for Syria to fight Bashar al-Assad.

September 2014
A dozen militants cross the border to Pakistan to deliver pamphlets in Pashto, Dari, and Farsi, calling on obedience to the Caliph of the Islamic State and jihad against the United States in Muslim lands.

October 2014
Taliban leader Abdul Rauf Khadem, a former adviser to Mullah Omar, visits Iraq.

January 10, 2015
Islamic State formally declares establishment of the Islamic State of Khorasan, with Hafiz Khan Saeed, a former Tehrik-i-Taliban commander in Orakzai, Pakistan.[622]

May 2015
ISIS Khorasan claims responsibility for a terror attack in Karachi, Pakistan, when six gunmen on motorcycles stop a bus, killing forty-five passengers with small arms fire.[623]

July 10, 2015
US DOD reports that Emir of Khorasan Hafiz Saeed Khan is killed by drone strike in Eastern Afghanistan. Three days later an audio recording indicates that he is still alive.

August–September 2015
ISIS pushes the Taliban out of Achin, Dih Bala, and Nazyan districts of Nangarhar Province, which are on or near the border of Pakistan.[624]

September 27, 2015

ISIS gunmen attack checkpoints in the Achin District of Nangarhar Province, killing nine policemen and wounding another eight. Afghan forces retaliate with attacks by air, killing eighty-five ISIS fighters, all of whom were Pakistani, according to Afghan National Directorate of Security statement.

September 29, 2015

US Treasury Department sanctions Hafiz Saeed Khan, despite reports of his death on July 10, 2015 by US Department of Defense.

November 6, 2015

Afghan Special Forces kill thirty-two ISIS members in the hillsides of Achin in Nangarhar province.[625]

November 20, 2015

Afghan forces kill twelve ISIS terrorists in Nangarhar province.[626]

December 6, 2015

Thirty-nine ISIS-Khorasan members were killed in combined air-to-ground combat missions by Afghanistan Special Forces and Air Force missions. Six ISIS were killed in Achin district by airstrikes. Thirty-three others were killed in a counterterror operation against their basecamp in Nangarhar Province. An ISIS radio communications network was also destroyed.[627]

ISIS IN SAUDI ARABIA

HISTORY

It has been estimated that 2,500 Saudis have recently traveled to Iraq and Syria to join the conflict there.[628] The country was seen as the largest source of foreign suicide bombers during the Iraq war.[629] At the same time, however, Saudi leaders have worked closely with American officials to successfully thwart terrorist plots and have been commended for de-radicalization efforts directed toward former terrorists.[630]

FIRST SIGNS OF THE ISLAMIC STATE IN SAUDI ARABIA

The fact that both Mecca and Medina lie within Saudi Arabia, and Abu Bakr al-Baghdadi's belief that the king of Saudi Arabia and his family are not legitimate custodians of Islam, are key reasons why ISIS, following in the footsteps of al-Qaeda, has targeted the leadership and the nation for destabilization.[631] In November 2014, Abu Bakr al-Baghdadi delivered a speech exhorting ISIS supporters to turn on Saudi leaders:[632]

> O sons of al-Haramayn [The two Holy shrines of Mecca and Medina] . . . the serpent's head and the stronghold of the disease are there . . . draw your swords and divorce life, because there should be no security for the Saloul.[633]

"Saloul" is a disparaging term used by the cultists to insult the Saudi leadership. In the same speech, al-Baghdadi also claimed to have accepted pledges of allegiance from supporters in Saudi Arabia and several other countries in the region.[634]

At the same time, Saudi Arabia's Interior Ministry noted a shift in ISIS online recruitment toward potential jihadists within the Kingdom to carrying out attacks in place rather than traveling to ISIS territory.[635] All of this was an indication that a Saudi-Takfiri civil war was gestating.

On April 28, 2015, Saudi officials announced that between then and the prior December, ninety-three people had been arrested on suspicion of links to ISIS.[636] By July, officials announced an additional 431 had been arrested.[637] Toby Matthiesen, a senior research fellow at Oxford University, is an expert on Saudi Arabia. He was quoted saying to the *Guardian*:

> Saudi Arabia may now have to choose between anti-Shia [sentiment] as a political tool at home and abroad and the very real threat that extremists taking anti-Shia [sentiment] too seriously will bring the fight back home—with unpredictable consequences for the stability of Saudi Arabia and the wider region.

ISIS PLEDGE OF ALLEGIANCE

On November 10, 2014, a group called Mujahideen of the Arabian Peninsula pledged allegiance to Baghdadi.[638]

It also appears that a number of unnamed, purportedly Saudi individuals have been posting images of written pledges of allegiance, including a cake in the shape of the ISIS flag.[639]

ORGANIZATION OF ISIS IN SAUDI ARABIA

There appear to be three wilayat proclaimed in Saudi Arabia: Haramayn, Najd, and Hijaz. According to the Soufan Group, ISIS's presence inside Saudi Arabia could be characterized as "meaningful and operational."[640] The identities of senior leadership are not publicly known at this time.

CAMPAIGNS

In November 2014, eight Saudis were shot to death in Al-Ahsa in one incident,[641] while a Danish citizen was killed in Riyadh.[642]

January 5, 2015

Two SPBIEDs killed two Saudi border guards and injured their commanding officer in Arar. Guards killed one of the two attackers but the second one detonated his vest when captured.[643]

April 18, 2015

Yazeed Mohammed Abdulrahman Abu Nayyan—aided by accomplice Nawaf bin Sarif Samir al-Enezi—opened fire on two police officers in Riyadh, killing both.[644]

Late May 2015

Two suicide bombers struck in the same week at mosques in Dammam[645] and al-Qadeeh[646] killing four people in the former and 21 at the latter.[647] Unlike previous "lone wolf" attacks, these attacks suggested coordination.[648]

August 2015

A new group calling themselves Hijaz Province of the Islamic State took responsibility for a mosque bombing in Abha, Saudi Arabia, targeting Saudi security forces.[649]

Abu Sinan al-Najdi martyrdom attacker on Saudi Special Emergency Forces Center in Asir killing 15

October 16, 2015

After a gunman attack that killed five, ISIS's claim of responsibility came via a branch named "Bahrain Province." The attack was carried out via a stolen taxi. One ISIS fighter was killed; the remaining two were arrested.[650]

FINANCE

In late 2010, the *Guardian* published a leaked cable in which Secretary of State Hillary Clinton wrote: "[D]onors in Saudi Arabia constitute the most significant source of funding to Sunni terrorist groups worldwide."[651]

Saudi officials have identified schemes by which ISIS solicits donations via Twitter and accesses them via Skype,[652] in which donors relay the numbers of international pre-paid cards to organization representatives.[653]

The images of Saudi individuals pledging support online serves evidence of a key source of funding.[654]

ISIS IN YEMEN

HISTORY

Background

Yemen is the poorest country in the Middle East.[655] It has longstanding divisions. From 1970 to 1990, southern Yemen was independent.[656] In

Terrorists in Yemen declare pledge loyalty oath to ISIS.

1994, a short civil war erupted.[657] In 2012 President Ali Abdullah Saleh, who had held power for thirty years, was toppled in an election during the Arab Spring.[658] His vice president, Abdu Rabbu Mansour Hadi, was voted in, the only candidate on the ballot.[659] This orderly succession was seen at the time as a "model for post-revolutionary Arab states."[660]

The Iranian-backed, Shi'ite Houthi tribes allied with Saleh[661]. They descended on Sana'a, Yemen's capital, in September 2014, a move that culminated in an assault on the presidential palace in January 2015 and the subsequent ouster of Hadi, who left Yemen entirely on March 25, 2015.[662] The Houthis are Zaydi Shi'ites and staunch opponents of al-Qaeda, and are viewed by Saudi Arabia to be so closely allied with Iran as to be an extension of Tehran.[663]

In the wake of Hadi's ouster, the country fell into a complex civil war[664] with eight factions. Saudi Arabia implemented a full-scale military intervention of Yemen called Operation Decisive Storm. Using GCC troops from Saudi Arabia, Qatar, Kuwait, the United Arab Emirates, Egypt, Morocco, Jordan and Bahrain they imposed a naval blockade and started air strikes in March 2015. The Saudi Army led a small footprint ground campaign to support the Hadi forces that has since enmeshed itself in a deep insurgency with the Houthis and exposed itself to terrorist attacks by both al-Qaeda and ISIS. Al-Qaeda in the Arabian Peninsula (AQAP), Al Qaeda's strongest branch,[665] comprised of Saudi and Yemini offshoots that consolidated in 2009,[666] used the confusion as an opportunity for a territorial grab.[667] Saudi involvement in Yemen's civil war helped ISIS gain traction.[668]

First Signs of the Islamic State in Yemen

In March 2015, ISIS affiliates claimed responsibility for the capture and execution of twenty-nine Yemeni soldiers, just days after ISIS had claimed responsibility for two mosque bombings that killed 137 Houthis. The mosque bombings represented the first indication that ISIS was massing sizable forces in Yemen[669] and represented the deadliest terrorist attack in Yemeni history.[670]

This was followed up in July with unverified images purportedly showing an ISIS training camp established in Aden, a seaside city in southern Yemen.[671]

If ISIS continues to grow in Yemen, it will be headed toward a direct confrontation with AQAP, a development which fundamentally threatens al-Qaeda overall.[672] Thus far, the two groups have not engaged in direct battle in Yemen,[673] and for the moment, it seems unlikely that they will any time soon.[674]

Yemen Pledges Loyalty to ISIS

In early February, a band of fighters supporting AQAP apparently transferred their loyalty to ISIS.[675] Their announcement wasn't verified:[676] "It is unclear how credible those reports are and whether they come from a faction of AQAP that would have any significance," according to a US State Department spokesperson.[677]

However, there is reason to believe that some AQAP leaders have indeed jumped ship—such as Maamoun Hatem, whose May 11 death via drone strike prompted ISIS members to eulogize him on Twitter.[678]

In an April 24, 2015 video, twelve masked men identifying themselves as "Soldiers of the Caliphate in Yemen"[679] pledged allegiance to the caliphate.[680]

ORGANIZATION OF ISIS IN YEMEN

It is thought that seven sub-wilayats fall under Wilayat al-Yemen:

1. Sana'a
2. Ibb and Taiz (the "Green Brigade")

3. Lahij
4. Aden
5. Shabwa
6. Hadramawt
7. al-Bayda[681]

LEADERSHIP

The head of ISIS in Yemen is reportedly the Saudi Nasser al-Ghaydani, whose nom de guerre is Abu Bilal al-Harbi.[682]

OTHER SIGNIFICANT EVENTS

March 20, 2015

Two mosques are bombed by four suicide bombers in Sana'a, allegedly wearing explosive vests, killing 137. The first bomber at the al-Badr mosque detonated outside the gate when confronted by guards. The second bomber then detonated as the worshipers fled. The next two attacked at the al-Hashoosh mosque. This would be the largest attack in Yemen by ISIS.[683]

April 2015

ISIS executes fifteen Yemeni soldiers, four of whom are beheaded.[684]

April 23, 2015

The "Green Brigade" claims responsibility for an attack on Houthi in Yarim. No information on the group accompanies their message.[685] Seven ISIS attacks on religious sites in June 2015 kill approximately one hundred Houthi supporters. [686],[687]

June 17, 2015

Four car bombs target the Houthi headquarters in Sana'a. Of the four car bombs, two were suicide attacks.

June 30, 2015

ISIS claims responsibility for four additional attacks on Houthi sites (killing approximately thirty) and two car bombs, one set off near a mosque and the other in a Houthi-secured area in Sana'a.[688]

Aug 20, 2015

ISIS claims attack on government building, which was targeted against the governor in Aden.[689]

August 23, 2015

ISIS loads several Houthi prisoners onto a boat on the port of Aden and detonates it.[690] Video later released via Wilayat Aden.

September 2, 2015

Al-Muayad Mosque bombing kills at least twenty in the al-Jeraf area of Sana'a.[691]

September 24, 2015

Yemen mosque attack in Sana'a kills twenty-five at the al-Balili mosque.[692]

October 2015

ISIS conduct a number of bombings in Aden and Sana'a.[693] Targets include a hotel where government officials are staying, the headquarters used by soldiers of the nine-member Saudi-led[694] Persian Gulf coalition

ISIS Land cruiser 'technical' moves through the war torn streets in Yemen.

fighting against the Houthi rebels to restore Hadi to power, and a mosque.[695] The attacks use two SVBIEDs and rockets, with car bombs at the al-Qasr Hotel.

WEAPONS AND EQUIPMENT ORDER OF BATTLE

Immediately after the Houthi takeover of Sana'a and Hadi's ouster, the US military acknowledged that it has ceased being able to account for a large stash of equipment sent over to Yemen over a period of years.[696] According to the Guardian, this equipment includes "helicopters, night-vision gear, surveillance equipment, military radios, and transport aircraft."[697] It was believed at the time that Houthi rebels had taken control of the equipment, which totaled more than $500 million. "We have to assume it's completely compromised and gone," an anonymous legislative aide told the *Washington Post*. US officials maintained that the lost equipment would not meaningfully impact the conflict; guns and heavy weaponry have been and continue to be easily obtainable in Yemen.[698]

ISIS FORCES DEFECT IN YEMEN DUE TO ABUSES

Translation provided by the US Directorate of National Intelligence Open Source Center.[699]

. . . We, the soldiers of the Islamic State in Yemen, the undersigned, do hereby declare our pledge to the caliph of the Muslims, Ibrahim Ibn-'Awad al-Hussayni al-Qurayshi [refers to ISIL leader Abu-Bakr al-Baghdadi], and once again renew our pledge to the caliph in all matters, except in those matters in which we observe clear apostasy. We will state the truth and fear only God.

There are excesses and violations against sharia currently taking place in Yemen by the wali and his inner circle. Despite our efforts to advise and inform the caliph's office on matters happening in Yemen, the violations against the sharia remain present and continue to increase. They stopped working in accordance with the prophetic path regarding the resolution of many problems and issues. Most recently, the following took place:

First: The dismissal of a number of soldiers of the Islamic State after they filed a lawsuit against the military commander on the pretext that there is no need for them now, knowing very well that some of them are fugitives wanted by the enemy.

Second: The death of many Islamic State soldiers during the "Sir and Shibam" incident in Wilayah Hadramawt due to the lack of basic resources for the battle, including:

- Lack of a plan of retreat
- Lack of support detachments for the fighters
- Lack of scouts and guides with knowledge of the area
- Lack of a medical team and supplies
- The adjustment of the battle plan hours before zero hour to attack two barracks instead of one
- The prevention of some of the fighters from gaining access to necessary weapons for the battle by the military commander
  . . . and many others.

This led to the loss of many more brothers on the roads and the killing of almost half of the soldiers participating in the battle. The martyrs' corpses were not retrieved for a period of two days so that they might be buried among the Muslims. Despite all this, no official measure was taken to hold the military official to account.

Third: The wali of the coast, Abu-Muhammad al-Najdi [from the Najd region of Saudi Arabia], refused to accept the arbitration of a sharia court in the matter of the Al-Tawasul tribe. This had been the demand of the relatives of the slain in order to prove the apostasy of their sons [as received]. Despite this, the wali informed them that he refused this arbitration without any consequences. Sharia officials wrote to the wali more than once but he never responded to them.

Other violations included:

- Oppressing the downtrodden
- Expelling the muhajirin [refers to foreign fighters]
- Segregating most of the Ansar [refers to local fighters] who harbored and took care of [members of] the [Islamic] State, even when the State lost most of the land that had sheltered it.

These [things] have caused us to adopt the following stance and profess before God the Exalted and Sublime the following:

Removing the Wali of Yemen and his retinue, stating as Ibadah, may God be pleased with him, said: "By God, I do not accompany him in his soldiers a black night."

*Warning: Do not disseminate the statement to anyone other than to the soldiers of the Islamic State.

ISIS IN OTHER GULF STATES

Other Gulf States are members of the Gulf Cooperation Council,[700] consisting of Kuwait, the United Arab Emirates, Oman, Qatar, and Bahrain. The GCC is a mutual defense organization that came into being in 1981 in the shadow of the Iranian revolution and the Iran-Iraq war.[701]

Abu Sulayman al-Muwahid suicide bomber at Kuwaiti mosque.

FIRST SIGNS OF THE ISLAMIC STATE IN THE GULF REGION

On June 26, 2015, ISIS conducted a suicide bombing attack at the Imam Ja'far as-Sadiq Shi'a mosque, killing twenty-seven and wounding 227.

On the heels of the suicide bombing of a Kuwaiti mosque, ISIS announced it would be targeting Bahrain next.[702] Turki al-Binali, the Bahraini-born ISIS commander who went to Syria in 2014, made the announcement.[703]

On October 22, 2015, Bahraini officials announced they had arrested twenty-four people for links to ISIS, including the charge that they were trying to set up a terrorist cell.[704]

ISIS IN BANGLADESH

HISTORY

Despite Bangladesh's large Muslim population (146 million) and decades-long history of militant Islamic groups,[705] [706] ISIS activity in Bangladesh has been surprisingly limited until recently. Westerners with Bangladeshi backgrounds and ties to ISIS are sometimes arrested, but infrequently, and Bangladesh police have caught a handful of young ISIS-affiliated militants, usually while in transit to or from Bangladesh. Little is known about the leadership, structure, distribution, or capabilities of the self-titled "Caliphate in Bangladesh."

According to reports, US officials have warned Bangladesh authorities of evidence that ISIS is beginning to organize and become operative. Despite this, the Prime Minister of Bangladesh refutes ISIS's disruptive capabilities. Currently, the Caliphate in Bangladesh has not conducted any coordinated campaigns, preferring instead to conduct small hit-and-run attacks on police checkpoints, killings of foreign nationals, and isolated attempts to kill large numbers of the Shi'a minority on buses and in mosques. These attacks have grown in number and in casualties during late 2015, and may be an indication of growing sophistication, organization, and determination of the Caliphate in Bangladesh.

ASSASSINATION OF ITALIAN AID WORKER

Cesare Tavella, fifty, an Italian national working as a veterinarian for the Dutch church cooperative ICCO, arrived in Bangladesh in late August 2015 to work as a program manager on a rural food security and economic development project.[707] On September 28, 2015, three assailants on a single motorcycle approached him in the high-security Gulshan market diplomatic zone of Dhaka while he was jogging.[708] Two of the assailants shot him dead while one waited with the motorcycle. Witnesses heard at least three gunshots. The assailants got on the motorcycle and left immediately without taking anything from Tavella. Doctors declared Tavella dead after transport to a local hospital. Dhaka's Metropolitan Police Commissioner Asaduzzaman Mia speculated that the murder was planned in advance.

A day later, ISIS claimed responsibility for the attack in a statement saying that a security detachment had tracked Tavella and killed him with "silenced weapons," and that "citizens of the crusader coalition" in Muslim nations would receive similar treatment. It was the first time ISIS had claimed responsibility for a terrorist operation in Bangladesh.

On October 26, 2015, police authorities announced the arrest of four men for the assassination attempt. In a press briefing, Commissioner Mia said that three of the assassins were ordered to kill a Caucasian foreigner, but did not specify who gave the order. The fourth man provided the motorcycle. Although the political and religious affiliations of the men are unknown, Commissioner Mia cited "technology and other means, that the publicity was made saying IS did it was not authentic," and suggested that ISIS was protecting "the real culprits," whom he suggested were political opponents of Prime Minister Sheikh Hasina.

OTHER SIGNIFICANT EVENTS

August 7, 2014
Five militants pledge allegiance in video.[709]

September 7, 2014
Bangladesh police catch Indian youths entering Bangladesh to join ISIS.[710]

July 2, 2015
Bangladesh police catch twelve men with ties to al-Qaeda.[711]

October 2015
US officials tell Bangladeshi counterparts there are indications that the IS will intensify efforts within Bangladesh. Italian aid worker killed in Dhakar diplomatic zone. Japanese agricultural advisor shot in Northern Bangladesh.[712]

October 24, 2015
ISIS operatives throw three IEDs at Huseiniyat Dalan, a Shi'a mosque in Dhaka, killing one and injuring eighty.[713] [714]

October 28, 2015
Bangladesh PM Sheikh Hasina rejects reports of ISIS involvement in recent attacks: "Bangladesh is moving ahead and it'll do so . . . Let me say one thing: The march forward of Bangladesh can't be stopped by hurling two bombs or five eggs. Those who are thinking this are making a mistake."[715]

November 4, 2015
ISIS operatives on motorcycles ambush a police checkpoint in Baruipara, near Dhaka. The assailants stabbed and shot two police officers, then fled the scene.[716]

November 19, 2015
ISIS operatives shoot and critically wound Italian missionary Piero Parolari in Dinajpur province, 277 km (172 miles) northwest of Dakha.[717]

November 26, 2015
ISIS claims responsibility for an attack on worshippers at a Shi'ite mosque in Shibganj, northern Bangladesh, 125 km (78 miles) from Dhaka.[718]

PART III:
WHAT THEY BELIEVE

CHAPTER 9

SHADE OF SWORDS: THE ISIS WAR TO DESTROY ISLAM

UNDERSTANDING ISIS'S "EXTREMIST IDEOLOGY"

Everyone can understand the Who, What, When, Where, and How—experts abound in giving clarity to the horrific details, but the motivation of the terrorists is often lost in the debate as each spectacular attack is reported. Thousands of news reports and articles have been written asking "Who is ISIS and what do they really want?" However, a more important question finally being posed is "What was the Ideology that motivates the global Jihad?"

ISIS did manage to finally introduce into the media lexicon a word rarely heard in the debates on terrorism: ideology—the belief system of the jihadist terrorists. So when ISIS carried out its medieval rampage, pundits, opinion makers, scholars, and talking heads of all stripes started to pontificate on their interpretations of what beliefs and values were really driving the way the terrorists were waging war.

For over two decades the most important questions raised in the counterterrorism military and intelligence communities were on precisely what fueled the belief system of groups like al-Qaeda and ISIS. How could this ideology be disrupted? In Wood's article, he noted early on that American battle commanders including the US Special Operations Commander tasked to defeat ISIS, Major General Michael Nagata had commented, "We have not defeated the idea," he said. "We do not even understand the idea." If that is the case, General Nagata cannot be excused for not visiting the student library at the JFK School of Special Warfare in Fort Bragg or the US Army Combating Terrorism Center at West Point to pick up a copy of two books written almost a decade ago by the two most noted jihadi ideology experts in US intelligence, Will McCants and Jarrett Brachman: *The Militant Ideology Atlas* and *Stealing Al-Qaeda's Playbook*. Between these two books there is virtually nothing that has been written that could not clarify the philosophy, origins, and strategy behind everything that has guided the jihad movement since the eighteenth century, except the meaning of why the glue was so strong in the terrorists. For that, one must understand what Islam is and discern if ISIS meets the definition.

Observed as a whole for nearly thirty years there were few discussions about what the jihadist movement desired apart from only the most superficial readings of their statements. Few believe that they are more than an extremely orthodox variant of Islam. Taken at face value that could be true. The discussions of the belief systems, the spark in the heart and soul of the clockwork mechanism that makes the jihadist movement tick, were few and far between. Although it may appear that discussions on the ideology of ISIS, al-Qaeda, and the constellation of groups that make up the global jihad movement are relatively new, a very small subset of academics and intelligence officers have been studying the mechanism that motivated the raw foot soldiers to abandon their lives, join and desire nothing less than their own deaths in this movement. Yet, for all the years of dialog, analysis and debate about 'What the jihadist movement is' and 'what they really want' there really was no rigorous debate within the global community about their basic goals, intentions and what, in fact, they actually are.

Scholars, academics, policy advisors, media pundits, and even theologians could only describe the entire movement within the frame of the religion they purported to be fighting to defend—Islam. This narrative is wrapped so tightly into the mindset of virtually all observers that the global media will bend over backwards to the next great column or article that depicts the global jihadist movement as wholly Islamic, wholly un-Islamic, or wholly paper range targets.

Politically, opinions fall into one of three camps: The most prominent group believes that the terrorists are motivated by a radical or extremist form of Islam. To them the religion itself is the problem. They derisively refer to it as "Radical Islam" or "Islamic Extremism." This group insists that this faction of Muslims are fighting a wholly religious war, which may be apocalyptic in nature but is most definitely a legitimate clash of civilizations, Islam vs the West.

Graeme Wood, a political science professor at Yale University, wrote a widely read article for *Atlantic Monthly* where he leads the charge that ISIS is an unashamedly apocalyptic Islamic group which in turn fuels their acts of terror.[719] Other more conservative scholars and pundits say that because the terrorists themselves claim Islam, call themselves

Muslims, and quote texts from Qur'an, that Islam is the source of the problem. At the right extreme, Islamophobes in the West such as Pamela Geller and Robert Spencer hold the view that because al-Qaeda and ISIS are Muslim, they are the vanguard of the Muslim world's attack on the West. These ideologues believe that it is only a matter of time until all Muslims will join them and that Muslims, advancement must be checked. Any number of politicians and pundits attempt to legitimatize ISIS's deviance and urge the Muslim world to hurry up and join the jihadists. They want a clash of civilizations and unending war. Aayan Hirsi Ali, a former Muslim, wrote that she believed that Islam is completely violent and must be reformed and transformed into a modest version of Christianity.[720]

Hysterical rhetoric such as this is precisely what ISIS wants and desires and, God willing, the western chattering class will assist them in achieving that goal.

A second camp believes that though the terrorists say they are Muslims, labeling them and attributing their acts to the religion of Islam is incorrect. They assert that the terrorists' behaviors, ideology, and actions fall far outside of the norms of Islam and that technically makes them un-Islamic entities.

President Obama said, "Al Qaeda and ISIS and groups like it are desperate for legitimacy. They try to portray themselves as religious leaders, holy warriors in defense of Islam . . . We must never accept the premise that they put forth because it is a lie. Nor should we grant these terrorists the religious legitimacy that they seek. They are not religious leaders. They are terrorists."[721]

This opinion is echoed by many Muslim and world leaders who fear that labeling the terrorists as Islamic extremists or calling them Muslim radicals works in their interest. This group includes the highest ranking Muslims in Islam, the Muftis of Saudi Arabia and Egypt, monarchs including King Abdullah of Jordan, King Salman of Saudi Arabia, and King Hassan II of Morocco, and any number of Arab state prime ministers and Muslim theologians, intellectuals and communities.

A final group, embraced by military commanders at the US Department of Defense and NATO, takes an antiseptic view and labels the terrorists as criminals whose religious or political ideology is irrelevant. They simply want to put bombs and missiles on terrorist targets as effectively and accurately as possible.

Is it possible that all three camps could be considered correct? Yes, it is true that in the eyes of the global jihad movement the religion of Islam is the genetic basis of their being. Yes, Osama bin Laden conceptualized and disseminated an ideological perversion of Islam that is so un-Islamic that it could be called anti-Islamic. Yes again, they are terrorists who need a few thousand more accurate bombs placed on them. The arguments have merit but there is a fourth, unifying argument that is equally as accurate, incorporates all of the concerns of the above camps, and provides a satisfying explanation of the jihadist's ideology: The global jihad movement is arguably the most wealthy, influential, and virulent terror cult in the history of mankind.

Defining Jihad[723]

1— "Offensive Jihad is when the Muslims launch an offensive attack. If this attack is on the Kuffar who have previously received the message of Islam, then to call them toward Islam before commencement of the attack is considered preferable. However, if the message of Islam has not reached them, then the Kuffar will be invited toward Islam. If they reject this true faith, then they will have to pay Jizyah (Kufr tax). If they refuse to submit to the payment of Jizyah then the Muslims are to fight against them. With this type of Jihad the Kuffar who plot against the Muslims are repelled and their hearts are filled with fear, so that they do not succeed in their plans."

2— "Defensive Jihad is when the Kuffar enemy attacks the Muslims, forcing them into a defensive position. This is one of the most important obligations upon the Muslims. In researching and studying the Jihad work predecessors, we understand that Jihad is considered Fardh ayn under the following conditions: a) when the unbelievers attack upon a country or city belonging to the Muslims or if they gain control of a Muslim country; b) when the unbelievers take Muslims captives; c) when a Muslim woman is held by the Kuffar, to ensure her freedom is Fardh upon the whole Muslim Ummah; d) when the Imam (leader) of the Muslims orders the Muslims to go for Jihad; e) when the Kuffar and Muslims face each other in the battlefield and the battle takes place."

Contrary to what some scholars claim, Peter Bergen, by naming his book *Holy War, Inc.*[722] did not attempt to whitewash the religious nature of al-Qaeda but to correctly identify its corporate structure to hold itself to its original name, *al-Qaeda al-Jihad*, The Headquarters of the Holy War. The jihadist's ideology has always stressed its religious nature. Al-Qaeda and its modern adherents never once indicated that there was any semblance of secularism in their methods, thought, or strategy.

In fact, since well before Peter Bergen ever met bin Laden, al-Qaeda written or spoken doctrine never implied that they or any of their affiliate groups were anything but a religious order of the most extremist of orthodoxies. In fact al-Qaeda was unlike any preceding Arab terrorist groups. The PLO and even Hamas at their peaks embodied less Islamic fever than al-Qaeda/ISIS. None of the nationalist groups were even considered part of the jihadists. If anything jihadists were jealous of the discipline and religious fervor of the Shiite Hizballah group's capacity to fight and defeat the Israeli army in Lebanon, even if they considered them apostates worthy only of death.

Each of these labels has merit, and it is in fact critically important to adopt a proper label that accurately describes the origins, beliefs, and motivations of the men and women who are determined to change Islam, and afterwards, the world.

The ideology of many other smaller groups exist throughout the Balkans, Central Asia, the Caucasus, and Southeast Asia. Many thousands of self-radicalized individuals and supporters are sprinkled throughout most Western nations or self-convert from other religions. They adopt the words and beliefs of the cultists as spread through the Internet via YouTube video, Twitter, or DVDs.

Performing acts of ultraviolence, at the behest of the cult leader and in the name of God, allows for complete vindication from any moral code.

1,436 years after the death of the Prophet Mohammed, the cult of perpetual jihad and mandatory martyrdom seeks to enjoin a great clash of civilizations and, through the power to kill anyone and destroy anything, bring the entire world under the control of the new Islam. Then would come the judgment day. Like many aspects of the ideology of al-Qaeda, ISIS's strategic intentions, their ultimate goals, their esprit d'corps and other combatant force factors were dismissed as caricatures of the evil Islamic fanaticism.

Performing acts of ultraviolence, at the behest of the cult leader and in the name of God allows for complete vindication from any moral code.

Many observers believe that the ultimate aim of the group called the Islamic State of Iraq and Syria (ISIS)—and that has anointed itself as an Islamic caliphate with the grandiose name of "Islamic State"—views itself as being part of an apocalyptic global war which pits the Muslim world in a clash of civilizations with Christianity, Democracy and virtually all other global religions and cultures.

ISIS: A CULT OF JIHAD

In September 2014, the Prime Minister of Australia started referring to ISIS and its followers as a "terrorist death cult," and President Obama himself has used the phrase from time to time.[724] In 2004, Peter Bergen, the CNN terrorism expert, gave the ideology the moniker bin Ladenism. The US intelligence community often called it al-Qaedaism. Bin Laden called it the "Victorious Denomination" ideology. For simplicity it can be better described as the Cult of Jihad.

In my 2010 book, *An End to al-Qaeda*, I took up the challenge of defining and reframing the seemingly inexplicable behaviors of terrorists. I proposed that the most efficient way to disrupt their recruiting and support was to attack their belief system through Counter-Ideological Operations and Warfare (CIDOW).[725] That is, to directly attack the legitimacy of their beliefs on a global stage.

However, I quickly came to the conclusion that the global jihad movement is unquestionably a religious cult and discovered that there have been several like them before in Islam.

As an intelligence professional, I do not use this word in the run-of-the-mill way of insulting a group of seemingly brainwashed people. No, I assert that these groups meet the textbook psychological definition of cults.

Taken at their word, and given their actions, the global jihadi terror groups meet virtually every qualifying item on the mass–mind control checklist. Even the most cursory study the terrorist's "religious" ideology is so absolutely corrupt and violates so many laws, scripture, and traditions that it can never be considered legitimately Islamic.

The ISIS Cult of Jihad may not be monolithic, but its core values and ideology do have a single point of origin: Osama bin Laden. The current ideology was synthesized during the anti-Soviet war in Afghanistan and launched from Peshawar, Pakistan in 1988. It has spread like wildfire since 9/11 brought it to the global stage. Like an unstoppable hydra, it was designed to multiply each time it was attacked.

The ideology infects communities like a hemorrhagic virus. Initially it was rare and not very contagious unless ingested by a susceptible host. However, once it infects a community, it becomes extremely hard to check. Survive infection and it still affects one's life in a negative way. In al-Qaeda's time, it took direct contact with a member of the group and cajoling to become infected, but now the virus of the cult of jihad is spread virtually, through a bewildering myriad of social platforms, communications devices, and media. Anyone who wants the disease only needs to accept that they believe in it and then act on those beliefs.

To those who understood Osama's long term strategy, ISIS's ascension was not abandonment of al-Qaeda's mission but a sign that the plan worked much better than designed. Bin Laden not only foresaw the rise of ISIS but laid out the strategic framework in which multiple ISIS-like organizations would grow and spread across the Muslim world then unite into a Caliphate. Old men like Dr. Ayman al-Zawahiri, bin Laden's successor, were never destined to lead such a movement. Each generation of jihadist has always passed the terror torch on to younger, increasingly violent men.

The uniformity of the Cult's ideology is directly attributable to al-Qaeda's writings and speeches throughout the 1990s. Bin Laden based his doctrine on writings by ancient theologians like Mohammed ibn Abdul Wahab al-Tamimi, who established the form of worship popular in Saudi Arabia, called Wahabism. Other influences came from terrorists and radicals whose beliefs were read only in the most outer fringes, including Abu al-A'lal Mahdudi, Sayyed Qutb, Mohammed Abdu Salam al-Faraj, and others. He bound these ideas and concepts into a cult variant of Islam that would stress living like the companions of the Prophet (*Salaf*), exercising ability to determine who is and is not a Muslim (*Takfir*), perpetual Holy War (*Jihad*) and mandatory suicide martyrdom (*Shaheed*). From these he would create two new objectives for Muslims to aspire: establish a New Islamic Caliphate from Spain to the Philippines, and eliminate all tolerance and compromise of the last 1400 years from Islam. Then the path to a clash of civilizations against the West would bring about the blessed End of Times with the defeat of the Anti-Christ by the Prophet Isa or Jesus, son of Mary. These beliefs are scripture in Islam but form the raison *d'etre* of the Cult of Jihad. Technically one could say they *Jihad for Jesus*.

THE PROPHETIC METHOD

ISIS believes that it is carrying out a chain of events as prophesized by the Prophet Mohammed. All components of their belief system enjoins the words in the Qur'an, but instead of interpreting it the way that that it has been for the past fourteen centuries, they took another direction. From the very beginning of al-Qaeda, the mission of the organization was to accept with absolute belief that their actions are the physical manifestation of the will of God. They believe that everything they do, all acts, no matter how small, including all defeats and particularly all successes, are not in their hands but that of their maker.

This manifestation of faith by ISIS is the draw by which they recruit the most disinterested Muslims, and even non-Muslims. They speak and tell of an interpretation of Islam which is so convincing and extremely orthodox that it must be true. They can express their reinterpretation of Islam with almost unbelievable passion and ardor. They can spin the tale that the phrase "*Insha'Allah*" or God Willing is actually meant to be a divine prayer in which the answer to manifest the will of God is to harness the human capacity to perform actions with which He only could be pleased. Therein lies the rub. Once the listener is caught in the heat of the passion, the truth comes to the fore—God must have his wishes on earth brought to completion by the men who are willing to act in the will of God and do whatever is necessary. The only way to have the acts of God validated and wishes of God to come true is the purity of death. They believe that only the most extremely devout Muslim, a Muslim that eschews all comfort, rejects all changes, the century of interpretations and *Bidah*, the innovation that calls for tolerance and respect and accepts science and high art . . . these all must be cleansed to please God.

In the interpretation of ISIS, their ideology commits them to work solely in the belief that all God wishes is prayer and devotion to God and commitment to the literal words of the Qur'an and the events it predicts. Nothing less will satisfy. If Islam has been corrupt for 1,437 years, Allah wills that it be corrected. They believe the only way to convince 1.8 billion Muslims that God is pleased with the beheading of children and the rape of women is to characterize those acts as a form of worship. This is the interpretation of ISIS that defines their cultism. All mass murder, subjugation, slavery, death and more death is the highest form of worship to God. They are his instrument and absent direct orders they accept that they are fulfilling the events in the Qur'an's book of Tribulation (the Christian Book of Revelations).

ISIS has taken it upon themselves to bring about, on their own, the literal interpretation of the Qur'an. Instead of letting God's will happen, they are making their interpretation of His desires their own will.

Nowhere in the Qur'an does it state that men are to take into their own hands the will of God and make it happen. ISIS argues that since God does not intercede then it is his will. But who are they to tell Islam that God allowed them to pass judgement against the 1.8 billion that do not follow their corruption? Who are they to tell Islam that God told them to declare 210 million Shia' as apostates who must be killed? That's to be answered by the learned of Islam. When put to the average Muslim, they will tell you there is only one way, in their faith, that humans are incited to commit acts of evil and misadventure: These acts were inspired by Satan and his demons.

Islamic eschatology, or the study of the end of days, culminates with the *Youm al-Qiyāmah* or Judgement Day. This is the day where all life on earth ends and all stand before God in judgement. If it sounds familiar, it is nearly identical to the Christian and Judaic belief except in a few peculiar aspects. And like those faiths, many people have spent their lives trying to force Gods, hand and create the conditions of the judgement day.

In his mind, bin Laden was merely interpreting God's orders about the End of Times. This interpretation is the genesis of the group's pathology. But it was up to him and his fellow travelers to develop and implement the strategic plan that would lead to its success. Like the radical Christians who tried to breed a red cow, or destroy the Dome of the Rock mosque in order to bring about Judgement Day, so too do ISIS seek to force God's hand through direct action.

Thanks to the invasion of Iraq, al-Qaeda's ideology would not die in the mountains of Pakistan. In Iraq he got the most fanatical killers imaginable and had them managed by a chain of exceedingly ruthless commanders: Abu Musab al-Zarqawi, Abu Ayyub al-Masri, Abu Umar al-Baghdadi, and now Abu Bakr al-Baghdadi. The cultists would be spread in the geographic heart of the Middle East by the younger, faster, and more agile men who would man ISIS.

Why couldn't al-Qaeda seem to harness the energy and excitement of the world's youth like ISIS, Boko Haram, al-Shabaab, Ansar al-Dine, et al? In their day they did. The excitement of 2015 is just an illusion manifested through better social technology and the unleashing of the brand name. A major difference is al-Qaeda was selective and wanted terror professionals. In letters captured in Abbottabad by SEAL Team 6, bin Laden understood that the al-Qaeda brand was slipping from his ability to control who was and was not a follower. The ideology was becoming trendy and popular, almost too popular. Bin Laden wanted higher quality, professional fighters to run the al-Qaeda brand. Anyone can join ISIS or its affiliates. The era of professionals has given way to the terrorist mobster. No matter what one thinks of the ideology or the new wave of its embrace, with ISIS on the rise and al-Qaeda's older pros observing from the corporate skybox, Osama bin Laden has successfully managed to fight us from the grave.

The beauty of the ISIS Cult of Jihad is that they do not need bin Laden or Caliph Ibrahim alive to lead them. It is now a sentient and self-sustaining series of standing orders that has stood the test of time among the believers. Real jihadists individually believe that no one on earth can revoke or invalidate the variant of Islam they have been told will take them to Paradise. Indeed, now that the Caliphate has been declared, the cult is on autopilot.

The Four Commands of Caliph Ibrahim.[726]

Jammah—Gather (Together away from Infidels)

Ta'ah—Obedience (to Caliph Ibrahim and his commanders)

Sama'—Listen (to commands from ISIS)

Millah—Keep to the Path of Righteousness (Stay with us only)

YOLO! SEE YOU IN PARADISE!

If this is a cult, why do so many individuals seek out, join, and believe in this ideology? To those who join, the madness is a promise that they will be at the heart of something special. They offer everyone who is filled with hatred, boredom, or who believes that Islam is presently out of proper orbit to come and join. The video montages show heroic action, blissful death and a human paradise on earth.

The Caliphate's cult ideology has an appeal to the disenfranchised, the devout, the bored, the opportunist, and the criminally insane. Untold numbers of individuals and supporters are self-radicalizing through the Internet. Many abandon their birth religions to join. It offers a simple, appealing answer to the questions of how to advance in life or how to fill emptiness. ISIS says "Join us, kill for God, and take your rewards both here and in heaven!" And like all ideologies based on perversion and ignorance, the objectives they seek can only occur through human sacrifice.

The only real difference between al-Qaeda and ISIS is that the cultists have moved from hiding their intentions to bursting forth with a passion to let us know how they will kill us and why. There is almost no covert planning with them. The pride in their blood-soaked legacy is supported through a massive feedback loop of positive reinforcement spread across the globe by a legion of cheerleaders and fan boys. Everything done by ISIS and al-Qaeda followers—child rape, mass decapitation, sexual slavery, and burning humans alive—requires only the belief that such acts give God, *the cult's God*, the greatest pleasure and that such atrocities will be rewarded beyond imagination. And God can reward them only if they die.

The very act of joining a jihadi group affords the member special privileges in Paradise that all others will be denied upon their death or execution. Additionally, the cultists believe that the highest form of worship to God is not just death in battle but suicide sacrifice through explosive bombing.

They crave the bloodlust of jihad. They wrap themselves in the thinnest veneer of a legitimate global religion—and they have never been more popular.

This is not the first time experts considered the global jihad movement as a cult movement. In 1996, the first report I ever saw on a group called *al-Qaeda al-Jihad* described it as "an apocalyptic Islamic cult." Peter Bergen, one of the last journalists to interview bin Laden, wrote in his 2001 book, *Holy War, Inc.*, that al-Qaeda ranged somewhere "between a cult and a genuine mass movement." But many scholars view the word "cult" as a pejorative. Some tiptoe up to the line and say these groups are similar to Christian cults but won't call it as they see it. For example, in interviews after his recent *Atlantic* article, "What ISIS Really Wants," Graeme Wood equated ISIS's claim to speak for Islam to be similar to Christian cultists David Koresh and Jim Jones. Others have suggested it is more like Joseph Kony's child-stealing Lord's Resistance Army in Uganda or the Aum Shinrikyo's hybrid Christian-Buddhist cult in Japan. In fact, it may be argued that what is occurring in Iraq and Syria is closer to the Khmer Rouge, an atheist agrarian cult of Maoist communism that mass murdered almost a million.

Many scholars call the Jihadists Islamic extremists, but Christian death sects are not referred to by their religion but instead by the description of their behavior—cults. Why not apply this to religions equally? Why specifically limit the description to groups outside of Islam?

Death cultists of all religions are groomed and expected to kill perceived enemies and kill themselves, preferably both at the same time.

Terrorist cults have existed in many forms and in virtually every religion, but Muslims don't seem to embrace this word either. The Saudi religious authorities, the Ulema, dance around it. They often refer to the terrorists as "Deviants," "Misguided," or "Miscreants." Muslim authorities must know that by labeling the global jihadi movement as a cult, that means they are practicing apostasy and the punishments they would have to visit upon them would require a terrible and bloody effort on a global scale. They would have to issue a religious ruling, or fatwa, and declare an official Jihad, whereupon the average Muslim would have a personal obligation to stop or destroy the terrorists wherever they are found.

In any case, these events show exactly why the global jihadists who follow ISIS are precisely like the misguided and brainwashed apocalyptic cult followers of Jones, Koresh, Kony, and Asihara. They promote beig Declaring these people apostates also conflicts with the Saudi evangelism of the less violent forms Wahabism and "quietest" Salafist philosophy, whose orthodoxy is respected and practiced in Saudi Arabia. Some Muslim theologians believe that the neo-Salafism of ISIS is just a hair's breadth across the line and could be brought back into the fold. This is fantastical thinking. Yet, if the psychological characteristics of cults are analyzed and compared to their behaviors, it's clear the ISIS jihadist movement falls well into the definition of a cult.

CHAPTER 10

A CULT OF JIHAD: THE CONTEXT OF THE ISIS WAR TO DESTROY ISLAM

HISTORY OF ISLAMIC CULTISM

Many observers make a simple calculation that equates the terrorists to Islam because the terrorists identify themselves as Muslims, claim they are fighting for Muslims, or use phrases from Islamic texts in their statements. However, several cults have disrupted Islam in significant ways well before al-Qaeda or ISIS. Let us review the four most significant examples from the last fourteen centuries.

THE KHAWARIJ

In 658, during the first Islamic civil war, two great armies, one belonging to the governor of Syria, Mu'awiya, and the other under command of Caliph Ali, the third successor to the Prophet Mohammed, faced off near the village of Siffin in Iraq. Mu'awiya sent his soldiers into battle with pages of the Qur'an on their spear tips. This gesture forced Caliph Ali to parley rather than fight. After a negotiated truce, the battle was called off. Objecting to this decision, a group of twelve thousand soldiers decided to abandon both armies and start their own movement. In Arabic they were called the al-Khawarij—"those on the outside." Orientalists called them the Kharajites.

The Khawarij took a literalist reading of the Qur'an and believed that no man, neither Mu'awiya nor Ali, should be allowed to lead Islam. They decamped for Baghdad with the intention to spread their anarchist's interpretation of Islam. Both Caliph Ali and Mu'awiya knew this could not be allowed. Ali's forces intercepted them and convinced eight thousand to return. Four thousand chose battle and were slaughtered. Nine survivors escaped, formed a terrorist group, and finally managed to assassinate Ali in 661. It resulted in a split between Islam's followers. The Faction of Ali or "Shi'itul Ali" would branch off into Shi'ite Islam, which is now 13 percent of the Muslim world. The other 87 percent are called Sunnah.

The ideology of both al-Qaeda and ISIS are similar to the Khawarij. Even today some Muslims derisively call ISIS "Kharajites" on Twitter and in social media. It has so upset ISIS that they warned in a recent statement that they would behead opposition groups that referred to them as Khawarij.

The Khawarij pioneered the al-Qaeda/ISIS penchant for hijrah, or emigration to isolate members from other societies, and they exercised the right to practice takfir—to determine who is and is not a Muslim and execute them. They considered all people not in their cult to be kuffar—unbelievers. They mass-murdered all outside their group with impunity. They executed orders that women and children were not to be spared in any circumstance, so no bloodlines could avenge them. They operated in complete secrecy, preferring to use taqiyyah—the practice of lying to maintain their true beliefs, rather than proselytize. Small Khawarij family groups spread across the Arabian Peninsula and were eliminated by the next Islamic cult, the Qaramitah.

THE QARAMITAH

The Qaramitah was founded in 874. Referred to as Caramathians by Orientalist scholars, the sect formed after the Sunnah-Shi'ite split. Hamdan al-Qaramat of Kufa, a follower of the Shi'ite Ismaili sect, felt compelled to prepare Southern Iraq militarily for the return of the Mahdi. According to Islamic beliefs dictated by the Prophet Mohammed, the Mahdi, a redeeming savior, would return after three years of famine and turmoil, and rule for seven years. It's the Imam Mahdi's destiny to assist the Prophet Isa (Jesus) at the end of days to turn back the anti-Christ (Mashih ad-Dijjal) in a battle outside of the Saudi city of Medina. It is believed that Jesus will finally destroy the anti-Christ at Bab al-Lud near today's Ben Gurion airport in Israel.

To prepare for this eventuality, Qaramat formed armed, military-oriented communities along the eastern coast of Arabia. By 906 his Bedouin followers would occupy modern-day Bahrain. The Qaramitah started raiding and looting Hajj pilgrimage trains and settlements along the Eastern Arabian Peninsula. They attacked trade lines from Bahrain to southern Iraq. They even raided Basra, destroying mosques and killing hundreds, including the governor.[727] Ironically, their raids destroyed the last outposts of the Khawarij cult.[728]

The Abbasid caliphate paid tributes to stop the raiding, but when they were cut, the Qaramitah declared war on Islam. The new leader, Abu

Tahrir, ruled that the entire practice of hajj had devolved into Shirk, or idolatry. As evidence he stated that the hajj pilgrims were going to Mecca to worship an idol at the very central point of Islam, the Kaaba. Within the Kaaba was a black stone, a meteorite. Abu Tahrir decided he would put a stop to Muslims worshiping in its presence. Using their knowledge of the Arabian Peninsula, they set off and attacked Mecca.[729]

In 923 the Qaramitah surrounded Mecca and laid siege to the city and residents for seventeen days. They desecrated the Kaaba, destroying the structure and seizing the black stone. They then massacred worshipers and dumped their bodies into the holy well of Zem Zem. The Fatimid caliphate negotiated with the Qaramitah but would not get the black stone back until twenty years later in 950. They were finally exterminated in 1077.[730]

THE MAHDISTS OF SUDAN

In 1881 a cult movement formed in Sudan under the leadership of Muhammed Ahmed, a forty-year-old Nubian from the Sufi sect who later proclaimed himself Mahdi. Sudan was under an oppressive Turkish Caliphate, ruled by Egyptians and British civil servants, including the former British General Charles "Chinese" Gordon. Muhammed Ahmed called on a local Sufi religious assemblage to name him Mahdi. He subscribed to the philosophy that Sudan needed to return back to Salafism, a state of Islam equal to that of the immediate companions of the Prophet Mohammed. He also sought to recapture the entirety of the Muslim world from the Ottoman Empire and bring it under his rule as its Caliph. Ahmed was scoffed at by Islamic scholars for having none of the physical characteristics of the Mahdi—high brow, fair skin, pointed nose, and a dark spot on both the right cheek and hand—nor had any signs of the tribulation occurred, as prophesied.

Despite the details that did not fit the Mahdi narrative, many Sudanese looked for salvation, and armed revolt was their choice. The Mahdists soon decimated the Egyptian forces in Sudan and took control of a swath of territory that dwarfed ISIS's recent seizures. They controlled an area of almost 700,000 square miles—much larger than the entirety of

Iraq, Jordan, Lebanon, and Syria. The British were forced to evacuate the remnants of the Egyptian army and foreigners from the capital, Khartoum. Despite great effort, "Chinese" Gordon was killed defending the city when it fell to Mahdist forces in 1885.

The Sudan uprising under Muhammed Ahmed may be considered cultist in nature because of the radical changes he forced onto Islamic law and religious practice. He dictated that salvation was not found through direct appeal to God but through himself as the "Savior." He was ignored by the Egyptian and Ottoman religious leaders, the Ulema, as were his claims of direct lineage to the Prophet Mohammed. That did not stop him from adopting changes based on his whims. He even went so far as to give himself the title of "Khalifat Rasul Allah" or "Successor to the Prophet Mohammed."

As "savior of Islam," he ordered changes be made to replace two of the five pillars of Islam. The Shahada, or recognition of the monotheistic nature of God, is an obligatory statement of belief: "There Is No God but God and Mohammed Is His Messenger," was corrupted to include ". . . and Muhammed Ahmed is the Successor to the Prophet Mohammed." Additionally, he removed the obligation of Hajj, or pilgrimage to Mecca, and substituted an obligation to Jihad, or holy war.

All of these were astonishing to the traditional Ulema and the Ottoman Caliphate. Muhammed Ahmed was quickly ruled a heretic and his followers apostates. In turn, Muhammed Ahmed then ruled the Ottomans were the real apostates. Like the Qaramitah (and later ISIS), he too went on a cultural cleansing of traditional Islam through book and manuscript burnings. Muhammed Ahmed died of typhus in 1885. Winston Churchill remarked on the death of Muhammed Ahmed that God "whom he had served, not unfaithfully, and who had given him whatever he had asked, required of Mohammed Ahmed his soul; and so all that he had won by his brains and bravery became of no more account to him."

Muhammed Ahmed's followers would not be stamped out until 1898 by the campaign that included a young Winston Churchill, assigned to the 21st Lancers under General Kitchener. Speaking on ending the Mahdists' influence, Churchill said many years later, "Now this is not the end. It is not even the beginning of the end. But it is, perhaps, the end of the beginning."[731]

THE UTEYBISTS

Juhayman al-Uteybi leader of the
Grand Mosque attack after capture.

In 1979, Juhayman bin Seif al-Uteybi was a former member of the Saudi National Guard and a devout practitioner of Salafism. He became convinced that an associate of his, Muhammed bin Abdullah al-Qahtani, bore the physical characteristics of the Mahdi. They formed a well-armed group named al-Jamaa al-Salafiya al-Muhtasiba, "the Salafist Group that Demand Right and Forbids Wrong."[732] An obsessively insane Salafist, he saw every aspect of Saudi modernism from televisions, to cars, to currency as anti-Islamic innovations. They decided to cleanse Islam and start anew, so they seized the Grand Mosque in Mecca and engaged in open warfare with the government. From the pulpit of the Grand Mosque in Mecca they proclaimed al-Qahtani as the Mahdi on the 1,400-year anniversary of Islam. They were immediately engaged by the Saudi army and fought a pitched battle that lasted two weeks. Hundreds of pilgrims, soldiers, and terrorists were killed in the shrine. The Saudis were so desperate to clear the terrorists from the labyrinth of underground chambers in the complex that they asked for France's assistance to drop nerve gas onto the Grand Mosque.[733] Sixty-three captured Saudi and foreign fighters were later beheaded, including al-Uteybi, however the links to the modern-day al-Qaeda and ISIS are astonishing. There were rumors that trucks from the largest construction contractor in Saudi Arabia working on the shrine were used to smuggle in weapons. That company was the bin Laden Group. At the time it was run by Salem bin Laden, brother to a young Osama. One of the survivors was a Kuwaiti named Abdel Latif al-Dirbas or Abu Hazza; he was brother-in-law of Abu Muhammed al-Maqdisi. Al-Maqdisi would become the most influential theologian in al-Qaeda. Maqdisi also shared a cell with Abu Mussab al-Zarqawi, the future leader of Al-Qaeda in Iraq and grandfather of ISIS.

CHARACTERISTICS OF ISIS CULTISM

To the Cult of Jihad (CoJ) there is practically no single more important guiding principle than one particular phrase from the Qur'an's Surat al-Baqarah 4:74—

> So let those fight in the cause of Allah who sell the life of this world for the Hereafter. And he who fights in the cause of Allah and is killed or achieves victory—We will bestow upon him a great reward.

This sentence guides virtually the entirety of jihadist ideology. Yet the rest of the Qur'an delineates numerous restrictions on jihad, war, apostasy, hypocrisy, and murder. The Prophet Mohammed himself repeatedly cautions and tempers all rash acts with compromise and respect of others specifically and through scholarly interpretations. Conflict, internal strife, and civil war are inevitable in any society but the Prophet Mohammed appeared to understand that the love of war could bring about a love of something greater than God. In Surat al-Baqarah he said "Fight in the cause of Allah those who fight you, but do not transgress limits; for Allah loveth not transgressors." The CoJ has reinterpreted this statement by changing the limits for their own purposes. As William Shakespeare quipped, "the Devil can cite scripture for his purpose."

Selecting one passage from the Qur'an to supersede all others to control their own pathological communities and justify mass murder belies any claims to religious legitimacy. Therefore one must seriously consider cultism.

Psychologist Robert Jay Lifton in his book *Thought Reform and the Psychology of Totalism* spelled out numerous clearly identifiable cult traits that may explain the jihadist's seemingly irrational behaviors.[734]

The jihadist's use of the Qur'an's eschatological doctrine to hone their followers into weapons is known as Milieu Control. This is Lifton's theory that control of communication, information, and the environment of followers can impact cognitive behavior. These controls set the cultists at odds with commonsense and normative human characteristics such as self-preservation or rational decision-making. In the Jihadist narrative this starts with creating entire communities isolated from all society and calling others to come join them.

The terrorist's adoption of the story of the Prophet Mohammed's hijrah, or "emigration" from Mecca to Medina to found Islam, has been coopted by the terrorists to mean leaving the modern world and one's family behind. Using the word hijrah in this way gives the prospective recruit a religious justification to run completely away from their past and join the CoJ. "Emigrating" to an ISIS or al-Qaeda base allows them to be free from all communication, influence, and ties with their family, friends, and the world outside of the cult. It offers a new reality in a new world where the rules, actions, and requirements are specifically designed for the cultist believer to be thoroughly indoctrinated. Within that community is the strict control of dress, behavior, and adherence to piety. These are common milieu control techniques most of us recognize when we remember the camps of other death cults such as Jonestown in Guyana, the Branch Davidian compound in Waco, Texas, or the Aum Shinrikyo compound in Tokyo.[735]

According to a study by psychologist J. M. Curtis, there are as many as nine identifying factors found in potential members who could join cults:

> [G]eneralized ego-weakness, emotional vulnerability, pro-pensities toward dissociative states; tenuous, deteriorated, or nonexistent family relations and support systems; inadequate means of dealing with exigencies of survival; history of severe child abuse or neglect; exposure to idiosyncratic or eccentric family patterns; proclivities toward or abuse of controlled sub-stances; unmanageable and debilitating situational stress and crises; intolerable socioeconomic conditions.[736]

Cult expert and survivor Steve Hassan associated ISIS recruiting as being similar to the People's Church cult, where almost a thousand follow-ers willfully committed mass suicide in Jonestown, Guyana by drinking cyanide-laced Kool-Aid. Hassan worked as an investigator on arguably the most dangerous pre–9/11 religious cult in the world, Aum Shinrikyo. This group sought to topple the government of Japan through developing and deploying sophisticated weapons of mass destruction such as Sarin gas and the Ebola virus. Hassan was called to Japan after their terror nerve gas attacks on the Tokyo subway, to help the CBS news program *60 Minutes* make sense of it all. He had full access to the Aum Shinrikyo compound and members where he learned their indoctrination techniques up close.

From his experience with Aum Shinrikyo and other groups, Hassan developed the B.I.T.E. model of cult identification,[737] an acronym identifying the master controls cults place on their recruits in Behavior, Information, Thought, and Emotions. His scale identifies four major areas of control and thirty-nine specific behavioral identifiers that characterize cults.

Behavior Control

This is exercised through regulating or dramatically altering their physical reality, associations and friends, clothing, food, and sexuality. Much like Lifton's milieu control, grooming the environment and incessant indoctrination dominates their time in the group through prayer, memorization, and rigid adherence to dogma in a highly controlled environment. The entire jihadist movement is framed on behavior acceptable only to the group's doctrine.

Information Control

This is practiced by withholding information detrimental to the group, limiting or forbidding communication with the outside world, and making all information a choice between belief of the dogma, or heresy and conspiracy with the enemies of the cult. They encourage spying and create dramatic, magnificent propaganda that glorifies the criminal excesses of the group. Jihadists also use an emotional control technique Lifton called "Mystical Manipulation," defined as the "manipulation of experiences that appear spontaneous but in fact were planned and orchestrated by the group . . . some special gift or talent that will then allow the leader to reinterpret events, scripture, and experiences as he or she wishes." The jihadists often demonstrate this in the post-mortem manipulation of the facial muscles of dead comrades' corpses to show them as smiling. This ghoulish trick allows jihadi cult leaders to convince others that the suicide bombers went to Paradise serene, and are happy even after death.

Thought Control

This technique requires members to internalize the ideology as the only pure truth and, Hassan says, "adopt the traffickers' map of reality" as the only reality allowed. The member is given a new identity and name. Hypnotic techniques are used such as rote memorization and practices to alter the mental state of the subject.

Cults demand purity of their members as a core component of Thought Control: The world around them is always dirty and corrupt. This purity requirement drives the self-cleansing internal security mechanisms of jihadist groups whereby they not only kill all others who do not join them, but they also kill members who do not maintain the same rigorous mindset. Each member strives to be purer than the next. Guilt or fear is then used to control their ability to do whatever is asked of them.

Emotional Control

Cults manipulate feelings by encouraging constant questioning of the sincerity of one's own identity, piety, and sincerity to evoke emotional responses that can be reoriented toward loyalty or to overcome decency. They foster in recruits a sense of deep guilt in not practicing the religion, ridicule them for being part of the enemy forces, and insist that salvation can only be found with the cult's guidance.

Lifton also identified many other cult identification factors including the rule that doubt or dissent is never, ever tolerated, and that rational or critical thinking is treated as dangerous and heretical. In an interview with *National Geographic*, Morten Storm, a Danish convert to Islam and ex-member of al-Qaeda, made it clear that the moment a cultist stops believing is the moment they are generally expected to be killed:

> I'd also begun to be deeply troubled by the killing or maiming of civilians in the name of Allah. The Bali bombings, Madrid, London—these were acts of violence targeting ordinary people. If this was part of Allah's preordained plan, I wanted no

part of it. But I also knew that if I told people how I felt, I could be killed for apostasy.[738]

The technique of "confession" of their past sins before joining the cult was a method of thought control as well. This practice is seen in virtually all Jihadist videos where people from a wide array of backgrounds and languages stand with their guns in hand to disparage their pre-Hijrah lives, their secular families, time spent among the unbelievers. They ultimately confess that their only salvation was to join the jihad and enter the Dar al-Harb—"House of War"—where salvation awaits them.

Punishment is also used as a powerful tool to affect behavior as well. Transgressors are punished severely and fear of being out of step. But the Cult of Jihad takes it a step further. They use the rare Islamic practice of takfir, declaring one is an infidel, as the ultimate threat of punishment and the ultimate exercise of human power. Lifton calls this "Dispensing of existence." It is the "prerogative to decide who has the right to exist and who does not." He believed that empowering members with this characteristic is the single most dangerous part of cult indoctrination.

The practice of takfir empowers the street-level terrorist to kill anyone at any time on the slightest whim by simply declaring that the victim is an unbeliever, an apostate, or a traitor. In the CoJ every individual in the world is considered an unbeliever, except the jihadists. Unbelievers have only two options: Join the jihad (which is almost never accepted) or death. It creates a mindset where each jihadi is forged into a weapon system imbued with the power of God himself. In December 2014 the leader of the Nigerian terror cult Boko Haram, Abu Bakr Shekau, declared the entirety of Nigeria's 85 million Muslims and the rest of the world as unbelievers destined for murder or slavery:

> Salafist are disbelievers. Tariqah Tijani (Sufis) are disbelievers. Al-Qadiriyah are disbelievers. The Naqshabandiyah are disbelievers. Shaziliya are disbelievers. Muta'zila are disbelievers. Sahiziliyyah are disbelievers. Shi'ite (Muslims) are disbelievers. Democracies are disbelievers. The Saudi Arabians are not Islamic they are the people of Saloul, not followers of the

Prophet! . . . They are Disbelievers! We will Kill! We will hold slaves! We will selllllllll . . . slaves!

He set about proving it by summarily executing as many as two thousand people in two major cities.

An innovation on "dispensing of existence" is the Boko Haram practice of mass murder of one's family before a suicide operation, so that they precede them in paradise. On January 6, 2016 Leena al-Qasem a resident of Raqqa was turned in for "Apostasy." She was brought out from her job at the Central Post Office and publically executed by her own son, Ali Saqr, in front of her co-workers. He shot her through the head. She was accused of trying to encourage her son to leave ISIS. Days later he wrote a letter to the media claiming he did not do it but implying that if it were in his power he would have. He then publically redoubled his oath of loyalty to ISIS. This violation is not just a capital crime against Sharia law—its indifference to common human decency is abhorrent.

THE ISIS RADICALIZATION METHODOLOGY

Before any individuals go to an ISIS jihad zone or are selected to represent the group in a home mission, they first need to go through a process that brings them officially into the organization. In the professional terrorist group al-Qaeda, they relied on talent scouts who would find already radicalized professionals and make face to face contact. Only then would they be brought to a training center and swear fealty to the group and dispatched to a mission.

The brilliance of the ISIS system is that its recruitment system is almost passive. The prospective jihadi must radicalize his/herself, then make contact with a talent scout, be passed onto a recruiter, and then finally they will travel under the guidance of a handler. After acceptance into the organization, they are trained and equipped for combat missions and deployed.

The ISIS radicalization pathway has some similarities to al-Qaeda in that they too inspire their members and bring them into the organization through recruiters, but the entire ISIS process is far less covert, has fewer counterintelligence checks on the background of the prospective recruit, and relies on placing the burden of proof of usefulness on the volunteer. Al-Qaeda's selection process was much more like the grooming and qualifications program of a military special forces or intelligence agency. Isis is more like a regular military volunteer. ISIS accepts a far lower level of proof by allowing the recruit to prove themselves simply by engaging with them on social media or through contacts among the already radicalized. Virtually anyone can be recruited into ISIS. Osama bin Laden himself worried about the adventurers, murderers, and fanboys who wanted to join al-Qaeda, but al-Baghdadi welcomes them all.

This is actually the process of recruiting intelligence assets used by spy agencies worldwide. It provides for security in the recruitment process and allows for the prospective jihadi to be isolated or disposed of if they are found to be spies.

ISIS IDEOLOGICAL RADICALIZATION PATHWAY

1. **Admiration**—Tweets, videos, films, or face to face discussions are used to show the strength and heroism of the cultists. This draws a level of admiration from some personalities.
2. **Inspiration**—The violent images and religious rhetoric overwhelms the individual and makes them feel that they could be part of the ISIS cult machinery.
3. **Radicalization**—The individual affiliates with the terrorist philosophy or the person who makes contact with them and aspires to become one of their ilk. This is generally the "fanboy" stage.
4. **Isolation**—The process of Hijrah, or emotionally departing and "emigrating" from the family, friends, and community secretly and planning to physically depart from the land of the Unbelievers.

5. **Identification**—Adopting the trappings, name, or behaviors of ISIS or its members.
6. **Dedication**—Swearing Bayah or oath of loyalty to ISIS and to obey the orders of al-Baghdadi.
7. **Operations**—The individual is now part of ISIS and trained to participate in the terror operations.

HOME-TO-HIJRAH PATHWAY

Once a person has proceeded through to at least the Identification part of the radicalization process, they generally will attempt to physically travel to join the group in one of its Jihad zones. This could be in Syria, Libya, or Yemen—or if they choose, they can remain behind "enemy lines" in their home nation.

1. **First Contact**—The prospective recruit reaches out to ISIS scouts who watch social media, explore video links, or have face-to-face chance encounters.
2. **Talent Scout**—The recruit is put into communication with a talent scout who remains in contact until the sincerity of the individual is assessed.
3. **Handler**—Once the recruit is validated a handler is assigned. It may be the talent scout him/herself or another professional handler who finesses the Hijrah process. Once near a jihad zone, ISIS will bring the individual to a site where they can be physically assessed and placed in isolation until transfer to an ISIS counter-intelligence unit can be accomplished.
4. **Logistician**—The ISIS staff who handle the transfer of recruits across borders will supply transportation, lodging, and meals before hand-over.
5. **Hand-Over**—The handlers will pass the recruit over to a counter-intelligence team who will interrogate and determine the truthfulness of the person's conviction.

6. **Induction**—A successful recruit will go through a rigorous religious and psychological training process before being transferred to a combat unit.

BI-POLAR WORLD OF ROMANTIC RELIGIOUS FANTASY

For an allegedly true Islamic movement, ISIS espouses jaw-dropping hypocrisy concerning mass murder. The jihadists ceaselessly complain in videos, writings, and tweets about the murder or deaths of children by Syria, the Kurds, Shi'ites, Israel, and America and in the same breath claim to carry out wholesale genocide, rape, and slavery in the name of the entire Muslim world.

To lure in those with a semblance of conscience they claim to be primarily a social movement that is forced to fight in defense of the defenseless. They claim to run a fully functioning nation that repairs power, runs nursing homes, and gives freely to charity, all the while mass-murdering Muslims with an intensity and hatred the Crusaders would respect. In fact, after taking Mosul, Abu Bakr al-Baghdadi may have bested King Richard the Lionhearted's famous massacre at Acre in 1191 of three thousand bound hostages by capturing and killing virtually every Muslim soldier, government worker, Yazidi, Kurd, and Christian they could lay hands on in Northern Iraq.

Among one another, the cult is described as an amazing movement that transcends the modern world and allows the jihadi to go back to what they believe is a more perfect time: the earliest days of Islam. It exists without consideration as to the modernity of the world or changes within Islam. In fact, every word they speak is as if they were actual companions of the Prophet Mohammed, sitting in the sand, eating dates at the battle of Badr, or passing him water in the trenches at Yathrib. They live as if the end of times and their role in it are happening in their seventh-century lives. They do not live in the twenty-first century, until they want a jar of Nutella or a case of Red Bull energy drinks. It's a dance between reality and imagination that does not exist among modern Muslims. The global jihad movement lives the fantasy, and each murder gives them paradise plus points (Ajur) toward a perfect future drawn from the past. It is a game of *Call of Duty* with real guns, real blood, and game over gets you directly into heaven filled with rewards.

Whether in print or in film, the constant drumbeat of a "holier than thou" message of piety is supreme in the strategic narrative of ISIS. Its members demand the listener adopt an unrealistic faith, often delivered through Nasheeds, or religious chants, in an intensely repetitive manner. These elements are present in virtually all the official videos and audio recordings produced by the organizations.

The jihadist cultists are not just mimicking the early days of the Qur'an; they are reliving the events and templating them over today's terror acts as a homage. For example, every terror attack or offensive combat action they perform is called a Ghazwah, the raids carried out by the Prophet Mohammed against opposing forces. In the modern day, as Iraqi forces planned to take back the city of Mosul, there were reports that the sectors of the city held by ISIS fighters started digging fighting trenches. Another such 17-km long trench was dug outside of their capital Raqqah. Many believe that they were attempting to recreate the conditions of a victory the Prophet Mohammed won in 626 against a larger force using a defensive trench at the Battle of Khandaq (the Trench). Even though this may seem an illogical tactical move in the face of American aerial firepower, it is more likely that ISIS believes the proper way to win a twenty-first century battle is to inspire their men by re-creating a seventh-century event.

> The CoJ empowers the terrorist to believe that they are each an individual weapon of God and that alone or combined they change the world to the way their God wants it.

ISLAMIC KABUKI THEATER

ISIS also exhibits a convincing version of Islamic Kabuki theater. To the jihadists Islam is a mask, and their role in it is a form of Kabuki theater—wearing black uniforms, beards, hair locks, expressing piety, and enforcing an unwavering religious drama in the face of the cameras, but they still drink Red Bull, rape women, and secretly drink alcohol among themselves. Swearing to follow al-Wala wal Bara—"allegiance to all thing Godly and forbidding of all ungodly"—but using un-Islamic Western inventions such as personal mobile phones, chatting with women on Facebook and Twitter, driving to battle in Cadillac Escalades, or showing off hijab-clad women posing on 2014 BMWs. All of the false piety is designed to lure the wannabe to the glimmering sexual and personal treasures of the Caliphate, all while mass-murdering Muslims.

In fact, by posting photos of themselves in combat action poses and praising images of smiling dead, the jihadis clearly harbor a deep narcissistic desire to be honored as heroes and martyrs. By their own definition their self-indulgence is a form of selfie Shirk—idolatry and worship of images—with the photos and videos of their heroes placing them above the average Muslim and next to God. They have killed other Muslims for less.

Evidence suggests that ISIS and al-Qaeda have been using cult recruiting and control models for more than just religious fanaticism. Intelligence, counterterrorist, and police agencies may make inroads by understanding this is a dehumanized cult. Steve Hassan believes that law enforcement requires extensive training on the methods of cult recruiting and to learn to identify how people become situationally susceptible, particularly through the Internet. As of now, the agencies are facing a behavioral control network that has perfected a mind-control subroutine that makes recruits impervious to family, love, intimidation, or death.

ISIS Cultist Demand Changes in Islam

The five obligations of Salat, praying towards five times a day; Zakat giving charity to the needy; Sawm, Fasting during the holy month of Ramadan; Hajj, the pilgrimage to the holy city of Mecca and Shahada; attesting publicly in their belief (Aqeed) that there is one god and the prophet Mohammed is his messenger. Perhaps the single great cult innovation inspired the Kharajites and the Sudan Mahdists was the elevation of Jihad into the sixth pillar of Islam. The Egyptian jihadi philosopher Mohammed Abdus Salam Faraj wrote a book that is extremely popular in the movement called *Jihad: The Absent Obligation*. He argued that Jihad is the greatest calling and should displace all other obligations of Muslims or at least be added as a sixth pillar to Islam, followed by a seventh—Martyrdom in Jihad.

In the end ISIS or any future variant will continue to be a vindication for the plan established a quarter century ago. Bin Laden's challenge to any and all jihadists contained three goals: (1) fight and die to establish a neo-Islamic Caliphate; (2) re-engineer Islam to topple the existing power structures through terror; and (3) provoke and fight the rest of the world to fulfill the prophecies of the End of Days.

WHAT THEY REALLY WANT: TO RE-ENGINEER ISLAM . . . AT GUNPOINT

It is far worse than heresy to work to destroy the 1436 years of Islam for their own amusement. In fact, where they believe the Qur'an is wrong or too accommodating for their tastes, they correct it. In their visually vibrant and slick online recruiting magazine, *Dabiq*, ISIS turns the words of the Prophet Mohammed as a religion of peace on their head. The February 2015 cover article was "Islam is the religion of the sword, not pacifism." What can be more un-Islamic than rejecting the Prophet's own teachings?

Clearly the usurpation of the Qur'an and Islamic history in this manner is not only crazy to any Muslim you would care to ask, it's a re-engineering of Islam. The members of this cult believe it is the other 1.8 billion Muslims who were corrupted by centuries of bad Islam.

The Cult of Jihad now led by ISIS and a close second al-Qaeda seek nothing less than the seizure, dismantling, and destruction of the entirety of Islamic thought, culture, jurisprudence, and tradition since 632. All of those centuries of tolerance, discovery, and compromise with the rest of the world are weakness to be ruthlessly eliminated. To them, little of Islam can be salvaged—the Muslim world is going to have to be burned to the ground to be saved for God.

The ideology has always been clear about one thing: For victory against the other world's civilizations, everyone under their mandate must vow themselves to two new pillars which do not exist as obligations in Islam—Jihad and Martyrdom. Not satisfied with the destruction of Islam, the CoJ intends to harness the slave nation it will build from Muslims and march with what remains for the destruction of all other religions, cultures, and national boundaries. When this mass march and slaughter is complete, only then will they be satisfied that the groundwork has been laid for the glorious end of days. Those jihadists left behind will be brought to paradise to be reunited with their dead comrades and sit next to the Prophet Mohammed and God.

CHAPTER 11

LIFE AND DEATH IN THE "ISLAMIC STATE"

فرحة المسلمين في مدينة هراوة بغزوة فرنسا

THE ISLAMIC STATE FANTASY

The image ISIS tries to foster among those traveling to Paradise on earth: A city filled with an internationalist body of Muslims living in peace and equality while their soldiers cleanse the Middle East of unbelievers. They portray the capital, Raqqa, as a land without prejudice, fear, or hunger; where infrastructure and security has come to the cities for the first time. They claim to fulfill the promises the governments of Iraq and Syria could not. There is no disease, and every death is a celebration. This rose-tinted projection is impressive for its ability to convince susceptible followers to abandon their lives in the West. One of the five pillars of Islam is the act of giving charity. In ISIS, they emphasize giving charity in all aspects of their daily lives. This necessity has become acute in ISIS-captured lands because the supply infrastructure has broken down and only those with wealth can afford to live as they had before ISIS seized control. A class of ISIS soldiers, war-profiteering merchants, smugglers, looters, and thieves are able buy their way through ISIS lines and live extraordinarily well, but the average citizen lives in horrifically abject poverty.

In a very real sense, ISIS runs the world's largest prison, with all aspects of life enthralled by a cult interpretation of the earliest days of Sharia law. As noted in Chapter 10 the interpretations of life in their lands is a strict interpretation from the earliest days of Islam. Their belief system brings twenty-first-century Muslims to live precisely as Muslims in the seventh century would, but with electricity and automatic weapons; a system designed to focus every aspect of the inhabitants' lives about what constitutes a proper diet, or how they should dress on the street in order to live solely for God, even when in violation of all previous fourteen centuries of Islamic law and tradition. ISIS controls all aspects of life, from price controls in the market to the elimination of all music, art, and culture not related to religious observances. They hold control with dictatorial grip, and allow only their own soldiers to administer justice, mediate civil disagreements, and determine what one can and cannot do in the Caliphate.

THE HISBAH

ISIS keeps its population in line though a brutal internal security police force called the "Hisbah," which is Arabic for "Accountability." In the Islamic State, this means accountability to God's doctrines and dogma according to ISIS's cultist interpretation of Islam. The Hisbah are a more orthodox and murderous version of the Saudi Arabian model of Committee for the Support of Virtues and the Prevention of Vice (CSVPV), also known as the Mutawwa'. They control every aspect of life. Their mission is to ensure that the people under ISIS control now live according to the observances of the seventh-century tribes of the Western Arabian desert. The Hisbah accomplish this with soft-spoken intimidation, arrest, trial, and punishment, up to and including death.

Any vice that is not sanctioned such as alcohol, drug use, smoking cigarettes, or Shisha (Hookahs), playing music, playing western games, wearing un-Islamic clothing, theft, non-sanctioned personal violence, slandering, blaspheming, having "illicit" sex (heterosexual or homosexual), or adultery falls under their pur-

view. The Hisbah also enforce religious rulings, price controls, mediate small-scale disputes, and essentially act as God's Sergeant-at-Arms. On a practical level, this manifests as a liberty to meddle openly in the details of day-to-day lives of passersby, and since the Hisbah is mainly a foreign contingent, they routinely undermine the sense of self-esteem and autonomy of Syrians and Iraqis.[739]

Hisbah units are organized into local battalions under the Emir of Sharia law, and operate in one- or two-man vehicle police squads. They dress in white Dishdashas that end above the ankle, black vests, and carry a Mahsassil, or camel crop, so they can mete out drumhead justice for light offenses. They generally carry AK-47s and pistols, and in a manner similar to the Nazi Gestapo or the Soviet KGB, it is common knowledge that they can summon the might of the ISIS combat

أرسل جنودك إلى الأرض لتقاتلنا وجها لوجه لكنك تعرف أن جنودك جبناء

A noteworthy member of the ISIS Hisbah police force is a British subject named Omar Hussein. The former resident of Wycombe, Buckinghamshire made videos begging for the US and UK to send forces into Syria.

machine as easily as they do fear and dread. As a paramilitary force they fill the role of police as well as light combat infantry.

There has been some backlash against the Hisbah's brutality and pervasive influence in ISIS life. Resistance forces and militias routinely target them for execution, to convey the message at the street level that the pre-ISIS way of life can be achieved. The Syrian Observatory for Human Rights claims that it is not possible to say how many members of Hisbah have now been kidnapped or killed by the "resistance." Assailants not only decapitated the assistant commander of Hisbah in Mayadin, but they also posed his head with a cigarette in his mouth and a pious ISIS-like note at his side, exclaiming that smoking is a sin.[740]

The Internationalist Paradise that is Raqqa, the ISIS Capital

"Muhaajirat families in Raqqa live in peace and are untouched by hunger, the cold winds, or frost. The Caliphate fairly divides money among all the people, migrant and non-migrant, so that there is no difference between Arabs and Persians, blacks or whites. All are under the rule of Islam.

It is not possible to live in this Islamic way in any place ruled by tyrants, who implement nationalism over religion and patriotism over Shariah. People in these lands are obligated to pay a sum (iqamah) as if they were People of the Book, as if they are not equal to the people of the country in work, in healthcare, in social life, and everything else. To hell with these laws, to hell with nationalism!"[741]

ROLE OF WOMEN

The Islamic traditions regarding the freedoms of women, which developed over fourteen centuries, are completely eliminated in the Islamic State. In ISIS society women are subordinated to a level of oppression and brutality that was last seen in the eighth century; they are essentially slaves. Many compare ISIS's control of women to Saudi Arabian or Afghan culture, but the role of women in Raqqa and occupied cities makes those societies seem relatively liberal.

Women are regarded as virtual non-entities, apart from acting as nursemaids to the children of jihadist fighters, and preparing the boys to become child soldiers and the girls to become marriage chattel. The women are expected to constantly keep their education limited to waging Jihad and maintaining only ISIS's version of Islamic cultism. As one woman said, "Jihad brings the promise of a heavenly reward . . . Women are primarily tasked to assist their men in their jihadist duty."[742]

Any and all digressions from the rules for women are considered a religiously punishable offense, called Hudud. Leaving one's home without a mahram or a blood/marriage related male chaperon, even to cross an alley to speak to another woman or doing so without being 100 percent covered, is one such Hudud. Any violation can provoke an arrest or a beating from a male or female police brigade member.

WOMEN RELIGIOUS ENFORCERS: AL-KHANSAA AND UMM RAYHAN BRIGADES

ISIS maintains two all-women forces to conduct social controls against the female population and to root out men infiltrating their lines dressed as women. The *al-Khansaa* brigades and its sister organization, the *Umm Rayhan* brigades, act as paramilitary police forces in support of the Hisbah religious police force. Each of the brigades operates its own all-female police stations in order to avoid the mixing of male and female officers, or women prisoners. The brigades use Kia passenger vans to hide themselves and their victims during transport.[743]

To join the force the women must be age 18–25 and must be a virgin. They get paid $75 per month and are authorized to carry AK-47

rifles. The brigades have two types of units: Morality Police, and a counterintelligence combat support unit. European volunteers join the combat support arm at checkpoints and search the bodies of women to detect female-disguised male infiltrators. However, Arab women patrol the streets and enforce the oppressive laws against their own.

Local Raqqa women make up the unit, along with the wives of regional fighters who have traveled to Syria, including about sixty British members who handle the English-speaking women and children who emigrated to Syria.[744] The development points to a burgeoning sort of "'jihadi girl power' subculture" on social media, according to some analysts. A Glaswegian named Aqsa Mahmoud was known to be a senior leader.[745]

A major role for the Khansaa/Umm Rayhan units is to beat women who wear proscribed clothes, make-up, any type of high heels, or anyone who dares talk back to a Hisbah officer. These women receive forty lashes of the cane. Women who attempt to escape receive more severe punishments, such as sixty lashes with a horsewhip, or are being beaten to death by the Hisbah or the husband of the victim.

Who was al-Khansaa?

Al-Khansaa was the first magazine for jihadist women issued in 2004 by al-Qaeda of the Arabian Peninsula in Saudi Arabia.[746] The name was derived from the famous seventh-century woman poet named Tumāir bint Amrāibn al-Harth ibn al-Sharīd al-Sulamīyah, a friend of the Prophet Mohammed. She has been referred to as the first "Mother of Martyrs." Nicknamed after the local Gazelle (al-Khansaa), she was well known for writing eulogies for martyred Islamic fighters. It is a legend that she sacrificed four of her sons to the founding of Islam in the battle of Qadisiyyah. She is regarded as one of the companions of the Prophet and a role model for woman in jihadist circles. The ISIS al-Khansaa brigade is named in her memory.

VOLUNTEER WIVES: THE SEX JIHAD

Despite such a high-minded and high-handed belief system, the cultists ceaselessly extol earthly rewards for their fighters. Many groups, including famous cults such as the Manson family, Aum Shinrikyo, and Jim Jones, used abduction, rape, and sex as control tools for women and enticements for men. ISIS has taken this to a new level by convincing thousands of single women that they have a spiritual obligation to come have sex and children with jihadists.

The term "Sex Jihad" or Jihad al-Nikah describes the waves of young women who volunteer themselves to come to the jihad zone and offer their bodies and children to the terrorists as their contribution to the holy war. Yes, the cult offers pleasure, flesh, and progeny in exchange for mass murder. The prospective jihadi bride's reward is to be "allowed" to marry a cult-sanctioned soon-to-be "martyr."[747] The women who volunteer to become sexual objects for the jihad are convinced they are giving their bodies and sexual favors to God's chosen men, and that the jihadist's sexual satisfaction is pleasing to God. This in turn brings in more men who want the fruits of labor along with the heroic image of a values-guided killer.

An FBI audiotape of an American recruiter for the Somali al-Shabaab terror group extols to Boston grad student Tarek Mehanne the fabulousness of the jihad zone with a passion of a spring break fraternity pledge. "Check this out. Come here. You don't even have to have a dime in your pocket. I will set you up with everything. I'll have people pick you up, a place for you stay and, heck, if you want, I can have a wife waiting for you!"[748]

The women of the cult accept the role as child producer and support system for men they have never met and are not allowed to marry unless the local "Emir" authorizes it. Usually the Emir makes the decision about who gets married to whom. In 2014 ISIS opened a marriage bureau near the Turkish-Syrian border crossing north of Aleppo for prospective women to travel and be placed into arranged marriages.

Not even the prospect of death deters the jihadi sex brides. Many send Twitter messages to their prospective beaus longing for death. One read: "True love doesn't end in death, if Allah wills it it'll continue in jenna (paradise) TOGETHER FOR JENNA." Many jihadi brides even complain that they cannot die in suicide attacks in order to be with their dead partners.

Hoda Muthana, 20-year-old student at University of Alabama in Birmingham was an American citizen of Yemeni parents. She became radicalized over the internet and in November 2014 she told her parents she was going on a school trip, but secretly fled to Syria and joined ISIS. Through her twitter account she became an active ISIS recruiter. She now offers advice to American Muslims who could not travel to a jihad zone on how to kill their fellow citizens: "Americans wake up! . . . Men and women altogether. You have much to do while you live under our greatest enemy, enough of your sleeping! Go on drive-bys and spill all of their blood, or rent a big truck and drive all over them. Veterans, Patriot, Memorial etc Day parades...go on drive by's + spill all of their blood or rent a big truck n drive all over them. Kill them."

This is not a Muslim phenomenon. Many western Christian women have abandoned their lives and joined the Sex Jihad.[749] Former UK punk rocker Sally Jones married a jihadi in Syria, renaming herself Sakinah Hussein. She further expressed the desire to behead Christians with blunt knives. Western and ex-Christian women become valuable propaganda tools and reliable recruiters by demonstrating that the sex jihadists have a good life and that other women should come and join them. This exodus to ISIS did not exclude Americans. According to Fordham Law School's Center on National Security, most of the American females attempting to aid and join ISIS are teenagers. Such was the case of three siblings from the suburbs of Chicago, and in another instance some high school girls from Chicago. In both cases, they had already made it out of the country before being stopped on their way to join ISIS.[750]

Former punk rocker Sally Jones, now member of ISIS.

Australian Zehra Duman posts regularly about life in the paradise that is ISIS's Syria. "Food is yummy!" she exclaimed in one tweet. Duman wrote in a chatroom discussion her views on how she feels about the West: "US + Australia, how does it feel that all 5 of us were born n raised in your lands, & now here thirsty for ur blood?"[751]

An interesting exchange occurred on an official ISIS website where a foreign fighter complained to women interested in marrying that they were choosing the wrong kind of men. He argued that prospective brides should avoid half-hearted jihadists who had time for chatting and courtship. Sex Jihadists were encouraged to come out to the farthest reaches of the war in order to find the real men who live in the combat outposts and fight daily. Many do just that.

DRESS CODE FOR WOMEN IN THE CALIPHATE

ISIS designed and sold its own variant of the Hijab and Niqab dress for all women under their control. It is even more oppressive then the most severe Saudi dress.

Dress laws under ISIS, which tightened after their declaration of a caliphate, require women to cover themselves over their entire body so that no skin and no female form may be apparent, or the women may be arrested and beaten by the religious police, al-Hisabah, or their all-female al-Khansaa and Umm Rayhan enforcer brigades.[752]

Islamic jurisprudence uses the quote from the Qur'an 66:13 as the sole basis for Islamic modesty and protection of chastity: "And [the example of] Mary, the daughter of 'Imran, who guarded her chastity, so We blew into [her garment] through Our angel, and she believed in the words of her Lord and His scriptures and was of the devoutly obedient."

In January 2015, an Arabic language document called *Women in the Islamic State: Manifesto and Case Study*, began appearing online after being uploaded by the al-Khanssaa police media arm.[753],[754] In contrast to the romanticized role of female participants in ISIS propagated on social media, this document outlines a more realistic depiction of the restrictive policies that govern women as subjects of the Islamic State.[755] It is likely that the document initially went untranslated by extremists in hopes of bypassing the more Western audience.[756]

The ISIS Manual for Women spells out the reason for making strict dress codes:

> After the establishment of the caliphate, coverings and hijab things returned to the country and decency swept the country. Now, women are able to travel to their people in Raqqa without having to show their face to the eyes of even one inspector. Respect for their bodies has returned and has been taken from the eyes of onlookers, with their corrupted hearts. Causes of their humiliation are prevented, revealing dresses were confiscated from shops and scandalous photos were banned from walls and shelves. Muslims, with the permission of God, were cleansed.[757]

Abaya: The Abaya is a long full-body black robe commonly worn though out the Middle East, particularly the strict interpretations of Saudi Arabia and Iran. Usually, the hands and eyes and even the face may be exposed. Under ISIS the woman must wear the most orthodox and strict interpretation with 100 percent covering of the body from neck to feet. After the June 2015 announcement of the Caliphate, a woman could not display any skin whatsoever. The face is to be covered with a sheer mask, hands must be covered with black gloves, and stockings must cover the legs. Absolutely no decorations are allowed, and the Abaya must be so loose as to show almost no female form.

Components of Women's Dress

The covering of women is a cultural tradition of pre-Islamic medieval Western Arabia that was incorporated into the religion. The tradition in Islam was brought into Sharia law as supported by the quote from the Qur'an "O Prophet! Tell your wives and your daughters, and the believing women, to draw their cloaks (veils) over their bodies. That will be better that they should be known (as respectable women) so as not to be annoyed. And Allah is Ever Oft-Forgiving, Most Merciful."[758]

Hijab: A headscarf that wraps around the entire face and head covering all hair and that drapes down over the top of the bosom. Traditionally it could be loosely worn and wrap under the chin to expose the face. Orthodoxy demands that it fit loosely over the hair and tightly around the face, with space for the niqab (see below) to cover the eyes.

Niqab: A short veil that covers the mouth and traditionally the forehead, but leaving the eyes exposed. In orthodox Islamic societies the Niqab with a double-layer semi-sheer veil is used to completely cover and hide the eyes of a woman. The purpose of the strict wear of a veiled Niqab is that in romantic Islam it is the Ayuun, or eyes, that lead one to love, much less than the female form. For centuries Islamic art and poetry extol the virtues of the eyes. (The great poet Rumi wrote: In The Heavens, I see your eyes. In Your Eyes, I see the heavens. Why look for another Moon? Or another Sun? What I see will always be enough for Me.)

ATTEMPTS TO ESCAPE ISIS

As has been widely reported, women from the West are joining ISIS at a surprising clip, though women's numbers overall comprise perhaps only about 10 percent of recruits to the Islamic State, a number smaller than historically found in terrorist groups such as the IRA and more in keeping with right-wing organizations.[759]

Luring women to the group is important for state formation, analysts say. As illustrated by Boko Haram's kidnapping of Nigerian schoolgirls, leaders of extremist groups also need to acquire and dole out young women as gifts for their fighters.[760] Earlier this year, reports surfaced that ISIS has instituted a policy forbidding women under forty-five from leaving the city of Raqqa, in order to keep them on hand as potential wives for their fighters.[761]

Still, westerners continue to willingly go, only to find that their circumstances are not what was promised. Some are told that that they might find themselves employed on social media or in hospitals, most women find themselves relegated to the role of homemaker and babysitter.[762] Major events such as marriage and pregnancy often prompt a re-evaluation of life in the Islamic State. Another disappointment is widowhood; although martyrdom is celebrated in ISIS, the loss of a husband has had a disillusioning effect on some Western converts.

Unsurprisingly, when Western women try to return home, they are detained against their will or murdered.[763] Even if they are able to escape, those who willingly travel from the West to the Islamic State often have huge legal hurdles to overcome in their home countries—many of which have laws in place stipulating that returnees could face imprisonment or in some cases be barred from re-entry.[764],[765]

For western women looking to defect, these can be overwhelming obstacles. Mia Bloom, a professor at the Center for Terrorism and Security Studies at UMass-Lowell notes, "[These members] have nowhere to go . . . They need a pathway out." [766]

CASE STUDY: ISIS EUROPEAN "POSTER GIRLS" BELIEVED EXECUTED

Austrian teenagers Samra Kesinovic, sixteen, and Sabina Selimovic, fifteen, left their homes in Vienna on April 10, 2014.[767] They were daughters of Bosnian refugees who immigrated to Austria in the 1990s. According to media reports, the message they left for their loved ones was brutally succinct: "Don't look for us. We will serve Allah—and we will die for him."[768]

Ill-fated teenagers Samra Kesinovic and Samina Selimovic.

They reportedly traveled to Raqqa, Syria, where they married Chechen fighters and possibly both became pregnant, which Selimovic personally denied on social media. While in Syria, their social media accounts remained very active, posting images of themselves posing with weapons and fighters, in addition to positive messages—so much so that they were dubbed ISIS "poster girls" and images of the pair were used to aid recruitment. [769],[770] At one point, Selimovic even tweeted her enthusiasm to Paris Match magazine, saying "Here I can really be free. I can practice my religion. I couldn't do that in Vienna."[771] However, there were suspicions at the time that the girls' accounts had been hijacked and that images posted there had been digitally altered.[772] Prior to their leaving, Kesinovic evidently had conversations with a relative about entering into an arranged marriage.[773] The two teens reportedly also attended a Viennese mosque presided over by Salafi preacher Mirsad Omerovic, a.k.a. Ebu Tejma, later arrested on charges he recruited the two teens as well as over 150 Europeans to join ISIS.[774] At some point between April and early October, the girls contacted their families and expressed the desire to come home. Austrian officials publically stated that doing so might be "impossible," due to Austrian laws preventing individuals returning from ISIS.[775] In September 2014, unconfirmed reports began to surface that one of the two had been killed in fighting, later identified as Selimovic.[776],[777] In late November 2015, the Austrian newspaper *Österreich* and other Austrian media outlets reported an unconfirmed document by government officials relating that the then eighteen-year-old Kesinovic was beaten to death with a hammer after trying to escape from Raqqa.[778],[779]

ISIS CHILDREN: BUILDING BETTER DEATH CULTISTS

What of the children who are born into the cult of Jihad? Like all large-scale cults, the control and indoctrination of children is critical to advancing the future survival of the group. From the Nazi "Hitler Youth" to Saddam Hussein's "Saddam Cubs," children are specifically and routinely cultivated as child soldiers and often into human guided weapons.

Our children are a
trust from Allah

It is a common form of exploitation to harvest the lives of child soldiers. Abducted or adopted children were staples of combat cults such as the Pol Pot's Khmer Rouge and the Lord's Resistance Army. Cults constantly challenge the children of recruits to prove their worth by dying or killing like their fathers. The ISIS "cubs of the caliphate" are the next generation of killers.

In August 2014, just two months after Abu Bakr al-Baghdadi announced the establishment of a new caliphate to be known as the Islamic State, a report on Syria from the Office of the United Nations High Commissioner for Human Rights (OHCHR) determined that the "so-called Islamic State" was taking a "devastating toll" in children's lives.[780] The report detailed ISIS's treatment of children and came to the unsurprising conclusion that their form of "education" was in fact a focused brainwashing and cult indoctrination campaign that constituted war crimes.

The ISIS methodology of brainwashing the vulnerable minds of their children and those of the people whose communities they occupy is critical to building a new generation of fighters and expanding the borders of the Caliphate. A core component is the necessity of deliberately depriving children of an education except in subjects they see as critical to maintaining their warfighting capacity and religious identity.[781] The educational system operates as a body mill for future soldiers and prospective wives for the fighters. It appears that with the exception of religious indoctrination, attendance in other courses is not mandatory.

ISIS schools are strictly gender-segregated; in fact, the education of girls is not a priority in occupied regions as much as the control of their bodies and morals.[782] Despite claims to the contrary, the education of girls is exclusively limited to Islamic studies and preparation for marriage. According to ISIS's Manual for Women, the following guidelines dictate female education:

> From ages seven to nine, there will be three lessons: Fiqh [Deep discussion of Islamic jurisprudence] and religion, Qur'anic Arabic (written and read) and science (accounting and natural sciences). From ten to twelve, there will be more religious studies, especially fiqh, focusing more on fiqh related to women and the rulings on marriage and divorce. This is in addition to the other two subjects. Skills like textiles and knitting, basic cooking will also be taught. From thirteen to fifteen, there will be more of a focus on Shariah, as well as more manual skills (especially those related to raising children) and less of the science, the basics of which will already have been taught. In addition, they will be taught about Islamic history, the life of the Prophet and his followers.[783]

An activist for the NGO "Raqqa is Being Slaughtered Silently" claims that there are at least two schools in Syria especially for English-speaking children, since hundreds have arrived in the country during the past year.[784]

CHILD SOLDIERS: THE "CALIPHATE CUBS" & THEIR TRAINING CENTERS

The most widely reported aspect of educational system in ISIS territory are the Sharia Camps, a cross between ISIS ideology school and a military camp. Trainees swear fealty to Abu Bakr al-Baghdadi as the Caliph,[785] watch sermons and videos, and receive training in practical combat skills. Boys attending the Sharia Camps are divided according to their strengths and abilities—for example, hand-to-hand combat or logistical

operations. Some children are selected to become informants among the general population, reporting to ISIS's Security Offices. These particular "soldiers" are referred to as the "Flash Memory," as they are trained to collect information on and betray anyone, including their families.[786]

These young soldiers are called the "Ashbal," or "cubs of the caliphate," in a reference to ISIS fighters calling themselves "lions," and are publicized as new generation of jihadists, part of ISIS's long-term plan for war.[787,788,789]

In one of the known main camps west of Raqqa, it's known that children spend some fifteen days studying the Qu'ran, Sharia law, and related subjects, then spend thirty days training for physical combat and weaponry.[790] A CNN report quoted a young boy (who had since fled from Syria), who said that for thirty days "we woke up and jogged, had breakfast, then learned the Qur'an and the Hadith of the Prophet. Then we took courses on weapons, Kalashnikovs and other light military stuff." This training included watching beheadings, lashings, and stonings, and encouraging children to participate in public brutality,[791] including

holding decapitated heads for public display or playing "football" with these heads. The final test of this education in loyalty is, apparently, the execution of a prisoner.[792] A source told the BBC that children received blond dolls in order to practice decapitation.[793]

This is not happening not only in Syria or ISIS controlled territory; in October 2015, a training camp for children was reportedly found in Istanbul after a raid of some eighteen different homes, which resulted in fifty people detained for suspected links to ISIS. Of this number, approximately half were children who had been receiving training in basement apartments.[794]

There are many ways in which a young boy can find himself on his way to becoming a soldier: through family or social ties, such as children of foreign and local fighters, as well as supportive locals; orphans in ISIS-controlled orphanages; runaways; and children who are taken from their parents or whose parents are coerced into "volunteering" them.[795] This is identical to the method that the Saddam Fedayeen used to create the "Saddam Cubs." In some cases, families give up their children for compensation. One figure quoted in reports cites prices between $250 to $350 per month per child, which is an inducement for many families in material need.[796] Some have referred to this method as bribes.[797]

The result of these recruiting campaigns can be seen in the many videos where dozens of boys engage in military training, where they are depicted waving the group's flag, praying, reciting verses from the Qur'an, performing exercises, and and chanting.

BRAINWASHING CENTERS OF EXCELLENCE

ISIS's hold over schools results in a process of indoctrination rather than education. Even when the teachers remain the same as before ISIS's control, they teach to a new curriculum.[798],[799] Such is the case of a grammar school in Raqqa, recently reopened by ISIS, where, according to reports, children are instructed from the age of three.[800] Dr. Mia Bloom at University of Massachusetts, Lowell, believes they operate by the "pedophile's playbook." She noted that ISIS indoctrinates children slowly over weeks or months into activities a child would never do, including murder, abuse, and preparation for suicide bombing.

The UN report goes on to accuse ISIS of having "established training camps to recruit children into armed roles under the guise of education."[801] ISIS's method includes stimulating competition between children, expecting that this sense of rivalry will incite them to do better and create a sense of prestige in being chosen.[802] This makes teachers "talent

ISIS toddler instructed by father to behead and immolate his own teddy bear.

scouts" of a sort, looking for star jihadist pupils to move up into the organization and as junior fighters to fill the officer ranks.

One of the filmmakers of a PBS *Frontline* documentary on children living under ISIS rule explained that though he expected the children to learn at least some basic knowledge—such as grammar or math—they are instead taught such things as what is jihad.[803]

There are many advantages to this system of recruiting and training—primarily the guarantee that their jihadists are ideologically pure.[804] There have been reports stating that since children are so easily brainwashed, they can be fully trusted to fulfill their orders, which has led to their being used in suicide missions.[805]

For the most part, the boy soldiers of the Ashbal Khalifa are engaged in a variety of combat support sessions that would be unwise to task to a adult, including acting as messengers and look-outs, assisting elder fighters, moving small quantities of rifle or mortar ammunition, and rear-area support functions such as cooking, cleaning, and carrying water. They also act as apprentice soldiers by participating in localized guard patrols and manning non-critical checkpoints and barriers.[806, 807] By October 2015 the blood requirements for hospitals was so dire that they were called upon to act as blood donors.[808]

The missions given to these young boys have become progressively more extreme, such as the fourteen-year-old boy who became a suicide bomber in 2014, a fate which has become somewhat commonplace, especially with mentally challenged children. As of mid-2015, as many as nineteen children had been used as suicide bombers.[809] These suicidal missions assigned to children exemplify how the violence is performed both by and to children.

They commit hideous acts of war, yes, but are also victims of extensive war crimes, and it is hard to see a way to break out of this cycle.

A report from the Syrian Observatory for Human Rights claims that in the year after the establishment of this new caliphate, ISIS in Syria had been responsible for executing more than three thousand people, among them seventy-four children.[810] This number may well be higher, since the Observatory has received information about dozens of other, unconfirmed deaths.[811] These deaths were due not only to explosions, clashes, and airstrikes, but also to suicide attacks and executions. The UN has also received at least nine reports of sexual violence against children by ISIS, though the number is also thought to be much higher.[812]

It is worth noting that this violence toward children is committed both against children who do not belong ideologically in ISIS's caliphate—like countless Yazidi children executed and left to die in ISIS's genocidal military maneuvers[813]—but also children supposedly on their side, like the twelve children executed for trying to flee from training, near the city of Mosul.[814] Other gruesome reports claim that children were crucified as punishment for not fasting during Ramadan,[815] or had a finger cut off for refusing to fight.[816]

The violence performed on video by ISIS's "cubs of the caliphate" has been escalating since January 2015, when a clip showed boys shooting two alleged Russian agents in the back of the head. According to the

Syrian Observatory for Human Rights, this was the first documented declared execution carried out by children. Other videos followed, showing boys performing a range of violent actions such as fighting in cages, witnessing executions, leading prisoners to their executions, handing knives to adult jihadists, and shooting enemy soldiers.[817],[818] In May 2015, a video emerged depicting a Roman amphitheater in Palmyra, where twenty-five children lined up and executed twenty-five Ba'athist regime soldiers by shooting them in the back of the head, while a crowd witnessed.[819]

The most gruesome of these videos, however, might be the one released in July of 2015, where a young boy of perhaps ten years old is shown beheading an adult. This footage was also shot in or near the city Palmyra, a UNESCO World Heritage Site that has been under ISIS control since May of 2015. In this video, the unnamed captured soldier, apprehended by ISIS at the nearby Al-Bosayri army checkpoint and believed to have been a regime leader, is forced to lie on the ground, on his stomach. The boy approaches him from behind, pulling back his head and using a small knife to cut the man's throat and behead him. He celebrates the beheading by raising the victim's head and then placing it on top of the cadaver's back.

This is believed to be the first time a "cub of the Caliphate" has been recorded performing a beheading. The boy does not bother to cover his face in a mask, and is filmed wearing camouflage and a black headdress.[820] Before the video ends, an older militant appears on camera to threaten any Westerners watching, vowing that ISIS's goals are "not only Palmyra or Homs or Damascus, rather our goal is to conquer Bayt al-Maqdes [Jerusalem] and Rome, God willing." [821]

ISLAMIC STATE HEALTH SERVICE & HOSPITALS

The first feature of the Islamic State Health Service that needs to be mentioned is that, as the following headline reveals, it is a copy of the British health system; even its logo is so patterned: "ISIS mimics Britain's NHS with 'Islamic State Health Service ISHS'"[822] The content of the same article also begs the question whether the system really exists or its existence is only propaganda designed to convey the notion that ISIS is a functioning state meeting its obligations toward its citizens.

Writing for the London-based counter-extremism think tank Quilliam Foundation, researcher Charlie Winter wrote that "radical preacher Anjem Choudary said that according to a strict interpretation of Sharia law, Islamic authorities personified by the self-styled caliph have the onus to provide housing, food, clothing, and all services to their subjects in return for their obedience."[823] Thus, the first question about the ISIS Health System is about its creation and existence. A health system requires an infrastructure, but the infrastructure does not seem to be there:

> It is difficult to see how an operational health system that will provide services to all of the citizens can be built given the fact that according to . . . statistics compiled by the Syrian American Medical Society and the WHO: approximately 60 percent of hospitals have been destroyed, 90 percent of the local pharmaceutical industry has been destroyed, 78 percent of ambulances

are severely damaged, and 70 percent of whatever medical staff is left cannot access their workplaces (Al-Jadda). In certain provinces, upwards of about 90 percent of all physicians have left or have been killed, and in the stronghold of Aleppo, less than 250 physicians are left, creating a physician-to-patient ratio of about 1:500,000.[824]

The article quoted above also reveals that the "system" lacks the human resources necessary to be effective. This is probably true of all the levels of the "system" from the policy and leadership level to the level of the healthcare providers. There are three emergent infectious diseases that are occurring at an epidemic level in the ISIS: polio, HIV/AIDS, and leishmaniasis. The Syrian civil war has allowed major outbreaks of previously manageable diseases due to a complete collapse of the healthcare system. United Nations–managed disease prevention and immunization programs were stopped, abandoned, or prevented by almost all parties. ISIS takes this a step further. It does not manage captive populations or peoples outside of ISIS's own hospitals, where almost all healthcare resources go to the families of fighters and then trickles down to the local populace. Polio had not been seen in Syria for over twenty years, but returned in 2013 and is spreading rapidly.[825] Insects spreading disease such as leishmaniasis, a flesh-eating infection of the skin that can be fatal if untreated, have cropped up because of ISIS's poor post-combat disposal of corpses in active combat areas. Flies in the corpses may have spread the disease.[826] Media reports state that cases of HIV have been discovered among women who emigrated to the Islamic State. A complete loss of the Syrian HIV/AIDS prevention system has allowed that disease to silently spread. Apart from anecdotal evidence from refugees, and despite great efforts by the United Nations and Syrian groups, little is known about everyday medical care or daily management of chronic disease under ISIS rule. Since ISIS has limited resources, eschews science, purchases weapons over medicines, and routinely implores "the Will of God," the mortality rate for manageable diseases such as diabetes, hypertension, asthma, and so on must be astronomical.

However, assuming it exists and functions as a system, then there are a number of questions; the first may be about access. According to sources in Syria, ISIS fighters and their families receive free healthcare,

---

Summary of ISIS Health Care

1. Approximately eight million people live under the self-styled "Islamic State" (ISIS).
2. Healthcare delivery in ISIS is characterized by a very low doctor/patient ratio of 1/500,000.
3. Most doctors and healthcare professionals have left or have gone underground.
4. Modern medical practice is secular and often incompatible with theocratic directives. Practitioners of the modern secular style in ISIS can be subjected to intimidation, abuse, and even death.
5. Only a few dozen healthcare professionals have immigrated to join ISIS. They are medically insignificant, but represent a powerful propaganda tool for ISIS.
6. Most hospitals in ISIS-controlled areas have been closed, destroyed, or repurposed as military headquarters.
7. Advanced services appear to have gone offline as trained and properly equipped personnel to use, maintain, and repair them have declined.
8. There is a paucity of public health measures in ISIS, resulting in spread of endemic diseases and resurgence of epidemic diseases.
9. Combat medicine in ISIS appears minimal. Basic interventions such as IVs, saline, and wound care are likely absent, except for high-value individuals. There appears to be no medical corps in ISIS infantry forces.
10. Survivability is expected to be low for ISIS combat casualties.
11. ISIS probably transfers its high-value personnel to Turkey for modern (and secular) medical care.

---

but the average person does not. Most have to rely on private doctors, charity clinics, or receive no services at all.[827]

Making the same assumption as above, it may be said that the "system" coexists with a "private-non-governmental system" that seems ready to exploit the situation for its own benefit, forcing the issuance of a decree from the "Islamic State Office of Health" that attempts to control the profit being made.

DOCTORS & NURSES RUSHING FOR THE EXITS

Another critical issue for the ISIS Caliphate is that the educated hospital staffs are leaving the country in massive numbers. Syrians and Iraqis who were not caught in the ISIS takeovers are dragooned into their health systems and forced to abandon the people and communities that they served. There are reports that Iraqi ISIS-controlled provinces confiscate the homes and property of medical workers unless they return.[828]

The third issue of the Islamic State's English-language online magazine *Dabiq* called for emigration to Muslim lands. Its message was directed to Muslims in the West and invited them to come and aid in the formation of this nascent Islamic state. The basic argument was as follows:

> Therefore, every Muslim professional who delayed his jihad in the past under the pretense of studying Shari'ah, medicine, or engineering, etc., claiming he would contribute to Islam later with his expertise, should now make his number one priority to repent and answer the call to hijrah, especially after the establishment of the Khilafah [caliphate]. This Khilafah is more in need than ever before for experts, professionals, and specialists, who can help contribute in strengthening its structure and tending to the needs of their Muslim brothers. As for the Muslim students who use this same pretense now to continue abandoning the obligation of the era, then they should know that their hijrah from darul kufr [land of unbelief] to darul Islam [Islamic lands] and jihad are more obligatory and urgent

than spending an unknown number of years studying while exposed to doubts and desires that will destroy their religion and thus end for themselves any possible future of jihad.

Public appeals for skilled workers come from higher-ranking ISIS officials and from online recruiters who already reside in the Islamic State.[829] To attract foreign medical professionals, besides the religious argument, ISIS has created a promotional video for a health care system operating out of the Syrian city of Raqqa. Despite the earnestness of the video participants, the conditions appear to be a sham.[830] The number of medical professionals immigrating to ISIS, numbering maybe a few dozen, is insignificant in terms of altering the medical landscape.[831] For obvious reasons, they have value as propaganda.

CHAPTER 12

PUNISHMENTS, VIOLENCE, AND POLICE STATE CONTROLS

SLAVERY & RAPE

Among the countless atrocities committed by ISIS since their inception, the issue of slavery and sexual violence against women and children may be the most grievous. The US State Department has claimed, in a statement by its Ambassador-at-Large for Global Women's Issues, that the "de-humanization of women and girls is central to ISIL's campaign of terror. . . . A coalition that fights ISIL must also fight this particularly egregious form of brutality."[832]

In order to fight the brutality of slavery and sexual violence against women and children, which are often intertwined, it is necessary to understand how it takes shape within the world dominated by ISIS.

The crest of the ISIS war crimes tide can be traced back to August 2014, when ISIS forces took control of the northern Iraqi Yazidi town of Sinjar, in Nineveh governorate. The territory was home to Iraq's Yazidis, a rural semi-isolated community whose members practice a religion that ISIS has declared apostasy, and therefore subject to mass murder and enslavement.

As part of Operation "Asdullah Balawi," ISIS combat forces that took parts of Northern Iraq turned their attention to capturing and ethnically cleansing the region. On August 3, 2014 ISIS forces blitzed the area, pushed the few Yazidi militiamen out of the town, and proceeded to conduct a pogrom that would make the Czars blush. Within a matter of days, mass murders of all captured Yazidi men would begin; as many as five thousand were summarily executed. Almost five hundred thousand Yazidis fled to Iraqi Kurdish areas or tried to escape across the Turkish border. Despairing Yazidi women and children struggled over mountains with ISIS in hot pursuit. After being denied passage by Turkey, they began to starve on the mountaintops. As US, Australian, and UK aircraft struck ISIS tanks, an allied airlift brought in food. American and Iraqi air force helicopters worked tirelessly to save as many as they could, and an Iraqi general would die in a crash after saving hundreds in his dozens of helicopter flights to get out as many as he could. While many Yazidis managed to escape to the mountains or to Kurdish territory, thousands of men, women, and children were captured and killed by ISIS. The UN estimated that some twenty-five hundred women—some still girls as young as twelve—had been taken by jihadists.[833] The US State Department has quoted this number of captured women to be between 1500 and 4000.[834] The number of total captives or murdered captives reported by the UN in 2016 is estimated to be as many as 3,500, which would include mainly women, children, and the elderly who could not move quickly enough to escape.[835]

After Sinjar was retaken from ISIS in November 2015, it was apparent that countless women and children were seized, moved, and whose whereabouts remain unknown. Soon after liberation, Yazidi forces started

Why Does ISIS Hate the Yazidis?

Yazidis were already a small minority in Iraq, with only an estimated 500,000 people, or less than 1.5 percent of the population.[836] According to the Qur'an, Yazidis are not one of the protected "People of the Book"—Muslims, Jews, and Christians.[837] Their religion incorporates elements from other faiths like Judaism and Zoroastrianism, in addition to Islam.[838] In the eyes of ISIS the Yazidis are worshippers of Satan, who plays a bit part in their religious belief. Yazidis themselves are also strictly conservative, and cannot marry into other religions. A 2007 video showed the stoning of a girl by a Yazidi crowd for wanting to marry a Muslim.[839] In this way, ISIS is well aware that sexual violence, forced conversions, rape, and marriages carry a much deeper layer of subjugation.

to find mass graves of mainly elderly women and men, but the young women were abducted and made slaves in ISIS households. The Yazidis are not the only minority being brutalized and taken into slavery. For Christians, Alawites, Druze, Turkmen, Shia Shabaks, and Sunnah tribes, any woman can be pointed out, declared an infidel, and sold, though all were guaranteed protection by traditional Islamic jurisprudence.[840] ISIS cares not a whit about that.

For the women who suffer this fate, sometimes the greater dishonor might be in the sexual violence than in slavery,[841] since by virtue of their community, a woman's privacy and virtue must be guarded and determines her standing in the community.[842] This makes for yet another reason why violence against women and girls, including rape, may be under-reported.[843]

Shockingly, ISIS shows great pride in how they justify committing their crimes. They claim that raping a prepubescent virgin is a form of worship to God, with the same justification they use for beheading, suicide bombing, and slaughtering children. In the cultist view of ISIS, all human atrocities can be accounted for as love of God.

PEDOPHILIC RAPE

In addition to claiming rape and slaves as God's rights to fighters on earth, child rape and group-sanctioned pedophilia are considered highly desired benefits of these rewards, despite all being forbidden in Islam. In contradiction to traditional Islam, and according to ISIS's own written rulings, sex with children, particularly prepubescent girls, is allowed and encouraged: "It is permissible to have intercourse with the female slave who hasn't reached puberty if she is fit for intercourse . . . However, if she is not fit for intercourse, he (the owner) can only enjoy her without intercourse." In this respect, ISIS allows oral and anal rape.

Rape of captured women is likewise permissible so long as they too are considered slaves or unbelievers.

ISIS views sexual conquest and slavery as a right owed to fighters just as it did in the time of the Prophet Mohammed. However, the Prophet tempered the rash actions and behaviors of his followers and exercised respect towards religious minorities and the chastity of women. ISIS scoffs in the face of Islam and spits on the words of the Prophet while reveling in the murder, rape, and sodomy of children. Accepting and worshiping God with these defilements, they reject Islam completely.

SLAVE AND HUMAN TRAFFICKING SYSTEMS

Through their online language magazine, *Dabiq*, ISIS announced to the world how they delighted in having captured, enslaved, and marketed Yazidi women and children. Not only that, they find themselves justified in this by their cult interpretation of the Qur'an and Sharia Law.[844] One such article, published in October 2014, is titled "The Revival of Slavery Before the Hour,"[845, 846] and goes on to claim that the abandonment of traditions like slavery—and toward women in particular—had resulted

in the spreading of sin, with men being tempted without this alternative to marriage.[847] Needless to say, countless Muslim scholars over centuries have repudiated this very literal interpretation of the Qur'an.[848]

ISIS issues official price lists for females, from the ages of one to fifty. The ISIS purchase list report talks about the female slave's market "decrease" and how this has affected "revenue and financing." Top price goes to younger women, with the value being $172 dollars. [849] Also according to the price list, it is forbidden to purchase more

than three slaves unless they are foreigners like Turks, Syrians, and Gulf Arabs.[850]

Their "Research and Fatwa Department" has also issued a pamphlet titled: "Questions and Answers on Taking Captives and Slaves."[851] These instructions can be very clear: "It is forbidden to have intercourse with a female captive if [the master] does not own her exclusively." Or: "A man may not have intercourse with the female slave of his wife, because [the slave] is owned by someone else." And: "He can't sell her if she becomes the mother of a child . . ." and other such rules.[852] These rules explicitly condone child rape.[853]

One of these many rules—which prohibit a man from having sex with a pregnant woman[854]—has grim implications for some captives. According to source quoted by CNN, some men bring along doctors to the slave markets to verify if the women are virgins and to provide abortions, if the slave buyer deems it necessary.[855] Part of the reason for these official documents regarding slavery and violence against women is ISIS's necessity to justify its actions to its own members is to cloak it within Islamic jurisprudence, and to squelch any questioning by jihadists.[856] Another curious aspect of this bureaucracy is that ISIS created a legal mechanism to set slaves free. Freedmen receive Certificates of Emancipation signed by an actual judge of the Islamic State, and their previous owners are said to receive a heavenly reward for doing so.[857] This occurs mainly when a slave converts to Islam.

ISIS has also established a sizeable internal infrastructure to accommodate the ownership, sale, and transportation of slaves in the form of sales "infrastructure," "networks," and a slave bus system. Like any major commercial enterprise looking to expand, ISIS has turned slavery into a commercial institution along the lines of the Nazis. All of these activities chillingly fit into the larger strategy of ISIS's self-proclaimed caliphate.[858]

There are countless witnesses who have managed to escape ISIS after being submitted to slavery and sexual violence, and though each must be taken independently, the consistency of their testimonies throws light into the how the ISIS machine operates.[859]

In practice, this system of slavery, human trafficking, and the sanctioned sex trade works roughly like this: Younger women and girls who are captured are separated from their families, often according to whether or not they are married or have children.[860] Though some of the victims are children themselves, they are the most desired. The women are detained in several locations for short periods due to fear of detection; lines of chained women could indicate official ISIS buildings, which may then be targeted for air strikes.[861] The slaves travel in trucks and buses to slave warehouses in the cities of northern Iraq near the border with Syria and in eastern Syria. They stay in schools, prisons, military bases, government offices or, as they are sold, private homes. These places are usually crowded and disgusting affairs, but there seem to have been prior preparations for receiving them. In many cases, they are starved and water is withheld to weaken them and limit their chances for escape.

The ISIS slave network is a well-oiled machine where leaders and their fighters can have their pick of the women to buy. The remaining women are bid on and bought by others or given as gifts for fighters in combat actions who have distinguished themselves.[862] The NGO "Raqqa is Being Slaughtered Silently" believes that members of ISIS initially took only virgins as sex slaves, but the scope of the program and number of estimated captives belies that.[863]

Generally women and girls are sold in public slave markets. Those who are not sold as virgins can expect to be raped multiple times and later be passed off to other fighters.[864] The girls and women can be placed on the block and auctioned off or they are photographed with identification number and sold online and at auction houses.

This market-like approach to slavery has given rise to a counter-industry, that of smugglers, who attempt to free these women and children—at a price, of course. The *New York Times* related the case of a family who paid $15,000 to have their daughter back.[865] There is even a highly controversial Canadian organization, Liberation of Christian and Yazidi Children of Iraq (CYCI) that works to fund the rescue of women in captivity. They claim to have done so for some 130 women, paying at most $3,000 a head. Their purpose and results have been questioned, as it can be seen as not only funding terrorism, but also fomenting sex trade.[866]

FORCED MARRIAGE

To some fighters, the prospect of a Muslim wife is high on their expectations for reward of service. To this end they employ the un-Islamic practice of forced marriage. There are many such accounts, and in some reports these "weddings" are even celebrated with parties, the women dressed as brides and forced to fake happiness for pictures. The price for those who refuse to take part can be extreme: in August 2015 Iraqi news agencies reported that ISIS executed nineteen women for refusing to have sex with their jihadist "husbands" after forced marriage.[867]

As for the women who have managed to escape or be freed—and whose testimonies help reveal the ISIS system—Human Rights Watch claims that there have been attempted and successful suicides among them, during and after their captivities.[868, 869] They are in need of urgent medical and psychosocial care to deal with eventual pregnancies and children born as result of rape, stigma, and reintegration.[870]

Some have received immediate treatment while others had to wait weeks. Even those who received treatment were often tested without being told what for, or informed of the results. This is all complicated by the fact that many of them can be reluctant to receive support due to their upbringing or traumatic experiences, and that the treatment they do receive may not be sufficient without specially trained professionals or the necessary equipment.

ISIS PROSTITUTION

ISIS declared that as a component of its sexual Jihad that its fighters have the religious right to "temporary marriages." Called Muta'ah marriage, it is a form of sexual transaction in which one can "marry" a woman after paying her or her male guardian a "dowry". Then the "marriage" is consummated" by having have sex with her for an hour. Once the allotted time is finished the man "divorces" her by stating it three times according to Islamic law. Surprisingly this is a common practice in Shi'ite Islam but which ISIS has adopted as just and acceptable.

ISIS SOCIAL PUNISHMENTS (HUDUD)

Hudud is a word used in Islamic law to describe the acceptable practice of issuing punishments for crimes that violate the social order. The word Hudud is plural of the Arabic word *had,* which means "limitations" or "restriction." The reason that the word is drawn from the word "limitations" is less to define the border of transgressions than to describe the minimal requirements for the application of punishments. Islamic jurisprudence is meant to work within the belief that God is the ultimate accountant of transgressions and that man-made laws simply control the basic behaviors but do not pardon sins. That is God's role.

Except in Saudi Arabia, it is rarely applied, or rarely applied strictly. The crimes with a well-defined punishment under Saudi religious law are: (a) theft—amputation of a hand; (b) having illicit sex—one hundred lashes; (c) accusing someone of having illicit sex with insufficient proof—eighty lashes; (d) drinking alcohol—eighty lashes; (e) apostasy—exile or death; and (f) banditry—death.[871]

In the modern day, Sharia law coexists alongside modern laws, as most Middle East nations have a basis in British or French colonial law.

The form of Hudud ISIS practices could be best described as "Hudud Ultra." They have arranged for all punishments to be carried out in the precise manner of seventh-century Islam. In fact ISIS has codified an excessive form of Hudud in order to eliminate any tolerance or compromise that was adopted since the Qur'an was written. That makes the ISIS variation far more inflexible than even the most the stifling extremes of the Qur'anic- and Hadith-based Hudud found in Saudi Arabia.[872],[873]

Each ISIS organization has a Sharia law advisory committee and a judiciary. The Sharia court for each level from the highest command to the street level brings the transgressor before them, listens to the case, and doles out the punishment. Usually the prisoners are held for some time in a Hisbah jail, as there is often a long waiting list for punishments.[874]

EXECUTION METHODOLOGIES

When it comes to the execution of people under their variation of Hudud, ISIS's leaders have a broad and vivid imagination. They have created a wide variety of diabolical methods even more vicious than those of the medieval period. Like gifted "artists" who do not simply steal, but who "steal with genius,"[876] they are willing to take a normalized mode of execution such as the Saudi capital punishment of beheading[877] and allow all of their men to apply it to those they see fit.

All actions in ISIS are religious and prophetic in nature and in which the punishment has to fit the Hudud. If there is a method to their madness it is the method described in the divine comedy of Dante Alighieri's *Inferno*. They take the phrase "eye for an eye" quite literally. If you have burned someone (or bombed them from the sky), you will be burned

There are variations of punishment which are even more strict then the regular ones in most provinces. On December 16, 2014 the ISIS chapter in Aleppo issued its own version of Hudud:

Blaspheming against God: Death

Blaspheming against the Prophet: death, even if one repents

Blaspheming against the Muslim faith: death

Adultery: Stoning to death (if one is married or 100 lashes and exile if one is not)

Sodomy (homosexuality): Death

Theft: The cutting off of one's hand

Drinking: 80 lashes

Slander: 80 lashes

Spying for the infidels: Death

Apostasy: Death

Banditry:

Murder and theft: Death and then crucifixion

Murder alone: Death

Theft during an act of banditry: Cutting off the left leg and the right hand;

Terrorizing others: Exile[875]

alive; if you have blown up a person with an RPG rocket, you will be killed with an RPG.[878] However, truly clever and inspired executions are carried out for the ISIS media machine, such as lacing explosive detonating cord around the neck of ten victims to have all of their heads fly off in a row. Islamic law allows precisely none of these punishments, and they are so vile and contemptuous to the religion as to be not only un-Islamic, but anti-Islamic:

Gun execution: Shooting a victim or victims in the back of the head.[879]

Beheading one or more victims:[880] Beheading can be done by the traditional Kalashnikov bayonet or by the ceremonial Islamic swords (Saif) carried by the religious police.

Decapitation through explosive detonation cord: ISIS rigs explosive detonation cord around the necks of their victims and decapitates them in a ring of fire.[881]

Death by dragging: Victim is chained to a vehicle and dragged at high speed until he dismembers.

Death by drowning: in one instance a steel cage containing five victims was submerged into a swimming pool. Cameramen filmed the victims when they were above the water as well as with underwater cameras when they were below it, until all five of them drowned one by one. The men's mouths spewed with white foam when the cage was lifted from the water.[882]

Immolation: Victims are placed in cages or trenches filled with flammable liquids and then set aflame.[883]

Immolation (human torch variation): ISIS hangs victims face down by their feet with chains so they looked like human "swings." They then light lines of a flammable substance on the ground so that the flames moved slowly toward them. When the fire reached the squirming victims they ignited and began to burn. Quickly engulfed by flame, they become human torches. In one instance, four men were burned alive, they were shown a video of an ISIS fighter who had been fried over an open pit by Shia militia in Iraq. The message in the video was simple: any man whose allies kill an ISIS member by fire will die by fire as well.[884]

Explosive execution: ISIS executes individuals and groups using explosive detonations of various fashions. The simplest method is to sit victims over explosive charges or and mines and set them off using a re-mote detonator. This has been seen in Syria, Iraq and Afghanistan. Oth-er variants have included rigging mortar shells looped over the victim's necks so that they hang over the chest or placing victims in a vehicle or small boat filled with explosives and detonating them as has been seen in Yemen. In Syria ISIS has executed groups of victims by placing them in a vehicle and shooting it with RPG-7 rocket launchers until it burns.

Death by burial: this was done to Syrian children by ISIS religious police for breaking the fast during Ramadan, according to the UN Com-mittee on the Rights of the Child.[885]

Death by "mashing" or "mutilation" of a man or woman's body: one "crushes" either part of it or all of it, either lightly, severely, or almost entirely via stoning, falling from a roof, or being run over and flattened.

Stoning to death a man or woman who is an adulterer: i.e., bruis-ing his or her skin, "mashing" his or her flesh, and even breaking a few bones; comparatively, this is a far milder way of "crushing" a man or woman's body.[886] The first publicized instance of an ISIS execution by in general, put methods in alphabetical order stoning was that of a married woman who allegedly committed adultery in the Syrian city of Hama. In this instance ISIS officials asked the woman's father if he was willing to forgive his daughter. For whatever reason, he refused. As a further humil-iation for her, he joined five ISIS "officials" and pummeled his daughter with fist-sized stones. Her body was laid out in a shallow hole so that she could not flee, and that each blow would strike home. The participants threw solid stones at her from short range and with great force until she died.[887]

Death by falling: Gay men are to be thrown from a high roof after being dangled from the edge, then dropped: shattering his body, and frac-turing and breaking many of his bones via the fall; based on the height of the roof, this may amount to "crushing" a man's body significantly.[888]

Stoning to death a gay man who has survived after falling from a high roof: thereby shattering his body, and breaking many of his bones via the fall, and finally stoning his body to finish him off; comparatively, this amounts to "crushing" the human body far more than one could by merely stoning it.[889] [890]

Death by squashing: "Traitors" or an enemy fighter are run over and flattened by a tank. In one video the victim "confessed" on screen to having run over [four] ISIL fighters with a tank, though he was a Syrian infantryman.[891]

CRUCIFIXION

ISIS tends to lay out its victims, 'dead bodies in an aspect of crucifixion, to display the result of crossing the religious establishment. Usually a sign with the description of the transgression is placed over the body. Live crucifixions have yet to be recorded but no doubt have occurred. Ac-

cording to a report by the UN Committee for the Rights of the Child, there were "several cases of mass executions of boys [by ISIS], as well as reports of . . . crucifixions of children and burying children alive." Two children were reportedly "crucified" by ISIS for not having fasted during Ramadan in Mayadin in the province of Deir Ez-zor. "The two boys, who are assumed to have been younger than eighteen, were killed and then shown to the citizens of the town in a public display, each with a sign around his neck that revealed his 'crime'" said the Syrian Observatory for Human Rights. This is a perfect example of apostasy and the anti-Islamic nature of ISIS. It is well known that people traveling over 25 km, pregnant women, and children under the age of ten are allowed to eat and drink water during the daylight fasting hours of Ramadan.

EXECUTION OF HOMOSEXUALS

The execution of gays is a public spectacle for a more complete humiliation in front of one's friends, neighbors, and family members. Scores of people will often attend the event and, apparently, often cheer for the death of the "sodomite."[892] The method of choice for a gay man appears to be death by falling from on high, with an occasional variation. For instance, the victim will be dangled over the edge of a roof and then dropped to his death, or pushed over the edge of a roof while seated in a chair. The mode of execution is a ham-handed symbolization for the theological concept of a "fallen" man.

WHIPPINGS AND BEATINGS

Whippings are part of the new ISIS version of Hudud. Under the ISIS code of Hudud, the drinker and the slanderer receive eighty lashes as his or her punishment, while the unmarried "adulterer" receives one hundred lashes and exile as his or her sentence.[893] Whipping is carried out using a bamboo or solid wood Mahsassil, or a traditional camel crop of approximately one meter. The crop gathers enough momentum to raise welts on the body and break them open when enough strikes are administered. The crops bloody the victim and in most instances leave permanent scars on the back.

Beatings by ISIS are very similar to being "jumped in" to an El Salvadorian drug gang: a squad of men descend on the victim and punch, kick, stomp, or smash the rifle butt or barrel tip of a Kalashnikov until they are exhausted. In the ISIS edition, the victim is not allowed to protect himself or punch back.[894]

CHAPTER 13

PAYING FOR
THE APOCALYPSE:
ISIS FINANCIAL
MECHANISMS

THE ECONOMY OF THE ISLAMIC STATE

How does ISIS pay a battle force of as many as 20–30,000 fighters, and perhaps 100,000 or more widows, pensioners, construction workers, and government bureaucrats, and still manage to buy cases of Red Bull, Nutella, and 7.62 x 39mm ammunition for its foreign fighters? The leadership of ISIS has the firm conviction that ISIS is a state that can supply all of its citizens with the modern trappings of a sovereign entity. Public benefit programs such as universal healthcare (for some), manufacturing women's clothing, mandating primary school education, and arming and equipping a terror army requires an extraordinary amount of money.

The US Treasury Department's Undersecretary for Terrorism and Financial Intelligence, David Cohen, is tasked with managing the intelligence effort for keeping track of that money. ISIS is considered the world's best-financed terrorist organization due to the cash and natural resources they looted from the populations and regions they seized in Syria and Iraq. And they use a myriad of methodologies to raise money for their proto-state. Some funds come from the direct theft of gold and cash from the banks of Raqqa, Mosul, Fallujah, and Ramadi; more comes from stolen oil produced on stolen oilfields and distilled in stolen refineries, then sold on the black market in bordering states. But this is just the tip of financial iceberg.

THE THEFT PORTFOLIO

French novelist Honoré de Balzac wrote, "Behind every fortune there is a great crime." Accordingly, the ISIS fortune could be called a takfirist kleptocracy. They have actually managed to seize so many assets at the point of a gun that their business enterprise could easily be described as a neo-Crusader invasion, due to their demonstrated competency for raping and pillaging the wealth of the Muslim world.

ISIS has a wide and more diversified "theft portfolio" that includes the license and sale of antiquities, the seizure of cars and jewelry,[895] human trafficking of captured women as "wives" or sex slaves, and ransom from the kidnapping of the men.[896] While oil and fuel still provide ISIS with its most important day-to-day revenue stream, it was the initial seizures of assets by ISIS that enabled it to acquire the necessary seed capital to initiate the would-be caliphate in Iraq and Syria. By one conservative estimate, the total value of the assets they seized in the region is more than $2 trillion.[897]

Donations to the jihad for "humanitarian charity" by rich Muslim sympathizers may also arrive in a valise filled with cash by private plane or handed over at the border of the caliphate. Many of these come from a wealthy donor, or from donation bundlers based in Qatar, Kuwait, Saudi Arabia, or Dubai. Despite this, the US Treasury believes that ISIS does not depend solely on raising money across international borders for its revenue, but rather through domestic looting, levying taxes, and a vehicle and business license extortion racket imposed on a captive population whose only alternatives are to die or flee.[898]

The most important liquid assets that were stolen by ISIS, in this case cash, were robbed from a series of banks in Iraq. ISIS's bank thefts together dwarf the scale of the $70 million theft at the Banco Central in Brazil in 2005, the largest heist in the world to that point. The total sum stolen in this series of bank thefts is estimated to have been somewhere between $500 million and $1 billion.[899] More than any other economic action that ISIS has engaged in, before or since, this may have been the corporate-scale acquisition that was most responsible for its recent and sudden rise to prominence in the Near East.

ISIS has stolen or seized an immense amount of land, along with the agricultural assets found on it: entire silos of wheat and barley, tons of baled cotton and wool, and grazing animals. Many of these agricultural commodities were then sold within Syria or smuggled across the borders, adding an immense sum to the coffers of the caliphate. For example, ISIS acquired as much as $200 million in potential value from its newly confiscated wheat silos in Iraq alone. All told, ISIS now has land in its possession in the Tigris and Euphrates river region that in the past has generated around half of the wheat yield in Syria, about a third of the wheat in Iraq, and nearly 40 percent of the barley in Iraq. Even if the annual grain yield of this ISIS farmland were sold illicitly outside of the "Caliphate," it still might generate as much as

$200 million in income a year.[900] ISIS now uses its stolen wheat and barley to feed those who are still willing to adhere to its extreme Islamist tenets.

The problem with some or most of ISIS's "theft portfolio" is that it may not be sustainable. Banks can only be robbed once. ISIS's own Islamic-compliant banks will no longer be able to thrive, or even function minimally, before local businesses go under due to a lack of short-term loans, or before the citizens whose deposits were robbed no longer have enough money to spend. How long can the "theft portfolio" stay up and running? Not long. ISIS has already eaten its seed corn. As American strikes hit home and isolate ISIS combat forces, and allied forces such as the Kurds, Iraqi Army, and Free Syrian Army make gains, ISIS will lose its grip on the population. The consequence of an economic collapse would be a second mass exodus to Turkey and Europe to avoid poverty, starvation, and death.

ISIS OIL

When ISIS seized a large swath of Iraq in 2014, they came to control numerous small Iraqi oilfields including the Ajil, Hamrin, Jawan, Taza, Najma, Qasab, West Tikrit, and Qayarah. In addition to the oil under the ground they acquired oil wells, small refineries, oil pipelines, and oil storage depots. The Iraq Energy Institute estimates that at one point ISIS had around 350 oil wells in Iraq alone, 45 of which it then lost as a result of US airstrikes and/or recapture by the Kurdish pershmerga. As it retreated, ISIS set fire to some of the wells that it lost.[901]

According to an International Energy Agency report in October 2014, when ISIS first seized its oil assets, it acquired a fair amount of initial oil supplies. Since 2014 ISIS has controlled around 60 percent of Syria's ability to produce oil production capacity and 80 percent of Syria's stored "prewar oil."[902] It began by draining around 3 million barrels of oil from four oil pipelines as well as from a series of storage depots and pumping stations.[903] The ISIS "oil ministry" claimed that it has 253 oil wells in Syria.

The oil assets ISIS stole are now being used to create a supply of fuel for its own cars, trucks, tanks, and armed personnel carriers; to generate electricity for ISIS territories; and to provide fuel to the 8–10 million Iraqis and Syrians under their control. This stolen oil also furnishes ISIS with a source of revenue from the sales to a variety of parties: the Assad regime, the Kurds, other Syrian rebels, international aid agencies, Turkey, and the other nations that currently share a border with the ill-defined and shifting landscape of the "Islamic State."

US intelligence agencies estimate that ISIS collected black market oil revenue of approximately $100 million dollars in 2014 after seizing major parts of Iraq and acquiring oilfields and pipelines in both Iraq and Syria.[904] After a year of almost unmolested operations, the US Treasury Department intelligence estimates these ISIS-controlled oilfields have generated around $500 million in 2015.[905] This estimate is convincing, as a document taken from ISIS's Ministry of Finance—the Diwan al-Rakaaez—reveals that they took in approximately $46.7 million in April 2015, which gives an annual average of approximately $560 million.[906] Former US ambassador Peter Galbraith, who was an informal advisor to the Kurdish Regional government on oil matters, believes that the amount is possibly higher than $800 million per annum because ISIS may be selling oil for as high as $200 a barrel in areas where oil is especially scarce, including to the government of Syria itself.[907]

MOVING THE OIL . . .

ISIS has no working oil pipelines at this point and its only large refining facility often requires repairs in order to function as a result of continuing air strikes. ISIS lacks a sufficient number of skilled maintenance personnel, technicians, and engineers to be able to pump at capacity, and as a result, is known to pay a certain premium for such services when they do become available. Because of the intermittent air attacks, ISIS at first had to rely on giant oil tanker trucks in order to transport its fuel and crude oil supplies to sites within the caliphate, or to a changing array of drop-off points within Syria, Iraq, and the surrounding countries. Those giant oil trucks seemed too vulnerable to air attack, so ISIS began to rely on smaller and more discreet oil trucks.[908]

. . . DESTROYING THE TANKERS

On November 16, 2015, US smart bombs hit 116 of those smaller oil trucks at the Syria oil collection depot of Abu Kamal, Syria. On November 23 it struck 280 trucks in one attack alone.[909] [910] This sustained campaign to destroy the infrastructure has begun to impact ISIS's ability to effectively supply its military trucks and its population with enough fuel to meet daily needs. At the same time, the campaign also limits ISIS's principal source of "state" revenue: overseas oil sales. After the Russian Metrojet bombing in November 2015, the Russian Federation joined in and started attacking hundreds of ISIS oil infrastructure and transport targets.

In the face of a sustained campaign, ISIS may move away from the tanker convoy model and attempt to make use of even smaller makeshift oil tankers such as the ubiquitous Kia Bongo, 5-ton military trucks, and dump trucks filled with oil barrels. It would take an armada of tens of thousands of vans, pickup trucks, and medium-sized delivery trucks with small oil tanks or barrels to take up the slack for even a few hundred oil tankers. Although it may be initially difficult for intelligence to detect these movements, the presence of small fleets of minivans and flatbed trucks lining up at the same mobile refineries, wellheads, and border crossings would eventually betray their intent. Even though oil could be loaded into such vehicles far more quickly, their presence would create a very solid intelligence signature and expose them to attack. Even if every small car and truck in ISIS's territory were to be designated to fill in for the oil tanker convoys, the volume of oil conveyed wouldn't be sustainable. Protracted combat against the oil industry will starve the caliphate's infrastructure, and the economy would likely grind to a halt if the effort was stepped up across all aspects and areas of the petroleum industry. These convoys will have to be destroyed, which may cause civilian casualties. Leaflet drops should be made notifying them that moving oil classifies them as ISIS logistics and opens them to attack without warning.

As they lose petroleum products ISIS will predictably impose driving restrictions and may stop movement of private vehicles altogether except bus, minibus, and licensed taxi-for-hire transport. The loss of mobility will have an exceptionally negative effect on the population. Black market sale of oil to the civilian population will likely increase, as there is money to be made, but ISIS will predictably crack down on this and start to execute participants. Again, this will remove the only avenue outside of ISIS's control for the people to buy gasoline and diesel to run their cars and electricity generators.

The loss of oil will also make ISIS's combat mobility even more vulnerable to attack from the air. ISIS's military power will be degraded and its ability to mobilize will be brought down to the level of getting ten men into a Toyota Hilux. Though ISIS excelled in this way they cannot move enough manpower and combat resources to stave off a heavy concerted incursion into their territory. Tanks require transporters and they have a large intelligence footprint that makes them exceptionally vulnerable to airstrikes.

IMPROVISED, JURY-RIGGED, AND BACKYARD REFINING

When the US began smart-bombing the ISIS oil refineries, the group started to rely more and more on an array of miniature oil refineries, including modular refineries made up of pre-packed trailers that can be set up anywhere to break down crude oil, mobile refineries based on vehicles, and backyard home refinery pits that just heat crude to

Jeribe Modular Oil Refinery

gain the byproducts. Although these are springing up across the Syrian and Iraqi desert, they can only fulfill a fraction of the need for the civil populace.[911]

The more sophisticated modular refineries are portable diesel fuel processing plants small enough to fit on purpose-built tractor-trailers. They can be built inside of ISIS territory using salvaged materials from oilfields and allow small-scale processing capacity. These modular refiners have a unique intelligence signature due to their location in oilfields near wellheads, and the protective 2-meter high dirt berms built around them. They can refine from 1,000–10,000 barrels per day, depending on the size. US intelligence has started to identify and strike these modular refineries, thus removing another source of ISIS income.

Mobile refineries are similar to modular platforms but are generally jury-rigged military and commercial vehicles with palletized machinery to perform the chemical process of breaking crude down to its components. The refining is conducted onboard while connected to a small physical plant to generate heat, and pumps to sustain pressure. Some of these can be quite small.

Backyard refineries are cropping up all over Syria and Iraq to supply fuel from barrels of crude, even in government-controlled areas. Like roadside falafel stands, these "refineries" are all over the highways and towns. People can acquire a barrel of crude and burn off the majority of it to create Mazut, a raw variant of diesel, as well as kerosene and gasoline. The operators refine the crude oil by simply putting oil in an open fire pit or a fuel tank over a high flame. The refining takes place as it heats up; it breaks down the crude and the byproducts are siphoned off into a linear chain of water-cooled pits. The cooling pits flow down in a fuel stream. The differing densities of diesel, kerosene, or gasoline flow from a spigot on the barrel and drip down into four dirt slit trenches. They are then scooped up in buckets, poured through a strainer and into plastic olive oil jugs or metal tins. It is then sold on the street. The whole process can be done in the open. Many locations have crude pits burning oil in the oilfields themselves. This production can also be done in burn pits behind a farm or along the highway so they can sell the crude diesel to passing truckers and cars. Roadside gas stations usually consist of kids guarding plastic containers and tin cans of diesel, which sell at a much higher rate than the official gas stations but which are plentiful on the roads. It generally takes two barrels of crude to produce one barrel of diesel due to the waste of the burn pits.[912]

Local Syrians and Iraqis may be harnessing a micro economy of refining used food oil into biodiesel for vehicles. Kerosene is a critical need as a home heating fuel in ISIS-controlled areas, as temperatures can fall to as low as 15 degrees Fahrenheit in winter, and it is also useful as a cooking fuel. Unfortunately the price of a barrel of crude to process this in the backyard can be as high as $200 or more, and the health affects are horrendous in the long term, but the financial returns from a desperate population can be extremely high. Like community electrical generators, these sites are built with multiple investors to collectively create a refinery with what little money they have. However, ISIS allows nothing to go unregulated, so this system is most likely under their control and heavily taxed, with priority going to ISIS-affiliated vehicles.

ISIS generates over $30 million per year just in taxes that they charge for commodities to move from their "caliphate" to other regions. In this way they generate cash for operational expenses while also continuing the flow of food and consumer goods to their zone of control.

THE BUYERS

ISIS is reportedly selling oil and fuel to some of its rivals and enemies—including the Assad regime and the Kurds—as well as to some international aid agencies. The US and its allies should, above all, be seeking to ensure that its Kurdish allies in both Syria and Iraq as well as the international aid agencies that are now active in the region are being furnished, on a regular basis, with oil supplies whose price is competitive with the black market oil and fuel that the Kurds and the aid agencies are now buying either from ISIS or from non-ISIS middlemen who are providing the caliphate with an oil revenue stream.

TURKEY AND SYRIA'S DOUBLE GAME?

Without question a major portion of ISIS's oil is reportedly being sold in Turkey. At this point, the Turkish border with Syria and Iraq is nowhere near as well-policed as the border between Saudi Arabia and Iraq, with its 30,000 Saudi troops.[913] Shoring up the policing capability of the Turks on their border with the Islamic State and increasing Turkey's access to US and allied satellite intelligence is an essential component in the strategy to reduce the major ISIS revenue stream. ISIS relies almost exclusively on their products and food market through Turkey. This is being paid from the smuggling of oil, fuel, and other contraband into Turkey, such as stolen grain, cotton, antiquities, etc. Given Turkey's main strategic aims in the region, specifically with respect to containing the Kurds, achieving this might be rather difficult.

ISIS needs the refined fuel products such as petrol and diesel, and exchanging crude for food and gasoline is lucrative to middlemen in western Syria and Turkey, as well as in Iraqi Kurdistan, where some Kurdish citizens, security personnel, and political figures in the regional government have been arrested for smuggling with their own enemy.[914]

At the same time the US might also need to make concessions to Ankara concerning US policy toward the Kurds in Syria and Iraq. None of this will be easy to do or in any way forthcoming, but if the US does not have the cooperation of Turkey on its cross-border oil trade with ISIS, then any attempt to effectively undermine the main revenue stream of the Islamic State will become far more problematic.

In their previous alias—Al-Qaeda in Iraq—ISIS found itself utilizing the same black market smuggling networks sponsored by Syrian intelligence agencies acquired or adopted from Saddam Hussein's embargo networks through Turkey, Syria, and Jordan. While not conclusive, the evidence on the framework of the pathways is strong. The oil-smuggling operation in the Islamic State is run along well-established food, weapons, and suicide bomber smuggling routes, some of which date from the Saddam Hussein era of the UN's Oil-for-Food program. These pathways across the Iraqi, Syrian, and Turkish borders also sustained the insurgency during the US occupation. Many of the same individuals and families who were involved in the illicit oil trade during that era are now once again involved.[915]

Many reports indicate that ISIS oil ends up passing through Turkey by truck and is exported by ship from the port of Ceyhan.[916] Once the oil reaches Turkey it has no nationality. Surprisingly, it is most likely sold to many of ISIS's mortal enemies, including the Assad government in Syria and Israel.

VIRTUAL OIL TRADING & SALES

A noticeable portion of the ISIS oil trade is being enabled by the use of mobile messaging apps such as Whatsapp and Kik for communications between buyers.[917] Doubtless this has come to the attention of intelligence agencies such as the National Security Agency, and the British General Communications HQ identify the locations of participants and help to diminish the ability of ISIS oil traders and non-ISIS middlemen to arrange deliveries both within and outside the confines of the caliphate.

Information warfare can be carried out as well. For instance, a combination of cyberwarfare, regulation, or pressure by the Treasury Department on the firms that developed these apps could result in widespread "cyberbans." Anything to cut the communications pipeline would to some degree assist in shrinking the revenue stream from the ISIS oil trade.

BATTLE OF THE GAS STATION: DEFEAT THE OIL AND PETROL CHAIN

Since oil is the primary source of revenue for ISIS, a comprehensive effort to undermine the oil revenue stream in every conceivable way should perhaps be the number-one priority for any US counterterrorism operation.

Since ISIS is only able to pump around a fifth of the total capacity of its oil fields and the campaign against oil is removing even that, the terrorists may not even be able to come close to meeting their daily needs. According to Luay al-Khatteeb at Brookings Doha, supplying fuel to 40,000 or more fighters and the eight million–person populace requires an estimated 70,000 to 80,000 barrels of fuel per day available at the least. However, a more sustainable supply of fuel for a combat force that is fighting an ongoing ground war would be 170,000 to 200,000 barrels a day.[918]

Since ISIS uses crude as currency, they are most likely exchanging the crude for refined petrol and diesel at an extortionate rate in order to meet even basic needs. Subduing or vanquishing ISIS in Syria and Iraq will likely require that its revenue stream be either severely limited or eliminated.

Initially, US air power struck the pipelines and storage depots, but only at key nodes in order to limit damage to the refineries and wells. This was done at the request of US allies and Syrian opposition so as to allow this vital infrastructure to available after the war. US Army Colonel Steve Warren, spokesman for the multinational forces in Iraq, has said that in some instances the damage to these ISIS oil facilities has been so light that at times they can be operational a mere day or two after US air strikes.[919] Those days are over. After the ISIS bombing of a Russian airliner over Egypt and the terrorist attacks in France, November 2015 became the month that the gloves were taken off by the coalition and Russia. Russia started the attacks with strikes on trucks and oil storage tanks. Frants Klintsevich, head of the Defense Committee in the upper house of the Russian Duma, has said that Russia will "level everything" that ISIS now has in hand.[920] The US upped the ante by systematically destroying several hundred fuel trucks and by coordinating British, French, and American strikes on the oil industry. As ISIS facilities are now target priorities, the balance of power on the ground in Eastern Syria may begin to shift dramatically, as the terror regime loses a significant portion of the daily revenue.

In the long term the destruction of the ISIS oil system will make the economic model of the caliphate unsustainable and could foster a level of hardship on the population that ISIS cannot control. Unfortunately, this may push ISIS to show a heavy hand in their willingness to squeeze the captive population by seizing more farmland and grain silos, impose more and higher taxes, dig up more valuable antiquities, kidnap more locals, and execute dissenters. In WWII the sustained hardships of Nazi Germany should be a reminder that economic pain rendered on the populace is worthless without fundamental destruction of their army and seizure of their lands.

It's time to create massive shortages of fuel within the boundaries of the "Islamic State." The caliphate is highly susceptible to fuel shortages. In November 2014, there was such a shortage of kerosene in Mosul from the interruption of the flow from the nearby Nejm and Qayayyah oilfields that the businesses were at the point of economic collapse.[921] ISIS quickly stepped in and returned the supply. This should not be allowed to happen again.

Additional strikes on easy targets could ratchet up the pressure, making the oil usage chain dangerous and unmanageable. Additionally, we should make life the in paradise that is the "caliphate" both unlivable and unbearable.

Public gas stations and fuel points are easy to identify. The lines for fuel extend for miles in some Iraqi cities and culminate in massive traffic jams. Drop leaflets and strike each gas station systematically and simultaneously. In fact, one single B-2 Spirit bomber could strike up to eighty Mosul gas stations and fuel points in a single strike. Hitting the gas stations at their lowest usage time, 2:00 am, could eliminate ISIS's resupply for that city. Done correctly, the leaflet drop warning of the strike should be accompanied by a small wave of ADM-160 Miniature Air-Launched Decoys that could fly over any designated city at low altitude in order to make ISIS think they are under sustained air attack by low-flying jets. This decoy strike could allow MQ-9 Reaper drones and strike aircraft flying safely above the target city the ability to observe and engage any ISIS anti-aircraft gun technicals firing at the decoys. Thus the fuel reservoirs for the city could be eliminated and dozens of ISIS mobile vehicles could be removed. This micro campaign should be carried out against Raqqa, Mosul, and other towns as an example of how "shock and awe" is not designed to make the fighter surrender, but to reveal themselves, lose resources, and be killed at the same time.

ISIS'S CURRENCY AND EXCHANGE SYSTEMS

Before the announcement of its new gold, silver, and copper coins, the ISIS's so-called "Islamic State" had three other currencies that it had been using to do business entirely outside of the framework of formal, local, and international banking institutions: Oil, illicit goods, and paper money in Syrian pounds, Iraqi dinars, and US dollars.[922]

In such a volatile economic environment, middlemen insist on cash payment. This is ISIS's currency of choice, since they seized and extorted so much of it from the population in their territory. A valise filled with paper money worth millions might be given to an ISIS agent or middleman in exchange for oil, fuel, cotton, wheat, barley, an entire silo filled with grain, farm animals, or looted antiquities. With this money ISIS pays its men to buy an electrical generator, a car or jewelry, a bride or a sex slave.

In November of 2014, ISIS announced that it intended to create an Islamic currency in order to combat the "satanic" global economic system based on paper money and the pre-eminence of the dollar, and that by their estimation has led to the misery and enslavement of Muslims

---

The ISIS Currency

The 21 carat gold 5 dinar coin, which weighs 21.25 grams, is said to be worth around €125 and has (a) a map of the world on its "tails" side and (b) an inscription on it "heads" side that reads: "The Islamic State—A caliphate based on the doctrine of the prophet."[926, 927] Thus, the 21 carat gold one dinar coin, which weighs 4.25 grams, will presumably be worth around €25. It will have an image of seven wheat stalks on it, which is a reference to the Koran that means "the blessing of spending one's money in the way of Allah."[928, 929]

Additional would-be coins of the new caliphate include the silver dirham, which has three distinct values and weights: a 10 dirham coin that weighs 20 grams; a 5 dirham coin that weighs 10 grams; and 1 dirham coin that weighs 2 grams.[930] The third variety of ISIS currency is a copper penny, which also has three distinct values and weights.[931]

at the hands of "Jews and Crusaders." According to ISIS, the dawn of their new caliphate will bring an end to the worldwide domination of the US economy and its worthless paper currency, the American dollar. At the center of the new currency system of ISIS is a gold dinar that can be seen as a new version of the legal tender used in the era of the Caliphate of Uthman, a major figure in the history of Sunni Islam in the seventh century. ISIS claims that its new currency will be "inflation proof."[923] [924]

The day-to-day feasibility of this millenarian currency scheme appears dubious. How will the new caliphate, a state within a state that is unrecognized internationally, ever be able to prevent its gold and silver coins from being smuggled, little by little, into other countries that are not Muslim? There is virtually no way to prevent these gold and silver coins from simply being melted and sold on the open market.[925] The voracious appetite of the Middle East gold market will simply swallow any of these coins whole and they will cease to exist if they ever do exist. This is why the ISIS currency is simply a propaganda ploy to announce its independence from the West.

PRIVATE DONORS & HAWALA BANKING

Using the ancient regional banking systems or hand carrying cash to Turkey, wealthy donors or "bundlers" of donations can send a rather ample sum of money in a single valise: i.e., from $1 to $2 million. When donor money is sent by private plane to Turkey or Lebanon to make its way to Raqqa, the airport or customs officials do not tend to check the content of the valises. At least in many instances, this is how a certain number of everyday business deals are still being done in the Mideast: cash, with no questions asked. As a result, this same form of transnational cash-in-hand deal-making can at times also help to facilitate the provision of donor money to ISIS.

A rather ample "gift" or "bundle" of donations from likeminded sympathizers can always be justified by a donor impresario as being a gift of "humanitarian aid" to orphans and refugees, under the Islamic precept of Zakat or charity. Illegitimate Islamic charities can be used to launder money, outside a donor's home country.[932] At times shameless donors will openly combine the idea of "humanitarian aid" with the idea of ISIS's caliphate and the righteous jihad. This false intermingling of jihad and Islamic charity may become more or less indistinguishable in the mind of the prospective donor, but it is not allowed in Islam. Zakat is to provide food for the poor, not to provide ammunition for a Kalashnikov.

It is likely that wealthy donors, often from the Gulf States, are able to find a sincere or at least seemingly sincere religious justification for their donations to the jihadis, even if—not infrequently—to their own ends. Gulf State donors to ISIS may be more open to geopolitical rather than religious arguments, i.e., they may wish, above all, to think they are countering the influence of Shi'ite Iran in the Levant by balancing it out with Sunnah fighters, no matter how extreme.

Some of the Gulf donors to ISIS are apparently Sunni clerics, some may be earnest or not-so-earnest Salafists, while others perhaps are openly drawn to the more extreme takfirism of ISIS that will allow a Sunni Muslim to freely cast an anathema onto an impure Sunni as well as onto a Shia apostasy.

How much money are the private donors or "donor bundlers" actually sending to ISIS? Compared with ISIS's other sources of revenue or theft, the sums seem to be relatively low, perhaps in the low millions of dollars annually.[933] Many of the donations appear to originate in Kuwait and Qatar, while Saudi Arabia at least is apparently now cooperating more or less convincingly with the US Treasury.[934]

TAXES AND OTHER REVENUE IN THE ISLAMIC STATE

By establishing their "caliphate," ISIS has gone from being a terror guerrilla army to an Islamist mafia state along the lines of the Somali pirate kingdoms. Since they have claimed to re-establish the caliphate, they had to initiate a finance system for the state to function.

According to US officials, presumably from the Office of Terrorism and Financial Intelligence at the US Treasury, "hundreds of millions" of dollars are filling the coffers of the ISIS each year either as a result of taxes or "shakedowns" of its millions of citizen-subjects.[935] According to some

Western estimates, the total could reach nearly $1 billion a year.[936] Daniel Glaser, Assistant Secretary of the Treasury for Terrorist Financing, says that ISIS is bringing in hundreds of millions a year in taxes on commerce alone.[937] In the ISIS capitol of Raqqa for instance, ISIS taxes all goods that are being imported, exported, or transported. This includes a tax on items being smuggled, such as looted antiquities, an illicit activity that is in violation of the tenets of Islam.[938]

ISIS is known to have a variety of other active "taxing," "fee," or "shakedown" schemes. For instance, some citizen-subjects of ISIS have to pay a 10 percent tax on their bank withdrawals (besides having their banks robbed from time to time by ISIS),[939] while police, soldiers, and teachers are allowed to "repent" for having served under a secular Ba'athist regime by getting their own "atonement ID" for a mere $2,500 with an added annual fee of $200 a year for good measure.[940]

ISIS is also gaining revenue from income taxes, a 10 percent zakat charity fee on small businesses, taxes on crops and farms animals,[941] taxes on those who provide humanitarian aid,[942] rent on the former regimes' buildings, profits skimmed from the businesses it now runs, textbook fees, road tolls and driving fines, cleaning fees for stall merchants, taxes on water and electrical bills, as well as fines for "inappropriate" clothing or for lighting up a pipe or a cigarette.[943]

STEALING FROM THE QUR'AN

If all of these "fees" were not eough, ISIS decided that they would reinstate the jizya, a tax on "sane" non-Muslim men, generally all Christians and Jews who are protected communities in the Qur'an who were "free" (i.e., not slaves). [944] While this revenue formed a primary source of funds for some Muslim nations in centuries past, this tradition, along with the Islamic tax on agriculture known as the kharaj, had nearly vanished in Muslim nations in the twentieth century.[945] [946] ISIS has revived the jizya, at least in some places in the Islamic State, requiring the well-to-do Christians in Raqqa, for instance, to either convert to Islam or to pay the value of half an ounce of gold, twice a year, with the poorer Christians paying one fourth as much.[947]

Yet it does not seem that the revival of the jizya is going well. For one thing, as of the end of 2014, most Christians had already fled from Raqqa, while 30,000 of them left Mosul soon after the ISIS seized it. It did not help that many of their churches were razed in both cities or converted to administration buildings.[948] There have also been atrocities associated with this practice. In Mosul, when an Assyrian Christian told the three ISIS soldiers who entered his home uninvited that he was unable to pay the jizya, they decided to take payment by raping his wife and daughter in front of him. Later, in a state of anguish, he killed himself.[949]

Is most of the current "tax base" of ISIS in any way sustainable? It seems as if much or a good part of it may not be. For one thing, ISIS cannot tax the non-Muslims who flee, whom they behead, or who have cause to kill themselves. ISIS cannot tax the traffic in looted antiquities once the ancient sites in the ISIS have been emptied of their artifacts. ISIS cannot tax the oil trade if they no longer have enough trucks to transport the illicit oil in as a result of US and Russian air strikes. ISIS cannot keep taxing the account withdrawals of their citizen-subjects by 10 percent, since, in time, some or most of them may simply decide to leave the ISIS with their remaining funds or run out of cash.

At some point, the local economies will likely cave one by one as the loans for big and small businesses begin to dry up and people will be forced to poverty and charity, or moved to rebellion.

CHAPTER 14

ISIS CULTURAL CLEANSING: THE PRECURSOR TO ETHNIC CLEANSING AND GENOCIDE

Raphael Lemkin, the Polish-born American jurist and author of the sem-inal book *Axis Rule in Occupied Europe*, was also the originator of the term genocide. Genocide is the elimination or attempted destruction of a class of people, or of ethnic groups as a whole. Not only did Lemkin champion the legislation to classify this as a crime against humanity, he also identified the preliminary steps regimes use to implement genocide. According to Lemkin, one of the indicators of genocidal intent is the elimination of culture, and with it, the entire history of a people from the earth. The 2013–15 combat operations of ISIS reveal a strategic com-ponent of their cult never seen on this scale in the history of Islam. ISIS groups are not only eliminating or selling other people within ISIS terri-tory, but also removing every vestige of their religions and cultures, both past and present.

The ISIS terror group follows a long-held tradition by totalitarian regimes, political juntas, and religious cults to attempt to desecrate icons, places of worship, burial grounds, museums, and libraries as a precursor to genocide. As we have seen in earlier chapters, ISIS harbors an un-Is-lamic hatred for religions that have enjoyed over fourteen centuries of sanctuary in Islam such as Christians and Jews. The Prophet Mohammed himself decreed these two religions should have special status and that its followers be allowed to live in peace. Rejecting the Prophet's orders, ISIS has spent a fair amount of time attempting to eliminate every aspect of other religions, apart from their own corrupt interpretation. ISIS inter-prets al-Wala Wal Bara—stay with that which is godly and reject all that is ungodly—should apply to history as well. As far as they are concerned, any image, symbol, or material, whether modern or ancient, which makes reference to or originates from another culture must be destroyed. That includes the culture and heritage of all other peoples.

Islam's tradition of art, culture, and worship has a special place in their pantheon of chaos. It is also ISIS's religious doctrine to eliminate through physical destruction all Islamic art, music, graves, tombs, shrines, and even religious sculpture and signage in every mosque, university, and public building. With the exception of Nasheeds, medieval chants of Qur'anic text, ISIS espouses that Islam must be cleansed of all forms of art, the study of nature, and all but the most basic study of math and science. One ISIS manual states, ". . . the ideal Islamic community should refrain from becoming caught up in exploring [science], the depths of matter, trying to uncover the secrets of nature, and reaching the peaks of architectural sophistication." [950]

As far as they are concerned, the rest must be thrown into the dustbin of history.

The real extent of ISIS's destruction of cultural heritage is as yet unknown. Scholars say that what has been destroyed in the zones of conflict is debatable. But what is not debatable is the fact that ISIS harnessed the weapons of the Syrian civil war to implement this first step to genocide. All wars bring cultural loss. Damage to historic places with military value such as the crusader castle of Krak des Chevaliers, which was remilitarized and bombarded during combat, is a terrible tragedy. The thousand-year-old al-Medina souk in Aleppo, which was destroyed in heated combat between the Syrian army and rebels, is regrettable. Yet the Islamic State takes this to a new level. That ISIS continues its destruction of the history of Northern Iraq and Syria underscores a serious concern that the region they call a "Caliphate" will be culturally as well as ethnically cleansed.

ISIS ATTACKS ON CULTURAL HERITAGE

IRAQ

July 2014

Destroying Jonah's Tomb: On July 24, 2014, the Islamic State posted a video showing ISIS members destroying Jonah's Tomb, a sacred site that is said to be the burial place of the prophet Jonah.[951] The tomb was located inside the Mosque of the Prophet Yunus, which is situated on top of a hill in eastern Mosul. The hill is one of two mounds that form part of the city of Nineveh.[952] In the Biblical book of Jonah, Jonah descended into the belly of a great fish.[953] Jonah is also known in the Qur'an as a prophet. There is still a dispute of the exact location of the tomb and the origins of the story.[954] The civil defense stated that the ISIS militants planted explosives around the tomb and remotely detonated them producing a cloud of dust, fire, and smoke.[955]

February 2015

Mosul Central Museum: Mosul, the second largest city in Iraq, is 249 miles north of Baghdad. The Mosul Central Museum held over 173 original pieces. As the second largest museum in the country, many of the artifacts in its collection originated from the city of Nineveh and the city of Hatra. When the Islamic State took over Mosul, they also gained access to approximately two thousand registered Iraqi archaeological sites.

On February 26, 2015, ISIS issued a two-minute long video showing their forces destroying cultural relics and artifacts from the Mosul Central Museum and an adjacent archaeological site. Though some reports claim that the overwhelming preponderance were modern copies, the remainder were invaluable and irreplaceable.

The video footage showed a squad of twelve men inside the museum with simple implements such as sledgehammers, commercial drills, air-powered jackhammers, and crowbars as they destroyed priceless statues, immovable monuments, and wall reliefs. As well as using tools, some were seen pushing statues to the ground from their pedestals to shatter on impact. The men then cut through a plastic protective layer covering a replica Assyrian bust from Hatra. The wrecking crew finished by smashing statue sections into rubble and kicking over other statues, then breaking what remained into unrecognizable pieces with an air powered jackhammer. As the iconoclasts destroyed a lamassu, or Assyrian winged bull, in the background, a bearded man in a white robe and black, armless sweater of the Hisbah—the ISIS religious police—spoke:

> Oh Muslims, the remains that you see behind me are the
> idols of people of previous centuries, which were worshipped

instead of Allah . . . The Assyrians, Akkadians, and others took for themselves gods of rain, of agriculture, and of war, and worshipped them along with Allah, and tried to appease them with all kinds of sacrifices. The Prophet Mohammad shattered the idols with his own honorable hands, when he conquered Mecca. The Prophet Mohammad commanded us to shatter and destroy statues. This is what his companions did later on, when they conquered lands. Since Allah commanded us to shatter and destroy statues, idols and remains, it is easy for us to obey, and we do not care what people think, even if this costs billions of dollars.

Other footage showed Lamassus, one of the Balawat gates with some bas relief depicting chariots and the reception to a tribune, and various relief sculptures being destroyed.[956] A museum sign indicated that one broken statue was a statue of Sargon II of Assyria.[957] The majority of the artifacts fell into two categories: Sculptures from the Roman period from the city of Hatra, and Assyrian artifacts from the city of Nineveh.[958] Some artifacts come from adjacent cities such as Khorsabad and Balawat.[959]

The British Museum issued a press release stating that none of the artifacts featured in the video were authentic.[960] Asil Nujaifi, the banished governor of Mosul, confirmed that most of the ancient artifacts were duplicates of genuine pieces that were relocated to the Baghdad Museum during the 2003 Iraq war. He also stated that seven original pieces might have been looted. The museum might have had more original pieces than was previously known.

The Mosul museum contained pieces from Assyrian and Akkadian history dating back three thousand years. Some artifacts in the footage were distinctive, with portrayals of the robe, beard, and headpieces of Assyrian royalty, including the statue of an unidentified, rarely studied Assyrian king. Other pieces included steles and wall reliefs, enormous figure statues erect and seated, the famous winged lamassu, Annunaki statues, bas reliefs representative of historical accounts of Assyrian and Akkadian wars, offerings to the Assyrian gods, and an Assyrian king demonstrating victory and power. The genuine artifacts in the Mosul Museum

collection that had survived three millennia were obliterated.

Mosul Library: On February 26, 2015, ISIS launched a second attack on another cherished cultural site, the Mosul Central Library. There they ransacked and burned over eight thousand ancient religious and cultural manuscripts and books.[961] The Mosul Library was established in 1921 by the British and was seen as a symbol of the birth of modern Iraq.[962] In addition to the books were one-of-a-kind newspapers from the twentieth century, maps, historic collections from the Ottoman Empire,[963] religious manuscripts from the eighteenth century, nineteenth-century Syriac books printed in Iraq's first printing house, and treasured antiques such as an astrolabe and a rare sand hourglass.[964]

When they were done the vandals rigged the library with explosives and blew it sky-high.[965],[966] It was not the first time that ISIS militants burned books. In December of the previous year, militants had burned Mosul University's Central Library, and in Anbar Province, they burned 100,000 books.[967]

March 2015

Demolition of Khorsabad: Khorsabad is one of the three cities where the Assyrian king Sargon II built a palace. It was abandoned after the kings' death.[968] Khorsabad was said to be significant among the Assyrian palaces due to its stylistic innovation, preservation of its paint on its wall relief, the extensive written documentation regarding the building projects,[969] and for its colossal statues of winged bulls.[970] The city lies about 19 kilometers northeast of Mosul. On March 11, 2015, fighters from ISIS razed parts of the city, knocked down the palace walls, and to some extent destroyed the temples.[971] The antiquities director Qais Rasheed told Reuters that the site was widely looted before the razing took place.[972]

March 2015

The Destruction of Nimrud: Founded in the thirteenth century BC, Nimrud was the second Assyrian capital and flourished under the reign of Ashurnasirpal.[973] The city lies 19 miles south of Mosul in Northern Iraq. Archaeologists excavated three royal tombs in the 1980s along a huge stony wall.[974] The Iraqi government rebuilt the palace grounds during the 1970s and 1980s.[975]

Tribesmen in the area said that the militants made entry to the archaeological site and plundered the valuables first. After all the pillaging, they proceeded to level the site with a bulldozer.[976] [977] The status of the bas reliefs and lamassus that were left in their original places and the palace grounds is unknown, but the worst should be expected.

Destruction of Hatra: Hatra was one of the best-preserved examples of a Parthian city. Hatra is a large, fortified city that lies 67 miles southwest of Mosul.

The history of Hatra dates back to the Parthian Empire and capital of the first Arab Kingdom.[978] Due to its strong fortification and watchtowers, the city withstood the invasion by the Romans in 116 AD and in 198 AD.[979] The city of Hatra had temples that were a composite of Hellenistic and Roman architecture.

On March 8, 2015, the day after the Islamic State destroyed the remains of the ancient Assyrian city of Nimrud, they moved on to destroying the city of Hatra. Residents said they heard two explosions and witnessed militants bringing bulldozers to the site.[980] [981] It is also reported that ISIS stole the ancient currencies in gold and silver coins stored inside the city that were used by the Assyrian king.[982]

Leveling of the Green Church: The green church was a seventh-century Christian site located in Tikrit, Iraq and belonged to the Assyrian church of the East.[983] The green church was located inside the presidential palace compound at the center of the city.[984]

The church was built by the Metropolitan of Tikrit, His Holiness Dinkha II, and was called the church of Saint Ahoadamah in remembrance of the Patriarch who was killed by the Persian King Khosrow I.[985]

Inside the church were the graves of Mar Dinkha II and his successors Daniel, Thomas, Basilious III, and John II.[986]

A source told Iraqi News that the Islamic state blew up the church using improvised explosive devices planted in the surrounding area.[987] The entire church was leveled.

August 2015
Destruction of Tomb of Sheikh Qadeeb Al-Ban Al-Mosuli: The tomb of the Sheikh Qadeeb al-Ban al-Mosuli dates from the thirteenth century and is the resting place of a sultan who was a scholar and patron of the arts. It has long been considered one of Mosul's holy places. Christopher Jones described the splendor of the tomb in his Near East history blog *Hyperallergic:*

> The interior walls are richly decorated with several brick geometric panels. A marble band, carved with flowers and leaves in high relief, wraps around the interior walls at eye level, with a ceramic inscription band on top. This elaborate carving contrasts with the flat terracotta panels located on the plain brick walls above. There is another inscriptive band below the dome muqarnas, which is derived from cross-shaped plan. The mihrab is situated at the southwest corner of the tomb because the building is not oriented towards Mecca.[988]

On August 25, 2014, the Islamic State released photographs of the tomb being demolished through explosive demolition, and reduced to rubble.[989]

SYRIA

Citing satellite evidence, the United Nations stated in a recent report that approximately three hundred cultural heritage sites in Syria have been destroyed, damaged, and/or looted since the start of the civil war in 2011.[990] This report focused on eighteen areas, of which six are part of UNESCO: The ancient city of Damascus, site of Palmyra, ancient city of Bosra, ancient city of Aleppo, Krak des Chevalier (Saladin's Castle), and the ancient byzantine villages of northern Syria.

UNITAR satellite images indicated that 24 sites were completely destroyed, 189 severely damaged, and 77 sites possibly damaged. All six of the World Heritage sites have been damaged due to the civil war, including the complete loss of the Roman ruins of Palmyra.[991]

May 2014

Carlton Citadel Hotel: Ottoman Sultan Abdul Mahid built this historic Aleppo landmark in 1883. The structure was the first public hospital before becoming a school for nurses. After restoration, the building became a hotel.[992] It faced the entrance to the thirteenth-century citadel.[993] In 2014, the rear section of the hotel suffered extensive damage from bombing. In February, Islamic Front rebels made a tunnel under the building and placed explosive charges, which they detonated on May 8. The hotel suffered almost complete destruction.[994]

Mass Looting of Dura Europos: Dura Europos is an important site that dates back to the third century BC and was occupied until the third century AD. Also known as Fort Europos, it was a Hellenistic Roman walled city. Founded by Seleucids (succesors to Alexander the Great) on the intersection of a trade route, it was part of a military colony that was abandoned after a Sassanian siege in 257 AD.[995] The site is located high above the Euphrates River in southeastern Syria, and is currently under the control of the Islamic State. The ISIS looters gutted the site with heavy machinery, leading to an estimated 80 percent destruction of the site. They removed everything; wall frescos, tiles, pottery, glass, silver and bronze coins, gold jewelry, and stone statues.[996] The looting also caused extensive damage to the necropolis.[997]

Sufi Shrines: The Islamic State destroyed several Sufi shrines and tombs in eastern Syria in the province of Deir Ez-zor. The Syrian Observatory

for Human Rights, based in the UK, reported that vandals destroyed two shrines and two tombs devoted to the Sufi sheiks.

August 2015
Destruction of the Roman City of Palmyra: In September 2015, ISIS forces started the destruction of the Roman ruins at Palmyra. The first building to be destroyed was the 2,000-year-old Temple of Bel. One month later, they blew up the Arch of Triumph. The Roman amphitheater remains as a mass execution spot for ISIS victims.

LIBYA

Sufi Shrines: Soon after the capture of the Libyan city of Sirte, images emerged showing ISIS's Hisbah religious police destroying Sufi shrines and a man attacking a shrine with a sledgehammer. Later images showed a bulldozer leveling the shrine and reducing it to a pile of rubble.[998] Sufi shrines had occasionally been targeted by other mainstream Libyan extremist groups such as Ansar al-Sharia who have been known to destroy mosques and shrines, and to loot graves.

Sheikh Abdul Salam Al Asmari Shrine: In August 2012 ISIS-backed rebels destroyed the shrine of Sheikh Abdul Salam Al Asmari as well as the Sheikh Abdul Salam Al Asmari mosque. In addition, they burned a collection of centuries-old manuscripts from a nearby library.

EGYPT

Although Egypt has not yet seen destruction of its cultural heritage as in Syria and Iraq, it is on the hit list. Several recent bombings reveal the same pattern of heritage-targeting, as seen in other nations. ISIS called for the obliteration of all ancient Egyptian culture. Bombings at the entryway to the Giza plateau and at Luxor by the ISIS-allied Ansar Beit al Maqdis occurred in 2015 but did no damage. Yet it is not just the Islamic State who wants to see the obliteration of the pyramids and the sphinx; a Kuwaiti Islamist and an Egyptian cleric echoed the calls for the destruction of these priceless historic edifices. The cleric wanted the antiquities to be demolished just as Prophet Mohammed destroyed the idols in Mecca, and said that the tourism ministry should be abolished, comparing it to "prostitution and debauchery."[999]

June 2015

Bombings at Giza: On June 3, gunmen on speeding motorcycles opened fire outside the Giza Pyramids, killing two police officers.

Suicide Bombing at Luxor: On June 10, a suicide bomber detonated a bomb, killing himself and wounding four people, including two police officers. The bombing occurred at one of the most popular tourist attractions, the ancient Egyptian Karnak Temple.[1000]

Three men in a car tried to enter the Temple's parking lot. The Luxor police grew suspicious when the occupants refused a police search of the car trunk. One of the attackers set off his explosive vest outside the

Karnak Temple, as police shot one accomplice dead and injured the second. During the subsequent investigation, the police took bags containing nineteen fully loaded rifle magazines into evidence.[1001]

Although no group claimed responsibility for the attack, the assailants' methods bore the hallmarks of an ISIS operation.

July 2015

On July 14, two police officers and two security guards were injured trying to dismantle a bomb outside a Cairo hotel near the pyramids. Passersby informed security guards of suspicious packages outside the Meridian Hotel adjacent the Great Pyramids of Giza, and quickly sent a bomb squad to inspect the packages. It was discovered that the packages were improvised explosive devices. This incident is one among many others that have occurred in the region.[1002]

LOOTING & SALE OF BLOOD ANTIQUITIES—TACTICS, TECHNIQUES, AND PATHWAYS

Despite financial and trade sanctions on groups doing business with ISIS, the group has combined cultural cleansing with the antiquities black market. They sell to their enemies what they steal. Finance is the only reason the Islamic State loots and sells artifacts. If they executed their full strategy, they would destroy each object as an anathema to their cult ideology. Still, they understand that the West values antiquities, and elect to fund their jihad with the money of the rich and self-interested.

ISIS seeks the financial means to administer the eight million people under its control, and likewise needs to maintain its tens of thousands of fighters. In part, by looting and smuggling antiquities out of Syria and Iraq, the Islamic State raises money to finance its operations and ideologies.[1003] By selling plundered antiquities, it gets rid of "idols" that run afoul of their radical understanding of Islamic law, while obliterating the cultural identity of minority groups.[1004]

Blood antiquities are nothing new. During the invasion of Iraq in 2003, former US Marine Colonel Matthew Bogdanos was investigating the looting of artifacts from Iraq's National Museum when he discovered the link between illicit sale of artifacts and weapons. It came in the form of a cache of weapons mixed with stolen antiquities.[1005]

Bogdanos explained that the Islamic State obtained the artifacts through looting. Accompanied by an armed escort, smugglers conveyed them across borders along established routes. The antiquities then appeared in the back rooms of souvenir shops of Damascus, Beirut, and Amman. If the antiquities are to go abroad, the smugglers find an individual in the antiquities industry who will "authenticate" the items, and even create a legal provenance through official documents.[1006] Then the antiquities are smuggled into western countries as legitimate goods.

ISIS MINISTRY OF LOOTING

Over a third of Iraq's twelve thousand archeological sites are under ISIS control, as well as many more sites in Syria. The group has been looting and selling artifacts as old as from 9,000 BC to 1,000 AD. Anything of great significance is dug up.[1007]

After the sale of oil, looting has the potential to become a large source of income for the Islamic State. ISIS even established a "Ministry of Antiquities," which is in fact a ministry for the looting and destruction of antiquities. They are tasked to oversee the process of looting and maximize the profit from looted artifacts from the territories it controls.[1008]

This ministry is subordinate to the "Ministry for Precious Resources."

Any locals that want to dig must get authorization from ISIS's Ministry of Antiquities or from the local emir, who issues stamped licenses. With this license, the locals are allowed to dig at

ancient sites as long as they give a percentage of the monetary value of anything found to the Islamic State. The local emir governs how the militants treat the antiquities, whether by destroying them, selling them, or protecting them. ISIS often partners with professional looters and smugglers as long as they also pay a 12.5–20 percent non-interest- bearing Islamic "tax," called Khums, for what they find and smuggle.[1009]

Any Islamic items looted can have a tax as high as 50 percent or higher. Local looters are paid as much as 700 Syrian pounds or US $3.87 per day by the local emir to dig for antiquities.[1010] On occasion, the locals can sell the objects to the smuggler directly if they pay the Islamic State 20 percent of the profit. If the equipment used in the looting belonged to ISIS, then ISIS takes 40–50 percent of the proceeds. It's common practice for the emir or authorities to confiscate the antiquities plundered by locals, then sell them to smugglers themselves.

Archeologically speaking, two factors dictate what can be looted and what needs to be destroyed. The first factor is whether an item can be transported to a location where a buyer exists, and the second factor is whether the antiquities sold can be recognized as legitimate. What ISIS can't sell they destroy, such as immovable monuments like shrines, Shi'ite mosques, or the giant lamassus (winged bulls) they blew up at the ancient Assyrian Capital of Nineveh in Iraq.

Pieces such as bas-reliefs taken from Nimrud weigh over three or four tons. These they usually cut up into smaller pieces for easy transport and sale. On Lamassus sculptures, they cut the head off as it's more portable, and believed to be more valuable to Western buyers. Smugglers take the cut pieces, along with everything else, across borders where they are

warehoused. In many instances the dealers put the cut-down pieces in storage for years, then reassemble them once a buyer comes forward. The dealers may or may not be aware that all of those pieces were part of a bigger piece.

According to the Department of Defense, ISIS's financial mastermind Abu Sayyaf was involved not only in military operations, but also illicit oil, gas, artifact, and financial machinations. After a US-led raid resulting in his death, soldiers found a cache representing some of the looted objects from the sites in Iraq and Syria. It encompassed a variety of archaeological artifacts and fragments, historical objects, modern/contemporary items, and replicated or faked antiquities. Most of the artifacts were property of Mosul Museum, and Iraqi experts are trying to determine the provenance of each object.[1011]

ISIS relies on a complex system of underground networks to manage its financial situations. It is said that most of the illicit artifacts go to Europe via the Turkish cities of Antakya, Gaziantep, Mardin, and Urfa,[1012] which serve as the main conduit for looted artifacts. The next largest markets for stolen artifacts are in Lebanon and Jordan.[1013] Well before World War II, Germany became a major transit hub for antiquities, and many still make it there.[1014] ISIS can find buyers all around the globe from the rich Arabs in the Gulf Region, to the nouveau riche of China and India.

WESTERN BUYERS

The question remains as to how international buyers become aware of available artifacts conveyed from the Middle East. There are many ways in which the middlemen can get in contact with buyers. The first way is by social network. The Islamic State has been using social media, including the two most common, Facebook and Twitter.

It has been acknowledged that the group likely created and used its own social network called Khelafabook.[1015] Social networking is the best-established means to find buyers, as it is difficult to distinguish between what is stolen versus what is not. In one case of alleged artifact trafficking, Facebook had to deactivate certain pages. Some of the alleged artifacts for sale were golden statues, Hebrew and Aramaic scrolls, clay tablets, and coins.

Matt Steinfield, a Facebook privacy spokesman, pointed out that not all artifacts and objects can be identified as stolen; however, when a person reports the contents, the pages are removed.[1016] Facebook is just one among other networks used by ISIS to find buyers who are willing to purchase looted artifacts. The Internet remains a convenient means to conduct illicit activities, and it should come as no surprise that the Islamic State uses it to sell plundered artifacts. The second way middlemen can contact buyers is likely through antique and tourist markets situated around the globe. Once the antiquities have been handed to European antiques merchants, those merchants communicate with other dealers in Europe and throughout the world. Europeans and foreigners alike come and buy the object without having knowledge that it was stolen.[1017]

MOVEMENT OF ANTIQUITIES BY TRUCK OR BY FOOT

Traffickers have devised clever solutions to import cultural antiquities to Europe and the United States. A common technique to mask archaeological materials is to classify them as legal "antiques." Some of the methods are as simple as labeling objects as handicrafts; attaching "made in place" stickers on ancient pots, or making them appear modern.[1018] Using these timeworn tricks, ISIS can make the hunt for illicit antiquities even more complicated.

Another way of smuggling antiquities is by means of refugees. Lieutenant Colonel Nicholas Saad, the head of Lebanon's Bureau of International Theft, said that as refugees pour into Turkey and Europe from Syria, the smugglers exploit this movement by mixing the objects with the refugees' belongings.[1019]

ISIS is a main player in the refugee smuggling network. One smuggler claimed that ISIS controls the business and that they have connections abroad, which permit them to ship antiquities out of the country.[1020] Most if not all of the antiquities that appear on the market are small and portable and as such are the easiest to smuggle out of countries. These include coins composed of gold, silver and bronze; pottery, glass, ivory, stone, and leather; and jewelry, figurines, bowls, and manuscripts.

Refugee smugglers tend to deal with small, high-value antiquities such as earrings, rings, small statues, and stone heads.[1021] The middlemen

Five Players in Blood Antiquities Trade	
Looters	The looters as seen above can either be the militants from the Islamic states, the locals, or professionals
Smugglers	People who participate in the illegal transportation of antiquities. They usually know the area very well.
Middlemen	A person across the border who buys the antiquities from the Islamic State or locals and sells them to dealers and merchantmen.
Dealer	The dealers are the merchantmen who work in antique shops. They can be found globally.
Buyers	The buyers can be either private collectors, museums, tourists, or millionaires.

or the "go-betweens" coordinate with dealers and distributors in Lebanon, Turkey, and Gulf States before they pass them on. Smugglers are usually well-known to each other, and place cash bonds to show they are trustworthy.[1022] Middlemen also travel to dealers in Turkey and Lebanon, who in turn sell the "fake" objects to fake "tourists" who then bring them into central Europe.

Despite international awareness, antiquities have been found in New York, California, London, Japan, Australia, France, Switzerland, Italy, and other industrialized countries. Antiquities have also been shipped to the UAE, Iran, Syria, and other Gulf States. The looted artifacts pass through many hands before making it to the market, and at the end of the journey are rich private collectors, CEOs, other dealers, and unlucky tourists. The artifacts that make it to museums come from collectors, who tend to wait few years for the suspicion to die down before donating or selling the object.[1023]

By 2011–2013, American imports of potentially illicit antiquities rose 133 percent. Secretary of State John Kerry hosted a press conference at the Metropolitan Art Museum in New York. There he released a red list of Syrian and Iraqi cultural objects at risk, to raise awareness of threats to the Syrian and Iraqi culture.[1024] Nonetheless, ISIS is not the sole culprit in such lootings. During the Syrian civil war, Syrian government forces were recorded taking funerary statues from Palmyra and Apamea. Groups fighting the Assad regime are also known to be plundering archaeological sites. One group is the Free Syrian Army and when confronted, they indicated that it was to raise money and weapons.[1025]

No one knows the exact estimate for revenue from the plundering and selling of antiquities. The Financial Action task force put the figures at tens of millions dollars.

It's hard to quantify the actual amount of money that ISIS makes as the antiquities are passed from hand to hand, and it can take years before a plundered artifact makes it to the market. For example, Cambodian antiquities from Angkor Wat turned up in auction forty years after the end of the Khmer Rouge.[1029] Illicit antiquities can be found pretty much on any continent as long as there is a buyer to pay. Scotland Yard announced four major investigations related to Syrian antiquities.[1030] In March 2015, US Immigration and Custom Enforcement recovered sixty artifacts. Among them was a head of the Assyrian King Sargon II, worth $1.2 million, but the value documented in Turkey was $6,500. [1031] An Egyptian funerary boat valued at $57,000 was also recovered.

Turkish authorities also have confiscated hundreds of antiquities, particularly in cities adjacent to the border, but are unwilling to disclose

---

Delta Force Raid in Syria Opens Trove of Antiquity Smuggling

On May 15, 2015 US Army Special Forces conducted a daring raid on the base of the chief of ISIS finances, Abu Sayyaf in al-Amr, also known as Abu Bakr. Housed on a large oilfield in Deir Ez-zor, Syria, they seized the financial records of the group. Soldiers also discovered a stockpile of hundreds of intact and broken antiquities for sale.[1026] During a raid at Abdulrahman al-Bilawi's house by Iraqi forces, a treasure trove of 160 computer flash sticks contained detailed information, including the names of foreign fighters, senior leaders, sources of inside ministry, and finances. The group made $36 million in looted antiquities just from Al-Nubuk.[1027] It was alleged that Westerners traveled to Turkey to purchase antiquities ranging from $100 for a Roman-era coin all the way to $100,000 for statues and rare manuscripts.[1028] The raid also revealed that senior ISIS commanders possessed artifacts for sale on the black market in order to enrich themselves.

information about the objects. The lack of transparency indicates that either Turkey doesn't take the illicit trade of antiquities seriously, or it fails to keep tabs on the smuggled objects it has recovered.[1032] Attorney Eyup Sabri Tinas from the border city of Urfa opined that smuggling cannot be entirely prevented, as many smugglers have political connections and relationships with the authorities in charge of monitoring them.[1033]

DEFEATING ISIS CULTURAL CLEANSING

Despite the loss of three major World Heritage sites to ISIS's cultural cleansing campaign, none of the opposing participants have made an effort to stop the marauding through military means. The airpower and intelligence capacity exist. Global political conferences and diplomats have discussed the damage to no end. There is a disgracefully insufficient level of cooperation between the world of heritage protection practitioners, the world's governments, and the American military coalition fighting ISIS. There must be an urgent revolution to identify, protect, and preserve the significant cultural artifacts in the Middle East combat zones. To that end some of the solutions that could  slow or stop the march of ISIS's attempts to culturally cleanse the Middle East and North Africa are clear.

INFLUENCE PUBLIC OPINION

The World Heritage protection community must band together and harness the world media to bring attention to what is happening on the ground in the Middle East, as well as link the destruction of heritage and culture to the next step—ethnic cleansing.

Historic heritage professionals must create coalitions with global citizens to bring awareness to the world in an effort to stop the destruction, vandalism, theft, and sale of historic artifacts and cultural objects. Some organizations have already taken up the banner. The Washington DC–based nonprofit group called the Antiquities Coalition is

spearheading and coordinating a global campaign against cultural cleansing. By harnessing the expertise of heritage experts, including archaeologists, anthropologists, art historians, curators, and archivists, the Antiques Coalition is attempting to mobilize others who will support the global effort to document, publicize, and identify the parties responsible for what the United Nations characterizes as "war crimes."

In April 2015, UNESCO, the Antiquities Coalition, and the Asia Institute held a ground-breaking conference called "Cultural Property Under Threat." The meeting brought together all of the Arab League cultural ministers in Cairo to discuss for the first time how to unify their efforts to stop ISIS from destroying the region's priceless cultural treasurers. They have started the process of a global movement, but far more needs to be done to make the general public as aware of blood antiquities as they are of blood diamonds.

Anyone who loves cultural treasures, art, and music must understand that the destruction of heritage is just a first step toward killing thousands and removing them from the history of the region.

RESTART THE "MONUMENTS MEN" PROGRAM

During World War II, Allied authorities recognized the significance of assigning specialized army officers to inform, advise, and assist combat commanders to identify and protect historical and archeological treasures. They were also to document the theft of stolen art, find caches of stolen archeological artifacts, and protect World Heritage with their lives. Today, we need another organization with the same mandate. The US Army recently investigated a renewal of this program, and one of their chief architects is Major Tommy Livoti. Major Livoti is an archeologist who was a combat-experienced Marine Force Reconnaissance officer and is now a US Army reserve officer specializing in heritage protection. A PhD candidate at the University of Montana, he received an assignment to investigate the feasibility of restarting the Monuments Men program and training Special Operations personnel on heritage protection. He believes that getting "Monuments Men" onto the staff of the Special Operations Task Force in Iraq and on the Joint Staff in Washington is imperative:

> The operational archaeologist will demonstrate to military leadership that implementing the simplest methods of cultural resource management into the military decision making process can protect cultural property and do so without compromising mission success, intelligence, and most importantly, protecting and saving human life in the combat zone.

The challenges that archaeologists and other heritage protectors will face in preserving cultural property in an asymmetric environment are the same challenges that face the Special Forces soldier on the ground. They must achieve a goal using precise applications of expert power. The new Monuments Men (and women) must fully integrate all resources into the military plan of action. This includes providing direct recommendations to the Pentagon's intent and schedule of operations. These efforts will help the military-political-diplomatic and intelligence decision makers and the heritage protection community to identify the crimes, interdict

distributors and middlemen who traffic in blood antiquities, and deny ISIS a major funding source.

FIGHT CLEANSING FROM THE SKY

To impact world opinion and incite horror, ISIS knows that they only have to get into a Toyota truck filled with explosives, enjoy a leisurely breakfast, and destroy a millennium-old icon while under the full view of US intelligence. Wide-area collections platforms such as the U-2 Dragon Lady reconnaissance aircraft as well as the Global Hawk drone with the Gorgon Stare long-look time video imager are already hovering over the battlefield, and it only takes reorienting some of the imagery analysis toward known heritage sites to detect unusual activity. When it comes to World Heritage sites, tasking a Predator or Reaper drone over the site and stopping destruction efforts are worth more than the cost of the operations time and weapons release. The target signature of ISIS forces is relatively easy to identify: Large collections of vehicles and armed men operating in proximity to World Heritage sites. Even individual units such as ISIS guards and looting-license checkers should be eliminated individually to make them aware that the site has now been designated as a kill zone. Should ISIS continue to press these sites, it makes the effort to destroy their local forces all that much easier.

The long-range and long-look advanced imagery systems such as gorgon stare do not give a "look through the straw" appreciation of the battlefield, but blanket the area with dozens of cameras simultaneously, and over time, and fuses these views of all observed activity into one large image. The sensors on the MQ-9 Reaper drone can be oriented to detect destruction preparations, looting, or propaganda events on or near World Heritage sites without taking any resources away from intelligence collection. When analysts have identified a threat to a World Heritage site, Pentagon planners must give strike priority to this threat. We must demonstrate to ISIS that war crimes against cultural heritage can have terminal consequences.

PART IV:
HOW THEY FIGHT

CHAPTER 15

GLOBAL STRATEGY OF ISIS

Our enemy is very adaptive. He may be an irregular
and he may be an insurgent, but he isn't dumb. These
are very, very clever people.[1034]
—Col. Len A. Blasiol of the U.S. Marine Corps
Concepts and Doctrine Division

UNDERSTANDING THE APOCALYPTIC RELIGIOUS BASIS OF ISIS

THE MANAGEMENT OF SAVAGERY

Ninety-six years ago, T. E. Lawrence, a brilliant English Arabist known as Lawrence of Arabia, laid out clearly what was going to happen to America in Iraq. He called it "a trap from which it will be hard to escape with dignity and honour."[1035] It is astounding how accurate he was in his assessment of the people of Mesopotamia. A veteran of the World War I Hejaz campaign on the Arabian Peninsula that made him famous, he had lived as an Arab. He knew the spirit of the people Britain was fighting in the 1920 Iraq insurgency and predicted it would not be a fair fight. In 2003, America and Britain chose to fight the same people, on the same ground, and in the exact same fashion. Accordingly in 2016 the same result is occurring. We are barely containing ISIS, once known as Al-Qaeda in Iraq. The rawness of their furious breakout from their Syrian civil war sanctuary in 2014 has given all pause to reassess if they really knew what the stakes were and what this enemy wants and will die for.

Small wars are brutal, dreadful affairs in which far more women and children are killed than the guerrillas or terrorists. An entire trove of historical studies exists in the Pentagon on the efficacy and difficulty of fighting this type of fight. America has fought similar wars in Nicaragua, Philippines, Dominica, Lebanon, and Somalia but somehow, in the face of the fresh memory of the enormous losses suffered in Vietnam, those histories were ignored in Iraq. That ignorance of the mindset of the enemy, the devotion to a cult ideology and their strategic goals have brought us back full circle to where we are trying to contain a new generation of Al-Qaeda in Iraq combined with the multi-decade veterans of the Saddam regime to create the most vicious insurgency since Pol Pot's Khmer Rouge.

The theo-political strategy of ISIS worldwide is the most important facet in understanding why they carry out tactical military operations the way they do. Like the rest of the Muslim world, they view their religion as a core component of their daily political and civil interactions. This is stipulated by the Qur'an. However, it's the attainment of

ISIS's doctrinal goals for a unified Muslim nation that will engage in a clash of civilizations with the West, rule with absolute control over all aspects of people's lives, and impose a variation of religion that scarcely resembles Islam.

Starting in 2003 with the opportunity of an American invasion of Iraq, then-Al Qaeda in Iraq, now ISIS, has been guided by a consistent and unwavering military strategy since al-Qaeda was founded in 1988. In my book *An End to Al-Qaeda: Destroying Bin Laden's Jihad and Restoring America's Honor*, I detailed the ideological underpinnings that led to the creation of the neo-Salafist philosophy and the religious motivations of why they fight. One aspect of that is the manual that all members of ISIS are required to study, Abu Bakr Naji's *Management of Savagery*. Actually named Muhammad Khalil al-Hakaymah, the manual was published by al-Qaeda in 2004 and was translated by Will McCants, one of the preeminent scholars on Salafist jihadist terrorism in the world. *Savagery* is a doctrine manual used by both groups to operationalize the goals of reestablishing the Caliphate and bringing about the end of days. The book is not about how to be a savage, though there is a section on how to be a cruel, heartless mass murderer and why it's necessary. Naji wrote that the collapse of empires after World Wars I and II and recent collapse of post-colonial governments creates "savagery" or chaos. Where there is Western initiated chaos and where nation-states fail then ISIS and its fighters fill the void. They view America as the last superpower and perceive perceive the United Nations as a global machine designed to keep Arab regimes in line.

The savagery they wish to manage is that of Western influence, chaos, and how to bring about the collapse of Western-backed Arab state so that they can fill the voids once chaos ensues.

Most importantly, *Savagery* spells out the political weaknesses of the United States and the West and explains how they must be exploited. Abu Bakr al-Baghdadi and ISIS are voracious consumers of Naji's doctrines. It reads more like a playbook for regional domination and the final clash of civilizations bin Laden so longed for. They make clear that their goals are medieval in origin but they use advanced social media, technology and of the modern world to spread the word.

Management of Savagery was not about how to be savages but to resist the savagery of the political world in the Islamic world. Dar al-Kuffar, Land of the Unbelievers and its political structures in the last century create "savagery." The Islamic knights are to confront the savagery and chaos of the West and "manage it" by providing stability, security, humanitarian aid, and Islamic law (Sharia) . In other words, the civilizations of the West are the Savages and must be destroyed.

9/11—THE SEPTEMBER OPERATION

Management of Savagery captures perfectly the doctrinal method enunciated by Osama bin Laden in his words, deeds, and writings, to force a confrontation by neo-Salafist forces throughout the Muslim world with America. The purpose of the 9/11 attacks was to force America to come to Afghanistan and to defeat them militarily in a clash of civilizations in the same way as the Afghan and Arab Mujahideen have done to the Soviet Union. Right up until his death in 2011, bin Laden believed this war caused the collapse of the Soviet Union (Naji refers to them as "the collapsed superpower") and that sustaining a Middle East–wide jihad would do the same to the West.

Starting with the 9/11 attacks bin Laden believed that by forcing the West, particularly the United States, to fight land wars throughout the Muslim world and bringing down what he saw as illegitimate Muslim governments, especially Saudi Arabia, would lead to their economic and political exhaustion. Once their economies were brought to the brink through extreme oil prices, war weariness from fighting his jihadis across the Middle East and Africa, and lack of political will, there would eventually be a political collapse of Western Christian civilization. After that a new Muslim world would flourish and neo-Salafist Islam would be the last religion standing. As the previous chapters have shown, the military strategy was to confront, engage, and kill to achieve these goals.

The terror spanning across Iraq, Syria, and other parts of the Levant,—carried out by the Islamic State of Iraq and Syria (ISIS), the jihadi Al-Nusra Front in Syria and the usurpation of Saddam's most evil henchmen as their most trusted advisors—is a critical part of creating the neo-Salafist state led by al-Baghdadi.

To the terrorists of ISIS, the Iraq-Syria battlefield is yet another of the expanding "new fields of Jihad." As far as the individual fighter is concerned, he is engaged in spreading a new variation of Islam that is both originalist and radical.

They believe they are living a lifestyle in the direct footsteps of the original companions of the Prophet Mohammed. This is called Salafism and is popular in Saudi Arabia. However, the way they interpret it is that the companions of the Prophet would be ruthless mass murderers who should have killed all before them. They have taken up the mantle and they believe that this is pleasing to God. That is called neo-Salafism. Add this to their own cult practice of declaring Muslims infidels and killing them, or Takfir, one finds their interpretation of Islam is almost wholly unrecognizable from mainstream Islamic practices apart.

In ISIS, this unwavering devotion to mayhem and destruction of the armed Jihad as a form of worship to God holds the key to saving Islam from itself and bringing about the cleansing of the earth through judgement day.

To further their strategic goals, ISIS doctrine believes that they will assist in the following prophetic events:

1. **Establish**—ISIS announces the return of the caliphate with the purpose of joining the Muslim world under the control of its caliph, who will be the only voice of Islam.
2. **Conquer**—ISIS believes it has created the first of three expeditionary armies to prepare the Muslim world for war with the Christian world. They will use these forces to provoke a clash of civilizations with the West. They will seize countries one by one to expand the Islamic caliphate and provide a base of operations for the Muslim people. They will also eliminate all borders and agreements dictated by the 1916 Sykes-Picot Treaty.
3. **Prepare**—They will prepare their Armies of Islam to fight against the polytheists of India and then await the prophecy on the return

of the Christian armies of the West and await the return of the Mahdi (Savior).

4. **Arrival**—With the arrival of the Mahdi they will await the signs of tribulation and fight the Army of Rome at the Battle of Dabiq.
5. **Dabiq**—The Muslim army, with the Mahdi, will confront Christianity in the Battle of Dabiq.
6. **Dijjal**—The Masih al-Dijjal (False Savior) or anti-Christ will come from Khorsan (Persia).
7. **Rejoice**—The Misih Isa (The Savior Jesus) will return to Damascus to lead the war against the Dijjal. Peace and harmony will rule till judgement day (Youm al-Qiyamah).

GLOBAL "LONG WAR" STRATEGY

ISIS strategic battle plan is based on the execution of what they believe is God's will as prophesied in the Qur'an. However, though some politicians think this is part of a global Islamic plan, it is in fact a microcosm of men who believe that they can change the world to fit the Qur'an's writings in opposition to all that the rest of the book stands for.

ISIS has hyper-operationalized Osama bin Laden's strategic plan to restore the Islamic caliphate and prepare for the tribulations that would make the end of days. They formulated two strategies: a military strategy, which encompassed their political structure, and a media strategy (see Chapter 19).

To effect this they are conducting a worldwide campaign to defeat traditional Islam and change it into a extremist variant where bin Laden's holy war is never ending and every Muslim must be prepared to die in suicide terrorism. Recruits are exposed and buy into the ideology, they abandon their families and eschew all belief in moderate Islam. They each desire only to worship God through a swift, explosive death that kills others in the process. This is what we are dealing with and it cannot be stopped by military force alone.

Neo-Salafist ideology claims Islam has not been pure since the seventh century and they will do the purifying even if it means destruction of centuries of the tradition. Additionally, a core tenet of al-Qaedaism is the direct confrontation and destruction of Shi'ite Islam wherever it is found. They believe Shi'ite worshipers are not Muslims at all but religious traitors. They do not believe they can ever be converted back to the Sunnah interpretation or live a repentant neo-Salafist life so they are worthy only of extinction. This is why the foot soldier of the ISIS jihad feels nothing at slitting the throat of Shi'ite Iraqis. In spite of what the Qur'an states, the same fate has befallen Christians, Alawites, Druze, Jews, Hindus, Buddhists, and any Muslim they decide is not part of their confession.

Well before his death, bin Laden saw the American invasion of Iraq as a blessing, even consequential than their presence in Afghanistan. An al-Qaeda jihad in Iraq had the potential for creating a true Islamic state based on al-Qaeda doctrine deep in the heart of the traditional, Sunnah Islamic bastion while confronting the apostates of Shi'ite Islam. In 2011 the Syrian civil war allowed ISIS to leapfrog into Central Syria and erase the border between Sunnah Iraq and Sunnah Syria. Oxford scholar Aymenn Jawad al-Tamimi notes: "The issue is that ISIS is defining itself as the one and only true Islamic state; in their view, waging war on ISIS thus constitutes waging war on 'God and His Messenger.'"[1036]

Many political scientists, pundits, and even some scholars believe that this has little to do with religion and more to do with achieving power, wealth, resources, and control over people. The argument goes they may be Muslims but they are just power-hungry madmen. There is some strength to this because human failings are the cause of all strife. However, the ISIS brand of cultism is based on a corrupted interpretation and only the cult leader, or in this case God himself, can stop the process.

Spectacular terror attacks are necessary to keep the West in a state of terror, keep their recruiting base motivated, and keep the suicide bomber rolls full.

Bin Laden called his religious struggle against the West, and particularly America. the "long war." The "Islamic State" is but one example of a potentially permanently inflamed Muslim world unless we assist in curbing the extremists, 'attempts to invoke God's pleasure through murder. America must step up to the plate and help Muslim governments and groups to cut that string. We must help the Muslim world propagate ISIS's spiritual illegitimacy in Islam.

In fact the strategy of ISIS is to use Islam as a disguise to inflict terror and pain on innocent people in order to achieve cult goals which offend the average Muslim. ISIS depends on the wordy exhortations and smooth delivery of Qur'anic quotes to deceive the people into believing that their strategy to jumpstart the end of times is not only what God wants, it's what he commands.

New York Times journalist David Rohde, a hostage of the Taliban, wrote about the ignorant mindset of his captives. Rohde wrote, "When I asked him why he wanted to die, he replied that living in this world was a burden for any true Muslim. Heaven was his goal, he said. Earthly relationships with his parents and siblings did not matter." This is an example of how ISIS makes men into cultists. Islam rejects suicide bombing in all its forms, and rejection of the family breaks the bonds of Islamic brotherhood and love of family for God's sake, which is held in the highest esteem in God's eyes. The doctrine of the cult is to care not a whit for the actual tenets of Islam.

Since 9/11 we have spent almost two decades re-learning all of our glaring weaknesses in facing asymmetric guerrilla operations. So few of our politicians, warriors, or citizens understand or can explain the actual spiritual and political basis that makes the enemy so motivated to kill that the enemy's mere image in social media is force multiplier. They are so feared in some quarters that there has been a small but vocal movement to start negotiating with the Islamic State as if it is actually a state. Others feel it is better to walk away rather than confront this threat. They are deluded and should not be taken seriously. ISIS's religious and apocalyptic vision is the heart of the military strategy of ISIS. It is also their most vulnerable aspect and is critical to defeating them.

ISIS'S MILITARY STRATEGY

The first component of ISIS's military strategy to achieve their religious goals is to perform asymmetric combat, or terrorist judo, to strike the west in such a way that large forces which cannot be sustained are forced to spread throughout the region. This will give ISIS "home court" advantage.

With this in mind it is clear that ISIS is not striking at America out of desperation. The calculation of a Christmas day massacre with a bomb over a major city or the slaughter of disabled people and their nurses is not just to punish the West or project strength. They are acts carefully designed to incite Western hatred against traditional Islam and innocent Muslims. With this hatred harnessed, Muslims may see ISIS as an only option. Joining ISIS would hasten the apocalypse they so desperately long for.

Force America to Be Humiliated and Disrespected

Al-Naji channeled bin Laden's understanding of the critical necessity of making the United States and the West spread its fear of Islam across the Middle East without any thought or consideration to their their actions. The after-effects of political and military conflict are stupendous and ISIS relies on political tirades that are boorish, racist, and xenophobic. Naji stated "Destroy a large part of the respect for America and spread confidence in the souls of Muslims . . . ." He also recommended harnessing the strength of the Western media and making them a plaything in the hands of the insurgent.

America Abandons the Muslim World

The next goal is to get America so deeply embroiled that they will be broken economically and retreat into isolationism. This is a key goal as ISIS wants the weaken and topple allies and unify the lands that they seize. The best way to achieve that is to attack the West so forcefully that it will "Force America to abandon its war against Islam by proxy and force it to attack directly . . ."

Force America to Fight

ISIS believes it is their duty to reveal the inherent weakness of the US protection in the Muslim world. They amplify this weakness though mastery of social media and baiting the US to fight them directly. Undermining

---

Apocalyptic Basis of ISIS's Expeditionary Warfare Operations

Allah's Messenger said: You will attack Arabia and Allah will enable you to conquer it, then you would attack Persia (Iran) and He would make you to conquer it. Then you would attack Rome (Italy/Europe) and Allah will enable you to conquer it, then you would attack the Dajjal (in Israel) and Allah will enable you to conquer him.

American resolve is a key lesson bin Laden learned in Iraq, and ISIS is capitalizing on it through their absolute information dominance of social media and their capacity to steer the global news narrative. Breaking American resolve through "anti-willingness" campaigns is a core component of the doctrine:

> If the number of Americans killed is one tenth of the number of Russians killed in Afghanistan and Chechnya, they will flee, heedless of all else. That is because the current structure of the American and Western military is not the same as the structure of their military in the era of colonialism. They reached a stage of effeminacy which made them unable to sustain battles for a long period of time and they compensate for this with a deceptive media halo.[1037]

Combat Doctrine for Achieving Strategic Goals

To achieve a foothold in regions where there is "savagery," ISIS establishes itself in locations where the vacuum is greatest. For example, they set up operations in Afghanistan in Nangarhar province, which has some of the toughest terrain in the Hindu Kush; in Libya they were in Derna halfway up the coast between Benghazi and Tobruq; in Egypt they moved into the remote parts of the Sinai peninsula. Once there, they arm themselves, create a community, and then start destabilization ("vexation") operations against the government security forces and personalities. Once the group has been firmly entrenched and a weapons and personnel pipeline has been established, they will then strike in multiple locations and seize terrain and then cities. The process is repeated in the next nation where chaos and political instability give them another opportunity. Usually this process takes many years, but for ISIS they were handed Iraq on a silver platter by the 2003 invasion. The Syrian civil war, the Libyan post-war dithering, and the Yemeni rebellion gave them a foothold in the chaos that followed the collapse of the regimes in the 2011 Arab Spring uprisings.

Tribal aspects of their doctrine must be considered as well. The al-Qaeda tactic of marrying into tribes and having children is now considered mandatory policy throughout the "Islamic State." In political vacuums of failing states, there is always an amalgam of religious, tribal, or monetary undercurrents that make safe bets disasters and impossible deals surprisingly doable. What you see is almost always what you do not get. As the Kipling poem says, "... and the epitaph drear: A Fool lies here who tried to hustle the East."

BRUTALITY IN ISIS OPERATIONS

The question so often asked is why does ISIS behead innocent people, kill whom they please, and rape and sell women into slavery? Again, it's not pleasure so much as it is written doctrine on how to conduct combat and post-combat behavior. ISIS believes that they must be as brutal as possible if only to show that they have the depth of spirit and commitment to fight to restore the caliphate. Using a circular logic they instruct their commanders to "Conduct warfare in a brutal method in order to lessen the brutality of the West." The ends most certainly justify the means in ISIS doctrine so long as it achieves the goals of provoking a clash of civilizations and bringing America to their home turf. They also stipulate that so long as the killings are within the laws of Sharia then they are fully authorized. This allows a wide range of tortures and behaviors that are literally medieval.

Another component is what I call the "Colonel Kurtz" school of warfare. ISIS is like the insane the movie "Apocalypse Now" officer in the movie *Apocalypse Now* who surrendered all rules and abandoned all common decency in order to achieve his goals of making the enemy "fear us."

ISIS too believes that as men they must act and behave beyond the pale in order to remove softness and maintain the physical and mental toughness to perform the acts that must be done to bring about God's will. *Savagery* section 4 notes, "If we are not violent in our jihad and if softness seizes us, that will be a major factor in the loss of the element of strength ..."

IN THEIR OWN WORDS: GOAL OF THE KHALIFA

The goal of establishing the Khilafah has always been one that occupied the hearts of the mujahidin since the revival of jihad this century. It was always a hope the mujahidin were certain of attaining, for Allah's Messenger (sallallahu 'alayhi wa sallam) had promised them with it. He said, "There will be prophethood for as long as Allah wills it to be, then He will remove it when He wills. Then there will be Khilafah on the prophetic methodology and it will be for as long as Allah wills, then He will remove it when He wills. Then there will be harsh kingship for as long as Allah wills, then He will remove it when He wills. Then there will be tyrannical kingship for as long as Allah wills, then He will remove it when He wills. Then there will be Khilafah on the prophetic methodology" [Ahmad]. It was also reported that Anas Ibn Malik (radiyallahu 'anh) said, "There will be prophethood and mercy, then Khilafah and mercy, then harsh kingship, then 35 dabiq tyrannical kingship, then tawaghit" [As-Sunanul- Waridatu fil-Fitan - Abu 'Amr ad-Dani]. However, the question that engaged some of the mujahidin was how they would achieve their goal. During the jihad in Afghanistan against the communists, many of the muhajirin found themselves fighting a war similar to the one being fought in Sham now. Parties with different backgrounds fought a "common" enemy, ignoring all matters that distinguished them from each other, even if those matters were an obstacle in the pursuit of Khilafah. The biggest of these distinguishing factors were nationalism that tainted many of the banners and parties in Afghanistan, in addition to serious innovations that destroyed the creed and healthy body of the Muslim jama'ah required for reviving the Khilafah. Still Allah ('azza wa jall) blessed the jihad, and many of its leaders and soldiers would later become the bridges upon which jihad would pass over towards the awaited Khilafah. One of these many important bridges was that of the mujaddid (reviver) Abu Mus'ab az-Zarqawi (rahimahullah). Learning from the lessons he gained from Afghanistan and elsewhere, he knew that Khilafah could not be established except through a jama'ah that gathered upon the Kitab and Sunnah with the understanding of the Salaf, free from the extremities of the murji'ah and khawarij. This jama'ah's most important goal would be to revive tawhid especially in matters ignored and abandoned by "Islamic" parties in our times – matters relating to wala', bara', hukm (ruling), and tashri' (legislation). The jama'ah would use the absent obligation of jihad as its fundamental means for change, implementing Allah's command, {And fight them until there is no fitnah and [until] the religion, all of it, is for Allah} [Al-Anfal: 39]. Its jihad would be based upon hijrah, bay'ah, sam' (listening), ta'ah (obedience), and i'dad (training), leading to ribat and qital (fighting), then Khilafah or shahadah.—*Dabiq* magazine

TERRORISM STRATEGY

A DJINN THAT DETESTS ITS BOTTLE

The West and America in particular have become blind to the fact that these insurgents, no matter how despicable or savage their acts, are human beings engaged in mortal combat. They will do what they must to achieve their goals. If we insist on ignoring their strategies, tactics, and goals and continue to underestimate their determination to kill us, then we will be fighting them for a very, very long time.

I know personally that terrorism is effective in guerrilla war. When conducted with forethought and malice, terrorism can produce astounding casualties and have strategic impact no matter how small the victim base. On my first overseas intelligence collections mission in Beirut, Lebanon, in 1983, America lost seventeen diplomatic staff among the sixty-three people killed at the Embassy. A few months later 241 Marines would die in a single terrorist SVBIED in less than one minute. On September 11, 2001, almost three thousand Americans were murdered in a matter of hours. The avoidable losses in these and other instances were because the political decision makers either never studied the history of the threats, felt impervious to the threat, or had ignored the warning signs from their own intelligence about the threat.

Even now as ISIS storms across the Middle East we appear to have forgotten that America lost more soldiers in the Iraqi insurgency than we did civilians in the 9/11 attacks.

Historians will not be hard-pressed to determine if the invasion of Iraq was actually the heart of a well-thought-out plan for transforming the Middle East writ large, or if it was a massive form of ill-conceived national revenge. Whatever the intent, good or bad, the invasion of Iraq was not part of what should have been priority number one—a plan to get the true perpetrators of the 9/11 attacks. ISIS is well aware that provocation attacks work very well on the American psyche. As we have learned, it is core doctrine to to draw Americans into an apocalypse-inciting disaster. In order to fulfill al-Qaeda's and ISIS's apocalyptic vision, they need a ground war. They use terrorism strategically and tactically to achieve this goal. This is why ISIS has executed over 3,500 people since they took over parts of Iraq and Syria in 2014. The shock value of terrorism is a force multiplier. They have set the standard for people they confront—accept subjugation or death.[1038]

The invasion of Iraq created a perfect storm of vicious, battle-hardened anti-American terrorists. They are presently a source of global terrorist weapons supply, and their "caliphate" is a crucible in which to forge a new generation of terrorist leadership in the Middle East. The invasion did not meet its primary goal of finding and disarming Iraq from of WMDs, but it did create the opportunity for both Iraqi and foreign fighters to develop operational terrorism experience and test their mettle in combat on a scale that could never have been possible after the loss of Afghanistan in 2001. US intelligence was well aware of the potential. In 2005 the CIA's National Intelligence Council stated, "Iraq has now replaced Afghanistan as the training ground for the next generation of 'professionalized terrorists' providing a recruitment ground and the op-portunity for enhancing technical skills."[1039]

With regard to terrorism, the CIA report also believed that "the urban nature of the war in Iraq was helping combatants learn how to carry out assassination, kidnappings, car bombings, and other kinds of attacks that were never the staple of the fighting in Afghanistan during the anti-Soviet campaigns of the 1980s."

Somehow, these prescient assessments, written by some of the best minds in the intelligence community, were discounted by many Washington decision-makers and attacked by politicians as "failures."

ISIS counts among its number the terror veterans of Al-Qaeda in Iraq, the best jihadist fighters from Syria's al-Nusra Front, as many as ten thousand fresh foreign fighters from across the world, and the entirety of the Iraqi Sunnah insurgents, most of whom were ex-Ba'athist fighters in groups like the Jaysh al-Mujahideen and Ansar al-Sunnah, among others. They have created an effective army of cultist foot soldiers and a terrorist force of "Ghost Soldiers."

Not all of these groups were motivated by al-Baghdadi's vision for a Sunnah caliphate, but over time they had to yield in order to survive. For the Sunnah Muslims of Syria and Iraq, the image of a Sunnah state from Damascus to Baghdad was not hard to resist. In the end they all joined ISIS and helped them become the most experienced and ruthless terrorists in the Middle East by incorporating all of the civil controls Saddam's intelligence agencies learned over forty years. The one skill they brought to the table was decades of government intelligence agencies' expertise at fomenting both state and political terrorism.

TERROR SHOCK VALUE (TSV) IN ISIS OPERATIONS

A fanatical, corrupt, religious passion informs the profound belief of ISIS is that they will die in jihad and go to heaven, or rule and impose their version of Islam on earth. This passion is stoked by the inherent belief that that only the fighting members of their group are allowed to truly understand what they believe is the purest, truest form of Islam—neo-Salafist cultism. Harnessed and given weapons, they are trained to tap into an unquenchable thirst to constantly prove their loyalty by killing all opposition at the street level and create an effect called Terror Shock Value.

Terror Shock Value (TSV) is often seen in the urban-warfare phase of irregular terror-based forces such as Boko Haram, Shabaab of Somalia, the FARC of Colombia, the Taliban, the Tamil Tigers, and the Vietcong to name a few. Using terrorism in a combat or near-combat environment gives the attacker a powerful combat multiplier that enhances the psychological impact of anything they do, be it negotiations or executions. In Iraq and Syria, the TSV of ISIS gave them the ability to affect political decisions on a tribal, regional, and national scale. This allowed them to seize large parts of both nations. After beheading two hundred Syrian soldiers captured in Raqqa, no one wanted to cross them or become a victim of their behaviors.

TERROR AS OPERATION TOOL IN *THE MANAGEMENT OF SAVAGERY*

In the jihadist playbook *Management of Savagery*, terrorism is considered just another tool in the apocalyptic vision tool belt. It can act as both bait and trap for all of the enemies of the Caliphate. Naji wrote that it was the mission of the jihadists to conduct themselves in such a masterfully murderous manner as to save the world from the horrific fate of living like Westerners. In their estimation, it's better to destroy the entire world and end Islam than to allow one Muslim to live a peaceful life in the land of the unbelievers. Naji wrote:

> The management of savagery [a.k.a. chaos of western democracy] is the next stage that the [Muslim people] will pass through and it is considered the most critical stage. If we succeed in the management of this savagery, that stage (by the permission of God) will be a bridge to the Islamic state which has been awaited since the fall of the caliphate. If we fail—we seek refuge with God from that—it does not mean end of the matter; rather, this failure will lead to an increase in savagery!! [1040]

This is why ISIS will use any and all weapons at their disposal. The terror and brutality of 9/11 and the al-Qaeda playbook are just the beginning; it must be a start to save all others. They believe they must burn down Islam and the West to save the world. This cult interpretation of the Tribulations predicted in the Qu'ran is a clear reason why the West must be destroyed. Again Naji makes this clear:

> This increase in savagery, which may result from failure, is not the worst thing that can happen now or in the previous decade (the 1990s) and those before it. Rather, the most abominable of the levels of savagery is (still) less than stability under the order of unbelief [niz'm al-kufr] by (several) degrees. [1041]

CLASSES OF TERROR OPERATIONS

ISIS and al-Qaeda interpret terror operations to be of two classes: Strategic Strikes and Qualitative Operations.

Global Impact Terrorism Operations (Amaliyat al-Strategiya)

Strategic strike missions such as the September 11, 2001 attacks are seen by the jihadist movement as being of such global import that virtually all groups are ordered to not carry them out. As a strategic planner with a vision, Osama bin Laden wanted to steer the West toward extreme decisions implicating several generations, such as the invasion of Iraq and the financial meltdown of 2008. He learned that his plan worked very well and that these missions must be used sparingly so that the full commitment of the United States would not be harnessed.

Qualitative Terrorism Operations (Amaliyah Na'awiyyah)

Terrorist operations that have a localized impact but have globally measurable metrics, such as the bombing of Beirut in November 2015 and the October 2015 suicide bombing that killed ninety-five people in Istanbul, were of high quality but did not have global impact. They made their point that the nations bordering ISIS's caliphate will bear the same damage as the Americans and Europeans.

Naji called regional terrorist attacks "qualitative attacks." These are missions where the political impact is measurable and thus of high quality in the mission to tame the West.

> I do not mean qualitative operations like the operation of September. Thinking too much about doing something like the latter might impede the undertaking of qualitative operations that are smaller in size. Likewise, if there is an opportunity for doing something like it, it is better not to do so in haste without knowing the opinion of the High Command . . . [1042]

This did not mean that terror missions had to be on the scale and size of 9/11 to have strategic impact. In fact, 2015 has seen five qualitative terror operations of small scale that approach the strategic impact of the 9/11 attacks for the victim countries: the March 2015 attacks on Europeans, the June 2015 massacres of British subjects in Tunisia, the October 2015 Metrojet bombing over the Sinai, the November 2015 Paris attacks, and the December 2015 massacre in San Bernardino. These attacks are indicative that ISIS is clearly carrying out a strategic terror campaign they have yet to publicly reveal; they love campaigns. Carried over into 2016, this may well be called Operation "Provoking the Crusader Alliance."

CHAPTER 16

THE WEAPONS OF ISIS

HISTORY

Unlike conventional armies, which utilize weapons and vehicles manufactured from factories and supported by various nations, ISIS doesn't have that capacity or logistics, and so the weapons and the materials used by the militants were all captured from conflict regions in Syria, Iraq, and Libya or exported to the region via middlemen through borders from Turkey. *Huffington Post* reported that the most common sources of weapons used by ISIS militants were manufactured in the United States and captured in Iraq, and Russian-made goods captured from the Syrian army.[1043] Conflict Armament Research suggests that many arms given to the moderate Syrian rebels by the allied nations are now in possession of ISIS, who overran the rebels. Much of the ammunition was manufactured in Russia but distributed to allied nations by the US. Nevertheless, weapons from other nations are also in the ISIS arsenal:

1. Austria
2. Belgium
3. China
4. Croatia
5. France
6. Germany
7. Iran
8. Italy
9. Poland
10. Romania
11. Russia
12. South Africa
13. Soviet Union
14. United Arab Emirates
15. United States
16. Yugoslavia

The weapons utilized by ISIS were overwhelmingly captured from the Iraqi military and police headquarters and checkpoints, the Assad regime military, the Free Syrian Army, or from other major players fighting in the Syrian conflict. ISIS has also acquired weapons from the black market, but it's simpler to get them from arsenals and depots. ISIS also acquired or captured weapons destined for its rebel opponents.

According to Bellingcat Investigative Project, ISIS had access to a variety of weapons such as rocket launchers, grenade launchers, and American-made M60 machine guns from Saudi Arabia. According to Bellingcat founder Eliot Higgins, weapons were first sold to Saudi Arabia and then flown to Turkey, then smuggled into Syria, where they were either sold or given to ISIS by sympathizers in other rebel groups.[1044] In 2013 the *New York Times* examined air traffic data composed of 160 cargo plane flights by Jordan, Qatar, and Saudi Arabia that had all landed in Turkish airports. Reports suggest that these contained equipment for the Syrian rebels fighting the Assad regime. Despite having no indication suggesting that those nations support ISIS by supplying equipment, the militants still get their hands on them.[1045]

The number of weapons in the hands of ISIS is hard to estimate and not easy to come by. Anthony Cordesman, a security analyst at the Washington-based center for Strategic and International Studies, said that the weapons and equipment taken by ISIS is worth roughly three to four divisions' worth of equipment and was stored in at least three depots.[1046] During the capture of the city of Mosul in 2014, ISIS took 2,300 Humvees, over 100 wheeled vehicles, and tons of tracked vehicles. Most of the vehicles were acquired from Camp Speicher near Tikrit.[1047] One estimate totaled the loss at $656.4 million, but this is only a fraction of the cost, as much more US-made equipment is in ISIS's hands[1048] and does not include the amount of equipment given to the Free Syrian Army and other factions that subsequently went to ISIS.

Equipment	Amount	Per Unit Price	Total Price
Humvee armored vehicles	2,300	$70,000	$161 million
M1A1 tanks	40	$4.3 million	$172 million
M198 howitzer	52	$527,337	$27.4 million
Army machine guns	74,000	$4,000	$296 million

VEHICLES

TOYOTA TRUCKS & TECHNICALS

The LandCruiser 70 and the Hilux are a series of compact pickup trucks marketed by the Japanese manufacturer Toyota. The Toyota pickup has a reputation for toughness and does particularly well in the tough terrain of Syria, Iraq, Libya, Yemen, and Afghanistan. It also makes regular appearances in ISIS propaganda videos.

When ISIS paraded through the center of its capital, Raqqa, two-thirds of all the vehicles were Toyota pickup trucks. Despite having confiscated all of the heavy military vehicles from the Iraqi forces, ISIS has remained a low-tech force that can hide in the urban areas by using civilian vehicles and converting them into "technicals" when necessary. "Technical" is an African term to describe the hybrid civilian/military vehicles made popular by the Somali militias of the *Black Hawk Down* era. It is usually an open-backed civilian pickup truck with a machine gun, antiaircraft gun, or a piece of light artillery mounted in the truck bed. Other popular vehicles are Land Rovers, Isuzus, Mitsubishis, Hyundais, and Chinese Great Wall Deer pickups.[1049]

US officials asked Toyota how ISIS got their hands on numerous new SUVs and Toyotas. The company doesn't know, but Iraqi military spokesman Brigadier General Saad Maan believes that the "vehicles have been smuggled into the country by middlemen."[1050] During 2014–2015, an Australian newspaper reported that 800 Toyota trucks were missing from regular inventories and might have been exported to Iraq.[1051] After the 2003 invasion and the withdrawal of our troops in 2011, the coalition gave Toyotas and technicals to the Iraqi police. In April 2014, Public Radio International published a report noting that the US State Department also delivered forty-three Toyota LandCruiser 70 trucks to the Free Syrian Army as part of the non-lethal aid to Syrian rebels.[1052] The US was not the sole supplier, as the British government also supplied the rebels with Toyotas. As ISIS advanced to different regions in Iraq, police and military units retreated, leaving behind an array of vehicles, including the Toyotas given to the Iraqi police forces. The vehicles given to the Free Syrian Army by the US and British governments were likely captured by ISIS.[1053] Oubai Shahbander, a Washington-based advisor to the Syrian National Coalition, said that the pickup trucks represent a "force multiplier" that could be used for both humanitarian and military purposes.[1054]

The ISIS militants in Iraq, Syria, Egypt, Yemen, Afghanistan, and Libya have all been using both the older and newer versions of Hilux. Toyota has a strict policy against selling vehicles that could potentially find a home in the hands of paramilitary or terrorists, but ISIS still managed to get them into their arsenal. Mark Wallace, former US ambassador to the United Nation, stated on TV that those Toyota trucks became "almost part of ISIS brand."[1055]

ISIS uses the Toyotas to convey militants and as technical vehicles by screwing a variety of heavy weapons on the rear of the truck bed and adding the seal of the "caliphate." The number of Toyotas used by ISIS is unknown, but could be anything from the hundreds to the thousands.

Technicals are commonly used by rebels, irregular armies, and terrorists due to their speed, mobility, and ability to strike enemies from unexpected directions. ISIS technicals could be compared with a lateen-sail armed dhow of the nineteenth century in terms of simplicity, capacity, and speed. The only disadvantage is that technicals are soft-skinned civilian vehicles that do not offer good protection to the crew and passengers, who are vulnerable to heavier weapons mounted on Humvees and MRAP's or even rifle fire.[1056]

Ford exported large quantities of the F-350 extended wheelbase double cab truck to the Iraq security forces, including the army, police, and oilfield police forces. Hundreds were fully armored. Hundreds fell to ISIS and created another fleet of technicals. Though not considered as reliable, they provide heavy lift capacity for squads of four to six men. Many editions are armored or semi-armored and can be used in a VIP protection role or as the basis for SVBIEDs.

ARMORED FIGHTING VEHICLES, TRUCKS, JEEPS, AND HUMVEES

ISIS has been known to use various US and allied nations–manufactured vehicles. The US vehicles include the M1114 armored Humvees, wheeled and tracked vehicles, and five- to six-ton trucks. The number and type of vehicles ISIS captured during the fall of Mosul is unknown, but various reports give colossal estimates. In 2008, the US and Iraq signed three contracts for the sale of vehicles and other equipment. On April 22, 2009, the US exported 5,000 Humvees and by July 2009, the Iraqi forces had 8,000 Humvees.[1057] During the withdrawal of US troops from Iraq in 2011, the US government sold the Iraqi government 3,500 Humvees, of which 3,000 were armored.

As ISIS captured wide swaths of Iraq and Syria, the spoils of war included US-manufactured armored vehicles left behind in Iraq and Syrian army armored vehicles supplied to the al-Assad regime from Russia. The list below is not comprehensive; the losses to ISIS may well be higher, and many of their vehicles may have been lost in fighting, inoperable due to a lack of parts, and destroyed by coalition air power.

Armored Fighting Vehicles			
Name	**Type**	**Manufacturer**	**Number Captured**
MT-LB	Armored Personnel Carrier	Russia	50
M1117 ASV	Armored Security Vehicle	USA	47
BMP-1	Armored Personnel Carrier	Russia	7
M113	Armored Personnel Carrier	USA	82
BTR-80	Armored Personnel Carrier	Ukraine	4

IEDS

SVBIEDS—SUICIDE VEHICLE-BORNE IMPROVISED EXPLOSIVE DEVICES (CAR BOMBS)

Not all of the vehicles captured by ISIS were used for conveying equipment and men. Many of the armored vehicles were transformed into Suicide Vehicle-Borne Improvised Explosive Devices (SVBIEDs). Insurgents used several hundred suicide car bombs against the coalition occupying Iraq and Afghanistan from 2003 to 2011. Frontal assaults with SVBIEDs and VBIEDs are a "poor man's" air strike. Daniel Gouré from the Lexington Institute stated, "What IS lacked with indirect fire support and airpower was made up with IEDs and VBIEDs."[1058] Marine Corps Brigadier General Thomas Weidley noted that SVBIEDs have functioned similarly as "high end strike weaponry" for ISIS.[1059]

When attacking well-defended bases, ISIS relied heavily on breaching gates and perimeters using SVBIEDs. Identical suicide truck bomb tactics have been seen by ISIS organizations in Iraq, Syria, Libya, Egypt, Nigeria, and Yemen. There are three main benefits of using armored vehicles as SVBIEDs:

- The main body of the vehicle safeguards the explosives.
- The driver is protected from direct fire before he can detonate the explosives.
- The vehicle can carry a large amount of explosives.

In Iraq and Syria, ISIS similarly captured roughly 100 vehicles. Most of the tracked vehicles were armored personnel carriers like M1113, which they did not want to operate as personnel movers, so they were changed into SVBIEDs.

ISIS SVBIEDs are varied in type, but they have been using primarily US-made equipment because the US vehicles are not as simple for mechanics to repair, and parts are scarce; therefore, they put these captured trucks into service as rolling bomb platforms. The types of trucks observed include:

Iraqi army Humvee captured by ISIS is paraded in Mosul. Iraq lost 2,300 Humvee armored vehicles when they abandoned their positions.

A captured Iraqi army M-113.

An M-35 truck captured in Iraq symbolically crosses the Sykes-Picot border between Iraq and Syria.

M-1152 Humvee captured from Iraq.

An Iraqi army MTVR heavy truck. These have been converted into suicide truck bombs or SVBIEDs.

Captured Iraqi army M-1114 up-armored Humvee.

SVBIED—Sedan: Most suicide bombs are sedans with a large payload of explosive hidden in the trunk and under the back seat. This gives them a distinctive lower-to-the-ground profile over the rear axles, a key sign of an SVBIED.

SBVIED—Bongo: The ubiquitous KIA Bongo flatbed truck is also a larger-capacity payload carrier, but the explosives are more susceptible to small arms fire.

SVBIED—Minivan: The minivan taxi is found everywhere in the Middle East, Asia, and Africa. They can carry unusually high numbers of people, but can also move over a ton of explosive material. If disguised as a "women's only" taxi, they can close on a target discreetly.

SVBIED Dumptruck/Cement Mixer/Water Tanker: Large-scale industrial construction vehicles have been used to attack structures and

ISIS converted this water tanker into a massive suicide bomb. The grating is to stop anti-tank rockets and the steel plate is to ram through gates.

ISIS converted this dump truck into an armored suicide truck bomb.

An Iraqi police Ford F-350 truck converted into an armored suicide truck bomb.

A Caterpillar 789 mining dump truck converted into a massive suicide bomb. It has a capacity of 150 tons of explosives.

military bases in Syria, Iraq, and Libya. The Caterpillar 789 mining haul trucks can carry 150 of tons of explosives, and when steel plate covers the driver's cab they are impervious to gunfire. Even if they detonate far away from the target, the explosion can still bring down several apartment-block-sized buildings.

SV-BMP: Captured Syrian and Iraqi BMP armored personnel carriers have been used in Northern Iraq and Syria as highly mobile armored bombs. The SV-BMP is usually plated with sheet steel to protect it from direct hits by an RPG grenade launcher. These distinctive plates are a sure sign that the vehicle is a bomb.

SV-M 113: Like the Russian BMP, ISIS frequently uses the American M113 armored personnel carrier as a rolling suicide bomb. ISIS prefers the M113 for its ability to cross terrain rapidly and directly attack targets.

Bombvee: Uparmored Humvees are used with large flat steel plates on all sides and narrow view slit for driver. Filled with one ton of explosives, it is effective as a fast, short-distance suicide bomb.

A Caterpillar 950 Wheel Loader was armored as a dual-role combat breaching vehicle and suicide truck bomb.

An M-1114 up-armored Humvee is converted into a "Bombvee" variant suicide truck bomb. Armored plating on the front is to ram into gates.

A Caterpillar D9 earthmover converted into an armored suicide bomb. This has been disabled and set afire by RPG rockets.

SVB-LTVR: The Iraqi Light Tactical Vehicle is a large truck that ISIS cannot maintain easily, so due to their ten-ton cargo capacity they have been surrounded with large steel plates and converted into Mad Max–style car bombs

Bomb-Cat: The D9 Armored Earthmover/Combat Bulldozer Bomb: ISIS has used the armored D9 Combat Bulldozer as a slow-moving suicide bomb. Covered with steel plate and rolled chain links to ward off rockets, it can be a dual-use combat engineering truck to make holes in defenses or as a massive protected bomb.

Bomb-RAP: High-value US-made COUGAR Mine Resistant Armored Personnel vehicles: these Iraqi Army surplus items are too high maintenance for the ISIS inventory. ISIS has modified them into rolling SVBIEDs to assault Iraqi security force positions.

SPBIED—SUICIDE PEDESTRIAN-BORNE IMPROVISED EXPLOSIVE DEVICE (SUICIDE BOMBERS)

ISIS-Sinai fighters carry suicide bombs as part of their combat kit.

The standard operating procedure for ISIS and their predecessors in al-Qaeda is to equip select men with an improvised explosive device so they can kill themselves and others in a close-quarters battle or terrorist attack. There are generally three types of SPBIED:

Offensive Combat/Terrorist SPBIED (TSV): ISIS equips select men with SPBIED vests or belts in order to use them as a form of human extreme precision-guided weapons. Battlefield SPBIEDs are used to breach heavy fortification gates and barbed wire, to attack positions, and to lie in ambush for enemy forces. ISIS units in almost all regions tend to equip men with SPBIED vests in order to use them as human land mines. When an enemy breaches an ISIS location, the bombers blow up. This

A rare ISIS female suicide bomber with explosive belt.

tactic is also used in terrorist attacks, as seen in the Bataclan theater attack in Paris.

Child SPBIED: ISIS has used children as young as eleven as walking SPBIEDs and has even rigged both live and dead babies, held in another bomber's arms, as a method of infiltrating a bomb into a facility. Nigeria has seen large-scale use of young kidnapped girls who have been dishonored by sexual assault and subsequently recruited as bombers.

Women SPBIED: as many as eighty-five women and girl suicide bombers are affiliated with ISIS's Boko Haram in Nigeria, but not in other regions. In the ISIS Paris attacks in 2015, a terrorist special mission team used a female operative to lure French BRI commandoes to make entry by shouting from a window that she was a hostage. She died in the subsequent suicide vest explosion of a male operative standing immediately behind her.

TANKS & ARTILLERY

Of the 140 M1A1 Abrams tanks in the Iraqi army's arsenal, thirty were captured and destroyed by ISIS. Despite the fact that they were in good condition and functional, ISIS destroyed them after stripping them of their machine guns and ammunition.[1060] The M1A1 Abrams tanks have sophisticated fire control and operating systems and are more difficult to maintain, unlike the Russian tanks. In Egypt, ISIS could not operate the army's M60A1s and blew them up with grenades or explosives.

The Russian stockpile of tanks, including the T-55, T-62 and T-72, have all been put in the field by ISIS in Iraq, Syria, Libya, Egypt, and Yemen. Most of the heavy tanks used in the heart of the "Caliphate" provinces came from both the Syrian army and Iraqi forces.

Tanks			
Name	**Type**	**Manufacturer**	**Number Captured**
T-55	Main Battle Tank	Russia	87
T-62	Main Battle Tank	Russia	20–30
T-72	Main Battle Tank	Russia	5–10
M1A1	Main Battle Tank	USA	30
Type 653	Main Battle Tank	China	1
WZT-2	Armored Recovery	Poland	3
M88A1	Recovery Vehicle	USA	1
2S1 Gvozdika	Self-Propelled Artillery	Russia	3
Construction Machinery	Construction	Iraq	N/A

ISIS seems to be more comfortable with the Soviet era-tanks as they are easy to repair and less complicated to operate. No one is sure how many older tanks ISIS has in its stockpiles, but they are a high-value target for US air power and are easily destroyed.

ISIS militants have seized numerous artillery pieces from military bases and outposts from across the war-torn regions of Syria and Iraq. Some of them are experienced artillerymen and expert in the use of artillery. Kurdistan news reported on an ISIS artillery forward controller "ace" so skilled at hitting Kurdish positions that they were forced to launch an attack on the village of Kharbani to hunt him down. Once killed the fire immediately stopped.[1061]

The precise number of artillery pieces and rocket launchers in ISIS's arsenal is unknown. ISIS took fifty-two US-built M198 howitzers after the fall of Mosul.[1062] The artillery piece is a medium-sized towed unit that can shoot at a range of twenty miles. The *Washington Post* report

An Iraqi Army T-55 tank captured by ISIS.

A captured BMP armored personnel carrier forced off the road by ISIS in Ramadi.

An Iraqi army M1A1 Abrams forced into an unfightable position was abandoned and destroyed by ISIS.

Iraqi army 2S1 Gvozdika, a 122mm self-propelled artillery and a T-55 tank captured by ISIS is paraded though Mosul.

in 2014 suggested that ISIS has in fact been practicing with the seized M198 howitzer at a military airport near Aleppo. [1063] ISIS's M198s are a very high-priority target for the US air campaign.

Towed Artillery & Multiple Rocket Launchers			
Name	Type	Manufacturer	Number Captured
2A18 (D-30) Howitzer	Howitzer	Russia	2
Field Gun (D-74)	Field Gun	Russia	6
M198 Howitzer	Howitzer	USA	52
Type 63	Rocket Launcher	China	2
BM-14	Multi-Rocket Launcher	Russia	N/A

ISIS shooting the US-made M-198 artillery piece.

ISIS captured Russian D-20 152mm howitzer.

BM-21 122mm multiple rocket launcher, Syria.

ANTI-TANK WEAPONRY

Anti-tank weapon systems (ATGM) exist in greater numbers and have seen more success in combat but still on a limited scale. ISIS-Sinai acquired the 9M33 Kornet advanced ATGM and attacked an Egyptian coast guard vessel with a successful hit that set it on fire.

ISIS also uses a variety of anti-tank missiles. A video released by the group shows a US-manufactured BGM-71 TOW anti-tank missile being used against the Syrian regime troops in Palmyra.[1064] This weapon system was supplied by Saudi Arabia to the Free Syrian Army. ISIS not only acquired them but also learned to effectively put them together and fire them. They have used it against the Kurds in Hasakah.[1065]

Other anti-tank weapons used by ISIS are the Russian SPG-9 90mm recoilless rifle and the American M-40 105mm recoilless rifle seized from Syrian, Libyan, Afghan, and Yemeni depots.

Anti-Tank & Anti-Aircraft			
Name	**Type**	**Manufacturer**	**Number Captured**
9M17 Scorpion	Anti-Tank	Russia	3
M113 Konkurs	Anti-Tank	Russia	1
9M133 Kornet	Anti-Tank	Russia	2
KPV	Anti-Aircraft	Russia	90
ZPU-1	Anti-Aircraft	Russia	7
ZPU-2	Anti-Aircraft	Russia	1
2K12 Kub	Tracked Surface-to-Air	Russia	N/A
ZU-23	Anti-Aircraft	Russia	31
M-1939	Air Defense	Russia	1
Type 65	Air Defense	China	2
AZP S-60	Auto Cannon	Russia	1

ANTI-AIRCRAFT GUNS

The most often seen weapon is the anti-aircraft artillery (AAA) of the DSsK (Doushka) 12.7mm heavy machine guns and twin 23mm ZU-23 class, either in the two ZPU-2 configuration or the single barreled ZU-1. ISIS gunnery mechanics often strip 23mm aerial cannons from captured aircraft and jerry-rig them onto technicals with dubious aiming and firing mechanisms.

The overwhelming preponderance of these weapons are mounted on Toyota technicals for use in a direct fire role as an anti-infantry or anti-position weapon. They are rarely used against aircraft.

An SPG-9 mounted on a Toyota 70 pickup in Damascus, Syria area.

Captured Syrian army Ural-4320 truck with ZU-23-2 anti-aircraft guns.

ZPU-1 anti-aircraft machine gun on the back of a Toyota Hilux pickup.

ISIS parades Toyota LandCruiser pickups with ZPU-2 twin 14.5mm.

ISIS acquired the US-built Saudi-supplied BGM-71 TOW missile from the Free Syrian Army.

M-40 105mm recoilless rifle on a Toyota 70 LWB "technical" in Syria.

SURFACE-TO-AIR MISSILES—MANPADS

Surface-to-air missiles fired from the shoulder are called Man-Portable Air-Defense Systems or MANPADS. No one is sure of the exact numbers of MANPADS acquired by ISIS worldwide. Before the Syrian revolution, the Assad regime stockpiled an estimated 20,000 MANPAD systems, which were captured by the Free Syrian Army.

British security analyst Robert Emerson said that some of the weapons possessed by the militants are very capable, including the SA-24 and the Chinese FN-6.[1066] The limitation of MANPADS is their battery shelf life, which is essential to fire them. However, ISIS has improvised effective batteries.

Some Free Syrian Army units have the FIM-92 STINGER missile and ISIS may have captured some units. Chinese-manufactured MANPADS such as the FN-6 units, which may have been supplied to rebels from sources in Saudi Arabia or captured, may have led to the loss of an Iraqi army Mi-35M which killed two crew during the Battle of Baiji. [1067] [1068]

It is rumored that ISIS acquired between 250 and 400 anti-aircraft missiles systems such as the Russian SA-18 and SA-24 Grinch MANPADS when it seized Tabqa airbase in Syria.[1069] However, little evidence exists that they actually have many working units. ISIS has conducted a limited number of MANPADS attacks against the Syrian air force or US coalition air forces. ISIS-Sinai in Egypt has shot down two aircraft with SA-16 IGLAs—one was an Mi-17, killing five soldiers, and an AH-64 Apache helicopter gunship. These may have come from Libyan stocks.

ISIS posted an online guidebook that gave detailed instructions on how to shoot down American Apache helicopters using MANPADS. According to a report by Iraqi news, ISIS militants targeted US A-10

ISIS shooting a Chinese-built FN-6 MANPAD at an Iraqi Air Force Mi-35.

ISIS propagabnda showing the Strela 2 MANPAD.

ISIS-Sinai video showing an Egyptian army Mi-17 crashing to the ground after being hit by a MANPAD.

Thunderbolt aircraft using 9K32 Strela-2 MANPADS when the planes carried out air strikes on ISIS positions near Mosul, Iraq.[1070]

CHEMICAL ARTILLERY, BIOLOGICAL WEAPONS, AND CHEMICAL IED WEAPONS

In an investigation on the use of chemical agents by ISIS on the Kurds, it was reported by National Public Radio that an artillery barrage in the village of Sultan Abduallah on Kurdish troops contained suspected chemical weapons. The medical symptoms were consistent with being exposed to mustard gas.[1071] Many reports suggest that ISIS uses mustard gas and a crude form of chlorine gas. Officials said that the mustard gas is likely to be in powder form and packed into explosives such as mortar rounds and artillery shells.[1072] Officials are not certain of how ISIS managed to get their hands on mustard gas, but speculate that they recovered rounds that were launched at Syrian rebels by the Assad regime. It is possible that the militants manufactured it, but it is extremely difficult to produce effectively. Chlorine bombs have been seen in both Iraq and Syria. They have been placed in roadside IEDs to slow down the advance of Iraqi forces.

Improvised 100mm and 120 mm mortars with launcher in Kobane, Syria.

Scorpion Bombs[1073]

In the 198 AD defense of the city of Hatra, Iraq, during the second Parthian War, the Hatrians used "scorpion bombs" in terra cotta pots to break the formations of Emperor Septimius Severus' legions. [1074] Herodian the scribe, from the ancient Syrian city of Antioch, referred to them as "poisonous flying insects."

Now, ISIS actually uses hollow large mortar containers with thousands of Iraqi death stalker scorpions. The arachnids are generally harmless, but create psychological panic in the impact area. Hamish de Bretton-Gordon, a chemical and biological weapons expert, said that scorpions are robust, can withstand the flight, and disperse on impact.

SMALL ARMS & LIGHT INFANTRY WEAPONS

Conflict Armament Research (CAR), a non-government organization monitoring the international movement of weapons, concluded that most of the weapons used by ISIS militants were manufactured mainly in the United States, the Soviet Union/Russia, and China. The finding is not surprising at all, in consideration of the fact that these nations supplied weapons to fight ISIS, but ISIS overran numerous military bases and their weapons caches in Syria, Iraq, Libya, and Yemen.

The investigation by CAR in Kobane suggests that ISIS has been using M16 rifles in Syria as well as in Iraq. The American M16 rifle has yet to equal the Russian AK in the Iraq-Syria zone, as ISIS is believed to have captured fewer than ten thousand. The scarcity of the M16 rifles is unsurprising. The Kalashnikov is a common weapon in the Middle East and the ammunition is easy to obtain, especially when all of the armed forces there use it. When the Iraqi forces retreated, they left behind 30,000 Kalashnikovs. ISIS also likely captured AKs from Syrian troops and from the moderate rebel forces fighting Assad and his regime.

Weapons		
Type	Manufacturer	Number Captured
AK-47	Russia China Romania Hungary East Germany Bulgaria Poland Iraq Yugoslavia	30,000 +
M16	USA	7400
M4	USA	N/A
FN FAL	Belgium	2
CQ	China	2
AKM	Russia	N/A
PKM machine gun	China	N/A
Elmech EM-992	Croatia	N/A
Type 79 sniper rifle	China	N/A
FN Herstal Browning	Belgium	N/A
XM 15-E2S	USA	N/A
Glock G-19	Austria	N/A
HS 9	Croatia	N/A

ISIS Weapons Slang
Ak-47: "Russiss," "Kalash"   **LMG:** "Rashash"
M-4 Carbine: "Mister Bush"   **HMG:** "Doushka"

According to Reuters, 74,000 machine guns fell into ISIS's hands.[1075] This number most likely includes automatic rifles, as well as the M-2 .50 caliber and the M240 7.62 NATO, including ammunition scavenged from the thirty M1A1 tanks and the M113 APCs.

ISIS militants are sometimes seen using exotic assault rifles that were never in Iraqi or Syrian inventories, such as the FN FAL, CQ, and the XM-15. It's likely that these weapons were imported via black market or taken from private security contractors. CAR also documented two Chinese PKM M80 machine guns, a Croatian Elmech EM-992 sniper rifle, and a Chinese type 79 sniper rifle.[1076] Kurdish forces have seized pistols from ISIS fighters such as the Belgian FN Herstal Browning, the Austrian Glock G19, and the Croatian HS Produkt HS-9 pistol.[1077]

ISIS USE OF DRONES

Until recently, relatively few countries used surveillance drones—United States, Britain, Pakistan, China, Iran, Iraq, Nigeria, South Africa, Russia, Hamas, and Israel. Since then, drone technology has become cheaper and easier to obtain. Unlike other factions, ISIS has made good use of

ISIS drone with GoPro camera tapes positions of Syrian army at an airbase.

technology. Just as they pioneered the use of social networking for propaganda purposes, ISIS has incorporated drones with high-definition cameras into its intelligence-collection and artillery-spotting processes. ISIS has released numerous videos depicting battlefield drone footage. In August 2014, ISIS released a video showing its forces using a drone at the Syrian Army Brigade 93 Base. In April 2015, video footage emerged showing how they used drones to conduct surveillance on Iraqi security forces positions and to correct rocket and mortar fire at the Baiji oil refinery complex. According to Iraqi security analyst Alex Mello, ISIS also used drones in Zawbaa and Fallujah to coordinate fighting in those regions.[1078]

Christopher Hermer, a senior naval analyst, noted that even less-sophisticated unmanned aerial vehicles could be improvised into deadly weapons, much like a suicide drone.[1079] *Popular Mechanics* reported that Turkish forces shot down such a drone that was packed with small explosives, while a second drone managed to explode.[1080] Although this last case is unverified and anecdotal, the question of ISIS's use of a jerry-rigged drone bomb capable of breaching a security perimeter is a matter of when, not if.

Drones and video cameras are easily acquired from the civilian market, and it is relatively easy to affix a camera and fly a drone above enemy positions as seen in Syria and Libya. Most likely these drones do not

On March 25, 2015, ISIS Wiliyat of Barqa in Libya carried out a suicide bombing using a Ford F-350 filled with aerial bombs. They filmed the bomber and the target using a drone hovering approximately 1,000 feet above the target.

have live video links. A few of the drones used by ISIS are well known. The Syrian rebel Levant Front downed what appeared to be an X-UAV Talon drone constructed with plywood that could be purchased as a kit for less than $100. [1081] In October 2015, Iraqi security forces announced that they had downed a drone belonging to ISIS east of Ramadi.[1082] That was a fixed-wing drone similar to the RQ-9. Other reports cite use of the Phantom FC-40 Phantom QR-X350 programmable drones, and eyewitnesses have spotted Skywalker X7 and Skywalker X8 drones in Iraq.

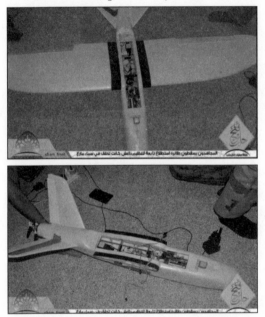

FSA rebels captured an ISIS radio controlled drone in Syria.

To date, CENTCOM reported that during Operation Inherent Resolve, coalition forces destroyed three ISIS drones.[1083] Kurdish forces are said to have downed numerous drones. One of them was a homemade attack drone that was believed to be packed with explosives. Kurdish YPG forces in Syria forces downed numerous DJI Phantom 3 quadrotors that apparently were used as artillery spotters, finding targets and correcting the fall or fire for mortar crews.[1084]

CHAPTER 17

ISIS IN BATTLE AND TERROR

GROUND COMBAT CAPACITY

HISTORY OF PROFESSIONAL STREET FIGHTERS

From its first days as Al-Qaeda in Iraq (AQI), the original members of ISIS had to learn on the fly. Living in safe houses in the city of Fallujah, they planned on maintaining a terrorist resistance through stealth, guile, and trucks full of plastic explosives. As the American military presence expanded, they found themselves alongside the Sunnah members of Saddam's security and intelligence apparatus, now gone underground. There, they found a secret army with thousands of safe houses full of weapons and ammunition, a logistical trail for ammunition and suicide bombers that extended back to Syria, and fully backed by the Bashar al-Assad government. However, just to move on the streets in Iraq was like moving around in the virtual game space of *Call of Duty*. Threats were everywhere, Americans dominated the air, and insurgent groups would frequently betray each other. This called for a new set of combat skills that could only be learned by OJT—On the Job Training. AQI had to learn to move in a hostile country with weapons and take on the strongest military power toe-to-toe. It was survival of the fittest, and no matter how strong your religious faith or how well you prepared, the US Special Forces, the Iraqi death squads, or even your deputy could remove you from the equation quickly unless a sixth sense for how to fight in this environment was not acquired, and quickly.

Learning to fight with rifles, hand grenades, and light machine guns means that the insurgent terrorist is only combat-effective out to a radius of 300 yards and really extends lethal effect out to 100–150 yards. These are the distances of fighting in an urban environment. If anything, AQI was an organization filled with fast learners and knew how to pass down the skills to infiltrate, do a blitz assault within 300 yards, and then disappear. Under the tutelage of the Saddam Fedayeen, known at the time as the Jaysh al-Mujahedeen, AQI became a lethal street combat force due to two factors that the other groups in Iraq did not have. The first was an absolute cult-level belief that their death was a form of worship to God and was welcome. The second was that attacks start with a suicide bomber . . . in fact, everyone in the group was a suicide bomber.

Like the communist terrorists of the 1970s, these rules applied only to the foot soldiers of the group. The leadership in both Afghanistan and Iraq knew they had to maintain a "combat nucleus" of personnel and leadership in order to train and deploy the international foot soldiers coming through Syria. This combat nucleus would stay alive as long as they could and pass down the tactics, techniques, and tradecraft to each successive new group of arrivals. Rarely did they write anything down, so their professionalization was more like a terror-mentorship. Each terrorist was responsible for the operational security of the group and was expected to give his life. If caught, just lie low. The Americans aren't the Saudis, and they eventually let everyone go. This would all change with ISIS. Documentation became the norm for all aspects of administration.

From the surviving nucleus came the current combat commanders of ISIS. After the fall of Eastern Syria, their Saddam Fedayeen and former Iraqi army generals and spies, now members of the team, would help them conduct a form of mobility warfare that al-Qaeda had never tried, or wanted to master. They would become like the marching army of the Prophet Mohammed. After defending at Yathrib he would march on Mecca, have many glorious battles, and take Arabia. This is the operational image and strategic vision of the ISIS battle commanders. Instead of camels, they would blitz, encircle, and lay siege to their enemies on the back of the Japanese Camel—the Toyota pickup truck.

RECRUIT READINESS & TRAINING

Dozens of ISIS recruit-training videos indicate that they are competent at teaching the basics of infantry combat, at least at the insurgent level. Their training curriculum is nearly identical to terror and insurgent groups worldwide. They start

with physical fitness and obstacle courses. They put them under six to eight weeks of brutal instruction and toughen them up for the rigors of running and moving through urban terrain. Most of this is like a soccer academy with lines and cycles of drills. It should be appreciated that this is not merely media fluff. ISIS has now had five years of full-time urban and expeditionary combat and thirteen years of terror experience against the greatest nations on earth.

As previous chapters have revealed, religious indoctrination is a major component of the recruit's day. The levels of incessant infusion of their ideology reinforce the brainwashing that they brought with them. The routines of combat formations, close contact combat drills, moving though trenches, and learning to shoot the AK-47 accurately at least to 100 yards is a daily affair.

EXPEDITIONARY WARFARE

ALPINE STYLE HYBRID TERROR COMBAT

ISIS entered the game of expeditionary warfare when they deployed their splinter unit, the Jebhat al-Nusra, to Syria in January 2011. The mission of this wing was to send terror fighters of Syrian origin back to capitalize on the political and security vacuum that came about when the civil war started. The objective was to enter quickly; seize police stations, military bases, and weapons stores; establish bases of operations; and start a training regime. The Jebhat did just that: They moved from their Iraq sanctuary and blitzed into Syria. Attacking at Deir ez-Zor and Raqqa they found that without the government to block them they could infiltrate as far as Aleppo. In Aleppo the city came under siege from the Assad forces and in assault after assault, ISIS's jihadi forces, who were really the only combat veterans present, established themselves as the "Special Forces" of the Syrian resistance. When a critical hole needed to be plugged they would blitz without regard to their safety and, screaming "Allahu Akbar," would seal the hole and then counterattack to take terrain. This would be repeated all over Syria till the battle lines favored their men. In 2013 they would take the city of Raqqa from the Syrian 93rd and 121st Mechanized Infantry Brigades. Those units would regret having surrendered. The 200 prisoners were summarily executed and their heads placed on spikes in Raqqa's center. The message went out all across Syria and Iraq—This was the resolve of ISIS. This is how they fought. This is how you will die.

ISIS learned to fight its street battles asymmetrically. They flip the firepower advantage of modern combat units by being the opposite: light, fast, and ruthless. They move in Toyota Task Force (TTF) columns on the roads that cannot be covered by tanks, and run circles around checkpoints. They don't have precision-guided weapons, so they used human-guided weapons. This way they managed to take over areas that actually had military dominance. They confidently employed what could be called Alpine-style warfare, where, like the mountain climbing technique, they move fast and light, hit an objective, and move to the next.

With the exception of a few sieges where they had terrain dominance; they used alpine-style combat to take a third of Iraq and half of Syria.

However, it doesn't always work. Trained forces that understand their strengths and have the right level of mental toughness have defeated ISIS's combat forces and when they do, it is a slaughter without exception. The Egyptian, Iraqis, Kurds, and Nigerians have at times stood up to the onslaught and swatted ISIS down like so many flies. Their techniques can be replicated.

ASSESSMENT OF COMBAT COMPETENCE

Discussions and analysis with over a dozen experienced combat veterans from the United States, Iraq, Syria, and Libya has revealed several common characteristics when fighting ISIS in ground combat.

ISIS by its nature is a soccer club turned Special Forces unit. They maintain tight, small unit cohesion and will stick to their battle buddies right up to the moment of death. In fact, their unit cohesion may be one of their faults, as they prefer to stick to squad-sized elements of six to ten men. However, unlike their opposition, they trust that the man next to them will fight like the devil for the team. This is an admirable quality that gives them the assurance that they will survive long enough to move on to the next battle.

Their biggest combat multiplier is the cult-like belief that they are killing Muslims for the betterment of the world. Their life and the strength of belief in God's capacity to see them through allows them to act rashly in lethal environments. This is generally where a competent force with accurate firepower can kill them quickly. However, an incompetent force or a paper tiger such as the Iraqi army divisions in Mosul will run or surrender in an attempt to cut deals to save their lives. This tactic has yet to work with ISIS.

ISIS fighters are trained that the strength of God gives them immunity or death, depending on the action. So they have honed a level of unit aggressiveness that the other forces do not have. That aggressiveness makes them feel touched by God. It explains rash behaviors like bouncing from behind a wall and calmly setting up an RPG shot in the face of multiple Syrian tanks, or creeping up to the barrel of the most advanced variant of the T-72 tank and rolling a hand grenade down the barrel, which causes it to blow up. These stories are legendary even if the jihadist

---

US Special Forces Soldier's Assessment on ISIS in Combat

We learned a lot fighting with Al-Qaeda in Iraq and the Iraqi insurgents. Then again ISIS learned a lot too. They watched us and observed carefully how we operate. Then they incorporated the best parts into their own tactics. This improved their fire and unit discipline. The newer ones do not use aimed fire, they just "spray and pray." They often expose themselves and bound out into the street spraying and praying. The biggest advantage they have is that they have no Rules of Engagement. They have no reason to take civilians' lives into consideration in any circumstance. That's why I tell everyone that if there is any situation where ISIS is involved, be prepared for them to carry out a suicide attack. They're not just going to fight, they are going to die and take you with them. —Randy Williams, former US Army Special Forces

dies. Everyone is a martyred lion and their heroism is retold or the videos of their actions are shown to the recruits.

This strength in mission allows ISIS fighters to take the initiative. When acting as a squad or driving the suicide bomb truck, they seem to strive for that moment when their action has decisive effect. This is a trait found in all soldiers, but with ISIS the effect is for God and sometimes the video camera that is surely watching. We would call their ability to take the initiative careless or foolish, but it has defeated armies thus far.

Intelligence collection before an attack is fundamental to their battle doctrine. This is where they make the best of young operatives who will crawl and sneak their way along the forward line of troops (FLOT) and conduct extremely dangerous reconnaissance. ISIS uses binocular and radio methods of intelligence collection, but now supplement it with the cell phone and quadcopter drone video (see chapter 16). More importantly, the ISIS commanders use intelligence almost immediately. They don't wait for orders from higher headquarters when they see an opportunity to kill enemy units or take a strategic position. Most professional soldiers would deem this rash, but in the right context it is boldness and daring. This audacity is part of the strategic plan as well. They need to fill the vacuums within the chaos of the battle space, so they do not wait for opportunity; they create it, even if it costs them men, and then they exploit it to the fullest.

On the attack they are like any trained soldier; they kill first and ask questions later. Like Western armies, the soldiers have it drilled into their heads that they can act as an Army of One if they are cut off and fighting alone. There is no escape and evasion, withdraw and regroup, just attack, reposition, or die.

As for prisoners of war, ISIS is designed to be a killing machine and unless specific orders are given to keep a prisoner or civilian alive, they will generally kill them and move onto the next objective.

The ISIS chain of command is clear and linear. This is design from the Saddam Hussein era where there is only one level of orders that matters to you: the next level. Like all armies' missions, orders are passed up and down the fighting units on battlefield via radio system. Each unit has an Emir who commands all the soldiers under him. He has deputy Emirs who carry out the action. Everyone knows the objective and the mission is carried out until they succeed or die. This is the way it has been since time immemorial.

ASYMMETRIC ROLES & TECHNIQUES

ISIS does have two unique traits that are different from regular armies. In their group everyone is expected to be a combat engineer/sapper and a human-guided weapons system. If trenches need to be dug out, everyone digs out, or someone will borrow an excavator and dig. If a line of razor barbed wire needs to be breached for the assault force to enter, then someone will be the designated suicide breacher and will throw himself on top of the wire and blow up. Much like the Japanese infantry of WWII, the ISIS fighter has obligations and death is at the top of the list. It's less taking one for the team and more taking one to meet God.

Meeting a hardened enemy force that has overwhelming firepower requires that the laws of asymmetries be adopted at every turn. ISIS has shown amazing adaptability at using whatever it has at hand to take advantage of the enemy's inability to predict it. The tunnel has come up as a favored ISIS technique to avoid US airpower. Ever since AQI was slaughtered in the battle of Fallujah in 2004, ISIS has learned to stop using just-breached walls for room-to-room aboveground movement. Like the Russians in Stalingrad, the Viet Cong at Cu Chi, and the Japanese at Tarawa, they went underground and created tunnels hundreds of meters long, chains of command posts, medical facilities, and ammunition stores in Ramadi, Sinjar, Raqqa, Fallujah, and Tikrit.

TUNNEL-BORNE IEDS
(A.K.A. TUNNEL BOMBS)

ISIS is starting to master the use of the tunnel bomb. The Joint Improvised-threat Defeat Agency (JIDA) reports that as many as forty-five tunnel-borne improvised explosive devices (TBIEDs) have been used in

Iraq and Syria. The technique of tunneling was widely used on the Egypt-Palestine border to smuggle goods past embargoes, but like its civil war-era use, ISIS now deploys it as an exceptionally deliberate direct-attack system.

Tricks and surprises are a regular feature of ISIS on the battlefield. If you have a massive defensive line dug in, they will dig a few kilometers of tunnels and conduct a massive suicide-bomber-initiated explosive breach that blows a hole in your perfectly prepared defenses or collapses an entire structure from the bottom.

Many in the leadership of ISIS are highly experienced Iraqi, Egyptian, Syrian, French, and Saudi military men and graduates of Arab war colleges. These are fighters who not only read history books but know the contents. They know full well how the twenty mines dug by British engineers at the Battle of Messines in WWI killed ten thousand Germans; they also know that the Battle of the Crater failed at Petersburg in the American Civil War because soldiers stopped to help the injured enemy. These old soldiers not only study this history but they know how to recreate it on a micro-scale.[1085] [1086]

IEDS ARE THEIR DEFENSIVE LINE

ISIS is not an army that takes retreat lightly. They live for the offensive, and when pushed into the defensive they behave with petulance and arrogance. Like a chained pit bull at a dogfight, they want to attack and not stay in a corner. However, they have decades of experience though their passed down historical base, which could be called the al-Qaeda Center for Terror Lessons Learned. When Saddam Hussein prepared for the insurgency in Iraq, he knew his artillery force would be decimated by American airpower. He initiated a program called the Ghafiqi project, to develop, package, and cache tens of thousands of artillery shells to be transformed into improvised explosive devices (IEDs). IEDs accounted for between half and two-thirds of the 4,815 US combat deaths in Iraq.

The tradition of using IEDs on the defense has been adopted heartily by ISIS. When ISIS seizes a position, IED factories in the rear start building loads of bombs for use along the flanks and for harassment tools when a fallback is necessary. After the battle of Tikrit in April 2015, the Iraqis found out the hard way that ISIS would slow the Iraqi forces' advance to a crawl by lining the road with hundreds of IEDs, some by themselves, others daisy-chained to make long lines of explosives more than a kilometer long.

Additionally, they use whatever tools they have at hand, including deploying captured mustard gas in IEDs and mortars taken from Syrian army stocks, as well as rigging chlorine gas IEDs in daisy-chain style to terrify and harass pursuers.

Dabiq Magazine: ISIS on How They Took Mosul

"By guidance from our leadership, the leadership of the ISIS, favored by Allah, the brothers in the ISIS camps began drawing up precise plans to conquer the entire Wilayat and purge it of apostates. This blessed battle began by intelligence jihad by the special detachments whereby the apostates' weak areas were studied and then the military force entered the city of Mosul from several directions and by the grace of Allah took complete control of their headquarters, including the Ghazlani HQ, the operations command, the second division HQ, Badush and Tasfirat prisons, and the headquarters of the battalions and brigades. Thousands of prisoners were also released as well as some female prisoners, and the praise and grace is to Allah. And now there is complete control over all internal and external access points to the Wilayat and with Allah's permission this series of blessed incursions that delight the eyes of the monotheists shall not cease either till Allah fulfills his promise or we shall perish...."[1087]

COMPLEX GROUND COMBAT AND LIGHTNING SEIZURE

ISIS has a very specific set-piece complex attack scenario that plays out in every serious offensive, with some variations thrown in to take advantage of geography, weather, and opposing forces. It can be summarized by the letters CSBS or Collect, Suppress, Breach, and Shock.

Collect: ISIS generally carries out very detailed human and video intelligence collections of enemy positions. They gain information about weapons emplacement and fields of fire and look for the flaws in an enemy's position that can be exploited by suicide bomber, their best offensive weapon.

Suppress: Tanks, rockets, technicals carrying 23 mm or 40 mm antiaircraft guns, and small units carrying SPG-9 recoilless rifles or anti-tank guided missiles stand off from 300–1000 meters and pound the enemy position until the main assault can make their way to the 500–300-meter range.

Breach: The principle ISIS breaching weapon is the suicide truck bomb or suicide bomber. Usually, a SVBIED speeds directly toward the main hard point or the most effective weapons location. The bomb must be large enough to not only blow holes into the enemy line, but to assist the shock value of the final assault. To take Iraqi positions in Ramadi in 2015, ISIS sent large front-end loaders and bulldozers to push the concrete T-Barriers of the defense perimeter, letting thirty car bombs penetrate Iraqi defensive positions.[1088] They attempted this technique again in the Battle of the Kurdish Line (see below), but airpower destroyed over a dozen excavators after they dug holes into the Kurdish berm.

Shock: Once they create a major breach, the ISIS infantry flows in and attacks at close quarters. Usually SPBIEDs are deployed to shock the opposition soldiers while they are shot down one on one. In the end, the ultimate shock is the systematic execution of the enemy soldiers by beheading or point-blank shots to the head.

IDENTIFYING & DEFEATING THEIR WEAKNESSES

The tactical weaknesses of ISIS are those found in all overconfident terrorist groups who move from covert action to expeditionary warfare to "nation" state. ISIS is an arrogant organization and that trait causes them to take chances that could be used against them. The way they perform infantry combat demonstrates a measure of skill, including the ability to make proper tactical movements on streets, proficient use of snipers and designated marksmen, and blitzkrieg offensive reach.

ISIS prefers the head-on battle and often neglects real flank security, or leaves the security to IEDs or one or two technicals. The technicals are generally placed to provide direct fire support and may forget to actually cover attacks coming from the flanks and rear. Tanks are used in defensive fire support, almost like mobile artillery platforms reminiscent of the Lebanese civil war, where they would sit atop a hill and fire down on enemy positions. They do not have a mobile tank warfare doctrine apart from drive up, try not to run over anyone, and lob shells from afar.

However, analysis of hundreds of their videos from all across the Middle East and Africa and debriefing of Special Forces personnel from the US and Iraq reveals they still make the amateur moves that every soldier calls "the idiot move." ISIS calls it the Shekel al-Butal, or the "Like a Hero" move. This move is performed by the bravest man, usually with the PKM machine gun, and it is an inspiration to watch. It may have a force multiplier effect because the shooters behind defensive positions generally are encouraged to get on the line and lay down a base of fire. This move generally gets the hero killed when he is fighting a competent opposition . . . No matter, even if they are killed, they are lauded as heroes who took chances and are buried smiling as ISIS legends. One tactic that is weapons-dependent is the ubiquitous "RPG bounce," where the gunner must spring from cover into the street to aim and fire an RPG-7 rocket at a target. American forces learned long ago to make the center line of any street the last resting place of the "idiot move." ISIS soldiers, particularly the most devout of them, will stand straight up over a berm or wall and attempt to go head-to-head with an enemy, but without careful aim.

For all of their years of combat experience, it appears that ISIS still disregards attacks from their rear. They could be easily ambushed, as the real fighters are placed on the point, always facing the enemy. Their bravest are given suicide belts or PKM machine guns (which are borne as as badges of honor). During offensives, the suicide bomb belt is issued on a one-in-ten basis to be used as human-guided breachers, and almost one-to-one during a desperate defense, like the battle at the Baiji oil refinery, where everyone was expected to try to kill as many enemy as possible by becoming a literal suicide squad. Like the Japanese at Tarawa or Iwo Jima, capture should never occur, and suicide bomb belts should be detonated at the last moment.

The Egyptian army learned the hard way in 2015 when ISIS's affiliate, the Ansar Beit al-Maqdis, launched a major offensive designed to seize the northern Sinai peninsula away from the Egyptian army. They attacked twenty fixed military bases and outposts simultaneously in a Mosul-style attack, using every aspect of firepower in the ISIS–al-Qaeda playbook. They failed spectacularly and videotaped most of it themselves.

They lack an ingrained tactical survival mindset, which is degraded by their ideology, and because they feel a sense of immunity. Like the Liberian militiamen who wear bamboo or tin voodoo-blessed body armor that makes them "invisible," and therefore impervious to enemy bullets, ISIS's Aqeedah, or faith in God, makes them immune to fear of death—until they are killed.

Operating in this manner, they are out in the open where their operations can be seen and where they can be killed. ISIS's desire for the "stand-up fight" has affected their numbers greatly in both ways. They recruit from their ability to play a live-fire version of the video game *Call of Duty*—indeed, there is even an ISIS video stating "This is our Call of Duty." Like the famous video of the 2006 massacre of an overconfident Jaysh al-Mujahedeen attack on OP Gray Skull of Marine Corps Charlie Company 3rd Amphibious Assault Battalion at Dulab, Iraq, their results often go very horribly wrong.

ISIS DEFEATED IN COMBAT

JULY 1, 2015—ISIS ATTEMPTS TO ATTACK THE SINAI *OPERATION SHEIKH ABU SUHAB AL-ANSARI A.K.A. THE BATTLE OF VENGEANCE*

ISIS–Sinai conducted a series of twenty simultaneously complex multidimensional attacks against Egyptian forces in the three cities of Sheikh Zuweid, Rafah, and Arish that left 21 Egyptian soldiers and 241 attackers dead. What was designed to be a version of the Iraqi seizure of Mosul left them struggling to survive. Poor intelligence led them to jump in scale from their previous small-scale attacks to challenge the government for control of the corridor from Rafah to al-Arish, much like ISIS did between Raqqa and Mosul. If they had succeeded they would have wrested control of most border posts at Keret Shalom and Bnei Netzarim in Israel. Such an event would have resulted in an immediate Israeli invasion of the area, which would play into the hands of ISIS. Additionally, it meant that the Gaza strip in Palestine would have had to rely on ISIS for resupply by tunnels, thus also allowing ISIS to challenge the authority of Hamas.

The tactics used in the attack follow the Collect, Suppress, Breach, Shock (CSBS) formula to the letter. It bore many of the hallmarks of the ISIS campaigns in Syria, Libya, Iraq, and Yemen, perhaps representing a flow of ideas and leadership between ISIS's Ba'athist strategists and the fighters of ISIS–Sinai.

The attacks began with a bold move, a suicide bombing at the al-Arish officer's club, where officers had barracks and a rest and recreation facility. The bomb prematurely detonated and killed the gate guards. Almost simultaneously, they carried out assaults on Sheikh Zuweid's police headquarters and a series of roadside outposts. The outposts were small citadel structures where soldiers would live and defend wide areas with infantry patrols. Each citadel had two to three M-60A1 battle tanks and M-113A4s, heavy machine guns, and twenty to thirty soldiers. The citadels were aligned linearly in a region between Rafah and al-Arish.[1089]

The first citadel checkpoint attacks began at 6:00 a.m. ISIS–Sinai had infiltrated hundreds of fighters from the desert in Toyota pickups to areas just outside of the visual range of the points. At a predetermined sign, they simultaneously attacked at dawn. Dawn was a good time to attack because Egyptian conscript soldiers had a reputation for being undisciplined and notoriously lazy. The most likely event was that they would be cooking a breakfast of *ful medames* or smoking shisha with their boots off and weapons away from them. They would be proven very wrong. ISIS attacked nearly simultaneously on the large al-Arif and Sheikh Zuweid citadels with large SVBIED truck bombs blowing up the Sedra and Refeai checkpoints. Then a dozen more were attacked by groups of as many as 100 fighters armed with light machine guns and suicide bomb vests. Almost all of them were struck with suicide bombs at some point.

By 10:00 a.m., Brigadier General. Mohamed Samir reported that a major ISIS attack was underway but failing with more than seventy terrorists killed.[1090] The fights continued throughout the day but ISIS started to withdraw as failure after failure to take all of the checkpoints sank in. Egyptian army quick reaction forces with tanks and APCs were starting to mobilize and move from bases in Qantara and Islamiliya, so ISIS cut and ran. They tried to blend into the local villages and hole up in small alleys. They did not have community support and several locals were summarily executed when they refused to allow ISIS to conduct ambushes from their roofs. By midday the Egyptians had launched AH-64 Apache helicopters and F-16 Falcon strike aircraft and were now hunting ISIS in the deserts. However, ISIS had packed their vehicles to move large amounts of weapons, ammunition, and explosives, so they were difficult to hide.

ISIS–Sinai claimed to have only conducted two attacks including two SVBIED attacks, led by "Kamal Alam," also known as "Sheikh Abu Suhab al-Ansari," which was the nom-de-guerre of the Ansar Beit al-Maqdis leader. Four teams of over 100 terrorists each took part.

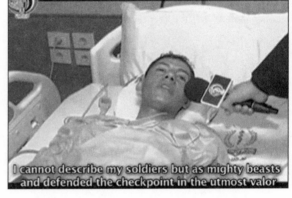
I cannot describe my soldiers but as mighty beasts and defended the checkpoint in the utmost valor

In Sheikh Zuweid, the attackers planted IEDs around the police station and down the road joining Sheikh Zuweid with al-Zuhour Army Camp. ISIS–Sinai fighters also planted IEDs to kill the fleeing soldiers and to ambush the quick reaction forces (QRF). The IEDs made al-Arish QRFs unable to pass quickly through Rafah and al-Arish.

In response to the attacks, the Egyptian army conducted raids July 1–5 and claimed to destroy four ISIS–Sinai headquarters, confiscated twenty-six vehicles, and disarmed sixteen IEDs. Additionally they seized machine guns, RPGs, mortars, and grenades. A few weeks later the ISIS–Sinai commander Selim Suleiman al-Haram was killed in Sheikh Zuweid, along with twenty other members.

DEFENSE OF THE ABU REFAEI CHECKPOINT—HOW THE EGYPTIAN ARMY DEFEATED SUICIDE WAVE ATTACKS

At 6:55 a.m., the Abu Refaei army checkpoint was attacked by a complex attack led by a suicide truck bomb. Egyptian army soldiers were not off guard as ISIS predicted, and intercepted the SVBIED before it reached the citadel. By engaging early, the suicide bomber detonated his truck prematurely, killing himself and the guards well outside of the intended blast zone, saving everyone in the garrison.

The troops in the barracks of the citadel immediately mobilized and went to their firing positions. By the time they arrived, ISIS fighters were laying down suppressing fire with heavy machine guns mounted on technicals and RPGs. They were starting to follow up the breach attack and preparing to storm the checkpoint. ISIS had surprising organization, including identical US-style "chocolate chip" battle uniforms, eight to ten magazines of AK-47 ammunition apiece, and suicide bomb belts. An estimated 200–300 terrorists armed with RPGs, grenades, and small arms took part in the attack.

The commanding officer of the checkpoint was Lieutenant Amro Ahmad Salah. Severely wounded in the attack, he gave interviews to Egyptian television from his hospital bed.[1091] Salah said, "My men were all heroes; they were all beasts . . . in particular, Private Abd El Rahman El Metwally." Private El Rahman was the unit sniper, and is credited with breaking the ISIS assault with precision gunfire and saving the checkpoint.

Abd El Rahman was born in al-Shal, a small village in the Egyptian countryside, near Mansoura, Daqhlia governorate. After being stunned by the suicide bomb attack, he ran to his firing position. As the designated marksman/unit sniper, he started to open fire on the bunched-up ISIS assaulters who were moving past the main gate. He was hit and wounded but continued to fire. According to Lt. Salah, he was killing terrorists left and right and he

was jubilant doing it, hardly believing himself. He shot one after the other of the main assault force and broke the back of the attack. At the time he was mortally wounded in his left side and bleeding heavily. Lt. Salah looked at the wound and told him to fall back with the wounded and wait for medical evacuation, but the private said, "I am not quitting, let's kill all the bastards," and resumed the fight. After seeing him kill fourteen on the assault force, the terrorists figured out where the accurate sniping coming from and concentrated their fire on him. He received a final bullet to the head, which killed him instantly. His precision gunfire held down the assaulters until the M60 tank and an M-113 APC could flank the attackers from the main road while Lt. Salah threw hand grenades down onto the terrorists. After forty-five minutes, the assault ended with twenty dead terrorist bodies abandoned around the site.

EXIGENT CIRCUMSTANCES—EGYPTIAN SAVES TEAMMATES FROM AN SVBIED WITH HIS LIFE.

Twenty-one-year-old Private Hossam Gamal was from the hamlet of al-Bashawat in the Faiyum Governorate. He was the front checkpoint guard at the Sedra-Abu Haggag checkpoint. As the men of the unit watched an ISIS SVBIED make its way toward them, they engaged with heavy machine guns and RPGs. As an RPG assistant gunner, Gamal held the spare rockets and watched in horror as the rockets failed to strike the target. After several attempts to hit the heavily armored suicide truck, he saw that the checkpoint was going to be hit. Taking an RPG, he sprinted out of the security perimeter and toward the suicide truck as it was trying to make its way over an obstacle to enter the post. Gamal saw there was a small observation slit in the heavy steel over the vehicle. He jumped onto the truck and shoved his rocket into the slit and fired. The truck blew up and skyrocketed into the air. Private Gamal was vaporized along with the truck bomb. His bravery and selflessness saved twenty-six of his teammates and broke the ISIS assault.[1092]

ISIS OFFENSIVE SLAUGHTERED ON THE KURDISH LINE & RAMADI

On December 17, 2015 at 4:30 a.m., Peshmerga forces aided by US and Canadian special forces and US airpower fought a massive assault by ISIS in northern Nineveh Province. After months of falling back slowly in Tikrit and Baiji, ISIS tried a dual combination attack against two regions they suspected were weak. They had been observing the Kurdish line east of Mosul and watched the Iraqi security forces (ISF) deploy and gradually take back Ramadi and cut off the last of their supply lines when they retook the Palestine Bridge. Their strategy was to make a serious operational push into the Kurdish region, flank the Kurdish defensive line, and perhaps blitz into Erbil, where they could confront the Americans and panic the Kurds. It was essentially a "paying the price" attack to relieve Ramadi, the ISIS strategy of attacking in lone location to save a force in another.

The ISIS Mosul command managed to mobilize and consolidate a combat battalion comprised of a Toyota task force supported by earthmovers, excavators, and suicide-bomb trucks. The objective was to carve through the Kurdish berm and assault through the breach using the CSBS strategy. They chose to attack in late afternoon at 4:17 p.m. in hopes of surprising the Kurds at a quiet time when they would be in siesta. ISIS would then use twilight and darkness to consolidate their gains and hold for follow-on forces.

Applying the typical assault tactics of deploying suicide bombers, VBIEDS, mortars, and rocket attacks, they attacked the areas of Ba'ashiqah, Nawaran, Tal Aswad, Khazir, Zardik, and Makhmour simultaneously.

ISIS started the attack with a possible decoy move. The Turkish army troops stationed at camp Ba'ashiqah were the first to come under

Katyusha rocket fire. Two Iraqi soldiers were killed and six others were wounded. The base was at the center of a recent dispute between Iraq and Turkey over involvement of Turkish troops against ISIS and an attack there would create confusion and suspicion between the Iraqis and Turks.[1093]

ISIS was able to temporarily penetrate each of the front lines briefly before being driven back by Peshmerga; the main force assault came from approximately 500 ISIS attackers.[1094] The Kurds fell back at a few of the penetration points, but that was to make room for US airpower to destroy the offensive. Coalition aircraft from five nations dropped over a hundred precision bombs on excavators, backhoes, and ISIS positions that attempted to breach the berms. ISIS infantry units were destroyed wholesale. As they attempted to assault Kurd positions, eleven VBIEDs were destroyed, as were several suicide bombers before they could strike their targets.

The resulting firefights lasted over seventeen hours, and by 9:00 a.m. the next day, the offensive was smashed and the ISIS forces had fled. The Joint Task Force Operation Infinite Resolve reported more than 187 ISIS fighters dead from airpower alone. At 20-to-1 ratio of ISIS to coalition casualties, this offensive was a resounding defeat.

Peshmerga commander Sarbast Trwanshi said that he had confirmed that ISIS leader Abu-Hamudia had been killed. Kurdish official Hemin Hawrami said that seven Peshmerga soldiers were killed.[1095]

ISIS made a strategic mistake attacking across the Kurdish forward line of troops. They believed their intelligence indicated that the Kurds would fold like paper tigers, and that an attack against a long geographical area would break through somewhere and allow them to assert pressure on Erbil, perhaps by taking Makhmour and the heights east of it. US forces are stationed on a base just north of Erbil. ISIS's greatest desire was to draw them out and go toe to toe with Americans. ISIS was overconfident that the thin Kurdish line wouldn't withstand their mixed-attack model. ISIS also assumed they could consolidate forces at night, and that Iraqis don't fight at night. In all likelihood they were pinned down all night, and the last thing you want to do is fight the US coalition at night.

KNOCKING DOWN SVBIEDS—ISIS MASSACRE AT PALESTINE BRIDGE

On the same day in Ramadi, ISIS was feeling the desperation of being quickly surrounded. To protect their last line of communications and supply to their forces in Syria, they attacked the Palestine Bridge north of Ramadi. The bridge crosses the Euphrates to the northwest of the city. The ISIS–Anbar province fighters attacked from north to south, using SVBIEDs, followed by infantry moving toward the direction of the Anbar Operations Center. The ISF counterattacked and destroyed the advancing SVBIEDs, using newly supplied AT-4 rocket launchers. Though the ISF contingent initially had the appearance of collapsing, they allowed the ISIS fighters and SVBIEDs to enter a kill zone, destroying the SVBIEDs and all the ISIS fighters. Coalition air support helped ISF to retake the bridge. Over fifty-nine ISIS fighters died.

MARITIME ATTACKS

November 12, 2014

ISIS-Sinai hijacked an Egyptian missile boat in order to attack Israeli vessels and offshore gas rigs. The American-built Ambassador MK III class missile patrol corvette was to deploy on a combat exercise when ISIS–Sinai members managed to commandeer the ship. There were reports a car accident was staged the week before to injure the captain Egyptian Navy Commander Mohamed al-Fujairy, forcing him to miss the movement of the vessel, and that the ship was seized by its executive officer, Navy Lieutenant Ahmed Mostafa Amer, who took it out to sea. Amer was the son of the port authority commander, Major General Mostafa Amer.[1096] The officer then allowed more Ansar Beit al-Maqdis (ISIS–Sinai) terrorists to board and forced the crew to sea. When at sea they killed five and threw eight of the sailors overboard,

where they were believed lost. Egyptian navy command noticed that the ship leaving Damietta port was not communicating, but saw its movement. When they realized that the vessel was underway but off track, they scrambled the Egyptian navy commando unit 777, the equivalent to the US Navy SEALs, and several other patrol craft were sent to intercept it. When they arrived, four fishing vessels with suspected terrorists were moving alongside. The navy opened fire on the corvette, and the 777 force stormed the vessel as well as the fishing boats.[1097] The vessel was supposedly hijacked to attack Israeli oil platforms and ships with its missiles and guns. The Egyptian navy tells a different story. They report that once the vessel was out of port, four small fishing vessels sent an SOS and, when the missile corvette responded, came under fire.[1098] The fishing vessels were sunk and dozens of ISIS members were believed to have died. Ten Egyptians and twenty-two foreign fighters were taken into custody. However, the official story doesn't address how the ship was initially taken over, and the SOS story does not correspond with the vessel already being seemingly hijacked and radio silent as it left port.

July 16, 2015

ISIS–Sinai attacked an Egyptian coast guard 26-meter Swiftships patrol vessel lying a few hundred meters off the Egyptian coast. An ISIS team using a Russian 9K129 Kornet, which may have come from Libyan army stock, struck the ship and set it afire. ISIS claims it killed everyone on board and issues a statement:

> Wilāyat Saynā' – On Thursday, Ramadān 29, the soldiers of the Khilāfah succeeded in destroying a ship belonging to the murtadd Egyptian navy in the Mediterranean Sea north of Rafah. They targeted the vessel with a guided missile and succeeded in completely destroying it and killing those inside.[1099]

That is doubtful as it did not sink, and managed to call for assistance, which quickly came.

ISIS COMBAT MEDICINE

There is little evidence of an organized combat medicine system in the ISIS forces, although there are isolated instances of battlefield care. The physicians and other personnel delivering battlefield care are not under any sort of special protection and incur the same risk as combatants. Many reports discuss the shortfall of ISIS medical personnel, for example "in June ISIS put out a call to recruit military officers, judges, managers, engineers and doctors. The call has met with some success. A Saudi Arabian newspaper noted that a doctor from that country joined ISIS . . . he either died in a booby-trap or while providing care to injured combatants."[1100]

The physicians that have joined ISIS have received no special training. That means a veterinarian or dentist or podiatrist could be dragooned into medical groups alongside general practitioners and nurses. The experienced doctors treating battlefield injuries and the critically wounded are centralized in urban hospitals, where they work under severe triage conditions. If they survive, the wounded have to be transferred to better medical facilities, which may not be available, thus ISIS most likely has a very high rate of mortality among the wounded.

Additionally, it is not clear if these facilities are designed to provide the care that the wounded need. And in these centers, combatants are treated before civilians. One report noted, "In Raqqa, the staff of local hospitals has been supplemented by the many foreign doctors and new medicine graduates—both Arab and Western—who have traveled to support the Islamic State. But they usually lack experience treating warzone injuries, so critically wounded IS fighters are transferred to Mosul, which has better medical facilities. And some medics take issue with how they handle emergencies. They force medical staff to treat combatants before civilians."[1101]

It is interesting to note that at least some of the wounded combatants have been transferred to Turkey for their medical care. An ISIS commander told the *Washington Post,* "We used to have some fighters—even high-level members of the Islamic State—getting treated in Turkish hospitals."

FIELD HOSPITALS

ISIS has few field hospitals and operates on an ad-hoc basis. One example comes from an Islamic State supporter named As-Soomaaliyyah, who claims to be a medic from Kenya. She tweeted a photo of a doctor in a

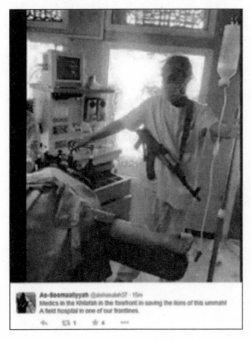

As-Soomaaliyyah @aishasalah37 · 15m
Medics in the Khilafah in the forefront in saving the lions of this ummah!
A field hospital in one of our frontlines.

field hospital sporting scrubs and an AK-47, captioned "Medics in the Khilafah in the forefront in saving the lions of this ummah! A field hospital in one of our frontlines." However, the stained glass behind the "medic," above and to his right, reveals that the "field hospital" is not a field hospital in the American sense—a portable installation relatively close to combat, where the wounded receive immediate care—rather, it is probably a permanent structure, either a civilian hospital adapted as a field hospital or a structure that was built for an entirely different purpose and is now being used as a field hospital. That it is an adapted civilian hospital does not seem likely, because the scene pictured is lighted through the glass windows and the windows or doors below them, rather than from above as it would be expected in a regular hospital or a field hospital.

CHAPTER 18

ABDUCTION, HOSTAGE ENVIRONMENT, AND RESCUE

ها هم أشبال الخلافة، سيقتلون من أرسله الموساد الغبي، ليتجسس على عورات المجاهدين والمسلمين

As for here in the Islamic State, here are the young lions of the Khilafah.

On July 3, 2015, President Obama signed an order for the US National Mission Forces to penetrate Syrian airspace to find and rescue American hostages. The primary consideration for the Commander-in-Chief: save the Americans or others, at all costs. A second consideration was that no US service members should be killed or harmed in this mission. There was no guarantee for zero casualties, but for the ISIS guards, that rule would certainly not apply.

The two most common hostages taken by ISIS are journalists and humanitarian aid workers. There have been a few innocent people who just ended up in the wrong place at the wrong time, like the French backpacker in Algeria, or in Libya where oil workers were accidentally left behind. For whatever reasons, wherever there are faction groups and Westerners, kidnapping is a good possibility.

So far, ISIS has taken twenty-five hostages from Western or industrialized countries, well below the seventy-six taken by Hezbollah in Lebanon during the 1980s. The *New York Times* has reported that a fair number of those hostages have been freed in exchange for ransom money, but what happens to the captives is contingent on factors in countries thousands of miles away. Either a concession deadline is met, or a ransom is paid, or a videotaped death is assured. The American policy to never negotiate or facilitate payment for the release of hostages is due to the belief that ransoms just fuel more hostage taking and fund more terrorism.[1102]

The western hostages taken by ISIS have provided the "caliphate" with two invaluable assets. This tried-and-true practice, ironically mastered by their Hezbollah enemies in the 1980s. One, it strikes fear in the Western public, and, two, brings them money or concessions. President Ronald Reagan actually negotiated with Iran to release Western hostages in Lebanon and supplied them with millions of dollars of advanced surface-to-air missiles. What could ISIS eventually get by taking Americans as captives? For them, it was easily worth the effort to find out. At a minimum cutting off heads are worth the terror they create through the news media.

ABDUCTION METHODOLOGIES

Capture of hostages by ISIS has been universally similar. Most of the captives met their fate when they crossed from Turkey into Syria. The abductions were either though a "snatch," a pre-planned on-the-road abduction where a vehicle overtakes the target and forces the hostage away at gunpoint, or a "checkpoint" abduction, where a roadblock is formed and the hostage is removed to a secondary captivity location.

A third type, the "walk-up" abduction, is generally rare. In this case the abduction takes place during a raid, when kidnappers simply walk up to the prospective hostage and guide them away on foot or to a waiting car. Doctors Without Borders reported that in January 2014, thirteen Doctors Without Borders members were abducted from their tents where they were working. Eight were Syrians who were released after a few hours, while the five international staff members were held captive for five months until their country paid a ransom.[1103]

Once the captives were abducted they were usually taken to an intermediate holding station. One was in a textile factory outside of Aleppo, Syria. There they were confined to individual cells. They would be questioned in an interrogation room. Eventually they would be taken to a permanent holding facility or cycled through several facilities in order to thwart rescue.

It's imperative to understand that when journalists and aid workers are captured, the initial hostage-takers were generally not ISIS members. In almost all cases the hostages were identified and captured by independent contractors like taxi drivers, translators, and "friends," or other terror groups such as Jehbat al-Nusra, who then "sold" the hostages to ISIS.

CONDITIONS

The conditions in which the captives lived were sparse and horrific. Universal ill treatment was the only right a hostage had in ISIS captivity. There was little hope for deliverance, as the hostages who were not released were executed in a spectacularly brutal way. The kidnappers, especially the English speakers, took relish in abusing the hostages in ways that mimicked the methods the US Army used to treat Iraqi prisoners at Abu Ghraib. The few hostages who were released recounted that they were made to wear bright yellow jumpsuits and were referred to by an Arabic number, so as to dehumanize as well as account for them.[1104]

One of the freed captives heard one of the jailers asking for a "password" to enter into the hostages' computers, cell phones, and Internet accounts. ISIS checked all accounts, including social networking and archives, for any signs of espionage.[1105] If a detainee was suspected of being a spy, the jailers would check for GPS chips in the prisoner's clothes and skin.[1106] ISIS believed all captives to be spies.

HOSTAGE TORTURE AND ABUSE

Several hostages, particularly those with military service, were waterboarded.[1107] If a captive was discovered to have had Western military service, ISIS would torture them, exploit them on video, and then execute them. David Haines and Peter Kassig were two such prisoners. One was betrayed by his LinkedIn account, while the other was featured on CNN. Other torture methods included close confinement in near total darkness, suspension by the ankles for long durations, horrific beatings, and repeated mock executions. Withholding food and water was standard; captives found themselves subsisting at times on as little as a "teacup of food a day."[1108]

While being held, a number of captives reportedly converted to Islam in the hope that it would improve their lot.[1109] James Foley was one such convert, whose conversion by all accounts was felt to be a sincere expression of faith.[1110] At least in the case of Foley, conversion seemed to temporarily convince his captors to ease up on the abuse, and at one point, Foley and British national John Cantlie, who has been featured speaking on behalf of the group in ISIS propaganda videos, were allowed to move about unchained inside their cells.[1111] This reprieve was short lived, as ISIS consolidated various foreign hostages together in one facility, handcuffed together. They were placed into two cells, one containing four women and one containing nineteen men.[1112]

James Foley

Steven Sotloff

Alan Henning

David Haynes

Haruna Yukawa and Kenji Goto

Magomed Khasiyev

HOSTAGE EXECUTIONS

There are a number of reasons why ISIS executes their hostages, but the three most likely reasons are, (1) to establish shock value through be-heading; (2) a refusal to pay ransom; and (3) concession deadlines were not met on time. Regardless of the reasons, all execution methods were gruesome. Execution was by either beheading or a bullet to the back of the head. With the exception of the immolation of Lt. Kassabeh, the majority of captives were beheaded. When American airstrikes began in June 2014, it sealed the fate of the American hostages. ISIS began to exe-cute them on video at the hands of Jihadi John, a British executioner.[1113]

The Americans and Brits were not the sole victims of execution. Fan Jinghui, a freelance consultant from China, and Ole Johan Grims-gaard-Ofstad, a Norwegian candidate for a master's degree in political science, were both killed by being shot in in head in November 2015.[1114] Kenji Goto, a freelance journalist, was captured in October 2014, while fellow Japanese countryman Haruna Yukawa was captured in August 2014. Yukawa was a security contractor acting as a consultant for Jap-anese companies.[1115] Goto and Yukawa were executed by beheading in January 2015. In these cases their governments declined to pay a ransom for their release. Just as with Foley, Haines, and Henning, these execu-tions occurred in front of a camera.

Frenchman Herve Gourdel was at the wrong place at the wrong time when backpacking in Djurdjura National Park in Algeria. He was kidnapped in September 2014 and subsequently executed when the French government continued airstrikes against ISIS. A Russian back-packer and blogger named Konstantin Zhuravlev also went missing in September 2014 while making an ill-advised crossing of the Syrian desert in a trek from Turkey to Egypt. He was abducted near Aleppo and has since disappeared.[1116]

In December 2015, Chechen Russian Magomed Khasiyev was the latest to be executed. It was reported by Radio Svoboda that he confessed to have been a spy been recruited by the FSB—the successor to the KGB—due to his connections with Chechen citizens in Syria before he infiltrated ISIS.[1117] In a theme common to all ISIS videos, he is wearing a bright jump suit with his hands tied behind him. A Russian-speaking

ISIS member dressed in paramilitary uniform then executed Khasiyev by decapitation.

Curiously, many hostages don't appear to struggle. It was reported by ex-ISIS militants that the captors conducted numerous "mock execution" drills that may have conditioned the hostages not to expect their death, resulting in a more relaxed appearance when the grim moment came.

The reason the militants behead some hostages while killing others with a seemingly more humane execution-style shot to the head appears to be linked to the degree of hostility the captive's government has toward ISIS. British and American governments refuse to pay ransoms and

Names of Persons Executed and Methods Used					
Name	**Occupation**	**Nationality**	**Date Captured**	**Date Executed**	**Means of Murder**
James Foley	Journalist	American	November 2012	August 2014	Decapitation
Kayla Mueller	Aid Worker	American	August 2013	February 2015	Unknown
Peter Edward Kassig	Aid Worker	American	October 2013	November 2014	Decapitation
Alan Henning	Aid Worker	British	December 2013	October 2014	Decapitation
David Haines	Aid Worker	British	March 2013	September 2014	Decapitation
Fan Jinghui	Consultant	Chinese	September 2015	November 2015	Shot
Sergey Gorbunov	Engineer	Russian	October 2013	April 2014	Shot
Steven Sotloff	Journalist	American	August 2013	September 2014	Decapitation
Lt. Muath al-Kasasbeh	Pilot	Jordanian	December 2014	January 2015	Immolated
Haruna Yukawa	PMC	Japanese	August 2014	January 2015	Decapitation
Kenji Goto	Journalist	Japanese	October 2014	January 2015	Decapitation
Ole Johan Grimsgaard-Ofstad	N/A	Norwegian	September 2015	November 2015	Shot
Herve Gourdel	Backpacker	French	September 2014	September 2014	Decapitation
Tomislav Salopek	Expatriate Worker	Croatia	June 2015	August 2015	Decapitation
Konstantin Zhuravlev	Backpacker / Blogger	Russian	September 2013	N/A	N/A

are actively engaged in destroying ISIS; subsequently British and American hostages get the worst treatment. The *Daily Mail* reported that Peter Kassig was executed by gunshot before being beheaded, suggesting that he might have resisted the captors.[1118] Above is a table showing the Western hostages that were executed in Iraq and Syria.

HOSTAGE RANSOMS AND OPEN SALES

ISIS does not usually execute hostages immediately after capture. Captives' families or governments receive demands for ransom in exchange for release. Alternatively, ISIS imposes impractical ultimatums on governments with strict deadlines. The prisoners are executed when a ransom is not forthcoming, or when the deadline passes.

Released ISIS Hostages			
Name	Occupation	Nationality	Released
Daniel Rye Ottosen	Photojournalist	Danish	June 2014
Didier Francois	Journalist	French	April 2014
Nicholas Henin	Journalist	French	April 2015
Pierre Torres	Photojournalist	French	April 2014
Edward Elias	Photojournalist	French	April 2014
Toni Neukirch	Citizen	German	June 2014
Fedirico Motka	Aid Worker	Italian	May 2014
Marc Marginedas	Journalist	Spanish	February 2014
Javier Espinosa	Journalist	Spanish	March 2014
Ricardo Garcia Vilanova	Photojournalist	Spanish	March 2014
Jejoen Bontinck	ISIS Jihadist	Belgian	October 2013

A debate started in 2015 about paying for hostages. Sharp international and internal criticism was levied against President Obama for the American policy of not paying or facilitating ransoms. ISIS was listening. Almost immediately they started offering "Hostage For Sale" pictures, taunting the West to buy hostages out of captivity. In the online magazine *Dabiq* in the eleventh issue on pages 64 and 65, the doomed hostages Fan Jinghui and Ole Johan Grimsgaard-Ofstad appeared in grim advertisements as being "for sale."[1119] Many European countries actually do pay ransom, including France, Italy, Germany, Austria, Spain, and Switzerland.[1120] Despite rebuke from countries that refuse to pay ransoms, most if not all of the hostages from those countries were freed. The Americans, British, Russians, Norwegians, Japanese, and Chinese were all executed.

According to reporting by the *New York Times*, ISIS captors would "triage" new hostages, with priority going to captives whose countries pay ransoms.[1121] Priority went to Spanish prisoners because their government had set a precedent by paying al-Qaeda €6 million for the release of aid workers.[1122] French citizens were the next most-prized.

MUSLIM AND CHRISTIAN HOSTAGE RELEASES

The group has taken a particularly hard-line stance in opposition to fellow Muslims who do not practice ISIS's strict brand of Sunni Islam.[1123] In the case of non-Muslims, on the other hand, the group has at times shown some mercy towards its hostages.

In March 2015, a Sharia judge for the organization ruled that nineteen Assyrian Christian captives held by ISIS should be sent home, on the grounds that they did not belong to militias and had not run afoul of Sharia law.[1124] They were instead required to recognize ISIS as their new leadership and pay a fine. This group was part of at least two hundred Assyrian Christians who were captured at the same time, and reportedly all later released.[1125]

This example stands in contrast to twenty-one Egyptian Coptic Christians beheaded by ISIS in February 2015.[1126] In April 2015, three

Sale sheet for Norwegian prisoner Ole Johan Grimsgaard-Ofstad. (*Dabiq*, Issue 11, page 64)

Sale sheet for Chinese prisoner Fan Jinghui. (*Dabiq*, Issue 11, page 65)

hostages taken in Libya who were all employees of the Austrian oil company VAOS were released. Two were staff from Bangladesh and one was from Ghana. The company did not comment on speculation that a ransom was paid.[1127]

HOSTAGE RESCUE AND RECOVERY

While the US doesn't pay ransom fees to terrorists as a matter of policy, they do try to rescue hostages. In June 2014, FBI officials traveled to separate locations in Europe to interview former captives of the Islamic State. US intelligence along with the FBI met with released hostages and collated their human intelligence to gain useful information on the whereabouts of missing hostages. When ISIS released three Western hostages, Daniel Rye Ottosen, a Danish photojournalist, and French citizens Didier Francois and Nicholas Henin gave descriptions of the prison where they were held.

Intelligence officials relayed the information gathered from the former hostages back to Washington, where the entire US intelligence community made a determined effort to find where the hostages would be located. Time was of the essence and the CIA, NSA, and National Geospatial intelligence agency worked with the US Army Intelligence and Security Command, and the Joint Special Operations Command pulled out all stops to plan a mission based on the location matching the description given by the former captives. Once isolated, the information was confirmed on the ground by other means. On July 3, 2014 executive order directed the US Special Operations Command to rescue American journalists James Foley, Steven Sotloff, and any captives held with them.[1128]

At approximately 2:00 a.m., several 160th Special Operations regiment MH-60 Blackhawk helicopters carrying national mission force soldiers of the 1st Special Operations Force-Delta teams left for Syria. They were supported by the bristling MH-60L Direct Action Penetrator helicopters, which carried a battery of hellfire missiles, rockets, and miniguns. They flew at incredibly low altitude and entered Syrian airspace heading toward the outskirts of Raqqa, Syria,

ISIS's capital. They were given overhead coverage by a MQ-9 Reaper drone carrying at least four AGM-134 Hellfire missiles and two GBU-12 500-pound laser-guided bombs, with a second drone carrying ten Hellfire missiles.

Once the Delta operators hit the ground, a gunfight ensued, killing two ISIS members. The operators stormed the building and cleared it room by room, but after a full search they found no sign of the hostages. They conducted a sensitive site exploitation and took whatever evidence they could find and flew back. The operation was a success, despite having not returned with the hostages.[1129]

The month after the attempted rescue, James Foley was executed by Jihadi John.

It has become evident that after the release of the European hostages, ISIS moves the rest of the hostages from location to location in order to foil rescue attempts, as they have done with Foley and the others. The mission has not ended; American soldiers have conducted numerous other rescues that resulted in freeing hostages from ISIS.

In May 2015, American and Kurdish forces raided a home in al-Shadadiya, Syria, where ISIS operated a sex trade in Yazidi women.[1130] Many young Yazidi captives were rescued in the operation.[1131]

On another 2:00 a.m. raid, a joint US Special Forces-Kurdish Pershmerga SOF descended on a an ISIS prison facility in northeastern Iraq. The Kurdish and American forces freed seventy-five hostages being held by the terrorist group,[1132] who were reportedly under immediate threat of execution.[1133] One Delta Trooper, Master Sergeant Joshua Wheeler, was killed in the raid; several ISIS fighters were killed, and five were captured.[1134]

Master Sgt Joshua Wheeler, US SFOD-D

CHAPTER 19

ISIS SOCIAL MEDIA: "OUR LIFE IN THE THRILL KILL CULT"

There has been a revolutionary shift in the media usage of jihadist groups such as al-Qaeda, ISIS, and their affiliates. Thirty years ago, al-Qaeda's first-generation membership promoted itself via audiocassette, printed pamphlets, and face-to-face sermons extolling the virtues of Holy War against the West. Today the modern ISIS terrorist straps on a GoPro action sport camera, sets up to edit on an advanced laptop, and rushes out to record a mass-murder campaign. While the techniques may appear sophisticated due to the improved technology, the motivation, the underlying methods and types of product, have remained constant over the past three decades of terrorism media. What has changed is technology.

From the founding of al-Qaeda in 1988 to about 2000, various forms of media spread al-Qaeda's ideological messages. The pamphlets and self-published books gave way to the audiocassette, which was ubiquitous in South and Central Asia and the Middle East. When circumstances dictated great secrecy, couriers used the Casio F-91 digital watch to carry messages, fatwas, and speeches. The storage media evolved from cassettes, VHS, and hi8, to smart cards, jump drives, and direct upload. By 1997, the DVD replaced other methods of media and was subsequently replaced by the World Wide Web. When jihadism was still starting, infant personal computers with dot matrix texts on bulletin board system forums (BBS) ruled the day. Networking has moved from BBS boards to BlogSpot, Facebook, Twitter, and WordPress, if not a standalone site. Online forums still have a strong presence on many jihadist sites and act as dump sites for video distribution.

Additionally, jihadis maintain file portals that contain hundreds of PDFs, MP3s, and videos of jihadist activities. Videos speak much more clearly and are easy to find with a little digging. The reason the jihadists of the past didn't upload photos or videos was due to the limitation of the technology of the time, not the ambition of the jihadist himself. That is why the advent of the CD-R and the early World Wide Web changed the face of messaging.

Today there are many ways to record video and post it immediately to the web. ISIS wants to avoid using cell phones to evade detection by authorities; however, it is still the most convenient way to record surreptitiously and produce the footage for others to edit at a later time.

Removal of the SIM card and Wi-Fi–only operation makes cell phones harder to detect.

Now that global extremists are transitioning from the underground al-Qaeda cells to aboveground ISIS platoons, we've seen a dramatic advancement in how the cult disseminates its message of bloodlust with the power and near-universal presence of the Internet. ISIS is formidable at harnessing social media for shock value simply because the media are now enmeshed in a revolutionary advanced-tech world. The message has definitely not changed, only the technology. Had Twitter existed, one can be sure al-Qaeda would absolutely have tweeted photos of the 9/11 attacks. The new generation of jihadist is raised in a world filled with graphic-rich video games, action movies, and the Internet's world reach at their fingertips in the form of the mobile phone and the portable tablet. The tools for terror have upgraded in line with available consumer goods, and this will always be the case for future terrorist organizations.

The driving purpose of terror videos is to simply transmit the threat of terror and to create a vision that the killer is omnipotent and coming next for the viewer. Whether this goal is successful or not is determined by the message narrative that the group creates about itself and a compliant mainstream media. The terrorist organization can no longer just be a flashy black mask and a hood; now they have terror spokesmen and stage media spectaculars. Other relevant factors are who is being killed, who is speaking, to whom they are speaking, the narrative they are trying to frame, and the distribution platform for the horror they wish to communicate. For example, the most sophisticated videos published by the al-Hayat Media Center—the English-language division of ISIS's media system—are directed at Muslims and non-Muslims in the West as well as an educated global audience. English is the language of business around the world, which makes it a second national language of many countries. ISIS understands that but carefully peppers each message with critical Islamic words and phrases that practicing Muslims should know and converts had better learn.

Virtually all of the terminology ISIS and other jihadis use is based on Islam and virtually identical, no matter where on the planet they espouse their beliefs. This characteristic causes many Western politicians, scholars, and pundits to wholeheartedly believe that the movement is unabashedly representative of Islam, despite the fact that virtually the entire the Muslim world disagrees. ISIS has never had more than tacit support in any country, as wholesale slaughtering of enemies and chattel slavery are now completely un-Islamic. The jihadis' myriad terms and justifications are all fraught with religious, military, and political contradictions. These signifiers create scholarly races to finally understand the meaning, origins, and motivation of these terrorists. ISIS plays this game gleefully by blasting out enormous quantities of Islamic-laden jibberish that speaks only to its terrorist adherents while befuddling the West.

For non-Muslims this fuses the image of ISIS as a wholly Islamic organization without any context as to accuracy or deviance. For more than a decade, a sizeable team of dedicated staffers crafted each message in al-Hayat publications, framing the message for the viewer in a cloak of piety or aggression, depending on the intended audience. Although the news media in the West is often focused on the violent messages as an accent to heightening outrage, al-Qaeda and ISIS have an industry-level understanding of the importance of filling the news cycle with what producers need, and shoot video for just that purpose.

The most sophisticated videos often have a singular message and may include acts of ultra-violence, or deep devotion laced with charity, each mixed with calm religious dissection and justification. The image created by al-Qaeda was of the itinerant Jihadi "knights" who travel the world, fighting injustice and striking terror into the hearts of the enemy. ISIS prefers the trappings of a transitional expeditionary force on the march, such as those led by the Prophet Mohammed in the seventh century. They show an army of Muslim heroes from around the world that have seized stolen lands, formed an army of God (Jaysh Allah), filled with actual soldiers of God (Jund Allah). These heroes have restored the Caliphate to Islam and are ready to sacrifice their lives to bring about the end of days as the prophecies foretold. These are two distinctly different narratives. They reveal al-Qaeda's preference for incremental change to achieve a "clash of civilizations" and ISIS's penchant for bloodlust in a revolutionary war.

For either group, the suicide bombings, executions, immolations, and crucifixions are designed to enrage the Western TV viewer and bring about the clash of civilization between the West and Islam so the terrorists can prevail and rule the world. They need the hatred, Islamophobia, xenophobia, and outrage to continue justifying their self-made image as defenders of Islam in order to eventually coopt and control all of Islam.

SOCIAL MEDIA FOR INTERNAL CONSUMPTION

However, the overwhelming majority of official terror media over the past three decades from both ISIS and al-Qaeda is internal propaganda aimed at recruiting new members and bolstering the determination of already-indoctrinated members. These audio/video bits include announcements of religious rulings (Fatwas), discussions of law, and sermons aimed directly at compelling the listener to feel guilty for their shortcomings before promising a salvation if they will renounce the world as they know it and enjoy the beauty of the Caliphate. If one doesn't speak Arabic, the media services have translations built into the stream that provide immediate translation.

VIDEO CALLS TO ABANDON PAST LIFE AND FAMILY

In a style typical of a destructive cult's indoctrination and brainwashing techniques, almost all ISIS videos call for the viewer to perform emigration (Hijrah) away from the lands of the unbelievers (dar al-Kuffir) and to come directly to Syria to join the caliphate. This misuse of Islamic history—the Prophet Mohammed performed Hijrah to leave Mecca for Medina to start Islam—is actually designed to divide the recruit from family members. The modern call to Hijrah is *always* a secret directive to leave one's corrupt past and prove fealty to Islam; if a family suspected radicalization they might intervene or call law enforcement.

In ISIS doctrine, Hijrah is described as the greatest of religious undertakings: no one should stop a prospective recruit except God. In fact, if one cannot leave the dar al-Kuffir, they can perform the emigration mentally and live ultraorthodox lives in their own homes or conceal it in their hearts. The San Bernardino killer Sayed Farook and his wife Tashfeen Malik are believed to have done just that. They concealed all about their radicalization from their families while performing mental Hijrah. Even his mother did not know he had radicalized to the point that they would abandon their six-month-old baby and carry out a mass murder.

TERRORISM AS SPECTACLE: WELCOME TO THE THRILL KILL CULT

The most sophisticated videos published by the al-Hayat Media Center—the English-language propaganda division of ISIS—are designed to influence the global media and potential Western recruits. However, the most popular videos among ISIS members and fanboys in the unofficial publications, web streams, forums, and internal storage dumps are the most brutal and barely watchable examples of mass murder, throat-cutting, and games with corpses. Once released into the Internet, these titles get instant global propagation as news outlets scramble to be the first to cover the latest threat from ISIS. There is an entire industry of security and media support companies that monitor terror video media just to be the first to get the latest atrocity into the news stream.

The most common ISIS videos are almost administrative in their dullness. They include province activity reports, unofficial publications, web streams, forums, and internal storage dumps. A handful of ISIS publications instruct how best to perform guerrilla mass marketing. The raw pages of many ISIS releases found on the extremely popular website *justpaste.it* indicate that ISIS intentionally spreads their message on as many platforms as possible due to the threat of interruptions through takedowns due to policy violations. A typical single post will often include a reference to the wilayat that created it, a custom graphic that represents the video, and a string of links to spread it around many media sources.

Most sources are based at archive.org, mediafire, Google Drive YouTube, and a very long list of file-sharing companies.

THRILL KILL CULT (TKC) VIDEOS

The videos reveal a Thrill Kill Cult (TKC) aspect of the entire ISIS ideological franchise. The members make videogame-like combat videos of merciless mayhem and bathe them with sacred mission rhetoric purposed by God alone to the tune of nasheeds or religious chants and hymns. To a man (and sometimes woman) they use the phrase "In the name of God" to justify whatever horror they are about to reveal. These videos are not just bragging, but allow the "cowards" (a.k.a. you the viewer) to bear witness to jihadists' mental strength and devotion to their God, no matter how horrible. The TKC videos are almost always intended to inspire fear in the non-faithful and jealousy from the co-denominationalist viewer who has not yet shown the guts to come to join the murderous rampage. The videos often mock the viewers directly and claim that they are not men, but cowards who eventually must either find the ISIS interpretation of Islam correct or die as the others. This is a cult-like core component of recruitment.

The TKC videos appear to intone the old British Army slogan "Come Be a Man among Men," and add "and Kill Anyone and Anything Not Like Us." Much of the cinematography is so well-executed, some scenes appear to have been cut from videos of gameplay in *Call of Duty* or *Medal of Honor*. The TKC component of ISIS videos show off how "fun" it is to kill kuffir (infidels), rafida (apostates), salibiyeen (Christian crusaders), or just about anyone who opposes ISIS. The raw video on reality sites such as Liveleak shows the bloody murder without any filter. This Thrill Kill Cult component of the terror videos exists within all ISIS jihadist groups from Yemen to Somalia to Nigeria, and is a key component of inspiring the mentally susceptible, the psychotic, and the fanatic to join the jihad and become a fellow murderer for their variant of God.

Whether it is in Mali, Chad, Libya, Syria, Pakistan, France, or Canada the videographer captures the horror in Kodachrome detail. Each terror subgroup performs in a precisely uniform manner and their actors say virtually the same thing:

1. They praise God for giving them the opportunity to fight.
2. They all extol the cult of jihad ideology that allows them to massacre innocents with utter impunity.
3. They issue the message du jour.
4. They perform a horrible act.
5. They praise God for allowing that horrible act to occur as His will.
6. They warn that more horrible acts are to come.

In reality these videos are a form of elite terrorist narcissism and convey their depth of devotion to compatriots; the highest form of worship to God. This is why groups such as al-Qaeda and ISIS seek to control the distribution of the media at strategic levels as often as possible. The raw footage that pops up on affiliate sites shows some jihadists behaving with hyena-like bloodlust. In fact the raw, uncut combat footage is shot to show off how fun it is to kill anyone who is opposed to them, which is not helpful to the strategic narrative of the group; the bloodlust must be carefully framed by a central media group.

TERROR MEDIA PRODUCTION UNITS

Al-Qaeda organized the first widespread use of professional centralized media groups around as-Sahab media in the mid-1990s. Though still strong and active—as-Sahab remains al-Qaeda Central Command's (AQC) official media wing and speaks with the voice of bin Laden's successor, Dr. Ayman al-Zawahiri—it has dramatically lost media share to ISIS after the 2014 declaration of the Caliphate. The heart and soul of the ISIS communications team is al-Furqan Media. It operates the currently popular al-Hayat Media Center for non-Arabic communications and propaganda. The various provinces have their own highly compartmentalized production teams directed by a media emir, who gives video assignments with instructions bearing the official IS logo and seal of the media emir.[1135]It would appear that all

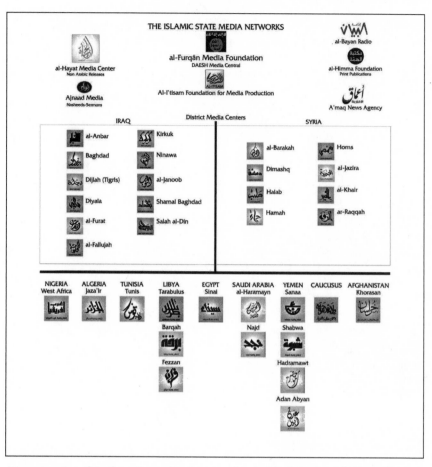

Approximation of the formal organizations associated with al-Qaeda and ISIS media worldwide.

Jihadi mass communications groups now maintain a few centralized production offices, followed by translation, repackaging, and transmission teams. These multimedia nodes are responsible for maintaining a globally linked multiplatform information technology network with subgroups monitoring, operating, and posting on web forums, Twitter, and other social media.

The most popular forums and press releases reveal that these groups are keen to avoid anyone modifying their work. Al-Furqan and as-Sahab remain the top generators of messages, with the al-Qaeda's al-Nusra Front in Syria following close behind. Releases then go to translation services to translate the messages, who then upload to the web at self-service storage sites. These translation and propagation groups include "INFORM" for Bosnians and Russians; "Global Islamic Media Front," who formed Al-Qadisiyyah Media for Urdu, Hindi, Bangla, Pashto, and Persian; and Fursan Al-Balagh Media, dedicated to English-language translations.

TYPES OF VIDEO PRODUCTION UNITS

ISIS utilizes three levels of video production as follows:

First Line Video

Body-, Helmet-, or Weapon-Mounted Cameras: The favorite camera of the fighting squads is the GoPro. Increasingly you can find first-person-shooter footage appearing on sites like LiveLeak that resemble video games as the fighters raid villages. One popular video shows a tank with a GoPro mounted as it launches an attack on the Kurdish city of Kobane. Another from Egypt shows a member of the Ansar Beit al-Maqdis terror group storming the remains of an Egyptian army barracks that had just been blown down by a suicide bomber. With a gun-mounted video camera he hunts, finds, and executes several wounded soldiers trapped in the rubble.

Second Line

Video Support Team (VSTs): These are the one- or two-man teams pioneered by al-Qaeda in Afghanistan that follow and shoot media like a military "Combat Camera" team. They never carry arms and exist solely to capture the footage for replay. Iraqi insurgents often co-located the VST with a suicide bomber supervisor who could also trigger the explosive by phone if the bomber backed out.

Third Line

Professional Newsmedia Teams (PNTs): These are high-quality media shot digitally and produced in a large format facility such as a newsroom or dedicated media site. The John Cantlie hostage news reports, such as his report from the Mosul souk, used this format and camerawork.

MESSAGING TYPOLOGY: ISSUE IDEOLOGICALLY SOUND MESSAGES

Consistent with the history of terrorism propaganda, the majority of multimedia produced and distributed by ISIS involves a call to action to prove one's faith. This tradition dates back through many movements to compel the viewer from watching to acting.

MAINTENANCE OF NARRATIVE CONTROL

There are hundreds of videos across the jihadist landscape. The tie that binds them all is the central message that the Islamic State or other jihad zones are the present utopias for all pious Muslims who emigrate from the land of the unbelievers. Getting to the utopia requires leaving a state of "ignorance" and understanding that the entire world except the AQ/ISIS-occupied lands are unclean.

Additionally, the image of a pastoral religious paradise with he-man fighting knights spreads quietly through systems of internal messaging in the ISIS/al-Qaeda franchise world. "Mujatweets" are Twitter messages that are archived and compiled for the benefit of prospective jihadis. Mujatweets are generally hidden from the news media and casual observers by dumping them into hidden folders. Though al-Qaeda and ISIS are believed to have issued over ninety thousand Twitter messages a day, the best and most representative for their media are kept from public view. Most Mujatweets are completely pastoral presentations of how wonderful life is in the self-named ISIS Caliphate and how brave the ISIS knights are to battle the entire world. On the other hand, the news media–style reports from the British hostage John Cantlie, detailing the "stability" of ISIS-controlled cities such as Mosul and Ar-Raqqa, are slick, convincing National Geographic documentary–style segments. The purpose of these media activities is to project a "nation" that is a paradise on Earth filled with images of cool water, a devoted Muslim community, and laughing mujahedeen children enjoying calm and stability, instead of the hellscape reality of the Syrian civil war and protracted aerial bombardment. To many Internet viewers, these ISIS media reports have as much validity as BBC or CNN.

One of the last but no less important uses of ISIS media is to maintain control and unanimity of effort in their jihad zone, be it the caliphate of the Islamic State or the combat regions of new ISIS provinces. This was especially prevalent when ISIS proclaimed itself the sole Islamic caliphate and government on earth. Many former al-Qaeda groups were exhorted to line up and swear an oath of loyalty to the new *Calife à la place du Calife*, Abu Bakr al-Baghdadi.

These publications also demonstrate cohesion of message in battlefield reports from the various district media centers that proclaim the enemies of monotheism have been conquered, or that repelled and wayward Muslims have confessed and are now ready to be part of the Islamic State.

Videos showing hostages and murder victims also validate the messaging. Hostage John Cantlie, a British journalist, "reported" on the conditions in Mosul under ISIS. At one point an Iraqi aircraft flew overhead and he shouted on camera "Here I am. Drop your bombs. Try to rescue me again . . . Rubbish." This was designed to show the viewer that Western forces were powerless with Cantlie standing out on a street. Although it may not have played well on CNN, in Iraq, Syria, and other parts of the Middle East it struck a chord.

HOSTAGE CONFESSION VIDEOS

Hostages who are not to survive captivity give coerced "last confession" videos. In a horrible routine, the victim is paraded before the camera to testify how ISIS helped them find the way back to pure monotheism and redemption, and they ask to be forgiven their sins. They never are. To the cultists, the terminal blessing of God is appointed the moment the victim confesses. To ISIS, the coming murder is an immediate reward for the victim wisely finding the way back to God. Usually, the camera shot is cut to reveal a gun at the back of the head or a large knife. The end is swift unless the victim is slated for "royal command performance" deaths such as immolation, drowning in a cage, decapitation by explosive detonation cord, stoning, or being thrown off a roof. Not one iota of this is Islamic in any way, but the novelty and barbarity is especially appealing to the consumers of terrorist propaganda.

There is a stark difference between the false humility of al-Hayat Media's highly polished propaganda videos and the raw combat footage. Al-Hayat seeks to maintain a positive and powerful image. The loose, individually shot combat reels show an undisciplined gang. Organized footage seeks to portray discipline in the ranks, while the loose footage reveals harassment and a lack of confidence in authority.

DEMONSTRATING THE PROJECTION OF POWER

First and foremost, the official media services of ISIS serve to project the constitution and viability of the organization on the world stage: "we are a force to be dealt with." A video will then bombard the viewer with a dizzying mashup of video team operations and proclamations of gains and glory, especially of future rewards. The narrative is laden with more than simply apocalyptic messages meant to signify what these propagandists believe; they are telling you what they want you to believe.

To prove their viability, the regional offices of the jihadist news services often applaud each other or themselves for hard-fought campaigns against enemies of the group. It is not unusual to see an al-Yemen media group congratulate a Boko Haram operation or vice versa. Within Syria the regional groups from one state will work to let each other know that the systems are working and that life is normal in the Caliphate.

DEVOTION THROUGH MARTYRDOM VIDEOS

From early on, ideological martyrdom videos of hyperbolic sermons overlaid with chanting ISIS music have been compelling recruitment tools. They usually have the same format, no matter which jihadi group issues it. The media centers give a brief clip of a suicide bomber before his or her mission. Without exception the young suicide bombers in martyrdom videos express unbridled joy about their coming death. Leaders then exploit their names in calls to other fighters to stay dedicated to the group's mission.

In the martyrdom video filmed by al-Qaeda follower Amedy Coulibaly—one of the early Paris attackers—the viewer can read of his path, see him work out with focus, express joy at the prospect of his future in heaven, and then watch muffled footage of the raid that ended his life. Prior to the London 7/7 al-Qaeda bombing operations, in their martyrdom videos, Mohammed Siddique Khan and Shezhad Tanweer told their families that they would miss them.

CORPSE MANIPULATION FOR MYSTICAL EFFECT

Whenever possible, particularly in post-combat martyrdom videos, if the head or body can be recovered, the videographers manipulate the face to look like it is peaceful or that the martyr died happy and is smiling. If the body or even just a hand is recovered they are posed and made to hold the forefinger up in the symbol of "One God."

THE BEHEADING VIDEO TRADITION CONTINUES IN HIGH DEFINITION

Despite the recent shock and disgust of the West, terrorists have documented their spectacles for decades now, yet the news media struggles to cover the latest atrocity with this historical context. Instead, they fixate on the glossy nature of the image.

The first viral video on the Internet was the beheading of Russian soldier Yevgeny Rodionov in

Unknown Russian Soldier

The first viral jihadist video on the web was of the decapitation execution of a Russian soldier, Yevgeny Rodionov.

1996 by Chechen jihadists. Six years later, al-Qaeda would release "The Slaughter of the Spy-Journalist, the Jew Daniel Pearl," after he was murdered. Nick Berg was murdered on camera by Abu Mussab al-Zarqawi in May 2004, followed by nine others including citizens of Japan, South Korea, Nepal, Egypt, Bulgaria, and the United Kingdom. The jihadists recorded and disseminated these for both shock value and as a recruiting device.

ISIS ADAPTIVENESS IN THE BEHEADING GENRE

The huge difference in response between the 2004 execution of Nick Berg, for instance, and the death of James Foley ten years later came by adding only a few changes to the original media style. The first change was to the venue. Berg's was in a basement and had all the appearance of murdering a trapped rat. ISIS conducted their murders outdoors in what they claimed was liberated land in a holy caliphate. They showed no fear of being caught or attacked from the air. The ISIS videos implied freedom to execute at will. The second change was that ISIS managed to get the victim to recite his message to the target audience, his people, and leaders. The third change was to select a native speaker from the victim's region of the world. Using Mohammed Emwazi or "Jihadi John" to speak in English and carry out the beheadings was powerful. Having him speak eloquent English and directly threaten the Western world demonstrated a degree of sophistication and caused a level of political emotional outrage that the murder of Nick Berg did not.

OFFICIAL VS UNOFFICIAL BEHEADINGS AND MURDERS ON VIDEO

Al-Qaeda leadership frowned on official beheadings after the globally negative impact of the Abu Mussab al-Zarqawi/Al-Qaeda in Iraq (AQI) videos of Nicholas Berg and other Western hostages. In fact, the use of official beheading videos from AQI was suspended after 2004. AQI knew that mass murders could continue in order to lure more Arab recruits, but

Islamic State boycott of Apple products.

not so publicly. When ISIS transitioned to all-Iraqi leadership, they wanted to reinstitute media spectacle as a form of Terror Shock Value (TSV) in order to subjugate the will of the victim populations and lure the Americans back in to a conflict with the Islamic State. Abu Bakr al-Baghdadi reinstituted official ISIS beheadings of Westerners with the murder of journalist James Foley in 2014.

It should be noted that before the Foley video, hundreds of beheadings were already occurring throughout Iraq and Syria. Videos of beheadings, crucifixions, hangings, and massacres proliferated on unfiltered sites like Live-Leak without notice by Western media. These were not official videos put out by al-Furqan for the polished presentation to the Western news stream, but unofficial documentation and recruitment videos, usually unpolished Handycam work revealing the gleeful pursuit of murderers admiring their handiwork.

CONTROLLING THE NARRATIVE

Individuals also act as self-generating media centers without editors or middlemen to the ISIS publication services, in a phenomenon similar to the Western "iReporter." Al-Furqan media tends to a carefully arranged message, even if this means reshooting a scene over and over. The self-generating individual doesn't have to adhere to criteria for official videos and may share footage that is insufficiently gory, or may overlook the necessity to remind the viewer there is only one God. This lack of editorial control has become troublesome for ISIS leaders, and they have told supporters and combatants to rein in unofficial video and to avoid giving away intelligence. Always wary of spying, ISIS leaders recently released a prohibition on Apple products, as the NSA and Mossad may use them to detect the whereabouts of leaders or units for attack by drone strike.

TRICKS OF THE TRADE FOR THE SOPHISTICATED MEDIA JIHADIST

Osama bin Laden, Ayman al-Zawahiri, and Abu Mussab al-Zarqawi all had to hide their video production in the shadows, and as a result, used a few familiar outside shots. Bin Laden used to have to summon a trusted videographer to come tape his latest lecture. It was also critical to the security of the group, since bin Laden had the famous Afghan warlord, Ahmed Shah Massoud, assassinated with a bomb in a video camera the day before 9/11 in order to hinder his assistance to the Americans. After the trusted videographers edited the product in a location far from the site of the shoot, they could then disseminate copies via courier to the world. The methods were advanced for the day.

During the Iraq insurgency, the *Washington Post* noted, "analysts said that as-Sahab is outfitted with some of the best technology available. Editors and producers use ultralight Sony Vaio laptops and top-end video cameras. Files are protected using PGP, or Pretty Good Privacy, a virtually unbreakable form of encryption software that is also used by intelligence agencies around the world." This changed when ISIS seized terrain. After conquering cities with large-scale television stations and production studios, they were more interested in exploiting full-scale media organizations and operating teams in captured newsrooms. They also seized all the electronic shops that sold cameras and gear, which provided them

Zarqawi makes plans "in secret" on camera.

with all the tools necessary to produce their media on a grand scale until destroyed or overrun.

ISIS'S MISSION: GO SMALLER, FASTER, PORTABLE, AND MAKE BROADCAST-READY MEDIA

HIGH DEFINITION CAMERAS— THE GOPRO GENERATION

In the 1980s and 1990s al-Qaeda used Sony Handycams with videotape cassettes of low-definition quality. Today, jihadis use many different types of camera systems, most of which are not level of quality found in al-Hayat publications, but have high enough digital quality for broadcast news.

Much of the first-level combat footage shows fighters using GoPro action cameras, iPad-styled tablets, smart phones, and an array of digital cameras. Examination of all the official publications by al-Hayat Media has shown that the quality of the cameras has simply gone up as they have kept pace with the average technology any of us can use to render a quality product. However, al-Hayat appears to be fixated on the quality of the video, because it is seeking to gain outside listeners to its message. Only the trained eye knows the best methods of capturing images. Most of the footage indicates that few quality videographers work for al-Furqan or as-Sahab, and none are working for the satellite groups like Boko Haram, AQAP, or lesser groups.

GOPRO AND THE CHARLIE HEBDO ATTACKERS

In the al-Qaeda inspired *Charlie Hebdo* Paris attacks of 2015, all the attackers had GoPro cameras. Two years previous, Medhi Nemmouche and Mohamed Merah also had GoPro cameras. Merah even had his strapped around his neck and wanted to have his footage played on Al-Jazeera.

According to a Paris police report, the Kouachi brothers never opened their GoPro camera box.[1136] That may indicate that the camera footage was an afterthought and they decided to carry out the attack and let the traditional media cover the result, rather than try to survive and issue their own footage. On the other hand, Amedy Coulibaly, who conducted the kosher supermarket siege, was pressing his hostages to upload video he had already filmed and edited on a laptop he had in possession.[1137] His video "Soldat du Califat" was, in essence, his martyrdom video. The laptop would indicate which software he used, and we know he used a jump drive from GoPro to computer, according to hostage accounts. Contrast this with the ISIS-directed terrorist attack at Stade de France and the Bataclan theater massacres. ISIS did not issue any media or send cameras with their teams. In a clever reversion to the fundamentals of terrorist propaganda propagation of the 1970s for the twenty-first century, they relied on the spectacular nature of the act to force global media to provide all the coverage they wanted and needed.

THE VIDEO SUPPORT TEAM VS INDIVIDUAL VIDEOGRAPHER

The extensive use of VST (Video Support Teams) in most operations continues to this day, but only in active war zones. We are seeing more and more self-driven first-person-shooter footage across the web portals we monitor. The ability to franchise the experience of adventure to a generation who grew up with the ability to play first-person-shooter war games is an obvious draw. This would also enable the fighter to be more than simply a fighter in combat, as they become part of the message-making mechanism.

RENDER HIGH-QUALITY EDITING

The quality of video has improved in most digital cameras over the past decade, enabling even the most unskilled videographer to capture moving images that would make their family and coworkers happy. The camera is only part of the work.

Editing is another discipline altogether. Simple editing suites are included with most new cameras, and in an examination of several of the major videos published by al-Furqan Media, there are areas where the editing is rushed unnecessarily, including bad edits in the November 16, 2014 video of Syrian soldiers and short edits in the Jordanian pilot video. In some cases, the frames listing the ISIS intended targets for attack were simply thrown in after the important names had been rendered.

GO HOLLYWOOD STYLE

The discussion in the media seems to often be focused on how advanced these operations are and whether professional filmmakers or Professional Newsmedia Teams (PNTs) are involved in the process. Al-Hayat products are called "Hollywood style" by most of the major media. While it may be easy to marvel at how advanced the techniques in these video productions may be, the videos examined so far could have been filmed with fewer than three cameras and edited on a standard laptop. The speculation about professional filmmakers assumes much about producing a film. Most of the videos are raw combat footage mixed with PowerPoint or inserts. If al-Hayat created one ubiquitous intro file and simply passed it along, it would only have to be made once. Once branded, the rest of the media outlets could more readily propagate the message instead of being caught up in the assembly of the message.

The average ISIS video clip usually lasts no longer than fifteen minutes. Two notable segments, one about the murder of Syrian soldiers and the other about the murder of Coptic Christians in Libya, were less than ten minutes apiece. To do this, the "directors" of these videos clearly conducted retakes and changes in angles. The preponderance of uninspired single-shot tripod-mounted camera videos dwarfs the number of sophisticated, well-made videos.

Despite speculation that the dozen or so high-quality films were produced on complicated platforms like Avid, it is also possible that they were created via Adobe Premiere with AfterEffects or Sony Vegas. In the past, many jihadists would use Sony Vaio laptops to edit their video, which leads one to suspect they are still PC-based and likely using pirated software.

DISTRIBUTION

ISIS has been conducting the same operations with al-Farqan as its predecessor al-Qaeda did with as-Sahab. Foot couriers are no longer necessary due to ISIS's advanced operational security systems, unless maintaining the most rigorous operational security, as al-Qaeda still does. Once the videographers have completed the finishing touches on their product, they enjoy innumerable options to disseminate their message. Most of the official media clips are readily available at Archive.org, a repository of video, PDF, and MP3 clips and other media from a wide variety of sources. Other sites used by jihadists for propagating their message include YouTube, Liveleak, Dailymotion, Facebook, Vid.me, MediaFire, badongo.com, extabit.com, rapidspread.com, easyshare.com, 2shared.com, and zshare.net, to name but a few.

ISIS released a video detailing precisely how it wants users to use hashtags (#) to project their message on the world stage. The video demonstrates a wrong way and a right way to do this. The right way includes jumping on to trending hastags that have nothing to do with the Islamic State. In other cases, the latest campaigns get a fresh hashtag that trends and shortly fades away.

Those who don't want to be found downloading the material use encryption, but the material can be often found without any protections in place on any number of download sites, supported by free blogs that host a repetitious updated list of links to download sites. Many of these sites are able to deal with copyright infringement, but not with terrorism propaganda. Twitter and YouTube actively remove posts and pages, but it only takes a few hours for another to pop up and republish the same material.

DABIQ MAGAZINE

ISIS moved into an arena that had been dominated by al-Qaeda for years, the slick online magazine. In 2010, al-Qaeda produced an English language magazine called *Inspire*, which featured articles about explaining their ideology, using counterintelligence tradecraft, and how to make homemade explosives. Their most famous article was called "How

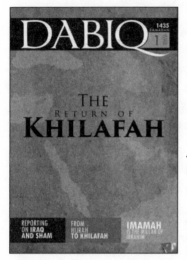

to Make a Bomb in the Kitchen of Your Mom."[1138] The Tsarnaev brothers used these simple instructions to carry out the Boston Marathon bombing that killed three and wounded 246.

After dominating the online world, ISIS debuted the first edition of *Dabiq* in July 2014. "Dabiq" is the location of the small Syrian village near Aleppo where an apocalyptic battle between Islam and "an Army from Rome" is supposed to take place before the return of the Mahdi and the second coming of the Prophet Jesus. The first edition of the magazine announced of "The Return of the Khilafah," followed by new editions monthly.

Each edition contains articles on how the Caliphate is challenging the unbelievers of the world, building infrastructure, and normalizing itself into statehood; stories of brave suicide bomber "martyrs" and great adventurous military campaigns; announcements of the most popular videos no fanboy should miss; and even advertising pages for hostages for sale.

The trend in the first twelve editions shows the expansion of ISIS from its central concerns in Iraq/Syria to its growth in Egypt, Yemen, Libya, and other regions where groups have sworn allegiance. Notably, there are sections devoted to the Islamic converts who are lauded as examples of good men who turned to Islam, left the West or Australia, and joined the Islamic State.

The magazine has become the official mouthpiece to take credit for terrorist attacks. Apparently working under deadline, they managed to complete a very fast five-day turnaround for the rapid release of edition twelve, "Just Terror," featuring the November 13, 2015 Paris attacks and the destruction of the Russian airbus over the Sinai. The publication featured a photo of the explosive device that allegedly blew up the airliner—a soda can filled with explosives—along with the claim that ISIS Sinai was behind the attack.

HOW YOU CAN HELP DEFEAT ISIS SOCIAL MEDIA

THE PRIVATE CVE CAMPAIGNS

The cyber hacking group Anonymous launched a global cyberwarfare campaign against ISIS and al-Qaeda, which flared first after the January 2015 *Charlie Hebdo* attacks and then again after the November 2015 Paris massacre. Called "Op ISIS," the secretive group harnessed the power of anonymous computer specialists they call "hacktivists" and collectively attacked ISIS's Twitter feeds, websites, and servers. Their methods—denial of service attacks, doxing, and other means—are no big secret, and the campaign has proven somewhat successful in bringing down the mundane posts of jihadi-fanboys and the most egregious images, but the Internet works so quickly that no non-government group could take down the majority of the real data without being fully integrated into the companies that host the content, like Facebook and Twitter.

Anonymous has identified ("doxed") tens of thousands of Twitter users it claims are ISIS followers and supporters. Critics have challenged the lists as improperly outing people who have nothing to do with ISIS, or innocent people who just post in Arabic or on Islam. Due to Anonymous's lack of expertise, innocents are treated the same as ISIS followers. In addition to Anonymous, there are many other small groups that employ other methods to engage ISIS online, from takedowns to parody.

BASICS FOR TAKING ISIS OFFLINE

The primary method used by Anonymous and small groups is to just use one's computer to make a complaint. This comes in the form of a "take down" notice being sent to Twitter, YouTube, Google, Facebook, and other online locations demanding that offensive or policy violation material should be "taken down." Though YouTube and Facebook have specific language related to terrorism content, Twitter and others only have general complaint forms with prescribed categories of concern. To make use of this, just find the email address for the company that is sponsoring the offensive material and send it to the abuse@ contact address for the site. Although this won't stop the posting of social media, if the thousands of watchers and users were to become hundreds of thousands, ISIS's ability to rapidly jump and continue to distribute widely would quickly come to an end.

On Twitter there are other methodologies such as filing complaints referencing "Not Interested in this account," "They are posting spam," "This account may be hacked," and "They're being abusive or harmful." After this point, the user must select a range of options to make their complaint so effective the server operators have no choice but to remove the data.

After choosing "They're being abusive or harmful," you can select "Pretending to be me or someone else," "Engaging in harassment or violence," and "This person might be contemplating suicide or self-harm."

If you select "Engaging in harassment or violence," the remaining two choices will be "Who is (name of Twitter user) targeting?" and the options are "Me" or "Someone else." Twitter then asks what the user is doing: "Being disrespectful or offensive," "Harassing me," or "Threatening violence or physical harm." At the end you will get the final tab, which is a general contact entry for additional commentary where you can give details of why this is an ISIS user and should be removed.

Then wash, rinse, repeat, hundreds of thousands of times.

Taking down Twitter accounts is Sisyphean at best. ISIS and their fanboys tend to crop right back up and the takedown must start all over. However, it does work. The ideal way to deal with these accounts would be for the hosting companies to use digital fingerprints on files to prohibit the uploads in the first place, or identify avatars commonly used by ISIS supporters, including the black shahada flag, or pictures of ISIS fighters, Osama bin Laden, and Zarqawi.

For example, with YouTube, one could easily identify ISIS material by using already-existing algorithms to compare the contents of new video uploads to previously flagged uploads. The system that YouTube currently uses to cross-match material with digital fingerprints is highly accurate and is distinct in behavior from direct takedown notices. Once an offensive video is discovered, it can be calculated, identified, and used to eliminate all the other copies found on YouTube, no differently than if you uploaded a clip from television and it matched existing material. Material is often instantly flagged at YouTube to check for copyrighted music alone.

CHAPTER 20

DEFEATING ISIS

ISIS is a monster fathered by al-Qaeda, birthed by the invasion of Iraq, whose DNA contains the worst parts of Saddam Hussein's police state. Since the 2003 invasion it has morphed from a small band of Jordanian terrorists into a full-fledged terrorist-run nation bent on dominating the world with a cult-based apocalyptic vision. What can be done? What can the world do that it is not doing now? How can America lead and take a tougher fight to the enemy in a way that does not grind the shattered Middle East into even smaller shards of chaos that are subsequently even more vulnerable to ISIS?

One suitable phrase is a possible answer: asymmetric warfare. Unfortunately for the West, only ISIS has taken advantage of this. They do not want a large army with a stifling national infrastructure. They only need the Qur'an, a rifle, and ammunition to flip the West time and again when attacked by heavy forces—the asymmetric war of the guerrilla. T. E Lawrence himself once stated that Arabs were not suited to large armies but to guerrilla warfare—attacking fast and quick with a rifle and a camel. Often it is the very image we think that is silly, the terrorist astride a horse, bearing a sword and leading men with black banners flying into battle against Apache helicopters and M1A1 tanks. We underestimated the asymmetric warrior in the Indian Wars, the Philippine insurrection, Vietnam, Afghanistan, and Iraq. We have had more success with intelligence to find, fix, and finish terrorist entities in Iraq, but what they possess and we do not is patience and a fervent ideological belief that they fight for God. They are the kamikaze of Islamic cultism and they embrace that role with passion.

The West is dealing with the ISIS threat by containment, a strategy that worked well for the Soviet Union, a rational self-preserving nation-state made up of hundreds of millions with a professional armed force. For dealing with al-Qaeda, the "Global War on Terrorism" was also a poor strategy. It elevated them to the status of national combatants and fostered their recruiting to the point where nineteen men killed three thousand citizens, and we invaded the wrong country in revenge. That forced error gave us ISIS.

The only possible hope is to play the game the way they play: use asymmetric warfare to our advantage. President Obama has taken an overly cautious approach to attacking ISIS, which has allowed them to take and maintain the initiative, at least in the news media. Since September 2014 ISIS has only launched one ground offensive, at Palmyra in Syria, but they have lost over 25 percent of the "caliphate." Settling in was bound to happen, but they are offensive fighters and they like to attack. With their proto-state under pressure they now lash out in Libya, Yemen, Egypt and Afghanistan

The White House clearly understands some components of the asymmetric fight—if ISIS wants a large national military footprint, deny it to them at all costs. If they want a ground war, give them an air war. If they hate the Kurds and Yazidis, arm them and support the ground forces who hate ISIS. The Department of Defense has conducted numerous such strike operations, and if it is to do so for the next few years, there is a way to make the Air and Special Operations campaigns even more lethal. Granted, taking on ISIS with small asymmetric forces designed to reign terror in their rear is not as exciting or sexy as invading Syria or re-invading Iraq with 150,000 men but the Small Footprint-Giant Strike approach is working—though it could be far more efficient and have much more dramatic impact. Since June 2014 the Pentagon estimates that as many as 23,000 ISIS fighters have been killed in combat action. That is a conservative number as it would only account for a little more than one fighter killed in each of the 17,000 airstrikes on targets to date, as well as their known combat losses in ground combat. The number is certainly higher and would likely constitute half of their combat power. Even with influx of an estimated 10,000 new foreign fighters and thousands of caliphate "cubs," ISIS is losing manpower and their best fighters are now pulling tedious mundane duties such as guarding bridges and highway checkpoints. They have also lost the initiative. In 2015 ISIS lost 25% of the territories they took in 2014 and with the exception of an offensive towards Palmyra, Syria, they have been pushed back into a defensive crouch. Like a cornered animal, that makes them dangerous, unless the entire narrative of "The Islamic State" is also flipped on its head.

In addition to military forces there must be a virtual war for the narrative of ISIS in both real space and cyberspace. Any combat operations without a global campaign of rejection against them would be futile.

They have had a battlespace ceded to them for almost a decade. Defeating ISIS means inciting a higher level of action in the Muslim world to reject their corruption of Islam.

ISIS has been shown that the asymmetry of power works both ways. The ISIS attempt to smash though the Kurdish line in December 2015 with their fast and loose convoys of suicide trucks and Toyota pickups found themselves under the foot of a much nimbler giant. The offensive was utterly crushed in one 13-hour battle where 187 ISIS fighters were confirmed killed just by air strikes from Reaper drones, fighter jets, and AC-130 gunships. In the same month ISIS wasted over 200 suicide bombers only to be defeated in Ramadi, the Nineveh governorate, and the Kurdish line.

If the West wants to fully engage ISIS on truly asymmetric terms they must re-tool the effort to encompass the natural asymmetries of the Special Operations and intelligence agencies into a broader scale that cuts across all components of government, from defense to diplomacy to communications. I call this strategy Full Spectrum Counter ISIS Warfare and Operations (FullSpec-CIWO, pronounced "see-whoa").

To the layperson, it may appear that we are already waging a full-spectrum military, political, and intelligence war against ISIS, but nothing could be further from the truth. We are currently using a small portion of our military airpower and an even smaller fraction of our diplomatic, intelligence, and communications soft power. While a limited number of warfighters fly missions and bomb their position and a few State Department staffers help the Secretary of State try to craft an alliance, the media, Congress, and the public stand off to the side and just watch like it's a reality TV show.

Because America and its allied citizens are not engaged and the asymmetries of the Western alliance are not even being considered, much less employed, America's hands are essentially tied. We are limited not only by rules of engagement and concern for civilian casualties, but also by indifference and governmental incompetence. One half of America would prefer that nothing be done until their candidate wins office. With these limitations and no authorization to use military force, the president can only contain ISIS from the air and wisely chose to limit ground forces, because ISIS fervently desires a large-scale expeditionary quagmire. Despite these limitations, America has actually badly damaged ISIS, but they have the gift of patience.

More lethal to America's interest is that they have the organizational ability to remember the historical lessons of the last 1,400 years and apply them quickly on the battlefield and cyberspace. By contrast, neither the American public nor the news media remembers that that we fought a war for eight years against the commanders and senior lieutenants of a group called al-Qaeda in Iraq, individuals who now lead ISIS.

What must happen—and quickly—is an unleashing of American asymmetric power, which I submit would be relatively easy to do and certainly politically and operationally less costly than a ground invasion. The highest levels of the national security apparatus must formulate a comprehensive multiyear strategy to craft a series of soft- and hard-power daggers against this beast. We must not only strike ISIS with airpower, but also deploy a tailored and unconventional ground force to retake the entire region-wide initiative back from ISIS and show that its time is limited. Instead of stomping on the terrorist puddle of mercury, it must be pressured to break up into manageable balls that can be mopped up and defeated in detail. ISIS's ability to reconstitute necessitates a massive diplomatic, financial, and cultural shift in each area to restore security, power, and livelihoods. Addressing the incredible multi-trillion-dollar problem of rebuilding these nations and clearing out the rats' nests requires open eyes, not bickering about the cost.

With FullSpec CIWO we must not only encircle the terrorists with combat and air forces, but with diplomatic power, alliances, and agreements. Most of all we must reengage the Middle East with the power of good ideas and values. For the Secretary of State's efforts to succeed, the entire State Department should be on a wartime footing and the primary message from America should be "unite with us to defend Islam and destroy ISIS worldwide." Defense Department operations, intelligence missions and counter-ideology warfare messaging should come together as part of the overall strategy of the military's six "Ds" of combat: Detect, Deny, Degrade, Disrupt, Defeat, Deceive, and Discredit our enemy.

The Muslim world is comprised of 1.8 billion people who want economic opportunity, good homes, families, and futures for their children. They place faith in their God and whichever government can provide stability, respect, and acceptance. They lived for fourteen centuries with relative peacefulness in their own world, achieved spectacular intellectual achievements, fostered a magnificent culture, and harnessed the fundamentals of science well ahead of Europe and Asia. It is Islam—a religion born of a tribal desert fight that settled into a peaceful coexistence with the world—that is at risk. ISIS is challenging all of their centuries of achievement, art, culture, and tolerance. By mimicking the religion's outward form, ISIS constitutes a cancer that has metastasized in the region. For many in America and some parts of Europe the afflicted patient, Islam, is being blamed for the cancerous lump that needs to be excised. Listening to certain American politics today on fighting ISIS is like watching a surgeon argue with a lumberjack over the relative merits of a scalpel versus a chainsaw. Let's make it simple: use the scalpel, and use it quickly.

ISIS has decided that the time of the centuries-old Great Game— the complex phenomenon that drew the borders and established empires and bureaucracies—will die in flames and be bloodily severed with a sword. Yet in America, Congress would not give the president so much as a dime, or permission, to fight. At the same time, Congress demands action and leadership but refuses to pay for bombs, fuel, and extra deployment pay because a certain president requests it, and they must deny him any chance of showing leadership at all costs. Observing this self-defeating political maneuvering from afar in Raqqa, ISIS's leadership is doubtless snickering in their teacups at their good fortune.

RE-ORGANIZE TO FIGHT LIKE ISIS

America must lead the world in a high intensity full-spectrum military, diplomatic, and counter-ideology war. Not against a nation-state but against fanatic human-guided weapons committed to a cult belief. It is akin to fighting the kamikaze gone rogue, without the Japanese empire, people, or armies behind them.

The West must unite into a coalition that is equally asymmetric: one that fights murderously well, is light on its feet, moves amazingly fast, and uses every trick and tactic that the enemy uses except mass murder. With optimized military footprints and massive coordinated strikes, we must apply pressure simultaneously on all fronts with withering intensity, and immediately follow it up by any force capable of moving forward. We need to make ISIS understand what it is like to be on the receiving end of their own blitz strategy.

Military

Unleash the inner OSS of the Special Operations Command. Like its WWII ancestor they need to embrace the same phrase that ISIS does: "the Gazwah," or "high speed raid." These missions are occurring, but on a small scale and in extremely limited numbers. While keeping up the training, intelligence, prisoner snatch and hostage rescue missions of the current Special Forces in Iraq, a slightly larger footprint and a return to some old missions could give the war an entirely new dynamic. At the same time, a massive air armada should be assembled to support the mission of drawing ISIS out at every point in the "caliphate" and confronting them using the local allied forces.

Social-Psychological

Social media, public diplomacy, information warfare, psychological warfare, and counter-ideology warfare should be harnessed and focused like a laser against ISIS's entire narrative that "We Speak for Islam. We are Changing Islam. We are Coming for You." The counter-ideology, information warfare, and propaganda effort should delegitimize their activities and harness the power of the global information space to shout down and reframe them as the cult they are. The effort should sow spiritual doubt and regret in those who have been forced to join.

Diplomatic

A global coalition of all nations, of all faiths, should be brought to bear against ISIS and its threat to both global stability and one of the great faiths. We should already be planning for a post-ISIS Nigeria, Syria, Iraq, Libya, Sinai, and Yemen.

The political theorist George Kennan developed a multidimensional diplomacy plan for what he called "organized political warfare." He defined this as "... the logical application of Von Clausewitz's doctrine in time of peace." It was to use all aspects of overt and covert action, political pressure, political funding, and propaganda to confront enemy political systems. In his time, communism was the adversary; today it is ISIS cultism. A revival of Kennan's policies should not be seen as radical but rational. This includes his deep belief in the policy of dialoging with our adversaries: in this case, not with ISIS's leadership, but with Iran, Hezbollah, and Hamas. Talking to these political opponents may prove critical, because ISIS has targeted each of those organizations for elimination (Hezbollah) or usurpation, particularly Hamas and Fatah in Palestine. This is a serious region-changing threat with potential devastating consequences that the world and the Israelis should take seriously.

Financial

Today we spend billions on the procurement of weapons and intelligence systems with contracting procedures that are so cumbersome that the Pentagon cannot even start to bid out contracts before the enemy shifts to entirely new strategy that nullifies the original purpose. FullSpec CIWO strategy should encompass all aspects of government and should be funded to the fullest, with the national commitment given to defeating communism but with a fraction of its budget.

PHASE 1—ASYMMETRIC WARFARE: DARK MATTER

Many of the political measures the US has taken so far in containing the ISIS terror network have proven to be ineffective. The political infighting and criticism of the containment strategy has only enhanced the image and prestige of ISIS, no matter how many of their men die on the battlefield. We cannot fight ISIS on the terms of the Iraq and Afghan insurgencies. We must switch the strategy to harness the same asymmetric techniques of ISIS but on our terms and harnessing our own asymmetric capability—we need to fight faster, lighter, and with old-school tactics coupled with total air dominance.

We have the technology, but the haphazard application of already-existing power systems in concert with a stunted political-diplomatic

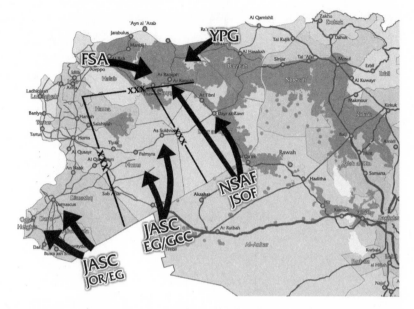

process prevents the success we seek in the battle space and cyberspace. We should hit ISIS on the ground, of course, but not on their terms. We should fight them in cyberspace but rig the game to our advantage so that we harness the world's social and financial energies against them. On every level we must attack their physical, spiritual, and ideological existence, simultaneously and repeatedly, until they run out of believers or wither in the face of the world's social rejection of any and all things ISIS.

It may sound like madness to the layman but we should craft a strategy to encourage ISIS to use their only effective tool in the box: the suicide blitz offensive. Like a bull that can only charge at the waving cape, ISIS cannot resist a fight on the ground if Americans might be involved. We should give them their chance, but on our terms. ISIS has two distinct disadvantages: they have no ability to stop airpower, and they detest defensive fighting unless they have massive quantities of improvised explosive devices (IEDs) and suicide car bombers. Without these tools to slow the advance of their enemies, they cannot hold ground at all against competent mobile ground forces combined with airpower. When surrounded, they fight to the death; these combatants never reappear at other battles. ISIS must be drawn out and encouraged to chase the flag and in doing so be destroyed with our own asymmetric advantage—unstoppable air and naval striking power. ISIS can be forced to dance to our tune. The battlespace at every turn should be shaped to our advantage on a daily basis. As we have seen in the December 2015 Battle of the Kurdish Line, ISIS should be allowed to come out and be defeated. If they adapt and remain in place then they can be defeated in situ as well. That is a foregone conclusion. Yet, given the nature of their ideology, they cannot sit still and their death wish must be accommodated at every turn. US and allied strategy should be planned so that every bomb dropped, every raid executed, should drive them mad with the desire to go on the offense.

In the first days of the 2001 war in Afghanistan, the CIA and US special operations sent small, mission-focused teams into Afghanistan to entice, cajole, and coordinate local forces that had the ground capacity to dislodge the Taliban and al-Qaeda. The first team was called JAWBREAKER, and its fast and light nature epitomized the concept of the WWII JEDBURGH teams of the CIA's predecessor, the Office of Strategic Services (OSS) and their English counterparts, the Special Operations Executive (SOE). The history of missions like this is rich but largely untapped today. In the Burma Theater the OSS Detachment 101 set up the Kachin Rangers to harass the Japanese behind their lines. The US–Canadian 1st Special Service Force practically created the concept of Special Forces in Europe. In Vietnam the Special Forces organized the Mobile Strike Command or MIKE Forces. These were small teams of indigenous forces armed and trained to attack the Viet Cong and North Vietnamese with their same tactics. Each of these historic units took extremely small teams on seemingly impossible missions deep behind the enemy's lines and gave the enemy a taste of their own medicine. In this way, the Jawbreakers and Special Forces teams used their small size and big firepower to topple the Taliban. This small team–high firepower mission must be reenergized and made the spear tip for all future thrusts against ISIS.

For the last decade the US Special Operations Forces (SOF) have been mentoring, training, and guiding indigenous forces, local allied Special Forces, and antiterrorism units to carry out very unconventional missions. Many mission profiles are not even considered by the Pentagon because they are extremely dangerous, will be deep in the rear of an adaptive and skilled enemy, and could cause political embarrassment if there is a cock-up. However, that's the exact reason we have a Special Operations Command, to plan and execute missions that ISIS is not ready for or believe we will never do. When the SOF experts are commanded by those who lack imagination or ignore the machinery of local intrigue, big mistakes happen. We cannot shy away from ISIS simply because we do not have heavy brigades to engage them in mobility warfare.

To go after ISIS properly, the president will need to redirect how we use the Special Operations Forces. President Obama's Secretary of Defense, Ashton Carter, announced some of those changes in December 2015 when he indicated that the SOF would be allowed to plan and carry out missions to capture and kill ISIS leaders as well as rescue hostages. This is a good first step but implementing an aggressive deep-penetration mission to fill many of the voids in ISIS territory with numerous special units, like the unseen force that binds the universe together, they could be called DARK MATTER teams. Done right, these forces could shatter the entire narrative of ISIS's homogenous "caliphate" being on the march with a single week of missions.

The current configuration of special operations forces in Iraq is adequate for the current mission of training and performing short duration tasking. An additional 1,000 soldiers, mainly an additional US Army Ranger Battalion, would bring the US footprint in Iraq up to 4,500. The Ranger Battalions are necessary because the strategic mission against ISIS would change from advising and assisting to assisting our allied forces to conduct full time raiding behind ISIS lines. The mission would be similar to the present operations, which is to attach US and allied Special Forces teams to Iraqi and Kurdish Special forces and Counter-Terrorism Units. The difference is that the US units will attach themselves to Iraqi and Kurdish Commando battalions and fight side by side, with the Americans holding the airpower keys and the national indigenous forces fighting to take back their lands. For a short period these units will conduct intense work-ups in the basics of running and shooting to prepare for unconventional, daring, multi-day, long-term missions behind ISIS's lines.

The objective of DARK MATTER would be to insert 100–150 fighters with heavily armed, fast, light vehicles with plenty of anti-armor weapons to interdict and then hold a position that cuts ISIS lifelines between major cities. These Allied SOF teams or Ranger companies could be introduced to the battle front in a myriad of ways designed to confuse ISIS as to how they will arrive—they could be jumped in by parachute drop, landed on improvised airports by Air Force C-17 or C-130 transports, or helicoptered in. They will seize an objective, be it an airbase, oilfield, or highway and then destroy all ISIS forces that seek them out. The practice of establishing temporary zones of control along major highways between ISIS-held cities for short periods of time would suddenly fragment the image of a consolidated nation-state with borders and reveal it is just a series of towns and villages occupied by thugs. Each DARK MATTER mission has the same terminal objectives: get soldiers on the ground behind enemy lines, kill any ISIS fighters present, and show that we will determine what moves in and out of the "caliphate," liberate towns temporarily, and gain intelligence.

For example, inserting massive raiding forces in the highways between Mosul and Tal Afar, between Raqqa and Deir ez-Zor, Rawah and al-Qaiem, Deir ez-Zor and al-Qaiem all on the same night would create mayhem among ISIS adherents. All movements would slow to a trickle as ISIS would not be able to safely secure night transport. Day transport and ISIS's extra security measures would be opened up to massive aerial attacks. Almost overnight the narrative of the war would show the US and allies on the offensive, on the ground with the right forces and smashing ISIS's economic lifelines.

Why send Iraqis and Kurds into Syria and not into Iraq? Syria is now a safe haven for ISIS and it needs to be confronted. Every truck and man that sits fat in the Euphrates Valley threatens Iraq indirectly. ISIS believes the border will be respected by the West—let us disabuse them of that notion. They are fair game wherever they are found. They like to brag that they erased the Sykes-Picot border so we should respect that and help erase ISIS within their newly defined "State."

With our assistance, our allied forces must disrupt ISIS long enough to coax them out of their cities, spoiling for a fight. Then we will have them right where we want them: out of their tunnels, away from their human shields and moving out in the open. At that point the Joint Tactical Air Controllers will bring down the air armada on anything that dares present itself. If ISIS manages to organize an overwhelming counter attack that forces the units to displace, just move them to a night extraction point, land C-17s, and depart. Of course ISIS's every step will be harried by drones and bombers.

The purpose of these missions is to raid and maraud, draw out the enemy, and force them to chase dozens of ghosts simultaneously all over the "caliphate." We can then let ISIS enjoy the fruits of the one asymmetric advantage we hold worldwide—precision bombing.

Deception and false deployments should be used extensively as well. False helicopter insertions could be accomplished using US Navy MQ-8B Navy Fire Scout Drones to bait ISIS into believing they are dropping off forces. In fact the US Army has retired an entire fleet of older OH-58 Kiowa helicopter airframes. A squadron of these could quickly be turned into remotely piloted armed drones to be used for the role of false helicopter insertions or anti-aircraft "bait" to draw out ISIS anti-helicopter defenses while real missions are performed elsewhere. Add an explosive payload and these drone helicopters they could also be modified to act as improvised flying explosive devices or "FLY-EDs." These drone helos could be launched from the Turkish border or secret desert bases and conduct armed missions directly over ISIS's most intense defensive zones, such as downtown Raqqa, to see just how intense they really are. If the enemy defensive environment is too intense to survive further flight they could perform a kamikaze profile to fly directly into the nearest high value ISIS positions or weapons system. If a helo is shot down or crash lands and is investigated by ISIS, its destruction payload can be detonated as an IED. Of course, given MQ-9 drone support, ISIS assets that approach or engage these FLY-ED missions could be directly attacked as well.

In WWII the OSS used "Beach Jumper" parachute decoys and on D-Day the "Rupert" parachute dummies simulated mass parachute jumps to fool our enemies into attacking fake landing sites. Today we can do the same and have drones or strike aircraft waiting for ISIS response. Additionally, false jumps could be simulated by mass air-dropping empty wood pallets by parachute. If ISIS takes the bait they could be followed up by drogue-chuted cluster bombs, drone attacks, or ambushes by the Marauder ground forces. Raqqa and Mosul could be placed on edge night after night by flying air-launched decoy flyovers; mixed within should be real raids of small units. We should make ISIS fear the night. Units should land, kill patrols, line up the bodies on the side of the highway, take their weapons and tweet the results. Real missions, false missions, and psychological warfare should occur from D-day to V-day. ISIS should feel no rest; going on night patrol, watching roadside checkpoints, and even coming out of the tunnels should make them think twice. The committed terrorists will come out fighting and be just as gladly killed. We should facilitate mass martyrdom at every opportunity.

Forces that have local investment should conduct the fighting, but the transport, targeting, and real-time support will have to come from America and its NATO allies. These Jawbreaker teams would ideally bring with them local forces on a ten-to-one basis; one Jawbreaker team would be assigned for every one hundred Iraqi or Kurdish Peshmerga commandos. They should give the appearance that the mission could appear out of the dark anywhere, and given the air power control and air mobility support, they can arrive just about anywhere between two major cities in multiple locations. Put these heavily armed platoons on ISIS's lines of communications with loads of anti-tank missiles and switchblade drone mortar rounds so that they can provide defenses against SVBIEDs and anti-aircraft gun wielding technicals. SOF's high-mobility vehicles move on desert or roads while they receive overwatch from armed drones and theater-level fire support. This will ensure that anyone that dares engage this force will not return to report a successful outcome.

The purpose of the DARK MATTER team is to not just guide and mentor allied raiders, but to fight side by side and bring down close air support, bomber artillery, and drone strikes on anything that comes near them. These teams should attack ISIS highways and lines of communication for periods of twelve to seventy-two hours; with the goal of establishing a bridge to other fast and light forces should the opportunity present itself. The teams should insert, establish control, and destroy any and all logistics life support for infrastructure serving ISIS cities.

Every battlefield advantage should be given to support these missions—creating drone strike corridors, landing LAV III wheeled armored vehicles that mount heavy anti-tank guns, and giving them priority calls for fire using MGM-140B ATACMS, the Army tactical missile system that can throw 275 submunitions over 80 miles. The result should be the same in every instance. Should ISIS engage they must be massively overwhelmed through firepower.

The enemy should be challenged to come out from their enclaves, get on the road, and attempt to engage these units. The ISIS provinces should be each stressed every night to the point that they cannot flow fighters from one province to the next to handle the threat the Jawbreakers would present. Of course ISIS is adaptive and clever and they will release intelligence or attempt to create an imagery signature that is designed as bait for an ambush. The response is simple: we choose where the missions will land. Should ISIS set an obvious trap by using their man-portable air defense systems then the airspace should be tested with helicopter drones, flown overhead at low altitude by Miniature Air Launched Decoys (MALDs). After the trap is "sprung" a follow-up drone and/or high altitude bomber strike should make them understand asymmetry of power works both ways.

If we executed these missions on a wide scale and coordinated them with US manned and remote air power, ISIS's Toyota task forces would take massive losses, and the myth of the invulnerability of their "caliphate" would be reduced to burning vehicles. We need to make them believe that they are surrounded and vulnerable to ground attack by forces unknown that swoop in from the desert nightly. When darkness arrives they could rest assured that their forces would be decimated somewhere. DARK MATTER missions could change the entire political military and diplomatic picture that ISIS has drawn. They will no longer be seen as invulnerable and that will make their global narrative of an unstoppable expeditionary army shatter overnight.

These missions can be replicated with virtually any force in any size in Libya, Egypt, and Yemen. Like the World War II Jedburgh teams, these small teams should be allowed to transit, attack, destroy and obliterate any force that dares come their way and make night driving on roads the last thing anyone in Syria or Iraq will attempt. If they feel they can sustain themselves and continue the mission past their scheduled return time, they should be encouraged, re-armed, and refueled remotely via air drop or clandestine resupply point. The demonstration of Iraqi, Syrian, and/ or Kurdish forces operating all across ISIS terrain would have a massive psychological impact on their supporters and the captive populace. ISIS won't know who will be attacking them, or from which direction, from one day to the next. The video of YPG Kurds fighting in the Iraqi city of al-Qaiem, Peshmerga cutting off roads between Syrian city of Deir ez-Zor and ISIS's capital of Raqqa, or a combined force landing in Palmyra and eliminating whole ISIS units would be a political/military coup that would hard to beat. The value of the panic that would ensue and the massive abandonment of Raqqa and other cities by civilians alone would be a game changer.

Make no mistake there will be casualties, but the small footprint of US forces means that losses will always be limited. And unlike the Invasion of Iraq, the disproportionate losses in this strategy will be borne by ISIS alone.

OPERATION LIGHTS OUT

In concert with the mass raids on the "caliphate" should be a strategy to cut off all life support for its most entrenched cities. All existing water and electricity service to the cities of Raqqa, Mosul, and Deir ez-Zor should be removed through direct attack. As in the non-destructive infrastructure attacks made on Belgrade, Serbia in 1999, graphite filament bombs could be dropped all over the occupied cities to short-circuit power lines, switching stations, and even small local electrical generators at the exact times they turn power on to the city, which is generally two hours per day. Where permanent results are required, JDAMs should be used to permanently remove power from the city. If any city deserves to be reduced to a dystopian hellhole it is Raqqa, ISIS's political center of gravity.

As this infrastructure is generally critical to the civilian population, losing power may force them to displace elsewhere within Syria. It would remove a critical financial and manpower pool from ISIS and reveal its utter vulnerability. ISIS intended to stay in Raqqa for years; there is no reason to allow them to enjoy electricity, fresh water, or sewage treatment. Discomfort must be brought upon their supporters in the population in order. At some point even ISIS families will want to leave, which could give critical intelligence about the group. If ISIS cannot quickly reestablish these utilities, then they will prove that they are merely toothless terrorists who stole the keys to the power plant.

PHASE 2: COUNTER-IDEOLOGICAL WARFARE

In my 2010 book *An End to Al Qaeda*, I outlined a limited Middle Eastern–focused psychological war for the mind and soul of the Muslim world. It was designed to attack the legitimacy of the ISIS cult's belief system. I called it a Counter-Ideological Operations and Warfare (CI-DOW) named CIRCUIT BREAKER. However, in that short half decade, while we quibbled over political differences and hogtied our government from doing anything against our existing enemies, ISIS sprang forth. Gains throughout the Muslim world show that ISIS is winning the battle of imagination and of cyberspace. They now have information dominance through their actions. It does not have to be this way. They unabashedly harnessed al-Qaeda's apocalyptic belief system and used Western technology to spread fear in a raw, easily consumable format that proved exceedingly popular.

Up to 2015 the US Department of State had been running a failing campaign called "Think Again Turn Away" through their Center for Strategic Counterterrorism Communications (CSCC). The information distributed through Twitter feeds and disseminated through American embassies and supporters was a good start but it was eclipsed by the media savvy of ISIS and al-Qaeda before it. The CSCC had a miniscule budget and was limited by political correctness and a lack of focus on the narrative. By the time they had a single decent video targeting the approval of our Middle East allies, ISIS would put out hundreds of videos from all across the Middle East targeting new recruits, bragging of their exploits, and threatening America. It was not that the US cannot develop nimble messaging or confront the ISIS counter-narrative challenge; it was operating with its hands tied behind its back before the fight started. The failure in US counter-ideology policy is that the US will not discuss the corruption of ISIS's Islam, nor discuss any aspect of Islam at all out of fear of alienating Muslims. To attempt to blunt that edge the State Department has worked with allies to establish their own Twitter feeds. The UAE was first to jump into the fray by establishing the Hedayah Center to develop Middle East–based strategies to counter violent extremism. A year after ISIS established its "caliphate" the UAE also established the Sawab Center for counter-messaging in Arabic. These efforts were well meaning but the bureaucracy was so staggering that ISIS managed to conqueror entire nations before one message from these organizations could reach the internet.

In January 2016 President Obama announced a new strategy intended to shake up the "propaganda war" against ISIS. The State Department's CSCC would be renamed the Global Engagement Center but would continue its faltering activities with a $5 million budget, which is the cost of less than one hour of fuel in the air war against ISIS. The US Department of Homeland Security would be tasked to create a domestic counter-extremism program to identify radicalization in the USA. All of the efforts are well meaning but the entire effort is meaningless because ISIS has centralized media campaign that understands its audience, understands its message and uses the best technology to disseminate it. The United States's counter-radicalization efforts remain akin to an elephant trying to balance on a tricycle.

President Obama stated in September 2015 that "we have to prevent [ISIS] from radicalizing, recruiting and inspiring others to violence in the first place. And this means defeating their ideology." On this point the president is correct and the effort announced still reflects the limited mindset towards the ideology of ISIS. Like the ground warfare strategy a new direction needs to be taken towards framing the narrative around ISIS. Make no mistake, the single best tool for changing the narrative for ISIS is to continue to erode their "caliphate" and lose territory. On the other hand we must help the Muslim world sow religious doubt about

ISIS's justifications of their actions and make them, and future recruits, fear for the sanctity of their souls.

As the second most important component of Full Spectrum CIWO, there needs to be a truly integrated counter-ideology campaign against ISIS on an international level, with the United States amplifying the message of the world to shout down the ISIS narrative, not just helping set up new slow offices in foreign countries. The president should order the establishment of a National Counter-Ideology Executive (NCIE). The NCIE would spearhead the combined military-diplomatic-intelligence war on ISIS's belief system in the real world and cyberspace but remove the bureaucratic hurdles to messaging, act as international coordination center and champion the counter-narrative that ISIS is illegitimate and that the world is coming to the defense of the Muslim world. The NCIE would be able to access all of the media and propaganda resources of the Department of Defense, State Department, and the intelligence communities, craft real-time counter-messaging and disseminate it quickly. Instead of running a political campaign war room to respond to ISIS media, the effort will be reoriented to craft a central narrative around ISIS's illegitimacy and cultism. The CSCC was criticized for using the actual images of ISIS's atrocities by stripping them from ISIS media. Instead of facing up to the facts, they stopped using images or videos from ISIS sources. This is a mind-boggling error. Imagine if President Roosevelt had removed all images and references to Nazi atrocities from the WWII propaganda effort. It surrenders the information battlespace to ISIS on the basis of political expediency. This is the heart of the problem. This may explain State Department's failure since they preemptively disarmed themselves by embargoing all visual references to ISIS's mass murder and genocide. When responding to ISIS videos and messages, the NCIE will absolutely use images and videos of their atrocities and make them regret that they made them. Even Osama bin Laden understood that the more their murders were publicized the greater difficulty they had in convincing the world of their mission.

The burning intensity of ISIS's ideology is a force multiplier for their terrorist cultists. It is a devotion to killing and love of suicidal death not seen since the Japanese kamikaze of World War II. Their belief in their success is all that matters to them. And like the kamikaze, they must be broken militarily and then discredited ideologically. In the words of al-Qaeda chief Ayman al-Zawahiri, they must fear being "crushed in the shadows" by a wave of Muslim social rejection.

However, the very idea of talking about Islam or to Muslims is a terrifying prospect to politicians. This year I met a staff member of New Jersey Senator Cory Booker. I was invited to give my views on why ISIS's social media was so virulent and how to stop it. When I explained that the only way to seriously damage them was to take on their belief system, I was told, "If you are talking about discussing Islam then I can see why your calls are not answered." My response was that Senator Booker, and by extension America, was then more than willing to surrender 1.8 billion people and allow ISIS to destroy their faith.

America has taken pains over the last fourteen years to avoid discussing Islamic illegitimacy of the terrorists. Only ISIS and its allies have gained from this silence. On the other hand, many politicians have taken great pains to antagonize the Muslim world and lump them together as part of ISIS or al-Qaeda in disguise. This pleases ISIS to no end.

George Kennan was right to encourage discussion as a way to attain understanding of our adversaries and grow closer to our allies. Discussing Islam is not just the domain of Muslims. It is an obligation of all people of good will to help our Muslim countrymen and allies combat a corrosion of their faith. Government officials and scholars who hide from fear of being considered Islamophobic or over-inclusive has been yet another reason that we cannot match ISIS in social media. ISIS uses their very vocal conviction asymmetrically against our desire to be rational and temperate in both the media and politics. In this way their narrative bulldozes over all rationality. We don't have to change how we discuss the terrorists or reject their religious nature; we just need to start an international dialog on the corrosion within the terrorist's belief system without falsely castigating the entire Muslim world and denigrating traditional Islam itself.

With US assistance, the Muslim world needs to stand up and amplify the best tenets of its faith to seriously challenge this gyrating, heretical, and hypocritical ideology. The very act of having a good-faith discussion by Muslims and other faiths on the true meaning of Islam would turn into a gross liability for ISIS, and given enough media exposure, could eventually help push the militants into an unrecoverable death spiral. ISIS never discusses the accuracy of their beliefs; they say submit or die. In fact, they would likely target any gathering of faith leaders to discuss their corruption, which is why holding monthly global conferences on the corruption of ISIS and how to reconcile their lost souls with God would degrade their legitimacy even more than any bomb could. The metrics of success would be relatively easy to identify—they would start verbally attacking these conferences in their magazines and threatening participants. They would then for the first time have to defend their corruption in the face of Islam. Having to explain their absolutism runs counter to their *modus operandi*; they speak with the sword for God. Introducing any doubt would break them apart. Let us sow those doubts deep and wide.

ISIS's rare supporters in the Islamic world do not see terrorists; they see seemingly pious fighters who want to help oppressed Muslims. They teach their children to kill because there is no alternative message that can overcome their cult messaging. In fact, their message is in direct conflict with the teachings of the Prophet Mohammed and the words in the Qur'an.

A way to start the dialog is to sponsor high-profile, globally-broadcast "Doha-style debates." These public forums should be supported and financed to discuss the corruption that took al-Qaeda and ISIS from being traditional Muslims to being Islamic cultists. The very question of how the sinful violations will be accounted for in the afterlife should be discussed in the open. Hiding from religious discussions when their every action is swaddled in religious justification is folly. These debates over traditional Islam versus ISIS cultism should be held all over the world and in many languages, because this is not a Muslim problem alone, nor an American problem. It is a global issue with global impact, and opinions should be heard from people of all faiths.

This may look like intellectual navel-gazing, but in the Muslim world such debates are highly regarded, and the participants are often young and vibrant with brilliant new ideas and perspectives. The Middle East is a place where the average person is a sharp student of political science and knows the history of America better than many Americans. The elder statesmen and scholars are world class and their depth of knowledge is incredible. Put these debates on US public television and build a knowledge and tolerance bridge across to the American and European peoples. Those who give the most coherent arguments should be offered positions where they can travel and speak to the world as a true voice of Islam against the oppression and corruption of ISIS cultism.

In social media, we should pick arguments and engage in debate between terrorist fanboys, apologists, and the traditional Muslim jurists and scholars about the heretical changes ISIS seeks in Islam, and the illegitimacy of mass murder and suicide in Islam. The goal of these discussions and public diplomacy should be to denounce and degrade street-level support throughout the world. No one should be willing to sell water to ISIS, much less Nutella and Red Bull. ISIS's ideology must become radioactive in the world that surrounds them. They should be more than secret pariahs; they must achieve public status and become named and shamed.

For all of the talk about using strong language and insults to damage ISIS, it appears there is a perception that they wish to keep about themselves. There are some words that they truly hate. The Arabic acronym *Daesh* does not truly bother them, but call them by the name of the first Islamic cult group that the Prophet Mohammed warned against, and they become unglued. In ISIS's early 2015 Ramadan audio recording, they demonstrated surprising sensitivity to allegations that they are un-Islamic and to being equated with the Khawarij. The ISIS spokesman al-Adnani took time out from his sermon about killing all of their enemies to make an astonishing admission. He appealed directly to God to complain about the bad word they were being called: "O Allah, deal with everyone who declares the blood of the mujāhidīn fighting for Your cause as halāl and wages war against them under the pretext that they are Khawārij." Clearly these insults hurt. Anything that brings this level of ire from ISIS should be used to the fullest.

We need to ask ourselves the question: do we have more heart than hate? We need to restore America's image as vanguard of freedom and liberty and fairness in the developing world in order to harness the goodwill necessary to support a new global counterterrorism and counterinsurgency campaign. We are not just seeking to tilt the hearts, minds, and soul of the Muslim world to support America's grievance, but to create an environment where the eyes of the Ummah will open and massively reject ISIS. Winning the hearts and minds of a people in wartime is proving to be harder than winning any military combat battle ever could be. ISIS's success has been the result of a well-calculated effort to subvert who and what America is in the eyes of Muslims around the world. American indifference to ISIS's long-term religious goals has already given them ten years of strategic advantage.

The ISIS leadership not only understands our rules, but studies our political systems, its limitations, processes, and behaviors. They keenly watch Western news media and observe the infighting and capitalize on it. In *Management of Savagery*, Abu Bakr Naji paraphrased a political scientist when he said, "A single political mistake [leads to] a result that is worse than one hundred military mistakes."

ISIS also is vulnerable to political mistakes, and it is their behavior in the face of these activities, which would be the metric to measure success. Ignore global surveys and interviews with the ISIS members, just watch how ISIS behaves in cyberspace. If they have to explain themselves, lash out against enemies with even more invective, and start naming individuals, then they are being negatively impacted. A police state will never let its guard down on the control of information, but like Hitler in the bunker, as the bombs start to take effect, the rants become more unhinged.

An adjunct method to stop this infectious spread was given to us by al-Qaeda themselves. They feared being publically branded when tied to "unjustified" atrocities. That may not seem so repellant to ISIS, which revels in the noteworthy deaths, but as an organization they reject negative press. Al-Qaeda leader Abu Yayah al-Libi warned in 2006 that publically shaming the leaders and foot soldiers as well as publicizing negative testimony from members who have left the organization had devastating effects on their supporters. They also feared being labeled apostates, and being shamed for murder of children. We should take al-Libi at his word and do just that.

In the same way that ISIS fanboys track individual enemy soldiers or diplomats and publish their addresses for supporters to attack them (called doxxing), we too could create a global campaign paid for out of the NCIE budget to publically identify and shame people who join the cult and leave for the "caliphate." No matter what country, including America, the community they come from should know who is fighting against them and be given an opportunity to broadcast their disgust on an international platform.

PHASE 3: DIPLOMACY UNLEASHED

PLAN NOW FOR A NEW SYRIA

The most painful lessons learned from the war in Iraq stemmed from the fact that US leadership never planned for postwar stability. The destruction of infrastructure, the dissolution of the army, the burning of all the historical records by the Ba'ath party, the refusal to recognize the insurgency, and the rejection of anyone who spoke Arabic or was an expert—all should be burned into our minds. This must never happen again. That said, we should harness political diplomatic engagement and relations across the Middle East, and make every effort to create an international framework that will call for establishing a larger Syrian government in waiting. Though the United States supports the Syrian Interim Government established in 2013, every Syrian worldwide, both refugee and in country, should be asked to place their futures on a new national unity government using the Syrian Interim Government as a basis for deepy detailed political and humanitarian planning for the future stability, security, and return of refugees to the region.

The Syrian people now come in two categories: trapped in a diaspora or captive to two brutally murderous regimes. Before the war the population was 22 million people. Count 200,000 less who were killed in the civil war. According to the UN's International Organization of Migration there are 4.5 million registered refugees in the Middle East alone. 53% of all refugees to Europe are Syrian. 1.9 million refugees live in Turkey and 7.6 million are internally displaced in Syria due to warfare. ISIS controls 8 million people, the Assad regime about an equal number.

It is time for the majority to create a third way. The world should be encouraged to establish the new Syrian government in exile and start now to draw up the plans, provide the resources, and encourage participation from the Syrian diaspora that has abandoned their country and migrated to the greater world. The citizens have suffered greatly over the last five years of war. They know full well what has happened there, what was destroyed, what it remains, and what the future could be. Instead of treating them like a plague that has descended upon Europe and America, we should welcome them as the Syrian government-in-exile. The international assets of the Assad government in Syria should be seized and distributed as social welfare to the refugees. Syrian political organizations should be funded to plan for their eventual return to the nation. We should encourage the future leaders who will be educated in Europe and the West to take the role of political guidance, using the lessons learned of both the oppressive Assad regime and ISIS. The Syrian community has lost enough to know that these two forms of government are just murder and mayhem behind the flag of two equally brutal dictators. The greatest fear of both groups is that of a democracy based on an informed electorate.

The new Syrian government should meet in the Middle East and establish a new constitution to be pro–rule-of-law, pro-education, pro-stability, pro-health care and focused on restoring electricity, water, sanitation and trade. Syria should operate as a true republic with democratic principles but safeguarding minority rights and representation that is fair and impartial. It should establish and guarantee special protected status for Kurds, Druze, Turkmen, and Alawites, and where necessary, give them autonomy. Like the Kurds, they should maintain the right to see after their own security and natural resources. Better to be a confederation than to return to the chaos that spawned ISIS.

FORM A NEW SYRIAN ARMED FORCES (NSAF)

The expatriate Syrian community can choose officers and train them at the joint Arab military force headquarters in Saudi Arabia or at the Zayed Military City in the United Arab Emirates. The best personnel can be brought in from around the world if there are promises of education and visa preferences to the Gulf Cooperation Council (GCC) states for those who join this force. The equipment should be purchased through the Gulf States' industries and suppliers well in advance of any intervention, and the logistical tail should be extensive. No derelict or ancient US equipment should be given. Pay top dollar, take care of their families, and provide excellent kit and you will get good solders. ISIS captured some the best equipment we had to offer and look at the results—even though the army was poorly led, badly paid, and essentially a welfare organization. The NSAF must have the burning desire to go home and stop ISIS and any other future terrorist group from destroying their nation. This army should be trained and equipped to be an undefeatable foe in the post-civil war.

The New Syrian Armed Forces should contain current loyalist units, rebel units and volunteers who should be offered a chance to be paid the highest military salaries in the Middle East. Currently ISIS pays $500 more per month than the Syria rebels. This same error was found in Libya. When the civil war ended the only jobs were in militias; the nation never formed a unified army because the army paid so poorly. The NSAF must be paid first-world salaries to perform dirty jobs that won't be performed by the US Army. It's worth the investment. In order to prevent wage theft or "ghost soldiers," an electronic payment system and European-standard debit cards that goes right to the families of the soldiers should be established. Should they die in training or combat, their families should receive death benefits that are the envy of the Middle East. As we saw in Libya, Iraq, and Yemen, despite the best intentions, military units did not maintain cohesion when salaries were cut or leadership, life support, family support, or health care was not provided. We must make a bold commitment to establish an entire system of soldier support to the NSAF before it is needed. With this system in place, it may perhaps be possible to entice entire military units from the al-Assad government to join loyalist units for the betterment of Syria. These programs for the NSAF should be given plenty of resources and time so that they may be implemented on day one, and be prepared to enter and fill all voids and vacuums.

If ISIS territory starts to fall, this force will be critical to establish unity and stop retaliation, as well as collect weapons, and secure military bases. This army would have two requirements: they must not run, and they must be ideologically committed to restoring the nation to greatness. They must have the best weapons, training, and commitment to defeat anyone that comes before them.

If a political settlement is achieved then the New Army can marry up with regime forces and reestablish security in the nation alongside of a pan-Arab stability force. Pro-Assad Syrian Arab Army military units, police, and militias should remain cohesive, given back pay and raises, improved life support, free family housing, and access to hospitals. Over fifty thousand local Syrians should be immediately hired and paid top dollar as contractors to clear and clean scrap, concrete debris, and war remnants, and to rebuild military bases and police stations. All of this was proposed to the Libyans in 2011, and despite a $160 billion bankroll they rejected it because they didn't want to "play favorites" to any group of people or tribe. As a result, the militias seized the bases and turned them into havens for pirates, human traffickers, and warlords. The NSAF should be the only dominant force in the nation.

ESTABLISH MIDDLE EAST–WIDE MARSHALL PLAN WITH GULF STATE BACKING

The Gulf States and an international coalition should prepare a Syrian, Libyan, Iraqi, and Yemeni Marshall-style plan for the restoration and reconstruction of these nations, just as they did for Lebanon after the civil war. The more prosperous these nations are, the better the Arabian Peninsula will become. Commit a plan to rebuild Syria, Libya, and Yemen, and make a commitment to the re-modernization of the Middle East. The next decade will present a chance to provide opportunity and remove the economic basis of radicalism. If the rich Arab states miss this chance, then they are next on the radicalization chopping block, and their money may not save them.

The humanitarian and medical needs in Syria will far eclipse all potential military missions. The United Nations, the International Red

Crescent, and other humanitarian organizations should prepare to assume the overwhelming responsibility of assisting the Syrian Red Crescent in saving Syria from a postwar humanitarian catastrophe. The United States can lead this effort by contributing a $1 billion grant to the international committee for the Red Crescent to bring an international pan-Arab medical assistance group to Syria that will take over, equip, and manage the Syrian medical system. Tens of thousands of Syrians can be trained to run the humanitarian cities and medical/nursing services to help return the millions of internally displaced persons to their homes.

All efforts should be made to establish a new Syria and guard against the immediate collapse into a failed state. The personnel and workers who maintain the national infrastructure, the army, the government bureaucracy, the school system, and the healthcare system should remain in place and expect not only to remain on the job, but to receive substantial increases in pay—even if not working—in order to retain the national intellectual capital. This should be met with an international effort to identify and categorize all refugee workers using UNHCR and IOM rolls. Critical skill workers should be prepared as part of a Syrian National Restoration Group, readied to return and start work when the political situation allows.

PHASE 4: A PAN-ARAB HUMANITARIAN INTERVENTION

It has been said many times before that the United States should not engage in a costly ground war in Syria, Iraq, or Libya. There are adequate regional land forces to do the mission under a United Nations or Arab League mandate of filling the void as ISIS starts to fall apart. No matter who organizes this, it will not be a clean mission, as we have seen from the sloppy Saudi-led GCC intervention in Yemen, but being prepared to fill the spaces that ISIS will eventually abandon is critical to any future Syria. Senator Lindsey Graham and Senator John McCain, the fiercest of hawks, have both proposed ground campaigns led by Arab forces. If this can be achieved, then US forces can remain in a small-footprint supporting role where they will act as air traffic control, strike coordinators,

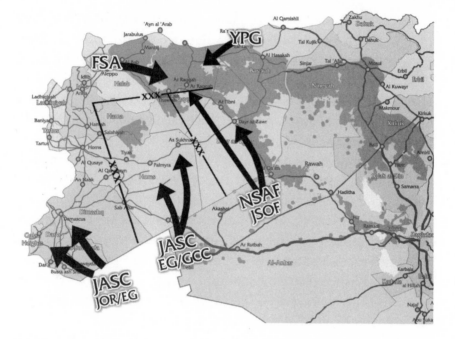

combat support, logistics, and training. Nothing would upset ISIS more than Arabs solving the problem of the Syrian civil war and the Americans bombing them without a massive ground invasion. So long as ISIS could not claim that the "Army of Rome" has finally arrived, their dependence on prophecy to fight the pan-Arab forces loses steam. They will try to fight but they lack the capacity to offensively move against the hammer of pan-Arab forces and the anvil of the Syrian army and a Kurdish/Iraqi army on the offense at the same time.

The United States and the West should join with Jordan, Egypt, and Saudi Arabia to rapidly establish, equip, and mobilize the proposed Joint Arab Stability Command (JASC) and prepare for humanitarian intervention in Syria and Iraq. A fifty-thousand-strong pan-Arab force drawn from Saudi, Emirati, Egyptian, Jordanian, Pakistani, and Syrian armies should prepare to intervene as ISIS starts to fall apart. Entering Syria through the Jordanian desert and western Iraq, their mission will not be to fight the al-Assad regime, but to separate the players, inject heavy stability and humanitarian forces between the warring parties, and act as a buffer to stop ISIS from moving further than at present.

This will result in temporarily separating Syria into three zones until the civil war stops and humanitarian aid comes in and ISIS is confronted. What to do with the al-Assad regime can be taken care of at a later date. However, the pan-Arab force will be covered by airpower that could devastate the remaining Syrian Arab Air Force and frontline army units even with Russia present.

West and south-central Syria will be the minority protection zone. The southwest, under Jordan, will protect the Druse and secure the Golan Heights. The central and eastern zone will cut ISIS off from the rest of central Syria and fill the voids when ISIS runs. At that point, ISIS would have to deal with extremely heavy forces and the Kurdish, Iraqi, and American-backed forces as well. They do not have enough manpower or equipment to handle it, and they would be destroyed by setting them up—asymmetrically—and forcing them to come out and fight on. The pan-Arab Special Forces units could be folded into the American-allied special marauding missions and assist in wreaking mayhem on ISIS's rear as well.

Doubtless the mission would be bloody, and as we have seen in Yemen, terrorism at a tactical level will abound, but the alternative is an "Islamic State" that eventually gets its act together long enough for its men to blitz Damascus and push Assad into a rump state comprised of Latakia and Tartus and seize a border with Israel. Unless Russia decides to intervene with 150,000 men to take ISIS on themselves and prop up al-Assad, this is a slow drip, but foregone conclusion. All the Russian bombing in the world cannot stop ISIS's terrorists from continuing their small-scale infiltration into Damascus and turning it into a Syrian version of Beirut in the Lebanese Civil War.

An important part of the plan is that the New Syrian Armed Forces will occupy Raqqa, Deir ez-Zor, and the ISIS oilfields. This force will have to prove themselves as the military saviors of Syria and fight for the most critical parts of the country against the worst foe but with the airpower of the USA and operational cooperation of the Iraqis and Kurds. Clearing ISIS could take as long as two years. If the plan is even marginally successful and the international bodies recognize the government in exile, the Syrian Arab Army too can play a role. Straight cash inducements should be offered to units of Assad's Syrian Arab Army to defect en masse and be folded into the New Syrian Armed Forces or the JASC to help cleanse the nation of ISIS, Jebhat al-Nusra, and any other Islamist extremist unit that want to fight. The cascading effect of the JASC, Iraqi, NSAF, and small, minority-led self-protection forces will erode al-Assad's ability to govern anywhere but his palace and the Russian-protected coast.

When ISIS is weakened and fragmented, then it will be time for the combatants to be separated into three corners. Northwestern Syria, the coast, and Damascus and the south must be separated with a military buffer force to ensure the stability and safety of the Druse, Alawites, and Christian communities, as well as to maintain the infrastructure of the government with or without al-Assad as its leader. JASC must protect the Syrian minorities at all costs.

One of the first objectives will be to de-weaponize the land and population of the explosive remnants of war and even scrap weapons systems. No one should be allowed to own military grade weapons in postwar Syria except the army, police, and regional militias. The 2003 de-Ba'athification law, written by L. Paul Bremer, opened a flood of illegal weapons sales that directly fueled the black market and funded al-Qaeda in Iraq and Iran. All government AK-47s were said to be legal for the protection of family but led to an endless circle of reprisal murders and fueled the insurgency. One way to ensure weapons are kept to a minimum is to implement realistic weapons buyback programs that pay top dollar for even the most simple rifle, pistol, or ammunition in any quantity with no questions asked. The Bremer–US Army program would only pay $50 for a rifle that was worth $200 on the street. A future program should pay 50% more than the street price for RPGs, rifles, and explosives.

Seizing, warehousing, and destroying the explosive remnants of war is also a critical requirement so that they are not used in a postwar insurgency as IEDs. Contracts to global unexploded ordinance disposal companies should be let out before the war so that the machinery for mass clearance is in place upon the stability operation. Tens of thousands of Syrians can be hired for this job alone.

An expatriate corps of experts spearheaded by Syrians who are specially trained in the Gulf states should reestablish the oil industry, use locals as oilfield workers and oilfield protection forces, as well as in antiquities protection. All expatriates should have a right to return to their homes in peace and stability. Jobs will be plentiful but the finances must be in place to hire and pay people to rebuild the economy as well. The global Syrian diaspora should have the chance to start a new nation on the ashes of ISIS's tyranny.

THE GULF STATES' AND ISRAEL'S SECURITY FROM IRAN & ISIS

ISIS is not considered Saudi Arabia's number one threat—that would be Iran—but intervening to ensure that neither ISIS nor Iran takes over Syria would go far to meet its goals of limiting Iranian influence to the parts of Lebanon they now occupy. Additionally, it keeps Israel from having to unilaterally intervene and occupy Damascus, a prospect that could actually happen if ISIS takes control of southern Syria or wins Damascus. That would set the table for a massive regional war that would absolutely require US ground forces, and in numbers larger than the Iraq war, to help defend Israel and Jordan. This can be avoided, but we would have to act quickly before ISIS could put their plans into effect.

With ISIS in existence, Israel is standing in a minefield of future trouble that they appear to be ignoring. Their blind obsession with Hamas and Iran/Hezbollah has completely precluded the realization of a real existential threat if the virus that is ISIS's cultism infects the Palestinian population. The greatest threat to the nation of Israel is not an Iranian atomic bomb, but millions of Palestinians deciding that the cult ideology of ISIS requires them to conduct suicide improvised weapons attacks in the tens of thousands. Israel may well soon be forced to consider what is now inconceivable: consulting with Hezbollah, Hamas, and Fatah as partners to counter the ISIS threat.

Should the ISIS "virus" infect Palestine, we will have a threat that will make Israel's current intifadas seem like the good old days. Such a

Syria will lessen the tension and allow for a Palestinian rapprochement.

THE MUSLIM WORLD MUST TAKE THE LEAD

THE STAKES FOR ISLAM

Obviously, any further academic debate on whether to call al-Qaeda or the ISIS terrorist groups Islamic or un-Islamic is pointless. Though wrapped in Islamic guise, the on-the ground reality of Osama bin Laden's cult ideology is that it poses an existential threat to Islam as we know it. Some Muslims seem to understand this. In September 2014 the former Grand Mufti of the Ulema, Abdul-Aziz ibn Abdullah Al ash-Sheikh, who was the highest ranking religious member in Saudi Arabia, excoriated the group's effrontery to Islam: "Extremist and militant ideas and terrorism which spread decay on Earth, destroying human civilization, are not in any way part of Islam, but are enemy number one of Islam, and Muslims are their first victims." Unsurprisingly he then called them "Kharajites," but refrained by the slimmest margins from calling them a cult.

An excellent step in the right direction is the Egyptian group Islam for Humanity Against Terrorism. Developed by the Dar al-Ifta or The House of Fatwas, an organization formed by the Grand Mufti of Egypt, Shawki Ibrahim Allam, Islam for Humanity Against Terrorism attacks the global jihad by delinking them from Islam and demanding that ISIS be called "QSIS" or the al-Qaeda Separatists in Iraq and Syria. Virtually every major religious leader in Islam has denounced the cult's actions as un-Islamic, but still Western news media ignore the Muslim world's efforts. Western governments need to make amplifying the Muslim rejection of cultists as priority number one. As far as many Westerners are concerned, no Muslim is willing to stop the cult of jihad and some believe that they are secretly in collusion with them. That narrative must be checked, reframed into a war against ISIS's cultism, and propagated on a global scale.

However, Muslims cannot condemn ISIS one day and validate their actions the next. The same Saudi Grand Mufti that condemned ISIS inadvertently validated their destruction of houses of worship (and tacitly gave approval to the destruction of antiquities) when he stated that all churches on the Arabian peninsula must be destroyed. Witness the power of personal interpretation: churches and synagogues are protected in Islam and their destruction is explicitly forbidden in the Qur'an. In fairness, the Saudis have been experimenting with rehabilitation of jihadists on a small scale.

Unfortunately, decades of high recidivism reveals that once members are infected with the ideology, they are generally irreconcilable. Until the Muslim world comes to terms with the lethality of this spiritual pathology they will live in an increasingly unstable political, military, and economic environment that will eventually infect their own youth. No amount of cash grants, new homes, or luxury car loans will stop the next wave, if left unchecked.

This cult ideology will not go away on its own volition. To the cultist, the specter of the Muslim world rising up and crushing them in the shadows, as Ayman al-Zawahiri worried in 2006, is not a concern. The terrorists believe they are gaining strength and will grow in numbers as they trend from the extremist fringe to toward the mainstream. When governments attempt to accommodate them, they gain confidence and strength that what they have been doing was just and correct. Accepting limitations only slows their chance to meet God in Paradise. They will only become more brutal and inhumane. Until one ideology, either traditional Islam or the cult of jihad, is eliminated, the battle will always be enjoined.

At the moment of death for Jordanian Air Force Lieutenant Muath al-Kasasbeh, it was clear that he was coached to look around him and behold the power and might of the ISIS force that held him captive. What was little noticed was that though he appeared resigned to his fate, he stood defiantly, unlike virtually any other victim seen in any other ISIS photo. He was well aware that the stage had been set and it was not a mock execution. His death was an example of true martyrdom in the greatest traditions of Islam. The uniformity of the faceless cultists was a testament to the deviance of the ISIS cult of jihad.

It will be up to the Muslim world to cleanse the world of this existential threat. Al-Qaeda and ISIS have stated over the years that it is their intention to destroy the existing power structure of political Islam and replace it with their absolutist cultism. Based on their behavior and statements about shrines and idolatry, they would be tempted to destroy shrines even as sacred as the Tomb of the Prophet Mohammed, and like the Qaramitah before them, the Kaaba in the Grand Mosque of Mecca too could be reduced to rubble.

The Muslim world does not have to lose its best traditions of Islam to fight this cult. Many countries have expended enormous amounts of effort to "deprogram" the jihadists, bring them back to Islam though spiritual guidance, and identify the holes in the cult ideology. Making the cultist fear for the sanctity of his or her soul is the best weapon at hand. However, until the Muslim world issues an ultimatum in the form of an official fatwa, the cult of jihad has little to fear.

The major Ulemic bodies must declare the ISIS cult members as a threat to Islam and who should be given no assistance or sustenance until they surrender. Only with Islam openly calling them out as enemies of the faithful can there be even a slight chance that spiritual fear and soul-searching will occur within themselves. Muslims are hesitant to claim apostasy so that the danger of acting for God is avoided but they can agree that ISIS is acting inhumanely—and perhaps not with God guiding them but evil cultism. The past Islamic cults were scattered to the winds by the Muslim world. The entire ISIS experiment could evaporate in an instant if the Muslim world starts to admit that the corruption has insulted Islam enough. Even introducing the word "cult" to the debate would be a radical start. The Muslim world already knows that these men directly challenge God and the Prophet Muhammed's own words. In India 70,000 imams and scholars signed a fatwa that found ISIS, al-Qaeda, and the Taliban were enemies of Islam. This must be replicated across the globe and be given a megaphone to shout that message down to the streets. In 2014, Sheikh Abdullah Bin Bayyah, a man called a "scholar's scholar," issued a fatwa against ISIS and Boko Haram. They should give them a chance to repent or face 1.8 billion true believers in a worldwide jihad against 50,000 religious deviants. As cultists, they are organizationally immune to outside influence, but if they resist the call to return to Islam, they will have been given their chance and may be truly called "apostates." Why not? ISIS refers to virtually every Muslim in the world by this word; perhaps it is time they suffered by its meaning as well.

The ISIS cult of jihad cannot be allowed to spread one step further. It must be stamped out and discredited completely. Small embers can start big fires; recall that just nine Khawarij split Islam into two. The Utaybists who survived the Grand Mosque siege managed to spread their apocalyptic message to members of al-Qaeda, and ISIS made that vision real.

In September 2015 ISIS assassinated a 30-year-old woman resident of Raqqa. Her name was Ruqi Hassan. ISIS assassination squads shot her in the head. ISIS accused her of being a spy because she dared write the truth about life in the fantasy of the "caliphate." Before her death she wrote of her despair on Twitter: *"im in Raqqa and I received Death threats and when #ISIS will Arrest me and kill me its ok Because they will cut my head and i have Dignity. its better than I live in Humiliation with #ISIS".* Her last words show the depth of strength and commitment of the people who have given their lives in resistance to ISIS.

The French philosopher Voltaire once remarked, "Those who can make you believe in absurdities can make you commit atrocities." ISIS is the epitome of this commentary. The absurdity of their cult ideology has caused the deaths of tens of thousands and subjugated millions under their rule. If the war to defeat ISIS could be fought with just the strength and moral fiber of Lt. Kasasbeh and Ruqi Hassan then the outcome would be the swift and utter destruction of this cult. Yet for all of the social power ready to be harnessed, a grand war promises not even the slightest chance of success until the ISIS cult's murderous mayhem is reframed, redefined, and revealed as the apocalyptic thrill-kill death cult that it is. Redefining and fighting this ideology with a single, damning word, "cult," is more accurate, readily consumable, and believable than hoping that ISIS will somehow contain itself or self-destruct.

ENDNOTES

1. Carter, Chelsea J. "Iraq developments: ISIS establishes 'caliphate,' changes name," CNN. Published June 30, 2014; accessed Nov. 22, 2015: http://www.cnn.com/2014/06/29/world/meast/iraq-developments-roundup/

2. Ferran, Lee and Rym Momtaz. "ISIS Trail of Terror," ABC News. Last updated Feb. 23, 2015; accessed Nov. 20, 2015: http://abcnews.go.com/WN/fullpage/isis-trail-terror-isis-threat-us-25053190

3. "Senior Iraqi al-Qaeda leaders 'killed,'" BBC News. Published April 19, 2010; accessed Nov. 21, 2015: http://news.bbc.co.uk/2/hi/middle_east/8630213.stm

4. "ISIS Fast Facts," CNN. Updated Nov. 17, 2015; accessed Nov. 22, 2015: http://www.cnn.com/2014/08/08/world/isis-fast-facts/index.html

5. Parry, Tony. "After leveling city, US tries to build trust," *Los Angeles Times* Jan. 7, 2005.

6. "ISI Confirms That Jabhat Al-Nusra Is Its Extension In Syria, Declares 'Islamic State Of Iraq And Al-Sham' As New Name Of Merged Group," Middle East Media Research Institute. Published April 8, 2013; accessed Nov. 21, 2015: http://www.memri.org/report/en/0/0/0/0/0/0/7119.htm

7. Shadid, Anthony. "Iraqi Insurgent Group Names New Leaders," *New York Times*. Published May 16, 2010; accessed Nov. 22, 2015: http://atwar.blogs.nytimes.com/2010/05/16/iraqi-insurgent-group-names-new-leaders/?_php=true&_type=blogs&_r=0

8. Reuter, Christoph. "Rational Monster: How Terror Fits into Islamic State's Plan," *Der Spiegel*. Published Nov. 20, 2015; accessed Jan. 12, 2016: http://www.spiegel.de/international/world/terror-a-means-to-an-end-for-islamic-state-a-1063454.html

9. "The Rise of Isis," *Frontline*. Originally aired Oct. 28, 2014; accessed Nov. 22, 2015: http://www.pbs.org/wgbh/pages/frontline/rise-of-isis/

10. Ibid.

11. "ISI Confirms That Jabhat Al-Nusra Is Its Extension In Syria, Declares 'Islamic State Of Iraq And Al-Sham' As New Name Of Merged Group," Middle East Media Research Institute. Published April 8, 2013; accessed Nov. 21, 2015: http://www.memri.org/report/en/0/0/0/0/0/0/7119.htm

12. Ibid.

13. "Isis Fast Facts," CNN. Published Dec. 28, 2015; accessed Jan. 12, 2016: http://www.cnn.com/2014/08/08/world/isis-fast-facts/

14. "Syria Iraq: The Islamic State militant group," BBC. Published Aug. 2, 2014; accessed Nov. 22, 2015: http://www.bbc.com/news/world-middle-east-24179084

15. Hubard, Ben. "Al Qaeda Breaks With Jihadist Group in Syria Involved in Rebel Infighting," *New York Times*. Published Feb. 3, 2014; accessed Nov. 20, 2015: http://www.nytimes.com/2014/02/04/world/middleeast/syria.html

16. "Terrorist Designations of Groups Operating in Syria," US Department of State. Published May 14, 2014; accessed Nov. 21, 2015: http://www.state.gov/r/pa/prs/ps/2014/05/226067.htm

17.   Glenn, Cameron. "The ISIS Primer," Wilson Center. Published Nov. 19, 2015; accessed Nov. 23, 2015: https://www.wilsoncenter.org/article/the-isis-primer

18.   Freeman, Colin. "Al-Qaeda seizes Iraq's third-largest city as terrified residents flee," *Telegraph*. Published June 10, 2014; accessed Nov. 22, 2015: http://www.telegraph.co.uk/news/worldnews/middleeast/iraq/10888958/al-qaeda-seizes-iraqs-third-largest-city-as-terrified-residents-flee.html

19.   Keating, Joshua. "Is the 'Islamic State of Iraq and Syria' a real country now?" *Slate*. Published June 10, 2014; accessed Nov. 22, 2015: http://www.slate.com/blogs/the_world_/2014/06/10/isis_takes_mosul_is_the_islamic_state_of_iraq_and_syria_a_real_country_now.html

20.   Ibid.

21.   "Isis Fast Facts," CNN.

22.   Ibid.

23.   Roberts, Dan and Spencer Ackerman. "US begins air strikes against ISIS targets in Iraq, Pentagon says," *Guardian*. Published Aug. 8, 2014; accessed Nov. 23, 2015: http://www.theguardian.com/world/2014/aug/08/us-begins-air-strikes-iraq-isis

24.   Accessed Nov. 22, 2015: https://en.wikipedia.org/wiki/Jihadi_John

25.   "ISIS Fast Facts," CNN.

26.   "Islamic State's 43 Global Affiliates Interactive World Map," IntelCenter. Published May 19, 2015; accessed Jan. 12, 2016: http://intelcenter.com/maps/is-affiliates-map.html

27.   MacFarquhar, Neil and Merna Thomas. "Russian Airliner Crashes in Egypt, Killing 224," *New York Times*. Published Oct. 31, 2015; accessed Nov. 22, 2015: http://www.nytimes.com/2015/11/01/world/middleeast/russian-plane-crashes-in-egypt-sinai-peninsula.html

28.   Yourish, Karen, Derek Watkins, and Tom Giratikanon. "Recent Attacks Demonstrate Islamic State's Ability to Both Inspire and Coordinate Terror." *New York Times*. Updated Nov. 17, 2015; accessed Jan. 12, 2016: http://www.nytimes.com/interactive/2015/06/17/world/middleeast/map-isis-attacks-around-the-world.html

29.   Abbas, Mushreq. "ISIS leader al-Baghdadi proves formidable enemy," *Al-Monitor*. http://www.al-monitor.com/pulse/originals/2014/02/iraq-isis-baghdadi-mystery.html#

30.   Lister, Charles. "Islamic State Senior Leadership: Who's Who," Brookings Institution. Research concluded Oct. 20, 2014; accessed Nov. 21, 2015: http://www.brookings.edu/~/media/Research/Files/Reports/2014/11/profiling%20islamic%20state%20lister/en_whos_who.pdf

31.   NB: This is an Arabic source. Accessed Nov. 24, 2015: http://www.syrianmasah.net/arabic/artical-details34130.html

32.   Abbas. "ISIS Leader al-Baghdadi proves formidable enemy." *Al-Monitor*

33.   Sherlock, Ruth "How a talented footballer became world's most wanted man, Abu Bakr al-Baghdadi." *Telegraph*. Published Nov. 2014; accessed Nov. 21, 2015: http://www.telegraph.co.uk/news/worldnews/middleeast/iraq/10948846/How-a-talented-footballer-became-worlds-most-wanted-man-Abu-Bakr-al-Baghdadi.html

34.   Childress, Sarah and the Soufan Group. "Who Runs the Islamic State?" Frontline/PBS.org. Published Oct. 28, 2014; accessed Nov. 21, 2015: http://www.pbs.org/wgbh/frontline/article/who-runs-the-islamic-state/

35.   Arango, Tim and Eric Schmitt. "U.S. Actions in Iraq Fueled Rise of a Rebel" *New York Times*. Published Aug. 10, 2014; accessed Nov. 21, 2015: http://www.nytimes.com/2014/08/11/world/middleeast/us-actions-in-iraq-fueled-rise-of-a-rebel.html?_r=0

36.   Wood, Graeme. "What ISIS Really Wants," *Atlantic*. Published March 2015; accessed Nov. 24, 2015: http://www.theatlantic.com/magazine/archive/2015/03/what-isis-really-wants/384980/

37.   Arango and Schmitt. "U.S. Actions in Iraq Fueled Rise of a Rebel." *New York Times*.

38.   Cockburn, Patrick. "Who is the Isis jihadi leader Abu Bakr al-Baghdadi?" *Independent*. Published June 16, 2014; accessed Nov. 24, 2015: http://www.independent.co.uk/news/world/middle-east/mosul-emergency-who-is-abu-bakr-al-baghdadi-9523070.html

39.   Walker, Hunter "Here is the Army's declassified Iraq prison file on the leader of ISIS" *Business Insider*. Published Feb. 2, 2015; accessed Jan. 12, 2016: http://www.businessinsider.com/abu-bakr-al-baghdadi-declassified-iraq-prison-file-2015-2

40.   Abbas, Mushreq. "ISIS leader al-Baghdadi proves formidable enemy," *Al-Monitor*. Accessed Jan. 12, 2016: http://www.al-monitor.com/pulse/originals/2014/02/iraq-isis-baghdadi-mystery.html#

41.   Hassan Abu Haniyeh, "Daesh's Organisational Structure," Al Jazeera Center for Studies, last updated Dec. 4, 2014; accessed Nov. 21, 2015: http://studies.aljazeera.net/en/dossiers/decipheringdaeshoriginsimpactandfuture/2014/12/201412395930929444.htm

42.   Reuter, Christoph. "The Terror Strategist: Secret Files Reveal the Structure of Islamic State," *Spiegel Online International*. Published April 18, 2015; accessed Nov. 21, 2015: http://www.spiegel.de/international/world/islamic-state-files-show-structure-of-islamist-terror-group-a-1029274.html

43.   "The Rise of ISIS," *Frontline*.

44.   Hubard. "Al Qaeda Breaks With Jihadist Group in Syria Involved in Rebel Infighting," *New York Times*.

45.   Daly, Michael "ISIS Leader, 'See you in New York,' "*Daily Beast*. Published June 14, 2014; accessed Jan. 12, 2016: http://www.thedailybeast.com/articles/2014/06/14/isis-leader-see-you-in-new-york.html

46.   Mandhai, Shafik. "Baghdadi's vision of a new caliphate," Al Jazeera. Published July 1, 2014; accessed   http://www.aljazeera.com/news/middleeast/2014/07/baghdadi-vision-new-caliphate-20147184858247981.html.

47.   "The Rise of ISIS," *Frontline*.

48.   "This is the Promise of Allah," English translation of statement by Abu Bakr al-Baghdadi. Published June 29, 2015; accessed Jan. 12, 2016: https://ia902505.us.archive.org/28/items/poa_25984/EN.pdf

49.   McCoy, Terrance. "How ISIS leader Abu Bakr al-Baghdadi became the world's most powerful jihadist leader," *Washington Post*. Published June 11, 2014; accessed Nov. 24, 2015: https://www.washingtonpost.com/news/morning-mix/wp/2014/06/11/how-isis-leader-abu-bakr-al-baghdadi-became-the-worlds-most-powerful-jihadi-leader/

50.   Nance, Malcolm. *An End to al-Qaeda: Destroying Bin Laden's Jihad and Restoring America's Honor*, St Martins Press, New York, New York, 2010.

51.   Burns, John and Dexter Filkins. "A Jihadist Web Site Says Zarqawi's Group in Iraq Has a New Leader in Place," *New York Times*. June 13, 2006: http://www.nytimes.com/2006/06/13/world/middleeast/13iraq.html?_r=0

52. Anonymous, "Statement from the Islamic State of Iraq." Accessed Jan. 12, 2016: http://www.kavka-zcenter.com/eng/content/2006/10/16/5985.shtml

53. Schmitt, Eric and Ben Hubbard. "ISIS Leader Takes Steps to Ensure Group's Survival." *New York Times*. Published July 20, 2015; accessed Jan. 12, 2016: http://www.nytimes.com/2015/07/21/world/middleeast/isis-strategies-include-lines-of-succession-and-deadly-ring-tones.html

54. Nance, Malcolm, *The Terrorists of Iraq: Inside the Strategy and Tactics of the Iraq Insurgency 2003-2014*. CRC Press, Boca Raton, Florida, December 2014

55. "Profile: Abu Arkan al-Amiri," Counter Extremism Project. Accessed Nov. 25, 2015: http://www.counterextremism.com/extremists/abu-arkan-al-amiri

56. Childress and the Soufan Group. "Who Runs the Islamic State?" Frontline/PBS.org.

57. Childress and the Soufan Group. "Who Runs the Islamic State?" Frontline/PBS.org.

58. McClam, Erin. "'Ideology Wouldn't Die' for ISIS, Even If Abu Bakr al-Baghdadi Did," NBC News. Published Nov. 10, 2014; accessed Nov. 25, 2015: http://www.nbcnews.com/storyline/isis-terror/ideology-wouldnt-die-isis-even-if-abu-bakr-al-baghdadi-n245401

59. Ibid.

60. "Profile: Abu Arkan al-Amiri." Counter Extremism Project.

61. TRAC graphic.

62. "Terrorist Designation of Abu Mohammed al-Adnani," US Department of State. Published August 18, 2014; accessed Nov. 25, 2015: http://www.state.gov/r/pa/prs/ps/2014/230676.htm

63. Ibid.

64. Barrett. *The Islamic State*.

65. Childress and the Soufan Group. "Who Runs the Islamic State?" Frontline/PBS.org.

66. Barrett. *The Islamic State*.

67. "ISIS declares creation of Mideast caliphate across Iraq and Syria," CBS News. Published June 29, 2014; accessed Nov. 25, 2015: http://www.cbsnews.com/news/isis-declares-creation-of-mideast-caliphate/

68. "Stephen Harper condemns ISIS audio urging attacks on Canadians," CBC News. Published Sept. 21, 2014; accessed Nov. 25, 2015: http://www.cbc.ca/news/world/stephen-harper-condemns-isis-audio-urging-attacks-on-canadians-1.2773636

69. Barrett. *The Islamic State*.

70. Barrett. *The Islamic State*.

71. "The Islamic State's organizational structure one year in," *Al-Monitor*. Published July 2, 2015; accessed Nov. 25, 2015: http://www.al-monitor.com/pulse/security/2015/07/islamic-state-caliphate-ministries-armies-syria-iraq.html#

72. Remnick, David. "Telling the Truth About ISIS and Raqqa," *New Yorker*. Published Nov. 22, 2015; accessed Nov. 25, 2015: http://www.newyorker.com/news/news-desk/telling-the-truth-about-isis-and-raqqa

73. Staff Writer. Al Arabiya News. "Abu Muslim al-Turkmani: From Iraqi officer to slain ISIS deputy," *Al Arabiya News*. Published Dec. 19, 2014; accessed Dec. 15, 2015: http://english.alarabiya.net/en/perspective/profiles/2014/12/19/Abu-Muslim-al-Turkmani-From-Iraqi-officer-to-slain-ISIS-deputy.html

74. Sanchez, Raf. "Islamic State's Deputy Leader Killed in US airstrike, White House Says," *Telegraph*. Published Aug. 21, 2015; accessed Dec. 15, 2015: http://www.telegraph.co.uk/news/worldnews/northamerica/usa/11817711/Islamic-States-deputy-leader-killed-in-US-airstrike-White-House-says.html

75. Sanchez. "Islamic State's Deputy Leader Killed in US airstrike, White House Says."

76. Childress and the Soufan Group. "Who Runs the Islamic State?" Frontline/PBS.org.

77. Thompson et al

78. "Profile: Abu Ali al-Anbari," Counter Extremism Project. Accessed Dec. 15, 2015: http://www.counterextremism.com/extremists/abu-ali-al-anbari

79. Mezzofiore, Gianluca. "Isis leadership: Who's who in the 'fluid, Islamic state structure of power," *International Business Times*. Published July 2, 2015; accessed Nov. 25, 2015: http://www.ibtimes.co.uk/isis-leadership-whos-who-fluid-islamic-state-structure-power-1509014

80. "Profile: Abu Arkan al-Amiri." Counter Extremism Project.

81. Moore, Jack. "ISIS Replace Injured Leader Baghdadi With Former Physics Teacher," *Newsweek*. Published April 22, 2015; accessed Dec. 15, 2015: http://europe.newsweek.com/isis-replace-injured-leader-baghdadi-former-physics-teacher-324082?rx=us

82. "Baghdadi's Advisor killed in Iraqi Raid," *Ara News*. Published Dec. 13, 2015; accessed Dec. 15, 2015: http://aranews.net/2015/12/baghdadis-advisor-killed-in-iraqi-raid/

83. Greene, David. "Hundreds Of Chechens Join ISIS, Including Group's No. 2 Leader" NPR. Updated Sept. 5, 2015; accessed Nov. 25, 2015: http://www.npr.org/2014/09/05/345997449/hundreds-of-chechens-join-isis-including-group-s-no-2-leader

84. Winfrey, Michael. "How Islamic State Grooms Chechen Fighters Against Putin," Bloomberg. Published Oct. 9, 2014; accessed Nov. 25, 2015: http://www.bloomberg.com/news/articles/2014-10-08/how-islamic-state-grooms-chechen-fighters-against-putin

85. "Profile: Omar al-Shishani aka Tarkhan Batirashvili," Terrorism Research and Analysis Consortium (TRAC). Accessed Nov. 25, 2015: http://www.trackingterrorism.org/group/omar-al-shishani-tarkhan-batirashvili-individual-profile

86. Mroue, Bassem. "Omar al-Shishani, Chechen in Syria, rising star in ISIS leadership," AP via *Christian Science Monitor*. Published July 3, 2014; accessed Nov. 25, 2015: http://www.csmonitor.com/World/Latest-News-Wires/2014/0703/Omar-al-Shishani-Chechen-in-Syria-rising-star-in-ISIS-leadership

87. Moore. "ISIS Replace Injured Leader Baghdadi With Former Physics Teacher," *Newsweek*.

88. Greene. "Hundreds Of Chechens Join ISIS, Including Group's No. 2 Leader," NPR.

89. Greene. "Hundreds Of Chechens Join ISIS, Including Group's No. 2 Leader," NPR.

90. Winfrey. "How Islamic State Grooms Chechen Fighters Against Putin," Bloomberg.

91. Cathcart, Will, Vazha Tavberidz, and Nino, Burchuladze. "The Secret Life of an ISIS Warlord," *Daily Beast*. Published Oct. 27, 2014; accessed Nov. 25, 2015: http://www.thedailybeast.com/articles/2014/10/27/the-secret-life-of-an-isis-warlord.html

92. Counter Extremism

93. Cathcart, Tavberidz, and Burchuladze. "The Secret Life of an ISIS Warlord," *Daily Beast.*

94. "Profile: Abu Arkan al-Amiri." Counter Extremism Project.

95. Cruickshank, Paul, Tim Lister, and Michael Weiss. "Who might lead ISIS if al-Baghdadi dies?" CNN. Updated July 2, 2015; accessed Nov. 25, 2015: http://www.cnn.com/2015/05/11/middlee-ast/isis-leadership/index.html

96. Suhaib Anjarini, "Chechen jihadists in Syria: The case of Omar al-Shishani," Al-Akbar English. Published May 1, 2014; accessed Nov. 25, 2015: http://english.al-akhbar.com/node/19615.#sthash.gr3Vpip2.dpuf

97. Sandberg, Britta. "Hashtags and Holy War: Islamic State Tweets Its Way to Success," *Spiegel Online.* Published Nov. 19, 2014; accessed Nov. 25, 2015: http://www.spiegel.de/international/world/inter-view-with-former-fbi-agent-and-islamic-state-expert-ali-soufan-a-1003853.html

98. Sandberg. "Hashtags and Holy War," *Spiegel Online.*

99. Barrett. *The Islamic State.*

100. Lister. "Islamic State Senior Leadership: Who's Who," Brookings Institute.

101. Childress and the Soufan Group. "Who Runs the Islamic State?" Frontline/PBS.org.

102. Lister, Charles. "Islamic State Senior Leadership: Who's Who," Brookings Institute.

103. Barrett. *The Islamic State.*

104. "Designations of Foreign Terrorist Fighters," US Department of State. Published Sept. 24, 2014; accessed Nov. 25, 2015: http://www.state.gov/r/pa/prs/ps/2014/09/232067.htm

105. Barrett. *The Islamic State.*

106. Casciani, Dominic. "Islamic State: Profile of Mohammed Emwazi aka 'Jihadi John,'" BBC. Published Nov. 13, 2015; accessed Dec. 12, 2015: http://www.bbc.com/news/uk-31641569

107. Sawer, Patrick. Who is Jihadi John? How did Mohammed Emwazi, a quiet football fan, become the symbol of ISIS?" *Telegraph.* Published Nov. 13, 2015; accessed Dec. 13, 2015: http://www.telegraph.co.uk/news/worldnews/islamic-state/11992681/Jihadi-John-profile-how-did-Mohammed-Emwa-zi-a-quiet-football-fan-become-the-symbol-of-ISIS.html

108. Mekhennet, Souad and Adam Goldman. "Jihadi John: Islamic State killer is identified as Londoner Mohammed Emwazi," *Washington Post.* Published Feb. 26, 2015; accessed Dec. 13, 2015: https://www.washingtonpost.com/world/national-security/jihadi-john-the-islamic-state-killer-behind-the-mask-is-a-young-londoner/2015/02/25/d6dbab16-bc43-11e4-bdfa-b8e8f594e6ee_story.html

109. "Mohammed Emwazi's father: no proof my son is Isis executioner," *Guardian.* Published March 4, 2015; accessed Jan. 12, 2016: http://www.theguardian.com/uk-news/2015/mar/04/moham-med-emwazi-father-proof-son-isis-executioner, 03/04/2015

110. "'Jihadi John': US 'reasonably certain' strike killed IS militant," BBC. Published Nov. 13, 2015; accessed Dec. 13, 2015: http://www.bbc.co.uk/news/uk-34805924

111. McCoy, Terrence. "How Douglas McArthur McCain became the first American to die fighting for the Islamic State", *Washington Post.* Published Aug. 27, 2015; accessed Dec. 13, 2015: https://www.washingtonpost.com/news/morning-mix/wp/2014/08/27/how-douglas-mcarthur-mccain-be-came-the-first-american-to-die-fighting-for-the-islamic-state/

112. Phillips, Sandra. "Former SD City College student killed while fighting for ISIS," Fox 5 San Diego. Published Aug. 26, 2014; accessed Dec. 12, 2015: http://fox5sandiego.com/2014/08/26/former-sd-city-college-student-killed-while-fighting-for-isis/

113. Hall, Matthew and Jeanette Steele. "Local Jihadist killed in Syrian Battle," *San Diego Union-Tribune*. Published Aug. 26, 2014; accessed Dec. 12, 2015: http://www.sandiegouniontribune.com/news/2014/aug/26/Douglas-McCain-ISIS-SanDiego-killed-Syria/2/

114. Dawah-Calling to Allah. Accessed Dec. 13, 2015: Facebook-https://www.facebook.com/Dawah-Calling-to-Allah-165739411623/

115. Koplowitz, Howard. "Who is Douglas McArthur McCain? American killed fighting for ISIS", *International Business Times*. Published Aug. 26, 2014; accessed Jan. 12, 2016: http://www.ibtimes.com/who-douglas-mcauthur-mccain-american-killed-fighting-isis-1670178

116. Ibid.

117. McCoy. "How Douglas McArthur McCain became the first American to die fighting for the Islamic State," *Washington Post*.

118. Vinograd, Cassandra and Ammar Cheikh Omar, "American Douglas McAuthur McCain Dies Fighting for ISIS in Syria," NBC News. Published Aug. 26, 2015; accessed Dec. 13, 2015: http://www.nbcnews.com/news/world/american-douglas-mcauthur-mccain-dies-fighting-isis-syria-n189081

119. Ibid.

120. Gartenstein-Ross, Daveed. "How Many Fighters Does the Islamic State Really Have?" *War on the Rocks*. Published Feb. 9, 2015; accessed Jan. 12, 2016: http://warontherocks.com/2015/02/how-many-fighters-does-the-islamic-state-really-have/ | Cockburn, Patrick (16 November 2014). "War with Isis: Islamic militants have army of 200,000, claims senior Kurdish leader," *Independent*. Published Nov. 15, 2014; accessed Jan. 16, 2015: http://www.independent.co.uk/news/world/middle-east/war-with-isis-islamic-militants-have-army-of-200000-claims-kurdish-leader-9863418.html

121. Nakhoul, Samia. "Saddam's former army is secret of Baghdadi's success," Reuters. Published June 16, 2016; accessed Jan. 12, 2016: http://www.reuters.com/article/2015/06/16/us-mideast-crisis-baghdadi-insight-idUSKBN0OW1VN20150616#byGi0oQijjekp85g.97

122. "UN says '25,000 foreign fighters' joined Islamist militants," *BBC News*. Published April 2, 2015; accessed Jan. 12, 2016: http://www.bbc.com/news/world-middle-east-32156541?utm_source=-Sailthru&utm_medium=email&utm_term=*Mideast%20Brief&utm_campaign=2014_The%20Middle%20East%20Daily | Burke, Jason. "Islamist fighters drawn from half the world's countries, says UN," *Guardian*. Published May 26, 2015; accessed Jan. 12, 2016: *http://www.theguardian.com/world/2015/may/26/islamist-fighters-drawn-from-half-the-worlds-countries-says-un*

123. Connolly, Amanda. "Canadian fighters killed in Syria pose paperwork problem for government families," *iPolitics*. Published Dec. 9, 2015; accessed Dec. 12, 2015: http://ipolitics.ca/2015/12/09/canadian-fighters-killed-in-syria-pose-paperwork-problem-for-government-families/

124. US Homeland Security Committee. "Terror Threat Snapshot," Published Dec. 2015; accessed Dec. 12, 2015: https://homeland.house.gov/wp-content/uploads/2015/12/December-Terror-Threat-Snapshot.pdf

125. The Soufan Group. "Foreign Fighters in Iraq and Syria," The Soufan Group. Published Dec. 9, 2015; accessed Dec. 12, 2015: http://soufangroup.com/wp-content/uploads/2015/12/TSG_Foreign-FightersUpdate3.pdf

126.   "89 Trinis Join ISIS fighters," *Guardian*. Published Nov. 16, 2016; accessed Dec. 12, 2015: http://www.guardian.co.tt/news/2015-11-16/89-trinis-join-isis-fighters

127.   The Soufan Group. "Foreign Fighters in Iraq and Syria."

128.   Van Ostaeyen, Peter. "Belgian Fighters in Syria and Iraq-Oct 2015," Pieter Van Ostaeyen blog. Published Oct. 11, 2015; accessed Dec. 13, 2015: https://pietervanostaeyen.wordpress.com/2015/10/11/belgian-fighters-in-syria-and-iraq-october-2015/

129.   Schmid, Alex P. "Foreign (Terrorist) Fighter Estimates: Conceptual and Data Issues.," Published Oct. 2015; accessed Dec. 12, 2015: http://icct.nl/wp-content/uploads/2015/10/ICCT-Schmid-Foreign-Terrorist-Fighter-Estimates-Conceptual-and-Data-Issues-October20152.pdf

130.   "125 Danish citizens have joined ISIS, returnees pose terror threat: Official," ARA News. Published Oct. 24, 2015; accessed Jan. 12, 2016: http://aranews.net/2015/10/125-danish-citizens-have-joined-isis-returnees-pose-terror-threat-official/

131.   The Soufan Group. "Foreign Fighters in Iraq and Syria."

132.   Kivimäki, Veli-Pekka. "Today's Finnish Security Intelligence Service event: 70 have departed for Syria, 15 killed, and about 20 have returned." Twitter. Published Dec. 3, 2015; accessed Dec. 12, 2015: https://twitter.com/vpkivimaki/status/661591870208872448

133.   "According to Germany's interior minister, 760 of the country's citizens have traveled to Syria and Iraq to join the Islamic State or terror groups." *Sputnik News*. Published Nov. 22, 2015; accessed Dec. 12, 2015: http://m.sputniknews.com/world/20151122/1030535022/german-citizens-join-militants-syria-iraq.html

134.   O'Shea, James. "Up to 40 Irish recruited by ISIS says ex-Minister for Justice," *Irish Central*. Published Nov. 23, 2015; accessed Dec. 12, 2015: http://www.irishcentral.com/news/politics/Up-to-40-Irish-recruited-by-ISIS-says-ex-Minister-for-Justice.html

135.   Il Sole 24. "Pinotti: 87 foreign fighers in the ranks of ISIS came from Italy," Il Sole 24. Published Sept. 20, 2015; accessed Dec. 12, 2015: http://www.ilsole24ore.com/art/notizie/2015-09-20/pinotti-file-dell-isis-87-foreigh-fighters-passati-dall-italia-170441.shtml?uuid=AC51QL1&refresh_ce=1

136.   Masini, G. "l'Italia è nel mirino della jihad; 10 jihadisti rimpatriati," *Il Giornale*. Published Jan. 15, 2015; accessed Dec. 12, 2015: http://www.ilgiornale.it/news/cronache/litalia-nel-mirino-jihad-dieci-foreign-fighters-rimpatriati-1083098.html

137.   Netherlands Ministry of Security and Justice. "Threat Level Continues to be 'substantial,'" Ministry of Security and Justice. Sept. 11, 2015; accessed Dec. 12, 2015: https://www.government.nl/latest/news/2015/11/09/threat-level-continues-to-be-substantial

138.   The Soufan Group. "Foreign Fighters in Iraq and Syria."

139.   Donn, Natasha. "Portuguese jihadist reported dead in Syria," *Portugal Resident*. Published March 12, 2015; accessed Dec. 13, 2015: http://portugalresident.com/portuguese-jihadist-reported-dead-in-syria

140.   The Soufan Group. "Foreign Fighters in Iraq and Syria."

141.   "Säpo: 125 Svenskar På Terroristidan," Sveriges Radio. Originally aired Oct. 3, 2015; accessed Dec. 12, 2015: http://sverigesradio.se/sida/artikel.aspx?programid=83&artikel=6270352Sverige Radio

142.   Dschihadistisch Motivierte Reisebewegungen. "Jihad-motivated travel movements-November Figures," VBS. Published Nov. 2015; accessed Dec. 12, 2015: http://www.vbs.admin.ch/internet/vbs/de/home/documentation/publication/snd_publ/dschihad.html

143. Neumann, Peter. "Foreign fighter total in Syria/Iraq now exceeds 20,000; surpasses Afghanistan conflict of the 1980s," Combating Terrorism Center. Published Jan. 26, 2015; accessed Dec. 12, 2015: https://www.ctc.usma.edu/posts/ethnic-albanian-foreign-fighters-in-iraq-and-syria

144. The Soufan Group. "Foreign Fighters in Iraq and Syria."

145. Ibid.

146. Ibid.

147. Ibid.

148. Mamon, Marcin. " The Mujahedeen's Vally: A Remote Region of Georgia Loses its Children to ISIS," *Intercept*. Published July 9, 2015; accessed Dec. 12, 2015: https://theintercept.com/2015/07/09/mujahedeensvalley/

149. The Soufan Group. "Foreign Fighters in Iraq and Syria."

150. Ibid.

151. Dusica, Tomovic. "Montenegro to Jail Fighters in Foreign Wars," *Balkan Insight*. Published Sept. 19, 2014; accessed Dec. 12, 2015: http://www.balkaninsight.com/en/article/montenegro-to-jail-fighters-in-foreign-wars

152. The Soufan Group. "Foreign Fighters in Iraq and Syria."

153. Ibid.

154. Bishkek/Brussels. "Syria calling: Radicalisation in Central Asia," Crisis Group. Accessed Dec. 12, 2015: http://www.crisisgroup.org/~/media/Files/asia/central-asia/b072-syria-calling-radicalisation-in-central-asia.pdf

155. Ibid.

156. Farooq, Umar. "Kyrgyzstand and the Islamists," *Diplomat*. Published Nov. 16, 2015; accessed Jan. 12, 2016: http://thediplomat.com/2015/11/kyrgyzstan-and-the-islamists/

157. The Soufan Group. "Foreign Fighters in Iraq and Syria."

158. Ibid.

159. Bishkek/Brussels. "Syria calling: Radicalisation in Central Asia." Crisis Group.

160. The Soufan Group, "Foreign Fighters in Iraq and Syria."

161. Ibid.

162. US Homeland Security Committee. "Final Report of the Taskforce on Combating Terrorist and Foreign Fighter Travel," Homeland Security Committee. Published Sept. 2015; accessed Jan. 12, 2016: https://homeland.house.gov/wp-content/uploads/2015/09/TaskForceFinalReport.pdf

163. The Soufan Group. "Foreign Fighters in Iraq and Syria."

164. Ibid.

165. Ibid.

166. Ibid.

167. Ibid.

168. Ibid.

169. Masbah, Mohammed. "Moroccan Foreign Fighters," SWP Berlin. Published Oct. 2015; accessed Dec. 13, 2015: https://www.swp-berlin.org/fileadmin/contents/products/comments/2015C46_msb.pdf

170. The Soufan Group. "Foreign Fighters in Iraq and Syria."

171. The Soufan Group. "Foreign Fighters in Iraq and Syria."

172. "South Africans return home from ISIS-held territory" News24. Published Sept. 11, 2015; accessed Dec. 12, 2015: http://www.news24.com/SouthAfrica/News/South-Africans-return-home-from-ISIS-held-territory-20150911

173. "Sudan says 70 of its nationals have gone to ISIS" *Sudan Tribune*. Published Oct. 13, 2015; accessed Dec. 12, 2015: http://www.sudantribune.com/spip.php?article56704

174. Ibid.

175. Martina, Michael. "About 300 Chinese said fighting alongside Islamic State in Middle East," Reuters. Published Dec. 15, 2014; accessed Jan. 12, 2016: http://www.reuters.com/article/us-mideast-crisis-china-idUSKBN0JT0UX20141215#jkot8pcc0PWcgY9s.97

176. IBNLive. "150 Indian youths under surveillance of security agencies for leaning towards extremist Islamic militant group ISIS," *IBNLive*. Published Nov. 18, 2015; accessed Dec. 13, 2015: http://www.ibnlive.com/news/india/150-youths-under-surveillance-for-leanings-towards-isis-1166108.html

177. Ibid.

178. Mezzofiore, Gianluca. "Kamikaze ISIS; Nine Japanese 'Joined Islamic State' Claims Israel," *International Business Times*. Published Sept. 26, 2014; accessed Dec. 13, 2015: http://www.ibtimes.co.uk/isis-nine-japanese-joined-islamic-state-according-israeli-official-1467375

179. Ibid.

180. The Soufan Group. "Foreign Fighters in Iraq and Syria."

181. Mallet, Victor, "The Maldives: Islamic Republic, Tropical Autocracy" *Financial Times*. Published Dec. 4, 2015; accessed Dec. 12, 2015: http://www.ft.com/intl/cms/s/0/aa9620dc-98f6-11e5-9228-87e603d47bdc.html

182. Ibid.

183. Fonbuena, Carmela. "FVR: Raw intel says 100 Filipinos training with ISIS," *Rappler*. Published Aug. 20, 2014; accessed Dec. 12, 2015: http://www.rappler.com/nation/66758-fvr-ramos-isis-filipinos

184. The Soufan Group. "Foreign Fighters in Iraq and Syria."

185. Senate of the Commonwealth of Australia. Legal and Constitutional Affairs Legislation Committee. "Title" Published Oct. 20, 2015; accessed Dec. 12, 2015: http://parlinfo.aph.gov.au/parlInfo/download/committees/estimate/b2ac3d04-3b49-4dbc-b8f5-568935767ea9/toc_pdf/Legal%20and%20Constitutional%20Affairs%20Legislation%20Committee_2015_10_20_3922.pdf;fileType%3Dapplication%2Fpdf

186. The Soufan Group. "Foreign Fighters in Iraq and Syria."

187. Barrett. *The Islamic State*.

188. Ibid.

189. Ibid.

190. Ibid.

191.   Ibid.

192.   "The Islamic State's organizational structure one year in," *Al-Monitor*. http://www.al-monitor.com/pulse/security/2015/07/islamic-state-caliphate-ministries-armies-syria-iraq.html, 07/02/2015

193.   Ibid.

194.   David Ignatius, "Al Qaeda affiliate playing larger role in Syrian rebellion," *Washington Post*. Nov. 30, 2012; accessed Nov. 28, 2015: https://www.washingtonpost.com/blogs/post-partisan/post/al-qaeda-affiliate-playing-larger-role-in-syria-rebellion/2012/11/30/203d06f4-3b2e-11e2-9258-ac-7c78d5c680_blog.html.

195.   Ibid.

196.   "Clinton visits Turkey for Syria talks as army pounds rebels in Aleppo," *Al Arabiya*. Aug. 5, 2012; accessed Nov. 28, 2015: http://english.alarabiya.net/articles/2012/08/05/230518.html.

197.   "Battle of Aleppo (2012–present)," *Wikipedia*. Last modified Nov. 19, 2015; accessed Nov. 28, 2015: https://en.wikipedia.org/wiki/Battle_of_Aleppo_%282012%E2%80%93present%29#cite_note-clintonvisits-88

198.   Ibid.

199.   Solomon, Jay and Sam Dagher. "Russia, Iran seen coordinating on Defense of Assad Regime in Syria," *Wall Street Journal*. Published Sept. 21, 2015; accessed Dec. 13, 2015: http://www.wsj.com/articles/russia-iran-seen-coordinating-on-defense-of-assad-regime-in-syria-1442856556

200.   Albayrak, Ayla, Joe Parkinson, and David Gauther-Villars. "Thousands of Syrian Kurds Flee Islamic State Fighters into Turkey," *Wall Street Journal*. Published Sept. 19, 2014; accessed Dec. 13, 2015: http://www.wsj.com/articles/thousands-of-syrian-kurds-flee-islamic-state-fighters-into-turkey-1411151657

201.   "ISIS hundreds of meters away from Kobane," Syrian Observatory for Human Rights. Published Oct. 2, 2014; accessed Dec. 13, 2015: http://www.syriahr.com/en/2014/10/the-is-is-hundreds-of-meters-away-from-ein-al-arabkobane/

202.   Butler, Darren. "Islamic State raises flag in eastern Kobani, Kurds say town has not fallen," *GMA News*. Published Oct. 6, 2014; accessed Jan. 12, 2016: http://www.gmanetwork.com/news/story/382418/news/world/islamic-state-raises-flag-in-eastern-kobani-kurds-say-town-has-not-fallen

203.   AFP. "Islamic State fighters capture Kurd HQ in Syria's Kobane" *Deccan Chronicle*. Published Oct. 10, 2014; accessed Dec. 14, 2015: http://www.deccanchronicle.com/141010/world-middle-east/article/islamic-state-fighters-capture-kurd-hq-syrias-kobane-monitor

204.   "The Islamic State's organizational structure one year in," *Al-Monitor*.

205.   Ibid.

206.   Pickles, Kate. "ISIS behead emir who ruled over Syrian region after discovering he was a drug dealer, and now face the wrath of his relatives, who are one of the group's founding families," *Daily Mail*. Published May 22, 2015; accessed Jan. 12, 2016: http://www.dailymail.co.uk/news/article-3093119/ISIS-behead-emir-ruled-Syrian-region-discovering-drug-dealer-face-wrath-relatives-one-group-s-founding-families.html

207.   "Assad vows to 'live and die' in Syria - Thursday 8 November 2012," *Guardian*. Published Nov. 8, 2012; accessed Nov. 28, 2015: http://www.theguardian.com/world/middle-east-live/2012/nov/08/syria-cameron-review-arms-embargo-live

208. AFP. "Jihadists expelled from flashpoint Kurdish Syrian town NGO says," *NOW.* Published July 17, 2013; accessed Nov. 28, 2015, https://now.mmedia.me/lb/en/nowsyrialatestnews/jihadists-expelled-from-flashpoint-kurdish-syrian-town-ngo-says

209. ["General Census 2004,"] [*CBSSYR*], [   ]. Published, 2004; accessed Nov. 28, 2015: http://www.cbssyr.sy/new%20web%20site/General_census/census_2004/NH/TAB08-15-2004.htm. [THIS NOTE WILL NEED TO BE VERIFIED AND FLESHED OUT BY AN ARABIC OR KURDISH SPEAKER].

210. "Syrian rebels clash with armed Kurds," *Al Jazeera.* Nov. 19, 2012; accessed Nov. 28, 2015: http://www.aljazeera.com/news/middleeast/2012/11/2012111917551517843.html

211. AFP. "Jihadist rebels in standoff with Syria Kurds: NGO," *Al Arabiya.* Published Nov. 22, 2012; accessed Nov. 28, 2015: http://english.alarabiya.net/articles/2012/11/22/251219.html

212. "Cessez-le-feu à Rass al-Ain," *ActuKurde.* Dec. 17, 2012; accessed Nov. 28, 2015: http://www.actukurde.fr/actualites/390/cessez-le-feu-a-rass-al-ain.html

213. AFP. "Islamists and Kurds end hostilities, to fight Syria regime," *NOW.* Feb. 19, 2013; accessed Nov. 28, 2015: https://now.mmedia.me/lb/en/nowsyrialatestnews/islamists-and-kurds-end-hostilities-to-fight-syria-regime

214. Gold, Danny. "Chatting about 'Game of Thrones' with Syria's Most Feared Militants," *Vice.* May 7, 2013; accessed Nov. 28, 2015: http://www.vice.com/read/talking-disneyworld-with-terrorists-in-syria

215. AFP. "Syrie: les Kurdes infligent une cuisante défaite aux jihadistes," *L'Orient le jour.* July 17, 2013; accessed Nov. 28, 2015: http://www.lorientlejour.com/article/824072/syrie-les-kurdes-infligent-une-cuisante-defaite-aux-jihadistes.html

216. "Al-Malikiyah: YPG seeks rapprochement with Free Syrian Army," *Kurdwatch.* Jan 15, 2013; accessed Nov. 28, 2015: http://www.kurdwatch.org/index.php?aid=2735&z=en&cure=1009

217. All4syria.info. "DAASH controls Mrkd, and mourns its leader from Hasaka," All4Syria. Published March 30, 2014; accessed Jan. 12, 2016: http://www.all4syria.info/Archive/139573

218. "The Islamic State's organizational structure one year in," *Al-Monitor.*

219. Ibid.

220. "ISIL re-enters Yarmouk refugee camp in Syria's capital," *AlJazeera.* Published April 4, 2015; accessed Dec. 15, 2015: http://www.aljazeera.com/news/2015/04/isil-enters-yarmouk-refugee-camp-syria-capital-150403124537528.html

221. "Syrian rebels defeat ISIS in Damascus," *Ara News.* Published April 20, 2015; accessed Jan. 12, 2016: http://aranews.net/2015/04/syrian-rebels-defeat-isis-in-damascus/

222. "IS militants enter Yarmouk refugee camp in Syrian capital," BBC. Published April 1, 2015; accessed Dec. 14, 2015: http://www.bbc.co.uk/news/world-middle-east-32147888

223. Aboud, Assaf and staff. "Syria conflict: Rebels evacuated from Old City of Homs," *BBC.* Published May 7, 2014; Nov. 28, 2015: http://www.bbc.com/news/world-middle-east-27306525

224. Ibid.

225. Benotman, Noman and Roisin Blake. "Jabhat al-Nusra, A Strategic Briefing," *Quilliam Foundation.* Accessed Jan. 12, 2016: http://www.quilliamfoundation.org/wp/wp-content/uploads/publications/free/jabhat-al-nusra-a-strategic-briefing.pdf

226. Makdesi, Marwan. "Syrian army moves into rebel-free Homs, starts de-mining operation," *Reuters*. Published May 9, 2014; accessed Nov. 28, 2015: http://www.reuters.com/article/2014/05/09/us-syria-crisis-homs-idUSBREA4806Q20140509

227. Freeman Spogli Institute. "Mapping Militant Organizations, Jabhat al-Nusra," Stanford University, Last modified Oct. 1, 2015; accessed Nov. 28, 2015: https://web.stanford.edu/group/mappingmilitants/cgi-bin/groups/view/493

228. Makdesi. "Syrian army moves into rebel-free Homs, starts de-mining operation," *Reuters*.

229. Blanford, Nicholas. "Retreat from Homs - Assad conquers cradle of revolution," *Times*. Published May 8, 2014; accessed Nov. 28, 2015: http://www.thetimes.co.uk/tto/news/world/middleeast/article4083611.ece

230. AP. "Rebel exodus from Old Homs marks end of the two-year siege," *Daily Star*. Published May 8, 2014; accessed Nov. 28, 2015: http://dailystar.com.lb/News/Middle-East/2014/May-08/255706-rebel-exodus-from-old-homs-marks-end-of-two-year-siege.ashx

231. "30 killed in Homs, Syria," *RTE News*. Published July 18, 2011; accessed Nov. 28, 2015: http://www.rte.ie/news/2011/0717/303800-syria/

232. Fahmy, Mohamed Fadel. "Arab League mission arrives amid violence in Syria," *CNN*. Published Dec. 26, 2011; accessed Nov. 28, 2015: http://edition.cnn.com/2011/12/26/world/meast/syria-unrest/index.html?hpt=hp_t2

233. "UN chief criticises 'atrocious' Homs assault," *Al Jazeera*. Published March 3, 2012; accessed Nov. 28, 2015: http://www.aljazeera.com/news/middleeast/2012/03/2012334752803236.html

234. Fadel, Leith. "Breaking: ISIS captures Maheen in East Homs; Christian city of Sadad in danger," *Al Masdar News*. Published Oct. 31, 2015; accessed Dec. 15, 2015: http://www.almasdarnews.com/article/breaking-isis-captures-maheen-in-east-homs-christian-city-of-sadad-in-danger/

235. Ibid.

236. "Islamic State 'seizes Syria town of al_Qaryatain' in Homs province," BBC. Published Aug. 6, 2015; accessed Dec. 15, 2015: http://www.bbc.com/news/world-middle-east-33806122

237. "The Islamic State's organizational structure one year in," *Al-Monitor*.

238. Ibid.

239. "Syria's Ramadan massacre," *Washington Post*. Published Aug. 1, 2011; accessed Nov. 28, 2015: https://www.washingtonpost.com/opinions/syrias-ramadan-massacre/2011/08/01/gIQAZHCKoI_story.html

240. AP and Reuters. "Activists Report Fierce Battles in Eastern Syria," *Haaretz*. Published Nov. 26, 2011; accessed Nov. 28, 2015: http://www.haaretz.com/middle-east-news/activists-report-fierce-battles-in-eastern-syria-1.397802

241. "Nine from one family among 10 killed in shelling as rebels kill 12 troops, *Al Arabiya*. Published May 1, 2012; accessed Nov. 28, 2015: https://english.alarabiya.net/articles/2012/05/01/211368.html

242. "Car bomb strikes near Syria military complex," *Al Jazeera*. Published May 19, 2012; accessed Nov. 28, 2015: http://www.aljazeera.com/news/middleeast/2012/05/201251973524973527.html

243. "Deaths reported in Syria police shooting," *Al Jazeera*. May 22, 2012; accessed Nov. 28, 2015: http://www.aljazeera.com/news/middleeast/2012/05/201252212505105610.html

244. Siddique, Haroon and Brian Whitaker. "Syria rebels overrun Aleppo police stations," *Guardian*. Published July 31, 2012; accessed Nov. 28, 2015: http://www.theguardian.com/world/2012/jul/31/syria-aleppo-fighting-goes-on-live

245. "Syrian government forces shell homes in town bordering Iraq," *Al Jazeera*. Published July 20, 2012; accessed Nov. 28, 2015: http://blogs.aljazeera.com/topic/syria/syrian-government-forces-shell-homes-town-bordering-iraq

246. "Dozens found shot execution-style in Syria," *Australian*. Published Jan. 29, 2013; accessed Nov. 28, 2015: http://www.theaustralian.com.au/news/latest-news/dozens-found-shot-execution-style-in-syria/story-fn3dxix6-1226564622261

247. Khalil, Ahmad. "Crossing the Bridge of Death in Deir Ezzor," *Syria Deeply*. Published Nov. 15, 2013; accessed Nov. 28, 2015: http://www.syriadeeply.org/articles/2013/11/2595/crossing-bridge-death-deir-ezzor/

248. Surk, Barbara. "Sunni extremist group expels jihadi rivals from provincial capital in eastern Syria near Iraq," *U.S. News*. Published July 14, 2014; accessed Nov. 28, 2015: http://www.usnews.com/news/world/articles/2014/07/14/officials-deadly-fighting-on-syria-lebanon-border

249. Saleh, Adam. "Isil compels FSA to evacuate Syria's Deir Ez-Zor," *ARA News*. Published July 16, 2014; accessed Nov. 28, 2015: http://aranews.net/2014/07/isil-compels-fsa-evacuate-syrias-deir-ez-zor/

250. Surk. "Sunni extremist group expels jihadi rivals from provincial capital in eastern Syria near Iraq," *U.S. News*.

251. Ibid.

252. Evans, Dominic. "Al Qaeda leaves east Syria strongholds to Islamic State–monitor," *Reuters*, July 3, 2014, accessed November 28, 2015, http://uk.reuters.com/article/2014/07/03/uk-syria-crisis-islamicstate-idUKKBN0F80SS20140703.

253. "The Islamic State's organizational structure one year in," *Al-Monitor*.

254. "Syrian rebels capture northern Raqqa city," *Al Jazeera*. Published March 5, 2013; accessed Nov. 28, 2015: http://www.aljazeera.com/news/middleeast/2013/03/201334151942410812.html

255. "Children 'killed' in Syrian army attack," *Al Jazeera*. Published Dec. 26, 2012; accessed Nov. 27, 2015: http://www.aljazeera.com/news/middleeast/2012/12/20121226102221539127.html

256. "Competition among Islamists," *Economist*. Published July 20, 2013; accessed Nov. 28, 2015: http://www.economist.com/news/middle-east-and-africa/21582037-one-islamist-rebel-group-seems-have-overtaken-all-others-competition-among

257. Oweis, Khaled Yacoub. "Syria opposition says captures eastern city of Raqqa," *Reuters*. Published March 4, 2013; accessed Nov. 28, 2015: http://www.reuters.com/article/2013/03/04/us-syria-crisis-city-idUSBRE92310920130304.

258. al-Hakkar, Firas. "The Mysterious Fall of Raqqa, Syria's Kandahar, *Al Akhbar*. Nov. 8, 2013; accessed Nov. 28, 2015: http://english.al-akhbar.com/node/17550

259. Harding, Luke and agencies, "Syrians tear down statue of al-Assad's father after rebel advance," *Guardian*. Published March 4, 2013; accessed Nov. 28, 2015: http://www.theguardian.com/world/2013/mar/04/syrian-rebels-statue-assad-father

260. Liam Stack and Hania Mourtada, "Syrian Rebels."

261. Reuters, "39 killed in air raids in Syria city of Raqqa as attacks intensify," *Independent*. Published June 3, 2013; accessed Nov. 28, 2015: http://www.independent.ie/world-news/middle-east/39-killed-in-air-raids-in-syria-city-of-raqqa-as-attacks-intensify-29114344.html

262. "Syrian refugee numbers may triple this year-UN," *BBC*. Published March 10, 2013; accessed Nov. 28, 2015: http://www.bbc.com/news/world-middle-east-21733331.

263. Namaa, Kamal. "Fighting erupts as Iraq police break up Sunni protest camp," Reuters. Published Dec. 30, 2013; accessed Jan. 12, 2016: http://www.reuters.com/article/us-iraq-violence-idUS-BRE9BT0C620131230

264. AFP. "Al Qaeda allies take over Fallujah, Iraq," *Deutsche Welle*. Published April 1, 2014; accessed Jan. 12, 2016: http://www.dw.com/en/al-qaeda-allies-take-over-fallujah-iraq/a-17341342

265. Morris, Loveday. "Islamic State attack on Iraqi base leaves hundreds missing, shows army weakness," *Washington Post*. Published Sept. 22, 2014; accessed Dec. 15, 2015: https://www.washingtonpost.com/world/middle_east/islamic-state-attack-on-iraqi-base-leaves-hundreds-missing-shows-army-weaknesses/2014/09/22/9a8b9e4d-0fea-4650-8816-5e720dbffd04_story.html

266. Varghese, Johnlee. "ISIS Militants in Iraqi Army Uniform Massacre Hundreds, capture 400 soldiers in Camp Saqlawiya," *International Business Times*. Published Sept. 23, 2014; accessed Dec. 15, 2015: http://www.ibtimes.co.in/isis-militants-iraqi-army-uniform-massacre-hundreds-capture-400-soldiers-camp-saqlawiyah-609729

267. AFP. "Jihadists launch onslaught on Iraq's Ramadi," *Hurriyet Daily News*. Published Nov. 12, 2014; accessed Dec. 14, 2014: http://www.hurriyetdailynews.com/jihadists-launch-onslaught-on-iraqs-ramadi.aspx?pageID=238&nID=74645&NewsCatID=352

268. Alkhshali, Hamdi. "ISIS on offensive in Iraq's Ramadi taking over mosque and government buildings," CNN. Published May 15, 2015; accessed Dec. 15, 2015: http://www.cnn.com/2015/05/15/middleeast/iraq-isis/

269. Arango, Tim. "Key Iraqi city falls to ISIS as last of security forces flee," *New York Times*. Published May 17, 2015; Dec. 15, 2015: http://www.nytimes.com/2015/05/18/world/middleeast/isis-ramadi-iraq.html?_r=0

270. "Al-Qaeda in Iraq claims deadly attack on Syrian troops," BBC. Published March 11, 2015; Dec. 14, 2015: http://www.bbc.co.uk/news/world-middle-east-21738613

271. "Heavy fighting rages in Iraq's Anbar province," *AlJazeera*. Published Oct. 2, 2014; accessed Dec. 14, 2014: http://www.aljazeera.com/news/middleeast/2014/10/isil-sunni-militias-battle-iraqi-town-201410281343980744.html

272. "Iraq conflict: Bomb kills two generals near Ramadi," Aug. 27, 2015; accessed Dec. 13, 2015: http://www.bbc.com/news/world-middle-east-34071169

273. "The Islamic State's organizational structure one year in," *Al-Monitor*.

274. Ibid.

275. Ibid.

276. Yacoub, Sameer and Adam Schreck. "Militants overrun parts of key Iraqi city of Mosul," *Yahoo News UK*. Published June 10, 2014; accessed Dec. 14, 2015: https://uk.news.yahoo.com/militants-overrun-parts-key-iraqi-city-mosul-132528918.html#keeS38M

277. Al-Sinjary, Zaid. "Sunni insurgents capture most of Iraq's second largest city," *Yahoo News UK*. Published June 10, 2014; accessed Dec. 12, 2015: https://uk.news.yahoo.com/sunni-insurgents-capture-most-iraqs-second-largest-city-112611507.html#umqK9mJ

278. Blender, Jeremy. "Saddam Hussein's Old Party Is Behind A Lot Of The Chaos In Iraq," *Business Insider*. Published June 18, 2014; accessed Jan. 12, 2016: http://www.businessinsider.com/saddam-husseins-old-party-is-behind-iraq-chaos-2014-6

279. "Iraq crisis: The battle for Mosul dam," *BBC*. Published Aug. 18, 2014; accessed Dec. 13, 2015: http://www.bbc.com/news/world-middle-east-28842515

280. Arango, Tim. "Sunni Extremists in Iraq Seize 3 Towns from Kurds and Threaten Major Dam," *New York Times*. Published Aug. 3, 2014; accessed Dec. 15, 2015: http://www.nytimes.com/2014/08/04/world/middleeast/iraq.html08/03/2014

281. "The Islamic State's organizational structure one year in," *Al-Monitor*.

282. "Iraq city of Tikrit falls to ISIL fighters," *AlJazeera*. Published June 12, 2014; accessed Dec. 12, 2015:   http://www.aljazeera.com/news/middleeast/2014/06/iraqi-city-tikrit-falls-isil-fighters-2014611135333576799.html

283. AlwasatNews-"Speicher Massacre-Relatives of Saddam's treachery started this, ISIS completed", 11/13/2014 accessed 12/12/2015

284. "Iraq Conflict: UN warns of possible Amerli 'massacre,'" BBC. Published Aug. 23, 2014; accessed Dec. 12, 2015: http://www.bbc.com/news/world-middle-east-28910674

285. Arango, Tim. "Escaping Death in Northern Iraq," *New York Times*. Published Sept. 3, 2014; accessed Dec. 14, 2015: http://www.nytimes.com/2014/09/04/world/middleeast/surviving-isis-massacre-iraq-video.html?_r=1

286. Siegel, Jacob. "The Iraqi Army's Alamo: Standoff in Tikrit," *Daily Beast*. Published July 20, 2015; accessed Dec. 14, 2015: http://www.thedailybeast.com/articles/2014/07/20/the-iraqi-army_s-alamo—standoff-in-tikrit.html

287. Mamoun, Abdelhak. "Hundreds of ISIS fighters arrive on Salahuddin outskirts," *Iraqi News*. Published April 14, 2015; accessed Dec. 14, 2015: http://www.iraqinews.com/iraq-war/hundreds-isis-fighters-arrive-salahuddin-outskirts/

288. AP. "Twin Suicide Blasts Kill Dozens in Beirut Suburb," CBS News. Published Nov. 12, 2015; accessed Dec. 11, 2015: http://www.cbsnews.com/news/isis-deadly-suicide-bombings-suburb-beirut-lebanon/

289. Masi, Alessandra. "Al Qaeda, ISIS Cooperate in Lebanon, But That's Just a Temporary Tactic," *International Business Times*. Published Feb. 2, 2015; accessed Dec. 11, 2015: http://www.ibtimes.com/al-qaeda-isis-cooperate-lebanon-thats-just-temporary-tactic-1828258?rel=rel2

290. "Over 1,000 ISIS Fighters Hide in Lebanese Mountains on Syrian Border—Security Chief," *Russia Today*. Published Jan. 4, 2015; accessed Dec. 11, 2015: https://www.rt.com/news/219663-islamic-state-lebanon-infiltrate/

291. Masi, Alessandria. "Christians Threatened by ISIS in Lebanon Turn to Hezbollah for Help," *International Business Times*. April 21, 2015; accessed Dec. 11, 2015: http://www.ibtimes.com/christians-threatened-isis-lebanon-turn-hezbollah-help-1889610

292. AP. "Twin Suicide Blasts Kill Dozens in Beirut Suburb," CBS News.

293. "Over 1,000 ISIS Fighters Hide in Lebanese Mountains on Syrian Border—Security Chief," *Russia Today.*

294. Ibid.

295. Malouf, Carol and Ruth Sherlock. "ISIS Is Building Strength on Lebanon's Doorstep," *Telegraph.* Published Jan. 20, 2015; accessed Dec. 11, 2015: http://www.businessinsider.com/isis-building-strength-on-lebanons-doorstep-2015-1?op=1

296. AP. "Twin Suicide Blasts Kill Dozens in Beirut Suburb," CBS News.

297. Malouf and Sherlock. "ISIS Is Building Strength on Lebanon's Doorstep," *Telegraph.*

298. Masi. "Al Qaeda, ISIS Cooperate in Lebanon, But That's Just a Temporary Tactic," *International Business Times.*

299. Ibid.

300. NOW. "Free Sunnis of Baalbek Pledge Allegiance to ISIS Caliphate," *NOW.* Published June 30, 2014; accessed Dec. 11, 2015: https://now.mmedia.me/lb/en/lebanonnews/553835-free-sunnis-of-baalbek-pledge-allegiance-to-isis-caliphate

301. AP. "Twin Suicide Blasts Kill Dozens in Beirut Suburb," CBS News.

302. Masi. "Al Qaeda, ISIS Cooperate in Lebanon, But That's Just a Temporary Tactic," *International Business Times.*

303. "ISIS Plans to Capture Lebanese Territories, Declare Emirate—Report," *Russia Today.* Published Feb. 23, 2015; accessed Dec. 10, 2015: https://www.rt.com/news/234859-isis-lebanon-islamic-emirate/

304. Ibid.

305. AP. "Twin Suicide Blasts Kill Dozens in Beirut Suburb," CBS News.

306. "Over 1,000 ISIS Fighters Hide in Lebanese Mountains on Syrian Border—Security Chief," *Russia Today.*

307. Masi. "Al Qaeda, ISIS Cooperate in Lebanon, But That's Just a Temporary Tactic," *International Business Times.*

308. Malouf and Sherlock. "ISIS Is Building Strength on Lebanon's Doorstep," *Telegraph.*

309. "Ceasefire extended in Lebanon's Arsal," *AlJazeera.* Published Aug. 6, 2014; accessed Jan. 12, 2016: http://www.aljazeera.com/news/middleeast/2014/08/ceasefire-extended-lebanon-arsal-201486152545936235.html

310. Mullen, Jethro, Greg Botelho, and Nic Robertson. "Source: Wife of ISIS Leader al-Baghdadi Arrested in Lebanon," CNN. Dec. 3, 2014; accessed Dec. 11, 2015: http://www.cnn.com/2014/12/02/world/meast/lebanon-isis-leader-family/index.html

311. Masi. "Al Qaeda, ISIS Cooperate in Lebanon, But That's Just a Temporary Tactic," *International Business Times.*

312. "ISIS Plans to Capture Lebanese Territories, Declare Emirate—Report," *Russia Today.*

313. Masi. "Christians Threatened by ISIS in Lebanon Turn to Hezbollah for Help," *International Business Times.*

314. AP. "Twin Suicide Blasts Kill Dozens in Beirut Suburb," CBS News.

315.   "Saja al-Dulaimi, Former Wife of al-Baghdadi Freed in Prisoner Exchange Deal," *Spec Ops*. Published Dec. 1, 2015; accessed Dec. 11, 2015: http://www.special-ops.org/14838/saja-al-dulaimi-former-wife-of-al-baghdadi-freed-in-prisoner-exchange-deal.html

316.   Reuters. "Beirut Bombing: Lebanese Authorites Arrest 11 People, Mostly Syrians, over Twin Bombings," Australian Broadcasting Corporation. Published Nov. 15, 2015; accessed Dec. 11, 2015: http://www.abc.net.au/news/2015-11-15/lebanon-arrests-six-people-over-beirut-bombings/6942598

317.   al-Arab, Mustafa and Tim Hune. "Widow of Beirut Bomb Attack Hero Adel Termos: 'He Made Us Proud,'" CNN. Published Nov. 16, 2015; accessed Dec. 11, 2015: http://www.cnn.com/2015/11/16/middleeast/lebanon-adel-termos-beirut-hero/index.html

318.   "Over 40 Killed, Dozens Wounded as Twin Suicide Bombings Rock Beirut," *Russia Today*. Published Nov. 12, 2015; accessed Dec. 11, 2015: https://www.rt.com/news/321723-lebanon-blast-suicide-killed/

319.   "5 Syrians, One Palestinian Detained Over Beirut Bombings," Press TV. Published Nov. 14, 2015; accessed Dec. 11, 2015: http://www.presstv.com/Detail/2015/11/14/437639/Lebanon-Beirut-twin-blasts-Daesh-ISIS-Syria

320.   Reuters. "Beirut Bombing: Lebanese Authorites Arrest 11 People, Mostly Syrians, over Twin Bombings," Australian Broadcasting Corporation.

321.   Ibid.

322.   Karasik, Dr. Theodore. "In Jordan, ISIS Hits a Wall . . . for Now," *Al Arabiya News*. Published June 30, 2014; accessed Dec. 10, 2015: http://english.alarabiya.net/en/views/news/middle-east/2014/06/30/Jordan-s-stand-ISIS-hits-a-wall-for-now.html

323.   Kenner, David. "The Men Who Love the Islamic State," *Foreign Policy*. Published Feb. 4, 2015; accessed Dec. 10, 2015: http://foreignpolicy.com/2015/02/04/islamic-state-jordan-zarqa/

324.   Dawber, Alistair, Christian Broughton, and Roisin O'Connor. "Isis Video Shows Death of Jordanian Hostage Muath al-Kasaesbeh," *Independent*. Published# Feb. 3, 2015; accessed Dec. 10, 2015: http://www.independent.co.uk/news/world/middle-east/isis-video-purports-to-show-jordanian-pilot-hostage-moaz-al-kasasbeh-being-burned-to-death-10021462.html

325.   Kenner. "The Men Who Love the Islamic State," *Foreign Policy*.

326.   Dawber, Broughton, and O'Connor. "Isis Video Shows Death of Jordanian Hostage Muath al-Kasaesbeh," *Independent*.

327.   Su, Alice. "It Wasn't Their War: Whatever Legitimacy the Islamic State Had in Jordan Was Incinerated Along with Muath al-Kaseasbeh's Body," *Atlantic*. Published Feb. 5, 2015; accessed Dec. 10, 2015: http://www.theatlantic.com/international/archive/2015/02/jordan-isis-pilot-response/385199/

328.   Khatib, Moufaq. "Jordan Moves 'Thousands' of Troops to Iraq Border: Jordanian Sources," NBC News. Published Feb. 10, 2015; accessed Dec. 10, 2015: http://www.nbcnews.com/storyline/isis-terror/jordan-moves-thousands-troops-iraq-border-jordanian-sources-n303441

329.   Al-Ghoul, Asmaa. "Gaza Salafists Pledge Allegiance to ISIS," *Al Monitor. Published* Feb. 27, 2014; accessed Dec. 11, 2015: http://www.al-monitor.com/pulse/tr/originals/2014/02/isis-gaza-salafist-jihadist-qaeda-hamas.html#

330. Issacharoff, Avi. "Gazans Nabbed in Sinai Were Hamas Naval Commandos en Route to Training," *Times of Israel*. Published Aug. 20, 2015; accessed Dec. 11, 2015: http://www.timesofisrael.com/gazans-nabbed-in-sinai-were-hamas-naval-commandos-en-route-to-training/?utm_source=dlvr.it&utm_medium=twitter

331. Varghese, Johnlee. "ISIS in Gaza: 100 Hamas Members Pledge Allegiance to Islamic State Leader Abu Bakr al-Baghdadi," *International Business Times*. Published Aug. 25, 2015; accessed Dec. 11, 2015: http://www.ibtimes.co.in/isis-gaza-100-hamas-members-pledge-allegiance-islamic-state-leader-abu-bakr-al-baghdadi-644149

332. Varghese, Johnlee. "4 Hamas Naval Commandos Who Went Missing in Egypt Abducted by ISIS, Say Reports," *International Business Times*. Published Aug. 21, 2015; accessed Dec. 11, 2015: http://www.ibtimes.co.in/4-hamas-naval-commandos-who-went-missing-egypt-abducted-by-isis-say-reports-643765

333. Withnall, Adam. "ISIS Accused of Beheading Captives in Palestinian Refugee Camp Yarmouk as Advance towards Syrian Capital Damascus Continues," *Independent*. Published April 7, 2015; accessed Dec. 11, 2015: http://www.independent.co.uk/news/world/middle-east/isis-accused-of-beheading-captives-in-palestinian-refugee-camp-yarmouk-as-advance-towards-syrian-10158061.html

334. Varghese, Johnlee. "Yarmouk Camp Beheadings: Hamas Arrests Prominent ISIS Preacher in Gaza," *International Business Times*. Published April 7, 2015; accessed Dec. 10, 2015: http://www.ibtimes.co.in/yarmouk-camp-beheadings-hamas-arrests-prominent-isis-preacher-gaza-628399

335. Ronen, Gil. "Hamas Arrests ISIS Man in Gaza after Yarmouk Beheadings," *Arutz Sheva*. Published April 7, 2015; accessed Dec. 10, 2015: http://www.israelnationalnews.com/News/News.aspx/193754

336. Varghese, Johnlee. "Gaza: ISIS Gives Hamas 72 Hours to Release Salafist Sheikh, Warns of Dire Consequences," *International Business Times*. Published May 4, 2015; accessed Dec. 11, 2015: http://www.ibtimes.co.in/gaza-isis-gives-hamas-72-hours-release-salafist-sheikh-warns-dire-consequences-631259

337. Varghese, Johnlee. "Gaza: ISIS Assassinates Senior Hamas Commander; Threatens to Kill More 'One by One,'" *International Business Times*. Published June 2, 2015; accessed Dec. 11, 2015: http://www.ibtimes.co.in/isis-assassinates-senior-hamas-commander-threatens-kill-more-one-by-one-634399

338. Varghese. "4 Hamas Naval Commandos Who Went Missing in Egypt Abducted by ISIS, Say Reports," *International Business Times*.

339. Issacharoff. "Gazans Nabbed in Sinai Were Hamas Naval Commandos en Route to Training," *Times of Israel*.

340. Zelin, Aaron, and Daveed Gartenstein-Ross. "How the Arab Spring's prisoner releases have helped the jihadi cause," *Atlantic*. Published Oct. 11, 2012; accessed Jan. 12, 2016: http://www.theatlantic.com/international/archive/2012/10/how-the-arab-springs-prisoner-releases-have-helped-the-jihadi-cause/263469/

341. Ashour, Omar. "Jihadists and Post-Jihadists in the Sinai," *Foreign Policy*. Published Sept. 5, 2012; accessed Jan. 12, 2016: http://foreignpolicy.com/2012/09/05/jihadists-and-post-jihadists-in-the-sinai/

342. "Public Notice 8689," US Department of Justice. Published Aug. 28, 2014; accessed Jan. 12, 2016: http://www.justice.gov/sites/default/files/eoir/legacy/2014/08/28/fr10apr14.pdf

343. Gartenstein-Ross, David. "Ansar Bayt al-Maqdis's Oath of Allegiance to Islamic State," Defend Democracy. Published Feb. 2015; accessed Jan. 12, 2016: http://www.defenddemocracy.org/content/uploads/documents/Ansar-Bayt-Al-Maqdis-Oath-of-Allegiance-to-the-Islamic-State-Wikistrat-Report.pdf

344. "Ansar Beit al-Maqdis declare allegiance to IS Emir Abu Bakr al-Baghdadi," *El-Balad*. Accessed Jan. 12, 2016: http://www.el-balad.com/1024731-

345. al-Shahed.net-" إخوان الكولبة التي اوقتلا الجهادي وبأ أيوي لمعد عاد شع "-http://www.alshahed.net/index.php?option=com_content&view=article&id=112365:2014-09-03-18-46-36&catid=478:01-09-04-2014

346. "Ansar Beit al-Maqdis denies pledging allegiance to ISIS," *Daily News Egypt*. Published Nov. 4, 2014; accessed Jan. 12, 2016: http://www.dailynewsegypt.com/2014/11/04/ansar-beit-al-maqdis-denies-pledging-allegiance-isis/

347. Al-Tamimi, Aymen. "Jamaat Ansar Bayt al-Maqdis' Allegiance to the Islamic State," *Pundicity*. Published Nov. 10, 2014; accessed Jan. 12, 2016: http://www.aymennjawad.org/2014/11/analysis-jamaat-ansar-bayt-al-maqdis-allegiance

348. Van Ostaeyen, Pieter. "Audio Message by Abu Bakr al-Baghdadi-Even if the Disbelivers Despise Such," Pieter Van Ostaeyen blog. Published Nov. 14, 2014; accessed Jan. 12, 2016: https://pietervanostaeyen.wordpress.com/2014/11/14/audio-message-by-abu-bakr-al-baghdadi-even-if-the-disbelievers-despise-such/

349. "Ansar Beit al-Maqdis loyalty to IS," *As-Safir*. Published Nov. 11, 2014; accessed Jan. 12, 2016: http://assafir.com/article/1/383372

350. Georgy, Michael. "Islamic State's Egypt affiliate urges attacks on judges in recording," Reuters. Published May 21, 2015; accessed Jan. 13, 2016: http://uk.reuters.com/article/uk-egypt-judges-militants-idUKKBN0O52NY20150520

351. Keating, Fiona. "Russian plane crash: Leader of Sinai Province group Abu Osama al-Masri named as bomber mastermind," *Sunday Times*. Published Nov. 8, 2015; accessed Jan. 13, 2016: http://www.thesundaytimes.co.uk/sto/news/uk_news/National/Terrorism/article1630319

352. Ministry of Interior Egypt. "A Statement from the Ministry of Interior," Published Nov. 9, 2015; accessed Jan. 13, 2016: https://www.facebook.com/media/set/?set=a.982292285147768.1073746477.181662475210757&type=3

353. African Commission on Human and Peoples' Rights. "Press Release on the execution of Mohammad Bakri Mohammad Haroun and five others," Published May 21, 2015; accessed Jan. 13, 2016: http://www.achpr.org/press/2015/05/d259/

354. "North Sinai tribal leader kills 4 Islamist militants," *Mada Masr*. Published Aug. 2, 2014; accessed Jan. 13, 2016: http://www.madamasr.com/news/north-sinai-tribal-leader-kills-4-islamist-militants

355. Xinhua Agency. "Egypt arrests Sinai leading militant," *Global Post*. Published Oct. 17, 2014; accessed Jan. 13, 2016: http://www.globalpost.com/article/6288896/2014/10/17/egypt-arrests-sinai-leading-militant

356. "ABM leader killed in N. Sinai: military," *Cairo Post*. Published Oct. 11, 2014; accessed Jan. 12, 2016: http://thecairopost.youm7.com/news/126843/news/abm-leader-killed-in-n-sinai-military

357. Gadher, Dipesh, and Miles Amoore. "Plane bombing mastermind unmasked as Egyptian cleric," *Sunday Times*. Published Nov. 8, 2015; accessed Jan. 13, 2016: http://www.thesundaytimes.co.uk/sto/news/uk_news/National/Terrorism/article1630319.ece

358. "Egypt crackdown delivers 'devastating blow' to Ansar, Brotherhood networks," *World Tribune*. Published Oct. 20, 2014; accessed Jan. 13, 2016: http://www.worldtribune.com/egypt-crackdown-delivers-devastating-blow-ansar-brotherhood-networks-2/

359. Fahim, Kareem, and Merna Thomas. "In Egypt, Jihadists Release Video of an October Attack," *New York Times*. Published Nov. 15, 2014; accessed Jan. 13, 2016: http://www.nytimes.com/2014/11/16/world/middleeast/in-egypt-jihadists-release-video-of-an-october-attack.html

360. AP Cairo. "Egypt militant group allied with ISIS claims it killed US Oil Worker in August," *Guardian*. Published Dec. 1, 2014; accessed Jan. 13, 2016: http://www.theguardian.com/world/2014/dec/01/egyptian-militant-group-us-oil-worker

361. Zaki, Menna. "State of Sinai' claim hundreds of killings in Sinai attacks," *Daily News Egypt*. Published Jan. 31, 2015; accessed Jan. 13, 2016: http://www.dailynewsegypt.com/2015/01/31/state-sinai-claim-hundreds-killings-sinai-attacks/

362. "Bombs kill two, wound others in Egypt's North Sinai," Reuters. Published March 10, 2015; accessed Jan. 13, 2016: http://www.reuters.com/article/us-egypt-violence-idUSKBN0M60DK20150310

363. "Separate attacks kill 2 women, injure policeman in Egypts Sinai," PressTV. Originally aired Oct. 6, 2015; accessed Jan. 13, 2016: http://www.presstv.com/Detail/2015/10/06/432257/Egypt-Sinai-Sheikh-Zuweid-Arish

364. "5 Police killed in al-Arish car bomb," *Daily News Egypt*. Published April 12, 2015; accessed Jan. 13, 2016: http://www.dailynewsegypt.com/2015/04/12/5-policemen-killed-in-al-arish-car-bomb/

365. Georgy, Michael and Stephen Kalin. "Islamic State's Egypt affiliate urges attacks on judges," Reuters. Published May 21, 2015; accessed Jan. 13, 2016: http://uk.reuters.com/article/2015/05/20/uk-egypt-judges-militants-idUKKBN0O52NY20150520

366. Thomas, Merna and Alison Smale. "Two Egyptian Policemen Shot Dead Near Pyramids of Giza," *New York Times*. Published June 3, 2015; accessed Jan. 13, 2016: http://www.nytimes.com/2015/06/04/world/middleeast/egypt-policemen-attacked-giza-pyramids.html

367. Lee, Ian. "Luxor suicide bomber, another assailant die in attack on temple, Egypt says," CNN. Published June 12, 2015; accessed Jan. 13, 2016: http://www.cnn.com/2015/06/10/middleeast/egypt-luxor-violence/

368. Fahim, Kareem and Merna Thomas. "Egypt's Top Prosecutor is most senior official to die in insurgency," *New York Times*. Published June 29, 2015; accessed Jan. 13, 2016: http://www.nytimes.com/2015/06/30/world/middleeast/roadside-bomb-injures-egypts-top-prosecutor.html

369. "241 terrorists killed in North Sinai in 5 days," *Ahram*. Published July 6, 2015; accessed Jan. 13, 2016: http://english.ahram.org.eg/NewsContent/1/64/134680/Egypt/Politics-/-terrorists-killed-in-North-Sinai-in--days-Militar.aspx

370. Dabiq 11-

371. Hall, John and Flora Drury. "ISIS brutally behead Croatian hostage kidnapped in Cairo after vowing to execute him unless 'all Muslim women' are freed from Egyptian jails," *Daily Mail*. Published Aug. 12, 2015; accessed Jan. 13, 2016: http://www.dailymail.co.uk/news/article-3195005/ISIS-brutally-behead-Croatian-hostage-kidnapped-Cairo-vowing-execute-unless-Muslim-women-freed-Egyptian-jails.html

372. AFP. "Islamic State Claims Killing of Egypt Police General," New Delhi Television. Published Sept. 17, 2015; accessed Jan. 13, 2016: http://www.ndtv.com/world-news/islamic-state-claims-killing-of-egypt-police-general-1218631

373. "Ansar Beit al-Maqdis kills Khaled Malki," *Albawabh News*. Published Jan. 10, 2015; accessed Jan. 13, 2016: http://www.albawabhnews.com/1526375001

374. "Ansar Bayt al-Maqdis posts video of deadly attack that killed 30 in Sinai," *Jerusalem Post*. Published Nov. 15, 2014; accessed Jan. 13, 2016: http://www.jpost.com/Middle-East/Ansar-Bayt-al-Maqdis-posts-video-of-deadly-attack-that-killed-30-in-Sinai-381854

375. Perry, Tom, and Sherine El Madany. "Egypt protests could turn more violent," Reuters. Published Feb. 5, 2011; accessed Jan. 13, 2016: http://uk.reuters.com/article/egypt-idUKLDE71400820110206

376. "Blast hits Egyptian gas pipeline," *AlJazeera*. Published July 4, 2011; accessed Jan. 13, 2016: http://www.aljazeera.com/news/middleeast/2011/07/2011740176861868.html

377. "Israelis killed in attacks near Egypt border," *Guardian*. Published Aug. 18, 2011; accessed Jan. 13, 2016: http://www.theguardian.com/world/2011/aug/18/israeli-bus-attacked-border-egypt

378. Lappin, Yaakov. "2 blasts shake Eilat; Salafi group warns Egypt ," *Jerusalem Post*. Published Aug. 16, 2012; accessed Jan. 13, 2016: http://www.jpost.com/Defense/2-blasts-shake-Eilat-Salafi-group-warns-Egypt

379. Greenberg, Joel. "Egypt-based Islamist militant group asserts responsibility for Israel border attack," *Washington Post*. Published Sept. 23, 2012; accessed Jan. 13, 2016: https://www.washingtonpost.com/world/egypt-based-islamist-militant-group-claims-responsibility-for-israel-border-attack/2012/09/23/abc05f24-058b-11e2-afff-d6c7f20a83bf_story.html

380. Zelin,   Aaron.   http://jihadology.net/2013/01/11/new-video-message-from-jamaat-an%E1%B9%A3ar-bayt-al-maqdis-the-battle-of-discipline-for-those-that-sacrileged-the-beloved-prophet/"-01-11-2013

381. Greenberg. "Egypt-based Islamist militant group asserts responsibility for Israel border attack," *Washington Post*.

382. "Sources confirm ex-army officer behind minister assassination attempt," *Egypt Independent*. Published Oct. 26, 2013; accessed Jan. 13, 2016: http://www.egyptindependent.com/news/sources-confirm-ex-army-officer-behind-minister-assassination-attempt

383. "15 dead, 134 injured in Egypt's Mansoura explosion," *Ahram*. Published Dec. 24, 2013; accessed Jan. 13, 2016: http://english.ahram.org.eg/News/89902.aspx

384. "Sinai's Ansar Beit al-Maqdis claim responsibility for Egypt's Mansoura blast," *Ahram*. Published Dec. 25, 2013; accessed Jan. 13, 2016: http://english.ahram.org.eg/NewsContent/1/64/89992/Egypt/Politics-/Sinais-Ansar-Beit-AlMaqdis-claim-responsibility-fo.aspx

385. Kirkpatrick, David. "Militants down Egyptian helicopter, killing 4 soldiers," *New York Times*. Published Jan. 26, 2015; accessed Jan. 13, 2016: http://www.nytimes.com/2014/01/27/world/middleeast/militants-down-egyptian-helicopter-killing-5-soldiers.html

386. Kingsley, Patrick. "Cairo hit by four explosions as Egypt insurgency escalates," *Guardian*. Published Jan. 24, 2014; accessed Jan. 13, 2016: http://www.theguardian.com/world/2014/jan/24/cairo-egypt-four-explosions-insurgency-escalates

387. Saleh, Yasmin and Shadia Nasralla. "Two Koreans and Egyptian driver die in Sinai tourist bus blast" Reuters. Published Feb. 16, 2014; accessed Jan. 13, 2016: http://www.reuters.com/article/us-blast-tourist-bus-egypt-idUSBREA1F0AW20140216

388. "Video shows beheading of four Egyptians in Sinai," *Al-Arabiya*. Published Aug. 28, 2014; accessed Jan. 13, 2016: http://english.alarabiya.net/en/News/middle-east/2014/08/28/Sinai-militants-claim-beheading-of-4-Egyptians.html

389. Kingsley, Patrick. "Attack on Egyptian military checkpint kills dozens," *Guardian*. Published Oct. 24, 2014; accessed Jan. 13, 2016: http://www.theguardian.com/world/2014/oct/24/attack-egyptian-military-checkpoint-kills-dozens

390. Kirkpatrick, David. "Militant group in Egypt vows loyalty to ISIS," *New York Times*. Published Nov. 10, 2014; accessed Jan. 13, 2016: http://www.nytimes.com/2014/11/11/world/middleeast/egyptian-militant-group-pledges-loyalty-to-isis.html?_r=1

391. "ISIS Planned to Attack Israeli Vessels After Commandeering Egyptian Missile Boat," *Algemeiner*. Published Dec. 1, 2014; accessed Jan. 13, 2016: http://www.algemeiner.com/2014/12/01/isis-planned-to-attack-israeli-vessels-after-commandeering-egyptian-missile-boat/

392. Shay, Dr. Shaul. "Egypt's War on Terror," *Israel Defense*. Published Oct. 20, 2015; accessed July 6, 2016: http://www.israeldefense.co.il/en/content/egypts-war-terror

393. "Egypt's army starts North Sinai Operation 'The Martyr's Right' reports 29 terrorists killed," *Ahram*. Published Sept. 8, 2015; accessed July 6, 2016: http://english.ahram.org.eg/NewsContent/1/64/139930/Egypt/Politics-/Egypts-army-starts-North-Sinai-Operation-The-Marty.aspx

394. Shaw, Mark and Fiona Mangan. "Illicit Trafficking and Libya's Transition," United States Institute of Peace. Published Feb. 2014; accessed Jan. 13, 2016: http://www.usip.org/sites/default/files/PW96-Illicit-Trafficking-and-Libyas-Transition.pdf

395. AFP. "Libya calls on neighbors to help lug pourous borders," *Ahram*. Published March 3, 2012; accessed Jan. 13, 2016: http://english.ahram.org.eg/NewsContent/2/8/35924/World/Region/Libya-calls-on-neighbours-to-help-plug-porous-bord.aspx

396. Karadsheh, Jomana. "Libya Rebels move onto Syrian battlefield," CNN. Published July 28, 2012; accessed Jan. 13, 2016: http://www.cnn.com/2012/07/28/world/meast/syria-libya-fighters/

397. Byrne, Eileen and Chris Stephen. "Tunis gunmen trained with Libyan militia, says security chief," *Guardian*. Published March 20, 2015; accessed Jan. 13, 2016: http://www.theguardian.com/world/2015/mar/20/tunis-gunmen-trained-libyan-militia-security-chief-bardo-museum

398. Swami, Praveen. "Libyan rebel commander admits his fighters have al-Qaida links," *Telegraph*. Published March. 25, 2011; accessed Jan. 13, 2016: http://www.telegraph.co.uk/news/worldnews/africaandindianocean/libya/8407047/Libyan-rebel-commander-admits-his-fighters-have-al-Qaeda-links.html

399. Bader, Gardy. "Libya announcement," Youtube. Published Dec. 13, 2012; Accessed Jan. 13, 2016: https://www.youtube.com/watch?v=tH7me_yigUs

400. Cruickshank, Paul and Nic Robertson. "ISIS comes to Libya," CNN. Published Nov. 18, 2014; accessed Jan. 13, 2016: http://www.cnn.com/2014/11/18/world/isis-libya/

401. Michael, Maggie. "How a Libyan city joined the Islamic State group," Associated Press. Published Nov. 9, 2014; accessed Jan. 13, 2016: http://bigstory.ap.org/article/195a7ffb0090444785eb814a5b-da28c7/how-libyan-city-joined-islamic-state-group

402. "Shura Council of Islamic Youth," Assakina. Published April 14, 2014; accessed Jan. 13, 2016: http://www.assakina.com/center/parties/42346.html

403.   Human Rights Watch. "Libya: Extremists Terrorizing Derna Residents," Human Rights Watch. Published Nov. 27, 2014; accessed Jan. 13, 2016: https://www.hrw.org/news/2014/11/27/libya-extremists-terrorizing-derna-residents

404.   "Saudi receives allegiance for DAASH from Libyans," *Al-Hayat News*. Published Nov. 3, 2014; accessed Jan. 13, 2016: http://www.alhayat.com/Articles/5450419

405.   "Islamic State moves in on Al-Qaeda turf," BBC. Published June 25, 2015; accessed Jan. 13, 2016: http://www.bbc.com/news/world-31064300

406.   Dabiq 5 p. 12

407.   Dabiq 5 p. 24

408.   Dabiq 5 p. 30

409.   Dabiq 11-Islamic State Magazine - page 62

410.   Morajea, Hassan. "Libyan gains may offer ISIS a base for new attacks," *Washington Post*. Published June 6, 2015; accessed Jan. 13, 2016: https://www.washingtonpost.com/world/middle_east/in-libyas-civil-war-the-islamic-state-shows-itself-as-the-main-threat/2015/06/06/65766592-0879-11e5-951e-8e15090d64ae_story.html

411.   Dabiq 11 - pg 60 - Sept 2015

412.   Meir Amit. "Spotlight on Global Jihad." Intellgience and Terrorism Info Center. Published Nov. 18, 2015; accessed Jan. 13, 2016: http://www.terrorism-info.org.il/en/article/20912

413.   "Abu al-Baraa el-Azdi profile," Counter Extremism Project. Accessed Jan. 13, 2016: http://www.counterextremism.com/extremists/abu-al-baraa-el-azdi

414.   "Islamic State leadership in Libya," *Maghrebi Note*. Published April 22, 2015; accessed Jan. 13, 2016: http://themaghrebinote.com/2015/04/22/islamicstateleadershiplibya/

415.   "IS said to have taken another Libyan town," *Times of Malta*. Published Feb. 10, 2015; accessed Jan. 13, 2016: http://www.timesofmalta.com/articles/view/20150210/world/is-said-to-have-taken-another-libyan-town.555481

416.   Ibid.

417.   Fryd, Jeremy. "Libyan Army Spokesperson to Assarigh: Tunisian IS Leader in Tripoli" *Tunisia Live*. Published Feb. 13, 2015; accessed Jan. 13, 2016: http://www.tunisia-live.net/2015/02/13/libyan-army-spokesperson-to-assarih-tunisian-is-leader-of-isis-in-tripoli/

418.   Paton, Callum. "ISIS In Libya: Who is Hassan al-Karami the spiritual leader of Islamic State in Sirte," *International Business Times*. Published Aug. 25, 2015; accessed Jan. 13, 2016: http://www.ibtimes.co.uk/isis-libya-who-hassan-al-karami-spiritual-leader-islamic-state-sirte-1517057

419.   "How a Libyan City joined the Islamic State Group," ABC News. Published Nov. 9, 2014; accessed Jan. 13, 2016: http://abcnews.go.com/International/wireStory/libyan-city-joined-islamic-state-group-26789640?page=2

420.   "ISIS-Libya Baghdadi proclaimed chief of Derna caliphate," *ANSAmed*. Published Oct. 31, 2014; accessed Jan. 13, 2016: http://www.ansamed.info/ansamed/en/news/sections/politics/2014/10/31/isis-libya-baghdadi-proclaimed-chief-of-derna-caliphate_28bc45c8-4ca3-48f7-94bb-fc9f75c6e39b.html

421.   Reuters. "Car bombs kill at least four in Libya as chaos mounts," *Times of Malta*. Published Nov. 13, 2014; accessed Jan. 13, 2016: http://www.timesofmalta.com/articles/view/20141113/world/Car-bombs-kill-at-least-four-in-Libya-as-chaos-mounts.543840

422.   Morajea, Hassan. "Libyan army gears up for Derna assault," *Middle East Eye*. Published Dec. 13, 2015; accessed Jan. 13, 2016: http://www.middleeasteye.net/news/libyan-army-gears-derna-as-sault-1618109392

423.   AP. "Al Qaida linked militants attack IS affiliate in Libya," *Yahoo News*. Published June 10, 2015; accessed Jan. 13, 2016: https://news.yahoo.com/al-qaida-militants-clash-libya-leader-killed-090144601.html

424.   Weyrey, Frederic. "Splitting the Islamists: The Islamic State's Creeping Advance in Libya," Carnegie Endowment for International Peace. Published June 19, 2015; accessed Jan. 13, 2016: http://carnegieendowment.org/syriaincrisis/?fa=60447

425.   "Libyan Islamists claim to drive Islamic State from port stronghold," Reuters. Published June 14, 2015; accessed Jan. 13, 2016: http://www.reuters.com/article/2015/06/14/us-libya-security-idUSKB-N0OU0P520150614#qxKoyjCMWM0hEUX0.97

426.   Zuber, Essam. "Libya officials: Jihadis driving IS from eastern stronghold," *Yahoo News*. Published July 30, 2015; accessed Jan. 13, 2016: https://news.yahoo.com/libya-officials-jihadis-driving-eastern-stronghold-140440469.html

427.   Farah, Waleed. "ISIS claim to take Nawfaliya town near Ben Jawad," *Libya Herald*. Published Feb. 9, 2015; accessed Jan. 13, 2016: http://www.libyaherald.com/2015/02/09/is-claim-to-take-over-libyan-town-near-ben-jawad/

428.   AFP/AP. "ISIS arm in Libya seizes Sirte airport from Tripoli," *National*. Published May 29, 2015; accessed Jan. 13, 2016: http://www.thenational.ae/world/middle-east/isil-arm-in-libya-seizes-sirte-airport-from-tripoli-forces

429.   "ISIS demands allegiance from Libya's sirte residents," *World Bulletin*. Published Sept. 15, 2015; accessed Jan. 13, 2016: http://www.worldbulletin.net/news/164282/isil-demands-allegiance-from-libyas-sirte-residents

430.   Cruickshank and "Robertson. ISIS Comes to Libya," CNN.

431.   "Libya bombings: Tobruk and al-Bayda attacked," BBC. Published Nov. 12, 2014; accessed Jan. 13, 2016: http://www.bbc.com/news/world-africa-30018894

432.   "ISIS: Libya, two human rights activists beheaded in Derna," ANSAmed. Published Dec. 1, 2014; accessed Jan. 13, 2016: http://www.ansamed.info/ansamed/en/news/sections/generalnews/2014/11/11/isis-libya-two-human-rights-activists-beheaded-in-derna_a801d4de-aa06-44e7-99a6-13c4ea4a9195.html

433.   "Massacre in Sukna: Report," *Libya Herald*. Published Jan. 2, 2015; accessed Jan. 13, 2016: https://www.libyaherald.com/2015/01/02/massacre-in-sukna-report/

434.   "ISIS Claims To Have Executed Two Tunisian Journalists," *International Business Times*. Published Jan. 8, 2015; accessed Jan. 13, 2016: http://www.ibtimes.com/isis-claims-have-executed-two-tunisian-journalists-1777782

435.   Karadsheh, Jomana and Hamdi Alkhshali. "Gunmen Attack Corinthia Hotel in Libya," CNN. Published Jan. 28, 2015; accessed Jan. 13, 2016: http://www.cnn.com/2015/01/27/middleeast/libya-corinthia-hotel-attack/index.html

436.   Dabiq7, Revenge for the Muslimat Persecuted by the Coptic Crusaders of Egypt,

437.   El-Gundy, Zeinab. "Islamic State publishes report on the Coptic Egyptian workers kidnapped in Libya," *Ahram*. Published Feb. 12, 2015; accessed Jan. 13, 2016: http://english.ahram.org.eg/NewsContent/1/64/122903/Egypt/Politics-/Islamic-State-publishes-report-on-Coptic-Egyptian-.aspx

438.   "Libya Violence: Islamic State attack kills 40 in al-Qubbah," BBC Africa. Published Feb. 20, 2015; accessed Jan. 13, 2016: http://www.bbc.com/news/world-africa-31549280

439.   Thornhill, Ted. "ISIS continues its desecration of the Middle East," *Daily Mail*. Published March 10, 2015; accessed Jan. 13, 2016: http://www.dailymail.co.uk/news/article-2987800/ISIS-continues-desecration-Middle-East-Islamic-State-reduces-Sufi-shrines-Libya-rubble-latest-act-mindless-destruction.html

440.   Amara, Tarek. "Senior ISIS commander killed in Libya," *Al-Arabiya*. Published March 18, 2015; accessed Jan. 13, 2016: http://english.alarabiya.net/en/News/africa/2015/03/18/Senior-ISIS-commander-from-Tunisia-killed-in-Libya.html

441.   "Islamic State militants claim suicide bombing in Libya's Benghazi: statement," Reuters. Published March 24, 2015; accessed Jan. 13, 2016: http://www.reuters.com/article/2015/03/25/us-libya-security-claim-idUSKBN0MK2RF20150325?mod=related&channelName=worldNews#c3XDuPSV02tS5Uzx.97

442.   AFP. "Four dead in Libya suicide bombing claimed by IS," *Yahoo News*. Published April 5, 2015; accessed Jan. 13, 2016: http://news.yahoo.com/four-dead-libya-suicide-bombing-claimed-114411970.html

443.   "Islamic State militants claim attacks on embassies in Libya," Reuters. Published April 12, 2015; accessed Jan. 13, 2016: http://www.reuters.com/article/2015/04/13/us-libya-bomb-idUSKBN0N401L20150413

444.   Westall, Sylvia. "Islamic State shoots and beheads 30 Ethiopian Christians in Libya," Reuters. Published April 20, 2015; accessed Jan. 13, 2016: http://www.reuters.com/article/2015/04/20/us-mideast-crisis-islamicstate-killings-idUSKBN0NA0IE20150420#6DAib8z6o4hc8VPm.97

445.   Al-Warfalli, Ayman. "Islamic State kills five journalists working for Libyan station-army official," Reuters. Published April 27, 2015; accessed Jan. 13, 2016: http://www.reuters.com/article/2015/04/27/us-libya-security-idUSKBN0NI1V820150427#APlS3zHuL4YsGbCP.97

446.   "ISIS Kidnaps 88 Eritrean Christians from Smugglers," *AlAlam*. Published June 9, 2015; accessed Jan. 13, 2016: http://en.alalam.ir/news/1710126

447.   AP. "Al-Qaida-linked militants attack IS affiliate in Libya," *Yahoo News*. Published June 10, 2015; accessed Jan. 13, 2016: https://news.yahoo.com/al-qaida-militants-clash-libya-leader-killed-090144601.html

448.   "Islamic State brutally crushes Sirte uprising." *Middle East Eye*. Published Aug. 15, 2015; accessed Jan. 13, 2016: http://www.middleeasteye.net/news/islamic-state-militants-step-reign-terror-massacre-libyan-town-1272577277

449.   "Abu Nabil al-Anbari not killed in US Derna attack," *Libya Herald*. Published Nov. 15, 2015; accessed Jan. 13, 2016: https://www.libyaherald.com/2015/11/15/abu-nabil-al-anbari-not-killed-in-us-derna-attack-report/

450.   Wescott, Tom. "IS seize Libya airbase after Misrata forces pull out," *Middle East Eye*. Published May 30, 2015; accessed Jan. 13, 2016: http://www.middleeasteye.net/news/seizes-sirte-airbase-after-misrata-forces-pull-out-67648483

451. Cousins, Michael. "ISIS starts to tax residents," *Arab Weekly*. Published Aug. 27, 2015; accessed Jan. 13, 2016: http://www.thearabweekly.com/?id=1746

452. "IS closes banks in Sirte; orders them to change to Sharia banking," *Libya Herald*. Published Sept. 13, 2015; accessed Jan. 13, 2016: https://www.libyaherald.com/2015/09/13/is-closes-banks-in-sirte-orders-them-to-change-to-sharia-banking/

453. Di Giovanni, Janine. "Tunisia's ISIS Connection," *New York Times*. Published June 16, 2015; accessed Jan. 13, 2016: http://www.newsweek.com/2015/06/26/tunisias-isis-connection-343295.html

454. Hirschfeld Davis, Julie. "John Kerry Says U.S. Will Give Tunisia More Financial Aid," *New York Times*. Published Nov. 13, 2015; accessed Jan. 13, 2016: http://www.nytimes.com/2015/11/14/world/africa/john-kerry-says-us-will-give-tunisia-more-financial-aid.html?ref=topics

455. Caryl, Christian. "Want to Beat the Islamic State? Help Tunisia," *Foreign Policy*. Published Nov. 21, 2015; accessed Jan. 13, 2016: http://foreignpolicy.com/2015/11/21/want-to-beat-the-islamic-state-help-tunisia/ | Holmes, Kim. "Tunisia Is Now a Hot Spot for ISIS Recruitment. How the US Could Help Change That," *Daily Signal*. Published Nov. 20, 2015; accessed Jan. 13, 2016: http://dailysignal.com/2015/11/20/tunisia-is-now-a-hot-spot-for-isis-recruitment-how-the-us-could-help-change-that/

456. Hirschfeld Davis. "John Kerry Says U.S. Will Give Tunisia More Financial Aid," *New York Times*.

457. Jemmali, Amira. "Why is ISIS targeting Tunisia?" *Type Writer*. Published Sept. 10, 2015; accessed Jan. 13, 2016: http://thetypewriter.org/2015/09/what-is-isis-targeting-tunisia-with-a-gunman/ | Di Giovanni. "Tunisia's ISIS Connection" Newsweek.

458. "The International Hotbeds of the Islamic State," The Soufan Group. Published July 22, 2015; accessed Jan. 13, 2016: http://soufangroup.com/tsg-intelbrief-the-international-hotbeds-of-the-islamic-state/

459. Elbagir, Nima. "The Tunisian town where ISIS makes militants," CNN. Originally aired July 3, 2015; accessed Jan. 13, 2016: http://www.cnn.com/2015/07/03/africa/tunisia-terror-attacks-kasserine/

460. Gartenstein-Ross, Daveed and Bridget Moreng. "Tunisian Jihadism after the Sousse Massacre," Combating Terrorism Center. Published Oct. 22, 2015; accessed Jan. 13, 2016: https://www.ctc.usma.edu/posts/tunisian-jihadism-after-the-sousse-massacre

461. Zelin, Aaron Y. "Tunisia's Fragile Democratic Transition," The Washington Institute. Published July 14, 2015; accessed Jan. 13, 2016: http://www.washingtoninstitute.org/policy-analysis/view/tunisias-fragile-democratic-transition

462. Jamaoui, Anouar. "The Development of Tunisian Terrorism," *Fikra Forum*. Published Sept. 25, 2015; accessed Jan. 13, 2016: http://fikraforum.org/?p=7733#.VmIdqmSrTow

463. Ibid.

464. Ibid.

465. Zelin. "Between the Islamic State and al-Qaeda in Tunisia," The Washington Institute.

466. Gartenstein-Ross and Moreng. "Tunisian Jihadism after the Sousse Massacre," Combating Terrorism Center. https://www.ctc.usma.edu/posts/tunisian-jihadism-after-the-sousse-massacre

467. Amit. "Spotlight on Global Jihad," Intelligence and Terrorism Info Center

468. AFP. "Friends shocked at Tunisian football fan turned bomber," *Tribune*. Published Nov. 28, 2015; accessed Jan. 13, 2016: http://tribune.com.pk/story/1000177/friends-shocked-at-tunisian-football-fan-turned-bomber/

469. "French Tourist Herve Gourdel abducted by Algerian militants," BBC. Published Sept. 23, 2015; accessed Jan. 13, 2016: http://www.bbc.com/news/world-europe-29319226

470. Shankar, Sneha. "Algerian Army Kills Leader Of Jund al-Khilafa Group That Beheaded French Tourist Herve Gourdel: Report," *International Business Times*. Published Dec. 23, 2014; accessed Jan. 13, 2016: http://www.ibtimes.com/algerian-army-kills-leader-jund-al-khilafa-group-beheaded-french-tourist-herve-1765668

471. Roussellier, Jacques. "ISIS: A Game Changer for Algeria," Carnegie Endowment for International Peace. Published Oct. 21, 2014; accessed Jan. 13, 2016: http://carnegieendowment.org/sada/?-fa=56981

472. "Algeria's al-Qaeda defectors join IS group," *AlJazeera*. Published Sept. 14, 2014; accessed Jan. 13, 2016: http://www.aljazeera.com/news/middleeast/2014/09/algeria-al-qaeda-defectors-join-group-201491412191159416.html

473. Lister. "Algerian beheading is sign of ISIS' growing impact—and of shrinking world," CNN.

474. Zelin, Aaron Y. "ISIS Has Declared The Creation Of Provinces In Several Countries," *Business Insider*. Published Nov. 14, 2014; accessed Jan. 13, 2016: http://www.businessinsider.com/aaron-zelin-isis-declared-provinces-in-arab-countries-2014-11

475. Shankar, Sneha. "Algerian Army Kills Leader Of Jund al-Khilafa Group That Beheaded French Tourist Herve Gourdel: Report," *International Business Times*.

476. AFP. "Algeria army kills 22 Islamists: defense ministry," *Yahoo News*. Published May 19, 2015; accessed Jan. 13, 2016: http://news.yahoo.com/algeria-army-kills-22-islamists-defence-ministry-205132414.html

477. Porter, Geoff D. "What to Make of the Bay'a in North Africa," Combating Terrorism Center. Published March 19, 2015; accessed Jan. 13, 2016: https://www.ctc.usma.edu/posts/what-to-make-of-the-baya-in-north-africa

478. Zelin, Aaron Y. "The Islamic State's Model," The Washington Institute. Published Jan. 28, 2015; accessed Jan. 13, 2016: http://www.washingtoninstitute.org/policy-analysis/view/the-islamic-states-model

479. "In the matter of the Designation of Jund al-Khilafa in Algeria as a specially designated global terrorist pursuant," US State Department. Published Oct. 1, 2015; accessed Jan. 13, 2016: https://www.federalregister.gov/articles/2015/10/01/2015-25004/in-the-matter-of-the-designation-of-jund-al-khilafah-in-algeria-aka-jak-a-aka-jund-al-khalifa-fi-ard

480. "Leader of Algerian 'beheading group' killed"- http://www.aljazeera.com/news/middleeast/2014/12/leader-algerian-beheading-group-killed-20141223132840215910.html, 12-23-2014

481. Elischer, Sebastian. "After this month's attack in Bamako, what do we know about fundamentalist Islam in Mali?" *Washington Post*. Published Nov. 30, 2015; accessed Jan. 13, 2016: https://www.washingtonpost.com/news/monkey-cage/wp/2015/11/30/after-this-months-attack-in-bamako-what-do-we-know-about-fundamentalist-islam-in-mali/

482. "Mali hotel attack: The unanswered question," BBC. Published Nov. 23, 2015; accessed Jan. 13, 2016: http://www.bbc.com/news/world-africa-34895019

483.   Fick, Maggie. "Why does Mali have a terror problem?" *Financial Times*. Published Nov. 22, 2015; accessed Jan. 13, 2016: http://www.ft.com/intl/cms/s/0/26ebca40-90fc-11e5-bd82-c1fb87bef7af.html#axzz3tH4mJXl0

484.   Barnard, Anna and Neil MacFarquhar. "Paris and Mali Attacks Expose Lethal Qaeda-ISIS Rivalry?" *New York Times*. Published Nov. 21, 2015; accessed Jan. 13, 2016: http://www.nytimes.com/2015/11/21/world/middleeast/paris-and-mali-attacks-expose-a-lethal-al-qaeda-isis-rivalry.html

485.   Lynch, Colum. "With the World's Gaze Fixed on the Islamic State, Mali's Islamists Return," *Foreign Policy*. Published Oct. 14, 2014; accessed Jan. 13, 2016: http://foreignpolicy.com/2014/10/14/with-the-worlds-gaze-fixed-on-the-islamic-state-malis-jihadists-return/

486.   Ibid.

487.   Schemm, Paul. "A look at Mali's Islamic extremist groups," Associated Press. Published Nov. 23, 2015; accessed Jan. 13, 2016: http://bigstory.ap.org/article/04fb938e48434ba983554bfeb891b7d9/look-malis-islamic-extremist-groups

488.   Lynch. "With the World's Gaze Fixed on the Islamic State, Mali's Islamists Return," *Foreign Policy*.

489.   Ibid.

490.   Ibid.

491.   Ibid.

492.   Lynch. "With the World's Gaze Fixed on the Islamic State, Mali's Islamists Return," *Foreign Policy*.

493.   Elischer. "After this month's attack in Bamako, what do we know about fundamentalist Islam in Mali?" *Washington Post*.

494.   Joscelyn, Thomas. "Confusion surrounds West African jihadists' loyalty to Islamic State," *Long War Journal*. Published May 14, 2015; accessed Jan. 13, 2016: http://www.longwarjournal.org/archives/2015/05/confusion-surrounds-west-african-jihadists-loyalty-to-islamic-state.php

495.   Ibid.

496.   "Al-Mourabitoun," Counter Extremism Project. Published Oct. 21, 2015; accessed Jan. 13, 2016: http://www.counterextremism.com/sites/default/files/threat_pdf/Al-Mourabitoun-10212015.pdf

497.   "CEP Releases Resources on Extremism in Mali Following Attack by Al-Mourabitoun and AQIM," Counter Extremism Project. Published Nov. 23, 2015; accessed Jan. 13, 2016: http://www.counterextremism.com/press/cep-releases-resources-extremism-mali-following-attack-al-mourabitoun-and-aqim

498.   Joscelyn. "Confusion surrounds West African jihadists' loyalty to Islamic State," *Long War Journal*.

499.   Withnall, Adam. "Boko Haram renames itself Islamic State's West Africa Province (ISWAP) as militants launch new offensive against government forces," *Independent*. Published April 26, 2015; accessed Dec. 11, 2015: http://www.independent.co.uk/news/world/africa/boko-haram-renames-itself-islamic-states-west-africa-province-iswap-as-militants-launch-new-10204918.html

500.   "Boko Haram," in *World Almanac of Islamism*. http://almanac.afpc.org/boko-haram unknown. Web. 11th December 2015

501.   Ibid.

502.   Ibid.

503.   "The Evolving Boko Haram War Machine," Council on Foreign Relations. Published Oct. 15, 2015; accessed Dec. 9, 2015: http://blogs.cfr.org/campbell/2015/10/15/the-evolving-boko-haram-war-machine/

504.   UNICEF. "Over 1.4 million children forced to flee conflict in Nigeria and region," UNICEF. Published Sept. 18, 2015; accessed Dec. 11, 2015: http://www.unicef.org/media/media_85551.html

505.   "Nigeria's Boko Haram pledges alliance to Islamic state," BBC. Published March 7, 2015; accessed Dec. 11, 2015: http://www.bbc.com/news/world-africa-31784538

506.   Weate, Jeremy. "Boko Haram's roots in Nigeria long predate Al-Qaeda era," *AlJazeera*. Published April 23, 2015; accessed Dec. 10, 2015: http://america.aljazeera.com/articles/2014/4/23/boko-haram-s-rootsinnigerialongpredatethealqaedaera.html

507.   "Nigeria's Boko Haram militants 'have new leader,'" BBC. Published Aug. 12, 2015; accessed Dec. 10, 2015: http://www.bbc.com/news/world-africa-33889378

508.   Zenn, Jacob. "Leadership Analysis of Boko Haram and Ansaru in Nigeria," Combating Terrorism Center. Published Feb. 24, 2014; accessed Dec. 10, 2015: https://www.ctc.usma.edu/posts/leadership-analysis-of-boko-haram-and-ansaru-in-nigeria

509.   Dorrie, Peter. "War is Boring. How Big is Boko Haram? " *Medium*. Published Feb. 3, 2015; accessed Dec. 10, 2015: https://medium.com/war-is-boring/how-big-is-boko-haram-fac21c25807#.ghzfzpt-vu

510.   Ibid.

511.   "The Evolving Boko Haram War Machine," Council on Foreign Relations blog. Published Oct. 15, 2015; accessed Dec. 9, 2015: http://blogs.cfr.org/campbell/2015/10/15/the-evolving-boko-haram-war-machine/

512.   Alfred, Charlotte. "How Boko Haram Used Female Suicide Bombers to Terrorize Nigeria," *Huffington Post*. Published Feb. 28, 2015; accessed Jan. 13, 2016: http://www.huffingtonpost.com/2015/02/28/boko-haram-female-suicide-bombers_n_6763386.html

513.   Varghese, Johnlee. "Nigeria: Isis-Style Boko Haram Video Shows Beheading of African Union Soldier," *International Business Times*. Published July 14, 2015; accessed Dec. 10, 2015: http://www.ibtimes.co.in/nigeria-isis-style-boko-haram-video-shows-beheading-african-union-soldier-639242

514.   Arcton, Ofeibea. "Boko Haram Takes a Page from ISIS Propaganda Playbook," NPR. Published March 5, 2015; accessed Dec. 10, 2015: http://www.npr.org/sections/parallels/2015/03/05/391024563/boko-haram-takes-a-page-from-isis-propaganda-playbook

515.   Ibid.

516.   "Islamic State ties broaden Boko Haram threat," BBC. Published Oct. 2, 2015; accessed Dec. 10, 2015: http://www.bbc.com/news/world-africa-34412956

517.   Laing, Aislinn. "Twitter suspends suspected Boko Haram account that tweeted pictures of child soldiers," *Telegraph*. Published Dec. 10, 2015; accessed Dec. 10, 2015: http://www.telegraph.co.uk/news/worldnews/africaandindianocean/nigeria/11387473/Twitter-suspends-suspected-Boko-Haram-account-that-tweeted-pictures-of-child-soldiers.html

518.   Zenn, Zacob. "Boko Haram's Dangerous Expansion into Northwest Nigeria," Combating Terrorism Center. Published Oct. 29, 2012; accessed Dec. 10, 2015: https://www.ctc.usma.edu/posts/boko-harams-dangerous-expansion-into-northwest-nigeria

519.   Smith, David. "More than 700 inmates escape during attack on Nigerian Prison," *Guardian*. Published Sept. 8, 2010; accessed Dec. 11, 2015: http://www.theguardian.com/world/2010/sep/08/muslim-extremists-escape-nigeria-prison

520.   "Bomb Blast kills 32 people in Nigeria, Boko Haram Blamed," *Nation*. Published Nov. 19, 2015; accessed Dec. 10, 2015: http://www.nation.co.ke/news/africa/Boko-Haram-explosion-kills-32/-/1066/2961836/-/h2vg76/-/index.html

521.   "Nigeria's Boko Haram Islamists Bombed Abuja Police HQ," BBC. Published June 17, 2011; accessed Dec. 11, 2015: http://www.bbc.com/news/world-africa-13805688

522.   "25 Killed in Beer Garden attack in Nigeria," *News*. Published June 27, 2011; accessed Dec. 11, 2015: http://www.news.com.au/breaking-news/killed-in-beer-garden-attack-in-nigeria/story-e6frfku0-1226082568954

523.   "Abuja Attack, Car Bomb hits UN Building," BBC. Published Aug. 27, 2011; accessed Dec. 11, 2015: http://www.bbc.com/news/world-africa-14677957

524.   Mark, Monica. "After Nigeria's Church Bombing: The Advent of Christian – Muslim Conflict," *Time*. Published Dec. 27, 2011; accessed Dec. 11, 2015: http://content.time.com/time/world/article/0,8599,2103163,00.html

525.   "Nigeria's Boko Haram suspected in Kano Police Attack," BBC. Published Jan. 30, 2012; accessed Dec. 11, 2015: http://www.bbc.com/news/world-africa-16786025

526.   Olukoya Sam. "Islamist Group Claims Responsibility for Cell Phone Tower Attack in Nigeria," Public Radio International. Originally aired Sept. 7, 2012; accessed Dec. 11, 2015: http://www.pri.org/stories/2012-09-07/islamist-group-claims-responsibility-cell-phone-tower-attacks-nigeria

527.   Abrak, Isaac and Mohammed Garba. "Suicide Bombs kill 11 at Military Church in Nigeria," Reuters. Published Nov. 25, 2012; accessed Dec. 11, 2015: http://www.reuters.com/article/us-nigeria-bomb-idUSBRE8AO05320121125 Ibid.

528.   Nossiter, Adam. "French Family Kidnapped in Cameroon," *New York Times*. Published Feb. 19, 2013; accessed Dec. 11, 2015: http://www.nytimes.com/2013/02/20/world/africa/seven-members-of-french-family-kidnapped-in-cameroon.html

529.   "Nigeria Unrest: Boko Haram Gunmen kill 44 at Mosque," BBC. Published Aug. 13, 2013; accessed Dec. 11, 2015: http://www.bbc.com/news/world-africa-23676872

530.   Parker, Gillian. "Yobe School Killing: Another Boko Haram slaughter, this time of children," *Christian Science Monitor*. Published July 8, 2013; accessed Dec. 11, 2015: http://www.csmonitor.com/World/Africa/2013/0708/Yobe-school-killings-Another-Boko-Haram-slaughter-this-time-of-children-video

531.   "Students massacred in Nigeria attack," *AlJazeera*. Published Sept. 30, 2013; accessed Dec. 11, 2015: http://www.aljazeera.com/news/africa/2013/09/gunmen-storm-nigerian-college-201392910646471222.html

532.   Nossiter, Adam. "Bako Haram Abducted Nigerian Girls One Year ago," *New York Times*. Published April 14, 2015; accessed Dec. 10, 2015: http://www.nytimes.com/2015/04/15/world/africa/nigeria-boko-haram-chibok-kidnapped-girls.html?_r=0

533.   "Hundreds killed in Boko Haram raid on unguarded Nigerian Town," *Guardian*. Published May 8, 2014; accessed Dec. 11, 2015: http://www.theguardian.com/world/2014/may/08/boko-haram-massacre-nigeria-gamboru-ngala

534. "Boko Haram release first beheading video since pledging allegiance to ISIS," *Al-Arabiya*. Published July 11, 2015; accessed Dec. 11, 2015: http://english.alarabiya.net/en/News/africa/2015/07/11/Boko-Haram-release-first-beheading-video-since-pledging-allegiance-to-ISIS.html

535. Hussain, Bukar and Abubakar Aminu. "Nearly 150 killed in suspected Boko Haram attacks in NE Nigeria," *Yahoo News*. Published July 2, 2015; accessed Dec. 11, 2015: http://news.yahoo.com/least-97-dead-boko-haram-attack-nigeria-witnesses-161053965.html

536. "Boko Haram Islamists Massacre Christian Villagers in Borno State, Nigeria," *Morning Star News*. Published Feb. 17, 2014; accessed Dec. 11, 2015: http://morningstarnews.org/2014/02/boko-haram-islamists-massacre-christian-villagers-in-borno-state-nigeria/

537. Botelho, Greg. "Boko Haram gunmen on horseback kill 79 in trio of attacks, locals say," CNN. Published Aug. 31, 2015; accessed Dec. 10, 2015: http://www.cnn.com/2015/08/31/africa/nigeria-violence/

538. Ibid.

539. Haruna, Umar and Adamu Adamu. "Teenage suicide bomber kills 5, injures 41 in attack in Nigeria," *Globe and Mail*. Published Aug. 25, 2015; accessed Dec. 10, 2015: http://www.theglobeandmail.com/news/world/girl-suicide-bomber-kills-5-injures-41-in-boko-haram-attack-in-nigeria/article26088132/

540. AP. "Chad Suspects Boko Haram in Island Attacks," *New York Times*. Published Dec. 5, 2015; accessed Dec. 10, 2015: http://www.nytimes.com/2015/12/06/world/africa/triple-suicide-bombings-at-lake-chad-kill-27.html

541. Chimton, Ngala. "Cameroon: At Least 6 killed in suspected Boko Haram Suicide bombings," CNN. Published Nov. 21, 2015; accessed Dec. 10, 2015: http://www.cnn.com/2015/11/21/africa/cameroon-violence/

542. Ejiofor, Clement. "Boko Haram's Source of Weapons Revealed," *Naij*. Published 2014; accessed Dec. 9, 2015: https://www.naij.com/66368.html

543. Ibid.

544. "Where Boko Haram Gets Its Weapons," *This Day Live*. Published May 15, 2014; accessed Dec. 9, 2015: http://www.thisdaylive.com/articles/where-boko-haram-gets-its-weapons/178579/

545. "Nigerian Troops Capture Monstrous Armored Tank From Boko Haram Insurgents," *Sahara Reporters*. Published Sept. 27, 2014; accessed Dec. 9, 2015: http://saharareporters.com/2014/09/27/nigerian-troops-capture-monstrous-armored-tank-boko-haram-insurgents

546. McCoy, Terrence. "Paying for terrorism: Where does Boko Haram gets its money from?" *Independent*. Published June 6, 2015; accessed Dec. 9, 2015: http://www.independent.co.uk/news/world/africa/paying-for-terrorism-where-does-boko-haram-gets-its-money-from-9503948.html

547. "Shekau: We Shot Down Nigerian Military Jet," *Nigerian News*. Published Oct. 2, 2014; accessed Dec. 9, 2015: http://thenewsnigeria.com.ng/2014/10/shekau-we-shot-down-nigerian-military-jet/

548. "The Evolving Boko Haram War Machine," Council on Foreign Relations blog.

549. Gambrell, Jon. "Oil bunkering threatens Nigeria's economy, environment," *Washington Post*. Published July 20, 2015; accessed Dec. 9, 2015: https://www.washingtonpost.com/national/oil-bunkering-threatens-nigerias-economy-environment/2013/07/18/e38cb4a0-e273-11e2-aef3-339619eab080_story.html

550. Adow, Mohammad. "The Looting and 'Cooking' of Nigeria Crude," *AlJazeera*. Published Aug. 3, 2012; accessed Dec. 9, 2015: http://www.aljazeera.com/indepth/features/2012/08/20128312530927823.html

551. McCoy. "Paying for terrorism: Where does Boko Haram gets its money from?" *Independent*.

552. Ikeke, Nkem. "US Officials Reveal How Boko Haram Gets Its Weapons & Finances Its Activities," *Naij*. Published June 6, 2015; accessed Dec. 9, 2015: https://www.naij.com/69044.html 2014.

553. Ibid.

554. Hafez, Mohammed M. *Suicide Bombers in Iraq: The Strategy and Ideology of Martyrdom*, United States Institute of Peace Press, Washington, DC, 2007.

555. Study Group Writer. Independent Strategy and Intelligence Study Group. http://isisstudygroup.com/ 15th December 2014. Web. 17th December 2015

556. Goldstein, Sasha. "Second Frenchmen identified as ISIS thug wielding knife in Peter Kassig beheading video," *New York Daily News*. Published Nov. 19, 2014; accessed Dec. 17, 2015: http://www.nydailynews.com/news/world/frenchman-id-isis-thug-peter-kassig-video-article-1.2015961

557. Study Group Writer. Independent Strategy and Intelligence Study Group. http://isisstudygroup.com/ 15th December 2014. Web. 17th December 2015

558. Allen, Peter. "Al Qaeda fanatic is dead: French serial killer jumps out his flat window with all guns blazing in dramatic end to 32-hour siege," *Daily Mail*. Published March 21, 2012; accessed Dec. 17, 2015: http://www.dailymail.co.uk/news/article-2118052/Toulouse-shooting-Mohammad-Merah-dead-jumping-flat-window-guns-blazing.html

559. "Paris attacks: What happened on the night" BBC. Published Nov. 13, 2015; accessed Jan. 13, 2016: http://www.bbc.com/news/world-europe-34818994

560. "Attentats de Paris : des proches d'un terroriste arrêtés," *Le Figaro*. Published Nov. 13, 2015; accessed Jan. 13, 2016: http://www.lefigaro.fr/actualites/2015/11/13/01001-20151113LIVWWW00406-fusillade-paris-explosions-stade-de-france.php

561. Blake, Andrew. "Bilal Hadfi, Paris terrorist, left social media clues before attacks," *Washington Times*. Published Nov. 20, 2015; accessed Jan. 13, 2016: http://www.washingtontimes.com/news/2015/nov/20/bilal-hadfi-paris-terrorist-left-social-media-clue/

562. "Paris attacks: BBC names Stade de France bomber as M al-Mahmod," BBC. Published Nov. 22, 2015; accessed Jan. 13, 2016: http://www.bbc.co.uk/news/world-europe-34896521

563. "Doubts about Syrian passport dropped by Paris attacker," *Deutsche Welle*. Published Nov. 17, 2015; accessed Jan. 13, 2016: http://www.dw.com/en/doubts-about-syrian-passport-dropped-by-paris-attacker/a-18856760

564. Reuters. "Paris nurse unwittingly tried to save suicide bomber Brahim Abdeslam, who detonated outside Comptoir Voltaire cafe," *New York Daily News*. Published Nov. 20, 2015; accessed Jan. 13, 2016: http://www.nydailynews.com/news/world/paris-nurse-unwittingly-save-bomber-brahim-abdeslam-article-1.2442302

565. Lichfield, John. "On the run from ISIS" Jihadists 'targeting Salah Abdeslam for chickening out of killings,'" *Independent*. Published Nov. 19, 2015; accessed Jan. 13, 2016: http://www.independent.co.uk/news/world/europe/paris-attack-eighth-attacker-salah-abdeslam-could-also-be-on-the-run-from-isis-amid-fears-the-group-a6740781.html

566. Faiola, Anthony and Souad Mekhennet. "Paris attacks were carried out by three groups tied to the Islamic State, official says," *Washington Post*. Published Nov. 15, 2015; accessed Jan. 13, 2016: https://www.washingtonpost.com/world/string-of-paris-terrorist-attacks-leaves-over-120-dead /2015/11/14/066df55c-8a73-11e5-bd91-d385b244482f_story.html

567. Safi, Michael. "Paris attacks: severed finger found at Bataclan theatre identifies attacker," *Guardian*. Published Nov. 15, 2015; accessed Jan. 13, 2016: http://www.theguardian.com/world/2015/ nov/15/paris-attacks-severed-finger-found-at-bataclan-theatre-identifies-attacker

568. Reuters. "ISIS claims Paris attacks and releases video threat," *Al-Arabiya*. Published Nov. 14, 2015; accessed Jan. 13, 2016: http://english.alarabiya.net/en/News/middle-east/2015/11/14/ISIS-releases-undated-video-threatening-France.html

569. Van Ostaeyen, Pieter, "Belgian Fighters in Syria and Iraq-Oct 2015," Pieter Van Ostaeyen blog. Published Oct. 11, 2015; accessed Dec. 13, 2015: https://pietervanostaeyen.wordpress.com/2015/10/11/ belgian-fighters-in-syria-and-iraq-october-2015/, 10/11/2015, accessed 12/13/2015

570. Clerix, Kristof. "Why are terrorists drawn to Belgium?" *Guardian*. Published Nov. 17, 2015; accessed Dec. 17, 2015: http://www.theguardian.com/commentisfree/2015/nov/17/terrorists-belgium-paris-attacks

571. Davidson, Colette. "Where are the guns in France coming from?" *AlJazeera*. Published Nov. 16, 2015; accessed Dec. 17, 2015: http://america.aljazeera.com/articles/2015/11/16/where-are-the-guns-in-france-coming-from.html

572. Ibid.

573. Ibid.

574. Axe, David. "This is How AK-47s Get to Paris," *Daily Beast*. Published Nov. 13, 2015; accessed Dec. 17, 2015: http://www.thedailybeast.com/articles/2015/11/13/this-is-how-ak-47s-get-to-paris.html

575. Davidson. "Where are the guns in France coming from" *AlJazeera*.

576. Oliver, Christian and Duncan Robinson. "Paris Attack: Belgium's arms bazaar," *Financial Times*. Published Nov. 19, 2015; accessed Dec. 17, 2015: http://www.ft.com/cms/s/0/33a2d592-8dde-11e5-a549-b89a1dfede9b.html#axzz3ueTBrYeY

577. Thomas, Joscelyn. "New Leader of Islamic Caucasus Emirate Killed by Russian Forces," *Long War Journal*. Aug. 11, 2015; accessed Dec. 10, 2015: http://www.longwarjournal.org/archives/2015/08/ new-leader-of-islamic-caucasus-emirate-killed-by-russian-forces.php

578. AFP. "Russia's Caucasus Islamists 'Pledge Allegiance' to ISIS," *Al-Arabiya*. Published June 24, 2015: accessed Dec. 10, 2015: http://english.alarabiya.net/en/News/middle-east/2015/06/24/Russia-s-Caucasus-Islamists-pledge-allegiance-to-ISIS-.html

579. "As Many as 5,000 Russians Join ISIS," *Pravda*. Published June 18, 2015; accessed Dec. 10, 2015: http://www.pravdareport.com/video/18-06-2015/131023-russians_isis-0/

580. Mukhopadhyay, Sounak. "Russian Militants 'Pledge Allegiance' to ISIS Forces," *International Business Times,* June 24, 2015, accessed December 10, 2015, http://www.ibtimes.com/russian-militants-pledge-allegiance-isis-forces-1981975

581. AFP. "Russia's Caucasus Islamists 'Pledge Allegiance' to ISIS," *Al-Arabiya*.

582. "ISIS Threatens to 'Liberate' Chechnya and Caucasus," *Russia Today*. Published Sept. 4, 2014; accessed Dec. 10, 2015: https://www.rt.com/news/184836-isis-putin-kadyrov-syria/

583. "ISIS Commander 'Omar the Chechen' Allegedly Killed," *Russia Today*. Published Nov. 13, 2014; accessed Dec. 10, 2015: https://www.rt.com/news/205239-russia-chechen-isis-killed/

584. "ISIS Issues Propaganda Magazine in Russian," *Russia Today*. Published May 27, 2015; accessed Dec. 10, 2015: https://www.rt.com/news/262545-isis-publishes-russian-magazine/

585. "As Many as 5,000 Russians Join ISIS," *Pravda*.

586. AFP. "Russia's Caucasus Islamists 'Pledge Allegiance' to ISIS," *Al-Arabiya*.

587. "8 ISIS Supporters Killed in N. Caucasus Special Op," *Russia Today*. Published Aug. 2, 2015; accessed Dec. 10, 2015: https://www.rt.com/news/311392-isis-killed-russia-caucasus/

588. Joscelyn, Thomas. "ISIS Has Claimed Responsibility for an Attack on Russian Military Barracks," *Business Insider*. Sep. 2, 2015; accessed Dec. 10, 2015: http://www.businessinsider.com/isis-attacked-russian-military-barracks-2015-9

589. "3 ISIS-Linked Militants Eliminated in Russia's Dagestan," *Russia Today*. Published Nov. 29, 2015; accessed Dec. 10, 2015: https://www.rt.com/news/323884-dagestan-isis-militants-elimination/

590. Ibid.

591. Gollom, Mark and Tracey Lindeman. "Who is Martin Couture-Rouleau?" CBC. Published Oct. 22, 2014; accessed Dec. 15, 2015: http://www.cbc.ca/news/canada/who-is-martin-couture-rouleau-1.2807285

592. Bostelaar, Robert. "Autopsies underway after Ottowa gun rampage," *Ottawa Citizen*. Published Oct. 23, 2014; accessed Dec. 15, 2015: http://ottawacitizen.com/news/local-news/autopsies-underway-after-ottawa-gun-rampage

593. Quan, Douglas. "Ottowa shooting by Michael Zehaf-Bibeau was 'last desperate act' of a mentally ill person, his mother writes,'" *National Post*. Published Oct. 25, 2014; accessed Dec. 15, 2015: http://news.nationalpost.com/2014/10/25/michael-zehaf-bibeau-mother-says-killing-was-last-desperate-act-of-a-mentally-ill-person/

594. Vidino, Lorenzo, and Seamus Hughes. "ISIS in America: From Retweets to Raqqa," Program on Extremism. The George Washington University. Published Dec. 2014; accessed Dec. 15, 2015: https://cchs.gwu.edu/sites/cchs.gwu.edu/files/downloads/ISIS%20in%20America%20-%20Full%20Report.pdf

595. Botelho, Greg. "Texas shooting: Outgunned traffic office stopped 2 attackers," CNN. Published May 5, 2015; accessed Dec. 14, 2015: http://www.cnn.com/2015/05/05/us/texas-police-shooting-hero/

596. Farrell, Paul. "Nadir Hamid Soofi: 5 fast facts you need to know," *Heavy*. Published May 4, 2015; accessed Dec. 15, 2015: http://heavy.com/news/2015/05/nadir-hamid-soofi-elton-simpson-phoenix-garland-muhammad-art-contest-shooting-suspect-terrorism-isis/

597. Holstege, Sean. "Phoenix man guilty of aiding terrorists," *AZ Central*. Published March 6, 2015; accessed Dec. 15, 2015: http://www.azcentral.com/news/articles/0306abujihaad0306.html

598. Weiss, Jeffrey and Kevin Krause. "2 Garland Shooters lives twined to tragic end," *Dallas News*. Published May 4, 2015; accessed Dec. 15, 2015: http://www.dallasnews.com/news/crime/headlines/20150504-2-garland-shooters-lives-twined-to-tragic-end.ece

599. "ISIS Jihadi linked to Garland attack had long history as Hacker" KTVQ. Published May 7, 2015; accessed Dec. 15, 2015: http://www.ktvq.com/story/28996661/isis-jihadi-linked-to-garland-attack-has-long-history-as-hacker

600. Botelho, Greg. "Man indicted for allegedly helping Mohammed cartoon contest attackers," CNN. Published June 16, 2015; accessed Dec. 15, 2015: http://www.cnn.com/2015/06/16/us/garland-texas-prophet-mohammed-contest-shooting/

601. Full Coverage, San Bernardino Terror Attack, Los Angeles Times, http://www.latimes.com/local/la-san-bernardino-shooting-sg-20151202-storygallery.html, December 2, 2015

602. Dabiq 13, Islamic State of Iraq and Syria, Page 3

603. Neubauer, Ian Lloyd. "A Teenage Terrorism Suspect Is Shot Dead in Australia After Attacking Police," *Time*. Published Sept. 24, 2015; accessed Dec. 15, 2015: http://time.com/3423975/isis-australia-melbourne-police-terrorism-suspect-abdul-numan-haider/

604. Silvester, John. "Melbourne terror shooting: Numan Haider 'planning to behead Victoria Police officers, drape bodies in IS flag," *The Age*. Published Sept. 24, 2015; accessed Dec. 15, 2015: http://www.theage.com.au/victoria/melbourne-terror-shooting-numan-haider-planned-to-behead-victoria-police-officers-drape-bodies-in-is-flag-20140924-10lb4i.html#ixzz3ECTsExXd

605. Sturmer, Jake. "Live Blog: Siege in Sydny's Martin Place," ABC News. Published Dec. 15, 2015; accessed Dec. 15, 2015: http://livenews.abc.net.au/Event/Live_blog_Siege_in_Sydneys_Martin_Place?Page=0

606. McAlister, Michell. "An Operator's Perspective on the Sydney Siege pt 4," *SOFREP*. Published Jan. 14, 2015; accessed Dec. 15, 2015: http://sofrep.com/39388/operators-perspective-sydney-siege-pt-4/

607. Dumas, Daisy. "Sydney siege: How the hostage drama played out," *Sydney Morning Herald*. Published Dec. 21, 2014; accessed Dec. 15, 2015: http://www.smh.com.au/nsw/sydney-siege-how-the-hostage-drama-played-out-20141220-12b1km.html, 12/21/2014, accessed 12/12/2014

608. Elliot, Tim. "Martin place gunman deranged, deluded and dangerous," *Sydney Morning Herald*. Published Dec. 16, 2014; accessed Dec. 15, 2015: http://www.smh.com.au/nsw/martin-place-gunman-deranged-deluded-and-dangerous-20141216-128j42.html, 12/16/2014, accessed 12/15/2015

609. Nazish, Kiran. "The Islamic State is Spreading into Pakistan," *New Republic*. Sept. 23, 2014, accessed Dec. 9, 2015, https://newrepublic.com/article/119535/isis-pakistan-islamic-state-distributing-flags-and-flyers

610. Jones, Seth. "Expanding the Caliphate," *Foreign Affairs*. June 11, 2015; accessed Dec. 9, 2015: https://www.foreignaffairs.com/articles/afghanistan/2015-06-11/expanding-caliphate

611. Craig, Tim and Haq Nawaz Khan. "Pakistani Taliban Leaders Pledge Allegiance to Islamic State," *Washington Post*, Oct. 14, 2014; accessed Dec. 9, 2015: https://www.washingtonpost.com/world/pakistan-taliban-leaders-pledge-allegiance-to-islamic-state/2014/10/14/34837e7e-53df-11e4-809b-8cc0a295c773_story.html

612. Agence France-Presse. "Islamic State Gaining Ground in Afghanistan: UN," *Yahoo News*. Sept. 25, 2015; accessed Dec. 9, 2015: https://news.yahoo.com/islamic-state-gaining-ground-afghanistan-un-235952988.html

613. Nazish. "The Islamic State is Spreading into Pakistan," *New Republic*.

614. Khan, M. Ilyas. "Can Islamic State Move into South Asia?" BBC. Jan. 31, 2015; accessed Dec. 9, 2015: http://www.bbc.com/news/world-asia-31022576

615. Nazish, Kiran. "The Islamic State is Spreading into Pakistan," *New Republic*. Sept. 23, 2014; accessed Dec. 9, 2015: https://newrepublic.com/article/119535/isis-pakistan-islamic-state-distributing-flags-and-flyers

616.   Rassler. "Situating the Emergence of the Islamic State of Khorasan," *CTC Sentinel.*

617.   Craig and Nawaz Khan. "Pakistani Taliban Leaders Pledge Allegiance to Islamic State," *Washington Post.*

618.   Nazish. "The Islamic State is Spreading into Pakistan," *New Republic.*

619.   Nazish. "The Islamic State is Spreading into Pakistan," *New Republic.*

620.   Sajid, Islamuddin. "Hafiz Saeed Khan: The Former Taliban Warlord Taking ISIS to India and Pakistan," *International Business Times.* Jan. 19, 2015; accessed Dec. 9, 2015: http://www.ibtimes.co.uk/hafiz-saeed-khan-former-taliban-warlord-taking-isis-india-pakistan-1484135

621.   Nazish. "The Islamic State is Spreading into Pakistan," *New Republic.*

622.   Rassler. "Situating the Emergence of the Islamic State of Khorasan," *CTC Sentinel.*

623.   Khan, M. Ilyas Khan. "Pakistan Gunmen Kill 45 on Karachi Ismaili Shia Bus," BBC. Published May 13, 2015; accessed Dec. 9, 2015: http://www.bbc.com/news/world-asia-32717321

624.   Faiez, Rahim and Lynne O'Donnell. "IS Loyalists Kill 3 Police in First Attack on Afghan Forces," Associated Press. Published Sept. 27, 2015; accessed Dec. 9, 2015: http://news.yahoo.com/afghan-official-islamic-state-fighters-kill-3-police-131134272.html

625.   "Afghan Army Kills 32 ISIS Militants in Eastern Province Nangarhar," *AlAlam.* Published Nov. 6, 2015; accessed Jan. 13, 2016: http://en.alalam.ir/news/1756770

626.   Ibid.

627.   "Forty ISIS Terrorists Killed," *AhulBayt.* Published Dec. 6, 2015; accessed Jan. 13, 2016: http://en.abna24.com/service/centeral-asia-subcontinent/archive/2015/12/06/723317/story.html

628.   Dickinson, Elizabeth. "The Islamic State Brings the War to Saudi Arabia," *Foreign Policy.* Published May 22, 2015; accessed Dec. 3, 2015: https://foreignpolicy.com/2015/05/22/isis-brings-the-war-to-saudi-arabia-qatif-mosque-bombing/

629.   "TSG IntelBrief: The Islamic State's Looming Fight with Saudi Arabia," The Soufan Group. Published Jan. 6, 2015; accessed Dec. 3, 2015: http://soufangroup.com/tsg-intelbrief-the-islamic-states-looming-fight-with-saudi-arabia/

630.   "Terrorist rehab: Rare look inside Saudi de-radicalization program," CBS. Published Nov. 18, 2014; accessed Dec. 3, 2015: http://www.cbsnews.com/videos/terrorist-rehab-rare-look-inside-saudi-de-radicalization-program/

631.   Obaid, Nawaf and Al-Sarhan, Saud. "The Saudis Can Crush ISIS," *New York Times.* Published Sept. 8, 2014; accessed Dec. 3, 2015: http://www.nytimes.com/2014/09/09/opinion/the-saudis-can-crush-isis.html

632.   "Islamic State leader urges attacks in Saudi Arabia: speech," Reuters. Published Nov. 13, 2014; accessed Dec. 3, 2015: http://www.reuters.com/article/2014/11/14/us-mideast-crisis-baghdadi-idUSKCN0IX1Y120141114#DbDUkeWcODVZIlJQ.97

633.   Ibid.

634.   Ibid.

635.   Dickinson. "The Islamic State Brings the War to Saudi Arabia," *Foreign Policy.*

636. "Saudi arrests 93 suspected of ISIS links," *Al-Arabiya*. Published April 28, 2015; accessed Dec. 3, 2015: http://english.alarabiya.net/en/News/middle-east/2015/04/28/Saudi-arrests-93-ISIS-linked-militants-.html

637. Ellis, Ralph. "Saudi Arabia arrests 431 with alleged ISIS ties," CNN. Updated July 18, 2015; accessed Dec. 3, 2015: http://www.cnn.com/2015/07/18/middleeast/saudi-arabia-arrests-431-with-isis-ties/

638. "Fighters in Saudi Arabia Pledge to the IS, Abu Bakr al-Baghdadi," SITE Intelligence Group Enterprise. Accessed Dec. 3, 2015: https://ent.siteintelgroup.com/Statements/fighters-in-saudi-arabia-pledge-to-the-is-abu-bakr-al-baghdadi.html

639. Al-Tamimi, Aymenn Jawad. "Bay'ah to Baghdadi: Foreign Support for Sheikh Abu Bakr al-Baghdadi and the Islamic State of Iraq and ash-Sham," *Jihadology*. Posted Aug. 22, 2014; accessed Dec. 1, 2015: https://azelin.files.wordpress.com/2013/08/gestures-of-support-for-sheikh-abu-bakr-al.pdf

640. "TSG IntelBrief: The Islamic State's Looming Fight with Saudi Arabia," The Soufan Group.

641. Dickinson. "The Islamic State Brings the War to Saudi Arabia," *Foreign Policy*.

642. Ibid.

643. "TSG IntelBrief: The Islamic State's Looming Fight with Saudi Arabia," The Soufan Group.

644. Dickinson. "The Islamic State Brings the War to Saudi Arabia," *Foreign Policy*.

645. Black

646. "Saudi Arabia: 20 people killed after suicide bomber strikes Shia mosque," *Guardian*. Published May 22, 2015; accessed Dec. 1, 2015: http://www.theguardian.com/world/2015/may/22/saudi-arabia-suicide-bomber-shia-mosque

647. Black

648. Ibid.

649. Pandey. "Saudi Arabia Mosque Attack: New ISIS Affiliate 'Hijaz Province' Claims Responsibility," *International Business Times*.

650. Alkhereiji, Mohammed. "Third ISIS branch emerges in Saudi Arabia" *Arab Weekly*. Published Oct. 23, 2015; accessed Jan. 13, 2016: http://www.thearabweekly.com/?id=2514

651. "US embassy cables: Hillary Clinton says Saudi Arabia 'a critical source of terrorist funding," *Guardian*. Published Dec. 5, 2010; accessed Dec. 3, 2015: http://www.theguardian.com/world/us-embassy-cables-documents/242073

652. Levitt, Matthew. "Here's how ISIS still has access to the global financial system," *Business Insider*. Published March 24, 2015; accessed Dec. 3, 2015: http://www.businessinsider.com/heres-how-isis-keeps-up-its-access-to-the-global-financial-system-2015-3

653. Ibid.

654. Al-Tamimi. "Bay'ah to Baghdadi: Foreign Support for Sheikh Abu Bakr al-Baghdadi and the Islamic State of Iraq and ash-Sham," *Jihadology*.

655. Todd, Brian. "ISIS gaining ground in Yemen, competing with al Qaeda," CNN. Updated January 22, 2015; accessed Dec. 3, 2015: http://www.cnn.com/2015/01/21/politics/isis-gaining-ground-in-yemen/index.html

656. Worth. "At Risk of Fragmenting, Yemen Poses Dangers to US," *New York Times*.

657. Ibid.

658. "Who Are the Houthis of Yemen?" *New York Times*. Published Jan. 20, 2015; accessed Dec. 3, 2015: http://www.nytimes.com/2015/01/21/world/middleeast/who-are-the-houthis-of-yemen.html

659. Kasinof, Laura. "Yemen's Election Ensures Leader's Exit," *New York Times*. Published Feb. 21, 2012; accessed Dec. 3, 2015: http://www.nytimes.com/2012/02/22/world/middleeast/yemen-votes-to-remove-ali-abdullah-saleh.html

660. Worth, Robert. "At Risk of Fragmenting, Yemen Poses Dangers to US," New York Times. Published January 21, 2015, accessed December 1, 2015: http://www.nytimes.com/2015/01/22/world/middleeast/yemen-at-risk-of-fragmenting.html

661. Worth. "At Risk of Fragmenting, Yemen Poses Dangers to US," *New York Times*.

662. Sharp, Jeremy M. "Yemen: Civil War and Regional Intervention," Congressional Research Service. Published Oct. 2, 2015; accessed Dec. 1, 2015: https://www.fas.org/sgp/crs/mideast/R43960.pdf

663. Worth. "At Risk of Fragmenting, Yemen Poses Dangers to US," *New York Times*.

664. Al-Batati et al and Fahim. "ISIS Takes Responsibility for Bombings in Yemen," *New York Times*.

665. Abdullah, Khaled. "Blood 'running like a river' in deadly mosque attack," Reuters via CBS. Updated March 20, 2015; accessed Dec. 1, 2015: http://www.cbsnews.com/news/yemen-suicide-blasts-target-shiite-houthis-in-sanaa/

666. "Al-Qaeda in the Arabian Peninsula," Council on Foreign Relations. Updated Jan. 19, 2015; accessed Dec. 1, 2015: http://www.cfr.org/yemen/al-qaeda-arabian-peninsula-aqap/p9369

667. Al-Batati and Fahim. "ISIS Takes Responsibility for Bombings in Yemen," *New York Times*.

668. Williams, Jennifer. "The Saudi Arabia problem: Why a country at war with jihadists also fuels them," *Vox*. Updated Dec. 1, 2015; accessed Dec. 2, 2015: http://www.vox.com/2015/12/1/9821466/saudi-problem-isis

669. Abdullah. "Blood 'running like a river' in deadly mosque attack," CBS.

670. Kavanaugh. "A Brief History of ISIS's Growing Presence in Yemen," *Vocativ*.

671. Ibid.

672. Al-Falahi. "Islamic State extends its tentacles into Yemen," *Al-Monitor*.

673. Ibid.

674. Ibid.

675. "Al Qaeda supporters in Yemen pledge allegiance to Islamic State: group," Reuters. Published Feb. 11, 2015; accessed Dec. 1, 2015: http://www.reuters.com/article/2015/02/11/us-yemen-security-qaeda-idUSKBN0LF0E720150211#we8JfUmtRJ5TEup7.97

676. "Al Qaeda supporters in Yemen pledge allegiance to Islamic State: group," Reuters.

677. "U.S. skeptical of shifts in loyalty to ISIS from Qaeda," Reuters via *Al Arabiya*. Published Feb. 12, 2015; accessed Dec. 1, 2015: http://english.alarabiya.net/en/News/middle-east/2015/02/12/U-S-skeptical-of-shifts-in-loyalty-to-ISIS-from-Qaeda.html

678. al-Falahi, Ashraf. "Islamic State extends its tentacles into Yemen," *Al-Monitor*. Published Nov. 30, 2015; accessed Dec. 1, 2015: http://www.al-monitor.com/pulse/originals/2015/11/islamic-state-expands-yemen-qaeda-aqap.html

679. "Caliph Soldiers in Yemen Pledge Allegiance to Al-Baghdadi + Video," *AlAlam*. Published April 25, 2015; accessed Dec. 2, 2015: http://en.alalam.ir/news/1697925

680.   Kavanaugh. "A Brief History of ISIS's Growing Presence in Yemen," *Vocativ.*

681.   Perkins, Brian. "Wilayat al-Yemen: The Islamic State's New Front," The Jamestown Foundation. Published Aug. 7, 2015; accessed Dec. 2, 2015: http://www.jamestown.org/single/?tx_ttnews%5Btt_news%5D=44263&tx_ttnews%5BbackPid%5D=7&cHash=901fe285861b27a174a00d29ee3b71ac#.Vl4hQWRY6kp

682.   Johnsen. "This Man Is the Leader In ISIS's Recruiting War Against Al-Qaeda In Yemen," *Buzzfeed.*

683.   Abdullah, Khaled. "US Pulling troups from Yemen after mosque attacks," CBS News. Published March 21, 2015; accessed Jan. 13, 2016: http://www.cbsnews.com/news/us-pulls-troops-yemen-suicide-bomb-attacks-mosques/

684.   Al-Falahi. "Islamic State extends its tentacles into Yemen," *Al-Monitor.*

685.   AFP Dubai. "Green Brigade of ISIS claims Yemen attack," *Al-Arabiya.* Published April 23, 2015; accessed Jan. 13, 2016: http://english.alarabiya.net/en/News/middle-east/2015/04/23/New-Green-Brigade-of-ISIS-claims-Yemen-attack.html

686.   Al-Falahi. "Islamic State extends its tentacles into Yemen," *Al-Monitor.*

687.   http://arabi21.com/story/843513/

688.   Al-Falahi. "Islamic State extends its tentacles into Yemen," *Al-Monitor.*

689.   Mukhashaf, Mohammed. "ISIS claims responsibility for explosion outside government building in Yemen," *Business Insider.* Published Aug. 20, 2015; accessed Jan. 13, 2016: http://www.businessinsider.com/isis-claims-responsibility-for-explosion-outside-government-building-in-yemen-2015-8

690.   Kavanaugh. "A Brief History of ISIS's Growing Presence in Yemen," *Vocativ.*

691.   AP. "20 Yemenis killed in bombings at Mosque," *New York Times.* Published Sept. 2, 2015; accessed Jan. 13, 2016: http://www.nytimes.com/2015/09/03/world/middleeast/yemen-red-cross-workers-shot-dead.html

692.   "Yemen suicide bombing in Sanaa mosque kills 25," BBC. Published Sept. 24, 2015; accessed Jan. 13, 2016: http://www.bbc.com/news/world-middle-east-34344648

693.   Al-Batati and Fahim. "ISIS Takes Responsibility for Bombings in Yemen," *New York Times.*

694.   Shaheen, Kareem and Stephen, Chris. "From Syria to Bosnia: Isis and its affiliates around the world, The Guardian. Published July 3, 2015, accessed December 3, 2015: http://www.theguardian.com/world/2015/jul/03/isis-and-affiliates-around-the-world

695.   Al-Batati and Fahim. "ISIS Takes Responsibility for Bombings in Yemen," *New York Times.*

696.   Ackerman, Spencer. "Pentagon loses track of weaponry sent to Yemen in recent years," *Guardian.* Published Feb. 3, 2015; accessed Dec. 1, 2015: http://www.theguardian.com/world/2015/feb/03/pentagon-loses-track-weapons-yemen

697.   Ibid.

698.   Whitlock, Greg. "Pentagon loses track of $500 million in weapons, equipment given to Yemen," *Washington Post.* Published March 17, 2015; accessed Dec. 1, 2015: https://www.washingtonpost.com/world/national-security/pentagon-loses-sight-of-500-million-in-counterterrorism-aid-given-to-yemen/2015/03/17/f4ca25ce-cbf9-11e4-8a46-b1dc9be5a8ff_story.html

699.   ONI, Open Source Center, TRO2015122158586912, The_Great_Defection_From_Al_Baghdadi_Group, Twitter, 16 December, 2015

700. "Profile: Gulf Co-operation Council," BBC. Updated Feb. 15, 2012; accessed Dec. 1, 2015: http://news.bbc.co.uk/2/hi/middle_east/country_profiles/4155001.stm

701. "Profile: Gulf Co-operation Council," BBC.

702. Atassi, Basma. "Bahrain tightens security amid ISIL threats," *AlJazeera*. Published July 3, 2015; accessed Dec. 2, 2015: http://www.aljazeera.com/news/2015/07/bahrain-tightens-security-isil-threats-150703062006728.html

703. Ibid.

704. "Bahrain charges 24 of forming ISIS cell," *Al-Arabiya*. Published Oct. 22, 2015; accessed Dec. 1, 2015: http://english.alarabiya.net/en/News/middle-east/2015/10/22/Bahrain-accuses-24-of-forming-ISIS-cell.html

705. Montero, David. "Are Terror Groups Finding a Haven in Bangladesh?" *Christian Science Monitor*. June 17, 2009; accessed Dec. 10, 2015: http://www.csmonitor.com/World/terrorism-security/2009/0617/p99s01-duts.html

706. Bayer, Michael D. *The Blue Planet: Informal International Police Networks and National Intelligence*, Washington, DC: National Defense Intelligence College Press, 2010, 80–81.

707. AP. "ISIS Says It Assassinated Italian Aid Worker in Bangladesh," CBS News. Sept. 29, 2015; accessed Dec. 10, 2015: http://www.cbsnews.com/news/isis-says-it-assassinated-italian-aid-worker-in-bangladesh/

708. Ali Manik, Julfikar. "Bangladeshi Officials Say 4 Arrested in Killing of Italian Aid Worker Were Not with ISIS," *New York Times*, October 26, 2015, accessed December 10, 2015, http://www.nytimes.com/2015/10/27/world/asia/bangladeshi-officials-say-4-arrested-in-killing-of-italian-aid-worker-were-not-with-isis.html

709. "ISIS in Bangladesh?" *Dhaka Tribune*. Aug. 7, 2014; accessed Dec. 10, 2015: http://www.dhakatribune.com/bangladesh/2014/aug/07/isis-bangladesh

710. "4 Indians Coming to Bangladesh to Join ISIS Held," *Dhaka Tribune*. Sep. 7, 2014; accessed Dec. 10, 2015: http://www.dhakatribune.com/crime/2014/sep/07/4-indians-coming-bangladesh-join-isis-held

711. Ali Manik, Julfikar and Nida Najar. "Bangladesh Police Arrest 12 Men Suspected of Qaeda Ties," *New York Times*. July 2, 2015; accessed Dec. 10, 2015: http://www.nytimes.com/2015/07/03/world/asia/bangladesh-arrests-al-qaeda-jihad-indian-subcontinent.html?_r=0

712. Barry, Ellen. "ISIS in Bangladesh: Contradictory Messages Deepen Anxiety," *Daily Star*. Nov. 2, 2015; accessed Dec. 10, 2015: http://www.thedailystar.net/op-ed/politics/isis-bangladesh-contradictory-messages-deepen-anxiety-165682

713. Agence Presse-France. "One Killed and Scores Wounded in Attack at Shi Site in Bangladesh Capital," *Guardian*. Published Oct. 24, 2015; accessed Dec. 10, 2015: http://www.theguardian.com/world/2015/oct/24/bomb-attack-on-bangladesh-shia-community

714. Reuters. "ISIS Claims Responsibility for Bangladesh Bombings," *Dhaka Tribune*. Oct 24, 2015, accessed Dec 10, 2015: http://www.dhakatribune.com/bangladesh/2015/oct/24/isis-claims-responsibility-bangladesh-bombings

715. Barry. "ISIS in Bangladesh: Contradictory Messages Deepen Anxiety," *Daily Star*.

716.   Najar, Nida and Julfikar Ali Manik. "ISIS Claims It Struck Police in Bangladesh," *New York Times*. Nov. 5, 2015; accessed Dec. 10, 2015: http://www.nytimes.com/2015/11/06/world/asia/isis-bangladesh-police-attack.html?_r=0

717.   Fahmy, Omar and Lin Noueihed. "Islamic State Claims Attack on Italian Missionary in Bangladesh," Reuters. Nov. 19, 2015; accessed Dec. 10, 2015: http://www.reuters.com/article/us-bangladesh-foreigner-killing-claim-idUSKCN0T81U220151119

718.   Agence France-Presse. "ISIS Claims Attack on Shiite Mosque in Bangladesh—SITE," *News Info*. Published Nov. 27, 2015; accessed Dec. 10, 2015: http://newsinfo.inquirer.net/743026/isis-claims-attack-on-shiite-mosque-in-bangladesh-site

719.   Wood, Graeme, What ISS Really Wants, The Atlantic, http://www.theatlantic.com/magazine/archive/2015/03/what-isis-really-wants/384980/, March, 2015

720.   Ali Hirsi, Ayyan. *Heretic: Why Islam Needs A Reformation Now*, Harper Collins, New York, NY, 2015.

721.   Obama, Barack. "Remarks by the President in Closing of the Summit on Countering Violent Extremism." Published Feb. 18, 2015; accessed Jan. 13, 2016: https://www.whitehouse.gov/the-press-office/2015/02/18/remarks-president-closing-summit-countering-violent-extremism

722.   Bergen, Peter. *Holy War Inc*, Free Press, New York, NY, 2001.

723.   Azhar, Maulana Muhammad Masood. *Definition and Ruling of Jihad*. Published Feb. 8, 2011; accessed Jan. 13, 2016: http://www.muftisays.com/blog/Seifeddine-M/1154_08-02-2011/definition-and-ruling-of-jihad.html, February 8, 2011

724.   Kenny, Mark. "Abbott declares war on the Islamic State 'death cult,'" *Sydney Morning Herald*. Published Sept. 15, 2014; accessed Jan. 13, 2016: http://www.smh.com.au/federal-politics/political-news/abbott-declares-war-on-the-islamic-state-death-cult-20140914-3fol3.html#ixzz3uZX-71Fjm

725.   Nance, Malcolm. *An End to al-Qaeda: Destroying Bin Laden's Jihad and Restoring America's Honor*, St. Martin's Press, New York, NY, 2010.

726.   Various, Dabiq 1, Return of the Khalifah, retrieved from database Terror Asymmetric Project for Strategy, Tactics and Radical ideologies

727.   Netton, Ian Richard (Ed.), *Arabia and the Gulf: From Traditional society to Modern States*, Croom Helm, London, 1986: pp 24.

728.   Kennedy, Hugh N. *Armies of the Caliphs*, Routledge, London and New York, 2001: pp 163.

729.   Carl F. Petry (Ed), The Cambridge History of Egypt: Islamic Egypt, 640-1517, Vol 1, Cambridge University Press, pp 106.

730.   Shaban, M.A. *Islamic History: A New Interpretation*. Cambridge University Press, London and New York, 1978.

731.   Churchill, Winston. *The River War,: An Account of the Reconquest of Sudan*, Prion, London, 1997.

732.   Lacey, Robert. *Inside the Kingdom: Kings, Clerics, Modernists, Terrorists, and the Struggle for Saudi Arabia*, Penguin, Oxford, 2010.

733.   Trofimov, Yaroslav. *The Siege of Mecca*, Doubleday, New York, NY, 2007.

734.   Lifton, Robert Jay. *Thought Reform and the Psychology of Totalism: A Study of "Brainwashing" in China*, Norton, New York City, 1961.

735. Lifton, Robert Jay. *Destroying the World to Save It: Aum Shinrikyo, Apocalyptic Violence, and the New Global Terrorism*, Owl Books, 2000.

736. Curtis, JM. "Factors related to susceptibility and recruitment by cults," *Psychological Reports*. Published Oct. 1993; accessed Jan. 13, 2016: http://www.ncbi.nlm.nih.gov/pubmed/8234595

737. Hassan, Steve. "Interview on BITE model of Mind Control and TerrorismCults," Freedom of Mind Resource Center. Published Aug. 2015; accessed Jan. 13, 2016: https://www.freedomofmind.com/Services/BITEModelTerrorism.php

738. Worral, Simon. "How Former Muslim Radical Helped U.S. Nab One of World's Top Terrorists," *National Geographic*. Published Sept. 12, 2011; accessed Jan. 13, 2016: http://news.nationalgeographic.com/news/2014/09/140911-al-qaeda-osama-bin-laden-yemen-anwar-al-awlaki-booktalk/

739. "The Islamic State (Part 4)," *Vice*. Aug. 13, 2014; accessed Dec. 14, 2015: https://news.vice.com/video/the-islamic-state-part-4

740. Mezzofiore, Gianluca. "Syria: Isis chief executioner found beheaded with cigarette in his mouth," *International Business Times*. Published Jan. 6, 2015; accessed Dec. 3, 2015: http://www.ibtimes.co.uk/syria-isis-chief-executioner-found-beheaded-cigarette-his-mouth-1482101

741. Winter, Charlie, trans. and analysis. *Women of the Islamic State: A Manifesto on Women by the Al-Khanssaa Brigade,* Quilliam Foundation. Published Feb. 2015; accessed Nov. 27, 2015: http://www.quilliamfoundation.org/wp/wp-content/uploads/publications/free/women-of-the-islamic-state3.pdf

742. Alami, Mona. "Women on the front lines," NOW. Feb. 15, 2014; accessed Nov. 27, 2015: https://now.mmedia.me/lb/en/reportsfeatures/535456-women-on-the-front-lines accessed

743. Moaveni, Azadeh. "ISIS Women and Enforcers in Syria Recount Collaboration, Anguish and Escape," *New York Times*. Nov. 22, 2015; accessed Dec. 14, 2015: http://www.nytimes.com/2015/11/22/world/middleeast/isis-wives-and-enforcers-in-syria-recount-collaboration-anguish-and-escape.html

744. Culzac, Natasha. "Isis: British women led by Aqsa Mahmood 'running sharia police unit for Islamic State in Syria,'" *Independent*. Sept. 8, 2014; accessed Nov. 27, 2015: http://www.independent.co.uk/news/world/middle-east/isis-british-women-running-sharia-police-unit-for-islamic-state-in-syria-9717510.html

745. Eleftheriou-Smith, Lula-Mae. "Escaped ISIS Wives Describe Life in the All-Female al-Khansa Brigade Who Punish Women with 40 Lashes for Wearing Wrong Clothes," *Independent*. April 20, 2015; accessed Dec. 14, 2015: http://www.independent.co.uk/news/world/middle-east/escaped-isis-wives-describe-life-in-the-all-female-al-khansa-brigade-who-punish-women-with-40-lashes-10190317.html

746. Usher, Sebastian. "'Jihad' magazine for women on web," BBC. Aug. 24, 2004; accessed Dec. 14, 2015: http://news.bbc.co.uk/2/hi/middle_east/3594982.stm

747. Agence France-Presse. "Sex Jihad Raging in Syria, Claims Minister," *Telegraph*. Published Sept. 20, 2013; accessed Dec. 23, 2013: http://www.telegraph.co.uk/news/worldnews/middleeast/syria/10322578/Sex-Jihad-raging-in-Syria-claims-minister.html.

748. Banfield, Ashleigh. "ISIS Operates Sophisticated Propaganda Machine," CNN. Originally aired on Sept. 17, 2014; accessed Oct. 7, 2014: http://www.cnn.com/TRANSCRIPTS/1409/17/lvab.02.html

749. "British Women Headed to Syria for Jihad al-Nikah: Report," *AlAlam*. Published Feb. 19, 2014; accessed Jan. 7, 2014: http://en.alalam.ir/news/1567279

750. Reitman, Janet. "The Children of ISIS," *Rolling Stone.* March 25, 2015; accessed Dec. 14, 2015: http://www.rollingstone.com/culture/features/teenage-jihad-inside-the-world-of-american-kids-seduced-by-isis-20150325#ixzz3sjSMPwpZ

751. Piokowski, Daniel. "We're thirsty for your blood," *Daily Mail,* March 17, 2015, accessed June 3, 2015, http://www.dailymail.co.uk/news/article-2999925/We-thirsty-blood-Playboy-jihadi-s-widow-poses-gun-toting-clique-female-fanatics-flash-BMW-boasts-five-star-jihad-lifestyle-Syria.html

752. Mahmood, Mona. "Double-layered veils and despair ... women describe life under Isis," *Guardian,* February 17, 2015, accessed March 3, 2015, http://www.theguardian.com/world/2015/feb/17/isis-orders-women-iraq-syria-veils-gloves

753. Winter. *"Women of the Islamic State."*

754. Ibid.

755. Ibid.

756. Ibid.

757. Winter. *"Women of the Islamic State."*

758. Qur'an, Surah 33:59. Accessed Aug. 9, 2013: http://www.usc.edu/org/cmje/religious-texts/quran/verses/033-qmt.php#033.059

759. Erlander, "In West, ISIS Finds Women Eager to Enlist," *New York Times.*

760. Dickey, Christopher. "The Boko Haram Bidding War," *Daily Beast.* Published May 5, 2014; accessed Nov. 27, 2015: http://www.thedailybeast.com/articles/2014/05/10/the-boko-haram-bidding-war.html

761. Jayoush, Kinda. "Prisoners in Their Own City: ISIS Bans Women Under 45 from Leaving Raqqa," *Syria Deeply.* Jan. 19, 2015; accessed Nov. 27, 2015: http://www.syriadeeply.org/articles/2015/01/6660/prisoners-city-isis-bans-women-45-leaving-raqqa/

762. Culzac. "Isis: British women led by Aqsa Mahmood 'running sharia police unit for Islamic State in Syria,'" *Independent.*

763. Canal. "What Life For ISIS' Female Recruits Is Like—And What Happens If They Try To Leave," *Bustle.*

764. Townsend, Mark, Tracy McVeigh, and Andrew Anthony, "Isis fighters must be allowed back into UK, says ex-MI6 chief," *Guardian.* Sept. 7, 2014; accessed Nov. 27, 2015: http://www.theguardian.com/world/2014/sep/06/richard-barrett-mi6-isis-counter-terrorism

765. Canal. "What Life For ISIS' Female Recruits Is Like—And What Happens If They Try To Leave," *Bustle.*

766. Ibid.

767. "Austrian ISIS poster girls 'want to return home,'" *Al-Arabiya.* Published Oct. 11, 2014; accessed Nov. 27, 2015: http://english.alarabiya.net/en/News/middle-east/2014/10/11/Austrian-ISIS-poster-girls-want-to-return-home.html

768. Charlton, Corey. "'We made a big mistake': Teenage Austrian poster girls for ISIS who moved to Syria to live with jihadis are now pregnant and want to come home ... but officials say that will be 'impossible,'" *Daily Mail.* Oct. 10, 2014; accessed Nov. 27, 2015: http://www.dailymail.co.uk/news/article-2788605/Teenage-Austrian-poster-girls-ISIS-moved-Syria-live-jihadis-pregnant-want-come-home-officials-say-impossible.html

769. Bacchi, Umberto. "Isis: Austrian Teenage Jihadi Bride Samra Kesinovic 'Wants to Return Home,'" *International Business Times*. Oct. 10, 2014; accessed Nov. 25, 2015: http://www.ibtimes.co.uk/isis-austrian-teenage-jihadi-bride-samra-kesinovic-wants-return-home-1469474

770. Piggott, Mark. "Isis: Teen Austrian 'poster girl' reportedly beaten to death for trying to leave Raqqa," *International Business Times*. Nov. 24, 2015; accessed Nov. 27, 2015: http://www.ibtimes.co.uk/isis-teen-austrian-poster-girl-reportedly-beaten-death-trying-leave-raqqa-1530343

771. Ibid.

772. Dickey, "The Boko Haram Bidding War," *Daily Beast*.

773. Ibid.

774. Rogers. "Revealed: Hate preacher terror 'mastermind' who recruited Austrian 'ISIS poster girls' sent 'another 160 to join jihad in Syria and Iraq,'" *Daily Mail*.

775. Sommers, Jack. "Isis 'Poster Girl' Samra Kesinovic Murdered For Trying To Flee Raqqa, Austrian Press Report," *Huffington Post*. Nov. 25, 2015; accessed Nov. 27, 2015: http://www.huffingtonpost.co.uk/2015/11/25/samra-kesinovic-isis-murdered-reports_n_8645622.html

776. Piggott. "Isis: Teen Austrian 'poster girl' reportedly beaten to death for trying to leave Raqqa," *International Business Times*.

777. "Wienerin von ISIS erschlagen?," *Das Bild*. Nov. 25, 2015; accessed Nov. 27, 2015: http://www.bild.de/news/ausland/isis/toetet-wienerin-weil-sie-fluechten-wollte-43539384.bild.html

778. "Wiener IS-Mädchen auf der Flucht erschlagen," *Österreich*. Nov. 25, 2015; accessed Nov. 27, 2015: http://www.oe24.at/oesterreich/chronik/wien/Wiener-IS-Maedchen-auf-der-Flucht-erschla-gen/213485094

779. Sommers. "Isis 'Poster Girl' Samra Kesinovic Murdered For Trying To Flee Raqqa, Austrian Press Report," *Huffington Post*.

780. Human Rights Council. "Report of the independent international commission of inquiry on the Syrian Arab Republic," UN General Assembly. Dated Aug. 13, 2014; accessed Dec. 14, 2015: http://www.ohchr.org/Documents/HRBodies/HRCouncil/CoISyria/A.HRC.27.60_Eng.pdf

781. Ibid.

782. Horgan, John and Mia Bloom. "This Is How the Islamic State Manufactures Child Militants," *Vice*. Published July 8, 2015; accessed Jan. 13, 2016: https://news.vice.com/article/this-is-how-the-islamic-state-manufactures-child-militants

783. Winter. *Women of the Islamic State*.

784. Raqqa is Being Slaughtered Silently

785. Hanoush, Feras. "ISIS Is Training an Army of Child Soldiers," *Newsweek*. Published Nov. 21, 2015; accessed Dec. 14, 2015: http://www.newsweek.com/isis-training-army-child-soldiers-396392

786. Ibid.

787. Horgan and Bloom. "This Is How the Islamic State Manufactures Militants," *Vice*.

788. Mullen. "ISIS' Use of Children: Propaganda and Military Training," CNN.

789. Boghani. "Why Afghanistan's Children Are Used as Spies and Suicide Bombers," *Frontline*.

790. Ibid.

791.   Office of the Special Representative of the Secretary-General for Children and Armed Conflict. "Syrian Arab Republic," Report to the Security Council. Issued June 5, 2015; accessed Dec. 14, 2015: https://childrenandarmedconflict.un.org/countries/syria/

792.   Raqqa is Being Slaughtered Silently

793.   "Islamic State Moulds Children into New Generation of Militants," BBC. Oct. 8, 2015; accessed Dec. 14, 2015: http://www.bbc.com/news/world-middle-east-34453476

794.   Bertrand, Natasha. "ISIS Training Ring for Children Discovered in Istanbul," *Business Insider*. Published Oct. 19, 2015; accessed Dec. 14, 2015: http://www.businessinsider.com/isis-training-camp-for-children-in-istanbul-2015-10

795.   Horgan, John and Mia Bloom. "This Is How the Islamic State Manufactures Militants," *Vice*. Published July 8, 2015; accessed Jan. 13, 2016: https://news.vice.com/article/this-is-how-the-islamic-state-manufactures-child-militants

796.   Hanoush. "ISIS Is Training an Army of Child Soldiers," *Newsweek*.

797.   "Islamic State Moulds Children into New Generation of Militants," BBC.

798.   Mullen. "ISIS' Use of Children: Propaganda and Military Training," CNN.

799.   Horgan and Bloom. "This Is How the Islamic State Manufactures Militants," *Vice*.

800.   Bloch, Hannah. "An ISIS School Teaches Jihad to Children at Age 3," NPR. Originally aired Nov. 19, 2015; accessed Dec. 14, 2015: http://www.npr.org/sections/parallels/2015/11/19/456508362/an-isis-school-that-teaches-jihad-to-children-at-age-3

801.   Human Rights Council, "Report of the independent international commission of inquiry on the Syrian Arab Republic," UN General Assembly.

802.   Horgan and Bloom. "This Is How the Islamic State Manufactures Militants," *Vice*.

803.   Bloch. "An ISIS School Teaches Jihad to Children at Age 3," NPR.

804.   Boghani. "Why Afghanistan's Children Are Used as Spies and Suicide Bombers," *Frontline*.

805.   Hanoush. "ISIS Is Training an Army of Child Soldiers," *Newsweek*.

806.   Boghani. "Why Afghanistan's Children Are Used as Spies and Suicide Bombers," *Frontline*.

807.   Hanoush. "ISIS Is Training an Army of Child Soldiers," *Newsweek*.

808.   "Islamic State Moulds Children into New Generation of Militants," BBC.

809.   Ibid. | AP. "Scores of ISIL Child Soldiers 'Killed' in Syria in 2015," *AlJazeera*. Published July 15, 2015; accessed Dec. 14, 2015: http://www.aljazeera.com/news/2015/07/scores-isil-child-soldiers-killed-syria-2015-150715132745980.html

810.   AFP. "Dozens of Child Soldiers Recruited by ISIL in Syria Killed Since the Start of 2015," *Telegraph*. Published July 15, 2015; accessed Dec. 14, 2015: http://www.telegraph.co.uk/news/worldnews/islamic-state/11741503/Dozens-of-child-soldiers-recruited-by-Isil-in-Syria-killed-since-the-start-of-2015.html

811.   Ibid.

812.   Office of the Special Representative of the Secretary-General for Children and Armed Conflict. "Syrian Arab Republic," Report to the Security Council.

813. "Obama authorises Iraq air strikes on Islamist fighters," BBC. Published Aug. 8, 2014; Jan. 13, 2016: https://web.archive.org/web/20140808001143/http://www.bbc.com/news/world-middle-east-28699832

814. Mamoun, Abdelhak. "ISIS Executes 12 Children in Mosul for Fleeing from the Training, Says Mamouzini," *Iraqi News*. Published Nov. 1, 2015; accessed Dec. 14, 2015: http://www.iraqinews.com/iraq-war/isis-executes-12-children-mosul-fleeing-training-says-mamouzini/

815. "ISIS Executed Scores of Children in a Year of Its Caliphate," Syrian Observatory for Human Rights. Published June 29, 2015; accessed Dec. 14, 2015: http://www.syriahr.com/en/2015/06/isis-executed-scores-of-children-in-a-year-of-its-caliphate/

816. "Islamic State Moulds Children into New Generation of Militants," BBC.

817. Dearden, Lizzie. "ISIS Video Shows Young Boy Beheading Syrian Soldier near Ancient City of Palmyra," *Independent*. Published July 17, 2015; accessed Dec. 14, 2015: http://www.independent.co.uk/news/world/middle-east/isis-video-shows-young-boy-beheading-syrian-soldier-near-ancient-city-of-palmyra-10397354.html

818. Boghani. "Why Afghanistan's Children Are Used as Spies and Suicide Bombers," *Frontline*.

819. "ISIS: Shocking Video Shows Islamic State Child Executioner Beheading Victim," Syrian Observatory for Human Rights. Published July 17, 2015; accessed Dec. 14, 2015: http://www.syriahr.com/en/2015/07/isis-shocking-video-shows-islamic-state-child-executioner-beheading-victim/ | "A Cub of the Caliphate Cubs' Carries out the First Beheading and IS Threatens to Conquer Rome," Syrian Observatory for Human Rights. Published July 2015; accessed Dec. 14, 2015: http://www.syriahr.com/en/2015/07/a-cub-of-the-caliphate-cubs-carries-out-the-first-beheading-and-is-threatens-to-conquer-rome/

820. Dearden. "ISIS Video Shows Young Boy Beheading Syrian Soldier near Ancient City of Palmyra," *Independent*.

821. "ISIS: Shocking Video Shows Islamic State Child Executioner Beheading Victim," Syrian Observatory for Human Rights. | "A Cub of the Caliphate Cubs' Carries out the First Beheading and IS Threatens to Conquer Rome," Syrian Observatory for Human Rights.

822. Bacchi, Umberto and Arij Limam. "ISIS Mimics Britain's NHS with 'Islamic State Health Service ISHS,'" *International Business Times*. April 24, 2015; accessed on Dec. 14, 2015: http://www.ibtimes.co.uk/isis-mimics-britains-nhs-islamic-state-health-service-ishs-1498183

823. Wood, Graeme. "What ISIS Really Wants," *Atlantic*. Published March 2015; accessed Dec. 14, 2015: http://www.theatlantic.com/magazine/archive/2015/03/what-isis-really-wants/384980/

824. Baskaran, Archit. "The Islamic State Healthcare Paradox: A Caliphate in Crisis," *Student Pulse*, Vol. 7, No. 7. Published 2015; accessed Dec. 14, 2015: http://www.studentpulse.com/articles/1054/the-islamic-state-healthcare-paradox-a-caliphate-in-crisis

825. Motlagh, Jason. "Fighting Polio Amid the Chaos of Syria's Civil War," *National Geographic*. Published March 5, 2015; accessed Dec. 14, 2015: http://news.nationalgeographic.com/2015/03/150305-polio-syria-iraq-islamic-state-refugees-vaccination-virus-jihad/

826. "ISIS dumping bodies behind spread of 'flesh-eating' disease in Syria," *Rudaw*. Published Feb. 12, 2015; accessed Dec. 14, 2015: http://rudaw.net/english/middleeast/syria/02122015

827. Bacchi and Limam. "ISIS Mimics Britain's NHS with 'Islamic State Health Service ISHS,'" *International Business Times*.

828. Al-Tamimi, Aymenn Jawad. "The Archivist: Critical Analysis of the Islamic State's Health Department," Rubin Center. Published Aug. 27, 2015; accessed Dec. 14, 2015: http://www.rubincenter.org/2015/08/the-archivist-critical-analysis-of-the-islamic-states-health-department/

829. Agron, A. "Wanted: Western Professionals to Join the Islamc State ISIS," Middle East Media Research Institute. Published May 15, 2015; accessed Dec. 14, 2015: http://www.memrijttm.org/content/view_print/report/8565

830. "ISIS Health Care Video an Ad or a Welfare State," *Vocativ*. Published April 24, 2015; accessed Dec. 14, 2015: http://www.vocativ.com/usa/nat-sec/isis-health-care-video-an-ad-for-a-welfare-state/

831. Townsend, Mark Marga Zambrana, and Muhammed Amahmoud. "What Happened to the British Medics Who Went to Work for ISIS?" *Guardian*. Published July 11, 2015; accessed Dec. 14, 2015: http://www.theguardian.com/world/2015/jul/12/british-medics-isis-turkey-islamic-state

832. Russell, Catherine M. "ISIL's Abuse of Women and Girls Must Be Stopped," US Department of State. Accessed Dec. 14, 2015: http://statedept.tumblr.com/post/97300225472/isils-abuse-of-women-and-girls-must-be-stopped

833. Oakford, Samuel. "Yazidi Women Captured by the Islamic State Suffer Terrible Fate," *Vice*. Published Oct. 12, 2014; accessed Dec. 14, 2015: https://news.vice.com/article/yazidi-women-captured-by-the-islamic-state-suffer-terrible-fate

834. Russell. "ISIL's Abuse of Women and Girls Must Be Stopped," US Department of State.

835. Semple, Kirk. "Yazidi Girls Seized by ISIS Speak Out After Escape," *New York Times*. Published Nov. 14, 2014; accessed Dec. 14, 2015: http://www.nytimes.com/2014/11/15/world/middleeast/yazidi-girls-seized-by-isis-speak-out-after-escape.html

836. Callimachi, Rukmini. "ISIS Enshrines a Theology of Rape," *New York Times*. Published Aug. 13, 2015; accessed Dec. 14, 2015: http://www.nytimes.com/2015/08/14/world/middleeast/isis-enshrines-a-theology-of-rape.html?_r=1

837. Ibid.

838. Semple. "Yazidi Girls Seized by ISIS Speak Out After Escape," *New York Times*.

839. "Iraq: Forced Marriage, Conversion for Yazidis," Human Rights Watch. Published Oct. 11, 2014; accessed Dec. 14, 2015: https://www.hrw.org/news/2014/10/11/iraq-forced-marriage-conversion-yezidis

840. Ibid.

841. McDuffe, Allen. "ISIS Is Now Bragging about Enslaving Women and Children," *Atlantic*. Oct. 13, 2014; accessed Dec. 14, 2015: http://www.theatlantic.com/international/archive/2014/10/isis-confirms-and-justifies-enslaving-yazidis-in-new-magazine-article/381394/

842. Ibid.

843. "Iraq: Forced Marriage, Conversion for Yazidis," Human Rights Watch.

844. McDuffe. "ISIS Is Now Bragging about Enslaving Women and Children," *Atlantic*.

845. Ibid.

846. Ibid.

847. "To Have and to Hold: Jihadists Boast of Selling Women as Concubines," *Economist*. Published Oct. 14, 2014; accessed Dec. 14, 2015: http://www.economist.com/news/middle-east-and-africa/21625870-jihadists-boast-selling-captive-women-concubines-have-and-hold

848.   Ibid. | Callimachi. "ISIS Enshrines a Theology of Rape," *New York Times*. | Yoon, Sangwon. "Islamic State Circulates Sex Slave Price List," *Bloomberg*. Published Aug. 4, 2015; accessed Dec. 14, 2015: http://www.bloomberg.com/news/articles/2015-08-03/sex-slaves-sold-by-islamic-state-the-younger-the-better

849.   "UN Official Verified IS 'Price List' for Yazidi and Christian Females," Defend International. Published Aug. 4, 2015; site accessed Dec. 14, 2015: http://defendinternational.org/is-price-list-for-yazidi-and-christian-females-verified-by-un-official/

850.   Webb, Sam and Khaleda Rahman. "The Price of a Slave . . . as Determined by Official ISIS Price List: Islamist Group Sets Prices for Yazidi and Christian Women—with Girls Under Nine Fetching the Highest Price," *Daily Mail*. Published Nov. 4, 2014; accessed Dec. 14, 2015: http://www.dailymail.co.uk/news/article-2820603/The-price-slave-determined-official-ISIS-price-list-Islamist-group-sets-prices-Yazidi-Christian-women-girls-nine-fetching-highest-price.html#ixzz3t0cpVvgc

851.   "Islamic State (ISIS) Releases Pamphlet on Female Slaves," Middle East Media and Research Institute. Published Dec. 4, 2014; accessed Dec. 13, 2015: http://www.memrijttm.org/islamic-state-isis-releases-pamphlet-on-female-slaves.html

852.   Roth, Kenneth. "Slavery: The ISIS Rules," *New York Review of Books*. Published Sept. 5, 2015; accessed Dec. 14, 2015: https://www.hrw.org/news/2015/09/05/slavery-isis-rules

853.   Callimachi. "ISIS Enshrines a Theology of Rape," *New York Times*.

854.   Callimachi. "ISIS Enshrines a Theology of Rape," *New York Times*.

855.   Shubert, Atika and Bharati Naik. "ISIS 'Forced Pregnant Yazidi Women to Have Abortions,'" CNN. Published Oct. 6, 2015; accessed Dec. 14, 2015: http://www.cnn.com/2015/10/06/middleeast/pregnant-yazidis-forced-abortions-isis/

856.   Callimachi. "ISIS Enshrines a Theology of Rape," *New York Times*.

857.   Ibid.

858.   Ibid.

859.   Ibid.

860.   Ibid.

861.   "Iraq: Forced Marriage, Conversion for Yazidis," Human Rights Watch.

862.   Yoon. "Islamic State Circulates Sex Slave Price List," *Bloomberg*.

863.   Sherlock, Ruth. "Islamic State Commanders 'Using Yazidi Virgins for Sex,'" *Telegraph*. Published Oct. 14, 2014; accessed Dec. 14, 2015: http://www.telegraph.co.uk/news/worldnews/islamic-state/11171874/Islamic-State-commanders-using-Yazidi-virgins-for-sex.html

864.   Brekke, Kira. "ISIS Is Attacking Women, and Nobody Is Talking about It," *Huffington Post*. Published Sept. 8, 2014; accessed Dec. 14, 2015: http://www.huffingtonpost.com/2014/09/08/isis-attacks-on-women_n_5775106.html?cps=gravity

865.   Semple. "Yazidi Girls Seized by ISIS Speak Out After Escape," *New York Times*.

866.   Wolf, Mat and Shira Rubin. "How to Buy a Slave Girl from ISIS," *Daily Beast*. Published Sept. 3, 2015; accessed Dec. 14, 2015: http://www.thedailybeast.com/articles/2015/09/03/the-isis-slave-girl-buyback-schemes.html

867. "ISIS Executes 19 Girls for Refusing Sex with Its Fighters," *The Quint*. Published Aug. 7, 2015; accessed Dec. 14, 2015: http://www.thequint.com/world/2015/08/07/isis-executes-19-girls-for-refusing-sex-with-fighters | Withnall, Adam. "ISIS Executes 19 Women in Mosul 'for Refusing to Take Part in Sexual Jihad,'" *Independent*. Published Aug. 6, 2015; accessed Dec. 14, 2015: http://www.independent.co.uk/news/world/middle-east/isis-executes-19-women-in-mosul-for-refusing-to-take-part-in-sexual-jihad-10443204.html

868. "Iraq: Forced Marriage, Conversion for Yazidis," Human Rights Watch.

869. Shubert, Atika and Bharati Naik. "'Hundreds' of Yazidi Women Killing Themselves in ISIS Captivity," CNN. Published Oct. 5, 2015; accessed Dec. 14, 2015: http://www.cnn.com/2015/10/05/middleeast/yazidi-women-suicide-in-isis-captivity/

870. "Iraq: ISIS Escapees Describe Systematic Rape," Human Rights Watch.

871. "Hadd," in *Oxford Dictionary of Islam*. Oxford Islamic Studies Online. Accessed Dec. 1, 2015: http://www.oxfordislamicstudies.com/article/opr/t125/e757

872. Ibid.

873. Saul, Heather. "Isis publishes penal code listing amputation, crucifixion and stoning as punishments—and vows to vigilantly enforce it," *Independent*. Published Jan. 22, 2015; accessed Dec. 3, 2015: http://www.independent.co.uk/news/world/middle-east/isis-publishes-penal-code-listing-amputation-crucifixion-and-stoning-as-punishments-and-vows-to-9994878.html

874. Ibid.

875. ISIS, Aleppo branch. "Clarification of the hudud," our version, based on a translation by the Middle East Media Research Institute, cited by Heather Saul in "Isis publishes penal code listing amputation, crucifixion and stoning as punishments—and vows to vigilantly enforce it," *Independent*.

876. Lenya, Lotte. "August 28, 1928," citing an unnamed friend, in Bertholt Brecht, *Threepenny Opera*, New York, Grove Press, 1960.

877. Withnall, Adam. "Saudi Arabia executes 'a person every two days' as rate of beheadings soars under King Salman," *Independent*. Published Aug. 25, 2015; accessed Dec. 3, 2015: http://www.independent.co.uk/news/world/middle-east/saudi-arabia-executions-amnesty-international-beheadings-death-sentences-rate-under-king-salman-10470456.html

878. Abu Mohammed. "ISIS executes a young man in Deir ez-Zor, using Bazooka (RBG) to kill him," Raqqa, *Raqqa is Being Slaughtered Silently*. May 21, 2015; accessed Jan. 13, 2016: http://www.raqqa-sl.com/en/?p=1184

879. Botelho, Greg. "ISIS video claims beheading of Russian spy, threatens Russian people," CNN. Updated Dec. 3, 2015; Dec. 3, 2105: http://www.cnn.com/2015/12/02/middleeast/isis-russian-beheading-claim/index.html?eref=rss_latest

880. Menezes, Alroy. "ISIS Kills 50 Syrian Soldiers, Beheads Many In Raqqa," *International Business Times*. Published July 26, 2014; accessed Dec. 3, 2015: http://www.ibtimes.com/isis-kills-50-syrian-soldiers-beheads-many-raqqa-1639948

881. Cleary, Tom. "New ISIS Video Shows 'Spies' Drowned in Cage, Blown Up," *Heavy*. June 23, 2015; 7:31, accessed Dec. 3, 2015: http://heavy.com/news/2015/06/isis-islamic-state-executes-drowns-in-cage-blows-up-spies-brutal-video-propaganda-uncensored-youtube-iraqi-espionage-men-killed/

882. Ibid.

883. "Jordanian Pilot Kaseasbeh Burned Alive by Islamic State; Jordan Executes IS Requested Prisoner Rishawi in Response," *LeakSource*. Published Feb. 4, 2015; Dec. 3, 2015: http://leaksource.info/2015/02/04/jordanian-pilot-kaseasbeh-burned-alive-by-islamic-state-jordan-executes-is-requested-prisoner-rishawi-in-response/

884. Withnall, Adam. "Isis releases graphic video showing four Shia 'spies' being burned alive in Anbar," *Independent*. Published Aug. 31, 2015; accessed Dec. 14, 2015: http://www.independent.co.uk/news/world/middle-east/isis-releases-graphic-video-showing-four-shia-spies-being-burned-alive-in-anbar-iraq-10479626.html

885. Dearden, Lizzie. "Isis 'crucifies children for not fasting during Ramadan' in Syria," *Independent*. Published June 23, 2015; accessed Dec. 3, 2015: http://www.independent.co.uk/news/world/middle-east/isis-crucifies-children-for-not-fasting-during-ramadan-in-syria-10338215.html

886. Mezzofiore, Gianluca. "Syria: Isis Stone Woman to Death for Adultery with Father's Help in Hama [GRAPHIC VIDEO]," *International Business Times*. Published Oct. 21, 2014; accessed Dec. 14, 2015: http://www.ibtimes.co.uk/syria-isis-stone-woman-death-adultery-fathers-help-hama-graphic-video-1471038

887. Ibid.

888. Segalov, Michael. "'Being gay in the Islamic State': Men reveal chilling truth about homosexuality under Isis," *Independent*. Published Aug. 25, 2015; accessed Dec. 3, 2015: http://www.independent.co.uk/news/world/middle-east/being-gay-in-the-islamic-state-men-reveal-chilling-truth-about-homosexuality-under-isis-10470894.html

889. Brydum, Sunnivie. "ISIS Executes Nine More 'Gay' Men," *Advocate*. Published Aug. 28, 2015; accessed Dec. 3, 2015: http://www.advocate.com/world/2015/08/28/reports-isis-executes-nine-more-gay-men

890. Senzee, Thom. "'Gay' Man Thrown From Roof by ISIS Survives Fall, Stoned to Death," *Advocate*. Published Feb. 4, 2015; accessed Dec. 3, 2015: http://www.advocate.com/world/2015/02/04/gay-man-thrown-roof-isis-survives-fall-stoned-death

891. "The 'Islamic State' carry out the first execution by tank against a regime force member because he 'run over the State's soldiers,'" Syrian Observatory for Human Rights. Published Oct. 24, 2015; accessed Dec. 3, 2015: http://www.syriahr.com/en/2015/10/the-islamic-state-carry-out-the-first-execution-by-tank-against-a-regime-force-member-because-he-run-over-the-states-soldiers/

892. Segalov. "'Being gay in the Islamic State': Men reveal chilling truth about homosexuality under Isis," *Independent*.

893. ISIS, Aleppo branch. "Clarification of the hudud," cited by Heather Saul in "Isis publishes penal code listing amputation, crucifixion and stoning as punishments—and vows to vigilantly enforce it," *Independent*.

894. "Shocking video allegedly shows ISIS beating fellow terrorists," *Daily Mail*. Accessed Jan. 14, 2016: http://www.dailymail.co.uk/video/news/video-1184932/Shocking-video-allegedly-shows-ISIS-beating-fellow-terrorists.html

895. Di Giovanni, Janine Leah McGrath Goodman, and Damien Sharkov. "How Does ISIS." Fund Its Reign of Terror," *Newsweek*. Published Nov. 6, 2014; accessed Dec. 4, 2015: http://www.newsweek.com/2014/11/14/how-does-isis-fund-its-reign-terror-282607.html

896. Simpson, Cam and Matthew Philips. "Why U.S. Efforts to Cut Off Islamic State's Funds Have Failed," *Bloomberg*. Published Nov. 19, 2015; accessed Dec. 4, 2015: http://www.bloomberg.com/news/articles/2015-11-19/why-u-s-efforts-to-cut-off-islamic-state-s-funds-have-failed

897. Brisard, Jean-Claude and Damien Martine. "Islamic State: The Economy-Based Terrorist Funding," *Thomson Reuters*. Published Oct. 2014; accessed Nov. 26, 2015: https://risk.thomsonreuters.com/sites/default/files/GRC01815.pdf).

898. Levitt, Matthew. *Terrorist Financing and the Islamic State*. Submitted to the House Committee on Financial Services Nov. 13, 2014; accessed Nov. 24, 2015: http://financialservices.house.gov/uploadedfiles/hhrg-113-ba00-wstate-mlevitt-20141113.pdf

899. Simpson and Philips. "Why U.S. Efforts to Cut Off Islamic State's Funds Have Failed," *Bloomberg*.

900. Ibid.

901. Di Giovanni, McGrath Goodman, and Sharkov. "How Does ISIS." Fund Its Reign of Terror," *Newsweek*.

902. Northam, Jackie. "Hitting ISIS Where It Hurts By Striking Oil Trucks," NPR. Originally aired Nov. 19, 2015; accessed Jan. 14, 2016: http://www.npr.org/sections/parallels/2015/11/19/456600398/hitting-isis-where-it-hurts-by-striking-oil-trucks

903. Middle East and Central Asia Department. *Iraq: Selected Issues*, International Monetary Fund, Washington, DC, Aug. 2015.

904. Smith, Grant, Ilya Arkhipov, and Henry Meyer. "Obama and Putin Agree on Bombing Islamic State's Oil Pipeline," *Bloomberg*. Published Nov. 19, 2015; accessed Nov. 26, 2015: http://www.bloomberg.com/news/articles/2015-11-19/obama-in-sync-with-putin-on-bombing-islamic-state-oil-riches

905. Ibid.

906. Hendawi, Hamza, and Qassim Abdul-Zahra. "ISIS is making up to $50 million a month from oil sales," AP via *Business Insider*. Published Oct. 23, 2015; accessed Nov. 26, 2015: http://www.businessinsider.com/isis-making-50-million-a-month-from-oil-sales-2015-10.

907. Ibid.

908. Ibid.

909. US Central Command. "Nov. 21: Military airstrikes continue against ISIL terrorists in Syria and Iraq" press release. Published Nov. 21, 2015; accessed Jan. 14, 2016: http://www.centcom.mil/en/news/articles/nov.-21-military-airstrikes-continue-against-isil-terrorists-in-syria-and-i

910. Miklaszewski, Jim. "U.S. Destroys 280 ISIS Oil Trucks in Syrian City of Deir ez-Zor," NBC News. Published Nov. 23, 2015; accessed Jan. 14, 2016: http://www.nbcnews.com/storyline/isis-terror/au-s-destroys-280-isis-oil-trucks-syrian-city-deir-n468126

911. Simpson and Philips. "Why U.S. Efforts to Cut Off Islamic State's Funds Have Failed," *Bloomberg*.

912. Syrian4all World. "Syria, Aleppo, Al-Bab Neighbourhood Detailed Explanation of Refining Oil with Local Expertise," YouTube. Published March 25, 2015; accessed Jan. 14, 2016: https://www.youtube.com/watch?v=TgeD_nBIS9k

913. Ibid.

914. Ibid.

915. Simpson and Philips. "Why U.S. Efforts to Cut Off Islamic State's Funds Have Failed," *Bloomberg*.

916.   Kiourktsoglou, George and Dr. Alec D. Coutroubis. "ISIS Export Gateway To Global Crude Oil Markets," *Marsec Review*. Published March 20, 2015; accessed Aug. 18, 2015: http://www.marsecreview.com/wp-content/uploads/2015/03/PAPER-on-CRUDE-OIL-and-ISIS.pdf

917.   Ibid.

918.   Di Giovanni, McGrath Goodman, and Sharkov. "How Does ISIS Fund Its Reign of Terror," *Newsweek*.

919.   Simpson and Philips. "Why U.S. Efforts to Cut Off Islamic State's Funds Have Failed," *Bloomberg*.

920.   Smith, Arkhipov, and Meyer. "Obama and Putin." Agree on Bombing Islamic State's Oil Pipeline," *Bloomberg*.

921.   Ibid.

922.   "Life under the ISIS Caliphate," *The Week*. Published Aug. 22, 2015; accessed Nov. 26, 2015: http://theweek.com/articles/572910/life-under-isis-caliphate

923.   "ISIL mints 'Islamic coin inspired by divine law,'" *Euronews*. Published June 24, 2015; accessed Nov. 26, 2015: http://www.euronews.com/2015/06/24/isil-mints-islamic-coin-inspired-by-divine-law/.

924.   Alarabi Albakri, Mohammed. "ISIL promotes for its new currency," Syrian Economic Forum. Published Sept. 2, 2015; accessed Nov. 26, 2015: http://www.syrianef.org/En/2015/09/isil-promotes-for-its-new-currency/.

925.   Ibid.

926.   Ibid.

927.   Ibid.

928.   Ibid.

929.   "ISIL mints 'Islamic coin inspired by divine law,'" *Euronews*.

930.   Alarabi Albakri, Mohammed. "ISIL promotes for its new currency." Syrian Economic Forum.

931.   Ibid.

932.   Di Giovanni, McGrath Goodman, and Sharkov. "How Does ISIS." Fund Its Reign of Terror," *Newsweek*.

933.   Swanson, Ana. "How the Islamic State makes its money," *Washington Post*. Published Nov. 18, 2015; accessed Nov. 26, 2015: https://www.washingtonpost.com/news/wonk/wp/2015/11/18/how-isis-makes-its-money/.

934.   Di Giovanni, McGrath Goodman, and Sharkov. "How Does ISIS Fund Its Reign of Terror," *Newsweek*.

935.   Hendawi and Abdul-Zahra. "ISIS is making up to $50 million a month from oil sales," AP via *Business Insider*.

936.   Rosenberg, Matthew, Nicholas Kulish, and Steven Lee Myers. "Predatory Islamic State Wrings Money from Those It Rules," *New York Times*. Published Nov. 30, 2015; accessed Dec. 4, 2105: http://www.nytimes.com/2015/11/29/world/middleeast/predatory-islamic-state-wrings-money-from-those-it-rules.html?_r=0.

937.   Hendawi and Abdul-Zahra. "ISIS is making." up to $50 million a month from oil sales," *Business Insider*.

938.   Di Giovanni, McGrath Goodman, and Sharkov. "How Does ISIS Fund Its Reign of Terror," *Newsweek*.

939.   Ibid.

940.   Simpson and Phillips. "Why U.S. Efforts to Cut Off Islamic State's Funds Have Failed," *Bloomberg*.

941.   Rosenberg, Kulish, and Myers. "Predatory Islamic State." Wrings Money from Those It Rules," *New York Times*.

942.   Di Giovanni, McGrath Goodman, and Sharkov. "How Does ISIS Fund." Fund Its Reign of Terror," *Newsweek*.

943.   Rosenberg, Kulish, and Myers. "Predatory Islamic State Wrings Money from Those It Rules," *New York Times*.

944.   Long, Matthew. "*Jizya,*" in *The Princeton Encyclopedia of Islamic Political Thought*, Princeton, Princeton University Press 2012, 283–284.

945.   Zarra-Nezhad, Mansour and Muhammad Reza Alam. "Estimation of Total Revenue of the Early Muslim Governments," *Journal La Pensée*, 76(3) (2014): 143, 152-153.

946.   Peri, Oded. *Ottoman Palestine, 1800-1914 : Studies in Economic and Social History,* ed. Gad G. Gilbar, Leiden, E.J. Brill, 1990, 287–288.

947.   Baker, Aryn. "Al Qaeda Rebels in Syria Tell Christians to Pay Up or Die," *Time*. Published Feb. 28, 2014; accessed Dec. 4, 2015: http://world.time.com/2014/02/28/al-qaeda-in-syria-extorts-christians/.

948.   "The Islamic State (Full Length)," *Vice*. Published Dec. 26, 2014; accessed Jan. 14, 2016: https://news.vice.com/video/the-islamic-state-full-length

949.   "2 Iraqi Christians, a father and a husband, Committed Suicide After ISIS Mercenaries Rape Wife and Daughter in Front of Them Because They Couldn't Pay the Jizya," *Syrian Free Press*. Published July 31, 2014; accessed Dec. 4, 2015: https://syrianfreepress.wordpress.com/2014/07/31/2-iraqi-christians-a-father-and-a-husband-commited-suicide-after-isis-mercenaries-rape-wife-and-daughter-in-front-of-them-because-they-couldnt-pay-the-jizya/ | the title of the article is in error; the source that the article quotes at length says that the "father" and "husband" are, in fact, the same person.

950.   Winter *Women of the Islamic State.*

951.   Jones, Christopher. "What is the Tomb of the Prophet Jonah?" Gates of Nineveh blog. Published July 11, 2014; accessed April 7, 2015: https://gatesofnineveh.wordpress.com/2014/07/11/what-is-the-tomb-of-the-prophet-jonah/

952.   Ibid.

953.   Ford, Dana and Mohammed Tawfeeq. "Extremists destroy Jonah's tomb, officials say," CNN. Published July 25, 2014; accessed April 7, 2015: http://www.cnn.com/2014/07/24/world/iraq-violence/

954.   Jones. "What is the Tomb of the Prophet Jonah?" Gates of Nineveh blog.

955.   Ibid.

956.   Ibid.

957.   Ibid.

958.   Ibid.

959.   Ibid.

960.   Ibid.

961. Fadhil, Muna. "Isis destroys thousands of books and manuscripts in Mosul libraries." *Guardian*. Published Feb. 26, 2015; accessed April 7, 2015: http://www.theguardian.com/books/2015/feb/26/isis-destroys-thousands-books-libraries

962. Ibid.

963. Ibid.

964. Haq, Husna. "ISIS burns Mosul library: Why terrorists target books," *Christian Science Monitor*. Published Feb. 25, 2015; accessed April 7, 2015: http://www.csmonitor.com/Books/chapter-and-verse/2015/0225/ISIS-burns-Mosul-library-Why-terrorists-target-books

965. Ibid.

966. Mohammad, Riyadh. "ISIS Burns 8000 Rare Books and Manuscripts in Mosul," *Fiscal Times*. Published Feb. 23, 2015; accessed April 8, 2015: http://www.thefiscaltimes.com/2015/02/23/ISIS-Burns-8000-Rare-Books-and-Manuscripts-Mosul

967. Ibid.

968. Tawfeeq, Mohammad, Hamdi Alkhshali, and Susannah Cullinane. "Tracking a Trail of Historical Obliteration: ISIS Trumpets destruction of Nimrud," CNN. Published April 13, 2015; accessed April 14, 2015: http://www.cnn.com/2015/03/09/world/iraq-isis-heritage/

969. Reuters. "ISIS Destroys Another Monument at Palmyra Ruins in Syria." *New York Times*. Published Oct. 4, 2015; accessed April 15, 2015: http://www.nytimes.com/2015/10/05/world/middleeast/isis-destroys-another-palmyra-ruins-monument-in-syria.html?_r=0

970. Evans, Dominic. "Islamic State ransacks Assyrian capital as Iraq appeals for help," Reuters. Published March 11, 2015; accessed April 13, 2015: http://www.reuters.com/article/2015/03/11/us-mideast-crisis-iraq-destruction-idUSKBN0M726Q20150311

971. Ibid.

972. Ibid.

973. World Heritage Convention. "Nimrud," UNESCO. Published July 7, 2000; accessed April 3, 2015: http://whc.unesco.org/en/tentativelists/1463

974. Ibid.

975. Shaheen, Kareem. "Outcry over Isis destruction of ancient Assyrian site of Nimrud," *Guardian*. Published March 6, 2015; accessed April 3, 2015: http://www.theguardian.com/world/2015/mar/06/isis-destroys-ancient-assyrian-site-of-nimrud

976. Ibid.

977. Shaheen. "Outcry over Isis destruction of ancient Assyrian site of Nimrud," *Guardian*.

978. World Heritage Convention. "Hatra," UNESCO. Accessed April 7, 2015: http://whc.unesco.org/en/list/277, Unknown

979. Ibid.

980. Shaheen, Kareem. "Isis video confirms destruction at Unesco world heritage site in Hatra," *Guardian*. Published April 5, 2015; accessed April 7, 2015: http://www.theguardian.com/world/2015/apr/05/isis-video-confirms-destruction-at-unesco-world-heritage-site-on-hatra, 5th April 2015, Web, 7th April 2015

981. Winsor, Morgan. "ISIS Demolishes Hatra, 2,000-Year-Old City In Ancient Iraq," *International Business Times*. Published March 7, 2015; accessed April 5, 2015: http://www.ibtimes.com/isis-demolishes-hatra-2000-year-old-city-ancient-iraq-1839750

982. Shaheen. "Isis video confirms destruction at Unesco world heritage site in Hatra" *Guardian*.

983. Blumberg, Antonia. "Islamic State Reportedly Destroys 7th Century Green Church In Tikrit, Iraq. One Of Middle East's Oldest Christian Sites," *Huffington Post*. Published Sept. 26, 2014; accessed April 14, 2015: http://www.huffingtonpost.com/2014/09/26/islamic-state-green-church_n_5887806.html

984. "Islamists Destroy 7th Century Church, Mosque in Tikrit, Iraq," *Assyrian International News Agency*. Published Sept. 25, 2014; accessed April 16, 2015: http://www.aina.org/news/20140925012701.htm

985. Ibid.

986. Mar Dinkha II, and his successors Daniel, Thomas, Basilious III, and John II

987. Blumberg. "Islamic State Reportedly Destroys 7th Century Green Church In Tikrit, Iraq. One Of Middle East's Oldest Christian Sites," *Huffington Post*.

988. Vartanian, Hrag. "Cultural Destruction by Islamic State Continues with No End in Sight," *Hyperallergic*. Published Aug. 25, 2014; accessed May 1, 2015: http://hyperallergic.com/143910/cultural-destruction-by-islamic-state-continues-with-no-end-in-sight/

989. Richter, Ash M. "Syria, in Ruins," *All Day*. Accessed April 18, 2015: http://allday.com/post/1426-syria-in-ruins

990. "UN: 300 cultural heritage sites destroyed, looted in Syria," *Al-Akhbar*. Published Dec. 23, 2014; accessed April 3, 2015: http://english.al-akhbar.com/node/22995

991. Ibid.

992. "Damage to Syria's Heritage 18 May 2014," Heritage for Peace. Published May 18, 2014; accessed June 9, 2015: http://www.heritageforpeace.org/syria-culture-and-heritage/damage-to-cultural-heritage/previous-damage-newsletters/damage-to-syrias-heritage-18-may-2014/

993. Ibid.

994. Ibid.

995. "Dura Europos, Syria," Sacred Destinations. Published 2005; accessed April 7, 2015: http://www.sacred-destinations.com/syria/dura-europos

996. Mack, David. "Here's A Look At Some Of The Ancient Sites Destroyed By ISIS And The Syrian Civil War," *Buzzfeed*. Published March 11, 2015; accessed April 3, 2015: http://www.buzzfeed.com/davidmack/a-look-at-some-of-the-world-heritage-sites-destroyed#.fi80GEPYx

997. Ibid.

998. [No Note Text]

999. Wood, Graeme. "Kuwaiti preacher, ISIS call for demolition of Egypt's Sphinx, pyramids," *Russia Today*. Published March 9, 2015; accessed Nov. 24, 2015: https://www.rt.com/news/239093-islamist-calls-destroy-pyramids/

1000. "Suicide attack outside Karnak temple in Egypt's Luxor," BBC. Published June 10, 2015; accessed Nov. 23, 2015: http://www.bbc.com/news/world-middle-east-33077862

1001. Ibid.

1002. "Giza bomb detonated by security forces causes 4 injuries," *Daily News Egypt*. Published Oct. 24, 2015; accessed Nov. 23, 2015: http://www.dailynewsegypt.com/2015/10/24/giza-bomb-detonated-by-security-forces-causes-4-injuries/

1003. Howard, Brig. Gen. Russell, Jonathan Prohov, and Mark Elliott. "Combating Terrorism Center, Digging In and Trafficking Out: How the Destruction of Cultural Heritage Funds Terrorism," Combating Terrorism Center. Published Feb. 27, 2015; accessed Nov. 29, 2015: https://www.ctc.usma.edu/posts/digging-in-and-trafficking-out-how-the-destruction-of-cultural-heritage-funds-terrorism

1004. Ibid.

1005. Wiser, Daniel. "Marine colonel: ISIS is institutionalizing the looting game," *Business Insider*. Published Sept. 14, 2015; accessed Nov. 23, 2015: http://mobile.businessinsider.com/isis-is-institutionalizing-the-looting-game-2015-9

1006. Ibid.

1007. Levitt. *Terrorist Financing and the Islamic State*.

1008. Loveluck, Louisa. "Islamic State sets up 'ministry of antiquities' to reap the profits of pillaging," *Telegraph*. Published May 20, 2015; accessed Nov. 29, 2015: http://www.telegraph.co.uk/news/worldnews/islamic-state/11640670/Islamic-State-sets-up-ministry-of-antiquities-to-reap-the-profits-of-pillaging.html

1009. "Following the trail of Syria's looted history." CBS News. Published Sept. 9, 2015; accessed Nov. 23, 2015: http://www.cbsnews.com/news/isis-looted-syrian-ancient-artifacts-black-market-us-and-europe/

1010. Howard, Prohov, and Elliott. "Digging In and Trafficking Out: How the Destruction of Cultural Heritage Funds Terrorism," Combating Terrorism Center.

1011. Cultural Heritage Center. "ISIL Leader's Loot," Bureau of Educational and Cultural Affairs. Published 2015; accessed Nov. 25, 2015: http://eca.state.gov/cultural-heritage-center/iraq-cultural-heritage-initiative/isil-leaders-loot

1012. Howard, Prohov, and Elliott. "Digging In and Trafficking Out: How the Destruction of Cultural Heritage Funds Terrorism," Combating Terrorism Center.

1013. Levitt. *Terrorist Financing and the Islamic State*.

1014. Mulder, Stephennie. "The blood antiquities funding ISIL," *AlJazeera*. Published Nov. 12, 2014; accessed Nov. 24, 2015: http://www.aljazeera.com/indepth/opinion/2014/11/blood-antiquities-funding-isil-2014119113948461658.html

1015. Shiloach, Gilad. "ISIS opens its own social network," *Vocativ*. Published Aug. 3, 2015; accessed Nov. 29, 2015: http://www.vocativ.com/world/isis-2/isis-opens-its-own-social-network/

1016. Spargo, Chris. "ISIS sells priceless ancient artifacts on FACEBOOK: Gold statues, scrolls written in Aramaic and coins up to 10,000 years old being peddled online by terror," *Daily Mail*. Published June 11, 2015; accessed Nov. 23, 2015: http://www.dailymail.co.uk/news/article-3120941/Facebook-purges-pages-offering-priceless-ISIS-plunders-sale-including-gold-statues-ancient-coins-Hebrew-scrolls-clay-tablets.html

1017. Cox, Simon. "The men who smuggle the loot that funds IS," BBC. Published Feb. 17, 2015; accessed Nov. 26, 2015: http://www.bbc.com/news/magazine-31485439

1018. St. Hilaire, Rick. "Conflict and the Heritage Trade: Rise in U.S. Imports of Middle East 'Antiques' and 'Collectors' Pieces" Raises Questions," Cultural Heritage Lawyer blog. Published Oct. 6, 2014; accessed Nov. 24, 2015: http://culturalheritagelawyer.blogspot.ro/2014/10/conflict-and-heritage-trade-rise-in-us.html

1019. Cox. "The men who smuggle the loot that funds IS," BBC.

1020. Ibid.

1021. Ibid.

1022. Ibid.

1023. Caulderwood, Kathleen. "How ISIS Pillages, Traffics And Sells Ancient Artifacts On Global Black Market," *International Business Times*. Published June 18, 2014; accessed Nov. 24, 2015: http://www.ibtimes.com/how-isis-pillages-traffics-sells-ancient-artifacts-global-black-market-1605044

1024. Mulder. "The blood antiquities funding ISIL," *AlJazeera*.

1025. Ibid.

1026. Cultural Heritage Center. "ISIL Leader's Loot," Bureau of Educational and Cultural Affairs.

1027. Chulov, Martin. "How an arrest in Iraq revealed ISIS's $2bn jihadist Network," *Guardian*. Published June 15, 2014; accessed Nov. 24, 2015: http://www.theguardian.com/world/2014/jun/15/iraq-isis-arrest-jihadists-wealth-power

1028. Howard, Prohov, and Elliott. "Digging In and Trafficking Out: How the Destruction of Cultural Heritage Funds Terrorism," Combating Terrorism Center.

1029. Watson, Andrea. "Islamic State and the 'blood antique' trade," BBC. Published April 2, 2015; accessed Nov. 24, 2015: http://www.bbc.com/culture/story/20150402-is-and-the-blood-antique-trade

1030. Ibid.

1031. Ibid.

1032. Trembley, Pinar. "Turkey major conduit for Syrian 'blood antiquities,'" *Al-Monitor*. Published Sept. 25, 2015; accessed Nov. 24, 2015: http://www.al-monitor.com/pulse/originals/2015/09/turkey-syria-cultural-heritage-turns-into-blood-antiquities.html

1033. Ibid.

1034. Agg, Cpr. J. "Marines Capitalize on Lessons Learned," *Marine Corps News*. Published May 5, 2005; accessed Jan. 14, 2016: http://www.military.com/NewsContent/0,13319,usmc1_050505.00.html

1035. Lawrence, Thomas E. "A Report on Mesopotamia" *The Times of London*. Published Aug. 2, 1920.

1036. Al-Tamimi, Aymenn Jawad and Johnathan Spyer, ISIS' use of Hudud punishments," Aymenn Jawad al-Tamimi blog. Published May 29, 2014; accessed Jan. 13, 2016: http://www.aymennjawad.org/14852/isis-use-of-hudud-punishments

1037. Naji, Abu Bakr, Adara al-Tawhish, Management of Savagery, translation by William McCants, John M. Olin Institute for Strategic Studies, Harvard University

1038. AFP "IS executes 3,500 in Syria since declaring 'caliphate': monitor," MSN. Published Nov. 29, 2015; accessed Jan. 14, 2016: http://www.msn.com/en-us/news/world/is-executes-3500-in-syria-since-declaring-caliphate-monitor/ar-AAfMYgC?li=BBnbcA1&ocid=SK2IDHP

1039. Priest, Ana. "Iraq New Terror Breeding Ground" *Washington Post*. Published Jan. 14, 2005; accessed Jan. 14, 2016: http://www.washingtonpost.com/wp-dyn/articles/A7460-2005Jan13.html

1040. Naji, Abu Bakr and Adara al-Tawhish. Management of Savagery, translation by William McCants, John M. Olin Institute for Strategic Studies, Harvard University.

1041. Ibid.

1042. Naji, Abu Bakr, Adara al-Tawhish, Management of Savagery, translation by William McCants, John M. Olin Institute for Strategic Studies, Harvard University

1043. Ahmed, Akbar Shahid. "3 New Findings On ISIS Weapons That You Should Know About," *Huffington Post*. Published Oct. 6, 2014; accessed Dec. 2, 2015: http://www.huffingtonpost.com/2014/10/06/isis-weapons-report_n_5942334.html

1044. Harress, Christopher. "ISIS Weapons Growing In Number, Sophistication: A Soviet, Balkan and American Mix, But The Group Can't Use All Of Them," *International Business Times*. Published Aug. 15, 2014; accessed Dec. 2, 2015: http://www.ibtimes.com/isis-weapons-growing-number-sophistication-soviet-balkan-american-mix-group-cant-use-all-1659176

1045. Ibid.

1046. Bender, Jeremy. "As ISIS Continues to Gain Ground, Here's What the Militants have in their Arsenal," *Business Insider*. Published Nov. 17, 2014; accessed Dec. 2, 2015: http://www.businessinsider.com/isis-military-equipment-arsenal-2014-11

1047. "Modren [sic] military hardware and Cold War weapons: Inside the ISIS arsenal," *Reveille*. Published Sept. 15, 2015; accessed Dec. 2, 2015: http://www.thereveillenwu.com/2015/09/15/modren-military-hardware-and-cold-war-weapons-inside-the-isis-arsenal/

1048. Pianin, Eric. "U.S. Shoots Itself in the Foot by Accidentally Arming ISIS," *Fiscal Times*. Published June 4, 2015; Dec. 2, 2015: http://www.thefiscaltimes.com/2015/06/04/Fog-War-US-Has-Armed-ISIS

1049. "ISIS Driving Toyotas a Little too often: US Treasury wonders why," *Russia Today*. Published Oct. 7, 2015; accessed Dec. 1, 2015: https://www.rt.com/usa/317886-toyota-isis-trucks-treasury/

1050. Engel, Pamela. "These Toyota trucks are popular with terrorists – here's why," *Business Insider*. Published Oct. 7, 2015; accessed Dec. 1, 2015: http://www.businessinsider.com/why-isis-uses-toyota-trucks-2015-10

1051. Pickard, Gabrielle. "Here's Why ISIS Terrorists Mostly Drive Toyota Trucks," *Top Secret Writers*. Published Oct. 25, 2015; accessed Dec. 1, 2015: http://www.topsecretwriters.com/2015/10/heres-why-isis-terrorists-mostly-drive-toyota-trucks/

1052. Snyder, Stephen. "This one Toyota pickup truck is at the top of the shopping list for the Free Syrian Army – and the Taliban," Public Radio International. Originally aired April 1, 2014; accessed Dec. 1, 2015: http://www.pri.org/stories/2014-04-01/one-toyota-pickup-truck-top-shopping-list-free-syrian-army-and-taliban

1053. Cartalucci, Tony. "The Mystery of ISIS' Toyota Army Solved," *New Eastern Outlook*. Published Sept. 10, 2015; accessed Dec. 1, 2015: http://journal-neo.org/2015/10/09/the-mystery-of-isis-toyota-army-solved/

1054. Snyder. "This one Toyota pickup truck is at the top of the shopping list for the Free Syrian Army – and the Taliban," *Public Radio International*.

1055. Engel. "These Toyota trucks are popular with terrorists – here's why," *Business Insider*.

1056. "Technical (Vehicle)," *World Heritage Encyclopedia* via Project Gutenberg Self-Publishing Press. Published 2002; accessed Dec. 1, 2015: http://self.gutenberg.org/articles/Technical_(vehicle)

1057. Wikiwand, "Forces Armées Irakienne," Wikipedia. Accessed Dec. 3, 2015: http://www.wikiwand.com/fr/Forces_arm%C3%A9es_irakiennes

1058. Gouré, Daniel. "ISIS, Ramadi and the Evolving IED Threat," Lexington Institute. Published June 16, 2015; accessed Dec. 2, 2015: http://lexingtoninstitute.org/isis-ramadi-and-the-evolving-ied-threat/

1059. Mehta, Aaron. "General: ISIL Using IEDs as Guide Munitions," *Defense News*. Published June 19, 2015; accessed Dec. 2, 2015: http://www.defensenews.com/story/defense/land/weapons/2015/06/19/isis-isil-ied-iraq-syria-coalition-pgm-suicide-truck-bomb/28984469/

1060. "Vehicles and equipment captured, operated and destroyed by the Islamic state inside Iraq," Oryx Blog. Published Nov. 22, 2014; accessed Dec. 2, 2015: http://spioenkop.blogspot.com/search/label/Iraq

1061. "Exclusive: Peshmerga hunt down ISIS artillery ace," *Rudaw*. Published May 28, 2015; accessed Dec. 3, 2015: http://rudaw.net/english/kurdistan/28052015

1062. Bender, Jeremy. "ISIS Militants Captured 52 American Made Artillery Weapons That Cost $500,000 each," *Business Insider*. Published July 15, 2014; accessed Dec. 2, 2015: http://www.businessinsider.com/isis-has-52-american-weapons-that-can-hit-baghdad-2014-7

1063. Lamothe, Dan. "Video: Islamic State fighters appear to fire U.S. made M198 Howitzer artillery," *Washington Post*. Published Aug. 27, 2014; accessed Dec. 2, 2015: https://www.washingtonpost.com/news/checkpoint/wp/2014/08/27/video-islamic-state-fighters-appear-to-fire-u-s-made-m198-howitzer-artillery/

1064. Weiss, Caleb. "Islamic State used US-made anti-tank missiles near Palmyra," *Long War Journal*. Published June 9, 2015; accessed Dec. 2, 2015: http://www.longwarjournal.org/archives/2015/06/islamic-state-used-us-made-anti-tank-missiles-near-palmyra.php

1065. Ibid.

1066. Sengupta, Kim. "It's not just the savagery of Isis that is shocking – its weaponry is too," *Independent*. Published Aug. 31, 2014; accessed Dec. 2, 2015: http://www.independent.co.uk/voices/comment/the-savagery-of-isis-is-shocking-and-so-too-is-its-weaponry-9700476.html

1067. Ibid.

1068. "ISIS fighters seen with advanced antiaircraft missiles," *Al-Arabiya*. Published Oct. 28, 2014; accessed Dec. 3, 2015: english.alarabiya.net/en/News/middle-east/2014/10/28/ISIS-fighters-seen-with-sophisticated-antiaircraft-missiles-.html

1069. Parish, Brent. "The Growing ISIS Arsenal pt. 1," *The Right Planet*. Published Aug. 29, 2014; accessed Dec. 2, 2015: http://www.therightplanet.com/2014/08/the-growing-isis-arsenal-pt-1/

1070. Cenciotti, David. "U.S. A-10 Thunderbolt Aircraft faces the Threat of Man Portable Air Defense Systems in Iraq," *The Aviationist*. Published Jan. 19, 2015; accessed Dec. 3, 2015: http://theaviationist.com/2015/01/19/a-10-strela-iraq/

1071. Bowman, Tom. "U.S. Investigates Reports ISIS Used Chemical Weapons in attack on Kurds," NPR. Published Aug. 14, 2015; accessed Dec. 3, 2015: http://www.npr.org/2015/08/14/432280662/u-s-investigates-reports-isis-used-chemical-weapons-in-attack-on-kurds

1072. Blake, Paul. "US Official: IS making and using chemical weapons in Iraq and Syria," BBC. Published Sept. 11, 2015; accessed Dec. 2, 2015: http://www.bbc.com/news/world-us-canada-34211838

1073. "ISIS launch Scorpion Bombs to spread Panic in Iraq," *Mirror*. Published Dec. 15, 2014; accessed Jan. 14, 2016: http://www.mirror.co.uk/news/world-news/isis-launch-scorpion-bombs-spread-4817241

1074. Mayor, Adrienne. *Greek Fire, Poison Arrows and Scorpion Bombs. Biological and Chemical Warfare in the Ancient World*, London, Duckworth Overlook, 2009, pp 181–186.

1075. Pianin, Eric. "U.S. Shoots Itself in the Foot by Accidentally Arming ISIS," *Fiscal Times*. Published June 4, 2015; accessed Dec. 2, 2015: http://www.thefiscaltimes.com/2015/06/04/Fog-War-US-Has-Armed-ISIS

1076. "Islamic State Weapons in Iraq and Syria," Conflict Armament Research. Published April 2015; accessed Dec. 2, 2015: http://conflictarm.com/wp-content/uploads/2014/09/Dispatch_IS_Iraq_Syria_Weapons.pdf

1077. Ibid.

1078. Weiss, Caleb. "Islamic State uses drones to Coordinate fighting in Baiji," *Long War Journal*. Published April 17, 2015; accessed Dec. 17, 2015: http://www.longwarjournal.org/archives/2015/04/islamic-state-uses-drones-to-coordinate-fighting-in-baiji.php

1079. Youssef, Nancy. "Is ISIS Building a Drone Army?" *Daily Beast*. Published March 18, 2015; accessed Dec. 17, 2015: http://www.thedailybeast.com/articles/2015/03/18/is-isis-building-a-drone-army.html

1080. Kee, Edwin. "ISIS Said to Pack Explosives in Drones," *Popular Mechanics*. Published Dec. 16, 2015; accessed Dec. 17, 2015: http://www.ubergizmo.com/2015/12/isis-said-to-pack-explosives-in-drones/

1081. Terror Monitor. "The Levant Front Rebel Group Shoots Down #ISIS Surveillance Drone At #Mare' City Of #Aleppo" Twitter. Published Sept. 12, 2014; accessed Dec. 17, 2015: https://twitter.com/terror_monitor/status/642892510302355456

1082. Sarhan, Amre. "Anbar Police Shoots Down ISIS Drone East of Ramadi," *Iraqi News*. Published Oct. 3, 2015; accessed Dec. 17, 2015: http://www.iraqinews.com/iraq-war/anbar-police-shoots-isis-drone-east-ramadi/

1083. Bier, Jeryl. "Three ISIS Drones have Been Destroyed in Iraq, Syria," *Weekly Standard*. Published Sept. 18, 2015; accessed Dec. 17, 2015: http://www.weeklystandard.com/three-isis-drones-have-been-destroyed-in-iraq-syria/article/1032670

1084. Hambling, David. "ISIS Is Reportedly Packing Drones with Explosives Now," *Popular Mechanics*. Published Dec. 16, 2014; accessed Dec. 17, 2015: http://www.popularmechanics.com/military/weapons/a18577/isis-packing-drones-with-explosives/

1085. *The History of WWI, Vol 3 Home Front Technologies of the War*, Marshall Cavendish Publications, Tarry Town, new york, 2002, p. 833.

1086. Catton, Bruce. *Grant Takes Command, 1863-1865*, Back Bay Books, New York, New York.

1087. Orden, Adaki. "ISIS statement details gains in Mosul," *Long War Journal*. Published Dec. 6, 2014; accessed Jan. 14, 2016: http://www.longwarjournal.org/threat-matrix/archives/2014/06/isis_statement_details_gains_i.php

1088. "The Devastating Islamic State Suicide Strategy," The Soufan Group. Published May 29, 2015; accessed Dec. 2, 2015: http://soufangroup.com/tsg-intelbrief-the-devastating-islamic-state-suicide-strategy/

1089. "Sky News Arabia: Chronology of attack on Sinai," Storify. Accessed Jan. 14, 2016: https://storify.com/zeinobia/sky-news-arabia-a-chronology-of-attack-in-sinai

1090. Egyptian military spokesman. Facebook. Accessed July 1, 2015: https://www.facebook.com/Egy. Army.Spox/posts/680778872053098

1091. Egypt Against Terrorism. "Egyptian Ministry of Defense," YouTube. Published July 5, 2015; accessed Jan. 14, 2016: https://www.youtube.com/watch?v=cUZCbCHqbBk&feature=youtu.be

1092. "Hero Martyrs of the Recent Sinai attacks," YouTube. Published July 3, 2015; accessed Jan. 14, 2016: https://www.youtube.com/watch?v=XSAVteYLKmM

1093. "Turkish Troops Wounded in ISIL Attack on Iraq," *News Telegraph*. Published Dec. 17, 2015; accessed Dec. 18, 2015: http://thenewstelegraph.com/2015/12/17/turkish-troops-wounded-in-isil-attack-in-iraq/

1094. "Pentagon Press Briefing with Col. Steven Warren," US Department of Defense. Published Dec. 18, 2015; accessed Dec. 18, 2015: http://www.defense.gov/Video?videoid=443314&videotag=Latest%20Videos&videopage=1&ccenabled=false&videopage=1&ccenabled=false

1095. Reuters. "ISIS fires rockets at base where Turkish troops stationed," *Newsweek*. Published Dec. 16, 2015; accessed Dec. 18, 2015: http://www.newsweek.com/isis-fires-rockets-iraq-base-where-turkish-troops-stationed-406208

1096. "Investigations underway with crew of Russian ship found nearby during attack against Egyptian navy vessel," *Egypt Independent*. Published Nov. 16, 2014; accessed Jan. 14, 2016: http://www.egyptindependent.com/news/investigations-underway-crew-russian-ship-found-nearby-during-attack-against-egyptian-navy-vess

1097. "ISIS planned to attack Israeli vessels after commandeering Egyptian missile boat," *Algemeiner*.

1098. "Military sources: Terrorists tricked Egypt's navy," *Egypt Independent*. Published Nov. 14, 2014; accessed Jan. 14, 2016: http://www.egyptindependent.com//news/military-sources-terrorists-tricked-egypt-s-navy

1099. Dabiq magazine issue #* 11

1100. Klugman, Craig M. Ph.d. "How medicine has fared under ISIS," Bioethics Blog. Published Feb. 25, 2015; accessed Jan. 14, 2016: http://www.bioethics.net/2015/02/how-medicine-has-fared-under-isis/

1101. "Under Islamic State's strictures, health care falls on harder times," *Christian Science Monitor*. Published Aug. 3, 2015; accessed Jan. 14, 2016: http://m.csmonitor.com/World/Middle-East/2015/0803/Under-Islamic-State-s-strictures-health-care-falls-on-harder-times

1102. Tisdall, Simon. "US ransom policy shift undermines UK's hardline stance," *Guardian*. Published June 24, 2015; accessed Dec. 14, 2015: http://www.theguardian.com/us-news/2015/jun/24/us-ransom-policy-uk-hardline-stance-obama

1103. Liu, Joanne. "Syria: An Unacceptable Humanitarian Failure," Doctors without Borders. Published March 11, 2015; accessed Dec. 14, 2015: http://www.doctorswithoutborders.org/article/syria-unacceptable-humanitarian-failure

1104. Callimachi, Rukmini. "The Horror before the Beheadings ISIS Hostages Endured Torture and Dashed Hopes, Freed Cellmates Say," *New York Times*. Published Oct. 25, 2014; accessed Dec. 14, 2015: http://www.nytimes.com/2014/10/26/world/middleeast/horror-before-the-beheadings-what-isis-hostages-endured-in-syria.html

1105. Ibid.

1106. Ibid.

1107. Ibid.

1108. Ibid.

1109. Ibid.

1110. Ibid.

1111. Ibid.

1112. Ibid.

1113. Ibid.

1114. Chin, Josh. "Islamic State says it has Executed Chinese and Norwegian Hostages," *Wall Street Journal*. Published Nov. 18, 2015; accessed Dec. 14, 2015: http://www.wsj.com/articles/islamic-state-says-it-has-executed-chinese-and-norwegian-hostages-1447865932

1115. Saul, Heather. "Isis Japanese Hostages: Who are Kenji Goto and Haruna Yukawa," *Independent*. Published Jan. 20, 2015; accessed Dec. 14, 2015: http://www.independent.co.uk/news/world/middle-east/isis-japanese-hostages-who-are-kenji-goto-and-haruna-yukawa-9989946.html

1116. "Russian traveler feared captured by Syrian militants," *Russia Today*. Published Oct. 12, 2013; accessed Dec. 14, 2015: https://www.rt.com/news/russian-abducted-syria-rebels-109/

1117. Oliphant, Roland. "'Russian Spy' beheaded by ISIL was an 'orphan pressured into spying,'" *Telegraph*. Published Dec. 3, 2015; accessed Dec. 15, 2015: http://www.telegraph.co.uk/news/worldnews/islamic-state/12031667/Russian-spy-beheaded-by-Isil-was-an-orphan-pressured-into-spying.html

1118. Hall, John. "US Hostage Peter Hassig was killed by Gunshot Before being beheaded, analysis shows, suggesting he may have resisted ISIS Captors," *Daily Mail*. Published Dec. 15, 2014; accessed Dec. 14, 2015: http://www.dailymail.co.uk/news/article-2874226/US-hostage-Peter-Kassig-killed-gunshot-beheaded-analysis-shows-suggesting-resisted-ISIS-captors.html

1119. Jorgensen, Katrina. "ISIS Reveals 2 New Hostage by Listing them as 'For Sale' Online," *Independent Journal Review*. Published Oct. 2015; accessed Dec. 15, 2015: http://www.ijreview.com/2015/09/416089-isis-reveals-2-new-hostages-listing-sale-online/

1120. Tisdall. "US ransom policy shift undermines UK's hardline stance," *Guardian*.

1121. Callimachi "The Horror before the Beheadings ISIS Hostages Endured Torture and Dashed Hopes, Freed Cellmates Say," *New York Times*.

1122. Ibid.

1123. Brumfield, Ben. "ISIS releases some Christian hostages -- but why?" CNN. Updated March 2, 2015; accessed Nov. 30, 2015: http://www.cnn.com/2015/03/02/middleeast/isis-hostages-why-now/

1124. Ibid.

1125. Mezzofiore, Gianluca. "Syria: Isis 'frees all Assyrian Christian Hostages,'" *International Business Times*. Published March 6, 2015; accessed Nov. 30, 2015: http://www.ibtimes.co.uk/syria-isis-frees-all-assyrian-christian-hostages-1490798

1126. "Islamic State Beheads 21 Egyptian Christians, Church Confirms," *Newsweek*. Published Feb. 15, 2015; accessed Nov. 30, 2015: http://www.newsweek.com/islamic-state-release-video-purporting-show-beheading-21-egyptians-306981

1127. Mosendz, Polly. "ISIS Releases Three Foreign Hostages in Libya," *Newsweek*. Published April 6, 2015; accessed Nov. 30, 2015: http://www.newsweek.com/isis-releases-three-foreign-hostages-libya-320025

1128. Shear, Michael D. and Schmitt, Eric. "In Raid to Save Foley and Other Hostages, U.S. Found None," *New York Times*. Published Aug. 20, 2014; accessed Nov. 30, 2015: http://www.nytimes.com/2014/08/21/world/middleeast/us-commandos-tried-to-rescue-foley-and-other-hostages.html

1129. Schmidle, Nicholas. "Inside the Failed Raid to Save Foley and Sotloff," *New Yorker*. Published Sept. 5, 2014; accessed Dec. 15, 2015: http://www.newyorker.com/news/news-desk/inside-failed-raid-free-foley-sotloff

1130. Neurink

1131. Ibid.

1132. Miklaszewski, Jim, Richard Engel, and Alastair Jamieson. "U.S. Special Operations Forces Commando Killed in ISIS Hostage Rescue," NBC News. Published Oct. 22, 2015; accessed Nov. 30, 2015: http://www.nbcnews.com/storyline/isis-terror/u-s-special-forces-troops-injured-rescuing-isis-hostages-sources-n449106

1133. Ibid.

1134. Ibid.

1135. Miller, Greg and Souad Mekhennet. "Inside the surreal world of the Islamic State propaganda machine," *Washington Post*. Published Nov. 20, 2015; accessed Dec. 13, 2015: https://www.washingtonpost.com/world/national-security/inside-the-islamic-states-propaganda-machine/2015/11/20/051e997a-8ce6-11e5-acff-673ae92ddd2b_story.html

1136. Burke, Jason. "Paris shootings: investigation launched into where gunmen got GoPro cameras," *Guardian*. Published Jan. 12, 2015; accessed Dec. 13, 2015: http://www.theguardian.com/world/2015/jan/12/paris-shootings-cameras-kouachi-brothers-amedy-coulibaly

1137. Albertini, Dominique. "Attaque du supermarché Hyper Cacher : un otage raconte l'horreur," *Liberation*. Published Jan. 11, 2015; accessed Dec. 13, 2015: http://www.liberation.fr/societe/2015/01/11/hyper-casher-de-vincennes-soudain-j-ai-entendu-une-tres-forte-detonation_1178435

1138. Al-Qaeda, *Inspire*, Issue #1, p. 33.

INDEX